Family Counseling and Therapy

Family Counseling and Therapy

SECOND EDITION

ARTHUR M. HORNE THE UNIVERSITY OF GEORGIA
J. LAURENCE PASSMORE INDIANA STATE UNIVERSITY
and Contributors

F. E. PEACOCK PUBLISHERS, INC.   Itasca, Illinois

Copyright © 1991
F. E. Peacock Publishers, Inc.
All rights reserved.
Printed in the U.S.A.
Library of Congress
Catalog Card Number: 90-63375
ISBN 0-87581-353-4
1 2 3 4 5 6 7 8 9 10
1991 1992 1993 1994 1995

This book is dedicated to Merle M. Ohlsen
and to our families:

> To the families of our past
> that contributed to making us
> who we are today;

> To the families of our present
> who provide our lives
> with meaning and happiness;

> To the families of our future
> who offer hope for continued
> meaning and happiness.

Outline of Book

Author	Model	Page	Definition	Historical Development	Tenets of the Model	Application	Case Example	Evaluation	Summary
Satir & Bitter	Human Validation Process Model		14	15	24	26	33	40	41
Papero	Bowen Theory		50	48	52	60	67	73	73
Colapinto	Structural Family Therapy		78	78	82	87	98	101	103
Keith & Whitaker	Experiential/Symbolic Family Therapy		108	108	111	121	130	134	139
Schilson	Strategic Therapy		142	147	149	160	173	175	175
Segal	Brief Family Therapy		180	181	183	189	199	202	203
Kilpatrick & Kilpatrick	Object Relations Family Therapy		208	209	215	221	226	229	230
Chaney	Milan Approach to Family Therapy		236	236	248	251	253	258	259
Kempler	Gestalt Family Therapy		264	264	267	280	289	296	297
Thayer	Person-Centered Family Therapy		302	303	310	316	333	338	340
Sherrard	Neurolinguistic Programming		348	349	350	362	377	380	380
Dinkmeyer & Dinkmeyer	Adlerian Family Therapy		384	384	386	390	397	399	400
Ellis	Rational-Emotive Family Therapy		404	404	408	417	422	429	430
Wubbolding	Reality Therapy		436	437	442	446	452	459	460
Horne	Social Learning Family Therapy		464	465	472	479	483	490	491
Erskine	Transactional Analysis		498	498	499	509	518	527	527
Loria	Integrative Family Therapy		532	533	536	543	553	560	561

Contents

PREFACE   xi

ACKNOWLEDGMENTS   xv

CONTRIBUTORS   xvii

CHAPTER 1.   INTRODUCTION   1
J. Laurence Passmore and Arthur M. Horne
    DEFINITION 3   HISTORICAL DEVELOPMENT 5
    TENETS OF THE MODEL 6   APPLICATION 7
    CASE EXAMPLE 8   EVALUATION 8
    THEORETICAL PLURALISM 9   A CAVEAT   10

CHAPTER 2.   THE THERAPIST AND FAMILY THERAPY:
                SATIR'S HUMAN VALIDATION PROCESS MODEL   13
Virginia M. Satir and James Robert Bitter
    INTRODUCTION 14   DEFINITION 15
    HISTORICAL DEVELOPMENT 15   TENETS OF THE MODEL 24
    APPLICATION 26   CASE EXAMPLE 33
    EVALUATION 40   SUMMARY 41

CHAPTER 3.   THE BOWEN THEORY   47
Daniel V. Papero
    INTRODUCTION 48   HISTORICAL DEVELOPMENT 48
    DEFINITION 50   TENETS OF THE MODEL 52   APPLICATION 60
    CASE EXAMPLE 67   EVALUATION 73

CHAPTER 4.   STRUCTURAL FAMILY THERAPY   77
Jorge Colapinto
    DEFINITION 78   HISTORICAL DEVELOPMENT 78
    TENETS OF THE MODEL 82   APPLICATION 87
    PRIMARY TECHNIQUES 91   CASE EXAMPLE 98
    EVALUATION 101   SUMMARY 103

CHAPTER 5.   EXPERIMENTAL/SYMBOLIC FAMILY THERAPY   107
David V. Keith and Carl A. Whitaker
    DEFINITION 108   HISTORICAL DEVELOPMENT 108
    TENETS OF THE MODEL 111   GOAL SETTING 118
    APPLICATION 121   ROLE OF THE THERAPIST 123
    TECHNIQUES OF FAMILY THERAPY 127   CASE EXAMPLE 130
    EVALUATION 134   SUMMARY 139

CHAPTER 6.   STRATEGIC THERAPY   141
Elizabeth Allan Schilson
    DEFINITION 142   HISTORICAL DEVELOPMENT 147
    TENETS OF THE MODEL 149   ROLE OF THE THERAPIST 157
    APPLICATION 160   TECHNIQUES 167   CASE EXAMPLE 173
    EVALUATION 175   SUMMARY 175

CHAPTER 7.   BRIEF FAMILY THERAPY   179
Lynn Segal
    DEFINITION 180   HISTORICAL DEVELOPMENT 181
    TENETS OF THE MODEL 183   APPLICATION 189
    CASE EXAMPLE 199   EVALUATION 202   SUMMARY 203

CHAPTER 8.   OBJECT RELATIONS FAMILY THERAPY   207
Allie C. Kilpatrick and Ebb. G. Kilpatrick, Jr.
    DEFINITION 208   HISTORICAL DEVELOPMENT 209
    CURRENT STATUS 214   TENETS OF THE MODEL 215
    APPLICATION 221   CASE EXAMPLE 226   EVALUATION 229
    SUMMARY 230

CHAPTER 9.   EVOLVING MILAN APPROACHES TO FAMILY THERAPY   235
Reece Chaney
    DEFINITION 236   HISTORICAL DEVELOPMENT 236
    TENETS OF THE MODEL 248   APPLICATION 251
    CASE EXAMPLE 253   EVALUATION 258   SUMMARY 259

CHAPTER 10.   GESTALT FAMILY THERAPY   263
Walter Kempler
    DEFINITION 264   HISTORICAL DEVELOPMENT 264
    TENETS OF THE MODEL 267   PSYCHOTHERAPY 270
    MECHANISMS OF PSYCHOTHERAPY 278   APPLICATION 280
    CASE EXAMPLE 289   SUMMARY 297

CHAPTER 11.   TOWARD A PERSON-CENTERED APPROACH TO FAMILY
              THERAPY   301
Louis Thayer
    DEFINITION 302   HISTORICAL DEVELOPMENT 303
    TENETS OF THE MODEL 310   APPLICATION 316
    CASE EXAMPLE 333   EVALUATION 338   SUMMARY 340

CHAPTER 12.   NEUROLINGUISTIC PROGRAMMING AND FAMILY
              THERAPY   347
Peter A. D. Sherrard
    DEFINITION 348   HISTORICAL DEVELOPMENT 349
    TENETS OF THE MODEL 350   APPLICATION 362
    PRIMARY TECHNIQUES 369   CASE EXAMPLE 377
    EVALUATION 380

CHAPTER 13.   ADLERIAN FAMILY THERAPY   383
Don Dinkmeyer, Jr. and Don Dinkmeyer, Sr.
    DEFINITION 384   HISTORICAL DEVELOPMENT 384
    TENETS OF THE MODEL 386   APPLICATION 390
    CASE EXAMPLE 397   EVALUATION 399   SUMMARY 400

CHAPTER 14.   RATIONAL-EMOTIVE FAMILY THERAPY   403
Albert Ellis
    DEFINITION 404   HISTORICAL DEVELOPMENT 404
    TENETS OF THE MODEL 408   APPLICATION 417
    CASE EXAMPLE 422   EVALUATION 429   SUMMARY 430

CHAPTER 15.   REALITY THERAPY   435
Robert E. Wubbolding
    DEFINITION 436   HISTORICAL DEVELOPMENT 437
    TENETS OF THE MODEL 442   APPLICATION 446
    CASE EXAMPLE 452   EVALUATION 459   SUMMARY 460

CHAPTER 16.   SOCIAL LEARNING FAMILY THERAPY   463
Arthur M. Horne
     DEFINITION   464   HISTORICAL DEVELOPMENT   465
     TENETS OF THE MODEL   472   APPLICATION   479
     CASE EXAMPLE   483   EVALUATION   490   SUMMARY   491

CHAPTER 17.   TRANSACTIONAL ANALYSIS AND FAMILY THERAPY   497
Richard G. Erskine
     DEFINITION   498   HISTORICAL DEVELOPMENT   498
     TENETS OF THE MODEL   499
     CURRENT STATUS AND OTHER SYSTEMS   505
     APPLICATION   509   CASE EXAMPLE   518
     EVALUATION   527   SUMMARY   527

CHAPTER 18.   INTEGRATIVE FAMILY THEARAPY   531
Bruce R. Loria
     DEFINITION   532   HISTORICAL DEVELOPMENT   533
     TENETS OF THE MODEL   536   APPLICATION   543
     CASE EXAMPLE   553   EVALUATION   560   SUMMARY   561

NAME INDEX   567

SUBJECT INDEX   575

Preface

When the first edition of *Family Counseling and Therapy* was published in 1982, several family changes were identified that affected families, including:

- the move from a rural to an urban environment;
- changing from a predominantly extended family system to a nuclear family arrangement;
- a breakdown of the nuclear family as defined in popular literature to diverse family forms including single-parent, multiple adult figures in the household, gay or lesbian parent families, and communal formats;
- smaller family sizes;
- a changing emphasis on life skills education from the family to schools and other community agencies; and
- power shifts from father-dominated to more democratically oriented family structures.

Besides the structural differences, a number of family changes were identified that also tax individual and family resources:

- People are living longer, needing emotional and financial support for extended periods of time.
- Mobility has provided freedom of travel but has increased contacts outside the family and separated many families.
- Mass media has influenced the family, defining new patterns of behavior and interaction our ancestors never experienced.
- Minority rights have resulted in changing family expectations and stresses, and multicultural issues have developed that were not a factor in family management in previous generations.
- The feminist movement has drastically altered family functioning and stress level.
- Changing sexual practices—particularly the Pill—have influenced families by providing for smaller family size and greater sexual freedom and impacting levels of commitment to family expectations.
- New or emerging diseases, such as herpes, AIDS, and other sexually transmitted diseases have led to family stress.

• Drugs, including alcohol and illicit drugs, have led to increased family tension and conflict.

The cumulative effect of the stressors identified has impacted individuals, families, and communities, resulting in concern from all elements of society. But unlike our scientific progress, families have not learned to adapt rapidly enough to cope effectively with the changing times. It may be that the lack of progress in helping families is due more to the inability to disseminate new knowledge on improved family living than to a lack of knowledge of what services are helpful. In the scientific fields, dissemination of knowledge used to require years, whether it was the development and ultimate use of a hybrid corn or the implementation of electronic developments; today the time from invention to utilization has decreased to months. Such is not the case in the social sciences. The period for development to testing to large-scale implementation is still thought of in terms of years or even generations.

Family therapy has attempted to provide the support and direction that families have needed as a result of the stressors and additional pressures that have accrued with the changes noted above. But just as there is not a clear picture of what the family is, there is not a single definition of family therapy. The hallmark of family therapy, though, is the belief that problems experienced by individuals indicate trouble within that individual and within the social system of that individual—usually the family.

The combining of societal stresses, marriage of people with different learning experiences in early family life situations, and developmental phases through which families go—courtship, marriage, children, moving, job changes, retirement—can lead to dysfunction within the family unit.

Families very seldom seek out family counseling. Generally, an identified patient is selected, often a child, and serves as the ticket of admission into therapy for the whole family. This may be the case for the mother who wants marriage counseling and fears asking for it, the alcoholic husband who wants help but doesn't know how to seek it, or the teenager who needs assistance developing into an autonomous individual. They enter family therapy through an individual who is identified as the patient; but in most family therapy, the family, not the individual, is treated as the dysfunctional unit.

The chapters selected for this book represent a broad array of approaches for treating troubled families, but all have as their emphasis a focus on the family, a definition of family interactions as the locus of problems for the individuals involved. Since publication of the first edition, several chapters have been added to represent the increased recognition that particular models have received: Milan family therapy, object relations family therapy, and strategic family therapy. The opening chapter and a final chapter on integrative family therapy are also new. Several chapters have been omitted since the first edition, for the models they described have either received less emphasis within the field or, more likely, their major tenets have been incorporated into other models that continue to evolve and develop. Some chapters have undergone only minor revisions because the contributors have determined that, while the approach remains popular and relevant, little new knowledge in the form of development of new techniques or refinement of research or theory has occurred. Other chapters have been drastically revised to represent the activity level of the theorists and clinicians of that particular orientation.

We believe that this text provides an introductory overview of the current status of family therapy. It does not attempt to provide material of a specific nature (e.g., family therapy with substance abusers, child molesters, gay parents, culturally diverse family structures, low-income family systems), for specific applications are beyond the scope of this book. The material presented, though, is an excellent introduction to the world of family therapy.

Acknowledgments

This book is the second edition of *Family Counseling and Therapy*. The first edition was coedited with Indiana State University Professor Emeritus Merle Ohlsen who provided leadership and enthusiasm for the project. Without his creative and energetic leadership, the book would have never been. We thank him for leading the way professionally and personally.

The contributors to this book were cooperative and helpful at all stages; they gave their time, energy, and resources to help bring their work to the readers. Their willingness to participate—to make the sacrifices necessary to meet deadlines, provide revisions, and do the detail work needed to complete their contribution—is greatly appreciated. They are a fine group of professionals who have given unselfishly.

Ted Peacock of F. E. Peacock Publishers, Inc., provided encouragement for the first edition and has remained a person of constant support. His enthusiasm for the first edition and prodding for the second led to the new version of the book. Leo Wiegman of Peacock Publishers provided much appreciated technical and production guidance, and John Goetz provided excellent editorial and design assistance. The contributions of all the Peacock staff have been extremely helpful.

Our colleagues and students in the Department of Counseling at the University of Georgia and at Indiana State University were very tolerant of the inconveniences caused them by our commitment to the book. Throughout the months of work, they continued to give support and encouragement.

Elaine Landes of Indiana State University provided the management skills necessary to bring the project to fruition. She was able to take the various manuscripts in their diverse forms, oversee the revisions in their various stages, and ultimately to put the manuscript into final form. Melinda Pass and Mary Cash of the University of Georgia assisted in the final stages of manuscript preparation.

Finally, our families tolerated the long hours we spent at desks rather than in other activities and, somehow, still seemed accepting of us.

To all who contributed, we thank you.

Contributors

JAMES ROBERT BITTER, PHD, Department of Counseling, California State University, Fullerton, CA 92634.

REECE CHANEY, PHD, Professor of Counseling Psychology, and Chair, Department of Counseling Psychology, Indiana State University, Terre Haute, IN 47809.

JORGE COLAPINTO, Licenciado in Psychology, Family Studies Inc., 114 East 32nd Street, New York, NY 10016.

DON DINKMEYER, JR., PHD, Associate Professor of Counselor Education, 236 Crest Lake Way, Western Kentucky University, Bowling Green, KY 42104.

DON DINKMEYER, SR., PHD, President, Communication and Motivation Training Institute, 4010 N.W. 99th Avenue, Coral Springs, FL 33075.

ALBERT ELLIS, PHD, Institute for Rational Living, 45 East 65th Street, New York, NY 10021.

RICHARD G. ERSKINE, PHD, Clinical Psychologist and Training Director, Institute for Integrative Psychotherapy, 500 East 85th Street, New York, NY 10028.

ARTHUR M. HORNE, PHD, Professor of Counseling, 402 Aderhold Hall, University of Georgia, Athens, GA 30602.

DAVID V. KEITH, MD, Associate Professor of Psychiatry, Family Medicine, and Pediatrics and Director of Family Therapy, State University of New York, Syracuse, NY 13210.

WALTER KEMPLER, MD, Director of the Kempler Institute, PO Box 1692, Costa Mesa, CA 92626.

ALLIE C. KILPATRICK, PHD, Associate Professor, School of Social Work, and Coordinator, Certificate Program in Marriage and Family Therapy, University of Georgia, Athens, GA 30602.

EBB G. KILPATRICK, JR., STM, Chaplain, Oconee Community Mental Health Center, Department of Human Resources, Milledgeville, GA 31061.

BRUCE R. LORIA, EDD, The Burlington Center for Human Growth, 464A S. Pemberton, NJ 08068.

DANIEL V. PAPERO, PHD, The Family Center, Georgetown University Medical Center, 4380 MacArthur Boulevard, NW, Washington, DC 20007.

J. LAURENCE PASSMORE, PHD, Professor of Counseling Psychology, Indiana State University, Terre Haute, IN 47809.

ELIZABETH ALLAN SCHILSON, PHD, Professor of Counseling Psychology, Indiana State University, Terre Haute, IN 47809.

LYNN SEGAL, MSW, Mental Research Institute, 555 Middlefield Road, Palo Alto, CA 94301

PETER A. D. SHERRARD, PHD, Assistant Professor of Counselor Education, University of Florida, Gainsville, FL 32611.

LOUIS THAYER, EDD, Professor, Department of Leadership and Counseling, 13 Boone Hall, Eastern Michigan University, Ypsilanti, MI 48197.

CARL A. WHITAKER, MD, Professor Emeritus of Psychiatry, University of Wisconsin Medical School, 5636 Pheasant Drive, Nashotah, WI 53058.

ROBERT E. WUBBOLDING, EDD, Department of Counseling, Xavier University, Joseph Building, 3800 Victory Parkway, Cincinnati, OH 45207.

CHAPTER 1

CHAPTER 1

Introduction

J. LAURENCE PASSMORE AND
ARTHUR M. HORNE

Mrs. Arno arrived for her first scheduled appointment at the outreach office of our mental health center. She assumed a seat across from me while Billy, her 7-year-old son, wiggled into an oversized chair. After introductions she began.

"You see, Billy has been soiling himself on and off since, well, for a long time now. He wets his pants, too, and sometimes wets the bed. He's having a real bad time at school. The kids all tease him."

I began to wonder if Billy had a medical problem. I further wondered if he had ever been adequately toilet trained. Mrs. Arno continued.

"We—my husband and I, that is— have had him to three pediatricians. They did all kinds of tests, tried different medicines, and, well, just nothing worked." I asked about toilet training. "Oh, yes, he was fully toilet trained at about 28 months and never had any 'accidents.'"

I thought about how some children who are encopretic are frequently angry; perhaps Billy's wetting and soiling were functional in some way. She proceeded.

"When I went back to work—I stopped working to have Billy and take care of him when he was an infant—I took Billy to the baby-sitter's. He didn't like the sitter. I told him he would have to go to the sitter's anyway since Mommy works now. I recall he told me that if I made him go back there, he would mess in his pants. Well, I did. And he did!"

Billy became increasingly nervous and squirmed in embarrassment. He got up on his mother's lap and lay across it as Mrs. Arno told me more. "We have tried making him clean up after he has an accident. He takes his clothes off in the bathroom, takes a shower, then dresses and puts his soiled clothes in the washer to be cleaned. He does this with his dirty sheets, too. We try not to get upset. But it's hard not to lose patience with him."

Later in the interview, Mrs. Arno revealed that she and her husband frequently quarrel over Billy's wetting and soiling and how best to deal with it. She also disclosed that Mr. Arno is an upwardly mobile, middle-level executive who is seldom at home and spends little time with Billy when he is present.

Reviewing the information Mrs. Arno provided, I ended the interview suggesting that she continue to use the behavioral clean-up procedure with Billy. I suggested several parental self-calming methods that perhaps she and her husband could employ. A second session was scheduled for Mr. and Mrs. Arno and Billy.

Every new therapeutic venture begins with the detailing of the client's life situation that stimulated the request for help. As a second step, the therapist must make some sense of the client's presentation. What sense do you, the reader, make of Billy and his wetting and soiling behavior?

Every practicing family therapist faces this general question: What is the best, most cogent, economical, practical way to understand my client-family? In the case of Billy, a number of ways to conceptualize the presenting complaint of wetting and soiling are possible. If a therapist works in a medical environment, it would not be uncommon to assume that some organic process or medication may be causing Billy's difficulty. Psychodynamically inclined practitioners may be sensitive to Billy's intrapersonal sphere and frame his problem as evidence of difficulty in object relations. The antecedent and consequent factors surrounding Billy's wetting and soiling may be the focus of learning theory-based behavioral therapy. A family systems therapist may view Billy's symptoms as a signal that the family is dysfunctional to some degree and not homeostatically balanced at the moment.

There is no "best" way to conceptualize Billy's case. The practitioner's ability to understand a case adequately is most likely a function of both the breadth and depth of his or her knowledge of family therapy theory. This introductory survey text presents a variety of theories in order to help the reader build a rich reservoir of conceptual frameworks for understanding (and making sense of) individual and family behavior as well as the process of family therapy.

Contributing authors present their theories according to a topical format, with corresponding headings. The topics, excluding summary and references, are definition, historical development, tenets of the model, application, case example, and evaluation. These same headings are used in this introductory chapter to orient you to the text.

DEFINITION

As this is a text devoted to the theory of family counseling and therapy, the terms *theory, family, counseling,* and *therapy* deserve elaboration. Additionally, an overview of the nature of the Definition section of subsequent chapters is provided.

Theory

For our purposes, theory can be loosely taken to mean points of view, or useful cognitive maps to guide the practitioner through the complexities of understanding human behavior, family dynamics, and processes of therapy. Theory represents a conceptual framework for making sense out of it all. Thus, theory in this regard does not necessarily exhibit the formal properties typically associated with so-called scientific theory.

The theories presented are not presentations of facts; that is, theory is both personal and projective. As such, theory constitutes a set of projected beliefs, observations, and constructs that are variously related or connected. These projected beliefs are connected in such a way as to help us find what we are looking for. Theory points us in certain directions. It tells us what to look for and what data to collect and attend to. In this regard, theory is self-confirmatory. Finally, theory does not state explicitly what it (we) chooses to ignore.

To put this another way: In the beginning there was the practice. Most but not all of the theories in this text were created by practitioners. Practitioners noted (superimposed) what they believed to be regularities in client presentation, family dynamics, and therapist-client-family interactions. The superimposed regularities became constructs that were discussed and eventually written about; so it happens that what we hear or read about theories of therapy is considerably removed from the practice of therapy. In short, what theoreticians do in practice is quite different from what they say they do. Does this mean theory is a lie? No! It does mean that theory is abstracted from the reality of doing therapy. Details are left out. We are all aware that we cannot speak about *everything* that we experience. (How do you tell someone what a chocolate tart with raspberry sauce *tastes* like?) The theories presented here are "maps of territories" (Johnson, 1946) in family therapy. There is some correspondence between these maps and the practice of family therapy.

Family

With some exceptions, the theories appearing in this text were generated from the study and treatment of the traditional family (the nuclear family or family of procreation). A once-married, never-divorced husband and wife with one or more children make up such a family. Reference may be made to the multigenerational family, which includes the nuclear family together with the family of origin of the mother and/or the father. Occasionally the extended family is mentioned—this includes the nuclear family and cousins, aunts, uncles, and so forth.

Several family forms are not specifically addressed by the models presented. With a divorce rate in the 1980s fluctuating between 40 and 50%, clearly there are many single-parent households, a majority headed by the mother. As rates of remarriage are substantial, there are indeed large numbers of stepfamilies, sometimes referred to as "blended" or "reconstituted" families. More recently, a small but growing number of gay and lesbian families have appeared.

The theories cited here tend to address rather generic aspects of personal and family living. While the models are use-ful for working with family forms other than the traditional family, they clearly do not specify special issues and dynamics found in alternate family forms (Chilman, Nunnally, & Cox, 1988).

Counseling and Therapy

Beginning in the late 1960s and continuing for at least a decade, a frequent question was, What is the difference between counseling and therapy? In a way, this is a trick question; it is posed without regard to who is asking and being asked, or to its context. As a result, there are many possible meanings and answers to the query.

The question can be a professional, sociopolitical one. As such, it suggests a hierarchy, or pecking order, of prestige, power, and influence. From highest to lowest, the hierarchy might look like this: psychoanalysis, psychotherapy, therapy, counseling, psychoeducation, and advising. The question may also tend to suggest variations in depth of client-family change. The depth gauge, from deepest to most shallow, can be represented somewhat as follows: personality restructuring, altered lifestyle, second-order family systems change, symptom removal, first-order family systems change, skill training, and education.

Where one conducts the therapy-counseling and who pays the professional may dictate whether one is considered to be doing therapy or counseling. Therapy is practiced in mental health centers and psychiatric hospitals. Counseling is done in university settings and public schools.

Some may argue that therapy is performed when the time frame under consideration is the (relatively) remote past, whereas counseling is done when the time frame is the proximal past or present. Others may contest that the two are distinguished according to process features.

Most factors that can be said to separate therapy from counseling tend to be differences that do not make a difference, if by this it is meant that the difference of interest is that of client-family change. For example, a full range of treatments now exists for tending to schizophrenia: pharmacotherapy, individual therapy, family counseling, and psychoeducational intervention. All have been shown to have some desired effect, singularly or in various combinations.

The overriding position in this text is that the two terms are interchangeable. They denote processes for aiding individuals and families in changing in identified and agreed-upon ways.

Chapter Definitions

In the Definition section of subsequent chapters, each author briefly delineates a model or concept of therapy. You may wish to be alert to the unit of focus for each theory. Theories vary considerably with respect to explicit attention to (a) client-family thoughts (cognitions), (b) client-family feelings (affects), and (c) client-family actions (observable behaviors). Further, theories focus differentially on the role of intrapsychic events (within individual phenomena), interpersonal events (dyadic transactions), and family events (systems dynamics) as explanatory bedrock for understanding human behavior.

Absent from the theories discussed are those that explain individual or family behavior as a function of existing medical conditions, including illness, and those attributable to medications (Levine & San-

deen, 1985), economic conditions (Chilman, Cox, & Nunnally, 1988), sociopolitical milieu, and ethnic-cultural context. Although these theories are important bases for understanding client-family behavior, they were judged to be beyond the scope of an introductory text.

HISTORICAL DEVELOPMENT

In *People in Quandaries,* Johnson (1946) wrote that "any statement you make about something at all refers in some measure to yourself" (p. 143). One may expand the comment to say that what one observes is in part a function of the total context (past and present) of the person making the observation. Taking this cue, each chapter author has included a section entitled "Historical Development." Each contributor presents some context for the theory—early life experiences, family life, professional training, special clientele studied or serviced, or research from other disciplines or within family therapy.

Early Experiences and Family Life

Some theories are very heavily influenced by the theoretician's early personal life. In a revealing account, Satir describes her experiences in her family of origin; as she suggests, there appears to be little differentiation between her personal, experiential accounting of herself and aspects of her theory. In a way, she *was* her theory. Satir represents one extreme of the projective-objective continuum. Rogers is noted to be a theorist whose formative years resulted in selected theoretical constructs. Perhaps his unconditional positive regard, genuineness, and the provision of core therapeutic conditions are outgrowths of his rural farm heritage and religious training. The early life of Adler, together with concurrent historical events in Germany, is reflected in his ideas about striving for excellence, making a contribution to the welfare of the group, and democratic family living and social equality among children and adults.

Types of Clients

A number of family therapists began to articulate models as a result of providing services to special or select populations. Glasser, confronted with delinquent girls in his consulting work at the Ventura School for Girls, was forced to rethink what he had previously learned. In the process, he developed reality therapy, which he found to be pragmatic, efficient, and effective when compared with the theoretical orientation of his training. Minuchin elaborated constructs of structural family therapy from work with highly disorganized inner-city families.

Research

Some models of family therapy are noted for their reliance on research and may be considered, in contrast to Satir's work, to be at the other end of the subjective-objective theory continuum. Brief family therapy is a fine example. Incorporating theory from cybernetics, communications, and biological systems, the constructs relate to research on the study of families with a schizophrenic child. Social learning family therapy also exhibits a tradition of research, dating to the initial theoretical work of Albert Bandura. A third example is shown in the early research of those associated with neurolinguistic programming.

TENETS OF THE MODEL

Tenets are principles that one considers to be true. In the description of models presented in this text, tenets are also central concepts. While the tenets as a whole vary greatly, they essentially relate to at least two important questions: How are the family and individual to be understood? What is to be changed? Though the question of how therapeutic change occurs may be addressed somewhat by some of the tenets, the section on application is more germane.

In the process of articulating central concepts, authors regularly provide their understanding of the healthy or functional family (individual) and of the unhealthy or dysfunctional family (individual). Additionally, some guidance about how to understand the presenting problem is frequently given. Beyond the concepts of functional or dysfunctional family and presenting problem, the models appear to have little in common regarding their core concepts. Philosophical premises along with clinical assumptions are presented. Genetic "givens" are postulated as well as family mechanisms such as multigenerational transmission.

The vocabulary is as diverse and wide-ranging as the tenets. Each model has its own argot and meaning. Proceeding from model to model, you may well wonder if there is indeed any commonality at all. Although considerable differences are apparent at the level of abstraction of a model, Frank (1981) has suggested that there are perhaps common domains across all theories of therapy. These are discussed now to help you identify likeness as well as uniqueness.

One domain is that of the client. The presenting family is viewed as bringing to the therapy both motivational and affective states that are embedded in their complaint(s). Typically, the family is in some state of demoralization, which is expressed as distress—a sense of alienation, poor self-regard, helplessness, or hopelessness. The Gestalt is that of a family that appears incompetent and unable to control their individual or collective lives, or both. Tenets having to do with healthy and unhealthy families relate to this common domain.

Structural components of theories share certain characteristics, according to Frank (1981). Of these four components, one is highlighted in the discussion of tenets. Frank suggests that each therapist has a conceptual schema for explaining to clients how they happen to be in their particular situation. Constructs related to how one views the client-family certainly provide the counselor with such schema. The remaining three structural components of theories of therapy include the therapist-client relationship, the setting wherein the therapy takes place, and a procedure or ritual for instigating and maintaining change. While select tenets may relate to these components, they are most especially addressed in the following section.

APPLICATION

In the Application section, the authors begin to bridge the gap between highly abstract theoretical constructs and the actual practice of family therapy. The *how* of therapy is addressed. Fundamental and practical questions are explored:

- What are the roles and responsibilities of the client?
- What types of clients with what types of problems are best treated from this orientation?
- What are the goals of treatment?

- What are the roles and responsibilities of the therapist?
- What specific techniques have been identified as effective?

Application and technique are designed to foster change in the client and family. Strupp (1973) has suggested that therapeutic change is due to three basic ingredients in therapy: the client-therapist relationship; a client who is adequately motivated, receptive, and capable; and specific techniques of therapist influence. He suggests that the first two ingredients are common to all therapies. Further, he believes that techniques specific to various theoretical orientations add little to the change process beyond the contributions attributed to the relationship and client factors.

Processes of change in therapy have been studied by Prochaska (1984), who has developed an interesting taxonomy, or categorization, useful in comparing and contrasting theories. Five basic processes are identified; the first three are commonly found among the so-called verbal therapies and the remaining two among the behavioral therapies. Each change process is conceived of as existing on both an experiential level and an environmental level. Essentially, the experiential level refers to change activated within the individual through direct experience. An environmental-level change process is stimulated extraindividually by changes in the environment.

Of the three change processes associated with verbal therapies, the first considered is *consciousness raising*. Experientially, consciousness raising is activated by feedback—clients monitoring their own behavior and achieving awareness of some habit, for example. Education, consciousness raising at the environmental level, is illustrated by a client being given normative information about the frequency of sexual relations among married couples.

Catharsis, suggesting emotional relief, is a second change process common to verbal therapies. Experientially, it is a corrective emotional experience in therapy. Environmentally, it may take the form of a client identifying with the character in a movie or play and experiencing relief.

Choosing is the last of the change processes common to many verbal therapies. After becoming aware of alternate choices and the consequences thereof, a client chooses in awareness and experiences self-liberation. At the environmental level, choosing takes the form of some type of social liberation. For example, choice becomes a reality through legislative change providing opportunities in education and employment for minorities.

Two change processes are associated with behavioral therapies (Prochaska, 1984): *conditional stimuli* (including counterconditioning and stimulus control) and *contingency control* (including reevaluation and contingency management).

As you read the theories contained in this text, you may want to compare and contrast them for their degree of emphasis on Strupp's basic ingredients and on Prochaska's mechanisms of change.

CASE EXAMPLE

The Case Example section provides, within the limits of the printed word, a glimpse of the actual world of therapy of each contributing author. Viewing a film or video recording of the work of each author would be perhaps the closest possible approximation to the theorist's real world of therapy. As the next closest approximation, each author provides a case in one of three formats: a typescript with or without written commentary, a case report supplemented with typescript excerpts, or a narrative case summary.

As you read each case example, you will want to assess for yourself the extent to which you believe the theoretical map provided by the author serves as a useful guide for the territory of the actual therapy. Can you "see" the theoretical constructs and applications in the case example?

EVALUATION

Is family therapy effective? This is the primary question addressed in the chapter section on evaluation. Researchers of individual and family therapy have been posing this question in various forms and attempting to answer it for more than four decades. Eysenck (1965) concludes that therapy is, for the most part, ineffective. Since his controversial study, outcome research has improved modestly in design, and better outcome measures are available. A review of outcome research in family therapy has been compiled by Gurman and Kniskern (1978, 1981). Enough research on the benefits of individual and family therapy has been done that the following generalization can be made: Persons receiving individual or family therapy are shown to benefit on several outcome measures when contrasted to no-treatment and wait-list control individuals. Additionally, a number of metanalytic studies, particularly a recent evaluation of family therapy outcome studies (Hazelrigg, Cooper, & Borduin, 1987), suggest that no one form of therapy is any better than another. That is, clients tend to benefit from therapy irrespective of the theoretical orientation.

Chapter authors address the evaluation of therapy for their respective theoretical orientations in a clinical rather than research manner, except those theories developed from research, not clinical practice. In the main, the evaluations contain valuable subjective statements collected from clients. Theoretical speculation, testimonials from professionals and laypersons, and personal impressions of the therapist or client are representative evidence of positive outcome. Referrals from patients, expressions of enjoyment by the therapist or client, and global judgments of benefit are reported. Few clinicians report systematically collected objective outcome and follow-up data.

You may ask what could or should you make of such a varied collection of reports concerning the effectiveness of family therapy? What you conclude will undoubtedly be a function of what you require as evidence. Just when you have decided what level of evidence you demand, consider that some (Haley, 1986) believe that between 40 to 60% of families may appear to get better from therapy but really improve because their life circumstances change and therapy was unrelated to the change (a condition called *spontaneous recovery*).

THEORETICAL PLURALISM

Most practitioners are not theoretical purists, nor are they true believers in one theory. Rather, they are theoretically plural—operating from some hybrid of theory. National surveys of practitioners, for example, that of Prochaska and Norcross (1983), illustrate this pluralism. A currently popular hybrid is that of object relations and cognitive behavioral approaches. Perhaps object relations theory aids the therapist in understanding the client-family, whereas cognitive-

behavioral theory guides interventions directed toward effecting client-family change.

Theoretical pluralism and eclecticism are supportable if one views theory as conceptualization. There are certainly many ways to view human behavior and therapy, and there exist a host of human behaviors to explain theoretically. Surely no one theory of therapy will adequately account for all the varieties of behavior of individuals and families. Eclectic models of therapy are beginning to appear; Norcross (1986) provides one sampling of such models.

Additionally, a theoretically well-grounded practitioner of family therapy will read beyond the confines of theory of individual and family therapy. Background reading in learning theory, social psychological theory, and group theory is warranted.

In preparing yourself conceptually for the work of family therapy, aim for broad preparation rather than narrow. Broad preparation better enables you to predict and control the therapy. You may be more able to explain, after the fact, why it made sense to do what you did in therapy, especially when in the moment of therapy you had no idea of the wisdom of your intervention. Consider the following case.

As a predoctoral intern in a college counseling center, I met Matthew, the client, about midfall 1967.

"What's going on, Matthew?" I inquired.

"Well, I'm getting worried. I've been on campus—I'm a freshman—for about two months, and now I'm real nervous."

"In what ways are you nervous, Matthew?"

"Ah, I smoke a lot now, lots more than I did in high school. And, my hands shake some. I don't get good sleep."

Matthew went on to tell me that he was missing his early morning classes (maybe making his 11:00) but was getting to his afternoon classes. Staying up late playing cards in the dorm accounted for his current sleep pattern. He had no regular exercise, was gaining weight, and was falling behind in his studies.

I asked what a typical week was like while he was a high school senior, just six months earlier. As a farm youth, he was up at 5 a.m., did his chores, ate breakfast, and went to school. Arriving home about 4 p.m., he would take a ride on his dirt bike, do farm chores, eat supper, study, and retire about 10 p.m.

I suggested that we attempt to work at reducing his nervousness by creating a schedule similar to the one he had followed most of his teenage years. Since he was going home the weekend after our session, I asked him to bring his dirt bike to campus. By chance, his roommate was teaching him how to lift free weights. I suggested that he lift weights during times he used to do farm chores, ride his bike each afternoon, and build his class and study time into a routine resembling his former high school schedule.

I saw Matthew twice after the initial session. The schedule worked well. His nervous complaints ceased, and he was going to class and completing his work.

I puzzled for some time as to why the intervention was so readily successful. Then I happened to read a book on circadian physiology (Luce, 1971) that reviews studies related to the physiological and psychological effects of changing activity schedules, prolonged isolation, gravity, and social stress. This was at a time before *jet lag* was a household term.

Wander—and wonder—in your readings.

A CAVEAT

Iatrogenic is an adjective roughly meaning physician-induced. Iatrogenic diseases for example, are attributed to the diagnosis and/or manner of treatment the physician provides to the patient. In applied psychology and family therapy, clients may incur iatrogenic psychosocial consequences from diagnosis and therapeutic treatment. Since diagnosis and treatment are in large part governed by the theories of therapy held by the practitioner, it may be said that all our theories contain iatrogenic potential.

Recall that in this text theory is considered to be an abstraction of experience, a cognitive map that only approximates the real territory of the client-family and the therapeutic process itself. The client-family risks some iatrogenic consequence of treatment, in part, to the extent that the family therapist loses sight of the fact that theoretical constructs are made up abstractions. Because we force the information we have about our client-family to conform to our a priori conceptualizations, we invite iatrogenic psychosocial disease.

A child psychologist told me a story that illustrates the caveat:

"As the 707 lifted off the runway of O'Hare on the flight to Denver, I thought about Jack. He and I had been high school buddies. And, although he went to Michigan to study engineering and I went to Missouri to study psychology, we had visited and written for some 20 years. I had not seen Jack in 2 years and was eager to visit with him and his family briefly before my conference began. I hoped the plane would be on time and Jack would be there to greet me at the gate.

Deplaning, I immediately saw Jack.

Collecting luggage after several hugs and back slaps, we made our way to his car, quickly resuming our boyish bantering. We were not in the car long when Jack told me about his 8-year-old son, Joey.

Joey had developed a 6-month history of difficulty with peers at school, conflict with teachers, and some destruction of property. As Jack related the events, I was alternately resentful in anticipation that he wanted a professional opinion from his ol' buddy and sorrowful as the parent in me empathized. Regretingly, I agreed to 'watch' Joey during my 2-day visit.

Shortly after arriving at the house, Sara, Jack's wife, showed me to my room. As I unpacked I became aware of birds chirping and shouts of children playing. Looking out the window, I surveyed the backyard and my eyes rested on Joey, who was sitting next to a large in-ground planter. He fingered pieces of chipped rock in an exploratory fashion. Eventually, he extracted a succulent night crawler and laid it out on the slate border of the planter.

As I saw him do this, flashing through my mind were all that Jack had told me about Joey and scenes and case accounts of disturbed children. I anticipated what Joey was about to do.

Joey lazily fingered the pieces of chipped rock again and selected a flat one with a sharp edge. Then, carefully, he cut the crawler in half.

(Flash: Recollections of mass murderer Charles Manson and others with an early childhood history of maiming and killing insects and animals.)

Then I heard these softly mumbled words from Joey: 'There, Mr. Worm. Now you have a friend.'"

Pathology, or empathy?

REFERENCES

Chilman, C. S., Cox, F. M., & Nunnally, E. W. (Eds.). (1988). *Employment and economical problems.* Beverly Hills, CA: Sage.

Chilman, C. S., Nunnally, E. W., & Cox, F. M. (Eds.). (1988). *Variant family forms.* Beverly Hills, CA: Sage.

Eysenck, H. J. (1965). The effects of psychotherapy. *International Journal of Psychiatry, 1,* 99–142.

Frank, J. D. (1981). Therapeutic components shared by all psychotherapies. In J. H. Harvey & M. M. Parks (Eds.), *Psychotherapy research and behavior change.* Washington, DC: American Psychological Association.

Gurman, A. S., & Kniskern, D. P. (1978). Research on marital and family therapy: Progress, perspective, and prospect. In S. L. Garfield & A. E. Bergin (Eds.), *Handbook of psychotherapy and behavior change: An empirical analysis.* New York: John Wiley & Sons.

Gurman, A. S., & Kniskern, D. P. (1981). Family therapy outcome research: Knowns and unknowns. In A. S. Gurman & D. P. Kniskern (Eds.), *Handbook of family therapy.* New York: Brunner/Mazel.

Haley, J. (1986). *The power tactics of Jesus Christ and other essays.* Rockville, MO: The Triangle Press.

Hazelrigg, M. D., Cooper, H. M., & Borduin, C. M. (1987). Evaluating the effectiveness of family therapies: An integrative review and analysis. *Psychological Bulletin, 101,* 428–442.

Johnson, W. (1946). *People in quandaries.* New York: Harper & Row.

Levine, F. M., & Sandeen, E. (1985). *Conceptualization in psychotherapy: The models approach.* Hillsdale, NJ: Lawrence Erlbaum Associates.

Luce, G. G. (1971). *Body time: Physiological rhythms and social stress.* New York: Pantheon Books.

Norcross, J. C. (Ed.). (1986). *Handbook of eclectic psychotherapy.* New York: Brunner/Mazel.

Prochaska, J. O. (1984). *Systems of psychotherapy: A transtheoretical analysis.* Homewood, IL: Dorsey.

Prochaska, J. O. & Norcross, J. C. (1983). Contemporary psychotherapists: A national survey of characteristics, practices, orientations, and attitudes. *Psychotherapy: Theory, Research and Practice, 20,* 161–173.

Strupp, H. H. (1973). On the basic ingredients of psychotherapy. *Journal of Consulting and Clinical Psychology, 41,* 1–8.

CHAPTER 2

The Therapist and Family Therapy:

Satir's Human Validation Process Model

VIRGINIA M. SATIR AND
JAMES ROBERT BITTER

INTRODUCTION

Virginia M. Satir was one of the early pioneers in family therapy. She began working with families when it was considered by many in the helping professions to be either a waste of time or even a detriment to clients. As a pioneer in a clinical field dominated by men and therapeutic notions that pertained mostly to the individual, she worked with the families of schizophrenics, hospitalized patients, and other people who were extremely hard to help. Satir used her personal presence and touch, an absolute faith in human potential, a penchant for detective work, a unique communication model, and an understanding of systems process shared by very few. And she was successful, making a difference in the growth of thousands of families all over the world.

A creative seeker and a visionary, Satir moved with the courage and determination of the profoundly and happily unorthodox. She liked to think of herself as a "homemade" family therapist in the sense that she had no formal training in family therapy. In the process of a life of discovery, Satir suggested that she simply "stumbled" on the possibility of working with the family as a treatment unit.

The authors thank two research assistants at California State University at Fullerton: Pari Pelonis for her invaluable work in preparing the typescript of the case example for the chapter, and Kim Stark for proofreading the entire manuscript.

To be sure, Satir was a role model for countless women in the helping professions. Indeed, she was a role model for all people who believed in the power of human contact and the possibility of change—people who, like herself, were more impressed with the potential for human health than the presence of human pathology.

Toward the end of her life, Satir dedicated much of her time and energy to promoting peace. The connected harmony she knew was possible in families was a metaphor for the peace she sought in the world. She believed that people centered in personal congruence and connected to others at peace with themselves could change a planet.

In July 1988, she had just returned from a month of training seminars in the Soviet Union; as she started her summer institute in Colorado, she became severely ill and was diagnosed with cancer of the pancreas and liver. Satir died September 10, 1988, as she had lived—at peace with herself and the world and full of wonder about all the possibilities in human life.

This chapter extends the original material Satir presented in the first edition of this text (Horne & Ohlsen, 1982). While change and rearrangement are inevitable, every effort has been made to stay faithful to Satir's beliefs, values, and therapeutic approach. Where possible, her model is presented in her own words, as it was in the original text.

DEFINITION

Virginia Satir used a number of different names to define her therapeutic approach, each one reflecting a slightly different emphasis in her work. When she first published *Conjoint Family Therapy* (Satir, 1983) in 1964, her emphasis was on making connections with and within families. She believed that an individual's self-esteem could be accessed through a supportive, nonjudgmental therapist's presence. It was the therapist's first task to reconnect people to the self-esteem inherent in the acknowledgment of their personal resources. Satir used her understanding of communication and metacommunication to help family members join with each other in the task of building a life together. Each connection added a piece to the whole and opened up possibilities that were blocked in the individual or the system. Therapeutic connections were the foundation of her work with families.

When Satir integrated posturing, sculpture, and movement into her therapy, the drama of families changing took center stage. She began to call her work "process therapy" (Satir, 1982), which highlights the dynamics of family interaction in a series of dramatic pictures, the system in the process of growth and evolution. Like a nurturing director of a play, the therapist is a guide, a leader in the process of change. The therapist and the family join forces to promote wellness. In Satir's model, the personhood of the therapist is more important than specific intervention skills. Therapists do not "cure" people or make change happen; they are process leaders in charge of the therapeutic experience, not the people in the experience.

During the last 10 years of her life, Satir wanted to emphasize the importance of nurturing the self-worth of people involved in the process of change. She began to call her work the "human validation process model" (Satir & Baldwin, 1983). She knew that she would encounter individuals and families who were experiencing pain and difficulty, but her focus was on wellness and growth. Therapy proceeded from all of the confirming and validating interactions and transactions, translated into methods and procedures, that moved the individuals in the family and the family system from a symptomatic base toward one of wellness.

Satir knew that all systems were balanced. The question is, what price does each part of the system pay to keep it so? The rules governing a family system are derived from the ways parents maintain personal self-esteem and, in turn, form the context within which children grow and develop their own self-esteem. Communication and self-worth are the basic components of a family system and the building blocks of the human validation process model.

HISTORICAL DEVELOPMENT

Precursors

Satir's early clinical training was essentially based on Freud's psychoanalysis. While she retained parts of this model (e.g., an acceptance of unconscious process in human behavior and defense mechanisms), she rejected its essence from the start of her professional work. Freud's emphasis on intrapsychic dysfunction and a deterministic model of pathology was essentially at odds with Satir's belief in human potential and human growth. While there is no evidence that Satir ever studied the approaches of Adler or Jung during her early training, later reviews noted parallels in her techniques to Adler's holistic orientation (Bitter, 1987) and the integrative possibilities with Jung's dynamic theory (Dodson, 1977).

Satir created her model largely from her phenomenal ability to learn from experience. Like all pioneers, she was charting unexplored territory, and she had to create the map at the same time that she entered into the unknown. Undoubtedly, she was also influenced by some of her fellow travelers, contemporaries forging change in therapeutic process and conceptualization.

The similarity of Satir's emphasis on the power of congruent communication to the work of Carl Rogers (1980) is obvious. In addition, both of these practitioners shared a belief in the importance of the fully functional and fully human person as therapist.

Satir's systems approach with families developed separately from, but at the same time as, the methodology of Murray Bowen. Gregory Bateson and Don Jackson, however, had the most direct influence on her conceptualization and utilization of systems theory in therapy.

During her life, Satir interacted with a wide range of therapists and thinkers who contributed to her growth and to the development of her model. Among them were Fritz Perls (Gestalt therapy); Eric Berne (transactional analysis); J. L. Moreno (psychodrama); Robert Assigioli (psychosynthesis); George Downing (body therapies); Ida Rolf (life-posturing reintegration); Alex Lowen (bioenergetics); Milton Erickson (hypnosis); S. I. Hayakawa (general semantics); Karl Pribram (brain research); Hans Selye (stress); Swami Rami and Alyce and Elmer Green (biofeedback); and several New Age theorists and practitioners (Brugh Joy, Jack Schwarz, Rolling

Thunder, Loma Govinda, Stan Kripner, Norman Sheeley, Carl and Stephanie Siminton, and business consultant Bob Tannenbaum) (Satir, 1982). In turn, most of these people knew and were influenced by Satir, thus fostering a cross-fertilization of thought and process that changed the frontier of therapy. Also, as always, experience was her guide in the discovery of meaning.

Satir's development was a quest. It was always at once a person-to-person pursuit and a world-transforming mission to her. It is a story told best in her own words (Satir, 1982, pp. 13–22).

Long before I had professional training, I had to work my way up from being a child. When I was 5, I decided to become a children's detective on parents. There was so much that went on between my parents that made little or no sense to me. Making sense of things around me, feeling loved, and being competent were my paramount concerns. I did feel loved, and felt I was competent, but making sense of all the contradictions, deletions, and distortions I observed both in my parents' relationship and among people outside in the world was heart-rending and confusion-making to me. Sometimes this situation raised questions about my being loved, but mostly it affected my ability to predict, to see clearly, and to develop my total being.

Becoming a detective meant becoming an observer. Naturally, I put all the clues I had together to make the best wholeness I could. This was my reality. The human brain has to make sense of what is going on, even if it is nonsense. In those days, faithfull to the format of detective stories, I needed to find out who was the "bad guy," to catch the person, then punish him or her, and subsequently bring about reform. Sometimes the culprit would be me, or one or both of my parents.

I was curious about everything, including those things I was "too young for," or that "weren't for girls." Accordingly, I developed a capacity for storing secrets, presumably without giving any clues. I loved school, was an insatiable reader, and got "very high" on ideas, particularly on knowing how things work, and what made things what they were.

Every once in a while, I would put words to some of my observations, and would tell my parents about their behavior. I got varying reactions: dismay, shame, amusement, surprise, or sometimes silence. I never knew what went into each variation. The same oral observation would get different reactions from each parent at different times. I handled this by making jokes, behaving as if I were deaf and dumb, and, many times, I behaved as though I had my attention elsewhere. I had twin brothers, 18 months younger than myself, who were quite useful in this regard.

Somewhere there was a whole world (inside human beings) that I meant to investigate. I felt a deep connection with all children. They were my troops. They were my focus. I was nearly 30 years old before it dawned on me that all adults were just children grown big. If they hadn't learned anything since childhood, they would still be doing childish things. This bit of insight helped me to understand adults a lot better.

The natural thing for me "when I grew up" was to be a teacher of grade school children. My education to become a teacher taught me about how children learn (learning theory), gave me a special appreciation and respect for the human capacity, and provided some inklings about the influence of parents on children. I was fortunate to have a group of very gifted and very human instructors who inspired me to continue to observe, listen, and draw my own conclusions. At this point, I enlarged my scope of understanding. These instructors helped me to keep a nonjudgmental attitude toward human beings. I felt like a humanistic scientist in the laboratory of children's lives.

I wanted to be a "real live" expert on children instead of an "armchair expert," so I arranged my 6 years of teaching experience in five different schools which were in different economic and social groups in widely scattered geographical areas. Some children were physically and mentally handicapped. Some

were gifted; some were racially different; and some were the so-called "average" children.

When I started teaching, it seemed natural to me that, if I wanted to help children, I needed to know their parents. So I proceeded to visit one child's home every evening after school. This home visitation program helped me develop strong bonds with over 200 hundred families during those 6 years.

Armed with a little more intellectual understanding from my undergraduate training, my observations became more focused. Through my contacts with individual family members, I soon began to put two and two together. For example, there was one youngster who seemed listless and uninterested in school and who looked like he needed help. When I got to know the family, I found that they were night owls. Everyone else could sleep late in the morning, but this lad had to get up early. I arranged a nap time for him and shared the situation with the family who then used their resources to help out. I know now that my nonjudgmental and human feelings drew them to helping me so I could help them. With their help, I was a better teacher to this little boy, and he was a better student with all of us helping.

Another lad came to school very dirty and hungry. When I investigated, I found out that his father went on binges. At night, he would lock his son out. I didn't "cure his alcoholism," but we were able to work it out so that the child was not locked out anymore.

A mother of another young boy, then 10, told me that the boy had been tied to a tree when he was 5, and genitally abused by other boys. The effect was that he often had lapses of consciousness. She asked me to protect him in woodshop so he would not injure himself while using the electric saw. He was passive and undersized. His mother told me that she had looked for help everywhere and had found none. My first response was to join her in becoming her friend. Then, feeling her support, I agreed to do what I could—knowing absolutely nothing technically about what to do to help the boy, yet trusting that somehow I would find something.

My way in teaching children was to create

an alive context, play games, do skits, paint ideas—in short, to do anything to touch their excitement and turn them on to learning. In the case of the 10-year-old boy, I initiated a project of making puppets, and then produced a fairy tale. I selected one that had a terrible "bad guy," and a "marvelously pure savior." I ended up with the young and meek little boy who had been abused playing both parts. He would stand behind the puppet curtain where no one could see him act, and he would become the most ferocious bad guy, with a voice that got bigger and bigger. And he could be a most competent good guy. After about 50 showings (we took the show around town), this child had physically grown nearly 2 inches, and his lapses of consciousness were gone. He later became a successful member of his varsity team in college and, still later, a successful professional person. It was many years before I understood what had happened.

What I was learning at this early stage was that:

1. Parents can be assets to their children if we know how to enlist their help;
2. If children have problems, something is going on in the family or has happened in the past which affects the child;
3. Difficult problems can be solved if we trust that they can and if we create a trusting atmosphere and work at gaining access to the necessary human resources.

My detective work was giving me more pieces, but I still didn't understand how they fit together. I knew that success had something to do with what goes on inside people as well as outside. I heard about something called social work, where one could learn about peoples' insides. I made plans, after 2 years of teaching, to enter summer sessions, and 4 years later entered as a full-time student. I then got caught up in the excitement of pathology, and essentially forgot what I had learned about the growing potential in people.

In graduate school, I learned about the world existing within people, and especially about something I interpreted as drives within ourselves that become powerful factors in our behavior. Since these drives are out of our awareness, they are also out of our control, as well as our understanding. In social work school, I learned intellectually about these "pathological" parts. I learned also that to help someone necessitated having rapport and investigating feelings, really a new intellectual concept to me. All of this was very exciting.

Prior to and following my graduation, for about 10 years, I worked with delinquent girls in a setting where I followed the same course I had in teaching school—that is, I attempted to get in touch with the girls' families. This job wasn't so "clinical." There were many who were listed as having either no parents at all, or mothers but no fathers. It seemed important to find out who and where their parents were. I played detective again, and I discovered the whereabouts of most of the parents, some of whom were still living, and some who had already died. In the cases where the parents were dead, I took the girls to the cemetery. The search for the parents brought me in contact with the very, very ugly part of life—mental hospitals, dirty rooming houses, death under horrible circumstances, poverty, neglect, morgues, hospitals. Regardless of all that, I had hope for everyone. I set about trying to reach the "little self-worths" in each person, which by now I knew, without any question, were present. Most of the time I succeeded in not only helping girls, but their parents too. I could enlist their help in their own behalf as well as that of their children.

I had developed a profound and unshakable belief that each human can grow. After 42 years, that belief is stronger than ever. My search is to learn how to touch it and show it to people so they can use it for themselves. That was, and still remains, the primary goal in my work. It means a special tailoring for each situation. I came to learn, upon starting clinical work, that that kind of detective work was called "diagnosis." What I had learned about awakening the hope in people was called "developing motivation."

In clinical work, I learned the psychiatric nomenclature. I could "diagnose" with confidence. This meant that I was "professional." It enabled me to talk "professionally" with my colleagues—"professional" jargonese—as well as to write impressive reports. It, however, did not always result in helping people very much.

Frequently, I felt that I was doing some kind of "name calling" when I diagnosed. My profession seemed to require it. The things in my clinical work that I was trained to look at were all negative. My sense told me that somewhere there had to be something positive. I certainly wasn't putting anything into anyone. It reached a point where I got a twinge every time I wrote a clinical diagnosis. It gradually dawned on me that it was because I was looking at only part of the picture. I began to understand why I felt so overwhelmed. I could not treat someone whom I labeled "paranoid" or "schizophrenic"; I could, however, help someone who felt empty and useless. It was the same person. By viewing that person as a person instead of a category, I could relate, and things would happen.

I learned nothing positive about other family members in my clinical training. At best, they were looked upon as dubious helpers; at worst, they were considered enemies. I had laid aside the experience I had gained as a teacher because then I was working with "healthy kids." Now, I was a clinician and was looking at sick people and their pathology. I was fast becoming a mental "ill-health" specialist.

Because I needed personal help, and because it was also felt to be beneficial professionally, I sought out the help of a classical psychoanalyst. I gained something, but the basic difficulty was never touched as I proceeded to make the same mistakes all over again. I knew there had to be something more. That search for something more put me in "no-man's land."

In 1951, at the urging of a close psychiatrist friend, I went into private practice. Now I was on the firing line. Being nonmedical, there was no liability insurance nor third-party payments for me. If I were to survive financially, I needed to get results; and if I were to survive professionally, I had to do it without making people worse, or even more scary, having my patients threaten to commit suicide.

To compound the situation, the people who initially found their way to me were either people whom no one else would touch or people who were "long-time alcoholics," "chronic schizophrenics," extremely dependent, or who had undergone treatment from others who had given up on them: they were all high risk.

Two things happened. First, knowing that all the classical treatment regimes had been tried, I realized that there was no point in my repeating them. I laid aside, for the time being, my "clinical professional self," and went back to my detective work of former years. Being a detective brought me back to observing, listening, and looking for health. Then one day, the second thing happened. After I had worked for 6 months successfully with a young girl who had been labeled "an ambulatory schizophrenic," I was called by her mother who threatened to sue me for "alienation of affection." That day, somehow, I heard two messages in her statement—a plea from her expressed in her voice tone, and a threat in her words. I responded to the plea and invited her in.

To my surprise, she agreed. I had been taught that she wasn't supposed to do that. When she came to join her daughter, lo and behold, the daughter was back at square one. When I got over my shock, I again began to observe and saw what I later came to know as the nonverbal cueing system, part of the double-level message phenomenon. This was the beginning of my Communication Theory (Satir, 1976 [1983, 1988; Satir & Baldwin, 1983]). It became clear that words were one thing, and that body language was something else.

Eventually, it occurred to me that the mother might have a husband and the girl, a father. I inquired. (In child guidance practice, fathers were excluded. Women had charge of the family.) There was a father, and he was still living. I extended an invitation to the wife and daughter to have the husband-father join. They agreed, and he came. Now I was privy to a new phenomenon. Mother and daughter had been doing well. With father's coming, a very different drama unfolded. I was now dealing with what I later came to know as the primary survival triad. This is now a conceptual cornerstone of my work. We all start life in a triad. The way this primary triad is lived is what gives us our identity. Somehow it had been assumed and seemed to be taken for granted everywhere that a triad had to be potentially destructive. The best one could hope for was to manipulate it so that it was benevolent rather than malevolent. I now know that this triad is the source of the destructive and/or constructive messages children receive. I know that in successful family therapy, the outcome rests on accomplishing a "nourishing triad" [Satir & Baldwin, 1983, pp. 170–175].

Thinking back to my brothers and sisters, I wondered one day whether there were other children in the family. Upon inquiring, I found there was a brother who turned out to be the "good guy" with his sister being the sick one. I was now in touch with what later I understood to be the family system [Satir, 1983]. I was to see this particular form many times in the future.

I was observing a new phenomenon and, being the detective that I am, I kept watching and listening, hoping to find some connection with previous experience. I extended the learning I gained with this family to all my other "patients." I eventually worked with people who were delinquent, alcoholic, psychotic, or handicapped, physically or mentally. I began to see different variations of the same theme. In the interest of survival, *people were conforming to something that worked against them.* A child would lie so mother would continue to love her; family members would say "yes" when they felt "no," and so forth.

During this period, I had a great deal of experience with people who were somaticizing. Here, I learned about the powerful link between body, mind, and feeling. The body is willing to accommodate itself to the most destructive directions issued by the mind. I began to see that the body said what the mouth denied, projected, ignored, or repressed. I saw this manifested in back problems, gastrointestinal disturbances, asthma, skin eruptions, diabetes, tuberculosis, propulsive vomiting, bedwetting, and other ailments. I also began to see that the body parts became a metaphor for psychological meaning.

It was while I was observing the body-mind-feeling phenomenon that I developed the communication stances which were later incorporated into literal body postures: placating, blaming, super-reasonable, and irrelevant (Satir, 1976, [1983]). Those stances gave a vivid picture of what was going on. When I put people into certain postures, I noticed they developed much more awareness. I know now that the physical act of posturing, which I extended into sculpting, activated the right brain experience so people could feel their experience with minimal threat. They were *experiencing* themselves, instead of only hearing about themselves. "Awareness" could be developed.

There are now many body therapies. I believe the body records all the experience one has. When the body is postured and sculpted, the old experience returns and has a chance for a new interpretation.

Once I began to get inklings that the body, mind, and feelings formed a triad, I began to see that if what one feels is not matched by what one says, the body responds as if it has been attacked. The result is physical dysfunction accompanied by either disturbances of emotion or thought.

I learned that I could see this discrepancy in the way people communicated with one another. I watched for the discrepancy between verbal and nonverbal levels of communication. I began to see that all nonverbal messages were a statement of the *Now.* The verbal part could come from anywhere, past, present, or future. Often this verbal component reflected the "shoulds" of the inhuman rules one had. The forms of discrepancy were manifest in (a) what one felt but could not say (inhibition); (b) what one felt but was unaware of (repression) and only reacted to in another (projection); (c) what one consciously felt, but since it did not fit the rules, one denied its existence (suppression); and (d) what one felt but ignored as unimportant (denial).

Out of the clear blue, in January 1955, I got a phone call from a man who was then a stranger to me, a Dr. Kalman Gyarfas. He was heading an innovative training program for psychiatric training. This was the forerunner of the Illinois State Psychiatric Institute, based in Chicago. Dr. Gyarfas was interested in the family relationship between identified patients and their family members, and he asked me to become an instructor in family dynamics for his residents.

By now, I had completed 4 years of working with families. They numbered over 300. I had been busy working with exciting ideas and had been having good results. Now to teach, I had to conceptualize what I had been doing. In doing so, I was able to clarify what I had been learning. Indeed, as I taught it, I also learned more about what I meant, and I became aware of the glaring gaps in my theoretical base.

Dealing with the psychiatric residents' experiences and their questions helped me greatly to fill in the holes and to clear up my fuzziness. New possibilities were revealed. All this training was done with state hospital patients, who were a mixture of persons in both acute and chronic states.

Here, I formulated that what I was doing was using the interaction between family members to understand the meaning and the cause of the symptom. I saw how family members cued each other on levels that they were unaware of.

I saw the need for developing an overview to understand the process. I developed something called the Family Life Fact Chronology [Satir, 1983; Satir & Baldwin, 1983] which featured what happened to a person's family over three generations: when events occurred, with whom, who went out, who came in, and other details. This was based largely on events and outcomes. I stayed away from subjective, emotional reactions. I put this chronology in a time frame so I could see the outcomes of family members' coping over time.

This chronology started with the birth of the oldest grandparents, and succeeding events were brought up through time. Since we live by time, I chronicled by time. Generally, most case and medical histories chronicled only the negative events which had emotional or medical impact. In my chronology, I wanted to have a firmly documented background with which to look at the context in which the current situation existed. This tool became the backbone of another basic technique called Family Reconstruction [Nerin, 1986; Satir & Baldwin, 1983; Satir, Bitter, & Krestensen, 1988]. Family Reconstruction is now part of my therapeutic tool kit.

Previously, when I took histories, I would file separate pieces of information, such as "when I was 5, I had several accidents." In one place, I might record: "in 1936, my brother was born," and in another place, I might read that "father lost his job when I was young," or that "mother became depressed and was hospitalized." When I put all of this into a specific time frame, it turned out "when I was 5, I had several accidents; it was also 1936. Mother was hospitalized shortly after the birth of my brother, and father lost his job at the same time." That makes a clearer picture of the stresses involved. I also began to see that outbreaks of symptoms often occurred around a clustering of stress factors.

All these facts produced a context in which one could understand better the meaning of the symptom. Instead of isolating facts, I put them in a time frame. Important new connections began to emerge. Patterns over generations became obvious. This also helped me to see people in the perspective of human life rather than only categories. Making a Family Life Fact Chronology became a requirement for those training with me. It aided them in coming to understand and appreciate the family as a context in which people lived, coped, and struggled as they responded to life events.

Sitting in my office reading a professional

journal one day in 1956, I became absorbed in an article entitled "Toward a Theory of Schizophrenia" (Bateson, Jackson, Haley, & Weakland, 1956). I remember the thrill of reading that other therapists' work affirmed what I had been seeing in my work with families. While I continued to have good relationships with my professional colleagues in Chicago, many of them later confided to me that what I was doing sounded "freaky" to them. Jackson and his associates were clearly supportive of what I was doing.

In the article, there was some information that helped me to understand better what I was doing and seeing, and some clues as to why it was working. I began combing the literature to provide a bibliography for the residents. I found a reference to Murray Bowen, Bob Dysinger, and Warren Brodey (Bowen et al., 1957), all M.D.'s who were engaged in research on schizophrenia that brought whole families to reside at the National Institute of Mental Health.

I immediately contacted Dr. Bowen. He graciously invited me to visit. He was probably as lonely as I was. At that time, working with families was unknown.

When I visited Dr. Bowen, I saw and heard so much that again validated what I had experienced and what I had conceptualized. Here was more support.

I continued to teach the residents for 3 years. Since my instructorship was only part-time, I continued my private practice. I regarded private practice as a kind of laboratory which gave me material to feed into my teaching. Then there came a significant turning point.

In 1958, I moved to California for personal reasons. Remembering "Toward a Theory of Schizophrenia," it was natural for me to contact Don Jackson when I moved to the San Francisco bay area in California. I had hardly begun to tell him about my work with families when he invited me to present my findings to his group at the Veterans Administration Hospital in Menlo Park. That group was composed of Gregory Bateson, John Weakland, Jay Haley, Bill Fry, and a few others. That was February 19, 1959. Don asked

me to come to Palo Alto and help him together with Dr. Jules Riskin to open an institute. On March 19, one month later, the Mental Research Institute was opened. It was originally conceived as an institute dedicated to researching the relationship of family members to each other, and how those relationships evolved into the health and illness of its members. The men involved agreed that family interaction seemed to behave like a system. Don Jackson and Gregory Bateson and their colleagues had studied one family in depth in which there was one "schizophrenic" member, and they had been able to conceptualize the rules of that family system and to dramatize them in a simulated family which, when heard on tape, sounded authentic. One of the rules of science is that when you replicate your experience you have discovered a new truth. Jules, Don, and I succeeded in getting a good research grant.

After a few months, I was keenly aware that research was boring to me. I felt that I needed to develop a training program, and I took it on as my next project. It was completed and opened to students in the fall of 1959. To the best of my knowledge, this was the first formal training program in family therapy. Actually, I was building on the experience I had had at the Illinois State Psychiatric Institute.

I developed a program which had three levels of training: beginning—6 weeks, one evening weekly; intermediate—twice monthly for 5 months; and intensive—1 year, 1 day per week. I started with 12 brave souls, a mixture of all the disciplines: psychology, social work, and psychiatry. (In those days, family therapy was still "freaky," and only genuine risk-takers applied.)

In 1964, at the suggestion of Gregory Bateson, I became acquainted with Eastern thought through Alan Watts and S. I. Hayakawa, a leader and student of general semantics. These contacts led to my discovering Esalen, a growth center in Big Sur, California, which had a profound effect on my professional thinking. Here I learned about sensory awareness, gestalt therapy, transactional analysis, altered states of consciousness and the so-called "touchy-feely" experiences: encounters, body therapies, and other nontraditional therapy modes.

Again, I found that the relationship between how one sees things, and how one interprets what one sees, determines the direction one takes.

I used to ask my students to state their views about (1) how growth takes place, (2) how growth becomes distorted or repressed, and (3) how the normal growth process is restored or established. The first question is related to healthy development, the second to symptom development, and the third to so-called "treatment."

I found, in the main, that most professional training had been based on pathology as being the center of attention, with health being a possible offshoot. Today, I see the strivings for health at the center with symptoms being a barrier or stumbling block to that health.

In my clinical training, I was taught to focus on ill health, which, if properly done, would result in the absence of a symptom. There was an underlying assumption that the absence of ill health was the same as the presence of health. I found this to be no more true than that the absence of hair on the female face was the same as the presence of beauty in that face.

While at Esalen, I was exposed to the concept of "affective domain" and the full use and experience of the senses, which were noted in my early training mostly for their dysfunction, but considered here in a different way.

I began to understand that seeing, hearing, and touching are experiences in themselves, and are not confined to the objects to which they are related. The experience of seeing, hearing, and touching which, in turn, is related to feeling, thinking, and moving is the essence of life. I learned that it is quite possible for a person to be so focused on what he or she is seeing that the experience of seeing is quite overlooked. For example, one may not be aware of smelling and tasting food, but only of eating it. This is probably the case with people who overeat. I observed that it is

possible to listen to the rhythm or lyrics of music without experiencing the music. I often heard people relate that they could wash their hands without the sensation of touching. I began to learn how to help people extend their awareness of their sensual reactions, and watched their sense of self-worth expand.

It was some time before I put together the idea that the right brain is the center of our feeling self and is linked to the experience of the senses; that well-being is directly linked to the feeling of vitality and, thus, directly to the development of self-esteem.

The central core of my theory is self-esteem. I now clearly see that without a direct link to the experience of the senses, there would be little change in feelings. Consequently, there would be little change in self-esteem, and therefore little real, dependable change in behavior.

This, of course, is a far cry from looking at individuals as masses of pathology. At this point, I was approaching a holistic model, the glasses through which I look at human beings. Since we were all born little, our concept of ourselves is made up of all the interactions around us, about us, toward us. We develop our concepts as a result of a system.

In 1964, I published *Conjoint Family Therapy* [Satir, 1983]. I wrote about what I had learned when I continued to use my most up-to-date glasses to view new experiences. I was always able to change my glasses when I came upon new things. Along the way, I discovered that growth was an ongoing process of sorting, adding on, and letting go of that which no longer fit.

I am compelled and impelled to understand the nature of life: what happens to stymie life, and what happens to transform it? What process makes it move and change? What factors nourish it, and what factors deplete or damage it?

Originally, I was taught that therapy was concerned with that which damaged life, and finding ways to repair it. I now see therapy as an educational process for becoming more fully human. I put my energies and attention on what can be added to what is present. To explain it in an oversimplified way, I find that when one adds what is needed to one's life, that which is no longer needed disappears, including the symptom. I call this process the concept of transformation and atrophy. I pay attention to the damage, but with the emphasis on what will develop health, instead of merely trying to get rid of what is wrong.

Many questions continue to present themselves: Does there have to be destruction in the human condition? Is it a precursor to developing strength? What are the best ways to restore health? The answers grow and change as my explorations of new possibilities continue. Exploring altered states, spiritual planes, and cosmic connections seem to be the next, natural steps to take in understanding the nature of life. What we learn may improve our day-to-day living experiences with ourselves, our intimates, and our society.

TENETS OF THE MODEL

The Human Validation Process Model is a communications/systems therapy that grew out of Satir's early work with families. Every part of Satir's approach is oriented toward growth with a belief in and focus on what people can become. Human beings are seen as unique, complex, whole individuals who grow up and live the majority of their lives in various human and organizational systems.

Satir's approach to both individuals and systems is holistic. Parts are always seen in relation to and interacting with other parts to create a dynamically changing whole. Rules are generated within individuals and among members of a system to govern the process and pattern of interacting parts.

Satir used the metaphor of the mandala to describe eight ways in which individuals grow and their life experience can be accessed (Satir & Baldwin, 1983). The first four are really the structural components of human life: the physical body; the intellect (or left-brain experi-

ence); the emotions, including intuition (or right-brain experience); and the five senses. The last four aspects are experiential needs that individuals must satisfy for ongoing growth and development: interactional or social needs, nutritional needs, contextual or life-space needs, and spiritual needs. At the center of each person is the self, the organizing, interpreting (meaning-making and esteem-processing) summation of the eight evolving aspects of the human mandala. Self-esteem is intimately linked to the meaning and value that people associate with the whole of their personal mandala.

The first task for all human beings is to survive. Indeed, survival is the main motivation for most of an infant's behavior. The first experiences of children are often characterized by alternating states of fear, satisfaction, want, helplessness, frustration, anger, striving, accomplishment, and joy. Their survival, however, is almost totally dependent on the care and nurturance provided by parents. Everything about parents (their words, tones, gestures, moods, attitudes, convictions, actions, etc.) takes on a special meaning to the baby, a survival meaning. It is the communication and posture of these important people that significantly affect the development of the child's self-esteem. Just as food, shelter, protection, and touch are essential for physical survival, parental validation nurtures the development of the self in the child.

The minute the child is born, a new system is created (Satir & Baldwin, 1983). The primary triad of mother-father-child is both an identity and a learning system for the child. Messages from parents about the child's self and behavior are interpreted and registered by the child as answers to "Who am I?"

and "What am I worth?" Within the family system, the child also learns about other people, the larger community, and relationships of inclusion and exclusion (boundaries) with both.

As Caplow (1969) and Bowen (1972) note, dynamics within a family triad can often be described as a coalition of two and the exclusion or isolation of the third person. The coalitions and isolations within triads are always changing and fluid. Caplow and Bowen seem to attach distinctly negative connotations (two against one) to triads in families. Satir did not.

While Satir recognized that negative experience is always possible, she also noted that coalitions could be formed *for* a third person as well as against that person. Indeed, infant survival often depends on the nurturing coalition the parents form for the child. High self-esteem in the parents makes a nurturing coalition (dyad) possible and provides the basis for a positive, nourishing triad with the child (Satir & Baldwin, 1983). Within a nurturing family triad, the child can find a place and a balance between personal power and cooperative effort (shared connections). The child's primary motivation of survival is replaced by the motivating desire for growth and maturation.

Growth, of course, is a lifelong process. In the same sense that Maslow (1987) refers to self-actualization as the motivation for human development, Satir knew that everything a person does is geared toward ongoing growth, "no matter how distorted [behavior] may look" (Satir, 1983, p. 24). Maturation, on the other hand, need not take a lifetime to achieve. Satir's definition of maturity is a guide for functional process and involves the effectiveness of personal congruence.

A mature person is one who, having attained his majority, is able to make choices and decisions based on accurate perceptions about himself, others, and the context in which he finds himself; who acknowledges these choices and decisions as being his; and who accepts responsibility for their outcomes (Satir, 1983, p. 118).

Again, it is the model that the parents present in the primary triad that enhances or detracts from the child's possibilities for growth and maturation. A life without problems is as impossible as a system without stress. Within families, what is experienced as a problem by one member exists as stress within the system for everyone else. For Satir, however, problems and stress are never "the problem." Coping is the problem. Functional family process and personal maturation are characterized by many of the same aspects: an openness to change, flexibility of response, the generation of personal choices or system options, an awareness of resources, an appreciation for difference as well as similarity, equality in relationships, personal responsibility, reasonable risk, freedom of experience and expression, clarity, and congruent communication.

When individuals discover effective ways of handling certain problems, they tend to return to those methods again and again. These patterns of individual coping take on the force of a personal rule: "When this . . . , do this . . ." Similarly, families develop rules that govern acceptable behavior and system process: rules about good and bad, right and wrong; rules about inclusion and exclusion; rules about required activity; rules about personal coping within the family group; and most importantly, rules about communication.

In functional families, rules are small in number, humanly possible, consistently applied, and relevant in new situations. When rules become fixed and rigid or arbitrary and inconsistently applied, when rules are invented to keep family members the same or bolster low self-esteem in the parents, the system quickly becomes dysfunctional. Chaos results, and the system loses its ability to cope. The system is in distress (Selye, 1974).

Satir used communication process to access the rules that exist within a family and to clarify the coping styles of individual members. Family members in distress are thrown back into survival mode; they invariably adopt communication patterns, defensive positions or postures, that Satir described as "blaming," "placating," "super reasonable," and "irrelevant" (Satir, 1976, 1983, 1988; Satir & Baldwin, 1983; Satir, Stachowiak, & Taschman, 1975). *Blaming* is an effort to avoid fault and put others on the defensive; it is expressed as criticism, irritation, anger, or aggressive acting out. *Placating* is an effort to avoid rejection and to make others happy; it is conveyed as constant agreement, pleasing, acceptance of fault, a willingness to follow any directive, anxiety, or self-sacrifice. *Super reasonable* describes an effort to avoid personal involvement and to gain control; it is demonstrated as an assertion of rational principles or right answers. *Irrelevant* is an effort to avoid stress and deny problems; it is manifested as distraction, distortion, changing the subject, and refusing to focus or take a stand. Each time a stance is used, the energy used to safeguard the self is diverted from the system's ability to handle problems. Still, a defensive stance is the family member's best effort at that moment in time at coping with and surviving the distress in the system. It deserves acknowledgment and an initial respect.

Satir (1976, 1988) believed in the power of *congruence* to handle stress without experiencing it as distress. Congruence is expressed in words that accurately match personal feeling and experience. There is a personal integrity in the communication, an emotional honesty. The person is alert, balanced, sensitive, and in touch with personal resources. The communication and the metacommunication match; there are no second-level, double-bind messages. "Anything can be talked about; anything can be commented on; any question can be raised; there is nothing to hold back" (Satir, Stachowiak, & Taschman, 1975, p. 49). Congruence is direct and clear; it frees energy in the system for generating options, problem solving, and creating new choices.

In its fullest sense, congruence is an expression of the personhood of the speaker. It is that personhood that Satir sought to access in every family member she encountered. Her goal was to help people find the resources they did not know they had and then to help them make full use of these new possibilities.

I equate the evolving, healthy person with a beautifully made and finely tuned instrument. Our instrument is finely made. We need to learn how to tune it better. That means developing a philosophy and an approach that are centered in human value and use the power of the seed which is based on growth and cooperation with others. (Satir, 1987, p. 68)

APPLICATION

Clients for Whom the Model Is Especially Effective

Even though this model grew out of work with clients who were extremely difficult to help and who were often highly disturbed, it is appropriate for everyone. All people start in a family. Their present outlooks reflect their early learnings in the family. Because the focus of Satir's work is on human validation and human communication, the therapist meets and works with family members as they present themselves. Whether the difficulties experienced are extreme or relatively minor, families who are in charge of their personal resources and connected to each other in a cooperative effort can face and handle whatever comes their way.

Adult life is often characterized by a striving to make a whole out of that which was a hole in the individual's early understanding. People who have serious difficulties in their present are still trying to create wholeness or make up for their past. This concept is as applicable to pairs and systems as it is for individuals.

Because the family system is the context in which people are born, raised, and live, it is essential to work with all parts of the system, the whole family. If one part is removed and isolated from the rest of the system, that part becomes alien to the primary system. Even if an individual family member is helped to change and improve, the person must eventually return to the system in which he or she lives. Once this is done, the system will either require a return to former ways of being or reject the changed member who no longer fits. When an identified patient is treated in isolation from other family members, therapy generally makes matters worse—except in unusual circumstances.

A whole family, physically present, can become a support network for all members. For the most part, the family contains the resources they need. When accessed and transformed, these resources can heal the family.

People seek therapy through many avenues, with behaviors or physical complaints that serve as a call for help or through voluntary or involuntary referrals. They may exhibit some obvious deficiency or behavior that is destructive to themselves or to others. Commonly used terms to describe such persons are schizophrenic, depressed, suicidal, delinquent, criminal, alcoholic, drug abuser, slow learner, poor and unmotivated, relationship problems, and organ difficulties (asthma, skin problems, back and intestinal problems, etc.).

People in pain may currently live in their families of origin, nuclear families, single-parent families, blended families (step-, foster, adoptive), or communal or social families. The initial unit seen in therapy may be the individual, a marital pair, parental-filial pair, a whole family, or a group. The people may be children, adolescents, adults, or geriatrics. Whatever description is appropriate, the therapist is always facing human beings who started out as children and received knowledge through learning, no matter who they are.

Satir never doubted that change was always possible. She would take whomever she could get at the onset of a therapy session; she would depend on her skills to encourage those present to bring in the rest of the family. When individuals were able to collect other members of the system for therapy, they were often exercising resources they didn't know they had, and the process change was well underway.

Goals of the Therapeutic Process

The goals and the process of therapy parallel Satir's picture of the process of change. Indeed, in a simplified sense, the entire goal and process of therapy is the facilitation of desired change in the family system. Change is learning. The context for change can always be different, but the process is the same.

The Status Quo. All people and all systems seek a balance, a homeostatic pattern of parts or transactions that allow people and systems to function in familiar ways. Once these patterns are established in the family, they become the status quo, the known and protected ways of being, participating, and belonging. Within the status quo, family members develop a set of assumptions, predictions, and expectations that help them handle the world and life. They live and count on the predictions governing the status quo.

The status quo does not have to involve happiness or functionality. To the contrary, it all too often involves pain, personal and psychological stress, abuse, or dysfunction. Unfortunately, familiarity is stronger than comfort. A symptom, for example, allows a person or system to predict; it is just based on hardened assumptions.

The status quo is always in balance. The question is, what price does everyone pay to keep the balance? In a healthy balance, everyone gives and receives to meet the collective needs of the whole. The thrust for change often comes when one or two members are paying all or too much of the price required for continued balance.

The Introduction of a Foreign Element. When anything happens to upset the balance of the system, a foreign element has been introduced. The foreign element is something new that cannot be ignored. It may be a personal or family crisis. It may be an illness or injury. It may be the intrusion of another system on the family. An initial meeting with a therapist is *always* the introduc-

tion of a foreign element into the family system.

A foreign element requires the system to address what will happen in new and largely unknown territory. At first, the system will attempt to expel the intruding element and return to the status quo. Failing this effort, a space, place, or context has to be made to help in receiving what is new to the family process. Most systems will attempt to integrate what is new into old and established patterns, as if nothing has really changed. A foreign element, however, changes everything.

Chaos. Anytime something new is added to the system, the whole configuration has to be rearranged. Family members experience this rearrangement as chaos, a highly vulnerable state characterized by fear and a loss of predictability. Everything seems out of balance and out of control. Chaos can last for a few seconds or even days.

Chaos is often experienced as being locked in an either-or (e.g., life-or-death) choice. Any movement seems at once absolutely necessary and dangerous. The resources needed to move effectively are not acknowledged or accessed within the person or the system. When confronted with or experiencing chaos, human beings first want to run to familiarity and safety. No change happens, however, without chaos. It acts as a demand on the person or system for coping. Seeing it through, with support and care, is the only chance people have for new possibilities.

New Possibilities. New possibilities exist beyond the vulnerability of chaos. They arise out of personal inspiration, a reconnection with personal resources, or a different approach when a shared effort is realized. On rare occasions, they occur simply with the passage of time or changes in environmental opportunities.

New possibilities take the person and the system out of the either-or deadlock. Real choice exists when there are at least three options for handling problems. Any new choice generated is only a possibility. Implementation involves risk, planning, a willingness to be awkward during first steps, and lots of practice. There is hope in new possibilities, and even a little excitement, but the person or the system will experience a need for concentration and a dedicated effort.

New Integration. New integration takes effect when the new possibilities implemented by the person or system become second nature. What was once new, awkward, and unfamiliar becomes with practice almost automatic. It is a recognized resource within the system. Change has occurred.

With a new integration, a new status quo is established. The system is in balance again, and predictability is newly restored. With a new integration, the person or the system experiences a state of rest and replenishment that lasts until a new foreign element requires another cycle of the change process.

With each successful cycle of the change process, the process itself becomes easier. Movement through the stages becomes known and somewhat predictable. The anxiety experienced when change is unfamiliar is less when change becomes an expected part of life.

Specific goals in therapy are related to the facilitation of the change process. The first goal is to generate hope and courage in the members of the family, to "reawaken old dreams or develop new ones" (Satir & Baldwin, 1983, p. 185). The second goal is to access, strengthen, enhance, or generate coping skills in family members. The third goal is to facilitate the development of choices and options, to develop health rather than merely eliminate symptoms, and to unlock the energy that is bottled up by symptoms or symptomatic behavior and to reorient that energy toward a positive outcome.

Therapist's Role and Function

The therapist's role and function is to guide the person or the family through the process of change. In this role, the therapist's personhood and humanness is more important than any particular set of skills. Faith in the ability of people and in systems to grow and change is essential. The therapist must know that people have the resources they need within them. The therapist's focus is on the whole of the system; problems and tasks are viewed from multiple perspectives. There are no one-directional causes in family dysfunction. Mostly, the therapist must model congruence and respond to family communication and metacommunication in a completely human and nonjudgmental manner (Satir & Baldwin, 1983).

This therapeutic posture infuses every stage of therapy with nurturance, human validation, and safety. The therapist is in charge of the therapeutic process. That leadership must be evident from the first meeting as well as when traveling through chaos with the family on the way to a new integration.

Making Contact. The first effort is to make real contact with the family via a meeting that demonstrates the feelings of value the therapist has for everyone involved in the process. This means the therapist shaking hands; focusing full attention on each person; and expressing a readiness to hear and listen, to be heard and be listened to, to see and be seen, to touch and be touched. This process sets the tone and the context for the human contact among the people who will work together.

Metaphorically, and sometimes literally, the therapist becomes a temporary companion, taking the hand of each family member and creating learning situations in which everyone can participate and benefit. This approach results in hope and trust, which in turn permits the risk of approaching life in a new, different way.

The therapist must trust that if people truly feel valued, they will allow themselves to be more fully seen. Initial contacts are aimed at engaging people as researchers of their own lives. In the beginning, the therapist may temporarily be the senior researcher. This approach counteracts the blaming that is so prevalent in families. Change in the family becomes like a puzzle—a puzzle that requires family members to become first-rate detectives, students of life, and experimenters.

Satir often visualized in images and made frequent use of metaphors. These images might be expressed directly to join with the family or be used as a basis for indirectly shifting focus. The therapist might say, "Right now, I feel as though I were in a can of worms. Does anyone else feel that way?" Most of the time, some family members do. In another instance, the therapist might relate a "family story" that is similar to what has been presented in the session but that has an ending that offers hope and encouragement.

As soon as possible, the therapist will usually make body postures of the current family communication pattern, then sculptures of their movement. People seem to find this method relatively non-threatening and are quicker to identify their underlying feelings. Within this frame, these sharings become more a statement of what is, rather than indictments of others.

Family therapy is experiential learning, a drama of real life, where many of the techniques of good theater are relevant. "I encourage people to come to know their masks and also to be comfortable enough to look at what is underneath, so they expand their universe of choice" (Satir, 1982b, p. 24).

In one sense, people present themselves as being made up of bad stuff—blame, incompetencies, and irrelevancies—that they protect through excuses, rationalizations, projections, denials, and ignorance. The therapist adds the parts that are present but in the background: the wish to be loved and valued, the wish to belong, the wish to feel and express their feelings without being judged, the wish to matter and to make a difference in the family or even in the world. The therapist reminds them of personal and family successes, however small. This expands the perspective so that background becomes more prominent in the foreground.

Chaos. Just describing the challenge (foreign element) facing the family system can initiate the stage of chaos. The therapist may be able to create hope that change can happen at this stage, but the family will not see any of the possibilities yet. Faith must come totally from the therapist-leader. It is important never to promise any specific outcome but to be willing to look for possibilities.

No matter how strong the desire in the family for retreat at this stage, the therapist-leader must not run. Chaos is an opportunity for the leader to be vulnerable, to touch and be touched, to cope from a centered position. It is important to breathe and stay grounded, to relax and find strength in the humanness and human resources present. Chaos is the leader's signal for a renewed openness to present, here-and-now experience.

When a person or system is in chaos, it is important to make no decision "that cannot be carried out in the next 10 to 15 seconds" (Satir & Baldwin, 1983, p. 219). It is not a time to decide about marriage or divorce, hospitalization, moving, changing jobs, or any other major event. In chaos, the survival fears or anxieties that people experienced as children may resurface. The risk of sharing fears, hurt, or worries—of speaking the unspeakable—is always a breakthrough in the journey through chaos.

Integration. When someone experiences something new, the therapist may look around and note that no one has dropped dead. Life is reaffirmed; new possibilities are highlighted; hope is being realized. To be sure, practice lies ahead, but the stage of integration is largely a time for temporary closure and emotional rest. It is also a time for celebration and the warmth of human connection.

A family is at once the weaver and the tapestry of the system's life. Working with a family is like weaving a new tapestry out of an old and cherished one. The therapist takes the threads from the used one, adds new ones, lets go of out-of-date ones, and together with the family's master weavers creates a new design.

Primary Techniques Used in Treatment

Family therapists must work their own life experience and professional skills and knowledge out of their own well-being and sense of being grounded. Part of their groundedness relates to their attitude toward all life and their commitment to use themselves to help their clients discover wellness within themselves.

It is important to remember that therapists are people, too, who may have faced difficulties and pain in their own lives similar to the people they are trying to help. This humanness is a significant awareness for the therapist, and it may even be important to share with family members. All of the therapist's ideals, values, and assumptions about family life get thoroughly tested when working with other families. When tested, the skills of the detective are especially important. What is going on and what would people like to have working better? What is present but not acknowledged? What change is possible? What resources are available? What wisdom is available in the therapist? How can the therapist join with the family in a human way? What skills, experiences, or techniques will make a difference? (Satir & Baldwin, 1983). Observation and intuition will usually point the therapist in an effective direction.

Throughout her life, Satir developed many tools and techniques to help her facilitate change in families. Most of her therapeutic interventions were created as spontaneous reactions to the special needs of the families or family members. Some of the techniques she developed (or used in a special way) for assessment or intervention are listed and described next.

Symptom Assessment. Any symptom signals a cessation in growth and has a survival connection to a system requiring blockage and distortion of growth in order to maintain a balance. The form differs in each individual and in each family, but the essence is the same.

Self-Esteem and the Mandala. Human beings have all the resources they need to flourish. Therapy helps people gain access to their nourishing potentials and learn how to use them. This is what creates a growth-producing system. The mandala represents eight levels of access: physical, intellectual, emotional, sensual, interactional, contextual, nutritional, and spiritual.

Family Maps. Family maps are diagrams or visual representations of family structure over three generations. Similar to genograms (McGoldrick & Gerson, 1985), a set of circles and lines is used to represent people and their relationships within the family. Three maps are used during family therapy: (a) father's family of origin, (b) mother's family of origin, and (c) the current family.

Family Life Fact Chronology (FLFC). FLFC is a holistic family history, a chronological listing of all significant events in the family starting with the birth of the oldest grandparents and proceeding through time to the present.

Ropes. Perhaps Satir's most unique intervention is her use of ropes to highlight process in family systems (Satir & Baldwin, 1983). Ropes can be used to manifest concretely the binds and pulls in the system and the many different ways in which family ties can be experienced. The feelings experienced by family members are often similar to those they have in daily life.

Sculpture. The use of sculpture often is paired with stress positions to illustrate family interactions and the ballet of the family system. People take physical postures, together with components of distance and closeness, that demonstrate their communication and relationship patterns.

Sculpture involves having all the people present (in spirit, if not in body) who impact one another. This may include, in addition to the nuclear family, the family of origin (grandparents and in-laws); significant others; household help; pets; and even, in a fitting way and at the relevant time, ex-spouses. When working with families or in groups, family members or role players can stand in for absent members.

Metaphor. Metaphor is an indirect, often parallel communication, used to speak to families symbolically or without threat. Because the metaphor creates a certain distance between the family and a threatening situation, the message is more easily heard. Metaphor may be used to convey an idea or feeling, to teach, or to suggest options that are not readily apparent. (Satir & Baldwin, 1983, p. 245).

Drama. Drama puts family metaphors, sculpture, stories, and events into motion. Through drama, the therapist is able to help family members reexperience and fully examine significant events or developments in the family's life. The process is especially important in helping children understand events that happened before they were born (e.g., their parents' first meeting or life in each parent's family of origin). "This allows them to look at the situation with new eyes and enables them to achieve new insights and develop new connections with the people they relate to" (Satir & Baldwin, 1983, p. 246).

Reframing. Reframing is often used to create a shift in the perceptions of family members. The therapist may use reframing to restructure a session away from a symptomatic focus and toward growth and change. Reframing may be used to create options or to defuse the potential for blame. "The therapist decreases threat of blame by accentuating the idea of puzzlement and the idea of good intentions" (Satir, 1983, p. 142).

Humor. Humor is an opportunity to develop perspective on ourselves, others, and events. A careful look at the human condition suggests that tragedy and comedy are often part of the same event. What is the tragedy of today can, when properly viewed, become the comedy of tomorrow.

I remember a woman who brought in her 8-year-old boy because he still ate with his fingers. When I asked her why she was concerned, her answer was that when he reached the age of 21, he would be in an important social gathering and would embarrass himself. I responded with mock incredulousness saying, "You mean in 13 years, he won't learn this!" We both laughed. Sixteen years later, this woman called to tell me that all had turned out well. Her son was now a successful psychologist. (Satir, 1982, p. 25)

Humor can add friendliness and relaxation to initial human contacts. It can be used to modify the intensity of difficult or confrontive situations; in such situations, humor often reduces the need for defensive reactions. By deliberately understating or overstating a perception, humor clarifies intent, nudges a family member in a new direction, or encourages a little movement or change. Natural humor emerges from everyday family interactions. It serves as a strengthening agent for families, giving them a new way to experience their joint difficulties.

Touch. Touch is probably one of the most healing and truly human aspects of therapy. For too long, helpers have tied their hands because too much of society associated touch only with sex and aggression. The power of touch in caregiving has been ignored. Through the use of hands, the therapist can give and receive information and provide comfort, reassurance, nurturance, and encouragement.

Satir developed two therapeutic processes specifically designed for multiple-family group therapy, each relying heavily on many of the techniques just described:

Family Reconstruction. Family reconstruction is a psychodramatic reenactment of significant events in three generations of family life. Based on the information generated through family maps and the FLFC, the experience is designed to clarify the source of old learnings and add a human perspective to parents who grew up in a different generation (Nerin, 1986; Satir & Baldwin, 1983; Satir, Bitter, & Krestensen, 1988).

Parts Party. A parts party is a drama that can be used to access and highlight the resources and characteristics of individuals within the family. Characters representing different parts of the individual are invited to a simulated party. The experience often dramatizes the inner conflicts that shackle and constrict the person's best efforts. The goal of a parts party is to acknowledge conflicting parts and transform them into a harmonious whole.

CASE EXAMPLE

The following case example is an edited typescript of a session Satir conducted with a blended family in 1968. The family is composed of Elaine, age 34, the wife and mother; Jerry, age 46, the husband and stepfather; Tim, age 16, the son; and Tammy, age 12, the daughter.

A year prior to this interview, the family decided to send the son to live with his biological father [Buddy]. His situation deteriorated to the point where he got all F's academically. The parents decided to bring the son back to this family unit. At the time of the interview, the new school year had been in progress for a month and a half. The boy refused to go to school or, when forcibly dropped at school, he refused to stay. The family was in the early stages of therapy at the time Virginia saw them. (Golden Triad Films, 1968, p. 11)

When the typescript begins, Satir has already met and greeted everyone in the family. She and the family are seated in chairs arranged in a circle.

Satir: Well, tell me: when you came here today, what did you hope would happen for you? (Turning to Jerry) Jerry, what did you hope would happen for you?

Jerry: I hoped that someone would give us more insight on what was going on, and I thought it would be to our benefit to be able to talk to you.

Satir: When you ask about some insight, it means to me that you have a puzzle of some sort that isn't very clear to you; and I wonder what that puzzle is for you, Jerry?

Jerry: Well, the insight I was talking about was, you know, the problem we're having with Tim.

Satir: Could you tell me as explicitly as possible what it is that you see Tim doing or not doing that gives you a problem?

Jerry: Well, #1. Not going to school. #2. Not wanting to work. And #3. I can't . . . beyond my wildest dreams, I can't believe a boy not wanting a car. He had the opportunity to have a car if he went to school, but he chose not to do that. The only other way to have a car is to work, but he chose not to do that. I don't care whether he goes to college or not, but I think it's very important to have a mini-

mum education. There's not too much that you can even do with that today.

Satir: Let me see if I can understand Tim not wanting a car. Were you saying that if he wanted a car badly enough that he would work or go to school? And since he isn't working or going to school, he must not want a car?

Jerry: Yes.

Satir: Well, the two might be related or not, but I think you are asking for something that you would like to see Tim have for his life somehow, that you feel he isn't doing. Is that right?

Jerry: Absolutely.

Satir: What would you like to have him have in his life that you're afraid he isn't going to get?

Jerry: I'm not sure what makes him happy, but you have to have a minimum of comforts to make you happy. Given the route he's going right now, he's not going to be able to afford them. In fact, he's not going to be able to support himself.

Satir: I picked up that you said you didn't know what made him happy. You've known Tim about 6 years? And what I hear you say is, "I haven't learned yet or found out how Tim lives inside himself, what has meaning to him."

Jerry: That's correct. I haven't.

Satir: Would you like to know that?

Jerry: I sure would.

Satir: Tammy, when you came today, honey, what had you hoped would happen for you?

Tammy: Well, I think he should be going to school.

Satir: OK. Now when your dad talked about it, that was a piece of it, but what he really came to was wanting to know what made Tim happy. Do you know what makes Tim happy?

Tammy: No.

Satir: You don't? Would you like to know?

Tammy: Yeah.

Satir: Do you know what makes Jerry happy, what makes him bubble inside and feel good about living? Do you know what makes Elaine, your mother, feel good?

Tammy: No.

Satir: So maybe in this family, people don't know how to find out what makes people happy. I don't know. Well, let's see. If you could find some ways to know what made Jerry, Elaine, or Tim happy, would you want to learn those ways?

Tammy: Yes.

Satir: Do you know what makes you happy?

Tammy: Usually.

Satir: Could you say one of the things you know for sure that when it happens you're really happy, bubbling inside with "Oh, isn't it great to be alive!"

Tammy: When I get an "A" on a test.

Satir: When you get an "A" on a test! Oh, there it is: I get an "A" on a test, and I feel, "Boy, I'm really OK." (Turning to Elaine) Well, when you came here today, Elaine, what did you hope would happen for you?

Elaine: I hoped that as a family we might get some insight. Right now, I don't want to turn down any possibility of any kind of help.

Satir: For . . . ?

Elaine: For all of us, Tim especially.

Satir: Well, let's see. You said all of us. What more would you like to find out or get in your relationship with Jerry?

Elaine: Maybe a better understanding of the best way to deal with the children.

Satir: Now, does that mean that you've noticed some ways that Jerry talks to or deals with Tim or Tammy that you wish he'd do differently?

Elaine: Jerry is basically a disciplinarian. He's very strict. Sometimes, I feel maybe a little too strict. So I maybe have a tendency not to be strict enough to maybe make up for it occasionally.

Satir: Would it go something like this? Jerry would say to Tim, "All right, Tim, I want you to do this or that." Then, you would go over to Tim and say, "Now wait. Come on, Jerry, don't be so hard on him." Is that a picture that might happen?

Elaine: Not directly to Tim. I wouldn't stand up and counteract whatever Jerry had done in front of Tim—and probably a lot of times, I wouldn't say anything. I would feel that it was too strict, but not necessarily say anything.

Satir: So here you would be with your feelings, and you would think, "Gosh, Jerry is so hard on those kids (I may be exaggerating a bit), but I can't tell him that I feel that way, because I don't want Jerry's image put down, but I feel that way, anyway." Is that kind of how it goes?

Elaine: Uh huh.

Satir: Is there any special area, any way Jerry handles situations in relation to Tim or Tammy, that you could let him know how you feel?

Elaine: Sometimes, they don't mind as well as they should. They're supposed to do, obviously, their rooms and clean up after themselves. They don't always do that, and Jerry gets very, very upset with those types of things.

Satir: Well, let's see. Would you like your house nice and clean?

Elaine: Yes.

Satir: So would you just wait longer? Or how would you handle it differently than Jerry?

Elaine: I would probably wait longer.

Satir: So you don't really differ in what you want. You differ in the way you deal with it.

Elaine: Uh huh.

Satir: So you'd like some way to get a little more clear or have Jerry hear you more about where you are on this?

Elaine: Uh huh.

Satir: Now, what changes would you like with Tammy?

Elaine: Yes. Tammy is getting a little mouthy lately. I haven't really had a problem with her in terms of discipline until Tim came back. She sees some of the things that Tim does, and I'm getting the "Well, Tim does it" or "Tim gets away with it." I really haven't had a problem with her before.

Satir: When my mother used to tell me I was "mouthy," she meant I was disagreeing with her. Is that what you're saying about Tammy?

Elaine: Talking back. Yes, disagreeing, I guess.

Satir: I have a feeling that you want to have the best-developed, best-equipped kids that they can be for life.

Elaine: Yes.

Satir: And one of the things they need to

know is when and how to disagree. We could get into something sticky here if we aren't careful, couldn't we? Something about how Tammy talks to you that makes you afraid?

Elaine: Maybe afraid of losing control.

Satir: So is it like this? "If Tammy doesn't listen to me, then she doesn't have very good judgment, and she might do some things that she would be sorry for." Is it something like that that gets into your fears?

Elaine: Yes.

Satir: OK. Is there something now that you're worried about: something that Tammy might do that you think would hurt her for life, or something like that, that you want desperately to stop her from doing?

Elaine: No, nothing *that desperate* right now. She's doing well in school. For the most part, it's her attitude, defying. She knows she's not supposed to leave the neighborhood, and she's done that a few times.

Satir: That's where the scary part comes in? What's happening to her? Do you get into that?

Elaine: Yes.

Satir: Have you ever talked with Tammy and shared with her about two things: you're scared when you don't know where she is and your worries about how she makes judgments about how to take care of herself?

Elaine: I've let her know the reason that I don't want her out after dark. Things could happen to her; so, yes, I've talked with her.

Satir: Do you think she hears you? And if she hears you, does she share the same fears you have?

Elaine: I don't think she probably shares the same fears, but I think she listens.

Satir: So that's a very important piece. You feel she listens to you. When you were growing up, and you were struggling with finding your own freedom, was there something similar that went on between you and your mother that goes on between you and Tammy?

Elaine: No, I don't think so. Mother worked quite a bit, and I started working when I was 14, so mother didn't really share a whole lot with me.

Satir: So maybe it was like Tammy not knowing what made you happy. You didn't

know what would make your mother happy—maybe not even what made her sad, only maybe what made her angry.

Elaine: Uh huh.

Satir: You didn't want to make her angry, I guess, so you learned how to say, "yes," oftentimes, when you meant "no"?

Elaine: Uh huh.

Satir: Are you still doing that in this family? Is that true here?

Elaine: Probably.

Satir: Would you like to change it?

Elaine: Yes.

Satir: OK. Now, what about Tim? We've talked about what you would like to have differently with Jerry and Tammy. What about Tim?

Elaine: I would like for Tim to go back to school. I think it's important that he get an education and prepare himself for life. At this point, he thinks that he would like to be out on his own.

Satir: Do you know what that could feel like? At 16, that feeling: "I'd just love to be out on my own!" Do you know what that feels like? Have you ever had that feeling?

Elaine: Yes, to a certain extent. I think that the difference is that I was working, and I'm not sure that Tim really knows at this point what he wants.

Satir: Could be. Could be. What I'm getting is that if you knew something about what Tim would want, you'd probably try to help him get it. Would you?

Elaine: Yes.

Satir: (Turning to Tim) Well, Tim, when you came here today, what did you want for you?

Tim: I didn't want to come.

Satir: You didn't want to come. But you got here.

Tim: I had to.

Satir: Somebody would be angry if you didn't come? Who would be angry?

Tim: Them . . . all of them.

Satir: And if somebody in the family gets angry at you, what happens for you?

Tim: I won't be able to go anywhere.

Satir: So if you can learn how to do what people in the family ask you to do, you'll get some privileges. Is that kind of how it goes?

Tim: I guess.

Satir: How does that feel to you? To feel that the only way you'll be able to get something is to do what other people tell you to do? It never went over very well with me when I was a kid. How does it feel for you? Maybe these are too hard to talk about. (Tim makes no response.) So at this point in time, am I to understand that you would like to work it out some way so that you could be more a part of the family and have more things to say about what happens to you? (Tim shrugs his shoulder slightly.) From the way you lifted your shoulder, I have a hunch that you feel it wouldn't matter what you wanted. There wouldn't be any use; it wouldn't matter. That's the feeling I got.

(Turning to Jerry) is that anything you know about, Jerry? The feeling that if I asked for something, it wouldn't matter anyway.

Jerry: Well, I think one of the problems is that he's had too much.

Satir: Too much what?

Jerry: Of everything. Whatever he wanted at the time, whether it would be from his mother or his grandparents. Up until he went to live with his father, he had everything he wanted.

Satir: Could you help me out, at least from your point of view, Jerry? What did you think would be helpful for Tim if he went to live with his father?

Jerry: Well, if it had turned out like Tim thought, and I thought it might, you know . . . (pause) My son came to live with us when he was 17, OK? And I'm not sure that a son doesn't need a father more at that age than he does a mother. I don't know, but I think that he could probably relate to a father better.

Satir: So you thought that maybe you could be helping Tim if he lived with his father a little bit, to support that idea?

Jerry: Well, I don't know whether it was that or whether I was just happy to see Tim go.

Satir: So were there already some ways in which you and Tim weren't seeing eye to eye by that time?

Jerry: Oh, I don't think Tim and I have ever seen eye to eye.

Satir: So it would be new if you ever did, huh?

Jerry: Yes.

Satir: Do you have at this moment any kind of clues at all what stops you and Tim from being able to see eye to eye, except your height?

Jerry: What prevents it?

Satir: Yeah. What do you think as you look with grown-up eyes?

Jerry: Tim is a taker, and unfortunately, I'm a giver. There's never any giving on his side that I've ever seen.

Satir: So you kind of feel that you've been putting out your gifts, and you're not getting anything in return. Is that it?

Jerry: Yes.

Satir: (Turning to Elaine) Did you know this was happening when you and Jerry were thinking about how to team up in a relationship? Because you must have had some hopes about what could happen between Jerry and Tim.

Elaine: I had hoped that Jerry would be a very positive influence on Tim.

Satir: In your experience, were you afraid that Tim didn't have enough strong influence from a man? Is that what you worried about? Because, let's see, when you came together, he was only 10. Just a young man, a very young man. But already you were worried about that?

Elaine: Yes.

Satir: (Turning to Jerry) Did you know what it was that Elaine was hoping about you coming in to father Tim?

Jerry: Well, I thought so at the time. I'm not sure anymore. As I see it, Elaine got married very young. She had Tim very young. She had a very domineering mother-in-law, who said "Jump!" and everybody would jump. And from the things that Elaine and the family have told me, Elaine had no support from Buddy as far as discipline is concerned. So I thought when she turned it over to me, and she will admit that she turned over to me the discipline of the children, that what she wanted was discipline, because they had not had any before. And I think it worked on Tammy.

Satir: So are you saying now that you feel

that maybe Elaine didn't mean that you should take it so seriously?

Jerry: I think that she did not participate, and it was left to me. She may have had feelings, but she didn't express them. And I don't do windows or read minds.

Satir: So you felt you were kind of off in left field.

Jerry: Yes.

Satir: (To Elaine) Is this a new idea that you are hearing from Jerry?

Elaine: No.

Satir: When you heard him just now, what went on inside you?

Elaine: It's basically true. It was kind of a relief for me to say, "Here are these two kids, and you kind of take over the responsibility as far as the discipline for a while." But on the other hand, I wanted it to be one, big, happy family.

Satir: I want to look at something. (To Elaine) Would you get up on this chair for me? (Virginia helps Elaine to stand on a chair.) Now, Jerry, would you stand up. I want you, Elaine, to look at Jerry, because it must be a long time that you've been looking up at him. And now I know that you are a little taller than he is, but I want you to look at him from up here. Tell me, Elaine, at this moment in time, what's you're feeling toward this beautiful man in front of you.

Elaine: Warm.

Satir: OK. Would you take a little bit of a risk and tell me what it is that you think Jerry is feeling as he's looking at you up here? Because he hardly ever sees people at his eye level.

Elaine: I think he's feeling the same.

Satir: Ask him. Would you check it out?

Elaine: (Turning to Jerry) How are you feeling?

Jerry: I feel the same.

Satir: We only have a short time together, and I want to share a hunch, OK? I heard Jerry say, "I did everything I knew to help you. And I did it in such a way, I think, that a boy I wanted to make friends with, I didn't succeed in making into a friend." (To Jerry) Is that true?

Jerry: Yes.

Satir: "And I feel bad about it at this point." (To Elaine) How do you feel hearing that from him?

Elaine: A little hurt.

Satir: OK, now, I'd like you to be aware that you, like Tim, like Tammy, like me and Jerry, at the moment we do something, it's the best we can do, or we'd do something different. What I'm hearing is that when you married Jerry, you needed so much, and you hoped for so much. I'd just like you to give yourself a forgiving message at this moment. You don't have to berate yourself. So right now, as you look at Jerry, can you think of telling him what you would like from him in relation to how he could be with Tim?

Elaine: (To Jerry) I would like you to be friends.

Jerry: And so would I.

Satir: Could you and would you be willing to remove from Jerry at this point the requirement that he be the only one who tries to give Tim help?

Elaine: I can try.

Satir: What does it feel like if you allow that to happen?

Elaine: Scared.

Satir: What do you get scared about?

Elaine: That I couldn't handle it.

Satir: Let's go step by step. Could you imagine asking Jerry to be a consultant to you—and you being a consultant to Jerry, and you and Jerry and Tim all becoming consultants to each other on how to make friends with each other where friends haven't existed for a while? Could you imagine that?

Elaine: Yes.

Satir: OK. I would like you to look at Jerry and see if you really feel you have a solid teammate.

Elaine: (Looking at Jerry) Yes, I do.

Satir: A few minutes ago, I remember you saying you'd like Jerry to do differently with Tim in some respects. Do you remember that?

Elaine: Yes.

Satir: Look at him now and tell him how you would like him to be different in relation to Tim.

Elaine: Well, I think you made one step

this week when you took Tim golfing, and I appreciated that.

Satir: Did you tell that to Tim?

Elaine: No.

Satir: Could you tell him that now? Because he may not know what in this family people appreciate and what they don't appreciate. Could you come down and tell him? (Virginia helps Elaine off the chair.) Just come close to him.

Elaine: (Sitting close to Tim, Elaine reaches to touch Tim's knee. He pulls it away from her.) I appreciated that you all went golfing together. (Tim says nothing.)

Satir: How does it feel to say that to Tim?

Elaine: It was fine.

Satir: How did you feel about Tim's response to you?

Elaine: It hurt.

Satir: What did you notice? What did you do that made you feel hurt?

Elaine: He pulled away when I touched him.

Satir: I saw you move toward his knee. I heard the feeling about it, and I saw him pull his leg away, but what did you make of that?

Elaine: He doesn't really want me around or near him.

Satir: He doesn't really want you around him. OK. Let's use that as a first working hypothesis. Could it be that at this moment Tim doesn't know whether to trust what's going on? Do you think that could be?

Elaine: Well, maybe.

Satir: Let's think of that as another possibility. Could we make another possibility that Tim would also like to participate in the choice of whether someone would touch him or not. Is that another possibility?

Elaine: Yes.

Satir: If you start thinking about those possibilities, then what happens to your feeling of being hurt by Tim?

Elaine: Maybe it was understandable.

Satir: Could you look at Tim as he is right now, and think of Tim as he is—as somebody who needs help along the road; and before we give people help, we have to know what kind they need. (Elaine nods.) And one of the funny things is that we sometimes offer help that we think other people need, but it may not *be* what they need. Has that ever happened to you? Maybe someone like your mother-in-law. "I know what you need, Elaine." Ever have that experience?

Elaine: Uh huh.

Satir: What did you feel like when your mother-in-law knew what you needed?

Elaine: I thought, "You don't know what you're talking about."

Satir: Can you imagine Tim feeling that way sometimes? "I don't know what she's talking about. How could she be asking that of me?" And when that thought comes to you, what are you aware of feeling?

Elaine: That he's probably very confused.

Virginia now turns to Tammy to check in with her. It becomes clear that in the absence of a positive feeling from Tammy, Elaine feels responsible for not being with her daughter.

Satir: I think that's been going on for you a long time. You have to be everywhere at once. I want to show you something I'm seeing. Will you get up? (They rise, and Virginia gets Jerry and Tim to stand on opposite sides of Elaine, holding her arms out and pulling.) Is that something you've ever felt in this family? (Elaine nods). Now, when you felt like this, what did you want to do?

Elaine: Hide.

Satir: OK. I want you to look over here. (Virginia takes her face and gently moves it.) My husband. My son. (Virginia reaches for a tissue and dabs the tears on Elaine's face.) What I was hearing earlier was that you were trying to bring your husband and your son together. Now, I want you to look at Jerry and say to him—we'll try this on for size—"Right now, Jerry, I want to turn all my attention to Tim." See what happens in your body when you say it.

Elaine: (To Jerry) I want to turn all my attention to Tim now.

Satir: (Virginia takes Elaine's hand from Jerry.) Now tell me how it feels to make this choice at this moment?

Elaine: Kind of cut off.

Satir: What do you think Jerry feels at this moment?

Elaine: Left out.

Satir: So if you gave your attention to Tim at a time when you were supposed to be with Jerry, you would feel cut off from him. And probably what Jerry would do is turn around (Virginia turns Jerry's back to Elaine), and he'd say he's not going to have anything more to do with you.

Elaine: Yes.

Satir: Now that's a very important thing to find out whether that's really true. Would you ask him if that's really true?

Elaine: Is it true?

Jerry: No.

Satir: Now look at him. Look at those eyes. Look at his shoulders. Look at what goes on in his face. Do you believe him?

Elaine: Yes.

Satir: Now, turn your full attention to Tim, and tell him that you're here.

Elaine: I'm here. (Tim smiles and turns head slightly away.)

Satir: What does it feel like to make that decision, because there are times when that decision needs to be made?

Elaine: It felt good.

Satir: Good. I want you to look at Tim and know that Tim and his relationship to you is a decision you make at a moment in time, and you don't lose Jerry.

Virginia now repeats the process with Jerry receiving Elaine's full attention when she turns away from Tim. Virginia continues to support the idea that Elaine can have a relationship with each man without getting in the way of their relationship.

When Tammy is asked where she fits in the family, she slowly takes a place between her mom and Jerry. Again, Elaine worries that Tim will feel left out.

Satir: Now isn't it funny. That's a worry you had. If you can't be with everyone, you'll leave somebody out, and you'll be to blame. But you know what? You can't go to the toilet that way. (Everyone laughs.) Are you ready to

go beyond that now? You notice you only got two hands.

Virginia now leads the family through all the possible triads in their system. She shifts the focus to looking at the dyads that are possible when any two people turn their full attention to each other. Finally, she asks:

Satir: Is it OK for people in this family at a moment in time to have their own special space? Can you imagine, Elaine, that you, Jerry, Tim, and Tammy can all have something, their own private space? Is that possible?

Elaine: Yes. I don't think it has been in the past.

In the last moments of the session, Virginia notes that the family will be continuing some work with their therapist:

Satir: I recommend this very strongly, because what I heard you say is that in the interest of trying to help each other, you've lost each other a bit.

Jerry: Yes.

Satir: And Tim got to be in charge, so to speak, without meaning to be. And I'd just like you to be in touch with that.

Virginia ends the session by expressing the closeness she's feeling for the family and by asking if she could share a hug with them. When she comes to Tim at the end, she asks:

Satir: I would like to hug you too, Tim. Are you ready for that? (Tim smiles and gets up slowly to hug Virginia.) I really appreciate that.

EVALUATION

Satir worked with more than 5,000 families during her lifetime. The families came in nearly every shape, form, nationality, race, income group, religious orientation, and political persuasion. She measured her effectiveness phenomenologically and clinically, using feedback from the families she helped. Like any therapist, she would meet a family from time to time with whom she could not facilitate meaningful change. These families were few and far between, especially toward the end of her career. Her personal presence and skill at human contact as well as a tenacious determination to enhance self-worth contributed to an extremely high rate of family engagement and completion of therapy.

Satir did a phenomenal amount of work in public, often before audiences of professional therapists and laypeople numbering in the hundreds—even thousands. Her public work provided a certain accountability through visibility. The human common sense of her approach was validated by the multitudes who were drawn to her presentations, demonstrations, and training programs.

Perhaps because of the tedium she associated with the pragmatics of research, Satir eschewed all but one formal study of her model and methods. In 1980, she joined the Family Research Project (Winter, 1989) in Richmond, Virginia. This project sought to assess the effectiveness of the models proposed by Bowen, Haley, and Satir. While these giants in the field of family therapy participated as consultants within the project, the delivery of family therapy services was left to practitioners specifically trained in the models under investigation. Satir chose members of her Avanta Network to implement her model.*

---

*The Avanta Network is composed of human-service providers from various disciplines who worked and trained with Satir. For more information about the training programs offered through the Avanta Network, write to: 139 Forest Avenue, Palo Alto, CA 94301.

More than 185 families were referred to practitioners working within the project. Sixty-four families were referred to the Satir group. Satir's practitioners engaged 59 families (92% of referrals) in therapy, of which 57 families (97%) completed therapy, both significantly high rates of involvement in family therapy. Families in the Satir group were seen for less than 10 hours of therapy each. Satir's practitioners used multiple-family group therapy as well as working with individual family units.

In general, the effectiveness of Satir's family therapy model was confirmed. Multiple measures of effectiveness and family change (improvement) were developed and used. Families who completed therapy made significant gains. Families who engaged in multiple-family group therapy improved more than families seen only as an individual unit. In some families, there were some differential results for individuals within the system. In the study, the differences in improvement in individuals are attributed in part to the brevity of treatment.

SUMMARY

The human validation process model grew out of Virginia Satir's lifelong quest to unlock the potential and self-esteem she knew was bottled up in every family system. There was always a detective in her who wanted to make sense out of the clues that people presented about themselves and the worlds in which they lived. Some of her training and all of her experience convinced her that a nurturing, nonjudgmental approach would unlock the meaning in human transactions and release the full potential and health of individuals.

Within this model, the therapist and the family members join forces to promote wellness. The heart of the human validation process model is the therapist's use of self as a leader of the change process and a facilitator of the family's movement from a symptomatic base to wellness.

All people are geared toward growth. A symptom is an indication that the freedom to grow is stalled by the rules in the family system, a blockage that limits the family's creative use of the context. The rules governing the family system are derived from the ways in which parents maintain their self-esteem. These rules in turn form the context within which the children grow and develop their self-esteem. Communication and metacommunication are the human vehicles by which rules are transmitted in the system and identity formation is affected and affirmed. Communication and self-worth are the foundation of the family system.

Functional family process and personal maturation are characterized by many of the same aspects. Among the most important are an openness to change, flexibility of response, the generation of personal choices or system options, an awareness of resources, an appreciation for difference as well as similarity, equality in relationships, personal responsibility, reasonable risk, freedom of experience and expression, clarity, and congruent communication.

When parents have high self-esteem, they can create an open context and a nurturing triad in which children can grow and learn to handle life. A life without problems is as impossible as a system free from stress. Within families, what is experienced as a problem by one member exists as stress within the system for everyone else. Problems and stress, however, are never the problem. Coping is the problem.

Low self-esteem will be reflected in defensive coping stances and communication patterns. Satir (1976, 1988) identified four dysfunctional communication patterns common in families: blaming, placating, super reasonable, and irrelevant. Congruence is the road to change within the family and the communication process that makes an open system possible.

The process of change always starts with a recognition of and an appreciation for the elements that constitute the status quo. The power of the status quo is its familiarity and predictability. Most often, change is motivated by the introduction of a foreign element that cannot be ignored (e.g., a family crisis, an illness or problem facing a family member, or even a session with a family therapist). A foreign element throws a person or a system into chaos and acts as a demand for a coping response. When people are helped to move through chaos, it is possible to generate new options for coping, growth, and development. With practice, these new possibilities can become fully integrated as a natural part of the person or the system.

Satir's therapeutic model is designed to facilitate and lead people through the process of change. The first task of the therapist is to make full contact with the individuals who make up the family, to build safety and hope, and to assess the status quo. When chaos surfaces, the leadership of the therapist is tested. A focus on the here and now and congruent communication are used to access the hidden family resources that are needed to create new possibilities. Integration is facilitated through practice, human validation, family celebration, and encouragement. As new and stronger processes are incorporated into the system, the family will be able to let go of what no longer fits.

The primary tool of the therapist is

the full presence of self, the complete use of one's senses, and the total interest of the "observer-detective." As the therapist engages the family, he or she may choose to assess any symptoms present for meaning; access self-esteem through the mandala; explore rules and family process through an assessment of communication and metacommunication; or examine the family system through maps, chronology, ropes, or sculpture. Throughout the process, metaphor, drama, reframing, humor, touch, family reconstruction, and parts parties can be used to promote change and free human resources.

The effectiveness of the model has been demonstrated in one major research project involving 57 families who completed therapy with the Satir group (Winter, 1989). It has also been validated clinically and phenomenologically with the thousands of families seen by Satir and members of her Avanta Network.

ANNOTATED SUGGESTED READINGS

Baldwin, M., & Satir, V. (Eds.). (1987). *The use of self in therapy.* New York: Haworth.

A collection of noted family therapists present their personal approaches to the use of self in therapy.

Bandler, R., Grinder, J., & Satir, V. M. (1976). *Changing with families.* Palo Alto, CA: Science & Behavior Books.

A collaboration on patterns of communication and the process of therapy. Bandler and Grinder later developed their concepts under the title "neuro-linguistic programming."

Bateson, G. (1972). *Steps to an ecology of mind.* New York: Chandler.

The papers and essays that first influenced Satir to adopt a systems perspective in her work, including classic works on schizophrenia.

Jackson, D. D. (Ed.). (1968). *Communication, family, and marriage.* Palo Alto, CA: Science & Behavior Books.

A collection of papers and research generated by the Mental Research Institute group in the 1960s, including papers by Satir, Jackson, and Haley.

Nerin, W. F. (1986). *Family reconstruction: Long day's journey into light.* New York: Norton.

Satir's family reconstruction process presented in detail with a forward written by Satir.

Satir, V. M. (1976). *Making contact.* Millbrae, CA: Celestial Arts.

Satir's communication model written for families and laypeople.

Satir, V. M. (1978). *Your many faces.* Millbrae, CA: Celestial Arts.

Satir's mandala and routes to self-esteem presented for families and laypeople.

Satir, V. M. (1983). *Conjoint family therapy* (3rd ed.). Palo Alto, CA: Science & Behavior Books. (Original work published 1964; 2nd ed., 1967)

The primary source for Satir's approach to family therapy that includes an essential chapter of how she met people and another on how she worked with larger systems.

Satir, V. M. (1988). *The new peoplemaking.* Palo Alto, CA: Science & Behavior Books.

An update of the original *Peoplemaking* (1972) and the last book Satir published before she died. An account of universal factors in families is presented simply to increase appreciation of what families are all about.

Satir, V. M., & Baldwin, M. (1983). *Satir: Step by step.* Palo Alto, CA: Science & Behavior Books.

The human validation process model presented. Part I is a typescript of a family therapy session with commentary added; Part II is theory.

Satir, V. M., Banmen, J., & Gerber, J. (Eds.). (1985). *Meditations and inspirations.* Berkeley, CA: Celestial Arts.

A collection of Satir's favorite meditations.

Satir, V. M., Bitter, J. R., & Krestensen, K. K. (1988). Family reconstruction: The family within—a group experience. *The Journal for Specialists in Group Work, 13*(4), 200–208.

A complete presentation in journal form of the theory, tools, and process of family reconstruction. Satir's last published work.

Satir, V. M., Stachowiak, J., & Taschman, H. A. (1975). *Helping families to change.* New York: Jason Aronson.

Based on presentations by the authors during a set of workshops, the book contains two chapters and a simulated family presented by Satir as well as an interview with her.

REFERENCES

Bateson, G., Jackson, D. D., Haley, J., & Weakland, J. H. (1956). Toward a theory of schizophrenia. *Behavioral Science, 1*(4), 251–264.

Bitter, J. R. (1987). Communication and meaning: Satir in Adlerian context. In R. Sherman & D. Dinkmeyer (Eds.), *Systems of family therapy: An Adlerian integration.* New York: Brunner/Mazel.

Bowen, M. (1972). Toward the differentiation of self in one's own family. In J. Framo (Ed.), *Family interaction: A dialogue between researchers and family therapists.* New York: Springer.

Bowen, M., Dysinger, R. H., Brodey, W. M., & Basmania, B. (1957, March). *Study and treatment of five hospitalized families each with a psychotic member.* Paper presented at the meeting of the American Orthopsychiatric Association, Chicago, IL.

Caplow, T. (1969). *Two against one: Coalitions in triads.* Englewood Cliffs, NJ: Prentice Hall.

Dodson, L. S. (1977). *Family counseling: A systems approach.* Muncie, IN: Accelerated Development.

Golden Triad Films, Inc. (1968). *Study guide for teaching tapes featuring Virginia Satir.* Kansas City, MO: Author.

Horne, A. M., & Ohlsen, M. M. (Eds.). (1982). *Family counseling and therapy.* Itasca, IL: F. E. Peacock.

Maslow, A. H. (1987). *Motivation and personality* (3rd ed., rev. by R. Frager, J. Fadiman, C. McReynolds, & R. Cox). New York: Harper & Row.

McGoldrick, M., & Gerson, R. (1985). *Genograms in family assessment.* New York: Norton.

Nerin, W. F. (1986). *Family reconstruction: Long day's journey into light.* New York: Norton.

Rogers, C. R. (1980). *A way of being.* Boston: Houghton Mifflin.

Satir, V. M. (1976). *Making contact.* Millbrae, CA: Celestial Arts.

Satir, V. M. (1982). The therapist and family therapy: Process model. In A. M. Horne & M. M. Ohlsen (Eds.), *Family counseling and therapy.* (Itasca, IL: F. E. Peacock.

Satir, V. M. (1983). *Conjoint family therapy* (3rd ed.). Palo Alto, CA: Science & Behavior Books. (Original work published 1964; 2nd ed., 1967).

Satir, V. M. (Presenter). (1968). *Blended family with a troubled boy* (Videotape No. 101). Kansas City, MO: Golden Triad Films.

Satir, V. M. (1987). Going behind the obvious: The psychotherapeutic journey. In J. K. Zeig (Ed.), *The evolution of psychotherapy.* New York: Brunner/Mazel.

Satir, V. M. (1988). *The new peoplemaking.* Palo Alto, CA: Science & Behavior Books.

Satir, V. M., & Baldwin, M. (1983). *Satir: Step by step.* Palo Alto, CA: Science & Behavior Books.

Satir, V. M., Bitter, J. R., & Krestensen, K. K. (1988). Family reconstruction: The family within—A group experience. *The Journal for Specialists in Group Work, 13*(4), 200–208.

Satir, V. M., Stachowiak, J., & Taschman, H. A. (1975). *Helping families to change.* New York: Jason Aronson.

Selye, H. (1974). *Stress without distress.* New York: J. B. Lippincott.

Winter, J. (1989). *Family research project: Treatment outcomes and results.* Unpublished manuscript, the Family Institute of Virginia, Richmond.

CHAPTER 3

The Bowen Theory

DANIEL V. PAPERO

INTRODUCTION

Human, feeling-based subjectivity manufactures innumerable explanations for why the human behaves in a particular manner at a particular time. Subjective explanations remain generally unsatisfying, and some people have sought a different, scientific understanding of human behavior to balance such subjectivity. As the 20th century turned, it seemed that a science of the human was within reach. Like a great *tsunami,* Darwin's ideas surged against and eroded the island of human uniqueness as people discovered and reluctantly acknowledged an ancient lineage. If evolution could become accepted as scientific fact, a foundation could be laid for a new human science. Freud's discoveries closely followed those of Darwin. Freud saw a new aspect of the person, and he worked toward a new theory. The secrets of human nature seemed about to open to scientific inquiry.

As the century nears its end, that early promise remains unfulfilled. A science of human behavior has not yet been achieved. The Bowen theory, however, is the product of one person's lifelong interest in such a science. While acknowledging that human behavior is not yet scientific, Murray Bowen wrote recently, "My life work has been based on an opposing viewpoint (to that which doubts the possibility of a human science). It says merely that the physical structure of the human is scientific, that the human brain *functions* to create feelings and subjective states, and that the brain is capable of separating structure from function. My premise merely states that the human is a passenger on planet earth and that sometime in the future the human can clarify the difference between *what the human is* from *what the human feels, imagines, and says"* (Kerr & Bowen, 1988, pp. 354–355).

HISTORICAL DEVELOPMENT

Bowen's lifelong journey toward a science of human behavior has been well chronicled elsewhere (Bowen, 1978; Kerr & Bowen, 1988). He reports a childhood interest and ability in science and in solving difficult puzzles. As a young physician, he explored many medical specialties. He had decided upon a residence in surgery when he entered military service presumably for 1 year in 1941. He remained for the duration of World War II. During the war years, he heard of a "new psychiatry" based on Freud that was reported to be scientific. He decided to forego the residency in surgery in favor of psychiatry. In 1946, he entered residency training at the Menninger Foundation, a center for the new ideas, in Topeka.

Bowen refers to the times in Topeka (1946–1954) as "the most important period in the development of a different theory" (Kerr & Bowen, 1988, p. 347). It became apparent to him that in spite of its many contributions, the body of ideas referred to as Freud's theory could not

48

gain acceptance as a science. The major problem concerned the subjectivity introduced when Freud selected terms to describe his thinking. His use of literary concepts moved him away from scientific facts that could be validated. No matter how valuable Freud's insights were for therapy, there was no way to bring his theoretical thinking in line with the accepted sciences.

Bowen completed the basic thinking for the new theory while at the Menninger Foundation. He refers to his movement toward a new theory as an "odyssey" and breaks it down into three phases (Kerr & Bowen, 1988). The first, *where theory has lost science,* involved much reading and working to understand recognized science's objections to Freud. The second phase, *clinical experience,* involved comparing the various concepts from literature with the actual clinical situation. During the third phase, *steps toward science,* he read extensively in all the professional disciplines concerned with humans. His goal was to understand the basic thought of each discipline and how these disciplines had managed to separate scientific fact from feeling.

A new theory emerged from this effort, that is, "a natural systems theory, designed to fit precisely with the principles of evolution and the human as an evolutionary being" (Kerr & Bowen, 1988, p. 360). He was ready to develop the new ideas in a planned manner and sought a research institution where this could be carried out. In 1954, he moved to the National Institute of Mental Health (NIMH) in Bethesda, Maryland.

Bowen spent approximately 5 years at the clinical center of the NIMH (1954–1959). He was able to bring entire families onto his research ward, which he directed in accordance with the principles of the new theory. He reports that the theoretical concepts of the emotional system and differentiation of self allowed him to predict in detail the sorts of abnormal behavior that might occur and to specify the required corrective action.

In essence, Bowen created a master theory that was always subject to revision when its predictions were inaccurate. When such inaccuracy occurred, either the theory had not been comprehensive enough or there had been an error on the part of the staff. When theory turned out to be incomplete, it was extended or modified. In this manner, the master theory developed continuously and spelled out actions to be taken. The staff's tendency to make decisions and change behavior in response to feeling could be avoided.

The new theory led to a host of new observations and findings. Concepts were developed to include in the theory alongside the emotional system and differentiation of self, among them triangles, the nuclear family emotional system, fusion, cutoff, the family diagram, projection to children, and overadequate-inadequate reciprocity. A derivative of the research was a method of family therapy based on the premise that "if the family is cause of the problem, the therapy should be directed to the family" (Kerr & Bowen, 1988, p. 361).

Recognizing that new theories and new ideas were slow to be accepted, Bowen attempted to use simple descriptive terms where possible and to avoid creating new words. Terms were borrowed from biology and used in a manner that closely approximated usage there. He kept his focus more on theory than on therapy, although the professions quickly made family therapy a major endeavor. The goal was to move toward science and to speak to researchers and basic scientists a century or two in the future, when a science of human behavior might be at hand.

Although the families involved in the NIMH research included a person called schizophrenic, Bowen's interest was in theory rather than in schizophrenia as a phenomenon (Kerr & Bowen, 1988). By 1957, Bowen was satisfied that the relationship patterns found in the research families could be seen in all families. Schizophrenia could be conceptualized, therefore, as one small piece of a broader process involving even people considered normal. The various clinical entities, each bearing a diagnosis, were part of a single continuum. As Bowen puts it, "the only difference between schizophrenia and the milder states was in duration and fixedness of the process of differentiation of self" (Kerr & Bowen, 1988, p. 367).

In 1959, Bowen moved from NIMH to the school of medicine at Georgetown University. With this decision he remained within the framework of medicine, a step he considered important for the further development of theory and the efforts to move toward the natural sciences. At Georgetown, he continued to expand on the developments at NIMH. He extended theoretical development beyond the family to work and social systems and even beyond to the larger systems of society.

Many of the theoretical concepts, initially defined separately, were integrated in the mid-1960s. This period of great effort and productivity resulted in a paper, "The Use of Family Theory in Clinical Practice" (Bowen, 1966), which Bowen notes as a milestone in his odyssey. The effort culminated in the visit to his own family (described in a well-known paper presented in 1967 to a national meeting of family therapists and published in 1972 with the authorship listed as anonymous), during which he knew he had found his way through the family emotional system. Bowen's report set off a national trend about the therapist's own family. In the rush to incorporate the extended family into the process of therapy, the professions tended to lose sight of the theoretical premises that guided the effort.

In 1968, the family faculty was formed at Georgetown. The faculty members were selected on the basis of their efforts in family research and volunteered their time. The first postgraduate training program began at this time, although the family faculty had no fixed location and conducted their activities in borrowed space at the medical center. In 1975, the faculty occupied the Georgetown University Family Center in office space located off campus but near the medical school.

During the 1970s, Bowen used the term *the Bowen theory* to refer to this work in place of family systems theory, because the latter term had come to be widely used to convey ideas that were not a part of his theoretical framework. In 1973, an additional concept concerning society was introduced to the Bowen theory. Society could be seen to go through cycles of better and poorer functioning, much as a family.

DEFINITION

A central piece of the foundation to the Bowen theory is the concept of the *emotional system*. Bowen explains what he means: "It [the emotional system] includes the force that biology defines as instinct, reproduction, the automatic activity controlled by the autonomic nervous system, subjective emotional and feeling states, and the forces that govern relationship systems. . . . In broad terms, the emotional system governs the 'dance of life' in all living things" (Bowen, 1975, p. 380). The emotional system is thought of as a guidance system, a product of a long evolutionary history, that forms the basis of behavior for all living things. The emotional system governs a creature's ability to exploit opportunities and to adjust to changes in its environment. While all organisms have such a guidance system, emotional systems differ among species and even among individuals.

A sunflower can model the operation of an emotional system. The sunflower's head follows the course of the sun across the sky; such behavior is governed by the emotional system of the species. Nevertheless, individual sunflowers may vary slightly in their ability to track the sun. Such slight variations, on a genetic level, form the basis of evolution. Living things reproduce themselves almost exactly, but the "almost" contains within it a wide range of variation when geological time and environmental factors are considered.

While genes are certainly considered a part of the organism's emotional system, that system is not seen simply as the inflexible development of a genetic code. The experience of individuals, those products of the organism's interaction with its environment that are retained, must also be included. To borrow an analogy from the world of computers, the emotional system includes both the operating system and the application programs that govern the behavior of the organism.

The emotional system of a species can work against the survival of individuals under certain circumstances. John B. Calhoun of the NIMH studies extensively the effects of population density on colonies of small mammals. From Calhoun's viewpoint, pathology can be defined as the inability to adjust to changing conditions. Any set of circumstances producing conditions with which the individual is unable to cope can be called an *ecological trap.*

As an example, Calhoun cites the lemming (Calhoun, 1967). The population of lemmings in arctic regions becomes extremely dense at regular intervals. Large numbers of these small mammals frequently die off, thereby solving the dilemma. Under some circumstances, however, the animals migrate en masse. These migrations generally serve simply to disperse the animals and relieve the population crisis. In Scandinavia, however, the tundra is marked by long valleys extending to the sea. The pressure for the lemmings to disperse (a function of their emotional systems) triggers the movement. The long valleys do not allow the animals to spread out, maintaining the pressure, with the result that the lemmings swim out to sea until they drown.

The physiological foundations of emotional systems vary considerably from early to more recently evolved forms. In single-cell organisms, chemical processes may well suffice to guide the creature through its world. With the addition of nerve tracts and a central junction (spinal column and ultimately brain), other sorts of capacities and complexities are added to the emotional system.

An obvious manifestation of the emotional system is the reactivity of the individual to its environment. It is likely that reactivity is rooted in physiology, in the cells and organ systems of the body and not just in the central nervous system. For the human, the tight stomach, sweating palms, pounding heart, and other characteristic signs of physiological reactivity frequently precede the psychological indicators of reactivity. Basic reactivity leads to reactive behavior with sufficient intensity. The organism acts automatically in a recognizable and often predictable manner. Such automatic or reflexive behavior impacts on other individuals who may react in turn. The result is a pattern of behavior for the group or unit as a whole.

Examples of human reactivity range from the subtle to the overt. A speaker's palms become damp as she hears her introduction to the podium. A mother scans her surroundings when she hears the cry of her child. A little boy cringes involuntarily when he hears his father angrily reprimanding a sibling. The muscles of a veteran tighten and his breathing becomes more rapid when he remembers a combat experience. In the middle of a difficult exam, a student begins to lose himself in sexual fantasies, and so forth.

The evolutionary course toward the family was set when sexual reproduction evolved. Mammals developed further the connection between the parent and offspring. It is characteristic for the human to form a mating pair and to live in a group comprised of the mating pair and offspring, the nuclear family. The tendency to form a family group is an aspect of the human emotional system.

Bowen observed that people vary greatly in their ability to manage reactivity. Some people seem to be continually reactive. Life tends for them to become primarily a matter of feeling well or feeling poorly. Minor changes in environment tend to produce intensely reactive postures. On the other hand, some people appear to have greater control of their reactive responses. While they react emotionally at times, they can make important decisions with careful thought

and little reactivity. Such people have a choice. They can respond to a situation emotionally or in a less reactive, more thoughtful manner.

TENETS OF THE MODEL

With this discussion of the emotional system, reactivity, and individual variation, we now approach the concept of differentiation of self. The basic idea is that different individuals have different capacities to adjust to changing conditions. Some have no choice but to yield to the environment. Others have some ability to compel the environment to adjust to them. Such a difference is a product of heredity and history.

Differentiation of Self

Bowen took the term *differentiation* from biology. From essentially the same material, cells develop, or *differentiate,* to perform separate yet related functions in the organism. In terms of the Bowen theory, differentiation of self refers to the degree to which an individual manages across a lifetime to separate emotional and thinking systems and therefore to retain some choice between behavior governed by thinking and by emotional reactivity.

One could attempt to present the distinction between the emotional system and the intellectual system in terms of objectivity and subjectivity. With the human brain dependent on a host of relays to convey information to it, complete objectivity is impossible. Nevertheless, one can distinguish between a narrowly subjective focus and a broader, objective view. Subjectivity defines self as the center of the universe, and all events and phenomena are interpreted in terms of the impact on self. The objective viewpoint sees the self as a responding part of a larger whole.

The distinction between emotional reactivity and thinking is often subtle and elusive. Some sorts of cerebration are clearly related to intense automatic processes. Easily recognized examples include the mental processes commonly called paranoia, the fantasies and mental events connected with falling in love, and those associated with intense anxiety and panic. A few characteristics of emotionally based mental processes include a narrowing perspective frequently marked by polarization (an either-or dichotomy), ambivalence, confusion, and a tendency to rely on what "feels right" and on whatever relieves discomfort. A kind of clear thought is also available to the human at least under some circumstances. A broad perspective with an appreciation of complexity is the hallmark of such thinking. Fact and knowledge are important ingredients. Feeling is recognized and respected but does not dominate the mental activity.

The basic level of differentiation of self is manifested in the degree to which an individual manages across a lifetime to keep thinking and emotional systems separate and to retain choice between thoughtful behavior and reactivity. Bowen theory postulates that the *basic level* of differentiation of self for any person develops and becomes relatively fixed early in life. For a particular individual, that level is roughly similar to that of the parents or primary caretakers. In a group of siblings, one child may be a little more differentiated than the parents and another a little less.

While the basic level is established early in life, it can be expanded in later life through disciplined effort. This is the basis of family systems therapy. The basic level of differentiation is solid and

not negotiable in the relationship system. In contrast, the *functional level* of differentiation changes in response to relationship variables. For example, one can appear principled and thoughtful with the support of a group, but when the group's approval shifts, so does the posture of the individual. With effort, one can always influence one's functional level of differentiation.

Among mammals a clearly visible movement toward group functioning can be noted, particularly in the presence of perceived threat, whether real or imagined. It is also evident in mating behaviors of a wide range of species. Bowen called this tendency in the human a *togetherness force*. Among humans, the togetherness force tends to heighten emotional functioning at the expense of intellectual functioning. The togetherness force can so intensify emotional system functioning that it overrides intellectual functioning altogether.

To value the intellectual system over the emotional misses the point, however. The human emotional system is as old as evolution itself. It incorporates within it the gigantic step that separated mammals from reptiles. Organisms need an internal guidance system operating beyond conscious awareness. Mating and attachment are as much emotional system functions as hostility and aggression. Togetherness, or the functioning of individuals as a unit, may be necessary under some circumstances for the maintenance of life itself. The blending of emotional functioning in a group, or the joining of one emotional system to another, may lie at the core of the concept of support for much of life.

Yet too much togetherness can create problems both for the individual and for the group. Individuals can become too reactive to one another. The group can so influence individual behavior that a life course becomes altered or impaired. Individuals can reach a point where they cannot function without one another, a fairly simple definition of *symbiosis*. Togetherness pressures can sweep people in directions they would have not chosen on their own and that may not be in their best interest.

Anxiety, the perception of real or imagined threat, is a critical variable affecting the balance of togetherness and individuation. Anxiety often triggers and intensifies the togetherness pressures, and the advantages of the group may not always relieve the anxiety. Differentiation has to do with the ability of the individual to maintain a degree of thoughtful autonomy in spite of the anxious pressures for togetherness. Differentiation does not deny the connectedness of people, but the well-differentiated person understands the advantages of both togetherness and individuation.

While the concept of differentiation of self occupies the center of the Bowen theory, the remaining seven concepts are closely associated with it. Each of the remaining seven concepts will be presented briefly in relationship to the concept of differentiation. Serious students of the Bowen theory will require a more thorough discussion and may consult Bowen (1978) and Kerr and Bowen (1988).

Triangles

The level of differentiation of any person governs his or her sensitivity to others, the intensity of the feeling states and responses that accompany such sensitivity, and the degree to which automatic or instinctive processes override or decrease that person's ability to guide behavior with careful reflection. The less well differentiated a person, the more his or her life decisions are rooted in the sensitivity and response to important others. The more such sensitivity governs the behavior of each party to a relationship, the more the pair acts as a unit rather than as separate individuals. When sufficient anxiety is present, such a unit behaves in a characteristic and predictable manner. The concept of the triangle describes this process.

A two-person relationship is essentially unstable. When sufficiently anxious, one of the two will automatically involve a significant third. This movement is predictable and can be known in detail. The effect of involving a third person in a tense two-person relationship can reduce anxiety. When anxiety is high, however, the basic triangle cannot contain and dissolve the tension, which results in further triangling and the activation of a web of interlocking triangles.

A clear example of the triangle exists in the affair. A spouse in a tense marriage can be involved in an affair of mild to moderate intensity that appears to have a calming effect on the marriage. The other spouse is generally not aware of the existence of a rival. Should the same affair become more intense, however, the uninvolved spouse becomes aware of it quickly and reacts by drawing others into the situation.

In a triangle, there are characteristically two relatively calm relationships and one anxious one. The intense relationship may shift around the three pairs of the triangle or may become fixed in a particular twosome. When free of anxiety, the participants may appear relatively autonomous and not intensely involved with one another. In the presence of anxiety, however, the characteristic interactions emerge predictably.

The system of interlocking triangles

comes into play when anxiety can no longer be contained within a single triangle. The system of interlocking triangles in a particular network can be mapped out with precision. When a fourth person is brought in, the original third is only discarded temporarily and can be reinvolved again. In this fashion, important others become involved in the process. Depending upon the level of anxiety in the network or family, various additional triangles are stirred up and become dormant in a regular pattern.

Nuclear Family Emotional Process

When two or more people function as an emotional unit, the greater the potential loss of autonomy for each. Pressures come into play for greater closeness and for greater distance, particularly when people are anxious. Bowen called the joining of two or more selves into a single self *fusion*. The greater the fusion of a unit, the more natural mechanisms are employed to manage the discomfort and anxiety produced by the togetherness. The greater undifferentiation in the individuals, the greater vulnerability of each to loss of autonomy to others.

Four such mechanisms or processes can be observed in the nuclear family. Generally, they involve the marital pair with others being drawn in as anxiety increases. Each of these mechanisms will be discussed briefly in the following paragraphs.

Emotional Distance. People often react to the intensity of emotional contact by pulling away. Emotional intensity, whether tinged positively or negatively, frequently produces distance, as if people were withdrawing from a hot stove. The distance can be actual, or it can be the result of a series of internal operations that effectively shield a person from contact with another. Where the distance is external, one may find a way to spend much time away from the other. He or she may seek employment that requires lengthy separations, but long work hours or great community involvement can produce the same result. In essence, opportunities for intense contact are reduced or avoided altogether. The internal processes leading to distance are often more subtle and difficult to see. Chronic irritability, involvement in an activity to the exclusion of all else, or simply "tuning out" another person all can manifest an internal shutting down of emotional contact.

Distancing occurs automatically and generally without the involved persons being acutely aware of it initially. As time passes, it comes to be an accepted way of living, so long as nothing increases the intensity of anxiety that the mechanism defuses. Efforts that one or the other makes to reduce the distance often increase it. Although distancing is a sort of safety valve built into the relationship system, it usually produces more distance than people want. What people actually seem to be avoiding is their own discomfort and reactivity to one another.

Marital Conflict. Marital conflict is generally recognized as a symptom of tension in a family, but its function as a mechanism to regulate anxiety and maintain equilibrium in a family is less well understood. Conflict can range from mild to severe. The critical variables are the degree of fusion in the relationship and the intensity of anxiety that propels the process.

Partners in conflict have high emotional reactivity to one another. Each tends to ruminate a great deal about the other, generally about the other's obstinacy and lack of caring. Conflict can flare up with little apparent provocation and escalate quickly in intensity. If the conflict exceeds the capacity of the relationship to manage it, others are brought in. In extreme examples, outside agencies (e.g., police or crisis intervention services) are attracted to the relationship and actively intervene. A familiar cycle involves conflict and ensuing distance. Conflictual episodes are followed by periods of warm togetherness. A subseqent increase in tension seems inevitable, and the closeness yields to distance and ultimately conflict once again.

One often hears concern expressed about children raised in a family with intense marital conflict. Yet from a theoretical perspective, the more anxiety that can be contained within the marital unit, the less likely it is to affect a child. Clinical observation suggests that children run a greater risk when a parent becomes anxious about the effects of marital interaction on the child. Such anxiety frequently leads to a parental effort to compensate the child in some manner. Such compensatory effort is based more in parental anxiety than in the child's need. The anxious involvement of the child with the parent is the basis for the third major mechanism of nuclear family emotional process.

Transmission of the Problem to a Child. All children become involved to a degree in the emotional process of their parents. An entire concept in the Bowen theory, the concept of the multigenerational transmission process, is based on that premise. In some families, however, the process is so intense and major that the child's functioning in life is impaired.

The process is relatively easy to describe. Anxiety in the primary caretaker is expressed in sensitivity and reactivity to a child. In effect, anxiety about the child affects the caretaker's abilty to provide basic care. The caretaker's involvement may appear as positive, loving involvement or as nagging worry and frustration. In the former, the caretaker has difficulty realistically assessing the child's behavior and development. Nothing is too good for the child, who can do no wrong in the eyes of the parent. In the latter version, the caretaker focuses on a real or supposed problem in the child. The caretaker, while wanting the child to be autonomous, appears afraid to allow the child to move beyond his or her range of guidance and control. The child comes quickly to behave as if she or he cannot function appropriately without such guidance.

To speak simply of caretaker and child is accurate but narrow. The primary caretaker is frequently one member of a breeding pair, usually the mother. Anxiety in the relationship between the parents directly relates to the involvement of the child. Lack of differentiation in the relationship directly impacts on each parent's ability to view self and the child objectively. Heightened emotionality between the parents often tends to result in the greater involvement of the caretaker and child.

To isolate the phenomenon in a particular generation of caretaker and child is misleading. That framework too easily allows the assignment of blame to the parent-caretaker and the status of victim to the child. The phenomenon sweeps across generations in a family, with each generation having some version of the relationship. Such a viewpoint also inadequately addresses the automatic, even physiological, proportions of the relationship between the caretaker and child. In intense forms, the union approaches symbiosis in the biological sense of the term. Each appears to have lost the ability to function and even to survive independently in the world.

Dysfunction in a Spouse. In many, perhaps all, marriages there are repeated compromises in which one spouse yields to the other to avoid conflict. This pattern is highly functional and is effective to a point in containing anxiety and preserving harmony. Often such adaptivity is two-sided, with each yielding to the other in different situations. In some marriages, however, the process becomes intense and relatively fixed. The result is increasing dysfunction in one partner and an apparent overfunctioning in the other. Bowen described the pattern in an early paper. "One denies the immaturity and functions with a facade of adequacy. The other accentuates the immaturity and functions with a facade of inadequacy. Neither can function in the midground between overadequacy and inadequacy" (Bowen, 1978, p. 19). In a sense, this arrangement is functional. Without someone taking charge, such families might never reach decisions. The price, however, is high.

Both people contribute to this outcome. The overfunctioning one may have been trained to decide for others in the family from which he or she came. The underfunctioning one may have been programmed to go along with the decisions of others. These postures are based in the relationship and not in particular personality flaws in one or both people. When the relationship changes, the pattern disappears. For example, when illness or injury incapacitates the overfunctioning one, the other will often display a dramatic improvement in func-

tioning that is maintained until the original relationship is reestablished.

When anxiety is low, the relationship pattern may not be evident. Under conditions of sustained chronic anxiety, the low-functioning individual may develop a physical, emotional, or social dysfunction. The course of the symptom may ebb and flow in response to levels of anxiety. The presence of such a symptom, however, across time can lead to new roles or postures for other family members in response to the dysfunctional one. Nursing and caretaker roles may ease interpersonal anxiety, but they also tend to make the symptom more intractable within the family system.

Family Projection Process

In a family, the primary caretaker's (generally the mother's) degree of emotional involvement varies among her children. Characteristically, her sensitivity and response is greater to one child than to the others. Anxiety increases her reactivity toward the child. She responds as if her anxiety were a problem in the child rather than in her. The involvement can begin even before the birth of the child. The caretaker's feelings can be intense and range from an overpositive, protective posture to revulsion. The child becomes sensitive to the anxiety in the mother and responds in ways that appear to justify her anxious concern.

Often the anxiety driving the process in a given generation rests between the parents. Each is sensitive and reactive to the other, but the basic problem between them is submerged in a concern about the child. The dysfunction of the parents as a unit leads to the inclusion of the child in the emotional process between them. When other mechanisms to regulate anxiety are effectively employed, a child may be only occasionally involved with little resulting impairment.

The process is marked initially by emotional shifts within the parental unit that are expressed in the mother's response to the child. If positive, she may overvalue, overprotect, and in general behave in ways that foster immaturity in the child. If negative, she may be overly harsh and restrictive. It is important to remember that the process appears to originate in the parent. The child quickly comes to play a role in triggering the caretaker's reactivity. While the emotional involvement is generally most observable between the mother and child, the father is equally involved in the process. The level of his own anxiety and mechanisms he employs to preserve his own functioning have great impact on the mother and the child. If he withdraws, the intensity between the mother and child increases. If he supports her concern, the problem tends to become more firmly fixed in the child.

Where the process involves only one child, other children remain relatively free from involvement. If anxiety is intense and prolonged, other siblings may become involved. The functioning of such compromised children is labile, tending to improve or deteriorate in response to anxiety in important relationships. Neither parent nor child is at fault in this process. Parents themselves have been involved with their parents to some degree, and their parents with their parents across the generations. The parents may have some awareness of the intensity of the relationships but find themselves unable to act differently. In short, the process in one generation represents the cumulative effects of what has happened in preceding generations. This is the basis for the fifth concept of the Bowen theory.

The Multigenerational Transmission Process

The family projection process, operating across the generations, results in branches of families that move toward greater and lesser levels of differentiation. People tend to pick as a mate a person of about the same level of differentiation of self. If a person, as a consequence of the family projection process, grows up with a lower level of differentiation than the parents and marries someone with a similar level, that next generation will emerge with a lower level of differentiation than that of the original parents. In this manner, across time, sections of families move toward greater and lesser levels of differentiation.

The most involved child is thought to have a slightly lower level of differentiation than that of the parents. The less involved children develop similar or slightly higher levels than their parents. This variation has important theoretical implications for life course. The higher the level of differentiation, the less vulnerable the person is to the effects of prolonged anxiety and reactivity.

The Bowen theory presumes that people marry partners with a level of differentiation similar to their own. Over the generations, therefore, the invested children of each generation marry partners with like levels of differentiation and operate with greater emotional intensity than did their parents. Their siblings create families with emotional levels as or less intense than those of the original family. From this perspective, in any family there are lines moving through time toward greater and lesser levels of differentiation. Fortuitous events in any generation can slow the process down. Similarly, unfavorable circumstances can speed it up. The ability of other mechanisms than the projection process to absorb anxiety is an important variable.

Sibling Position

In 1961, Walter Toman published *Family Constellation*. Drawing from studies of several hundred families, Toman presents a series of profiles of behavioral characteristics of individuals occupying specific sibling positions in a family. The work consolidates and clarifies an entire area of Bowen's thinking. The information about sibling position, along with the knowledge of triangles, makes it possible to see the mechanisms of the nuclear family clearly. It also makes it possible to work backward to reconstruct presumable relationship patterns in prior generations.

Toman's work involves "normal families," and it does not address the processes by which a child becomes involved in parental undifferentiation. Anxiety also plays a role in the expression of sibling position characteristics in a family. An anxious older brother can become more dogmatic and authoritarian than is the case when he is calmer. The youngest sister of several brothers may appear more helpless and needy when anxious than when not. In clinical practice, the knowledge of sibling position characteristics may provide a person a first glimpse of his or her own reactive behavior and its impact on another.

Emotional Cutoff

A basic element in the concept of differentiation of self is the notion of unresolved emotional attachment to one's parents. To manage the loss of autonomy in the relationship to the parents (and to other important figures in one's life), the person maintains a certain distance. The distance can be intrapsychic or actual. While the distance may insulate one from some of the discomfort of the attachment, he or she remains vulnerable to loss of autonomy in other important relationships.

The emotional cutoff is a natural process. On a simple level, people speak of the need for personal space or sometimes even freedom as a means of explaining their avoidance of others. Distance seems to be the safety valve of the emotional system. Yet distance also leaves people primed for but reactive to closeness. In extreme examples, people search continually for closeness but react intensely when it is at hand. Although the cutoff appears to handle the relationship to parents, the individual remains vulnerable to other intense relationships. In a marriage, a pattern and level of intensity can develop that is similar to that from which one cut off in the original family.

Emotional Process in Society

This eighth concept in the Bowen theory extends thinking to societal behavior. Bowen became interested in the way anxious, poorly differentiated parents deal with teenage behavior problems and in the way society, through its representatives, deals with the same phenomenon. The pressures for togetherness and individuation operate in society as in the family. The greater the level of societal anxiety at any point in time, the more togetherness erodes individuation. The primary generators of societal anxiety appear to be a burgeoning human population, dwindling resources, and humankind's propensity to defile its habitat.

Societal projection processes intensify in an anxious climate. Two groups join together and enhance their own functioning at the expense of a third. This is similar to the family projection process. The twosome can force the outsider into submission, the outsider can force the other two to treat him or her as impaired, or each can match the expectation of the other. It is difficult if not impossible to reduce the intensity of societal processes without first decreasing the anxiety that propels it.

The emotional climate and processes of society represent yet another element in the emotional climate of the family. The anxious society, like the anxious family, has difficulty resolving its problems without polarization, cutoff, reciprocal over- and underfunctioning, and so forth. The result is a series of crises, generally resolved on the basis of restoring comfort rather than with a thoughtful approach based upon principle, knowledge, and a degree of respect for differing viewpoints.

APPLICATION

The appearance of a symptom in an individual or in a relationship signals that anxiety within the emotional system in which the individual or relationship is embedded has exceeded the level that the natural mechanisms of that system can handle without difficulty. When anxiety can be reduced, the symptom will abate and even disappear. Whether the symptom disappears for good depends on whether the level of anxiety again reaches symptomatic range and whether more fundamental changes in the unit have taken place that reduce vulnerability.

Anxiety can be defined as the fear of real or imagined threat. More specifically, one can think of anxiety as the arousal of the organism preparatory to action to preserve the safety of the individual. Anxiety is also infectious. It spreads quickly among people, as the well-known injunction against crying fire in a crowded theater readily illustrates. The more anxious people are, the greater the tendency is for them to act automatically based on instinct and feeling. Any sort of clinical effort, therefore, must somehow initially assist the individual and the unit to reduce anxiety.

The methodology of family systems therapy is relatively simple. It is determined by theoretical considerations as much as possible. The most important goal or outcome of such therapy is improved differentiation of self (Bowen, 1974). Differentiation of self addresses the basic vulnerability of the individual and the unit to anxiety. Better differentiated people can tolerate greater levels of anxiety without losing the ability to think their way through situations. As you will recall, differentiation of self involves the ability of the individual to maintain separation of emotional and intellectual functioning, to preserve the ability to choose between reaction and intellectually directed action.

Family systems therapy attempts to assist each person to think and to gain some control of his or her reactivity. Often when people can begin to think about a situation, their anxiety decreases correspondingly. To the best of his or her abilities, the clinician attempts to relate calmly and neutrally to the family. There is no active attempt to make the family different. Interventions, or planned moves by the therapist to pressure the family to change, play little if any role. The clinician attempts to gather information, to maintain a thoughtful and broad perspective, to remain emotionally neutral, and to preserve an attitude of interested inquiry as much as possible.

The effort of the clinician to maintain an investigative or inquiring attitude is important and easily overlooked in efforts to apply the Bowen theory in clinical practice. The facts of the family are important. The facts lead to innumerable questions about the processes of the family. Real questions—that is, questions aimed only at acquiring information—assist the clinician to know more about the family and family to know more about itself. No single piece of information is particularly important, but each fact leads to further inquiry and a clearer view of how the emotional system of the individual and of the family operate to create the mosaic of life.

Family systems therapy does not require the presence of all family members. Often the two spouses, considered the responsible architects of the family, are seen together in clinical practice. This general guideline is not hard and fast, however. Other members of the family may be seen at different times as motivation shifts among family members and the clinician attempts to learn more about the family. In the late 1960s, Bowen's theoretical work led to an approach that included only one member of the family in the session. This development will be discussed later.

Bowen (1971) lists four main functions for the therapist with the spouses: (a) defining and clarifying the relationship between spouses, (b) keeping self detriangled from the family emotional system, (c) teaching the functioning of emotional systems, and (d) demonstrating differentiation by managing self during the course of therapy. Each function is rooted in theory and will be discussed more fully in the following paragraphs.

Defining and Clarifying the Emotional Process between Spouses

In a family, people become sensitive and reactive to one another. Spouses recognize each other's emotional sensitivities and reactivity quite well, knowing how to stir up the other's reactivity as well as how to calm the other down. Over time, the sensitive areas between people tend to be avoided in conversation and general interaction. When such areas are entered, an emotional chain reaction tends to occur with each reacting to the other in an increasing crescendo. The chain reaction can be loud or quiet, but it tends to hamper substantially the people's efforts to resolve differences and address problems.

The format of therapy aids the therapist in controlling the interchange between spouses. The clinician talks directly to one, often employing low-key questions, while the other listens. The questions and comments are directed to the thinking rather than the feelings of each person. They elicit observations about reactivity, both in self and in other. Often such a dialogue between clinician and spouse allows the listening partner to hear the other's views and thoughts about matters important to both. It is not unusual for one or the other to comment that his or her partner's views are particularly interesting and new to them. Spouses sometimes come to look forward to the sessions as an opportunity to learn more about one another.

When it becomes clear that feelings and reactivity are being stirred up, the clinician may increase the tempo of the questions, asking people to talk about the feelings rather than expressing them directly at the other person. For example, when tears come into the eyes of one, the clinician may ask the other if he or she noticed the tears and what kinds of thoughts the tears produced. When anger threatens to lead to direct conflict, the therapist can step up the pace and accentuate the low-key nature of the questions. What are the triggers that set off the chain reaction? What is there about self that makes the other so mad? What sort of formula have they worked out to slow the chain reaction when it threatens to run away with them? An important goal is to touch upon emotionally important issues and elicit thoughtful, calm responses (Bowen, 1971).

Keeping Self Detriangled from the Family Emotional Process

The emotional process between two people reaches out frequently to involve an important other. This is the process of the triangle described previously. When that third can remain in active contact with each of the others while remaining outside the emotional field between them, the emotional reactivity in the original twosome can resolve itself (Bowen, 1966, 1971). This is the theoretical basis for the task of maintaining emotional neutrality.

There are innumerable ways in which a clinician can take sides in the emotional process between the spouses. This can occur as easily when the clinician is quiet as when active. This is not much different from the manner in which he or she took sides in the process between his or her own parents. When one takes sides, one has joined the emotional process in the family. The effort to remain emotionally neutral is a central challenging task for the clinician in any clinical session. The effort to detriangle oneself from the family emotional process is the same as the effort to remain neutral.

When the clinician becomes absorbed in the content issues of the family, neutrality is easily compromised. A family can produce issues without end. When one such issue is apparently resolved, the family can produce another. The original issue can appear again at a later time

as if it were a new topic. General themes of content include sex, money, and children and tend to revolve around the emotional themes of right and wrong, fairness, and rights.

When the therapist can find a relatively objective, neutral position from which to relate to the family, the flow of emotion between people and patterns of reactivity become apparent. Bowen (1971) comments on a position that is neither too close nor too distant from the emotional process of the family. From that point, he is able to watch the emotional flow and view the process without becoming entangled. He is able to comment either seriously or with humor.

Such flexibility is the hallmark of the clinician who understands the nature of triangles and manages self well within them. It is not so much what the therapist says but his or her emotional position that is important. When caught in the family emotional process, almost anything he or she says produces reactivity in the family. When the clinician is neutral, almost anything he or she says aids thought and eases anxiety. To be neutral is more than being humorous. Often light humor can dissolve the tension of an overly serious presentation of content. But the pursuit of humor can mark the therapist's own reactivity to the family. The idea is to relate to the emotionally difficult areas for the family without becoming a part of its emotional system.

Demonstrating Differentiation by Managing Self during Therapy

The pressures toward togetherness operate between the clinician and family members just as within the family itself. When a person can state his or her convictions and principles clearly and then act in accordance with such beliefs, it is possible for the togetherness pressures to abate. In defining and acting on such a position, the clinician does not criticize the family or become involved in a feeling-laden debate. Bowen referred to this firm position for self as an *I-position*.

The I-position is more than a simple technique. It requires that the clinician have a clear grasp of his or her responsibility, particularly at times when the family emotional system is pressing him or her toward irresponsibility. The I-position is a movement to define and preserve self in the face of pressures to make all the same. With experience, a clinician can become familiar with routine sorts of situations that require a clear definition of self to a family. Nevertheless, anxious families can present unique situations without clear precedents, testing to the limits of the clinician's differentiation of self.

The I-position can be a simple statement of disagreement: "I'm listening to your words, but I don't agree with what you're saying." More complex and intense situations involve pressures for or against hospitalization, suicidal threats and gestures, pressures from the community, and a host of other efforts to press the clinician to behave in a manner contrary to his or her principles and responsibilities.

Teaching the Functioning of Emotional Systems

Teaching about emotional systems is a natural part of assisting people to think about their situation and to work at managing their reactivity. Timing plays an important role in teaching. Early in the course of therapy and when anxiety is high, the clinician teaches by example. I-positions are part of the effort, and stories can help make a point that could not be heard if stated directly. When anxiety is low, ideas and comments can be presented more directly without problem. At such times, family members can hear ideas and consider them thoughtfully.

While the effort with two spouses remains an effective method of family therapy, it is not the only method derived from the Bowen theory. In the late 1960s, Bowen presented an account of his efforts to manage himself in his own family to a conference of well-known family therapists. The ideas presented there began to enter his teaching efforts at Georgetown. He soon observed the students were applying these ideas in their own families and were making faster progress in their nuclear families and in clinical work than others, including those in weekly family therapy. They were automatically transferring what they learned in their efforts with their families into their nuclear families and into their clinical work.

From such observations arose a new method of therapy called *coaching*. In this technique, the clinician functions more as a consultant and teacher than as a traditional therapist. Often coaching takes place with only one member of a family, although others may be seen as well. Sessions are often infrequent, with people seen generally once a month or at even less frequent intervals. The focus is on differentiation of self, with the coach assisting the direction of the effort. Progress comes from the person's own efforts at differentiation in the family and in other important relationships.

The following general guidelines help structure the process of coaching. The person works (a) to become a more accurate observer of self and the family, (b) to develop person-to-person relationships with each member of the family, (c) to increase the ability to control emotional reactivity to the family, and (d) to remain neutral or detriangled while relating to the emotional issues of the family.

Becoming an Accurate Observer and Managing Reactivity

Recognition and regulation of one's own emotional reactivity are central to the effort to becoming a more accurate observer of self and family. The better control one has over reactivity, the more detached one can be from emotional process and consequently a more accurate observer. And the effort to observe more carefully, of course, leads to greater detachment and regulation of reactivity.

Any increase in objectivity about self and family that results from the effort to observe more accurately is of great benefit. One can see the interplay of people in the creation and maintenance of a problem. Taking sides becomes more difficult, and it becomes possible to understand emotionally that no one person is to blame for what happens in a family. When one understands that everyone plays a part, including oneself, it is difficult to be angry at anyone.

Developing Person-to-Person Relationships

"In broad terms, a person-to-person relationship is one in which two people can relate personally to each other about each other, without talking about others (triangling), and without talking about impersonal things" (Bowen, 1974, p. 79). What is so simply described appears difficult for people to attain. In general, conversations can stay on this personal level only for a few seconds before the discomfort in one or both parties shifts the content to other people or events.

The long-term effort to establish a person-to-person relationship to all living members of one's family is a significant challenge. Essentially an exercise in developing maturity and perspective, it requires that a person recognize and increasingly master the feelings and reactive behaviors that work against relating to another on a personal level. The specific behaviors and feelings are not the same for each person. For me, the effort highlights the mechanisms used to insulate self from others. One's own bluster and retreat cannot be overlooked as important factors in the inability to relate to another. Other people learn about physical responses to important others or about mental patterns that occur repeatedly, and so forth. The learning from such an effort is primarily for self, but the relationship system may benefit as well from the effort.

A variation of the effort to relate personally to each member of the family is to develop a person-to-person relationship with each parent. People often fail to see the point of such an effort. It is, indeed, very difficult. Relating tends to occur in well-established patterns of interaction. The parent tends to fall into parentlike behavior and the child into childlike postures and responses. Many people structure the relationship to parents to preserve a calm congeniality that blocks the person-to-person effort as effectively as conflictual distance. To relate personally to one's parents is a difficult place to begin to work on differentiation, and a coach may often suggest that a person begin with a more peripheral set of relationships surrounding the parents. A coach can be invaluable in embarking on and sustaining such an effort, particularly when the inevitable obstacles and diversions materialize.

Remaining Neutral

The effort to remain neutral in an emotional field is fundamentally the same as remaining detriangled, discussed earlier. Attention must be paid to interlocking triangles that constantly accompany the effort. One can seem to be progressing in a given triangle only to lose ground when an emotional onslaught comes from an unexpected direction. Allies are as much a problem as those who are antagonistic. The effort toward increased differentiation of self is by self, for self. It cannot be a joint project with another.

Frequent contact with family members, particularly when emotional reactivity is high, is important in the effort to remain neutral and ultimately to increase differentiation. Face-to-face contact is desirable, particularly during periods of anxiety. Generally, one is better off going alone to see family, at least when neutrality and differentiation are the goal. Spouses and children are obviously important people, but their presence can complicate the effort considerably. Bowen (1974) cautions that one cannot tell the family what one is trying to do and still make it work. Helpers and opponents can each stall a person's effort, and natural forces and processes can build into an insurmountable roadblock. A person who has some control of emotional reactivity and some ability to relate personally becomes important to everyone in the family.

Efforts with one's family should be undertaken with a great deal of thought and planning. Families are not all alike, and no general prescription can be given that will apply to all. Sometimes the effort to relate to one's family can lead to great personal reactivity. The coach needs to be aware of such possibilities and assist the person to think clearly about self, the family, and what can be accomplished. The effort to increase differentiation of self takes place minute by minute and day by day. When one can locate the effort in one's family, it is a plus. But it is not the only arena where the effort takes place.

Family systems therapy begins with a survey of the family emotional field or system. Much of the information is collected during the initial sessions, and the family and the clinician attempt to define the problem. The clinician gathers factual information producing a picture of how the family has functioned over time. Each nuclear family incorporates within themselves the processes characterizing the families of previous generations. The survey of the family emotional field serves as a road map or blueprint that the clinician can read and at times teach to the motivated family member.

As the information is collected, it is entered on the family diagram. A few general conventions guide the construction of a family diagram, making the information it contains accessible to a knowledgeable reader. Males are represented by small squares and females by circles. The husband and wife of a nuclear family are depicted with the male on the left and the female on the right. A solid line (three sides of a rectangle in shape with the male on the upper left corner and the female on the upper right) connects them. Each of the children produced by the breeding pair is connected to the marital unit by a straight line. The birth order of the children is represented by placing the oldest on the left, and each succeeding sibling is placed to the right of the older sibling preceding it. In this manner each successive generation is represented, with the most recent generation on the bottom of the diagram.

Basic information about each person is added to the diagram as it is collected. Where possible, the date and place of birth; date, place, and cause of death (where applicable); level of education completed; brief employment history; and a brief summary of the individual's health, including all major health problems and those of a chronic nature, should be included for each person represented on the diagram. Dates are important and should be noted for all events listed. Employment histories should include dates of job change, stated reasons for the change, and notable periods of unemployment. If health problems have been cited, the date of onset, the length and course of treatment, and the outcome should be added. A composite picture of the functioning of each family member is collected in this manner.

In addition to information about each person, the clinician gathers data about the functioning of nuclear and extended family systems. Each spouse has a perspective on the nuclear family. Their history has been marked by good and bad times, periods of tranquility and great upset. How does the family perceive the differences and account for the changes? Specific dates and events are always important. Separations and divorces are significant events in the history of a family. How does each person view such an event? What changes accompanied it, and how does each explain the change? Did people seem to function better or worse after the event? The composition of the household can change from time to time. Children grow up and leave home. Older family members come to live with younger ones. Births and deaths occur. How have such changes impacted on the family, and what does each person think about the changes?

In addition to information about a nuclear family, the extended family is also important. The clinician collects much the same information for the extended family. Furthermore, the frequency and the nature of contact between members of the nuclear and extended families is of interest. How does such contact influence the nuclear and extended family? Dates and accurate information about the nature of events in the extended family are important. Gradually the facts of a family across several generations can be collected, and a relatively accurate picture of its emotional functioning is produced.

The information of the family diagram need not be completed by the end of the first session. There are many ways to collect family information. Much of it is volunteered by informants in response to other questions asked by the clinician. The writer begins simply by asking what has brought them to the point of involving a stranger in their family. What is the problem, what has been done to this point, and what have been the results? How do people think about what is happening and what has occurred? People will frequently have different points of view about the problem and how it works. As people begin to describe the problem and their thoughts about it, the clinician can gather basic information rather easily.

For the thoughtful clinician, the family diagram is never completed. No problem or event is ever understood fully. As *nodal events* (events subsequent to which the functioning of the family has shifted) become clear, more questions are available about the nature of the event and its impact. It is always important to separate fact from opinion. Both are important. Family members have opinions and assumptions that govern their behavior, but the framework of fact can tell a different, sometimes conflicting story. The squares, circles, and lines of a family diagram are unimportant in themselves. The information is only useful alongside the theoretical thinking of the clinician. It is a part of the overall attitude of inquiry that the clinician seeks to maintain at all times. When linked to theory, the family diagram illustrates and illuminates the processes that have shaped a family's history and its present.

CASE EXAMPLE

The format of this volume requires that a case example be provided to illustrate the methodology of therapy. While such a report can be valuable to a serious student, the reader tends to focus on what the clinician does to change the family, to make a difference. The thoughtful reader will have already garnered the point of the preceding paragraphs. From the point of view of the Bowen theory, the clinician works mostly to manage self, not to change the family. While the general guidelines of such an effort can be described, it is not possible to illustrate with dialogue excerpts the processes within the clinician.

This point is worth discussing in some detail. There is a great deal of interest in the therapy community in changing the client or the family. This is generally expressed in terms of an intervention that the therapist and/or others plan and then implement. There are numerous techniques accompanying such an effort. Some involve how the therapist speaks to the person or family; others focus on what the therapist does (e.g., where he or she sits, how the therapist positions others in the room, etc.). Yet other technical applications involve who attends the clinical session and how it is structured.

The point to be made, however, is that a clinician following the guidelines of the Bowen theory does not think in terms of changing the family directly. Consequently, there is no preparation of an intervention and no active effort to make the family different. How the clinician thinks is extremely important from this point of view, as is how he or she uses thinking to manage self. The clinician does not know what is best for a family, at least from this perspective. It is each person's task to think for self and to determine what action incorporates his or her own best interest and fulfills his or her responsibility to others.

It would be inaccurate, however, to suggest that the clinician attempting to practice with the Bowen theory as a guide eschews technique altogether. Clearly, each clinician maintains an armamentarium of techniques that are employed under certain conditions to produce certain results. The clinician applies the technical side of his or her effort mainly to self, however, and not to the family. For example, I have a number of self-regulatory techniques learned from many sources to recognize and manage my own reactivity. I draw on these at any time to help manage self in the presence of others. For the clinician, the overriding goal is the maintenance of emotional neutrality and differentiation of self, and each approaches this in different ways based on his or her own level of anxiety and differentiation of self.

The following case summary will attempt to describe the clinical effort with one family over a 3.5-year period. Dur-

Figure 1. The W family's family diagram.

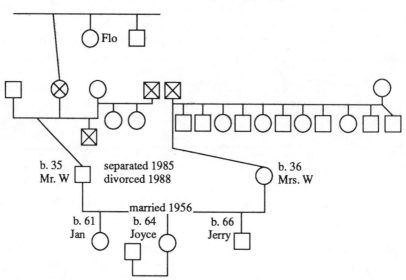

b. 35 Mr. W

separated 1985 divorced 1988

b. 36 Mrs. W

married 1956

b. 61 Jan

b. 64 Joyce

b. 66 Jerry

ing that time, only one person in the family was seen in 149 hour-long sessions. You may want to refer to the family diagram for orientation (Figure 1). Because of space limitations, nonessential information will be omitted, and additional important basic information will not be placed on the family diagram but will be given in the text. Three generations are represented. The Ws' three children, Jan, Joyce, and Jerry, represent the youngest generation. Mr. W's aunt (Flo) and Mrs. W's mother represent the oldest generation.

Mrs. W contacted the clinician in early 1986, about a year after she had left her husband of 30 years. The formal divorce negotiations had gotten underway poorly, and the tension level in the W family was very high. Mrs. W was extremely concerned about her children and their reactions to the separation and impending divorce. At that time, Jan, the oldest, was living with her father and was estranged from Mrs. W. Jan avoided all contact with her mother. Joyce, the

middle child, was equally distant from her father. Joyce had married and was a strong advocate for her mother's position. Jerry, the youngest, was a college student. When at home, he lived in his father's house and was the only child to have contact with both parents.

The Ws had met and married as young adults. Mrs. W reported devoting herself in the early years of the marriage to helping her husband progress through the ranks of a large national corporation. Marital conflict arose relatively early, roughly coinciding with the first pregnancy. From that point on, the Ws' marriage was generally tense and rocky. Mrs. W generally saw Mr. W's behavior as the problem. She believed him to be critical of her and unpredictable. During this same period, Mrs. W began what became a long series of visits to mental health professionals and clergy seeking help with the problem. Mr. W, in turn, found Mrs. W's behavior incomprehensible. Occasionally, he attended mental health consultations, but little relief was gained for either him or his wife in the process. Mrs. W did find it useful to talk to someone when tension levels in the family increased dramatically. A few years before reaching the decision to leave her husband, Mrs. W launched a small business that gave her purpose and some independent income. With her youngest child in college, Mrs. W decided the time had come to take action in the marital stalemate.

From the clinician's point of view, the W family was in a state of heightened anxiety manifested in intense emotional reactivity. The interlocking triangles of the W family operated in such a way that the anxiety came to be located primarily between the spouses and secondarily between Jan and Mrs. W and Joyce and Mr. W. Mrs. W was a central figure in the family drama. The clinician believed that if she could understand the role of her own anxiety and reactivity in the family and if she could do something about her part of the problem, she would function differently in the family and the family in turn could respond differently to her. Therefore, the initial task for the clinician was to manage himself in a way that was emotionally neutral while staying in contact with the emotional issues of the family as played out through Mrs. W.

The central reactive issues that Mrs. W presented during the first year and a half of consultation centered on her views of Mr. W's behavior, the difficulty of the divorce process, and the welfare of the oldest child, Jan, whom Mrs. W believed to be overly influenced by Mr. W. Mrs. W's frequent question was, "Will he [or she depending on the person referred to] ever see [Mrs. W's point of view and the reasons for her decisions]?" In short, her primary focus was to change the others, particularly Mr. W and Jan.

The clinician worked to maintain a position from which he could say whatever he thought to Mrs. W in a manner that minimized her tendency to overreact to him. He worked to communicate to Mrs. W that she had a choice in the reactive process between herself and her husband. She could act and react to him in a manner that stirred up the conflict, or she could work to manage herself in a more grown-up manner. The latter was the more difficult course initially, but it had within it the potential for a better resolution of the family problem. The choice was hers. She could remain mired in bitterness and anger; if she chose to pursue a different course, the clinician would do what he could to help her out. Mrs. W focused initially on revenge and "making him pay" for the problems in the marriage. The more she sought vengeance, the more Mr. W reacted, the more upset the children became, and the more complicated and stalled the divorce process became. Gradually, she understood the clinician's point, and despite many relapses she set out to manage herself less reactively to her husband.

In a similar vein, the clinician suggested to Mrs. W that she could view Jan as a helpless infant who needed her protection, or she could recognize that Jan was making important decisions and permit her the opportunity to bear the consequences of those decisions. On a practical level, that meant stopping the flood of anxiety directed at Jan in the form of pleas for togetherness, love, understanding, and closeness while simultaneously leaving the door open for Jan to approach if or when she chose. After considerable thought, Mrs. W began to challenge her own emotional view of her daughter.

Mrs. W slowly began to gain some control of her anxiety and reactivity. As she became less anxious, the clinician could act more as a coach and make further suggestions to her. One involved her own family. Mrs. W is the oldest of 12 children. Her parents had been relatively childlike people who assumed helpless postures toward the world. As the oldest, Mrs. W had stepped in to make the family function in the best way she knew how. She begged and borrowed food when the pantry was bare. She taught younger brothers and sisters, looked after their health, and did everything she knew to provide them with essential support.

Mrs. W's father died a few years prior to her separation, but her mother was still living. Mrs. W was highly reactive to her mother, frequently seeing her as deceptive, critical, and unpredictable. She never seemed to be able to please her mother. Although Mrs. W had remained involved with her family, generally as a figure of authority to be reckoned with, she had tended to avoid personal interactions with her mother. The clinician suggested that Mrs. W was fortunate to have two relationships of central importance in which she could practice managing her reactivity. Whenever Mr. W got the better of her, she could practice with her mother, and vice versa. Mrs. W slowly began to resume contact with her mother. As she learned more about managing her reactivity with her mother, Mrs. W appeared to translate what she had learned into her relationship with Mr. W. In fits and starts, the divorce negotiations began to progress.

A second suggestion concerned Mr. W's family, many of whom Mrs. W had known personally during the years of marriage. These people were unaware of the Ws' separation and impending divorce. The clinician suggested that Mrs. W might find it useful to resume her contacts with people in that family who had been important to her. The goal would not be to embarrass anyone or to reveal any secrets but to keep important people in contact with one another and to allow what resources the family could bring to bear on the situation to have full play. In early 1987, when a death occurred in the family, Mrs. W attended the funeral. She was well received by the family and reestablished contact with Mr. W's aunt, Flo. This became an important contact.

About a month after this event, a major shift took place in the divorce negotiations. Mrs. W dropped her notions of revenge and thought out a clear proposal for a settlement that met her needs and that allowed Mr. W room for negotiation. She presented her proposal to him immediately. Although negotiations continued with progress and regression, this proposal was essentially accepted and became the basis of the divorce decree a few months later. Various family members pressured Mrs. W to change her mind. Some argued she was being too harsh and others too lenient. Mrs. W thought her position was equitable and said so. Because she had developed her position carefully and clearly, she was able to maintain it under pressure, providing the stability for the divorce decree, which was arrived at without trial by mutual agreement.

Mrs. W had been plagued continually by an intense fear that she would "lose her children to her husband." This meant for her that her children would abandon her, accept her husband's viewpoint that she was the cause of the problem, blame her for the disruption of the family, and be unduly influenced by him in ways she considered unsound. Although she had begun to work on this anxiety with regard to Jan, it persisted after the divorce. In late summer 1988 following the divorce, Mrs. W traveled to spend a few days with Flo. She returned with a new sense of stability and perspective on the family and its problems. Shortly thereafter, Flo began to correspond with Jan and the other children. She had tended to function like a grandmother to the W children, who had not known why contact had decreased in recent years. Jan responded to Flo, and Mrs. W's anxieties about Jan decreased, even though Jan remained out of contact with her mother. Later that fall, Flo came for a visit. She made contact directly with Mr. W and with Jan. The Ws appeared to relax.

Early the following year, as a part of the final settlement of the divorce, the Ws were to exchange family mementos. Mrs. W had many from their wedding, and Mr. W had a collection of their children's items. The mementos were an emotional issue for Mrs. W, and the exchange became bogged down. Mrs. W became upset and threatened legal action. The clinician simply pointed out to Mrs. W that she had an interesting opportunity to approach the problem of her anxiety about the children. Over a period of several days, Mrs. W wrote Mr. W a detailed personal letter reciting her memories of the children. She realized, in fact, that she had the mementos in her memory. She reported to Mr. W that she had laughed and cried as she remembered the various objects and the episodes they represented. She knew he had always tried to be a good and responsible father, and she would leave the mementos with him because he would undoubtedly enjoy them. She took the letter and her own items to Mr. W at his house. She gave him the mementos and the letter, and they talked for a few minutes on the porch. Afterward she reported a great

sense of relief and the complete disappearance of the anxiety about the children. From that point on, she and Mr. W were able to establish basic communication with one another, particularly in matters concerning the welfare of the children. This has resulted over time in a gradual thawing of the estrangement between Joyce and her father, who now have created a shaky but nonetheless working relationship to one another.

Within a month or two of these events with Mr. W, Mrs. W had an opportunity to manage her own reactivity differently with her family of origin. Her youngest brother had always been a focus of her mother's concern. This brother, Jay, had been married and divorced and was at the time living in a trailer on the farm, not far from his mother, who occupied the farmhouse. Jay's life course had been difficult, and his functioning appeared marginal. His mother began to express indirectly her wish that the family farm be left to Jay when she died. This created a furor among the 12 siblings. The farm represented many emotional things to different members of the family. Those opposed to their mother's idea turned to Mrs. W to lead the fight. She had always been a proponent of "fairness" in the family, and she had always occupied an influential position within the family emotional network. Those favoring Jay's inheritance began to sound her out as well, trying to determine her position and how best to contend with her opposition.

Mrs. W initially reacted with anger at her mother's wish. As she thought about the situation, however, she began to recognize more clearly her emotional position in the family. She described that position as one of overresponsibility and "knowing what's best" for everyone. She thought through more carefully her own idea of responsibilty for herself and to the family. She composed a personal letter to her mother going over past emotional events and commenting on her changing understanding of her mother's position and the factors with which she had to contend. She concluded by communicating to her mother her own position on the matter of the inheritance, namely that it was her mother's responsibility to distribute her property as she saw the need and Mrs. W would support her wishes. She worked to retain a relatively neutral stance to her siblings. She did not tell them of her communication to her mother but encouraged each to think his or her position through independently and communicate it to their mother.

Events came to a head at a family reunion held at the farm. Mrs. W attended and worked to have personal contact with all of her siblings. She spent time alone with her mother on a more personal basis than for many years previously. Her oldest brother, the second child in the family, asked to see her. They met in the barn, where he demanded to know what she wanted and how she intended to influence the inheritance. Mrs. W was able to stay relatively calm. She told him she had communicated her views to their mother and that "fair was fair." Her brother remained angry, and Mrs. W disengaged herself from the conflict without attacking her brother in retaliation. From this point on, Mrs. W began to have more contact with this brother. Their old childhood rivalries surfaced in ways that Mrs. W could recognize more clearly than ever before. She was able to manage herself differently with him. Along with the more childish interactions, a different level of communication also occurred, one more mature and interesting to both. This brother

also had more interaction with their mother.

Following this series of exchanges, Mrs. W began a project of thinking through her relationship to each of her brothers and sisters and, as she called it, "letting them go." She spent much time thinking about herself and each of them. She wrote personal letters to each outlining her thinking about them and herself. As she progressed, she would report being increasingly calm. She reported a greater sense of aloneness, which she carefully distinguished from loneliness. The aloneness was at times uncomfortable, but it also made clear to her that she now had the responsibility only for herself and not for the others.

She also began to be interested in past generations of her family. She began a project to learn more about her grandparents and their lives. This led her to contact older members of the family, distant relatives with whom she had had little or no contact for years. She was generally well received, and she found the visits interesting and satisfying. In the process, she began to examine her own relationship to her paternal grandmother, an important figure in her early years whom she had tended to idolize. As she became more objective about her grandmother, recognizing her weaknesses as well as her strengths, she also began to see her own mother from a somewhat different viewpoint. This led to a further series of interactions with her mother. She was able to visit her grandmother's grave, which she had never done, and she reported a brief period of mourning that she had not experienced at the time of her grandmother's death.

Mrs. W continues her efforts with her families. Jan remains essentially out of contact, although she has seen her mother on two family occasions. These meetings did not result in conflict. Mrs. W is able to have contact with Mr. W when needed, and they can communicate about events in the family important to each other. Mrs. W is in ever-increasing and widening contact with her family. As she learns more about herself and her past, she behaves with less anxiety and reactivity. She describes her family as calmer than ever before.

Mrs. W reports that she is functioning better than she has ever previously. She is active, employed, and in contact with a great number of people. Her family comments on the difference in her but appear baffled by it. Some inquire if she is ill; others seem delighted. For the past 2 years, the role of the coach has been minimal. Mrs. W has developed a motivation and plan of her own, which she implements in her own way. Members of her family, with responsibility for themselves squarely on their own shoulders, appear to be functioning with greater stability than previously.

EVALUATION

A working theory is not static. As more thinking occurs and attempts are made to expand both theory and application, changes occur. The Bowen theory of 1990 is not the same theory as that of 1966, even though the major concepts remain the same. At any given moment in time, staff members are engaged in a variety of projects in theory development and application. The list of interesting areas is long, including a major area applying theory to chronic illness. Currently various staff members of the Family Center use the Bowen theory to guide their work with AIDS, cancer, and other difficult disease presentations. The use of various biofeedback devices is often a part of the effort, as staff work to understand more fully the operation of the human emotional system and reactivity.

A second area of interest applies the Bowen theory to processes in society. This interest appears particularly relevant as conditions in the world are expected to change over the next century faster than at any previous time in the history of life on earth. The pace of change will require living things to adjust at an apparently unprecedented rate. No one knows for sure what the outcome will be, but theory can help us predict how humans will adjust and how the anxiety generated by changing conditions may be manifested.

Any theory that aims toward a linkage with science must be consistent with the natural world. It must fit with what is known and developing as scientific fact. Consequently, there is a great deal of interest in the natural sciences, with various individuals pursuing avenues for contacting and connecting with researchers and thinkers outside the traditional disciplines of mental health. Often such people are invited to address Family Center meetings and to participate less formally in other activities. The list of distinguished guest lecturers at the annual Georgetown Symposium reflects this interest: J. T. Bonner, E.O. Wilson, Verner Suomi, Stephen Suomi, Melvin Konner, and Roger Payne, among others.

The potential for the applications of a natural system theory is vast. The descriptions given here are just a few of the various subjects and projects that surface at the Family Center. The results of such efforts are presented each year at various symposia sponsored by the Family Center and other organizations. Occasionally, the papers from such symposia are published as a group; but the effort is time-consuming and expensive, and many of these presentations never reach publication. Various individuals on the faculty and staff of the Family Center contribute sections to various anthologies of the family therapy literature and write more substantial pieces on theory.

The Family Center itself does not conduct formal research on the efficacy of psychotherapy. With limited time and resources available, individuals have directed their energies more toward the advancement, refinement, and extension of theory to new areas. Each investigator presents his or her findings at various discussion meetings, and each develops

ways for checking up on self. From time to time, Family Center staff agree to participate in various studies conducted by people outside the Family Center. Generally, the results turn up in someone's doctoral dissertation and are never published. In the late 1970s and early 1980s, however, faculty and staff participated in a therapy outcome research project sponsored by the court system of a large state. This research was designed and conducted by an outside organization and involved other clinical groups in addition to the Family Center. The results of this study have not yet been published by the responsible organization but should be in the near future.

ANNOTATED SUGGESTED READINGS

Bowen, M. (1978). *Family therapy in clinical practice*. Northvale, NJ: Jason Aronson.

The development of Bowen's ideas and the Bowen theory is traced through this collection of his published papers, arranged chronologically. The primary source for the Bowen theory.

Kerr, M. E., & Bowen, M. (1988). *Family evaluation: An approach based on Bowen theory*. New York: W. W. Norton & Company.

A detailed discussion of the Bowen theory culminating in a chapter on the clinical aspects of family evaluation. Bowen details the development of his ideas and his commitment to theory in an epilogue.

Papero, D. V. (1990). *Bowen family systems theory*. Boston: Allyn and Bacon. 1990.

This slim volume provides a basic introduction to the Bowen theory.

REFERENCES

Bowen, M. (1966). The use of family theory in clinical practice. *Comprehensive Psychiatry, 7,* 345–374.

Bowen, M. (1971). Family therapy and family group therapy. In H. Kaplan & B. Saddock (Eds.), *Comprehensive group psychotherapy*. Baltimore: Williams and Wilkens.

Bowen, M. (1974). Toward the differentiation of self in one's own family of origin. In P. Lorio & F. Andres (Eds.), *Georgetown Family Symposia: Volume I*. Washington, DC: Department of Psychiatry, Georgetown Medical Center.

Bowen, M. (1975). Family therapy after twenty years. In S. Arieti (Ed.), *American handbook of psychiatry*. New York: Basic Books, Inc.

Bowen, M. (1978). *Family therapy in clinical practice*. New York: Jason Aronson.

Calhoun, J. B. (1967). Ecological factors in the development of behavioral anomalies. In *Comparative psychiatry*. New York: Grune and Stratton.

Kerr, M. E., & M. Bowen. (1988). *Family evaluation: An approach based on Bowen theory*. New York: Norton.

Toman, W. (1961). *Family constellation: A psychological game*. New York: Springer.

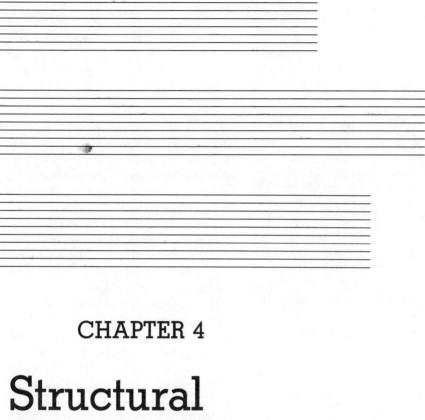

CHAPTER 4

Structural
Family Therapy

JORGE COLAPINTO

DEFINITION

Structural family therapy is a model of treatment based on systems theory that was developed primarily at the Philadelphia Child Guidance Clinic, under the leadership of Salvador Minuchin, over the last 25 years. The model's distinctive features are its emphasis on structural change as the main goal of therapy, which acquires preeminence over the details of individual change, and the attention paid to the therapist as an active agent in the process of restructuring the family.

HISTORICAL DEVELOPMENT

Structural family therapy was the child of necessity, or so the student may conclude in tracing the origins of the movement back to the early 1960s, to the time when Minuchin was doing therapy, training, and research at the Wiltwyck School for Boys in New York. Admittedly, our historical account does not need to start precisely there, but the development of a treatment model—no less than the development of an individual or a family—can only be told by introducing a certain punctuation and discarding alternative ones.

We could choose a more distant point in time and focus on Minuchin's experience in the newborn Israel, where families from all over the world converged carrying their bits of common purpose and their lots of regional idiosyncrasies, and found a unique opportunity to live the combination of cultural universals and cultural specifics. Or, reaching further back, we could think of Minuchin's childhood as the son of a Jewish family in rural Argentina of the 1920s and wonder about the influence of this early exposure to alternative cultures—different rules, different truths—on his conception of human nature. Any of these periods in the life of the developer of structural family therapy could be justified as a starting point for an account of his creation. The experiences provided by both are congruent with philosophical viewpoints deeply rooted in the architecture of the model—for instance, that we are more human than otherwise, that we share a common range of potentialities that each of us displays differentially as a function of our specific context.

But the Wiltwyck experience stands out as a powerful catalyst of conceptual production because of a peculiar combination of circumstances. First of all, the population at Wiltwyck consisted of delinquent boys from disorganized, multiproblem, poor families. Traditional psychotherapeutic techniques, largely developed to fulfill the demands of verbally articulate, middle-class patients besieged by intrapsychic conflicts, did not appear to have a significant impact on these youngsters. Improvements achieved through the use of these and other techniques in the residential setting of the school tended to disappear as soon as the child returned to his family (Minuchin, 1961). The serious concerns associated with delinquency, both from the point of view of society and of the delinquent individual himself, necessarily stimulated the quest for alternative approaches.

The second circumstance was the timing of the Wiltwyck experience: it coincided with the consolidation of an idea that emerged in the 1950s—the idea of changing families as a therapeutic enterprise (Haley, 1971). By the early '60s, family therapy thinking had become persuasive enough to catch the eye of Minuchin and his colleagues in their anxious search for more effective ways of dealing with juvenile delinquency. Finally, a third fortunate circumstance was the presence at Wiltwyck of Braulio Montalvo, whom Minuchin would later recognize as his most influential teacher (Minuchin, 1974, p. vii).

The enthusiastic group shifted the focus of attention from the intrapsychic world of the delinquent adolescent to the dynamic patterns of the family. Special techniques for the diagnosis and treatment of low socioeconomic families were developed (Minuchin & Montalvo, 1966, 1967), as well as some of the concepts that would become cornerstones in the model exposed a decade later.

Approaching delinquency as a family issue proved more helpful than defining it as a problem of the individual; but it should not be inferred that Minuchin and his collaborators discovered the panacea for juvenile delinquency. Rather, they experienced the limitations of therapeutic power, the fact that psychotherapy does not have the answers to poverty and other social problems (Malcolm, 1978, p. 70). Nowadays, *Families of the Slums* (Minuchin, Montalvo, Guerney, Rosman, & Schumer, 1967), the book that summarizes the experience at Wiltwyck, will more likely be found in the sociology section of the bookstore than in the psychotherapy section. But the modalities of intervention developed at Wiltwyck, and even the awareness of the limitations of therapy brought about by their application, have served as an inspirational paradigm for others. Harry Aponte, a disciple of Minuchin, has worked on the concept of bringing organization to the underorganized family through the mobilization of family and network resources (Aponte, 1976).

From the point of view of the historical development of Minuchin's model, the major contribution of Wiltwyck has been the provision of a nurturant and stimulating environment. The model spent its childhood in an atmosphere of permissiveness, with little risk of being crushed by conventional criticism. Looking retrospectively, Minuchin acknowledges that working in "a no man's land of poor families," inaccessible to traditional forms of psychotherapy, guaranteed the tolerance of the psychiatric establishment, which had not accepted Nathan Ackerman's approach to middle-class families (Malcolm, 1978, p. 84).

The possibility to test the model with a wider cross section of families came in 1965, when Minuchin was appointed director of the Philadelphia Child Guidance Clinic. The facility was at the time struggling to emerge from a severe institutional crisis—and, as Minuchin himself likes to remind us, the Chinese ideogram for "crisis" is made of "danger" and "opportunity." In this case the opportunity was there to implement a systemic approach in the treatment of a wide variety of mental health problems, and also to attract other system thinkers to a promising new pole of development for family therapy. Braulio Montalvo also moved from New York, and Jay Haley was summoned from the West Coast.

Haley's own conceptual framework differs in significant aspects from that of Minuchin, but undoubtedly the ideas of both men contributed a lot to the growth and strengthening of each other's models—sometimes through the borrowing of concepts and techniques, many times by providing the contrasting pictures against which the respective positions each became better defined. Together with Montalvo, Haley was a key factor in the intensive training program that Minuchin wanted and had implemented at the Child Guidance Clinic. The format of the program, with its emphasis on live supervision and videotape analysis, facilitated the discussion and refinement of theoretical concepts and has continuously been a primary influence on the shaping of the model. The preface to *Families and Family Therapy* (Minuchin, 1974) acknowledges the seminal value of the author's association with Haley and Montalvo.

While Minuchin continued his innovative work in Philadelphia, the clinical and research data originating in different strains of family therapy continued to accumulate, up to a point in which alternative and competitive theoretical renderings became possible. The growing drive for a systemic way of looking at behavior and behavior change had to differentiate itself from the attempts to absorb family dynamics into a more or less expanded version of psychoanalysis (Minuchin, 1969, pp. 179–187). A first basic formulation of Minuchin's own brand of family therapy was almost at hand; it only needed a second catalyst, a context comparable to Wiltwyck.

The context was provided by the association of the Philadelphia Child Guidance Clinic with the Children's Hospital of Philadelphia, which brought Minuchin to the field of psychosomatic condi-

tions. The project started as a challenge, in many ways similar to the one posed by the delinquent boys of Wiltwyck. Once again the therapist had to operate under the pressures of running time. The urgency, of a social nature at Wiltwyck, was a medical one at Philadelphia. The patients who first forced a new turn of the screw in the shaping of Minuchin's model were diabetic children with an unusually high number of emergency hospitalizations for acidosis. Their conditions could not be explained medically and would not respond to classical individual psychotherapy, which focused on improving the patient's ability to handle his or her own stress. Only when the stress was understood and treated in the context of the family could the problem be solved (Baker, Minuchin, Milman, Liebman, & Todd, 1975). Minuchin's team accumulated clinical and research evidence of the connection between certain family characteristics and the extreme vulnerability of this group of patients. The same characteristics— enmeshment, overprotectiveness, rigidity, lack of conflict resolution—were also observed in the families of asthmatic children who presented severe, recurrent attacks and/or a heavy dependence on steroids (Liebman, Minuchin, & Baker, 1974a, 1974b, 1974c; Liebman, Minuchin, Baker, & Rosman, 1976, 1977 [pp.153–171]; Minuchin, Baker, Rosman, Liebman, Milman, & Todd, 1975).

The therapeutic paradigm that began to evolve focused on a push for clearer boundaries, increased flexibility in family transactions, the actualization of hidden family conflicts, and the modification of the (usually overinvolved) role of the patient in them. The need to *enact* dysfunctional transactions in the session (prescribed by the model so that they could be observed and corrected) led therapists to deliberately provoke family crises (Minuchin & Barcai, 1969, pp. 199–220), in contrast with the supportive, shielding role prescribed by more traditional approaches. If the underorganized families of juvenile delinquents invited the exploration of new routes, the hovering, overconcerned families of psychosomatic children led to the articulation of a first version of structural family therapy.

In an early advance of a new conceptual model derived from the principles of general systems theory (Minuchin, 1970), the clinical material chosen as illustration is a case of anorexia nervosa. Although Minuchin's involvement with this condition was practically simultaneous with his work with diabetics and asthmatics, anorexia nervosa provided a special opportunity because in this case the implementation of the model aims at eliminating the disease itself, while in the other two cases it cannot go beyond the prevention of its exacerbation. In both diabetes and asthma, the emotional link is the triggering of a somatic episode, but it operates on a basic preexistent physiological vulnerability—a metabolic disorder, an allergy. Thus, the terms *psychosomatic diabetic* and *psychosomatic asthmatic* do not imply an emotional etiology for any of the two conditions. In anorexia nervosa, on the other hand, the role of such vulnerability is small or inexistent. Emotional factors can be held entirely responsible for the condition, and then the therapeutic potential of the model can be more fully assessed. Clinical and research experience with anorexia is the most widely documented of the model's application (e.g., Liebman, Minuchin, & Baker, 1974a, 1974b; Minuchin, Baker, Liebman, Milman, Rosman, & Todd, 1973; Rosman, Minuchin, & Liebman, 1975; Rosman, Minuchin,

Liebman, & Baker, 1976, 1977 [pp. 341–348]).

During the first half of the 1970s, with the Philadelphia clinic already established as a leading training center for family therapists, Minuchin continued his work with psychosomatics. In 1972, he invited Bernice Rosman, who had worked with him at Wiltwyck and coauthored *Families of the Slums,* to join the clinic as director of research. Minuchin, Rosman, and the pediatrician Lester Baker became the core of a clinical and research team that culminated its work 6 years later with the publication of *Psychosomatic Families* (Minuchin, Rosman, & Baker, 1978).

Also in 1972, Minuchin published the first systematic formulation of his model in "Structural Family Therapy" (Minuchin, 1972). Many of the basic principles of the current model are already present in this article: the characterization of therapy as a transitional event, where the therapist's function is to help the family reach a new stage; the emphasis on present reality as opposed to history; the displacement of the locus of pathology from the individual to the system of transactions, from the symptom to the family's reaction to it; the understanding of diagnosis as a constructed reality; the attention paid to the points of entry that each family system offers to the therapist; the therapeutic strategy focused on the realignment of the structural relationships within the family, on a change of rules that will allow the system to maximize its potential for conflict resolution and individual growth.

During this same period of time, the clinical experience supporting the model went far beyond the psychosomatic field. Under Minuchin's leadership, the techniques and concepts of structural family therapy were being applied by the clinic's staff and trainees to school phobias, adolescent runaways, drug addictions, and the whole range of problems typically brought for treatment to a child clinic. The model was finally reaching all sorts of families from all socioeconomic levels and with a variety of presenting problems.

In 1974, Minuchin presented structural family therapy in book form (Minuchin, 1974), and the Philadelphia Child Guidance Clinic moved to a modern, larger building complex together with Children's Hospital. A process of fast expansion started: the availability of services and staff increased dramatically, and a totally new organizational context developed. The visibility of the Philadelphia Child Guidance Clinic, which reached international renown, brought a new challenge to the model in the form of increasing and not always positive attention from the psychiatric establishment. In 1975, Minuchin chose to step down from his administrative duties and to concentrate on the teaching of his methods and ideas to younger generations, at the specially created Family Therapy Training Center.

This move signaled the beginning of the latest stage in the development of the model, a period of theoretical creation driven by the need to develop a didactically powerful body of systemic concepts consistent with the richness of clinical data. The current status of structural family therapy (Minuchin & Fishman, 1981) is characterized by an emphasis on training and theoretical issues. In the delivery of training, increasing attention is being paid to the therapist's epistemology—concepts, perspectives, goals, attitudes—as a "set" that conditions the learning of techniques. In the development of theory, the trend is to refine the early systemic concepts that served as foundations of the model, by looking into ideas developed by systems thinkers in other fields.

TENETS OF THE MODEL

Structural family therapy is primarily a way of thinking about and operating in three related areas: the family, the presenting problem, and the process of change.

The Family

The family is conceptualized as a living open system. In every system, the parts are functionally interdependent in ways dictated by the supraindividual functions of the whole. In a system AB, A's passivity is read as a response to B's initiative (interdependence), while the passivity-initiative pattern is one of the ways in which the system carries on its function (e.g., the provision of a nurturant environment for A and B). The set of rules regulating the interactions among members of the system is its structure.

As an *open* system the family is subjected to and impinges on the surrounding environment. This implies that family members are not the only architects of their family shape; relevant rules may be imposed by the immediate group of reference or by the culture in the broader sense. When we recognize that Mr. Brown's distant relationship to Jimmy is related to Mrs. Brown's overinvolvement with Jimmy, we are witnessing an idiosyncratic family arrangement as well as the regulating effects of a society that encourages mothers to be closer to children and fathers to keep more distance.

Finally, as a *living* system the family is in constant transformation: transactional rules evolve over time as each family group negotiates the particular arrangements that are more economical and effective for any given period in its life as a system. This evolution, as any other, is regulated by the interplay of homeostasis and change.

Homeostasis designates the patterns of transactions that assure the stability of the system, the maintenance of its basic characteristics as they can be described at a certain point in time; homeostatic processes tend to keep the status quo (Jackson, 1957, 1965). The two-way process that links A's passivity to B's initiative serves a homeostatic purpose for the system AB, as do the father's distance, the mother's proximity, and Jimmy's eventual symptomatology for the Browns. When viewed from the perspective of homeostasis, individual behaviors interlock like the pieces in a puzzle, a quality that is usually referred to as *complementarity*.

Change, on the other hand, is the reaccommodation that the living system undergoes in order to adjust to a different set of environmental circumstances or to an intrinsic developmental need. A's passivity and B's initiative may be effectively complementary for a given period in the life of AB, but a change to a different complementarity will be in order if B becomes incapacitated. Jimmy and his parents may need to change if a second child is born. Marriage, births, entrance to school, the onset of adolescence, going to college or to a job are examples of developmental milestones in the life of most families; loss of a job, a sudden death, a promotion, a move to a different city, a divorce, a pregnant adolescent are special events that affect the journey of some families. Whether universal or idiosyncratic, these impacts call for changes in patterns and in some cases—for example, when children are

added to a couple—dramatically increase the complexity of the system by introducing differentiation. The spouse subsystem coexists with parent-child subsystems and eventually a siblings subsystem, and rules need to be developed to define who participates with whom and in what kind of situations, and who are excluded from those situations. Such definitions are called *boundaries;* they may prescribe, for instance, that children should not participate in adults' arguments, or that the oldest son has the privilege of spending certain moments alone with his father, or that the adolescent daughter has more rights to privacy than her younger siblings.

In the last analysis, homeostasis and change are matters of perspective. If one follows the family process over a brief period of time, chances are that one will witness the homeostatic mechanisms at work and the system in relative equilibrium. Moments of crisis in which the status quo is questioned and rules are challenged are a relative exception in the life of a system; when crises become the rule, they may be playing a role in the maintenance of homeostasis. Now if one steps back so as to visualize a more extended period, the evolvement of different, successive system configurations becomes apparent, and the process of change comes to the foreground. But by moving further back and encompassing the entire life cycle of a system, one discovers homeostasis again: the series of smooth transitions and sudden reaccommodations of which change is made presents itself as a constant attempt to maintain equilibrium or to recover it. Like the donkey that progresses to reach for the carrot that will always be out of reach, like the aristocrats in Lampeduzza's *Il Gattopardo* who wanted to change everything so that nothing would change, families fall for the bait that is the paradox of evolution. They need to accommodate in order to remain the same, and accommodation moves them into something different.

This ongoing process can be arrested. Families can fail to respond to a new demand from the environment or from their own development: they will not substitute new rules of transactions for the ones that have been patterning their functioning. AB find it impossible to let go of the passivity-initiative pattern even if B is now incapacitated; Jimmy and his mother find it impossible to let go of a tight relationship that was developmentally appropriate when Jimmy was 2 but not now that he is 18. Maybe Jimmy started showing trouble in school when he was 12, but the family insisted on the same structure with the mother monitoring all communications around Jimmy and the school, so that Jimmy was protected from his father's anger and the father from his own disappointment.

When families get stagnated in their development, their transactional patterns become stereotyped. Homeostatic mechanisms exacerbate as the system holds tightly to a rigid script. Any movement threatening a departure from the status quo is swiftly corrected. If the father grows tougher on Jimmy, the mother will intercede and the father will withdraw. Intergenerational coalitions that subvert natural hierarchies (e.g., the mother and son against the father), triangular patterns where parents use a child as a battleground, and other dysfunctional arrangements serve the purpose of avoiding the onset of open conflict within the system. Conflict avoidance, then, guarantees a certain sense of equilibrium but at the same time prevents growth and differentiation, which are the offspring of conflict

resolution. The higher levels of conflict avoidance are found in *enmeshed* families—where the extreme sense of closeness, belonging, and loyalty minimize the chances of disagreement—and, at the other end of the continuum, in *disengaged* families, where the same effect is produced by excessive distance and a false sense of independence.

In their efforts to keep a precarious balance, family members stick to myths that are very narrow definitions of themselves as a whole and as individuals—constructed realities made by the interlocking of limited facets of the respective selves, which leave most of the system's potentials unused. When these families come to therapy, they typically present themselves as a poor version of what they really are. For example, the white area in the center of Figure 1 represents the myth, "I am this way and can only be this way, and the same is true for him and for her, and we cannot relate in any other way than our way," while the shaded area contains the available but as yet not utilized alternatives.

The Presenting Problem

Structural family therapy conceptualizes the problem behavior as a partial aspect of the family structure of transactions. The complaint, for instance, that Jimmy is undisciplined and aggressive, needs to be put in perspective by relating it to the context of Jimmy's family.

For one thing, the therapist has to find out the position and function of the problem behavior: When does Jimmy turn aggressive? What happens immediately before? How do others react to his misbehavior? Is Jimmy more undisciplined toward his mother than toward his father? Do the parents agree on how to handle him? What is the homeostatic

Figure 1. A model of structural family therapy.

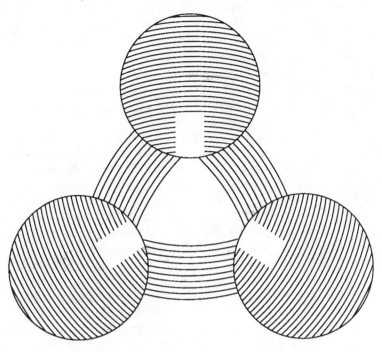

benefit from the sequential patterns in which the problem behavior is imbedded? The individual problem is seen as a complement of other behaviors, a part of the status quo, a token of the system's dysfunction; in short, the system as it is supports the symptom.

The therapist also has to diagnose the structure of the family's perceptions in connection with the presenting problem. Who is more concerned about Jimmy's lack of discipline? Does everybody concur that he is aggressive? That his behavior is the most troublesome problem in the family? What are the other, more positive facets in Jimmy's self that go unnoticed? Is the family exaggerating in labeling as "aggressive" a child that maybe is just more exuberant than his siblings? Is the family failing to accommodate their perceptions and expectations to the fact that Jimmy is now 18

years old? Does the system draw a homeostatic gain from perceiving Jimmy primarily as a symptomatic child? An axiom of structural family therapy, illustrated by Figure 1, is that a vast area of Jimmy's self is out of sight for both his relatives and himself, and that there is a systemic support for this blindness.

So the interactional network knitted around the motive of complaint is the real presenting problem for the structural family therapist. The key element in this view is the concept of systemic *support*. The model does *not* claim a direct causal line between system and problem behavior; the emphasis is on maintenance rather than on causation. Certainly, one sometimes observes families and listens to their stories and can almost see the pathways leading from transactional structure to symptomatology. But even in these cases, the model warns us that we are dealing with current transactions and current memories as they are organized *now,* after the problem has crystallized. Thus, instead of a simplistic, one-way causal connection, the model postulates an ongoing process of mutual accommodation between the system's rules and the individual's predispositions and vulnerabilities. Maybe Jimmy was born with a "strong temperament" *and* to a system that needed to pay special attention to his temper tantrums, to highlight his negative facets while ignoring the positive ones. Within this context, Jimmy learned about his identity and about the benefits of being perceived as an aggressive child. By the time he was 9, Jimmy was an expert participant in a mutually escalating game of defiance and punishment. These mechanisms—selective attention, deviance amplification, labeling, counterescalation—are some of the ways in which a system may contribute to the etiology of a "problem." Jimmy's cousin Fred was born at about the same time and with the same "strong temperament," but he is now a class leader and a junior tennis champ.

Discussions around etiological history, in any case, are largely academic from the perspective of structural family therapy, whose interest is focused on the *current* supportive relation between system and problem behavior. The model shares with other systemic approaches the radical idea that knowledge of the origins of a problem is largely irrelevant for the process of therapeutic change (Minuchin & Fishman, 1979). The identification of etiological sequences may be helpful in *preventing* problems from happening to families, but once they have happened and are eventually brought to therapy, history has already occurred and cannot be undone. An elaborate understanding of the problem history may in fact hinder the therapist's operation by encouraging an excessive focus on what appears as *not* modifiable.

The Process of Therapeutic Change

Consistent with its basic tenet that the problems brought to therapy are ultimately dysfunctions of the family structure, the model looks for a therapeutic solution in the modification of such structure. This usually requires changes in the relative positions of family members; more proximity may be necessary between the husband and wife, more distance between the mother and son. Hierarchical relations and coalitions are frequently in need of a redefinition. New alternative rules for transacting must be explored. The mother, for instance, may be required to abstain from intervening automatically whenever an interaction between her husband and son reaches a certain pitch, while the father and son should not automatically abort an argument just because it upsets Mom. Frozen conflicts have to be acknowledged and dealt with so that they can be solved, and the natural road to growth reopened.

Therapeutic change is then the process of helping the family to outgrow their stereotyped patterns, of which the presenting problem is a part. This process transpires within a special context, the *therapeutic system,* that offers a unique chance to challenge the rules of the family. The privileged position of the therapist allows him or her to request from the family members different behaviors and to invite different perceptions, thus altering their interaction and perspective. The family then has an opportunity to experience transactional patterns that have not been allowed under their prevailing homeostatic rules. The system's limits are probed and pushed, and its narrow self-definitions are questioned; in the process, the family's capacity to tolerate and handle stress or conflict increases, and their perceived reality becomes richer, more complex.

In looking for materials to build this expansion of the family's reality—alternative behaviors, attitudes, perceptions, affinities, expectations—the structural family therapist has one primary source from which to draw: the family. The model contends that beyond the systemic constraints that keep the family functioning at an inadequate level, there exists an as yet underutilized pool of potential resources (see Figure 1, the shaded areas). Releasing these resources so that the system can change, and changing the system so that the resources can be released, are simultaneous processes that require the restructuring input of the therapist. The therapist's role will be discussed at some length in the following section.

APPLICATION

In discussing the practical applications of structural family therapy, the first point to be made is that the model is not just a cluster of techniques with specific indications, but rather a consistent way of thinking and operating, derived from the basic tenet that human problems can only be understood and treated in context. As such, the model is in principle applicable to any human system in need of change.

The family, however, presents some unique characteristics that make it a comparatively accessible and rewarding field of application. A natural group with a history and a future, family members tend to remain associated even under circumstances that would be lethal for the fate of other human groups—such as high levels of ongoing conflict, extreme negative feelings, and ultimate dysfunctionality—and can then be expected (more than as members of other groups) to endure the challenges of therapy. Families usually have the motivation to invest time, money, energy, and affect for the sake of one of their members. They also offer a prospect of continuity for the changes initiated during therapy.

In actual practice, structural family therapy has been mostly applied to—and has grown from—families where a son or daughter is the identified patient. This context offers some additional advantages, in that cultural expectations define the family as a most relevant environment for a child, and the parents as directly responsible for his or her well-being. The extent of the bias, if any, built into the model's current formulations by virtue of the specifics of child psychotherapy will only be measurable on extensive application of structural family therapy to "adult" problems.

There are no specific requirements that families or problems should meet for the model to be applicable. True, the family needs to be motivated and resourceful, but a systemic understanding implies that any family can be motivated and no family is resourceless—otherwise the point of meeting the therapist would never have been reached. Similarly, the problem must be a transactional one, but this according to system thinking is a matter of how the problem is defined, described, or framed. In addition to the work with low socioeconomic families, delinquency, and psychosomatic illness (already mentioned in connection with the historical development of the model), the literature on structural family therapy includes case material from many different origins. School-related problems (Aponte, 1976; Berger, 1974; Moskowitz, 1976), drug abuse (Stanton, 1978; Stanton & Todd, 1979; Stanton et al., 1978), mental retardation (Fishman, Scott, & Betof, 1977), specific symptoms such as elective mutism (Rosenberg & Lindblad, 1978), and encopresis (Andolfi, 1978) are some examples. Although not a complete list, these cases give an idea of the variety of clinical contexts to which the model has been applied.

While it is difficult to imagine a family problem that could *not* be approached from structural family therapy, there are nonetheless certain contexts, of a different sort, that limit the applicability of the model. Hospitalization of the identified patient, for instance, hinders the efforts to restructure the family because of the unnatural isolation of a key member, the confirmation of the family's definition of the problem, and the naturalization of a crucial source of energy for family change. By artificially removing stress from the family's reality, hospitalization tends to facilitate and reinforce the operation of homeostatic mechanisms; the resulting therapeutic system is one in which the therapist's power to challenge stereotyped transactional rules effectively is greatly diminished. A similar constraint is typically associated with medication and generally with any condition that appeases crisis and takes the motivation for change away from the system.

Another crucial variable in determining the applicability of structural family therapy is the therapist's acceptance of the goals set by the model for the therapeutic enterprise and of the function prescribed for him or her. These are areas in which structural family therapy

departs considerably from some other approaches, as will be described in the following discussion.

Goals and Function of Therapy

The basic goal of structural family therapy is the restructuralization of the family's system of transactional rules, such that the interactional reality of the family becomes more flexible, with an expanded availability of alternative ways of dealing with each other. By releasing family members from their stereotyped positions and functions, this restructuralization enables the system to mobilize its underutilized resources and to improve its ability to cope with stress and conflict. Once the constricting set of rules is outgrown, individual dysfunctional behaviors, including those described as the presenting problem, lose their support in the system and become unnecessary from the point of view of homeostasis. When the family achieves self-sufficiency in sustaining these changes without the challenging support of the therapist, therapy comes to an end.

This statement of goals may appear as too ambitious an objective; after all, the presenting problem was perhaps originally characterized as one aspect in the behavior of one out of seven family members. But from the model's point of view, the structural relationship between system and problem behavior is not just a far-fetched conceptual connection—it is an observable phenomenon. Whenever the "problem" is enacted in a session, the structure of related transactions is set in motion with the regularity of clockwork. Again, the presenting problem ultimately *is* the structure of relationships, and each occurrence of the problem behavior or symptom provides a metaphor for the system. Changing one of the terms in this equation implies changing the other, not as a prerequisite but as a covariation. In structural family therapy, it is not necessary to postpone consideration of the original complaint in order to pursue structural change. On the contrary, it is possible, and frequently inescapable, to weave the fabric of the one with the threads of the other.

The therapist's function is to assist the family in achieving the necessary restructuralization. The position prescribed for him or her by the model is similar to that of a midwife helping in a difficult delivery. Once change is born and thriving, the therapist must withdraw and resist the temptation to rear the "baby." Some therapists are specially vulnerable to this temptation because of the tradition in psychotherapy that calls for a complete, ultimate "cure" of the client—an improbable goal whose equivalent cannot be found in other health disciplines (an internist will hardly tell a patient that he or she will never need a doctor again). The concept of an ultimate cure is unthinkable in structural family therapy, which emphasizes constant growth and change as an essential feature of the family system. Hence, the structural family therapist is encouraged to limit his or her participation to the minimum that is necessary to set in motion the family's natural healing resources.

It certainly may happen that as a result of the therapist's intervention the family is helped not only to change but also to metachange—that in addition to overcoming the current crisis, the family will also be better able to deal with future events without external help. This high level of achievement is, of course, desirable, but that does not mean that other, more modest accomplishments are valueless. A restructuralization that allows Danny to go back to school while Dad takes care of Mom's depression and emptiness may be a perfectly legitimate outcome, even if the family comes back 4 years later when Jenny runs into adolescent trouble. From the point of view of structural family therapy, this prospect is more sensible, natural, and economic than the protracted presence of a therapist accompanying the family for years, unable to separate because of a need to make sure that things are developing in a satisfactory way.

In yet another sense, the therapist's role as prescribed by structural family therapy runs contrary to psychotherapy tradition. Much of the confessorlike behavior encouraged by other approaches is here regarded as therapeutically irrelevant, and mostly counterindicated. The therapist is not there primarily to listen to and answer sympathetically the clients' fantasies, secrets, fears, and wishes, but to assist in the development of a natural human context that can and should provide that kind of listening. He or she is not there to provide extensive one-to-one reparative experience for this and that family member but rather to operate an intensive tune-up of the natural healing system.

By limiting the duration and depth of the therapist's incursion into the family system, the model places restrictions on the therapist's curiosity and desire to be helpful, and ultimately on his or her power to control events. This loss of control is an inevitable consequence of the broadening of the therapist's scope (Minuchin, 1970).

Therapist's Role

The therapist's role, as prescribed by the structural therapy model, includes an element of paradox. The therapist is asked to support while challenging, to attack while encouraging, to sustain while undermining. A crucial conceptual distinction is necessary here to protect the therapist from confusion or hypocrisy: he or she is requested to be *for* the people in need of help and *against* the system of transactions that cripple them.

The first task for the structural family therapist is to enter the system that needs change and to establish a working relationship. This requires a certain degree of accommodation to the system's rules—but not up to a point in which the therapist's leverage to promote change is lost. Too much challenge to the system's rules at the entry stage would lead to the therapist's dismissal; too much accommodation would void his or her input by absorbing it into homeostasis. The therapist has to find the right equation of accommodation/challenge for each particular family through a process of probing, advancing, and withdrawing that guides his or her entrance while at the same time providing clues about the family structure.

So the therapist is actively engaged in a dance with the family right from the beginning of their contact. There is little room in this model for neutral listening or floating attention. The therapist approaches the family with a series of initial hypotheses built on the basis of minimal intake information and proceeds to test, expand, and correct those hypotheses as he or she joins the family. Attention is selectively oriented toward process and away from content; he or she is more interested in how people relate than in what they have to say, listening to content mostly as a way of capturing the language of the family, the metaphors that will later help catch the ears of the clients. As processes and themes unravel, the therapist's selective attention privileges some of them and discards the others. A map of the family depicting positions, alliances, hierarchies, and complementary patterns begins to emerge.

Soon the dancer turns into stage director, creating scenarios where problems are played according to different scripts. The embedding of the symptom in family transactions is explored and highlighted. Family members are invited to talk to each other or are excluded from participation. Distances and positions are prescribed, alternative arrangements tried. The therapist-director uses whatever knowledge he or she is gaining about the actors to create situations that will uncover hidden resources or confirm suggested limitations. He or she is looking for the specific ways in which this system is keeping its homeostasis in order to disrupt them and force a new equilibrium at a higher level of complexity. But the therapist is also searching for the system's strengths that will indicate possible directions to follow. The stage director is out to make trouble for the cast.

While the model prescribes activity, initiative, and directiveness, it also warns against centrality. The therapist is supposed to organize a scenario and start the action, but then to sit back as a spectator for a while. If he or she becomes too central, the system cannot fully display its limitations and potentialities; the therapist may get trapped in a stereotyped position and most probably be absorbed by homeostasis. The therapist needs to be mobile, to redefine his or her position constantly, displacing him- or herself from one role to another, from one alliance to another, from one challenge to the next—while at the same time maintaining a focus, a thread, a relevant theme connecting all of the moves together and to the presenting problem.

Now the structural family therapist resembles a camera director in a television studio who decides to air the close-up take from one of the cameras. Far from indulging in self-praise for the beauty of the achieved picture, he or she is already planning the next take—knowing also that from time to time the total picture will be needed to remind the audience what it is all about.

In short, the role of the therapist is to move around within the system, blocking existing stereotyped patterns of transactions and fostering the development of more flexible ones. While constantly negotiating the immunological mechanisms of the family organism in order to be accepted, the therapist behaves as a strange body to which the organism must accommodate by changing and growing.

PRIMARY TECHNIQUES

Over the years, structural family therapists have developed and adapted a variety of techniques to help themselves carry out their function as prescribed by the model. They can be classified, according to their main purpose, into (a) those that are primarily used in the formation of the therapeutic system and (b) the larger group of techniques more directly aimed at provoking disequilibrium and change.

Joining Techniques

Joining is the process of coupling that occurs between the therapist and the family and that leads to the formation of the therapeutic system. In joining, the therapist becomes accepted as such by the family and remains in that position for the duration of treatment. Although the joining process is more evident dur-

ing the initial phase of therapy, the maintenance of a working relationship to the family is one of the constant features in the therapist's job.

Much of the success in joining depends on the therapist's ability to listen, capacity for empathy, genuine interest in the clients' dramas, and sensitivity to feedback. But this does not exclude a need for technique in joining. The therapist's empathy, for instance, needs to be disciplined so that it does not hinder his or her ability to keep a certain distance and to operate in the direction of change. Contrary to a rather common misunderstanding, joining is not just the process of being accepted by the family; it is being accepted *as a therapist*, with a quota of leadership. Sometimes a trainee is described as "good at joining, but not at pushing for change"; in this case, what in fact happens is that the trainee is *not* joining well. The trainee is accepted by the family, yes, but at the expense of relinquishing his or her role and being swallowed by the homeostatic rules of the system. Excessive accommodation is not good joining.

Maintenance is one of the techniques used in joining. The therapist lets him- or herself be organized by the basic rules that regulate the transactional process in the specific family system. If a four-generation family presents a rigid hierarchical structure, the therapist may find it advisable to approach the great-grandmother first and then proceed downward. In so doing, the therapist may be resisting his or her first empathic wish—perhaps to rescue the identified patient from verbal abuse—but by respecting the rules of the system, he or she will stand a better chance to generate a therapeutic impact.

However, in order to avoid total surrender, the therapist needs to perform maintenance operations in a way that does not leave him or her powerless; the therapist does *not* want to follow the family rule that Kathy should be verbally abused whenever somebody remembers one of her misdoings. As with any other joining technique, maintenance entails an element of challenge to the system. The therapist can, for instance, approach the great-grandmother respectfully but say, "I am very concerned because I see all of you struggling to help, but you are not being helpful to each other." While the rule "Great-grandma first" is being respected at one level, at a different level the therapist is creating a position one up in relation to the entire system, including the great-grandmother. The therapist is joining the rules to his or her own advantage.

While maintenance concentrates on process, the technique of *tracking* consists of an accommodation of the therapist to the content of speech. In tracking, the therapist follows the subjects offered by family members as a needle follows a record groove. This not only enables the therapist to join the family culture but also to become acquainted with idiosyncratic idioms and metaphors that he or she will use later to endow directive statements with additional power—by phrasing them in ways that have a special meaning for the family or for specific members.

At times the therapist will find it necessary to establish a closer relation with a certain member, usually one that positions him- or herself or is positioned by the family in the periphery of the system. This may be done through verbal interventions or through *mimesis*, a nonverbal response where the therapist adopts the other person's mood, tone of voice, or posture or imitates his or her behavior—crossing legs, removing a jacket, lighting a cigarette. In most of the occasions, the therapist is not aware of the mimetic gesture itself but only of his or her disposition to get closer to the mimicked member. In other cases however, mimesis is consciously used as a technique; for instance, the therapist wants to join the system via the children and accordingly decides to sit on the floor with them and play.

Techniques for Disequilibration

The second, larger group of techniques encompasses all interventions aimed at changing the system. Some of them, like enactment and boundary making, are primarily employed in the creation of a different sequence of events, whereas others, like reframing, punctuation, and unbalancing, tend to foster a different perception of reality.

Reframing is putting the presenting problem in a perspective that is different from what the family brings and more workable. Typically this involves changing the definition of the original complaint from a problem of one to a problem of many. In a consultation (Minuchin, 1980) with the family of a 5-year-old girl who is described by her parents as "uncontrollable," Minuchin waits silently for a couple of minutes as the girl circles noisily around the room and the mother tries to persuade her to behave, then he asks the mother, "Is this how you two run your lives together?" If the consultant had asked something like "Is this the way *she* behaves usually?" he would be confirming the family's definition of the problem as located in the child. By making it a matter of two persons, the consultant is beginning to reframe the problem within a structural perspective.

In this example, the consultant is feeding into the system his own reading of an ongoing transaction. Sometimes a structural family therapist uses information provided by the family as the building materials for a frame. Minutes later in the session, the mother comments, "But we try to make her do it," and the father replies, "I make her do it." Minuchin then highlights this brief interchange by commenting on the differences that the family is presenting: Mother cannot make her do it, Father can. The initial "reality" described just in terms of the girl's "uncontrollability" begins to be replaced by a more complex version involving an ineffective mother, an undisciplined child, and maybe an authoritarian father.

The consultant is reframing in terms of *complementarity*, a typical variety of the reframing technique in which any given individual's behavior is presented as contingent on somebody else's behavior. The daughter's uncontrollability is related to her mother's ineffectiveness, which is maintained by the father's taking over, which is triggered by the mother's ineffectiveness in controlling the daughter. Another example of reframing through complementarity is the question, "Who makes you feel depressed?" addressed to a man who claims to be "the" problem in the family because of his depression.

As with all other techniques employed in structural family therapy, reframing is based on an underlying attitude on the part of the therapist. He or she needs to be actively looking for structural patterns in order to find them and use them in communicating with the family. Whether the therapist will read the 5-year-old's misbehavior as a function of her own "uncontrollability" or of a complementary pattern depends on his or her perspective. Also, the therapist's field of observation is so vast that he or she cannot help but be selective in perception. Whether he or she picks up that "I make her do it" or lets it pass by unnoticed amid the flow of communication depends on whether his or her selective attention is focused on structure or not. As with joining and unbalancing, reframing requires from the therapist a "set" without which the technique cannot be mastered.

The reframing attitude guides the structural family therapist in the search of structural embeddings for "individual" problems. In one case involving a young drug addict, the therapist took advantage of the sister's casual reference to the handling of money to focus on the family's generosity toward the patient and the infantile position in which he was being kept. In another case, involving a depressed adolescent who invariably arrived late at his day treatment program, the therapist's reframing interventions led to the unveiling of a pattern of overinvolvement between the mother and son: she was actually substituting for his alarm clock. In an attempt to help him, she was instead preventing him from developing a sense of responsibility.

The intended effect of reframing is to render the situation more workable. Once the problem is redefined in terms of complementarity, for instance, the participation of every family member in the therapeutic effort acquires a special meaning for them. When they are described as mutually contributing to each other's failures, they are also given the key to the solution. Complementarity is not necessarily pathological; it is a fact of life, and it can adopt the form of family members helping each other to change. Within such a frame, the therapist can request the family members to enact alternative transactions.

Enactment is the actualization of transactional patterns under the control of the therapist. This technique allows the therapist to observe how family members mutually regulate their behaviors and to determine the place of the problem behavior within the sequence of transactions. Enactment is also the vehicle through which the therapist introduces disruption in the existent patterns, probing the system's ability to accommodate to different rules and ultimately forcing the experimentation of alternative, more functional rules. Change is expected to occur as a result of dealing with the problems rather than talking about them.

In the case of the uncontrollable girl, the consultant, after having reframed the problem to include the mother's ineffectiveness and the father's hinted authoritarianism, sets up an enactment that will challenge that "reality" and test the family's possibilities of operating according to a different set of assumptions. He asks the mother whether she feels comfortable with the situation as it is—the grown-ups trying to talk while the two little girls run in circles screaming and demanding everybody's attention. When the mother replies that she feels tense, the therapist invites her to organize the situation in a way that will feel more comfortable, and he finishes his request with "Make it happen," which will be the motto for the following sequence.

The purpose of this enactment is multileveled. At the higher, more ambitious level, the therapist wants to facilitate an experience of success for the mother, and the experience of a successful mother for the rest of the family. But even if the mother should fail to make it happen, the enactment will at least fulfill a lower-level goal: it will provide the therapist with an understanding of the dysfunctional pattern and of the more accessible routes to its correction.

In our specific example, the mother begins to voice orders in quick succession, overlapping her own commands and hence handicapping her own chances of being obeyed. The children seem deaf to what she has to say, moving around the room and only sporadically doing what they are being asked to do. The consultant takes special care to highlight those minisuccesses, but at the same time he keeps reminding the mother that she wanted something done and "it is not happening—make it happen." When the father, following the family rule, attempts to add his authority to the mother's, the consultant blocks his intervention. The goal of the enactment is to see that the mother makes it happen by herself; for the same reason, the consultant ignores the mother's innumerable violations to practically every principle of effective parenting. To correct her, to teach her how to do it, would defeat the purpose of the enactment.

The consultant keeps the enactment going on until the mother eventually succeeds in organizing the girls to play by themselves in a corner of the room, and then the adults can resume their talk. The experience can later be used as a lever in challenging the family's definition of their reality.

If the mother had not succeeded, the consultant would have had to follow a different course—typically one that would take her failure as a starting point for another reframing. Sometimes the structural family therapist organizes an enactment with the purpose of helping people to *fail*. A classical example is provided by the parents of an anorectic patient who undermine each other in their competing efforts to feed her. In this situation, the therapist may want to have the parents take turns in implementing their respective tactics and styles, with the agenda that they should both fail and then be reunited in their common defeat and anger toward their daughter—now seen as strong and rebellious rather than weak and hopeless.

Whether it is aimed at success or at failure, enactment is always intended to provide a different experience of reality. The family members' explanations for their own and each other's behaviors, their notions about their respective positions and functions within the family, their ideas about what their problems are and how they can contribute to a solution, and their mutual attitudes are typically brought into question by these transactional microexperiences orchestrated by the therapist.

Enactments may be dramatic, as in an anorectic's lunch (Rosman, Minuchin, & Liebman, 1977, pp. 166–169), or they can be almost unnoticeably launched by the therapist with a simple "Talk to your son about your concerns; I don't know that he understands your position." If this request is addressed to a father who tends to talk to his son through his wife, and if mother is kept out of the transaction by the therapist, the structural effects on behavior and perception may be powerful, even if the ensuing conversation turns out to be dull. The real power of enactment does not reside in the emotionality of the situation but rather in the very fact that family members are being directed to behave differently in relation to each other. By prescribing and monitoring transactions, the therapist assumes control of a crucial area—the rules that regulate who should interact with whom, about what, when, and for how long.

Boundary making is a special case of enactment, in which the therapist defines areas of interaction deemed open to certain members but closed to others. When Minuchin prevents the husband from "helping" his wife to discipline the girls, he is indicating that such specific transaction is for the mother and daughters to negotiate and that the father has nothing to do at this point. This specific way of making boundaries is also called *blocking*. Other instances of boundary making consist of prescriptions of physical movements: a son is asked to leave his chair (in between his parents) and go to another chair on the opposite side of the room so that he is not "caught in the middle"; a grandmother is brought next to the therapist and far from her daughter and granddaughter, who have been requested to talk; the therapist stands up and uses his or her body to interrupt visual contact between father and son; and so forth.

Boundary making is a restructuring maneuver because it changes the rules of the game. Detouring mechanisms and other conflict avoidance patterns are disrupted by this intervention; underutilized skills are allowed and even forced to manifest themselves. The mother of the 5-year-old is put in the position of accomplishing something without her husband's help; the husband and wife can and must face each other without their son acting as a buffer; the mother and daughter continue talking because Grandma's intervention, which usually puts an end to their transactions, is now being blocked; the father and son cannot distract one another through eye contact.

As powerful as the creation of specific events in the session may be, their impact depends to a large extent on how the therapist punctuates those events for the family.

Punctuation is a universal characteristic of human interaction. No transactional event can be described in the same terms by different participants because their perspectives and emotional involvements are different. A husband will say that he needs to lock himself in the studio to escape his wife's nagging; she will say that she cannot help protesting about his aloofness. They are linked by the same pattern, but when describing it they begin and finish their sentences at different points and with different emphases.

The therapist can put this universal to work for the purposes of therapeutic change. In structural family therapy, punctuation is the selective description of a transaction in accordance with the therapist's goals. In our example of enactment, the consultant organized a situation in which the mother was finally successful, but it was the consultant himself who made the success "final." Everybody—the mother included—expected at that point that the relative peace achieved would not last, but the consultant hastened to put a period—punctuate—by declaring the mother successful and moving to a different subject before the girls could misbehave again. If he had not done so, if he had kept the situation open, the usual pattern in which the girls demanded the mother's attention and the mother became incompetent would have repeated itself, and the entire experience would have been labeled a failure. Because of the facts of punctuation, the difference between success and failure may be no more than 45 seconds and an alert therapist.

Later in the same session, the consultant asked the parents to talk without allowing interruptions from their daughter. The specific prescription was that the father should make sure that his wife paid attention only to him and not to the girl. Given this context for the enactment, whenever the mother was distracted by the girl, the therapist could blame the *father* for the failure—a different punctuation from what would have resulted if the consultant had just asked the mother to avoid being distracted.

A variety of punctuation is *intensity,* a technique that consists of emphasizing the importance of a given event in the session or a given message from the therapist, with the purpose of focusing the family's attention and energy on a designated area. Usually the therapist magnifies something that the family ignores or takes for granted as another way of challenging the reality of the system. Intensity is achieved sometimes through repetition: one therapist put the same question about 80 times to a patient who had decided to move out of his parents' home and did not do so: "Why didn't you move?" Other times the therapist creates intensity through emotionally charged interventions ("It is important that you all listen, because your sister can die") or confrontation ("What your father did just now is very disrespectful"). In a general sense, the structural family therapist is always monitoring the intensity of the therapeutic process, so that the level of stress imposed on the system does not become either unbearable or too comfortable.

Unbalancing is a term that could be used to encompass most of the therapist's activity since the basic strategy that permeates structural family therapy is to create disequilibrium. In a more restricted sense, however, unbalancing is the technique where the weight of the therapist's authority is used to break a stalemate by supporting one of the terms in a conflict. Toward the end of the consultation with the family of the "uncontrollable" girl, Minuchin and the couple discuss the wife's idea that her husband is too harsh on the girls:

Minuchin: Why does she think that you are such a tough person? Because I think she feels that you are very tough, and she needs to be flexible because you are so rigid. I don't see you at all as rigid, I see you actually quite flexible. How is it that your wife feels that you are rigid, and not understanding?

Husband: I don't know; a lot of times I lose my temper I guess, right? That's probably why.

Wife: Yeah.

Minuchin: So what? So does she. I have seen you playing with your daughter here, and I think you are soft and flexible, and that you were playing in a rather nice and accepting way. You were not authoritarian, you had initiative, your play engaged her. . . . That is what I saw. So why is that she sees you only as rigid and authoritarian, and she needs to defend the little girls from you (punches father's knee)? I don't see you that way at all.

Husband: I don't know, like I say, the only thing I can think of, really, is because I lose my temper with them.

Wife: Yes, he does have a short fuse.

Minuchin: So what? So do you.

Wife: No, I don't.

Minuchin: Oh you don't. OK, but that doesn't mean that you are authoritarian, and that doesn't mean that you are not understanding. Your play with your daughter here was full with warmth and you entered very nicely, and as a matter of fact she enjoyed the way in which you entered to play. So, some way or other your wife has a strange image of you and your ability to understand and be flexible. Can you talk with her? How is it that she sees that she needs to be supportive and defending of your daughter? I think she is protecting the girls from your short fuse, or something like that. Talk with her about that, because I think she is wrong.

Wife: That's basically what it is. I'm afraid of you really losing your temper on them, because I know how bad it is, and they are little, and if you really hit them with a temper you could really hurt them; and I don't want that, so that's why I go the other way, to show them that everybody in the house doesn't have that short fuse.

Husband: Yes, but I think when you do that, that just makes it a little worse because that makes her think that she has somebody backing her, you know what I mean?

Minuchin (shakes husband's hand): This is very clever, and this is absolutely correct, and I think that you should say it again because your wife does not understand that point.

In this sequence, the consultant unbalances the couple through his support of the husband. His focus organizes him to disregard the wife's reasons, which may seem unfair at first sight. But it is in the nature of unbalancing to be unfair. The therapist unbalances when he or she needs to punctuate reality in terms of right and wrong, victim and villain, actor and reactor, in spite knowing that all the comings and goings in the family are regulated by homeostasis and that each person obliges with his and her own contribution, because the therapist also knows that an equitable distribution of guilts and errors would only confirm the existing equilibrium and neutralize change potentialities.

While unbalancing is admittedly and necessarily unfair, it is not arbitrary. Diagnostic considerations dictate the direction of the unbalancing. In the case of our example, the consultant chooses to support the husband rather than the wife because in so doing he is challenging a myth that *both* spouses share: initially the husband agrees to his wife's depiction of him, and it is only through the intensity of the consultant's message that he begins to challenge it. At different points in the same session, the consultant supports the wife as a competent mother and questions the idea of her unremitting inefficiency—again, a myth defended not only by her husband but by herself as well. In the last analysis, unbalancing—like the entire structural approach—is a challenge to the system rather than an attack on any member.

CASE EXAMPLE

The Murphy family is composed of Joe, the father, 33 years old; Connie, the mother, 30; Jenny, 7; and Kevin, 4. On the telephone, Connie stated that Kevin is very aggressive, throws toys at his sister, and screams for no apparent motive. Last week he pushed Jenny and caused her to injure her eye. Connie's sister Pat, 28 years old, who lives in the same apartment building and is a schoolteacher, has always thought Kevin to be hyperactive, and some time ago she arranged for a neurological examination. The test found nothing wrong with Kevin. The Murphys own a small grocery store where both work.

When the family (including Pat) enters the room for the first interview, Kevin and Jenny (who has a patch on her right eye) go directly to the toys; the therapist follows them and starts his joining by inquiring about Jenny's condition. He finds out that the lesion is not serious and also that Pat intervenes frequently in his dialogue with the children—adding to or correcting the information provided by them. It turns out that Kevin pushed Jenny while playing, and then Jenny hit a counter corner. As the therapist stands up from the floor and sits on a chair, the children quickly organize themselves to play; Kevin does not—and will not—show any of the typical signs of hyperactivity. The therapist proceeds then to explore the family structure and to reframe the problem.

Therapist: So you had a scare.
Connie: Yes. Thank God she is going to be

OK, but I still—I don't know, it is scary, the things that can happen, and I—(Looks at Pat).
Pat: Yes, well, I was the one who started this I guess, so maybe I should say something. (Connie nods.) You know, I had been noticing, like Kevin was always too active, and I wondered whether I should say something, but then Connie came up with the same thing and—
Therapist: Connie? What did you come up with?
Connie: Like she said, he was always difficult, but then he started to give more and more trouble and it got to a point—he is impossible. One minute he can be playing, and the next thing you know he is yelling and he will not stop. I don't know, the doctor says he doesn't need any medicine but I—
Therapist: You can't control him, eh? (After some exploration, Jenny has started to build a tower with blocks; Kevin follows her leadership.)
Pat: He is really uncontrollable when it comes to it.
Therapist: So Connie and Pat find Kevin difficult. How about you, Joe?
Joe: I don't know, he does get on his mother's nerves, but he doesn't give me any trouble.
Pat: Well, but you—you are different.
Joe: Yeah, maybe, but...well, I don't know.
Therapist: You think you are different?
Pat: He is more patient.
Therapist: Are you?
Joe: I don't know, she says that but... (Therapist signals that he should talk to Pat.) You say that I don't pay them enough attention.
Pat: It's not that. (To therapist) I feel it's easier for Joe because he can tune himself off, like when Kevin is hyper.
Therapist (to Connie): What do you think?
Connie: Pardon?
Therapist: Your sister is saying something about your husband.
Connie: Is it easier for him? Yes, in a way I think it is easier. Like, the kids can be playing rough and it is like OK with him, he doesn't care, he says kids are kids. But I cannot see

them going on like that; someone has to stop them, or everybody gets crazy.

Therapist: Everybody or just you?

Connie: Everybody. You know, Mr. Murphy here has his temper too.

Therapist: Then you stop them, eh? You mean you need to help him to keep his patience? Are you making things easier for him?

Connie: I guess, yes, I guess I am.

Therapist: That must be a hell of a lot of work. Is your sister helpful?

Connie: What do you mean?

Therapist: I mean, it must be very difficult to protect your husband's patience if he has a temper. Does your sister help you with that?

Connie: Well, she helps with the kids, they listen to her—that helps, a lot.

Therapist: That helps with Jenny but not with Kevin, because you two together cannot cope with him, right? It takes your husband's temper to control Kevin?

Connie: Well yes, when it gets real bad he is the only one.

Therapist: And I bet Kevin knows that. Kevin? Your daddy is tough? Is he tougher than Mommy? (Kevin nods and goes back to his play with Jenny.) So you have a nice arrangement here. You two take care of Joe's patience, and Joe only intervenes when it is really necessary. Only that then (to Joe), maybe sometimes Kevin has to get tougher if he wants you rather than Connie or Pat?

During this sequence the therapist has had a chance to assess the extent of Pat's involvement in the life of the Murphys. He is not challenging her interferences; rather, he is accepting the rules of communication of the family. At the same time, the therapist has been reframing the problem from a complaint about Kevin into a situation involving at least four people. Now the therapist is ready to initiate his challenge to the family's arrangement.

He sets the stage for an enactment by asking the parents to bring Jenny to talk with the grown-ups but to leave Kevin playing. At this point he thinks that

Jenny also has a function in keeping Kevin busy and that the separation of the children will trigger Kevin's "hyperactivity." When Kevin, as expected, begins to protest loudly about the unfair discrimination, the therapist asks Connie to protect Joe's patience.

Connie: You stay there playing for a while, Kevin; the doctor wants to talk to Jenny.

Kevin: No! (Stands up and moves toward his mother.)

Connie: No Kevin, I told you to stay there. You cannot come here now.

Pat (to Kevin): It is only for a while.

Kevin: Is he going to see her eye?

Pat: No, I don't think so. (Looks at the therapist who looks at the ceiling. Kevin leans on Pat.)

Connie: (to therapist): Is it OK if he stays here?

Therapist: I don't know. (To Joe): Is it OK that he should disobey your wife? She just told him to stay there.

Joe: Yeah, but that is it, you see, they keep doing it. Connie and Pat, they do it all the time.

Therapist: Tell that to your wife.

Joe: But I tell her. I tell you, don't I?

Joe and Connie now initiate a rather low-key discussion about what should be done when Kevin does not respond to their requests, with Joe espousing a more stern position and Connie advocating for more understanding. Pat alternates between trying (not too forcefully) to send Kevin back to the toys and listening to the couple's dialogue. Jenny watches silently. After a minute or two, the therapist interrupts the sequence and steps up the challenge.

Therapist: You are not going to get anywhere, because you are asking your wife to send Kevin back but she can't do it.

Joe: Yes, I know. Well, I wasn't—

Therapist: But you know why? You know why your wife can't do it? Because she does not have Kevin right now, Pat does.

Joe: How do you mean?

Pat: He means I'm stealing your son, like we used to say—

Therapist: No, you are not stealing anything; you are trying to help. But you are not being helpful, because all the time that you take care of Kevin they don't have to agree. You see, they can't finish this argument, they don't need to, because you are protecting them from Kevin, and Kevin from them.

Pat: But I am not keeping him.

Therapist: Oh yes you are, by being so available. I'll tell you what, I'll ask you to take a rest.

The therapist then invites Pat to move her chair next to him and spend the next minutes observing her relatives. So Pat is being defined as a well-meant, helpful person—which she most probably is—but the boundaries are being set all the same.

The therapist is also punctuating the triadic relationship by placing the emphasis of his description on Pat's helpfulness toward the Murphys. The same transaction could alternatively have been described as the Murphys helping Pat to feel useful, or as the two women forming a coalition against Joe, or as Connie being the middlewoman between her husband's and her sister's demands, and so forth. In fact, these different versions of the same reality are equally true and will eventually be emphasized in later sessions. At this point, however, the therapist chooses the angle that seems to be less threatening for Pat, because he has assessed the power held by the sister in the family.

The rest of the first session is employed in discussing the differences in personality between Jenny and Kevin and other issues where the children are the focus of attention. Joe is asked to "interview" the children for the therapist, in a move that anticipates the direc-

tion of the unbalancing that will be initiated in the second interview. At the end of the session, Pat is invited to share her observations with the family.

The Murphys were in treatment for a total of 18 weekly sessions. The early scene where Joe and Connie fruitlessly disagreed while Kevin clung to Pat could be used as an illustration for different stages of the treatment—provided the scene was photographed from many different angles and with many different lenses, so that it could render a variety of themes. The first therapeutic goal was to make room for an unobstructed relationship between Joe and Kevin. They should be able to establish their own rules without interference from Connie or Pat. This objective was made difficult by the myth that Joe was unable, either because of his temper or his indifference, to sustain such a relationship. The therapist had to unbalance by pushing Joe to exercise his rights and obligations, challenging Connie's opinion and maintaining Pat as a nonparticipating observer.

As Joe gained in assertiveness, he began to bring his own challenges into the picture. He insisted that Kevin should go to nursery school and successfully refuted his wife's objections. (Kevin had been spending most of his days with Connie at the store, a small place that constrained his activity and where Jenny's accident occurred.) The complaints about Kevin's behavior gradually disappeared, and, simultaneously, Pat began to lose interest in the sessions and even missed some. The therapist decided to temporarily excuse the children from attending the sessions and to shift the focus toward her.

Pat, the younger of the two sisters, was single and divided her life mostly between her job as a teacher and the Murphys. She and Connie talked a lot, mostly about the children and probably about Joe as well. Pat was also the family's favorite baby-sitter. With Joe assuming a new role in the family, the pattern of coalitions underwent a change: Connie moved closer to her husband and away from her sister. Pat began to feel depressed and to withdraw even from the children, which brought about a reversal in the sisters' relationship. While before Pat had been the knowledgeable teacher and Connie the troubled mother, now Connie was being the fulfilled family woman and Pat the lonely single. Connie grew solicitous about Pat, which only helped to increase Pat's feelings of depression and inadequacy.

The therapist introduced his own framing in this arrangement by pointing out that Connie was being intrusive; Pat had a right to her own privacy, including the right to feel depressed and lonely without interference. Connie could indicate that she would be available if Pat needed company or advice, but she should not impose herself on her sister. At Pat's own request, the therapist held a couple of individual sessions with her alone.

The content of these two sessions is not nearly as important as the fact that they took place, reinforcing the message of differentiation. Following them—and although the subject had not been discussed between Pat and the therapist—Pat announced in a somewhat solemn manner her "resignation" as the Murphy's baby-sitter. The Murphys, particularly Connie, were distressed at the possibility that Pat could be acting out of a feeling of rejection; the therapist supported Pat in her stand that she was just making what she thought was a good decision for her.

The last sessions, in which the children were again included, were devoted to monitoring the adjustment of the Murphy family to the new set of rules. At that point, Kevin was doing well in nursery school (after a somewhat difficult start), while at home he did not present any problem that his parents could not handle. The parents had reopened a discussion about the future of their grocery store, an issue on which they had conflicting points of view. Dealing with the conflict had been impossible before because of Connie's fears of making Joe feel incompetent and his fears of upsetting her; now, from their new perceptions of each other, a conflict-solving approach was possible. Finally, Pat's private life remained wrapped in a mystery that the therapist had to respect because his restructuring intervention had come to an end.

However, 8 months later, the therapist called for a follow-up, and, according to Connie, the only news worth mentioning was that Pat was dating somebody whom she—Connie—did not like at all. "But," she hastened to add, "Joe keeps telling me it's her life and it's none of my business. And I tell him if I don't like the guy, I'm sorry, I don't like him, and that's none of *his* business either."

EVALUATION

Treatment models tend to resist evaluation, not only because of the methodological difficulties that plague the definition and control of relevant variables, but mainly because of the decisive effect of value judgments on the selection and interpretation of data. Outcome criteria, which are crucial in assessing the efficacy of treatment, ultimately reflect the ethical choices of a culture or subculture; "empirical evidence" is just a relative truth (Colapinto, 1979).

Structural family therapy enjoys in this respect a comparatively enviable status, because one of its areas of application—psychosomatic illness—facilitates the formulation of objective criteria for the evaluation of outcome. Symptom remission is a more precise indicator when the issue is labile diabetes than when we are talking about a depressive reaction. In the first case, it is possible to count the number of hospitalizations, whereas in the second, one has to rely more on subjective reports.

Minuchin and his collaborators have periodically published their research findings in the field of psychosomatics (see, e.g., Baker et al., 1975; Liebman, Minuchin, & Baker, 1974c; Minuchin et al., 1975; Rosman et al., 1976, 1977). The most complete report (Rosman, Minuchin, Liebman, & Baker, 1978) summarizes information on 20 cases of labile diabetes, 53 cases of anorexia, and 17 cases of intractable asthma.

In the case of labile diabetes (operationally defined as severe, relapsing ketoacidosis, chronic acetonuria, and/or extreme instability in diabetic control), 88% of the subjects (aged 10 to 18 years) recovered—this meaning that no hospital admissions for ketoacidosis occurred after treatment and/or that diabetic control stabilized within normal limits. The remaining 12% showed moderate improvement: some symptomatology persisted after treatment, but there was a marked reduction in the number of hospital admissions and/or a more stable diabetic control. The diabetic group was in therapy for periods ranging from 3 to 15 months, with a median of 8 months, and was followed up for 2 to 9 years, with a median of 4.5 years.

Of the 53 anorectics (aged 9 to 21 and with a median weight loss of 30%), 86% achieved normal eating patterns and a body weight stabilized within normal limits; 4% gained weight but continued suffering the effects of the illness (borderline weight, obesity, occasional vomiting), and 10% showed little or no change or relapsed. Treatment lasted between 2 and 16 months, with a median of 6, and follow-up was done between 1.5 and 7 years, with a median of 2.5 years.

Finally, the 17 asthmatics (suffering severe attacks with regular steroid therapy or an intractable condition with steroid dependency, aged 7 to 17 years), achieved recovery (little or no school days lost, moderate attacks with occasional or regular use of bronchodilator only) in 82% of the cases. An additional 12% improved moderately (weeks of school lost, prolonged and severe attacks, and some use of steroids but with symptomatic improvement), and the remaining 6% stayed unimproved (more than 50% school loss, need for special schooling, persistent symptoms, dependency on regular steroid therapy). Duration of treatment was between 2 and 22 months, with a median of 8, and follow-up was done between 1 and 7 years later, with a median of 3.

Psychosocial assessment of the 90 cases, based on the degree of adjustment to family, school, or work, and social and peer relationships, showed results that paralleled these data.

The systematic and sustained application of the model in the Philadelphia Child Guidance Clinic over the last 25 years—in which thousands of families were served—provides an additional, although admittedly indirect, indication of its validity. The same applies to the sustained enrollment in the training programs offered at the Clinic by the Family Therapy Training Center. In addition to workshops and other continuous education activities, the Center offers an 8-month extern program, where an average of 40 family therapists are trained each year, and 3 summer practica, which provide an intensive experience to another 70 professionals. The intensive use of live supervision and videotapes encourages and facilitates the evaluation of treatment process.

SUMMARY

Structural family therapy is a model of treatment primarily characterized by its emphasis on structural change and on the therapist as an active agent of change. Its origins can be traced back to Salvador Minuchin's work with delinquent boys from poor families at the Wiltwyck School in the early 1960s. Its consolidation coincided with Minuchin's tenure at the Philadelphia Child Guidance Clinic, where he was appointed director in 1965. The successful application of the model to the treatment of psychosomatic conditions, documented through research, was primarily responsible for the interest aroused by Minuchin's approach; but structural family therapy can be and has been applied to the entire range of emotional disorders.

The model conceptualizes the family as a living open system whose members are interdependent and that undergoes transformation of an evolutionary nature. Family process is regulated by the multilevel interplay of homeostasis and change, and it can be arrested—in which case the family fails to adjust its rules to changing environmental or intrinsic demands, and homeostasis becomes dominant. Intergenerational coalitions, triangulations, conflict avoidance, and lack of growth and differentiation characterize these families, which then come to therapy as caricatures of themselves.

The problem behavior is seen as a partial aspect of this family stagnation. The diagnostic endeavor consists of assessing the transactional and perceptual structure that is supporting (rather than "causing") the symptom. Accordingly, therapeutic change depends on the modification of the family structure: positional changes, increases and reductions in distances, redefinition of hierarchical relations, exploration of new alternative rules, and conflict resolution are required so that the natural road to growth can be reopened. A special context, the therapeutic system, is created to this effect, where the therapist pushes the system limits in a quest for its potential strengths and underutilized resources.

The therapist, whose function is to assist the family in restructuralization, participates subject to boundaries both in terms of depth and time. In a paradoxical role, he or she needs to find the right equation of accommodation and challenge. At different times, the therapist's role can be compared to the job of a dancer, a stage director, a camera director, and a strange body in the family organism. The model provides the therapist with techniques for forming the therapeutic system and for creating disequilibrium and change: joining techniques such as maintenance, tracking, and mimesis; and disequilibrating techniques such as reframing, enactment, boundary making, punctuation, and unbalancing.

Structural family therapy has been validated directly through research in the fields of psychosomatics and indirectly through its application to thousands of families presenting all sorts of different problems. The sustained demand for training from mental health practitioners provides another indirect measure of the model's validity.

ANNOTATED SUGGESTED READINGS

Minuchin, S., Montalvo, B., Guerney, B. G., Rosman, B. L., & Schumer, F. (1967). *Families of the slums.* New York: Basic Books.

A summary of the experience at Wiltwyck. It reports on research focused on the structure and dynamics of poor and disorganized families with more than one delinquent child, and it includes some of the early instruments developed by the group to assess family interaction.

Minuchin, S. (1974). *Families and family therapy.* Cambridge, MA: Harvard University Press.

The first systematic presentation of structural family therapy. It discusses the basic concepts in the model and their implications for therapy, with the help of excerpts and transcriptions from interviews with normal and problem families.

Minuchin, S., Rosman, B., & Baker, L. (1978). *Psychosomatic families: Anorexia nervosa in context.* Cambridge, MA: Harvard University Press.

Presents the specifics of psychosomatic disorders, including the characterization of the psychosomatic family, the treatment program and the outcome, with a special emphasis on anorexia nervosa. It also includes long excerpts from family sessions.

Minuchin, S., & Fishman, H. C. (1981). *Family therapy techniques.* Cambridge, MA: Harvard University Press.

An updated account of the model that draws from the experience accumulated in the course of several years of teaching at the Family Therapy Training Center. Emphasis is on the analysis of techniques and the theoretical and philosophical rationale behind the techniques.

Umbarger, Carter C. (1983). *Structural Family Therapy*. New York: Grune & Stratton.

Beginning family therapists will find in this book a simple yet not oversimplified step-by-step explanation of the major moves and interventions in structural family therapy, preceded by a coherent presentation of the underlying concepts. Provides an excellent introduction to Minuchin's own writing.

REFERENCES

Andolfi, M. (1978). A structural approach to a family with an encoprectic child. *Journal of Marriage and Family Counseling, 4,* 25–29.

Aponte, H. J. (1976). Underorganization and the poor family. In P. Guerin (Ed.), *Family therapy: Theory and practice.* New York: Gardner Press.

Baker, L., Minuchin, S., Milman, L., Liebman, R., & Todd, T. C. (1975). Psychosomatic aspects of juvenile diabetes mellitus: A progress report. In *Modern problems in pediatrics* (Vol. 12). White Plains, NY: S. Karger.

Berger, H. (1974). Somatic pain and school avoidance. *Clinical Pediatrics, 13,* 819–826.

Colapinto, J. (1979). The relative value of empirical evidence. *Family Process, 18,* 427–441.

Fishman, H. C., Scott, S., & Betof, N. (1977). A hall of mirrors: A structural approach to the problems of the mentally retarded. *Mental Retardation, 15,* 24.

Haley, J. (1971). A review of the family therapy field. In J. Haley (Ed.), *Changing families.* New York: Grune and Stratton.

Jackson, D. D. (1957). The question of family

homeostasis. *Psychiatric Quarterly Supplement, 31,* 79–90.

Jackson, D. D. (1965). The study of the family. *Family Process, 4,* 1–20.

Liebman, R., Minuchin, S., & Baker, L. (1974a). An integrated treatment program for anorexia nervosa. *American Journal of Psychiatry, 131,* 432–436.

Liebman, R., Minuchin, S., & Baker, L. (1974b). The role of the family in the treatment of anorexia nervosa. *Journal of the American Academy of Child Psychiatry, 13,* 264–274.

Liebman, R., Minuchin, S., & Baker, L. (1974c). The use of structural family therapy in the treatment of intractable asthma. *American Journal of Psychiatry, 131,* 535–540.

Liebman, R., Minuchin, S., Baker, L., & Rosman, B. (1976). The role of the family in the treatment of chronic asthma. In P. Guerin (Ed.), *Family therapy: Theory and practice.* New York: Gardner Press.

Liebman, R., Minuchin, S., Baker, L., & Rosman, B. (1977). Chronic asthma: A new approach to treatment. In M. F. McMillan & S. Henao (Eds.), *Child psychiatry treatment and research.* New York: Brunner/Mazel.

Malcolm, J. (1978, May 15). A reporter at large: The one-way mirror. *The New Yorker,* pp. 39–114.

Minuchin, S. (1961). *The acting-out child and his family: An approach to family therapy.* Paper presented at the William Alanson White Institute, New York.

Minuchin, S. (1969). Family therapy: Technique or theory? In J. H. Masserman (Ed.), *Science and psychoanalysis* (Vol. 14). New York: Grune and Stratton.

Minuchin, S. (1970). The use of an ecological framework in the treatment of a child. *International yearbook of child psychiatry* (Vol. 1). New York: Wiley.

Minuchin, S. (1972). Structural family therapy. In G. Caplan (Ed.), *American handbook of psychiatry* (Vol. 2). New York: Basic Books.

Minuchin, S. (1974). *Families and family therapy.* Cambridge, MA: Harvard University Press.

Minuchin, S. (1980). *Taming monsters* [Videotape]. Philadelphia: Philadelphia Child Guidance Clinic.

Minuchin, S., Baker, L., Liebman, R., Milman, L., Rosman, B., & Todd, T. (1973). Anorexia nervosa: Successful application of a family approach. *Pediatric Research, 7,* 294.

Minuchin, S., Baker, L., Rosman, B., Liebman, R., Milman, L., & Todd, T. C. (1975). A conceptual model of psychosomatic illness in children. *The Archives of General Psychiatry, 32,* 1031–1038.

Minuchin, S., & Barcai, A. (1969). Therapeutically induced family crisis. In J. H. Masserman (Ed.), *Science and psychoanalysis* (Vol. 14). New York: Grune and Stratton.

Minuchin, S., & Fishman, H. C. (1979). The psychosomatic family in child psychiatry. *Journal of the American Academy of Child Psychiatry, 18* (1), 76–90.

Minuchin, S., & Fishman, H. C. (1981). *Family therapy techniques.* Cambridge, MA: Harvard University Press.

Minuchin, S., & Montalvo, B. (1966). An approach for diagnosis of the low socioeconomic family. *American Psychiatric Research Report, 20.*

Minuchin, S., & Montalvo, B. (1967). Techniques for working with disorganized low socioeconomic families. *American Journal of Orthopsychiatry, 37,* 380–387.

Minuchin, S., Montalvo, B., Guerney, B. G., Rosman, B. L., & Schumer, F. (1967). *Families of the slums.* New York: Basic Books.

Minuchin, S., Rosman, B., & Baker, L. (1978). *Psychosomatic families: Anorexia nervosa in context.* Cambridge, MA: Harvard University Press.

Moskowitz, L. (1976). Treatment of the child with school-related problems. *Philadelphia Child Guidance Clinic Digest, 5,* 1.

Rosenberg, J. B., & Lindblad, M. (1978). Behavior therapy in a family context: Treating elective mutism. *Family Process, 17,* 77–82.

Rosman, B. L., Minuchin, S., & Liebman, R. (1975). Family lunch session: An introduction to family therapy in anorexia nervosa. *American Journal of Orthopsychiatry, 45,* 846–853.

Rosman, B. L., Minuchin, S., & Liebman, R. (1977). Treating anorexia by the family lunch session. In C. E. Schaefer & H. L. Millman (Eds.), *Therapies for children: A handbook of effective treatments for problem behavior.* San Francisco: Jossey-Bass.

Rosman, B. L., Minuchin, S., Liebman, R., & Baker, L. (1976). Input and outcome of family therapy in anorexia nervosa. In J. C. Claghorn (Ed.), *Successful psychotherapy.* New York: Brunner/Mazel.

Rosman, B. L., Minuchin, S., Liebman, R., & Baker, L. (1977). A family approach to anorexia nervosa: Study, treatment, outcome. In R. A. Vigersky (Ed.), *Anorexia nervosa.* New York: Raven Press.

Rosman, B. L., Minuchin, S., Liebman, R., & Baker, L. (1978, November). *Family therapy for psychosomatic children.* Paper presented at the annual meeting of the American Academy of Psychosomatic Medicine, Atlanta, GA.

Stanton, M. D. (1978). Some outcome results and aspects of structural family therapy with drug addicts. In D. Smith, S. Anderson, M. Buxton, T. Chung, N. Gottlieb, & W. Harvey (Eds.), *A multicultural view of drug abuse: Selected proceedings of the national drug abuse conference—1977.* Cambridge, MA: Shenkman.

Stanton, M. D., & Todd, T. C. (1979). Structural family therapy with drug addicts. In E. Kaufman & P. Kaufman (Eds.), *The family therapy of drug and alcohol abuse.* New York: Gardner Press.

Stanton, M. D., Todd, T. C., Heard, D. B., Kirschner, S., Kleiman, J. I., Mowatt, D. T., Riley, P., Scott, S. M., & Van Deusen, J. M. (1978). Heroin addiction as a family phenomenon: A new conceptual model. *American Journal of Drug and Alcohol Abuse, 5,* 125–150.

CHAPTER 5

Experiential/Symbolic Family Therapy

DAVID V. KEITH AND CARL A. WHITAKER

DEFINITION

Experiential/symbolic family therapy is essentially clinical. It has evolved from an effort to intensify the family's organization and assertive competence so that they can better handle their own relationship to the community, both as a whole and in reference to a particular member, whether it is one of the kids or one of the parents. It is not ecological, communications oriented, or anchored in any specific psychological theory. It is not guided by research, nor is it organized around the community's demands.

We presume that it is experience, not education that changes families. The main function of the cerebral cortex is inhibition. Thus, most of our experience goes on outside of our consciousness. We gain best access to it symbolically. For us, "symbolic" implies that some thing or some process has more than one meaning. While education can be immensely helpful, the covert process of the family is the one that contains the most power for potential changing.

HISTORICAL DEVELOPMENT

The background of our style of family therapy is best defined by the evolution of Carl Whitaker's career, which began

This chapter was supported in part by NIMH grant No. MH 14971-03.

An earlier version appeared in Gurman and Kniskern (1980), *Handbook of Family Therapy,* New York: Brunner/Mazel.

with a deficit in psychiatric training related to personnel shortages in World War II.

In 1938 and 1939, he worked as the resident psychiatric administrator in a small diagnostic hospital operated under an antiquated custodial care system. He was taught nothing about dynamic or psychoanalytic psychiatry. Instead he learned hospital care maneuvers, thereby escaping the fear of insanity so prevalent among those who learned psychiatry in the midst of the big state hospital and the masses of "deteriorating" patients. His previous training as an obstetrician/gynecologist was credited toward board eligibility in psychiatry.

Whitaker's subsequent training was in a child guidance clinic. He learned play therapy and was supervised by the chief social worker, who had been trained in the Rankian tradition. She interviewed each mother, while he interviewed the child. The two interviews were conducted separately and then reviewed. No effort was made to involve the father, and there was no cotherapy. He was steeped in the power dynamics of experiences that result from interacting with children as the process of change is lived out in the playroom. The use of symbols and nonverbal communication are dominant in child therapy; playing on the floor, playing with toys, talking Melanie Klein (1932) talk, struggling with problems of discipline and boundary control—all encouraged learning process talk. The child who was bored with toys

108

was obviously ending psychotherapy; the child who talked about the little boy next door who needed help was ready to leave therapy.

In addition to learning from patients, Whitaker was forced to learn by teaching. The psychiatry faculty at the University of Louisville were overseas, and this young child-psychiatry resident became a "faculty member" who taught medical students to do psychotherapy. He knew nothing about psychotherapy and not much about psychiatric patients. Medical-student interviews with emotionally disturbed patients pressured him to adapt child therapy to work with neurotic adolescent and adult psychosomatic patients.

A subsequent 3 years with delinquent teenagers in an inpatient home and an outpatient clinic again focused on behavior rather than intrapsychic problems. Play therapy with these teenagers included the use of toys, amputation dolls, clay, and checkers. He kept compulsive reports, and his written notes usually included every word from the beginning to the end of the entire psychotherapy.

During the next 2 years (1944–1946) in Tennessee at Oak Ridge Hospital, the seven staff psychiatrists were under massive pressure from the Army and from the 75,000 industrial workers in the huge atomic plant. (Oak Ridge National Laboratory was the sight of the Manhattan Project during World War II.) The entire three plants and the living city were fenced. There were three gates, and only those with a pass could enter or leave. Whitaker saw 20 patients a day back-to-back in half-hour interviews. This kind of intensity led to an absence of metadiscussion, of intellectual formulation, or of learning adroit ways of talking about therapy.

Whitaker's inexperience and the psychological stress of the setting led to the use of cotherapy. With Dr. John Warkentin he began to see patients conjointly. Psychologically, they were both rather naive, given Whitaker's surgical and play therapy experience and Warkentin's PhD in psychophysiology. They taught each other, and they learned with patients.

One unique experience expanded Whitaker's orientation forcefully. He had been seeing a 5-year-old and treating him with using a baby bottle filled with warm milk. It happened that the next patient was an acute manic-psychotic brought in from the 10-bed inpatient ward. He spied the bottle and became tremendously excited. Sucking it was an orgastic experience. The next 12 daily interviews, each one preoccupied with the intense bottle-feeding experience, pulled him out of his psychosis, and he was discharged back to his job. For the next 3 years Whitaker said he was convinced that every patient could benefit by sucking on a baby bottle. Most patients accepted the offer, and a large percentage rocked in his lap. He became their play therapy or primary process mother. It made no difference whether they were psychotic, neurotic, or had psychosomatic problems. However, once he had developed his own capacity to be a symbolic "mother," the technique became useless—like an old joke. The patients would not accept it apparently because it was not consonant with his then-current (1950) emotional state. However, the technique was adopted by several of the clinic staff until it also became sterile and useless in their psychotherapy.

During the subsequent 2 years, the psychotherapy group, supported by cotherapy and constant consultation, evolved an interactive pattern including an aggressive give and take with patients—arm wrestling, leg wrestling, and confrontational episodes. Whitaker thinks of it now as developing his paternal competence. After 2 years, that pattern also became nonfunctional for the group. These experiences convinced him that each technique is a process whereby the therapist is developing himself and using the patient as an intermediary; that is, the therapist is interacting in a primary process mode as did Slavson in his group therapy with delinquents.

Concurrent with the emergence of these techniques was the development of a kind of functional pyknolepsy in Whitaker. In the middle of an interview he would fall asleep and dream about his relationship with the patient in front of him. Sharing the dream with the patient became a part of the interview. It took years to get over the embarrassment, but it became more and more clear that a therapeutic process was taking place. He has been able to continue this dream technique over the years, although lately it seems less frequent. It happens now only when he is under pressure, when therapy is not succeeding, or when he cares deeply about the family he is working with.

Warkentin and Whitaker moved to Emory University in Atlanta in 1946 in order to establish a department of psychiatry in the medical school. There had been no previous department of psychiatry, and they were allowed to inaugurate their own system. It was organized around the process of being successful in interpersonal relationships and a process psychotherapy that followed the Rankian brief therapy model (Rank, 1936) rather than models focused on insight or psychopathology. All medical students had weekly group psychotherapy throughout their first 2 years. Addi-

tionally, in the sophomore year the group became the collective psychotherapist for a patient. Thus, the medical students were taught to be people in relationship to each other during their first and second years and to be physicians doing psychotherapy in their second year. In their third year, they functioned as though they were resident psychotherapists for three patients each afternoon, two afternoons a week for 6 weeks. Warkentin's background in psychophysiology helped them to remain aware of the somatic correlates of their work.

Dr. Thomas Malone joined the group in 1948. His PhD in psychoanalytic psychology and his analytic training with Dr. Ernst Simmel added another facet to the group orientation. They deliberately taught the process of psychotherapy rather than psychodynamics during the 9 years spent developing a department of psychiatry. All the while they were pressing for a core theory to explain the process of individual therapy. In 1953 they published *The Roots of Psychotherapy* (Whitaker & Malone).

During these same years, 1946 to 1955, their involvement in treating schizophrenia with an aggressive kind of play therapy was expanding. The addition of cotherapy made the experience of treating individual schizophrenics in a rented home with a recovered schizophrenic as live-in attendant a creative and exciting process. Two therapists, who functioned as "coparents," helped reactivate a regressive process in the schizophrenic. They strove to induce a full-fledged infantile condition and disrupt the pseudoinfantile state of the schizophrenic. As an infant he could be nourished, his affect hunger satiated, and the psychotic transference served to facilitate recovery.

The early development of this methodology rested on a pragmatic approach to psychotherapy as a symbolic experience. In Atlanta, the medical students were trained to take everything said by the patient as symbolically important as well as realistically factual. The use of cotherapy with students allowed for open communication about the experience going on between the two therapists and the single patient.

Whitaker's interest in schizophrenic patients eventuated in a series of ten 4-day weekend conferences on the treatment of schizophrenia involving members from his group and several from Philadelphia, including Ed Taylor, John Rosen, Mike Hayward and, on some occasions, anthropologist George Devereux. The conferences centered on intensive treatment of one schizophrenic, or a schizophrenic and his family, for the 4 days. Two interviews were carried out each day by a subgroup, while the rest watched through a one-way mirror. The rest of the day and night were spent discussing the interviews. The 10th conference was held at Sea Island, Georgia (1955) and included Gregory Bateson and Don Jackson. This meeting led to the publication of *The Psychotherapy of Chronic Schizophrenia* (Whitaker, 1958).

Whitaker left private practice in 1965 to become a professor of psychiatry at the University of Wisconsin Medical School in Madison. At this point he defined himself as a family therapist.

Gus Napier came to Madison from Georgia in 1968 to do an internship in clinical psychology in the department. He stayed to do a postdoctoral year, then moved into private practice in Madison. David Keith became a resident in psychiatry at the University of Wisconsin in 1971 and joined the faculty in 1975 after completing a fellowship in child psychiatry.

Neither Napier nor Keith enjoyed the advantage of insufficient training. Both hooked up with Whitaker as apprentices and worked their way into the position of colleagues. They formed an informal group to do cotherapy, to teach, and to develop some conceptual framework for their ideas and methods.

In 1978, Napier completed the *Family Crucible*, an in-depth, book-length review of psychotherapy with a family. The book is an excellent description of their style of family therapy. Retreating from Wisconsin's harsh winter weather in 1979, he returned to Atlanta to do private practice and teaching.

There are several important themes behind the evolution of Whitaker's career in psychotherapy: (a) the use of cotherapy in clinical work as well as in teaching and writing; (b) the use of symbolic, nonverbal methods or play; (c) a steady effort to depathologize human experience; and (d) a pragmatic nontheoretical approach to psychotherapy. Whitaker likens himself to a garage mechanic; Keith describes himself as a psychotherapeutic bush pilot.

TENETS OF THE MODEL

The foundation for experiential/symbolic family therapy can best be understood by looking at both the healthy or self-actualizing family and the dysfunctional or growth-inhibiting family.

The Healthy or Well-Functioning Family

Health is a process of perpetual becoming. When Warkentin coined the term *growing edge therapy,* he pictured an open wound healing in from both sides.

The operation of a family, healthy or not, is covert and implicit. Their rules and regulations are not expressed in a formal manner; they develop out of the operation of the family. They are largely expressed in living rather than in words. Health has neither a past or future. Most important in the healthy family is the sense of an integrated whole. The healthy family is neither a fragmented group nor a congealed group. The whole functions as the leader and the control system both in supporting the family's security and in inducing change. The healthy family will utilize constructive input and handle negative feedback with power and comfort. The group is also therapist to the individuals, rotating the security blanket and serving as goad when needed by persons or subgroups.

The family as a three- to four-generation whole is longitudinally integrated. That is, the family, the subgroups, and the individual members relate to an intrapsychic family of three-plus generations. Interaction within the extended family is related to this sense of their historical ethos.

The healthy family maintains a separation of the generations. The mother and father are not children, and the children are not parents. The two generations function in these two separate role categories. Members of the same generation have equal rank. However, there is a massive freedom of choice in periodic role selection, and each role is available to any member: Father can be a 5-year-old, Mother can be a 3-year-old, the 3-year-old can be Father, Father can be Mother, depending upon the situation; each family member is protected by an implicit "as-if" clause.

A basic characteristic of all healthy families is the availability of this as-if structure. Play characterizes all metacommunication. For example, the 6-year-old son says to his father, "Can I serve the meat tonight?" and Daddy says, "Sure, you sit over on this chair and serve the meat and the potatoes, and I'll sit over in your place and complain." Daddy does this and probably gets more out of making believe he's 6 than the son does out of pretending he's Mother's husband, the father of the family, and an adult man. Metacommunication is considered to be an experimental process, an offer of participation that implies the clear freedom to return to an established role security rather than be caught in the tongue-in-cheek as-if microtheater. That trap is the context that pushes a son into stealing cars or a daughter into incest with her father while her mother plays the madame. The whimsy and creativity of the family can even be exaggerated to where family subgroups or individuals are free to be nonrational or crazy.

The power distribution within the healthy family is flexible, with a casualness evolved through the freedom to express individual differences, to renegotiate role structure and role expectations, and to reevaluate past experience. There is great freedom of choice in each individual's right to be him- or herself. He or she may develop uniquely with encouragement and very little counterpressure. This freedom for aloneness or belongingness is protected by the group.

The normal family does not reify stress. Some families stay connected by such weird rituals as the evening meal fight. The healthy family is one that continues to grow in spite of whatever troubles come their way. The family lives with the fact of their inconsistency and acknowledges the passing of time. The healthy family always seeks to expand their experience. All families have myths; myths are part of the definition of a family. One of the problems for dysfunctional families is that they are unable to tolerate changes in their myths. In contrast, the healthy family has an evolving myth. The evolving myths permit them to travel through the cycles of regression and reintegration. Symptoms are not absent from the healthy family, but they are a way to increase the family's experience and thereby growth.

Roles are defined by a panorama of conditions in the family: past history (the family of origin), present history (age of the kids), and ideas about the future (the mother's plan to return to teaching). The family roles are further defined by interactions with each family member, with the extended family demands, and with the culture. The roles are also defined by the individual's own growth experiences. The guiding myth evolves; it is not fixed. Sometimes roles are defined by covert needs of the parents determined before the child's birth in order to reestablish for the parents a sense of being back at home in their family of origin, whether that was a good or a bad world; home is home. We believe roles are defined interactionally in vivo, not by deliberate decision making. The mother's need for the comforting of her mother may establish the role of the first child, or the role of the first child may be defined by the mother's need to care for the real, live dolly of her 3-year-old fantasy with the daddy. As the mother becomes more involved with taking care of the later children, the third child or the fourth child may be given the role of the father's girlfriend or the father's mother as his need and the mother's need are integrated. A friend of ours says, "We get the children we need."

Problems are solved in the normal family by marshalling customs, myths, family rules, hopes, taboos, and facts. There are many covert assumptions and some overt rationalizations, but basically problems develop as impasses and get resolved by the standard process of thesis, antithesis, and synthesis. Father wants a new convertible; Mother says, "We can't afford it." Time resolves this, and they buy a less expensive car with a tape deck in it.

Problem solving is often accomplished by realigning the Gestalt. The realigning is accomplished in a complex systems way. The family's process of deciding is similar to that of each of us. Decision making is based on those factual realities brought to bear on the situation and the methodologies that worked in the past. These may be impulsive, irrational, ambivalent, and dependent, strongly influenced on a covert level by watching the mother and father make decisions, by watching schoolteachers or others who have been important to them. Living problems are like calculus problems with multiple variables. The constants are the long-term family values of both spouses. The decisions include influences from the next-door neighbor, the parents' work situation, and each child's school situation. These cultural influences, language-bound limitations, restrictions, and processes from the families of origin of the two parents result in a compromise end point, with many pressures of varying quantitative effect in an algebraic summation of taboos, rules, mythologies, and realities. All of this sounds complex and ponderous, but the human mind and its combinations in the family operate with computerlike precision, handling an infinite variety of stimuli.

The family life cycle is a great model of evolution in a system, changing while simultaneously maintaining its integrity. The clearest markers in the family life cycle are birth, death, and marriage. The developmental periods of the children in large part define family process. For example, the new baby pulls all three generations together, whereas adolescents push the parents into middle age. Some other life cycle markers include changes in income, family moves, Father quitting drinking, and Mother turning religious. These are important events that the family therapist must listen and watch for. They are frequently understated and underestimated in significance; however, it is common for important life events to cluster in the family history. We learn from families that life cycle stress is cumulative within the system as a whole. For example, Father's fight with his mother may produce tension in the marriage, which causes depression in his wife and school phobia in the 9-year-old. The clearest example of cumulative stress in the family life cycle occurs in the family with adolescent children. The kids are individuating and in an identity crisis, the parents are frequently suffering a midlife crisis, and the grandparents are in an old-age crisis related to retirement, illness, or another change in self-image. The healthy family acknowledges the stress in all members and does not concretize it in one of them.

Another way to look at the family life cycle is as serial impasses. The primary "we" of courtship is ruptured; the secondary "we" of living together emerges and develops stress. The stress is resolved either by repression, by struggling through it in the open, or by various other means such as accidents or change of focus; thus, we-ness is reestablished. The stress between unification and separation of the individuals is repeatedly erupting and resolving.

The healthy family becomes increasingly strong as a group, therapeutic in its role to itself and its components, and flexible, casual, and covert. Organic functioning of the whole resembles phys-ical skills, like the psychomotor stage of cognitive development. Coordination is confused by the long circuiting of awareness. The high level of affect that is established in the beginning gradually becomes part of the fiber of the family, and individual freedom to separate and return crystallizes an increasing wholeness within the family. The component parts contribute to the whole, and the whole contributes to the component parts.

The healthy family changes through identity crisis (self-doubt, illness, struggling with the children). Frustration is a useful enzyme for accelerating change. The processes are assimilation and accommodation. On another scale, the process is regression then reintegration, falling apart then reorganizing. Episodes of laughing, crying, and other orgasmic equivalents serve that function in individuals.

Passion and sexuality are the current in a family system. When the flow is free, things go well. When the flow is impeded, the system heats up and the possibility of damage is always present. Passion describes our sense of the feeling juices in the family. *Passion* arises out of a Greek word meaning "to struggle"; thus, it defines a process and not a state. It includes sadism and hatred as well as lovingness. The kernel of affective energy at the center of family living process is the core of psychosomatic living, an undifferentiated germ plasm. The behavior in the family is an emanation, always with interpersonal and metaphorical components. In effect, we assume the biological basis of family therapy. The culture thinks of a healthy family as one with a lot of positive affect. We agree, but we also think that children hate and ought to know that they are hated (Winnicott, 1949). The failure to have an easy flow of affect often results in at least migraine headaches, if not peptic ulcer or high blood pressure.

Feelings in the family in whatever form or degree are handled in nonverbal and symbolic pulses, mediated by the as-if clause noted earlier. The as-if clause makes it possible for the mother and child or the father and child to play out quasi-sexual roles. Mother and son may go on a date while Dad stays home, complaining jealously and insisting that Junior bring Mom home before 10 p.m. Father and his daughter go to the gradeschool dance. Father catches himself being absurd in a temper tantrum and switches to playing a roaring buffoon. The healthy family knows the difference between murder and play murder, between sexual play and intercourse. This as-if clause was demonstrated dramatically when one child-abusing family began to play fight with rubber bats in our office. The whole family had great fun with a symbolic slugfest, transcending the danger of real murder.

Love, sexuality, and hatred are lived out through touching, nonverbal intimacy, fighting and making up, subgrouping and resubgrouping, triangulation and detriangulation, teaming, and fantasies.

Case Example

Bob and Harriett completed therapy just before the birth of their first child. They asked for another appointment when the baby was 4 months old. He felt that she had grown cold toward him, and she said he was too distant and mechanical with her. He was frustrated with her constant refusal to have sex. He was sympathetic with her feelings about herself, her fatigue, and her attachment to the new baby. One Sunday afternoon, he attempted to turn her on, but she stayed cold. He went to the kitchen to get something to eat but returned to the bedroom. She was sitting on the bed, thumbing through a magazine. He had a visual image of himself bashing her ribs in with his fist. He relaxed, changed his shirt, and went out to mow the lawn. His conscious experience of this fantasy had somehow facilitated an existential shift in his head. It permitted him more open, less demanding lovingness.

It is the physical sexuality combined with lifetime commitment that makes marriage a unique, nearly biological relationship. We think the whole family is involved in the family sex life in one way or another. Sex is more open and fun if it involves all the generations. One of the best ways is by sexual joking. In the early marital years half of the couple's sex life is fighting about it. Unfortunately, we don't learn that until after we are married. Family sexuality is obviously conveyed in a preverbal, experiential manner. Middelfort (1976) says that sex education does not occur in the schools; it is not a vocabulary course. Real sex education is in the parents' eyes. When the mother in a pseudomutual family declares their sex life is "just lovely," the therapist thinks of a funeral parlor visitation where the lady is saying that the corpse is "just lovely."

In this section on the healthy family, we have emphasized that family process is covert and nonverbal. In our method of doing psychotherapy, we distrust communication training methods because they often cool (acting out) rather than increase (acting in) interpersonal stress. In our method of therapy, affective expression is a natural process that is *allowed* rather than taught.

Increases in intimacy and separateness must go hand in hand. Neither can increase without an increase in the other. One can only be as close as one can be separate, and one can only be as separate as one can be close. Family rules define the tolerable degree of this pressure, and the unspoken family barometer is very accurate. In a healthy family, a wide range of intimacy and separateness levels are found. The levels are also movable without inducing panic in a healthy family. The size of the family space bubble and each individual's space bubble is determined by experience and the historical perspective that the family have inherited via their "social genes" (Grinker, 1971).

Real dependency is linked to real autonomy in the same way that intimacy and separateness are linked. A symbiotic relationship is one in which there is a fixed emotional distance. Each member is dependent on the other not to alter the distance; the relationship controls the two persons. Thus, two married persons may appear to be quite autonomous, but if the relationship heats up in some way, such as having a child or one member becoming ill, the other members may experience quite a bit of stress because they rely on this relationship remaining distant. In a marriage, the wife may appear dependent while the husband appears autonomous and independent. However, on the covert side it may be quite different; the wife carries a lot of power, while the husband is really a little boy whose power is in his tantrums or his good behavior.

Case Example

Bob and Gloria had been married for 23 years. The marriage was unsatisfactory but stable. Gloria stayed at home, took care of the kids, and seemed quite dependent. Bob was a successful businessman who spent a lot of time away from home and characterized himself as being strongly independent. During the marriage, he maintained a close relationship with his mother who lived nearby. The couple divorced 1 year after his mother's death. We assume that the marriage was not able to absorb his covert dependency needs.

The healthy family is a subculture established over several generations. The power of this subculture is well structured, and the struggle between that subculture filtering down from the mother's family of origin is gradually integrated with the power of the subculture handed down from the father's family of origin.

Relationships with extended families, however, are secondary to the healthy nuclear family. It is possible to visit the extended family of origin without double-crossing the nuclear family. Troubles develop when there is a fixed relationship with someone in the extended family—for example, two sisters having a closer relationship between themselves than either has with her respective husband. In the healthy family, the relationships are also variable and responsive to specific needs. Grandma may be able to take care of the kids once in a while if the second generation needs it, but she is also free to turn them down. The 40-year-old son is able to go home to take care of his mother after she falls and strains her hip. He does not double-cross his wife in doing this.

Extended family relationships are troublesome when they are not updated. In other words, the extended family relationships are in-the-head-projections left over from age 5 or 15.

The boundaries of the family are flexible, and here the custom and historical perspective are as important as they are in the family dynamics. Information regarding who is allowed in, when, under what conditions, for how long, on whose OK is all programmed covertly. The interdigitating of the two family cultures evolves over time and endless experiences in vivo. The family is in a constant flux between the culture of the two families, modified by reality stresses and their resolution.

The healthy family has the capacity

for outside relationships and the ability to move in and out without being a counterbalance to family struggles. That is, the wife may choose to play bridge on Wednesday evenings because she likes to play bridge, not only to get even with her husband. Members need not have joint access to nonfamily members. The husband need not share in all of his wife's relationships and vice versa.

The Pathological or Dysfunctional Family

Our general orientation toward pathological functioning is related to the concept of craziness, which can be colored pink by calling it "creativity." We include both of Minuchin's (1974) concepts of disengaged families and enmeshed families in this category—that is, the family with excessive callouses and no craziness but massive inhibitions, or the family with "nobody in it" in which the family members live back-to-back. The dysfunctional family is characterized by a very limited sense of the whole. In a more specific way, it is frequently true that the only person who believes in the spirit of the family is the family scapegoat who may, of course, be either the black sheep, the delinquent, or the member who is crazy or disorganized in some way that stresses the family. On the other hand, she or he may be the "white knight" or the socially overadapted family hero, often a workaholic and the one used by the family to cover up their anxiety and extol their health. Family craziness is denoted in the same way as individual craziness—that is, through a nonrational functioning process that may show up as silliness or as chaos. The schizophrenogenic family is dedicated to a state of chaos. In general, the degree of craziness is measured by an integration of the creative, nonrational impulsive-

ness in the family and psychosocial adaptability. Some families are highly creative, but like individuals who are crazy, they disconnect themselves from the social structure. Some others are creatively exciting and are more socially adapted and integrated. The summation of these two adaptations to creativity is one way of measuring the dysfunction. Indications for lack of integration are expressed by way of fixed triangles and fixed subgroups. When the family has unresolved oedipal triangles or a feud between the males and females, the functioning of the family as a whole is disrupted. It disrupts the marriage and many times even more the relationship of the two extended families from which it originated. Pathological functioning in a family is largely a nonverbal process, and we assume that the verbalization is mostly a facade, a kind of sociopolitical sop to the culture.

Craziness in the family may be compared to several of the individual diagnostic categories. The catatonic family imitates the New England patterns of rigidity and emotional constriction; there are paranoid families who are profoundly suspicious, very much as the lower socioeconomic "have nots" are about the "haves." A surprising number of families operate like the simple schizophrenic in that they make decisions without any content and in a very fogbound manner. They roam into decisions; their behavior apparently has no basic understructure that is perceptible or even intellectually available to them.

The craziness of the individual can be divided easily into three general categories. First, there is the *driven crazy,* who has been driven outside the family and is trying to find a primary process mother in the community. Another type of craziness we call *going crazy,* that is, craziness that emerges out of the profound acceptance, or unconditional positive regard, that Carl Rogers spoke of. Falling in love can be a metaphor for this process. This is identical with a therapeutic psychosis, a kind of intensified version of the therapeutic neurosis. A third variety of craziness, many times misidentified, is *acting crazy*. This pattern comes about when one who has been crazy is faced with an intolerable anxiety and regresses into crazy behavior. It is not a process craziness but a reactive craziness, in the same sense that there is process schizophrenia and reactive schizophrenia.

Causes and Development of Family Dysfunction

We think that dysfunction is related to the struggle over whose family of origin this new family is going to model itself after. One way to view etiology assumes there is no such thing as marriage; it is merely an arrangement whereby scapegoats are sent out by two families in an effort to re-create themselves. There are also family growth impasses that lead to dysfunction—the arrival of a new child, the death of a family member, invasion from the outside culture, development dynamics relating to the growth of children, aging of parents, or other natural phenomena related to time.

Dysfunction also arises following the father's retirement or one child leaving for college, or other time or space wars. Time and space conflicts can produce stress without becoming apparent to those involved. Who gets the nicest bedroom as the children come along, who occupies the living room or the parent's bedroom, to what degree do friends belong in the family living space, and who has territorial rights to the car, the garage, and so forth—these decisions may be important literally and as symbolic expressions of family power dynamics.

GOAL SETTING

The goals of family therapy are to establish the members' sense of belongingness and simultaneously to provide the freedom to individuate. In our system of therapy, social adaptation is not a goal; we seek to increase the creativity (what we call craziness or right-brained living) of the family and of the individual members.

These goals are accomplished by the aggregate effect of the following subgoals:

1. *Increase the interpersonal stress.* We assume that all families can tolerate any increase in anxiety. The homeostatic power of the family is massive in comparison with the therapist's input. Raising stress can be accomplished in several ways. One way is to convert individual symptoms into systems problems that increase the interpersonal stress. As an example, a young mother had a phobia about being dangerous to her husband and daughter. She refused to describe the content, and she never acted anything out. We said that if she was so selfish with her crazy thoughts we could not stand working with her. The problem was not her intrapsychic thoughts but her depriving the family of excitement. The second method is to expose another unacknowledged problem, like the father's obesity or the mother's tearfulness. In other words, the anxiety is not expanded in the same territory as the presenting symptom but is expanded horizontally.

2. The family's administrative competence and power emerge from shared anxiety in the *development of a family nationalism*. The family becomes more of who they are, a team with increased morale.

3. We push to *expand the family's relationships with the extended family.* The

relationship to the extended family has a psychic introject of at least three generations, probably more.

4. We push to *expand the family's relationship to the culture and community members*. In this way the family establishes an interface with the culture, accentuating their sense of belonging to the culture and simultaneously maintaining the freedom to move in and out of it.

5. We push for a *sense of the family boundaries* with joint understanding of and connection with family expectations.

6. An effort to *separate the generations* is critical. Although the mother and father should be able to play at being children from time to time and the children should be able to play at being adults, there are real differences between the generations and a separate structure for each. Especially dangerous are cross-generational triangles, because they disrupt the separation between the generations. When the child carries the delusion that he is Mother's peer or when Mother completely deserts her adult role and becomes a bonded partner with her son against her husband, it is more dangerous than the triangle between three children, between the father, mother, and her sister, or between the father, mother, and his secretary.

7. Simultaneously with the clearer structure, *the family must learn how to play.* This goal sounds simple, but family groups often have great difficulty with it. To be more specific, families need to differentiate between playful sadism and real murder. They need to differentiate between sexual intercourse and flirting. Play is universal. It must be present to maintain health and facilitate growth (Winnicott, 1971). One manifestation of playfulness is the role availability in the family. All roles should be available to

each person depending on the situation and with the family's agreement.

8. We strive to develop a we-they union between the therapeutic team and the family with the *constant cycle of separation and rejoining.* In this way we model the we-ness of the children to the parents, and model for the parents a relationship to their own two families of origin.

9. We want to *explode the myth of individuality.* We want the family to believe in themselves as a unit, but it is important that this belief be flavored with a strong sense of its absurdity.

10. Each family member ought *to be more of who they are,* with added access to themselves.

The more specific ultimate goals involved in work with a family tend to evolve out of the process of the therapy. That is, they are often established without any verbal definition by the cotherapists, evolving out of their interaction with the family. Those goals established by the therapist nonverbally have an advantage because the usual intellectual thinking tends, in both the family and the therapy team, to divert, dilute, and avoid change. Methods that bypass this intellectual game playing are more effective. As parents need to maintain their roles, therapists assumably will remain faithful to their role responsibilities while at the same time using the self to the fullest possible effect.

The goals of treatment are evolved by the therapist and the family, both jointly and separately. Many are largely unconscious and can only be acknowledged in retrospect. The family usually has goals that vary from those to which the therapist aspires. The therapist's early goals are usually covert but dominant. For example, the therapist may merely try to help the patients stay in treatment, or he or she may elect to invade greatly in hopes of accomplishing what is needed within the first few interviews. In essence, our goal as therapists is to become more human in the context of the family.

The piano teacher metaphor is useful in defining the family's ongoing expectations and interests. The pupil may come the first time just because her parents send her, or she may stay on for a brief time to learn a few techniques and then decide she does not want to know anything about piano. On the other hand, she may gradually change from being a reluctant victim of her mother's interest to becoming an enthusiastic student, even going on to play Beethoven. This metaphor accurately describes the range of what is available in our style of family therapy. The difference in goals between therapists and family are often resolved in a mutual experience with learning one another's language as the therapist highlights significant interpersonal events. In some way with each family, we try to create a new culture or a new family with us as grandparents. We work at developing a dream Gestalt with the family. However, it is valuable for the family to know explicitly the personal agenda of the therapist. The most honest way of revealing the therapist's personal agenda is to admit we do family therapy as a way for us to aid our own growth. We do not operate altruistically out of any saintly inner wish to help the patients change to counterbalance the gargantuan pressures of the culture.

Usually the family's painful symptom is only a ticket of admission. Symptom relief is certainly valuable in itself or as a cultural goal, but we assume there is always a more serious distress. Relief of the symptom too soon may prevent a more adequate handling of the hidden stress. For example, one patient came in for treatment of sexual impotence. His symptom disappeared when the therapist exposed a delusion that he would get the Nobel prize. As a result, the interpersonal lifestyle that generated the two symptoms was not modified, only diverted.

Our goal is to bring about change in the patient so that we can thereby alter ourselves. Psychotherapy, like a courtship, demands some understanding of the investment the therapist has, the vulnerability he or she hopes to establish in him- or herself, the respect for both the family's rights and his or her own rights. The goals of the therapist should be overt because therapy is a test of the teaming established between the family and the therapist. Any deliberate dishonesty tends to weaken that bond. The way we discuss goals depends on the developmental age of the family. If we give the family objective information at the beginning or end of the first interview, we often find later that they have completely forgotten it. We usually discuss goals when the family asks for them. We don't always respond in the frame of their question. Sometimes we define goals in a double-binding way or invent a Zen-style koan, or paradox. When one drug addict asked what Keith was trying to do, Keith told him that he was trying to teach him how to suffer. A rigid, standoffish couple returned for three very boring interviews. Near the end of the third interview, the wife, a behavioral therapist, asked, "What are your goals? I don't know what you're up to." The therapist responded, "I'm not up to anything; I'm just trying to get through the third carbon copy of the first interview."

The impression may have been given here that we refuse to talk straight about goals, but that is not the case. We do wait until the family asks, and we respond according to the terms in which they ask. The terms, of course, have both verbal and nonverbal components, with the nonverbal carrying the greatest importance. As much as possible our goals are established in metaphorical language—a language that incorporates more than one level of meaning, that expands meaning rather than narrowing it. Thus, another goal is to reactivate metaphors in the family process, to use expanded meanings. The use of metaphorical language and visual or pictorial metaphors is most valuable because they can be left incomplete. Overextended metaphors may lose their power for stimulating creativity. The open Gestalt or the nonverbal component in any metaphor makes it less easy for the family to memorize it and then dismiss it, making it one more thing they recognize but don't learn from. An incomplete Gestalt makes for learning rather than recognition only.

APPLICATION

The main contraindication to family therapy is the absence of a family therapist. There is also a relative contraindication—the absence of a family, that is, the absence of relatives. (Clinicians will understand this humor.) Our method of clinical practice is family therapy. *We do not simply do family therapy; we are family therapists.* Any psychotherapy venture ought to begin with a family interview. If the whole family is not available, then someone from the patient's world should be there at least for the first interview. The presenting problem is not what determines the suitability for family treatment. Suitability depends on the extent to which the family shares our culture's implicit belief that the world works best with people who believe in families and less well with people who do not believe in families.

Families with Susceptibility to This Approach

The following types of families are most likely to experience successful experiential/symbolic therapy:

1. Crazy families who are in for fun and/or involved in a dilemma that is multifaceted and multipersonal.
2. Therapists who would like a family therapy experience or families with psychological sophistication.
3. Nonsubjective families with psychological problems. The system is not based on intellectual understanding but rather on interactive process in the family, metaphorical language, and personal interaction between therapists and family members.
4. Families in crisis.
5. Families with a serious scapegoat—for example, schizophrenia (pre-, acute, or chronic) or juvenile delinquency in a family.
6. Families with young children—they seem to get more from working with us. We become parents to these new families.
7. Families with multilevel problems.
8. High-powered or VIP families.
9. Families with a psychosomatic problem.
10. Families who are disorganized by the culture, for example, a family who has a probation officer, a social worker, or an alcoholic counselor overattached to them. Our effort is to increase the family's unity so that they can get rid of intruders.

Families Immune to Infection

The families for whom there is no take in experiential/symbolic therapy are idiosyncratic. We have no way of predicting a priori what families will and will not work well. The approach has developed in work with biologically intact families and operates best when all three generations are available. It works less well when members are not available by reason of death, distance, or a simple refusal to come. We assume such a denial to be a family ploy. We adapt our work to all sorts of situations, but the likelihood of a take is reduced by compromise. We work with extended families, social networks, divorcing couples having simultaneous affairs, divorced couples with a child in crisis, and lesbian and homosexual couples. Still, families who seem immune to infection by this method of family therapy are:

1. Those that are panicked by spontaneous feelings, such as postdivorce situations where wounds are still healing and are too tender for reexploration.
2. Those with long-standing pathology and no strong inducement to change.
3. Those in which the scapegoat is an adopted child.
4. Manic psychotics who are new to us, although we often work with acutely psychotic schizophrenics outside the hospital and without drugs.

"No Treatment" Advised

1. When there has been a completed treatment case, the family has had a therapeutic experience and ended. When a new symptom emerges or an old one reemerges, we have the family come back for a single-visit consultation. If there is excitement in the whole family and they are handling the symptom well, then it is not useful to reactivate treatment. These situations are like fire drills. The family is testing their ability to respond to a crisis and is checking out our availability.

2. Families who have had too much therapy, so-called professional patients, are advised that they should stop looking for treatment. They are to come in if a crisis arises.

3. Families who are seeing a good therapist and come to us out of a negative transference response are sent back with the suggestion that we act as consultants if the therapist so desires.

There are some situations where we are not likely to continue or to begin treatment, but not because treatment is not indicated. If the family is only willing to send a segment—that is, the husband and one child; husband and wife; or husband, wife, and one child only—then we suggest they find someone else. If the father is against psychotherapy, we would rather not be involved. The family is free to do whatever they want with our refusal. We leave the opportunity open to return to family therapy at any time the father may decide that he is willing. The same is true if there is not enough anxiety in the family to make psychotherapy worthwhile. Then it is our preference to decline the referral rather than to try to carry their part of the anxiety load.

Responsibility of Patients

Somehow, patient responsibility is not an important issue for us. We expect patients to grow up and leave home. They have responsibility for their own living and for changing. Whether they change or not has to do with their level of desperation, which must outweigh the pressure for homeostasis or remaining the same.

The patients are responsible for their own secrets. They may expose them or continue with them as they see fit. We do not look for additional background information from other sources. We let the family describe the problem and their needs. If they say they do not need therapy, we take their word for it and terminate immediately.

As the therapist sees more patients and gains confidence, the question of the client's responsibility diminishes. The family is more and more free to come to the office and regress, like the grown-up adolescent who returns home for a weekend.

ROLE OF THE THERAPIST

The therapist is like a coach or a surrogate grandparent. Both roles demand structure, discipline, and creativity, as well as caring and personal availability. Balance between these components is established through experience. Our availability is different from that of the biological parent in that it does not involve the whole self of the therapist.

We are very active as therapists. We don't exclude being directive; on the other hand, we may use silence as one unusual activity for increasing anxiety. The therapist overtly controls the first few sessions of family therapy. He or she is active, both in infiltrating the family and exposing anxiety-laden territory, but usually without being directive. We expect to be part of the family's interaction. Although we do not forbid family members to talk to each other, we assume the main process to come from the family's interaction with the therapeutic team.

We always prefer to work as cotherapists. (Cotherapy is discussed in detail in the next section.) The therapeutic team is modeled after a marriage with children. The family is seen as a new baby who, with luck, grows to be a child, an adolescent, and finally leaves home. The two "parents" ordinarily assume the complementary roles described in the small-group literature as executive or educational director (father) and the supportive or nurturant individual (mother). These roles with the family can be stabilized, but ordinarily they alternate during a single interview or from the early part of therapy to the later part. The third therapist, the cotherapy "we" (or, from the other side, the paranoid "they"), functions as a decision-making discussion center.

The evolving role of the therapy team moves through several stages. In the early part of therapy, the parental team is all-powerful, but they quickly define themselves as impotent, unable to push the whole family around. The therapeutic team declines all efforts to be regarded as magic or possessing supraknowledge of how that family should live. We assume that each family has a unique culture style and that our function is to help perfect it and give it more explicit and specific direction defined by the family's own functional patterning. It is like teaching tennis to an advanced player. The entire game cannot be made over; rather, the player's strong points are consolidated and emphasized, and weak points are corrected.

In the second interview, the family says, "What should we talk about?" The therapist replies, "I don't know. What do you want to change?" "Well, we told you last time." "I know, but that has probably altered since then. You carry the ball, and we'll be glad to try to help."

In the midphase of therapy, the parental therapeutic team functions as a stress activator, a growth expander, and a creativity stimulator. In this phase, when the family is secure, the therapist may say, "By the way, Jane, when you spoke like that to your husband, you sounded like you were talking to your mother or your father. I wonder if you really want to let him get away with that." This implies that it is a joint arrangement between the two spouses. She is being infantile not only because she wants to be but also because the husband needs her to be infantile.

In the adolescent or late phase, the team has no function except to be there and watch. They provide a time and place for the family to get together. Of course, they are available for deeper involvement as needed. The therapists depend on the family to carry all of the initiative, and they do not try to interfere even if they see they can contribute. In this later phase, the therapeutic team functions as a proud parent, watching the family while mitigating their own role. This follows the patterning of parents' relationship to a late adolescent who is about ready to leave home. Parents who try to continue educating their children at this late stage are making a serious mistake. The adolescent's independent functioning should be more than respected—it should be revered. The therapeutic team needs to do this with a late-stage family. For example, the mother says to the father, "I think I may end up divorcing you." The therapist is tempted to say, "You've never done it all these 18 years; I don't see why you think you could do it now," or, conversely, "It looks like you two are more loving; I cannot see why you talk about divorce." These are helpful in the early or mid-phase of therapy, but not in the late phase.

We often use self-disclosure, sharing minutia in a metaphorical manner, imposing on ourselves the limits of our own role models. We use it in specific ways, usually sharing fragments or facets of our lives that we have worked over in our own therapy or through our living (Fellner, 1976). Going beyond the role model must be carefully monitored by the therapist to avoid a role change in which he or she becomes an organizing educator while the family is not allowed full opportunity for its own initiative. Personal disclosure is used to increase the interpersonal focus or to shatter a Gestalt that is becoming too set, never to diminish anxiety.

Later in therapy, the therapist's participation can at times be increased, moving toward fragments of his or her fantasy as they occur during the interview or bits of the personal history. As the family becomes more secure in handling the input, the therapist can feel free to be increasingly nonrational, free associative, fantasy organized, confronting, or paradoxical in any one of many different models. For example, "Dad, I don't think you have to worry about the family getting along so much better. It's not going to last anyway. They'll go back to isolating you and beating on Mother by next week or at least the week after." Or, on another occasion, "Mary, I'm certainly glad I'm not married to you the way you take off after your husband. I think I would run for the hills if you were my wife." Or, to one of the kids, "Hey, you know the way your father looks at you when he tells you to either clean up your room or he's going to paddle your behind, I would be tempted to head for San Francisco and probably get on drugs just to get back at him." Noting physical responses to interactions can be extremely powerful. "The way you glared at me just then gave me a prickly feeling in the back of my neck."

Another method of self-disclosure that we use is interaction between the cotherapists. It may be in the form of a private joke or a comment about our outside life. We may share a childhood recollection with our cotherapist, or we may ask if we are too judgmental.

Therapists do not have a choice about joining the family. If the family continues to come to the clinic, they do so because they have given the therapist some role. We actively join the family. We assume our transference to them to be the anesthesia that enables them to tolerate the anxiety precipitated later in the middle phase. Ongoing therapy demands both joining and distancing sequences. That is, the therapist must be able to leave the role by his or her own initiative and later to reenter it. It's as though the cotherapists take turns jumping over Wynne's (1958) "rubber fence" into the family, holding hands with the partner and jumping back. They thus take turns being "in" and "out." They model the basic problem in family growth. The process of uniting and individuating is both a group stress and the fluctuating experience of individual members as well as family subsystems. The cotherapy team joins the family and in so doing forms a therapeutic suprafamily of which they are a subgroup.

The sequence of joining and distancing is important. It is a lot like being with children. A father can get furious with his kids one minute, then be loving the next. We take the same stance with families. If the therapist gets angry, he or she does not hold onto it; if the therapist jokes with the son about his flirtation with mother, he or she simultaneously retains the freedom to empathize with the father's sadness about being left out. Don Juan, Carlos Castaneda's teacher (Castaneda, 1975), is a good model. He is described in a number of quasi-real, quasi-metaphorical situations where Don Juan moves close and then away,

then disappears and suddenly reappears. This is a nice model for the family therapist. The joining/distancing sequence is a difficult, advanced technique for the therapist to master. Less experienced therapists often do not have a sense of when they are in and when they can afford to withdraw. There is a difference in the way that the two of us handle this. Whitaker can allow himself to be disinterested, suddenly become involved deeply with a family member, then just as suddenly change the topic or dissociate himself. Keith, with 30 years of experience behind Whitaker, operates more cautiously. He is apt to lead gradually toward a confrontation, engage in the interaction, and then move back more slowly.

The therapist's role changes throughout therapy. In the beginning, the therapist is a kindergarten teacher–shepherd. Within the therapy, he or she moves from being this dominant, all-giving parent of the infant to being the as-if pal, an age-mate of the young child, then to be the advisor and resource person of the older child, and eventually the retired parent of an adult. As the family becomes more independent, the therapist team can become more personal, more educational, and more outside the family as such. When a family moves toward ending therapy, we respect it as a real initiative, not a symbolic one. We always stand ready to end with them. We do not look at reasons why the family wants to leave but begin to help planning the termination as soon as it's mentioned.

Cotherapy

Cotherapy is a regular component of our work. Mostly, two therapists join together in a professional marriage for ongoing treatment; however, we use alternatives. A therapist may work alone but use a colleague as consultant along the way. The consultant comes into interviews on call. We also get together as therapists to share case fragments and problems.

There are a number of reasons for operating as a team.

1. Teaming allows more creativity and variability in functioning. At root this gives more power to the cotherapy team.

2. Psychotherapy is anticultural, and it is important to have a close colleague in order not to pay the price of being depersonalized. When two professionals are present in the name of therapeutic change, the spiritual power increases exponentially. When subjective perceptions are shared by two members, they are less easily disregarded.

3. The therapists' pathology intrudes less. This component may be less important if the therapist uses a structured method of working. In cotherapy, each therapist may use him- or herself and his or her subjectivity with a colleague there to counterbalance.

4. Cotherapy offers the freedom to think. While one therapist is working actively with the family, the second therapist may sit back, look at what is happening from a distance, think over what is said, and arrive at some differing conceptions.

5. Cotherapy helps prevent the therapist from stealing one family member for a therapeutic helper. Either the black sheep or the white knight, when used in this way, distorts the process of family unity and further isolates the scapegoat of the family.

6. We believe that cotherapy reduces

affect spilling outside the interview. There is less chance of the therapist being aloof during the interview and taking his or her affect out in a supervisory or curbstone consultation with another therapist, a spouse, or some unrelated person.

7. Cotherapy decreases the sense of loss at the family's leave taking. Protective withdrawal of the individual therapist from the next patient and the grieving that might distort the family's leave taking are minimized. When the family ends, the therapists have each other. The therapist's professional development, increasing competence, and growing enjoyment of family therapy is thus enhanced. More simply, it is much easier for two therapists to avoid compromising their integrity or their goals because of the impending departure of the family.

8. Finally, it is possible in the cotherapy setting for one therapist and one patient to have an extended experience in a one-to-one relationship while the family is present and still to avoid feeling extruded. This may take place either in a single interview or over a period of interviews. Such special empathy and interaction between one team member and one family member will not distort the therapeutic process as it does when one therapist wears several hats.

There are obvious disadvantages in working as cotherapists. It costs the patients more, there are more scheduling problems with a whole family, it reduces each therapist's grandiosity, and interpersonal complications between the therapists can arise. We use marriage as a metaphor to guide our work as cotherapists. At the heart of a prosperous marriage is the struggle between the two spouses to remain autonomous I's and at the same time to join in a dependent we. This same struggle is at issue for both the family and the cotherapy teams.

TECHNIQUES OF FAMILY THERAPY

We noted earlier that structuring in our therapy sessions is implicit. The first interview includes developing a systems history of the family. We actively attempt to learn about the family emotional system: Where are the stresses located? Who has had symptoms? What are the individual character structures? What about past stress episodes? We try to expose the personality of each individual as well as that of the total family and its subgroups. We ask about grandparents from each family of origin: Where are they? How are they? What do they think about the situation? We propose an extended family interview. When can they come?

We follow a pattern in our first interview. The family is told that we will talk with each member singly to get a multiple view of what is going on with the family. We start with the member who is psychologically most distant, most often the father. After the father, we go around to the different siblings, saving the mother for last. In most cases, the mother knows what is going on and is most available to be a symptom bearer. This style of interviewing may seem awkward and may go against the instincts of many therapists, but the interactions that develop around it and the messages that are sent often result in a big therapeutic payoff.

If another family member interrupts the talking person, we politely ask them to wait their turn and tell them that they will have their chance. If an argument breaks out that sounds like an ongoing one, we ask them to hold it because we are not trying to cause trouble but to find out what is up with the family. While we get the history, we are continually restructuring what the family says by their deciding who talks, minimizing some information, and highlighting other areas.

Joining the Family

The family therapist must develop a basic empathy with the family. We hope his or her transference feelings will include an identification, a feeling of pain, and a sense of the family's desperate efforts to self-heal.

We work hard to capture the family in the first interviews. If the therapist can develop a liaison with the father, there is a good chance that the family will continue in therapy; if not, chances are they will drop out. Additionally, the chance of losing the family increases if the therapist gets overinvolved with the mother too soon. The overinvolvement can happen in several ways: (a) sexually tinged seduction, (b) taking her on as the identified patient and thus stealing her from the family, or (c) making her angry.

Another way the therapist gains membership in the family is by the bilateral transference. We adopt some of their language, a softer accent or a special rhythm. The therapist's posture may be the same as someone else's in the family. We listen for the metaphorical set and attempt to make use of it.

Playing with the children is another important way to join the family. The play need not be explicitly significant, but often it turns out that way by surprise.

Specific Techniques

One of our standard early techniques is to precipitate in the family a taboo against the bilateral pseudotherapy that develops in every marriage. We give the parents full credit for what they have accomplished in straightening each other out. We declare an end to that therapy, because it is failing, and demand they turn the therapeutic function over to us. They are to allow no further crying on shoulders and no further talking about illness, symptoms, or their relationship except during the interview. Isolating the metacommunication to the interview setting induces a great reality to the home-edited interpersonal communication. The parentification typical of the ordinary marriage is interrupted. Blocking the parental (therapeutic) function in the spouses undercuts the secondary gain they accrued as each took a turn at being infantile. The technique is most ably activated in the middle of the first interveiw. When the father says, "You see, Mary, that's exactly what I was saying to you," the therapist may say, "Shut up! This is my project, I don't want you helping. You'll just make things worse. And think of the joy of not having to listen to her whining any more." This kind of specific interdiction models what we hope will happen outside the interview.

Changes in the family structure many times result from the therapist invading the family dynamic operation. We tend to emphasize noneducational, noninsightful patterns, such as paradoxical intention, the posing of dissonant models, teasing, deriding or reversing a family's statements, or presenting ego-syntonic arguments. For example, the mother says, "I am unhappy with my husband." The therapist suggests that the next time she should get a younger man since she looks more energetic than her husband. Maybe she could pick a professional athlete who likes a lot of exercise. She could consider taking all this husband's money and going to Chicago where life is very exciting and the possibility of happiness much greater.

We like to use personal confrontations, even presenting our own boredom. "Mrs. Zilch, the way you responded to your husband just then made me have the nicest feeling that I am not married to you. I don't know whether I would cringe and leave the house or move to counterattack, but it certainly was upsetting to me, and I'm just a visitor here." In like manner, if the mother, for example, is talking about how weak she feels in the family, we tease her by presenting contrary evidence. She has raised five children who were born 1 year apart, her husband was absent during most of that time, and it is a wonder that she is not flat on her back with battle fatigue or a psychosis.

Our intent with these techniques is to produce transcendent experiences, that is, to help the individual members or even the family as a whole move above their pain and stress to savor the laughable situations the therapist verbalizes, or to help them enjoy the experience of looking from a completely different frame. We hope to attain the kind of existential shift that Ehrenwald (1966) presents. Similarly, we call patients on praxis, that is, the accommodation the husband makes to the wife's projection. For example, she wants a mother and looks up to him, and he very obligingly agrees to play the mother game, even though both agree she gets pseudomothering.

With our emphasis on the power of the experience in the therapy hour itself, it is not surprising that homework is rarely used, except to interdict the generation flip as described above. We cave in their pseudotherapy work on each other. We also advise getting the extended family into the therapy and exert pressure until this is accomplished. We may suggest that each person visit the home of origin without the other so as to regress in the service of that family's ego. If the extended family cannot come in and a home visit is not possible, we suggest that the members of the marriage send empty audiocassettes to their families. The instructions are for the parents to dictate tapes describing their lives up until the kids were born.

These techniques are used gently and early in therapy to test out the family's tolerance. Later on, we push them more specifically. A partial list of the techniques we consider important follows.

Symptoms Are Redefined as Efforts for Growth. We then increase the pathology and implicate the whole family scene. The family scene is converted into an absurd one. Our effort is to depathologize human experience. The wife is complaining that her husband is trying to get rid of her. "He's never loved me you know," she says. "He said once that he would cut me up. Another time he threatened me with a gun." The therapist replies, "How can you say he doesn't love you? Why else would he want to kill you?" Psychosis in one of the family members can be defined as an effort to be Christ-like: "I'll be a nobody so that you and Father will be saved." Or the desperation felt by one member of the family can be redefined as a hopeful sign because it means the family cares enough. Just a mild tongue-in-cheek quality must be included with this technical play so that the confrontation will not be too painful.

Modeling Fantasy Alternatives to Real-Life Stress. A woman who has attempted suicide can be pushed to a fantasy. "If you were going to murder your husband, how would you do it?" or, "Suppose when you got suicidal you decided you were going to kill me. How would you do it? Would you use a gun or a knife or cyanide?" In a family with a schizophrenic son, the daughter's conversation with her father was understood by the therapist as a sexual pass. The family was embarrassed and perplexed by that. At the end of the hour, however, the father tenderly held his daughter and rocked her in his arms. Thus, teaching the use of fantasy permits expansion of the emotional life without the threat of real violence or real sexual acting out.

Separating Interpersonal Stress and Intrapersonal Fantasy Stress. For example, the patient who has attempted suicide can be encouraged to talk with the group about whom her husband would marry if she killed herself, how soon he would marry, how long he would be sad, how long the children would be sad, who would get the insurance, how would her mother-in-law feel, what would they do with her personal belongings, and so forth. This conversion of intrapersonal fantasy stress to an interpersonal framework is valuable since it contaminates the fantasy. It allows the family a new freedom in communication among themselves since they discover that such frightening words do not mean the end of the world.

Adding Practical Bits of Intervention. In one-to-one therapy these moves would be inappropriate. In the context of an operational suprafamily, they are safe since the family will utilize what it wants and is perfectly competent in discarding what is not useful. For example, the husband whose wife is having headaches can be offhandedly offered the possibility that if he were to spank her, the headaches might go away. Or the wife who is driven up the wall by her children's nagging or Dad's aloofness can casually be offered in the presence of the whole family the idea that she could run away to her mother's for a week and let the family make their own meals.

Augmenting the Despair of a Family Member. The family will then unite around that person. This technique is usually most efficient when used with a scapegoat. For instance, we might say to a schizophrenic son, "If you give up and become a nobody and spend the rest of your life in a state hospital, do you really think your mother and father will be happy with each other 20 years from now, or will they still be at each other's throats as they are now and you will have given up your life for nothing?"

Affective Confrontation. This is the kind of event that takes place vis-à-vis the parents, most often in defense of the children. It is the change in tone that occurs when the child in play therapy goes from knocking over a pile of blocks to throwing a block at a window pane. An 8-year-old boy and the therapist were mock fighting during a family interview. The parents viewed it as a distraction and continually interrupted as though the boy were the initiator when it was clearly the therapist. After several minutes of listening to the parents complaining to the boy, the therapist got angry and told them to bug off. He said he was playing with their son, and he did not want to be interrupted by them.

Treating Children Like Children and Not Like Peers. Younger children at

times like to tease us or to fight us physically. We enjoy taking them on and always overpower them. We are willing to be supportive and understanding of teenagers, but we also set strong limits with them. Despite our usual openness and acceptance, we can be very moralistic when chewing out a teenager for pushing us around.

CASE EXAMPLE

Background

The Cashman family was referred to us by an attorney. The son Mike, aged 15, had run away from home 10 months before our first contact. While on the run, he was involved in a car theft. After being apprehended, he went to boys' training school for 6 months, then was paroled to his father's custody. The father is a senior executive in a well-known local firm. The parents had divorced 12 years prior. Negotiating the first appointment was difficult. The mother, who had recently received an MBA, did not want to attend the therapy sessions. There was also a 17-year-old daughter, Carol.

In the first interview, all the family members filed in and sat down. The therapists sat in their usual seats, side by side, at the north end of the room. The father and Mike sat at opposite ends of a sofa on the south end, while the mother and Carol were perpendicular to them on a sofa on the west side of the room.

Keith: The first questions are how can we help, and what is it that you want from us? How about if you start us off, Dad?

Father: Well, my wife knows more of the details, why...

Keith: I know, it's always true that mothers know the most about families, but I like to pick on fathers, so why don't *you* say how it looks to you.

Father: Well, I should have some hard and fast answers for this, I guess, let's see, ah...

Whitaker (interrupting): Or maybe some tricky questions, instead. (His voice was challenging, yet indifferent.)

The father shifted gears in his head. He had started under the guise of a confused buffoon; the slight pressure of Whitaker's challenge now caused him to organize his thinking.

Father: My son Mike came to live with me. I'm scared to dert...ah...death that it's going to fail and I'd like to...ah...avoid failure. I want to make sure I can provide a good home and avoid the distance we feel right now. Right now our relationship is fragile. I want to find out how to make it work better.

Whitaker (while rummaging in his desk drawer): Just like that, huh?

Carol, the daughter, was working on a three-dimensional puzzle. It was made of clear plastic in the shape of an egg. No one addressed her, but at the pause in the father's speech several people in the room turned their attention to her.

Carol (defensively): I didn't take it all apart.

Keith: The question is how far to go with it.

Carol: I'm afraid to go much further or else it will all fall apart, and I would die of embarrassment if I couldn't get it back together.

Keith: So go ahead and take it apart some more. If you die, it won't be a big problem. I know the hospital mortician personally; I could call him, and he would come over right away so that you wouldn't have to lay here long. (Then addressing the father:) Can you tell us more how the family operates?

The father then related more of the family's unstable, dissonant history.

Father: Since all of this trouble, we've been back together more than ever.

Keith (directing his questioning to Carol): From the way your dad describes it, it sounds like an impossible situation. It's not very clear to me what you want from us. Do you think it would help if we taught your brother how to run away and not get caught?

Carol: I don't know what's needed. It's Mom and Dad's ball game right now.

Whitaker (still fumbling in his desk drawer): Just because you play second base, you don't count?

Carol: No, I'm more of a spectator.

Whitaker: How can you be a spectator on your own baseball team?

Keith and Whitaker are working as a team here. Keith has the job of a straight man. Whitaker moves in and out of the interview putting questions in a metaphorical frame of reference and dissociating himself as he rummages in his desk drawer.

The interview plodded on, not gaining any momentum of its own. We reviewed the history as we described earlier. We distorted the dynamics and made primary process observations and interpretations. It was a flat, tiresome interview. In rummaging, Whitaker had found four steel ball bearings that he began to roll Queeg-like in his hand as we talked.

As we neared the end of the hour, there was a prolonged silence of perhaps 2 minutes. Whitaker broke it: "The whole thing sounds discouraging from here. Sounds like a war over the size of the table. Nobody wants to negotiate, and everybody's afraid to put their cards on the table. Nobody is willing to put demands on the table. Everybody plays their cards so close to the vest, they aren't even sure if they're playing bridge or poker." There was another long silence. Nobody said anything. Whitaker's steel balls clicked in the silence.

Keith leaned back in his chair, reached over, and held the arm of Whitaker's chair as he said to Whitaker, "The other possibility is that they're afraid it's going to get worse."

Whitaker: I think they ought to be afraid of that. (Then to Mike:) Would you go to the men's reformatory at Quebec Falls next time? Or do you think you would go back to the Viroqua School for Boys again? Viroqua is kind of kid stuff, but they do treat you nice there. How was the food, by the way?

Mike: Oh, it wasn't very good.

Keith: I don't suppose it's very good at Quebec Falls, either. You could get a job in the kitchen. But even then I suppose most of the good food goes to the more experienced criminals in the kitchen. Maybe you could go crazy first, then you wouldn't have to go to jail. You could get off on a plea of innocent by reason of insanity. Then you would have to come back and see us, and it would be worse because the court would make you come. (There was more silence. The family was thinking; they weren't looking at each other or at the therapists. Their eyes seemed to be turned inward.)

Father: I think we have to figure out what game we're playing.

Keith: I doubt that you'll ever figure it out. So far it sounds like a game of secrets. (Another short silence.)

Whitaker: To say it more straight, it seems to us that the only time a family changes is when everybody is scared, and it doesn't feel like anybody is really very scared in this family.

Keith: It seems like you're concerned, but the concern is of such low voltage.

Father: It may appear that way, but I don't believe it.

Whitaker: I don't *believe* it either, but if the pain is hidden, it's hard to summate enough to make any difference. And worse than that, you can't find it if you run away from each other.

Father: I feel a sense of isolation. I tiptoe around in my house because I'm afraid of too much noise.

Whitaker: That's what I'm talking about. It feels like all four of you are tiptoeing around in here lest something happen.

That ended the first interview. The cross sections that we selected for use here represent portions where we attempt to increase anxiety, while the history segments are not included. From here we will summarize the case as it continued on. We picked this case in advance with the conviction that we would report wherever it went. It is one of the psychotherapies that cannot be regarded as a success or a failure; more accurately, it is a combination of both.

The Cashmans returned for two very flat interviews that were, in essence, continuations of the first interview. Then the mother moved to another city, as planned, to take on a high-level job, leaving the father and son to suffer with one another. Another appointment was not scheduled because the father planned to take Mike on a business trip to North Carolina. Two months elapsed before the father called back, in essence because things had gone sour between them and he was getting fed up.

The father was upset because he could not keep track of Mike. He had complaints from his school and the probation officer. Additionally, he was being psychologically tortured as only an adolescent can torment a parent. Mike would leave the house in a mess and never clean up after himself. His father's stereo was badly damaged by Mike's misuse.

One day the front door was locked, so Mike kicked it in. Mr. Cashman complained that he had to pay to get it fixed. We told Mike that he should kick in the back door and the side door too, just to keep his old man from getting uppity. They were an odd couple—this youthful, energetic, bright, 43-year-old executive and the cynical, indifferent, 15-year-old son. They made up a kind of Cain and Abel twosome.

We liked Mr. Cashman. He was quite lively and hated to act like an old fuddy-duddy. His father had been too strict with him, and he was dedicated to being a more lenient father than his had been. On the other hand, when he joined the second generation, he felt weak and impotent. He was afraid that Mike was headed for more trouble somewhere, although he didn't really have many facts at his disposal.

Mike (furious with his father): You interfere with everything. You want me to live like you do.

Keith (to Mike): Do you think he's trying to map out your life?

Father (joining in): That's probably true, I would like to map out his life because I'm afraid that he's going to let himself go down the drain.

Keith: The only problem with that is that he sounds like he's got a different map.

Father: I suppose I am being a nursemaid.

Whitaker: Not so much a nursemaid. I had a picture of a St. Bernard running to the rescue whenever Junior gets in a jam.

Father: I guess so. I'm a faithful friend alright. I'm always waiting for the alarm to go off. Then I go to offer my expert help, and he gets mad about it. What is it that St. Bernards carry around in that little barrel?

Whitaker: Brandy, I think.

Father: Yeah, that's it, brandy. I suppose I should just sit down in a snowbank and drink it myself.

Whitaker: That's an even better idea. You could become an alcoholic. Do you think you could be any good at it?

The hour ended shortly thereafter. We elaborated the plans for how helpful it would be if the father became an alcoholic. Then he wouldn't be expected to take care of this twirp son of his; in fact, if he was lucky, the Social Services would intervene and take the boy away. Or they could make him go back to the mother; that way the father could kill two birds with one stone. He could get rid of his son and torture his wife simultaneously.

Father: So you think I ought to be an alcoholic? (as he was headed out the door)

Keith: We think it's one way that you could help your son, but remember that it could be dangerous to your health. It's mainly a question of how self-sacrificial you want to be.

The father thought we were nuts to make a suggestion like that, but on the other hand, our distortion helped him to see some of the absurdity in the strange struggle he was having with his son.

The next interview began in silence. Mike tossed one of the Nerf frisbees to Keith, who tossed it back to the father and then it went back to Whitaker. The four of us tossed it around a few more times.

Father: Things haven't changed much. I haven't become an alcoholic, but I've been sort of upset with the idea that you think I'm a St. Bernard. I think I'm upset because it seems pretty accurate, but I can't think what the next step is. In some ways it is easy to turn my back on what he is doing, but I'm afraid to. How can I stop worrying about him? He is my kid.

Whitaker (comfortingly): Of course you can't stop worrying. He is your son, and you're stuck with the problem of worrying about him. But worrying is different from giving him your map for his life. I don't think parents ever get over worrying. In fact, yesterday afternoon we saw a family with 65-year-old parents, and the father was still worrying about his 40-year-old daughter and the path that her life had taken.

The father visibly relaxed. It looked as if he had shifted gears inside his head, as if he had suddenly settled the problem of how to be responsible and still not responsible for his son. He was still worried but not too worried. It would be simple to say that he was now able to laugh at himself, but there was more to it than that.

We had started therapy by being confronting with him, implicating the father in the family situation, laughing at his naivete and impotence. We had developed what we think of as a therapeutic double-bind. We cared about him and his life's predicament, encouraged him to try harder, but snickered when he did. He found himself in a logically impossible situation a little like a Zen student who is shown a stick and asked, "What is it? If you tell me it is a stick, I'll hit you; if you tell me it is not a stick, I'll hit you; if you don't tell me anything I'll hit you."

The therapy continued uncertainly with all the grace of a trained circus bear riding a bicycle. The father would say things like "I don't know what he's doing. I'm worried about him, but it's very clear to me that I can't make him do what I want him to."

Mike remained a kind of mystery for all of us adults, but he was cleared from probation. However, the father made no progress at all at becoming an alcoholic.

We met every other week or so for an hour. Once Mike had been off of probation for a month, the father began to get frustrated again. He came in one day without Mike. The father had been 10 minutes late to pick him up at school, and Mike did not wait. The father said, "God, I've had it with that little shit. I feel like he is constantly working to outmaneuver me. I want him to do better, so I'm always suckered out of position when he suggests that he is going to do something constructive. I don't know what I should do."

Whitaker: Maybe you ought to get your wife up here.

Father: What would she do?

Keith: I'm not sure what she'd do, but at least you would have a team. You're outmaneuvered because you're all by yourself. With a twosome you might have more luck.

Father (thinking for a moment, then speaking): But she's got a job, and I hear

that it is going well, and I don't think that she'd come back. But I have been thinking of something. I've been thinking of having my father come up here with us. I'm very certain that he wouldn't take any of this bullshit from Mike.

Whitaker: That sounds like a good idea to us. Single parenting is virtually impossible. From what you say it sounds like your father would make a good choice behind your wife. It would also probably go some way to upsetting this very careful dance that you and your son do with one another.

The father left the office again. He said he was going to think some more about having his dad come up. There, in midair, is where the situation is suspended.

EVALUATION

Effectiveness of the Approach

There is very little objective evidence for the success of this model of family therapy. The goodwill of the community, the fact that most referrals come from previous patients, the statements of families who have apparently failed but are later seen in the community and report their gains from the therapy are all clinical evidence of success, but they are very little help in research.

Probably the most solid proof is the enjoyment of the psychotherapist in his or her personal, ongoing change. It does not seem possible that the therapist could stay happy and fun loving or creative if the feedback on the covert level were not successful. Any therapist would become bitter, withdrawn, and suicidal if the therapy he or she did were not successful. Further evidence is the therapist's freedom to participate in the patient's change. The therapist's own change through the constructive-creative experiences of the family should be seen as evidence that the therapeutic process is useful for the family as well.

The Training of Family Therapists

Learning family therapy occurs in three different stages: (a) learning *about* family therapy, which is probably best done in seminars and workshops; (b) learning to *do* family therapy, which requires the pressure of clinical experience; and (c) *being* a family therapist, which involves orienting one's clinical work around families, a reorientation in which the therapist comes to believe in families rather than individuals.

A first question has to do with who should do family therapy. It is important that the persons have a background of some powerful existential experience—some kind of Zenlike explosion, a brief episode of craziness, individual therapy, or some other identity crisis or confrontation with him- or herself. These might include therapy, an extended work experience outside of psychotherapy, perhaps military service. One characteristic of such experience is that the person loses the sense of uniqueness while retaining fascination with his or her complexity (Fowles, 1977).

A background of clinical experience is essential. The people who make the best use of training include frustrated physicians or battle-experienced social workers who have come to the point of giving up without becoming nonsubjective. These people have an experiential sense of systems and have learned to work through and within experience more than ideas. They are acquainted with but not frightened by their own impotence. We think that this method of family therapy is best practiced by professional psychotherapists. The discipline of the therapist is not critical, but discipline is required.

There are problems with professionally qualified people attempting to learn family therapy. Physicians with training in the specificity of functioning may have the most to unlearn and also have more ambivalence about the switch to working with a group. A problem in their value orientation, however, is counterbalanced by their sense of systems and the massive load of intensive clinical experience behind them. Persons with PhD training often have trouble switching to family therapy because of their lock into research methodology and the need to stay with linear thinking.

Learning about Family Therapy. Learning is best initiated by reading and seminars, both of which introduce trainees to the new language that goes with family work. Exposure to the language also stimulates their thinking and helps interest them in conceptualizing about families and family therapy.

Some clinical experience is necessary in order to learn about family therapy. Experience can be acquired in several ways, such as by watching an experienced family therapist work or by seeing families in a context such as inpatient psychiatry service, a medication clinic, or a social agency. These experiences provide a look into the back window of family therapy. There is no great demand for change in the families seen in these contexts, but it is a way to learn about the power and functioning of the family.

Learning to Do Family Therapy. We think that one learns to do family therapy best in an outpatient setting. This is the kind of training we try to provide our general psychiatry residents. A person who is capable of doing family therapy should be able to do the following:

1. Take a family system history.
2. Understand basic systems thinking and the ways in which it complements and is related to clinical work in mental health areas.
3. Assess family structure and process.
4. Provide crisis intervention for couples and families.
5. Do long-term couples therapy.
6. Organize and construct a family conference around a crisis in a family or an illness in a family.
7. Know the potential use of family therapy in general psychiatric practice as, for example, in doing medication checks or in seeing patients with psychosomatic illness.
8. Utilize consultation in the practice of psychotherapy.

Being a Family Therapist. This is a more complicated, long-range process. As background, it should be understood that marital therapy is a psychosocial process and family therapy is a biopsychosocial process. Thus, the voltage is higher, the problems are more difficult, and the pressures are much greater in practicing family therapy. Individual therapy is also biopsychosocial, but it operates in an intrapsychic framework dealing with introjects. The model that we believe in for learning family therapy utilizes cotherapy. The cotherapy team should be imbedded in a cuddle group of other cotherapy teams. Our ideal sequencing of clinical experiences in becoming a family therapist is as follows:

1. We like to think that the process of learning begins with a cotherapy team treating a marital couple. This opportu-

nity is really a play at psychotherapy. The actual process is to supervise the bilateral pseudotherapy between the husband and wife, who are already deeply transferred to each other.

2. The cotherapy team treats a couples group. Here the process moves from the husband and wife supporting each other to a later effort to offer themselves as patients. The couples group also must resolve the male-versus-female subgroup and thereafter the emotional triangulation that challenges each couple.

3. The next stage in training to be a family therapist is for the cotherapy team to treat an individual, preferably an individual who is or has been in treatment with his or her family by another therapist. The patient could be someone who is residual from a family therapy success and wants to go on in intrapsychic development; it may be a person who has been working through a divorce in the family and who is now alone; or it might be an older adolescent who has individuated after family therapy and is living at a distance from the family.

4. The final stage is cotherapy with a family. With this stage completed, the trainee can go back through the whole process in several different patterns: (a) with a peer for cotherapist or (b) without a cotherapist but with a consultant who comes in on the second interveiw and is available from time to time to evaluate and help clarify the situation in therapy. Thus, the trainee should learn couples therapy first, individual therapy later, and family therapy last.

If the beginning family therapist does individual therapy too early, he or she becomes frightened of the symbolic transference experience and tends to play defensive games. The therapist operates out of a watered-down individual therapy theory such as a half-hearted psychoanalysis. However, it is important for family therapists to learn to do individual therapy. This one-to-one way of working is deeply entrenched in our language and culture. People who do family therapy exclusively from the start may misunderstand the way relationships provide healing. Individual treatment also gives therapists new to psychotherapy a way to learn about therapeusis (mutual therapeutic neurosis). A therapist without exposure to individual therapy may also risk becoming oversystemsatized (systems addicted).

Learning individual therapy should include individual therapy with children using the model we described earlier. It is difficult to become a family therapist without an extended experience with children. Doing therapy with children teaches the therapist nonverbal methods as well as extensive work with the use of fantasy in communication.

Therapy for the therapist is crucial. We don't think one is prepared to do psychotherapy until one has had the experience of being a patient. The family therapist should start his or her investment by having marital therapy and then family therapy with three generations. Where family therapy is not available, a useful substitution is to do a study of one's own family with a group of colleagues involved in the same project. After work with the therapist's own family, the therapist may decide to go into extensive intrapsychic therapy to increase access to his or her own creativity.

The reason for family therapy for therapists and the study of the therapists' own families is not only to get them individuated out of their families but also to help them develop more belongingness to their family. They need to gain a sense of the flexibility of the triangles in their own families. Jung (1961)

said of people who leave their families that their development stops at the point where they depart. This developmental arrest is profoundly damaging to family therapists.

We would like to expand some of the ideas generated earlier in this section. First of all, we are dedicated to cotherapy as the primary model of training. We operate our cotherapy training as peers. Some think that cotherapy should not be done except between equal and heterosexual peers. This is ideal but rarely available. We think that any cotherapy team develops a model for pairing that has therapeutic value to the family. Much of our cotherapy with trainees works out something like an older man's marriage to his young second wife. The less experienced members of the cotherapy team attach themselves to the more experienced. For example, when Keith works with Whitaker, Keith is much more likely to follow Whitaker's lead. On the other hand, Whitaker uses Keith's working time as a time to pull away from the family so that he may re-enter at a very different point. The same pattern pertains when Keith works with residents. They are more likely to match something that he is up to or to take a tangent from it, while Keith finds himself dissociating while they're working and then coming in on a completely new tack from theirs. When the cotherapy team is made up of peers of the same generation and experience, functioning is always much more mixed and provides more competition and more freedom for each. It takes time to develop a cotherapy team so that the team can work together and trust each other. One learns the most about cotherapy when working with the same cotherapist in different treatment settings.

The cotherapy method for training is

especially useful when family therapists are advanced in their training. Consider how a surgeon learns to do surgery: the resident performs surgery with the professor. There is a strong tradition for this model in medicine, which may have to do with why we prefer it. The method has much to do with an identification with the teacher. The Hippocratic oath suggests that the professor and student will live together as father and son. It is very clear to us that our investment in a resident has to do with his or her learning and vice versa. Many trainees ask if they can see a family; they do so, then drift away. Others become more invested in the work, and we naturally become more invested in them.

The core of our training is organized around the use of cotherapy. Regardless of where the trainee is in his or her experience, we operate our cotherapy training as peers. We do not invite the trainee in as a cotherapist so that we can provide him or her with an experience; we invite the trainee in because we need him or her. The best model for the cotherapy team is the marital relationship where the therapists function both as two separate I's and as a we. As teachers, we form cotherapy units with the trainees, the trainees develop cotherapy teams with each other, and we meet weekly as a group to discuss cases and conceptual issues. This cuddle group of therapists provides us a way to gain more personally from our psychotherapy work. It is here that we can celebrate our wins and mourn our losses. It also gives us a way to develop conceptually the basis of psychotherapy work.

It is important to mix up methods of training so that the therapist does not end up programmed to a set pattern. It is useful to watch and be watched from behind a one-way mirror and to use video-

tape so that the therapist can review the session after the fact. Keith recalls a day spent with Jill Metcoff watching Whitaker work from behind the mirror. She was interested in a process phenomenon that she called a microevent (Metcoff & Whitaker, 1982). During these interviews, we turned off the audio system and watched only the nonverbal behavior in relation to who spoke when. It was fascinating.

Something more needs to be said about the importance of using couples groups in training family therapists. It is a unique, valuable experience, especially when working with couples who may have been consulting with the therapist previously. In the beginning, it is best if couples are selected who are not too disturbed. Cotherapy with a couples group allows the trainee and supervisor to take part with other couples but simultaneously to operate in an administrative role and to lose themselves in or utilize personal involvement. The dynamics of the individuals supporting their spouses gradually weakens, and the war goes on between the four males and the four females. Once the battle of the sexes has been worked through, triangles between Husband 1, his wife, and Wife 2, or Wife 1, Husband 1, and Husband 2 preoccupy the couples group. The therapist has the opportunity to live through the experience of these family dynamics.

Does a family therapist need to have full child therapy training? We do not think so. As noted above, the more that the therapist knows about children, the better. He or she can also learn about children from having his or her own or from working part-time in a child-related agency such as a school or other treatment facility. The important factor is that the therapist learn how to relate to children, that he or she learn the importance of children and the special stresses that they generate and are exposed to in any multigenerational group.

SUMMARY

In this presentation of one method for helping families develop a quality change in their living pattern, we have not been able to describe fully the reciprocal effects of such efforts on a therapist as a person. Interaction obviously impacts on each interactor. As a father in a family so accurately put it at their ending interview, "Overall, I've really enjoyed coming here...but something must happen to you guys in all this, too. I mean, even if you just sat there, you would have to get something personal out of it."

Like becoming a parent in the nuclear family, the qualitative effects of becoming a family therapist are often dramatic. Treating families is both painful and deeply moving. Doing psychotherapy is change inducing in its symbolic effect on the therapist. The power of the family, like that of the infant, is seductive and threatening. The therapist and the conceptual framework that emanates from his or her work live between the pressure for constrictive narrowing toward more specific definition and the need for openness and vulnerability that lead to growth and reparative experience.

ANNOTATED SUGGESTED READINGS

Campbell, J., & Robinson, H. M. (1961). *A skeleton key to Finnegan's wake.* New York: Viking Press.

Campbell's masterful review of Joyce's masterpiece is a useful guided tour into the murky terrain of primary process language. The book provides an artful introduction to the schizophrenic lurking in each of us.

Garcia-Marquez, G. (1971). *100 years of solitude.* New York: Avon Books.

A fictionalized family chronicle weaving between history and dream in the way that we think families in treatment do. The images in this book are vivid and frequently come to mind when seeing families in the clinic.

Haley, J. (1973). *Uncommon therapy.* New York: Norton.

A series of brilliant case reports from Milton Erickson's work. We think that it teaches best how to make creative yet pragmatic interventions in common but complex clinical situations.

Napier, A., & Whitaker, C. (1978). *The family crucible.* New York: Harper & Row.

A review of a family's therapy experience in a case where Napier and Whitaker work as cotherapists. *The family crucible* complements this chapter perfectly.

Whitaker, C., & Malone, T. P. (1981). *The roots of psychotherapy* (2nd ed.). New York: Brunner/Mazel.

A reissue of the book first published in 1953. The book develops the experiential component of psychotherapy and adds historical depth to the ideas presented in this chapter.

REFERENCES

Castaneda, C. (1975). *Tales of power.* New York: Simon & Schuster.

Ehrenwald, J. (1966). *Psychotherapy: Myth and method, an integrative approach.* New York: Grune & Stratton.

Fellner, C. (1976). The use of teaching stories in conjoint family therapy. *Family Process, 15,* 427–433.

Fowles, J. (1977). *Daniel Martin.* Boston: Little, Brown.

Grinker, R. R., Sr. (1971). Biomedical education on a system. *Archives of General Psychiatry, 24,* 291–297.

Jung, C. G. (1961). *Memories, dreams, reflections.* A. Jaffe (Ed.). New York: Pantheon.

Klein, M. (1932). *The psychoanalysis of children.* London: Hogarth.

Metcoff, J., & Whitaker, C. (1982). Family microevents: Communication patterns for problem solving. In F. Walsh (Ed.), *Normal family processes.* New York: Guilford Press.

Middlefort, F. (1976). *Personal communication.* Conversation.

Minuchin, S. (1974). *Families and family therapy.* Cambridge, MA: Harvard University Press.

Rank, O. (1936). *Will therapy.* New York: Alfred A. Knopf.

Whitaker, C. (Ed.). (1958). *Psychotherapy of chronic schizophrenia.* Boston: Little, Brown.

Whitaker, C. A., & Malone, T. P. (1953). *The roots of psychotherapy.* New York: Blakiston.

Winnicott, D. W. (1949). Hate in the countertransference. *The International Journal of Psychoanalysis, 30,* 69–74.

Winnicott, D. W. (1971). *Playing and reality.* New York: Basic Books.

Wynne, L. C., Ryckoff, I. N., Day, J., & Hirsch, S. I. (1958). Pseudomutuality in the family relations of schizophrenics. *Psychiatry, 21,* 205–220.

CHAPTER 6

Strategic Therapy

ELIZABETH ALLAN SCHILSON

DEFINITION

Strategic therapy is family therapy in which the therapist devises and initiates strategies for solving the family's presenting problem. The strategic therapist is concerned with dysfunctional hierarchies and repetitive sequences of behavior between and among family members and, as appropriate, with other systems that support the presenting problem. The family is either attempting solutions to the problem at the wrong hierarchical level, denying the presence of a problem when one actually exists, or is creating a problem when there is none (Haley, 1987). The strategic therapist takes responsibility for directly influencing the family in order to bring about the altering and eliminating of the presenting problem.

Therapy is typically accomplished by the therapist's assessing and understanding the family's life cycle stage of development, the hierarchical dysfunction, and the repetitive sequence or cycle of family interactions, then correcting the hierarchy and breaking the cycle through straightforward or paradoxical directives. In order to increase the family's motivation for therapy, the therapist intensifies the presenting problem and the solvable symptoms. Clear goals are set that always include the presenting problem. Since each family is seen as unique, the emphasis is not on using strategies to be applied to all cases but on creating a step-by-step plan and designing strategies for each unique family.

Steps in Therapy

The general outline of therapy is described in the following subsections.

Establishing a Therapeutic Relationship. The main vehicle for change is the trust the family places in the therapist. Therefore, the therapist strives to develop trust from the first moment of contact with the family and continues to maintain it throughout the therapy.

Clarifying the Presenting Problem. The therapist must identify the dysfunction supporting the problem. Therefore, the therapist in assessing the presenting problem will track the behavorial sequence until he or she has a clear confirmation of who is involved in the presenting problem and in what ways.

Setting Goals. Once the therapist understands the dysfunctional hierarchy and sequences, he or she is in the position to set goals. The therapist establishes with the family clear goals for what life for the identified patient and the family will be like at the end of and after treatment. The simplest therapeutic goal is to change the presenting problem and sequences of behavior by preventing cross-generational coalitions (Haley, 1987).

Developing a Plan. The therapist needs to think in terms of two or three levels in the hierarchy and three stages in the sequence of change (Haley, 1987). In respect to the hierarchy, the therapist should first conceptualize the hierarchical dysfunction of the family and the stage it is in in the family life cycle as it enters therapy. Second, the therapist must consider how the hierarchy needs to be functioning when therapy is completed to determine what he or she is working toward. Third, the therapist needs to think of the intermediate interviews as the "work" of therapy, the bringing about of change in the family organization via interventions (directives), so the presenting problem will no longer serve a function. In other words, the family may not be able to be moved directly from the presenting problem to the functional goal. "Haley thinks of therapy in terms of a step-by-step change in the way the family is organized, so that it goes from one type of abnormal organization to another type before a more normal organization is finally achieved. By then, presumably, the symptom is no longer necessary" (Hoffman, 1981, p. 280).

Madanes (1981) has said:

Usually change is planned in stages, so that a change in one situation or one set of relationships will lead to another change in another relationship and then to yet another until the whole situation changes. Interventions are planned to involve family members with one another or to disengage various family members from one another. Often the therapist attempts first to create a new problem and to solve it in such a way that the change will lead to the solution of the problem originally presented by the family. (p. 22)

The therapist develops intermediate plans, substeps, and strategies and may or may not be verbalized to the family. If after a few sessions a particular plan is not successful in moving the family toward the goal of the therapy, the thera-

pist devises a new plan with different strategies.

This therapeutic approach allows the therapist to use as strategies any techniques from any other models of therapy thought to be useful in solving the presenting problem (Haley, 1987)—for example, child-management techniques from Adlerian, social learning, and behavioral models; bibliotherapy; P-A-C from transactional analysis. It is open to and includes working with social systems beyond the family in order to involve others who have power over the identified patient (e.g., school personnel, probation officers, family physician with control over medications, hospitalization admit and discharge procedures).

Madanes (1981) has stated that there are no counterindications in terms of client selection or suitability. The approach has been used with people representing the whole age range and all socioeconomic classes, with presenting problems of various kinds (e.g., marital problems, loneliness, fears, delinquency, psychosomatic symptoms).

Terms Used in Therapy

The following definitions are important to the understanding of strategic therapy.

Boundaries. A *boundary* is a delineation, border, or separation between the family system and other elements of the environment making it a distinct entity. Inside the family, it is a separation between the subsystems. Goldenberg and Goldenberg (1985) have explained boundaries in respect to family therapy in the following manner:

...members of families who function with poorly defined boundaries run the risk of overinvolvement with one another and the subsequent loss of autonomy and diminished potential or individual mastery of problems. Families whose boundaries are firmly delineated, impermeable and rigid tend to have members who go their own ways. Families are said to violate functional boundaries when members, crossing generations and subsystems, intrude upon functions that are properly the domain of other members. For example, children may be assigned long-term roles that are inappropriate, inflexible and ill-fitting; in some cases, children and their parents may even exchange family roles. (p. 72)

Circularity. Interactions between and among family members are not necessarily related in a simple cause-and-effect manner; rather, events take place in a circular manner. The behavior of one person influences that of a second, which influences that of a third, which may return to have an impact on either the first or second person and trigger a new cycle of similarly related events. Thus, the behavior of each person involved can affect and is affected by each other person's behavior (Watzlawick, Beavin, & Jackson, 1967).

Coalition. *Coalition* means a process of joint action against a third person, in contrast to an alliance, where two persons might share an interest not shared by the third (Haley, 1987, p. 116). A fundamental rule of social organizations is that an organization is in trouble when coalitions occur across levels of a hierarchy, particularly when these coalitions are secret. "When such a coalition happens occasionally, it is a minor matter. But when sequences of this kind become organized so that they repeat and repeat, the organization is in trouble and the participants will experience subjective distress" (Haley, 1987, p. 111).

Directives. A *directive* is an instruction or task that the family or individual

is to follow at the request or direction of the therapist, the main goal of which is to get the family to behave differently and to have different subjective experiences.

Dysfunctional. The dysfunctional family is characterized by repetitive and impaired or abnormal interactions. High hostility levels; incongruous beliefs; and difficulty coping with change, separation, and loss are often present. "Symptoms in any part of the family are viewed as evidence of dysfunction, whether the symptoms be emotional, physical, conflictual, or social" (Haley, 1971, p. 167–168).

Functional. The functional family is organized and operates in a manner considered to be normal or healthy in this culture. According to L'Abate, Ganahl, and Hansen (1986):

There are two crucial aspects of family functioning. First, there are the functional responsibilities assigned to the family by the environment, that is, meeting basic needs of survival, education, and upbringing of children; the creation of a psycho-bio social environment for growth; social control of its members; and the nurturance of emotional bonds to enhance emotional growth. (p. 16) ...The family system has to have enough stability, order, and predictability so that it can operate separately from yet interdependently with the larger system or society. Therefore, families are described as having their own organization, distribution of power, and sets of rules in order to function. There are discernable boundaries that separate the family from the outside world. The second phenomena, and of equal importance, are the dynamic movements from the inside to the outside and from the outside toward the inside. This leads to change and growth. (pp. 20)

Feedback. *Feedback* consists of those processes or exchanges of information responsible for receiving, interpreting, and transmitting information within the family and its environment.

Generation. In strategic therapy, *generation* signifies those persons constituting a single step in the line of descent from an ancestor.

Hierarchy. In any organization, there is hierarchy in the sense that one person has more power and responsibility to determine what happens than another person; that is, the members are not equal. In a functional family organization, the parents are higher in the hierarchy than the children (Madanes, 1981). There are certain characteristics of a malfunctioning organization if one thinks in terms of three levels and a triangular unit. First, the three persons responding to one another are not peers but members of different generations. Second, the member of one generation forms a coalition with one of another generation. In a two-generation conflict, one person joins another against the other's peer (e.g., the father joins the son against the mother). In a three-generation conflict, the person at the top forms a coalition with the person on the bottom against the person in the middle (e.g., the grandmother supports her grandchild against the child's mother, the grandmother's daughter). Third, the problem is most severe when the coalition across generations is denied or concealed. An organization is not malfunctioning because cross-generational coalitions exist but because such coalitions are repeated again and again as part of the system (e.g., a woman must save her child from her husband at times, but when this act becomes a way of life, the family organization is in trouble) (Haley, 1987).

Homeostasis. Once a system process is established, it tends to persist in that same process.

Paradox. Communication is paradoxical when it involves two messages that qualify each other in conflicting ways. The double-bind messages "Be spontaneous," "Don't be so obedient," "I want you to dominate me" are common paradoxes in human relationships (Haley, 1963). "They are paradoxical because if the receiver of the message complies with the request, he is not complying with the request. The paradox occurs because one directive is qualified by another, at a different level of abstration, in a conflictual way" (Madanes, 1981, p. 7).

Parental Child. In some families, there is a third generation that is not clearly a "generation," for instance, one-parent families with many children. There are a mother and her children, but in between there is an older child who functions as a parent for the younger children. He or she is not an adult but a child, yet functions as an adult insofar as he or she is taking care of the younger children (Haley, 1987).

Presenting Problem. A presenting problem is "a type of behavior that is part of a sequence of acts between several people" (Haley, 1976, p. 2). It is viewed as an interpersonal strategy or effort to define the nature of the relationships, often that of who is in control. The repeating sequence of the presenting problem is the focus of therapy (Haley, 1987).

Reframing or Relabeling. Reframing or relabeling is the most frequently employed of all methods in psychotherapy. To *reframe* means to change the conceptual or emotional viewpoint of the family in relation to the situation being experienced and to place it in another frame that fits the facts of the same concrete situation equally well or even better, thereby changing its meaning. Reframing alters perception, while the situation itself may remain quite unchanged. What turns out to be changed is the meaning attributed to the situation and therefore its consequences, but not its concrete facts (L'Abate, Ganahl, & Hansen, 1986). An example would be reframing a child's temper tantrums as the child's way of asking the parents to set firmer limits.

Resistance. Resistance is the reluctance displayed by families when they react against a therapist asking them to change. If the family is in a stable state, they are resistant to change because to change means instability and something new and unknown. If they are in a crisis with everyone upset, they will often follow directives more easily because they are trying to stabilize.

Structure. The family is organized, and this organization is reflected by characteristic family behaviors that are highly dependable and predictable, that is, patterned family behaviors. "A structure is composed of repeating acts among people" (Haley, 1987, p. 111).

Subsystem. The structure of the nuclear family system can be divided into four basic, smaller, dependent parts of a larger system, or *subsystems,* each with its own needs, boundaries, and expectations: the individual, husband-wife, sibling, and parent-child (Haley, 1976). Subsystems can be formed by genera-

tion, by sex, by interest, or by function (Minuchin, 1974).

Symptom. A *symptom* is a label for a sequence in the family organization. In strategic therapy, such symptoms as "depression" or "phobia" are viewed as a contract between people and therefore as adaptive to their relationships (Haley, 1987). Symptoms are "communicative acts that have a function within an interpersonal network" (p. 106). The symptom is an analogy for the identified patient's relationships with the other family member.

System. All families have a greater patterning in their communications than one would expect if these communications ruled by chance (Haley, 1971). "The family *is* a system in that a change in one part of the system is followed by compensatory change in other parts of the system" (Haley, 1971, p. 288).

Triangles. A two-person system under stress will form itself into a three-person system. As more people become involved, the system becomes a series of interlocking triangles. Haley (1987) has suggested:

if one thinks in terms of a triangular unit— such as mother and father and child, or mother-in-law and husband and wife—one can calculate how many triangles there are in the average family if we think in terms of three levels of a hierarchy. In a family with two parents, two children, and four grandparents, there are only eight persons, but there are 56 triangles (and this count does not include uncles, aunts, neighbors, employers, or therapists). Each person in the family is involved in 21 family triangles, and every one of the 21 triangles of parents and children carries the possibility of a coalition across generation lines and so the possibility of a malfunctioning structure. (p. 115)

HISTORICAL DEVELOPMENT

The philosophical roots of strategic therapy can be traced to contributions of Gregory Bateson and Milton Erickson to family therapy. Bateson in his early professional years was a research anthropologist. His interest in communication led to a research project for the study of schizophrenia (the Palo Alto Project) in which he brought together the group of Jay Haley, Don Jackson, John Weakland, and William Fry. Bateson contributed his ideas based on the theories of cybernetics, communication, and systems research. Haley was primarily interested in analysis of fantasy. Weakland, a chemical engineer, became involved with the group through his interest in anthropology. Jackson, a psychiatrist, joined the group as a clinical consultant and a supervisor of psychotherapy with schizophrenic patients. He had been working with schizophrenics and their families and was beginning to develop the concept of homeostasis. Fry, also a psychiatrist, was interested in humor as a therapeutic modality.

The members of this group had differing opinions and interests, but all were united by the idea of the importance of communication in the organization of the family. Their collaboration was important because it served as the beginning of the integration of communications theory and systems theory and provided the conceptual base for strategic therapy.

In 1956, Bateson, Jackson, Haley, and Weakland published an article entitled "Toward a Theory of Schizophrenia." Haley wrote about the research leading to this article in his book, *Changing families: A family therapy reader* (1971):

We had brought a schizophrenic patient together with his parents to try to find out why the patient could not be with them on visiting day for more than a few minutes without collapsing in an anxiety state. It was an information-gathering session, not a family treatment interview. Yet what we observed so changed our views about treating schizophrenics that by the beginning of the next year we had started a systematic program of treating families of schizophrenics. (p. 3)

This historic article introduced the concept of the double-bind as a factor in the etiology of schizophrenia. The concept of double-bind is that one person makes a statement to another that simultaneously contains two messages or demands that are logically inconsistent and contradictory. (See the definition for *paradox*). No matter how the individual responds, failure to please is inevitable. The double-bind is a particularly destructive form of paradoxical communication.

In the same year, the Bateson group received a grant from the National Institute of Mental Health to study family dynamics and worked until 1962, when the group disbanded.

During the years in which the Bateson group was together, two of its members, Haley and Weakland, were heavily influenced by Erickson, a psychiatrist. They spent their weekends traveling to Phoenix, Arizona, where Erickson maintained a small private practice, occasionally treating couples and families. Erickson was considered to be a highly innovative therapist who was mostly interested in teaching his ideas to others. His use of hypnosis and paradoxical instruction heavily influenced Haley and Weakland. His approach was pragmatic and flexible since he believed that people's problems are unique and infinitely variable. He believed people get "stuck" when they view their problems as having only one solution. His therapy, therefore, focused on provoking clients to behave in new, more adaptive ways.

Erickson assumed full responsibility for the outcome of treatment. He was powerful and directive in therapy and favored manipulation as a vehicle for change. Particularly relevant was his utilization of other family members in the treatment of problems traditionally viewed as individual, intrapersonal problems (Gurman & Kniskern, 1981). His hypnotic techniques typically required the therapist to assume full responsibility for the treatment and to issue directives, however subtle, as a way of gaining leverage with patients and ultimately manipulating them to change.

Haley became a student and interpreter of Erickson's extraordinary feats of observation and uncanny ability to tap unrecognized resources in his clients (Haley, 1973). Erickson was particularly skilled at encouraging resistance with clients; that is, he was able to encourage patients to maintain a symptom by not fighting it or to insist the client work at giving it up and then subtly introduce directions to induce change. Haley (1973) has stated that Erickson was thus able to avoid direct confrontation with the symptom, a tactic likely to have been met with resistance, and to utilize the client's own momentum to force symptom abandonment. This common hypnotic technique became the basis for the development of the paradoxical directive, a hallmark of the strategic approach (Haley, 1973).

During this time, Haley began his private practice of psychotherapy, specializing in brief treatment. He sought Erickson for supervision and began using hypnosis, communications and cyber-

netic systems theory, and the double-bind concept. This was the beginning of the strategic approach (Stanton, 1981).

In 1959, Jackson formed the Mental Research Institute (MRI) in Palo Alto, California, to continue to explore how these concepts could be applied to psychiatric treatment. Virginia Satir joined Jackson at this time from the National Institute of Mental Health, where she had been working with Murray Bowen (Satir, 1982). Haley and Weakland joined them in 1962. The assumptions of the group became (a) an underlying problem in the family is being exhibited by the pathology of the identified patient in the family; (b) the family behavior is governed by the cybernetic principles of homeostasis, feedback, and redundancy; and (c) treating the family involves changing its patterns of communication (Segal, 1982).

In 1967, Haley left Palo Alto to join Salvador Minuchin and Braulio Montalvo at the Philadelphia Child Guidance Center, where he worked as director of family therapy research for 10 years. In their work, primarily centered around training poor and black people to treat families, they focused on dysfunctional families with confused hierarchies and with cross-generational coalitions.

Several basic assumptions of strategic therapy resulted from this work: (a) Families are rule-governed systems that can be best understood in context. (b) The presenting problem serves a function within the family. (c) The concepts of boundaries, coalitions, hierarchy, power, metaphor, family life cycle development, and triangles are basic to the diagnosis of stuck families.

According to Hoffman (1981), Haley's position is actually more that of a structural strategist. His concern with family hierarchy and coalitions and other issues of family structure place him in the structural group, whereas his interest in paradoxical directives and other unobtrusive ways of managing resistance identifies him with the strategic group.

Haley returned to his own work with schizophrenics when he left Philadelphia in 1976 for Washington, DC, where he joined the faculty of the University of Maryland Medical School and established his own strategic family therapy institute. He was joined by his wife, Cloe Madanes, who has made significant contributions of her own to the strategic approach (Madanes, 1981).

Madanes had a degree from Argentina and went to the MRI in 1965 to pursue her interest in research. Though at first she was strongly psychoanalytic, she became influenced by Erickson's work. In 1971, she joined Minuchin and the others at the Philadelphia Child Guidance Clinic training professionals in family therapy. It was at this time that she met Haley (Simon, 1986). According to Simon, Madanes's predominant theoretical contribution to family therapy is the "idea that most symptoms, and the responses they evoke from other family members, are really metaphors that mirror, at the same time as they disguise, other problems whose direct expression might irreparably injure a family's status quo" (p. 22). She is probably best known for her pretend techniques, directives that instruct the identified patient to act as if he or she had the problem at the moment (e.g., stomachache). The family members pretend along with the identified patient.

Haley and Madanes present workshops around the country as well as train therapists in their Strategic Therapy Institute. They remain based in Washington, DC. MRI is still conducting research, and the Philadelphia Child Guidance Clinic is still on the cutting edge of structural therapy.

In summary, the strategic approach came of age with the family therapy movement. In the field of family therapy, strategic therapy's entry into mainstream thought was marked by publication of the seminal book by Watzlawick, Beavin, and Jackson (1967), *Pragmatics of Human Communication.* An earlier work by Haley (1963), *Strategies of Psychotherapy,* recorded the creative work of Milton Erickson and sought to demonstrate that paradox was a common factor in all approaches to therapy. Haley further articulated Erickson's hypnotic techniques in *Uncommon Therapy* (1973).

The strategic approach to therapy has evolved from both communications theory and general systems theory. The assumptions regarding intervention were based on the work of Bateson (1972) and Erickson together with Satir, Jackson, Watzlawick, Weakland, and Haley. Other contributors to the strategic approach over the years have been Mara Selvini Palazzoli, Luigi Boscolo, Gianfranco Cecchin, Guiliana Prata, Lynn Hoffman, Richard Rabkin, and Richard Fisch. Strategic therapy is also known by other descriptions, including problemsolving therapy, brief therapy, and systemic therapy.

This chapter will present strategic therapy as it is articulated, taught, and practiced by Jay Haley and Cloe Madanes and their followers.

TENETS OF THE MODEL

Since Haley and Minuchin worked together from 1967 to 1976, it seems only natural that strategic and structural approaches would share similar tenets. The following tenets are held in common.

1. Each family is viewed as unique, with their own rules and patterns that define identity and organization. All be-

havior is viewed as perfectly logical from the unique perspective of the particular family, and all families are viewed as functional in terms of their unique perspective.

2. The social context is emphasized in that strategic and structural therapists believe that problems involve at least two and usually three people. "When tension between members of a two-person system becomes high, a third person is brought into the picture" to stabilize the system (Stanton, 1981, p. 365).

3. Strategic and structural therapists foster the idea that functional families have an appropriate hierarchy of power, with parents having more power than children. Generally dysfunctional families have hierarchical confusion.

4. Therapy is symptom oriented. Haley (1963) defines symptoms as tactics used by one person to deal with another. These tactics are embedded in the relationships of the family and serve a very important function in maintaining complex, back-and-forth feedback mechanisms between and among family members (Haley, 1976).

5. Problems of individuals are manifestations of disturbances within the family. The presenting problem is understood within the context in which it occurs—the family—and the function it serves within the family. The identified patient (IP) is not the real problem; rather, the problem is the manner in which the family interacts. Therefore, an individual cannot be expected to change unless the family system changes. Since the problem exists in relation to other family members, it is assumed that the problem must be solved within that context.

6. As the family's understanding changes, the individual's behavior changes. There exists a problem in the family because of the way in which the family members perceive and conceptualize the situation, and the problem is the result of misguided attempts at solving or avoiding that situation. The therapist works to provide the family with a different way to perceive and conceptualize it. As the family comes to see the situation differently, the problem is dealt with differently.

7. The therapist assumes responsibility for determining the structure of the therapy process. The therapist takes a directive role. According to Madanes (1981):

The approach assumes that all therapy is directive and that a therapist cannot avoid being directive, since even the issues he chooses to comment on and his tone of voice are directive. In this therapy, directives are deliberately planned, and they are the main therapeutic technique. (p. 23–24)

The therapist must have the ability to avoid the family's efforts to triangulate him or her yet remain involved, persuasive, and active in the therapy process. The therapist must join the family's ongoing dysfunctional system and change it by participating within it and synchronizing his or her position with the direction of needed family change. Change is brought about by the shifts the family members make in interacting with each other because of the ways they are having to respond to the therapist (Haley, 1976).

Much emphasis is placed on giving directives for out-of-session change (i.e., homework), which is examined later for behavioral sequences. In this manner, the system is thrown into disequilibrium, and the homeostasis is disturbed by substitution of new behaviors into the circular system. In other words, this is not therapy where relationships are changed by talking about relationships; rather, relationships are changed by altering the ways family members respond to each other, thereby acquiring new behaviors that lessen or eliminate the presenting problem.

8. Process is emphasized over content. The therapist follows the family's examples or content "stories" regarding the problem until he or she understands the underlying process flowing consistently through the content stories. Once the therapist comprehends the dysfunctional process the family is experiencing (sometimes within only a few minutes of the initial interview), he or she can move to instigating change.

9. Strategic therapy is change rather than growth oriented. To the strategic therapist, change occurs not through insight and understanding but through the process of the family's carrying out directives issued by the therapist (Goldenberg & Goldenberg, 1985).

10. The general concepts of systems theory are used in the diagnosis of dysfunctional families (i.e., boundaries, circularity, coalitions, hierarchy, homeostasis).

11. The family life cycle is considered important in developing diagnosis and understanding of family dysfunction. Problem families often are seen as being stuck at a particular stage within the family life cycle; that is, the family has difficulty making the transition from one stage of the family life cycle to the next. They develop problems because they cannot adjust to transitions occurring in the family life cycle.

12. Families are rule-governed systems. In functional families, a nonsymptomatic process is system maintained and system maintaining. In dysfunctional families, a symptomatic process is system maintained and system maintaining. A family system operates by repeating the same interactional patterns, whether these be functional or dysfunctional. In families with dysfunctional patterns, the identified patient and family members cannot see a way to alter the situation through nonsymptomatic means. In functional families, the members are less preoccupied with themselves and their own motivations or problems. Erickson has said, "If you look over the lives of happy, well-adjusted people, they have never bothered to analyze their childhood or their parental relationships. They haven't bothered and they aren't going to" (Haley, 1973, p. 246).

13. Emphasis is on the present rather than on the past. The family members' history is not so relevant, since dysfunctional behavior is maintained by current interactions. Strategic therapists are concerned with what is going on in the family at present, not with why or how the family became this way. Simply, the family is believed to be the way it is because that is the way it is, not because of what happened to it in the past (Watzlawick, Weakland, & Fisch, 1974).

14. Because the problems are maintained by ongoing interactional processes, insight is not a necessary prerequisite for change. Problems cannot be alleviated through understanding alone because the problems are maintained by ongoing interactional processes. Effort is placed on reframing or relabeling rather than on producing insight.

15. Most strategic therapists follow a brief therapy model, and they terminate as soon as possible following positive change in the presenting problem. This is important in terms of not giving a mixed message to the family. If the presenting problem has been eliminated, the therapist wants to discontinue therapy soon. Unless a new contract is negotiated, the therapist may move to recess within one

to four more sessions. Haley (1980) believes that therapy works best when there is intense involvement and rapid disengagement rather than weekly sessions over years. The length of therapy is contingent on the presenting problem. Some strategic therapists limit treatment to 10 sessions as a standard procedure. Most strategic and structural therapists doubt the effectiveness of therapy that extends beyond 15 months. Early sessions are usually spaced a week apart, although they may be held more frequently with less frequent contacts near termination. Follow-up sessions are conducted to ensure positive change.

16. If therapy fails, it is the therapist's fault. If therapy succeeds, the therapist does not take credit for it but instead congratulates the family members for their success. This reinforcement of the family members' efforts helps to strengthen the positive effects of the treatment. Treatment is not considered to have been successful if there has been no beneficial change in the presenting problem.

17. Strategic therapists do not encourage the expression of feelings or emotions per se. Such display has not been found to be helpful and, in fact, can even retard progress by diverting attention from the needed change.

How do the strategic and structural approaches differ? Haley first used the term *strategic* to describe any therapy in which the clinician actively designs interventions to fit the problem (Hoffman, 1981). Strategic therapists are concerned with the specific problem brought to the first session, and they focus on it as the unit to be attacked, reframing it in such a way that it can be solved. They are therefore more *symptom focused* than structural family therapists. Using the model of the self-reinforcing sequence,

the strategic therapist assumes the symptom is being maintained by the very behaviors that seek to suppress it—that is, by the solution. It is assumed that symptoms characterize the ways family members relate to each other. A careful analysis of these behaviors will show that at the same time that the problem is being attacked by behaviors opposing it, it is also being supported covertly by eliciting behaviors. The importance of maladaptive behavioral sequences in the dysfunction is emphasized. The therapist looks for this cycle or sequence and is aware that the problem, as described by family members, gives clues about its conceptual framework and about solutions that they have attempted.

Strategic therapists stick with the presenting problem and assign responsibility for change to the therapist's ability to reframe it so the client can see it from a different perspective. Structural therapists believe the problem should be spread to other family members. This is the most basic difference between strategic and structural approaches. Strategic therapists believe that the presenting problem makes sense in the social context of which it is a part, and they emphasize the positiveness within the maladaptive solution. It is in this light that one can understand the strategic therapists' emphasis on reframing.

The strategic therapist is not concerned about other dysfunctional behaviors if the family members do not complain about them. In other words, the strategic therapist does not push into an area where he or she is not invited (Hoffman, 1981). Hoffman has said that "in the world of therapy, the strategic therapist is a minimalist" (p. 273). Strategic therapists believe that it is not necessary to change all behaviors in a self-reinforcing cycle to remove the problem.

They have a narrower focus than other types of therapists. Since they work systemically, they expect that a small change in an important family relationship will have a domino effect on other relationships.

Strategic therapists will generally see all significant family members in the first interview. However, during the course of therapy they often work with one or two members of a family. They do not worry about necessarily seeing all members of a household together, as do structural therapists. They may even prefer to see individuals or family subgroups separately, maximizing change by setting one group or person secretly against the other.

Strategic therapists are concerned primarily with four interrelated elements: (a) symptoms, (b) metaphors, (c) hierarchy and power, and (d) family life cycle development.

Symptoms

The emphasis strategic therapists place on the symptom or presenting problem is understandable when one looks back at the historical beginnings of strategic therapy. The Palo Alto group dealt initially with very difficult families, partly because of their strong interest in schizophrenic families and partly because it was usually these very difficult families who were referred to them. These families were very entrenched in their homeostatic patterns as well as very skillful in throwing therapists offtrack. To avoid being distracted, the therapist had to keep centered on the presenting problem; in this way, he or she could justify the therapeutic moves to the family as being consistent with their goals (Stanton, 1981).

Traditionally, symptoms have been ex-plained as expressions of intrapsychic conflict. Haley (1963), who is strongly opposed to intrapsychic explanations, defines symptoms as misguided tactics used by one person to deal with another. Therefore, in strategic therapy, symptoms are seen as interpersonal strategies or efforts to define the nature of relationships. They are embedded in the family's network of relationships. The family system works to maintain homeostasis in interactional patterns, and symptoms can be viewed simply as particular types of behavior functioning as homeostatic mechanisms that regulate family transactions.

The term *symptom* is a label for a circular set of dysfunctional behaviors occurring within the family. Symptoms are not caused. They evolve as the family attempts to find a means to establish or maintain the family equilibrium, usually succeeding only in making matters worse and becoming the presenting problem in therapy.

The strategic approach holds that for a symptom to develop only two conditions need to be fulfilled: (a) a difficulty in a relationship needs to be mishandled; and (b) when the difficulty is not resolved, more of the same solution is attempted (Szykula & Morris, 1986). Therefore, the symptom usually develops when the family becomes stuck in a particular situation and cannot find a nonsymptomatic way to get out of it. One member may be labeled as the problem, even though his or her contribution is but one part of a total family process. Most symptoms, and the responses they evoke from other family members, are really metaphors that mirror deeper problems at the same time as they disguise them, the direct expression of which the family fears would damage its status quo (Madanes, 1981). If the symptom persists, the family context is consistent with maintaining the dysfunctional behavior it is seeking to change (Stanton, 1981). It is important, therefore, that the therapist understand the family's thoughts regarding how the symptom is perpetuated and how, in all of its ramifications, it affects the family's life.

Metaphors

A *metaphor* is a statement about something that resembles something else. A pattern of interaction develops around a situation and becomes an analogy for the deeper issue in the relationship. A pain that has no organic cause can be understood as a metaphor about family life. Therefore, the symptom may often be a metaphorical means for conceptualizing the problem, as well as a solution, although usually an unsatisfactory one. According to Madanes (1981), a metaphorical message usually contains an explicit element—"I have a headache"—as well as an implicit element—"I want more attention" or "I am unhappy." Madanes (1981) discusses several ways symptomatic behaviors can be metaphorical:

1. A symptom may be a report on an internal state and also a metaphor for another internal state. For example, a child's headache may be expressing more than one kind of pain.
2. A symptom may be a report on an internal state and also an analogy and a metaphor for another person's symptoms or internal states. For example, a child who refuses to go to school may be expressing his own fears and also his mother's fear. The child's fear is analogical to the mother's fear (in that the child's fear symbolizes and represents the mother's fear).
3. The interaction between two people in a family can be an analogy and a metaphor, replacing the interaction of another dyad in the family. For example, a husband may come

home upset and worried, and his wife may try to reassure and comfort him. If a child develops a recurrent pain, the father may come home and try to reassure and comfort the child in the same way that the wife was previously reassuring and comforting him. The father's involvement with the son in a helpful way will preclude his involvement with the wife in a helpless way, at least during the time in which the father is involved with the son. The interaction between father and son will have replaced the interaction between husband and wife.

4. The system of interaction around a symptom in one family member can be a metaphor for and replace another system of interaction around another issue in the family. Mother, father, and siblings may helpfully focus on a child's problem in a way that is analogical to the way they focused on the father's problem before the child's problem developed. The focus on the child's problem precludes the interaction centered around the father's problems.

5. There may be a cyclical variation in the focus of interaction in families, sometimes centered on a symptomatic child, sometimes on the problem of a parent or on a marital difficulty; but the interaction remains the same, in that there is helplessness and incongruity. (pp. 225–226)

The strategic therapist assumes that families will behave in a manner logically consistent with their conceptual frames. Reality is based on perspective. Therefore, the therapist might ask a series of questions to gather data about aspects of the family's life that are analogic to statements about the presenting problem: for example, "Can you tell me more about that?" (to increase the flow of analogies) or "Do you have similar fears about other things?" (to bring out related analogies). The therapist will seek verbal descriptions of what is happening that is analogic to other things in the family's life, then he or she will respond with metaphors about the family or about other families (Haley, 1976). The therapist will work to ease the family out of the metaphors they are using and into more appropriate ones, or the therapist will block the metaphor so that more suitable ones must be developed. When therapy is done effectively, the family undergoes changes so that more normal communication is possible from everyone involved (Haley, 1976).

Hierarchy and Power

A struggle to control is implicit in every relationship. According to Haley (1963), it is a maneuver for power, not a struggle to control another person. Haley (1976) has stated:

All creatures capable of learning are compelled to organize. To be organized means to follow patterned, redundant ways of behaving and to exist in a hierarchy. Creatures that organize themselves form a status, or power, ladder in which each creature has a place in the hierarchy, with those above and those below. (p. 101)

Any group of creatures—in this case, a family—must deal with oganizing into a hierarchy. Haley (1963) commented:

Any two people are posed with the mutual problems: (a) what messages, or what kinds of behavior are to take place in this relationship, and (b) who is to control what is to take place in this relationship, and thereby control the definition of the relationship. . . . It must be emphasized that no one can avoid being involved in a struggle over the definition of his relationship with someone else. (p. 9)

Ways of relating must be worked out about who is primary in status and power and who is secondary. Once the hierarchy is organized, functional or dysfunctional, all participants work to maintain it, not because it is necessarily comfortable but because it is familiar. It is this repetition of behavior that defines the hierarchy and with this principle that systems theory and hierarchy come together. If a member deviates from the repeating behavior and attempts to define a different hierarchy, the others react against that deviation and try to shape the behavior back into the habitual pattern (Haley, 1976).

An individual showing dysfunctional symptoms indicates that the family has an unclear or inappropriate hierarchical arrangement. In an ambiguous organizational pattern, no one is quite certain who is peer or superior or when and under what conditions another will be peer or superior. In an inappropriate organizational pattern, a member in one level of the hierarchy forms a coalition with a member of another level against a peer. Haley (1976) has stated, "If there is a fundamental rule of social organization, it is that an organization is in trouble when coalitions occur across levels of a hierarchy" (p. 104). When this becomes a stable pattern of organization within a family, symptomatic behavior in one or more family members is highly probable.

In most societies, power or status is simplified into three levels: grandparents, parents, and children. In American culture's functional nuclear family, the power resides with the parents, and the grandparents move to more of an advisory role. This can be different in another culture. In the Asian cultures, for example, grandparents are higher in the hierarchy than parents and tend to have more power than either the parents or the children in decision making. In American culture, parents are expected to be in charge of their children, and cross-generational coalitions (e.g., one parent siding with a child against the other parent) are considered to be dysfunctional (Madanes, 1981). It is thought that a family member is likely to be more disturbed in direct proportion to the number of malfunctioning hierarchies in which he or she is involved (Haley, 1976).

There are many ways for a hierarchy to be corrected, the most effective being to incorporate into the therapy the family's theories regarding the symptom. In parent-child dysfunctional hierarchies, the strategic approach is to rearrange the hierarchy so that parents are in a position superior to their children. Parents are encouraged to state rules concretely to increase the likelihood that the rules will be followed. The rules must be practical, and there must be consequences if the rules are not followed. When the child obeys the rules, then he or she is placing the parents in a superior position in the hierarchy. However, when the child refuses to obey the rules, then he or she is struggling for superior power, to which the parents must respond by instigating consequences and thereby taking the higher level position of power in the hierarchy.

Madanes (1981) describes the difficulties parents in dysfunctional families experience in maintaining their superior position in the hierarchy. She states that parents typically use a series of communication maneuvers to avoid defining the hierarchy as one where they have power over the offspring. They do so because they think "they are losing or have already lost their superior position in the hierarchy, because the youth is more powerful than they, because society has intervened to take power away from them, because they are afraid to do the wrong thing or harm the youth, because they are afraid [they will] lose their child" (p. 129). It is these perceptions that the therapist must counteract so that the proper hierarchy can be developed.

Haley (1976) explains pathological systems in terms of dysfunctioning hierarchies, emphasizing that one way to design a strategy is to shift from the presenting problem to a different abnormal one before reorganizing the family in a more functional hierarchy. He gives the following examples to present this idea:

A mother may be too central to her children, so that there is no hierarchy in the family and all the children function through her as if she were the hub of a wheel. In such a case it may be appropriate to create a system where an older child relieves the mother by taking charge. Essentially, this change creates a parental child hierarchy [a family organization with an older child who functions as an adult by taking care of the younger children]. From this new abnormal state, it is possible to shift to a more reasonable hierarchy in the family, so that all children can participate with different responsibilities.

Conversely, if the family comes in with a parental child system, one possibility is to make the mother overly central as the first stage. This change frees the parental child, and from this new abnormal hierarchy it is possible to go to a more normal one.

If the sequence involves a grandmother who is crossing generation lines and siding with the child against the mother, one can follow the procedure of giving responsibility to the grandmother. One can then go from this abnormal stage to another abnormal one in which all responsibility is given to the mother and the grandmother cannot discipline the child at all. From this abnormal state one can go to the more normal one.

If mother and child are in an overly intense relationship and the father is peripheral, the first stage can be one where the father takes total control of the child and the mother is excluded. This is an abnormal system, and from it one can move to a more normal one. It might also be possible to use an older sibling as a parental child to disengage mother and child, thereby introducing a parental child system as the first stage. Similarly, one might introduce the grandmother and create that hierarchy as a first stage. (pp. 122–123)

Family Life Cycle Development

Haley (1973) and Erickson, along with Weakland, Fisch, Watzlawick, and Bodin (1974), have stressed the importance of the family developmental life cycle as a framework for explaining symptomatology. Much like an individual, a family can be viewed as going through a developmental life cycle as members age and fulfill a variety of successive roles. There are potential crisis points that, although sometimes difficult to get through, are usually transversed by most families without great difficulty. On the other hand, some families experience an inability to manage such transitions normally.

The first detailed description of the family life cycle from a systemic point of view was presented in Haley's (1973) book *Uncommon Therapy*. Haley expanded the therapeutic techniques of Erickson across six stages of the family life cycle. He highlighted the facts that (a) symptoms are likely to occur at points of transition between stages; (b) some families develop problems because they are not able to make the necessary transition from one stage to the next stage; (c) when there is a disruption or failure to move to the next stage in the family life cycle, dysfunction occurs; and (d) the failure or disruption is because the family is having difficulty mastering the tasks inherent in that stage of the life cycle. The problem then is not the identified patient but the way the family reacts and attempts to adapt to the next stage it is approaching or has entered (Haley, 1971).

Most intact families go through much the same developmental processes over time. They pass through the same phases, most of which are marked by a critical transition point—courtship period, early marriage, birth of the first child, rearing of the young, departure from home of the children, retirement, and old age. Progression is often more complicated for single-parent families, blended families, and families experiencing crises due to loss.

Viewing the specific family over the course of the life cycle places their symptoms or dysfunctions in context of the normal progression through the family life cycle of the healthy family. A family should be observed in terms of their past patterns of transition, the behaviors that are presently being maintained, and the projection to the future toward which they are moving (L'Abate, Ganahl, & Hansen, 1986). The presenting problem is likely a signal that the family is having problems mastering the tasks associated with the present stage of the life cycle (Haley, 1973).

From the developmental life cycle view of the family, the influence of the entire emotional system of at least three generations is taken into consideration. As well, the nuclear family is seen as a subsystem of the larger family constellation reacting to past, present, and future relationships. With this concept, the therapist can understand the family themes, triangles, and labels evolving in the family over the generations as well as the dimensions of the current life cycle. This concept emphasizes the enormous amount of vertical stress that can be passed down through generations of the family, as well as the situational pressures that occur on the family as they are moving forward through the transitions from one stage to another (L'Abate, Ganahl, & Hansen, 1986).

ROLE OF THE THERAPIST

The role of the therapist in this theoretical approach is one that requires that the therapist be directive, active, persuasive, warm, involved, and in control. While the therapist must be personally involved rather than distant and overly objective, the therapist's personality is downplayed. Joining with the family is essential, but it is not the sole basis on which change is produced. The therapist needs to be comfortable with being the expert and hold the expectation that the family will respond to him or her as the expert.

Initial Interviews

In strategic therapy, developing hypotheses and checking feedback from the strategies or interventions used is very important. As a result of the intake information, some hypotheses will have been generated in the therapist's mind. In the initial interviews, the therapist will be gathering data that will confirm or deny these initial hypotheses as well as developing a clearer perception of the presenting problem and dysfunctional hierarchy in the family. Therefore, the first therapeutic task is to approach the family in such a way that the overt/covert hierarchical structure, as reflected in the family's description of the presenting problem, can be identified. To do this, the therapist needs to listen to the verbal statements and watch the nonverbal behavior of the family members— who speaks to whom, how they seat themselves, who looks at whom, who speaks for whom, and so forth.

The therapist needs to diagram the hierarchy mentally, thinking in terms of three possible levels: the person having the most power or control at the top, or executive, level; the person or persons with the next amount of control in the middle; and then the person or persons with the least power on the lowest level.

The therapist should not side consist-ently with any one member of the family against any other member. That does not mean he or she should not *temporarily* side with one against another, because that is in fact the only way therapists can induce change (Haley, 1976). "Siding is unavoidable, for even if the therapist thinks he/she is maintaining a strictly neutral or objective position, the family still judges him to be partial. The problem of the therapist is to decide as a therapeutic tactic when and with whom to side intentionally" (Haley, 1971, p. 219). The therapist should also side with the identified patient toward the ultimate goal of helping the person out of his or her disturbing situation (Haley, 1976). By the manner in which the therapist forms coalitions from the higher status as an expert, the therapist interrupts the family's dsfunctional hierarchical system.

During the initial sessions, the therapist must focus heavily on the seriousnses of the presenting problem, thereby gaining leverage for bringing the family back to therapy. The therapist can "awfulize" the presenting problem: "If your son is in this much trouble now at the age of 12 and you are having trouble controlling him, can you tell me what it will be like for him when he reaches the age of 16? What will it be like for you, his parents? (To the daughter) If your brother refuses to attend school, what will become of him? (To the son) What will it be like for you when you are retained and must repeat this grade next year?" Emphasizing how serious the presenting problem is leaves no doubt in the family members' minds that they were correct in bringing their problem to therapy and that much work needs to be done in order to make changes.

The therapist also gives the family hope that they will be receiving some help. The critical task is to help the parents feel empowered in their executive function and view the presenting problem in terms of a manageable task for which they have the necessary coping resources. The therapist reframes the presenting problem in a conceptual framework that the parents believe they can handle (Haley, 1987).

Compulsory Therapy

If the therapist knows in advance that the case is court or school ordered and has cooperation from court or school personnel, the best way to begin is to have a representative of that system at the first interview. Because the court replaces the family in the executive function when a family member is placed on probation, the major task of the therapist is to help the parents take charge of their child so the court will not have to be involved again in the future (Haley, 1976). Emphasis is placed on developing a functional hierarchy in the family with the parents in the executive role. The parents are helped to develop appropriate rules and consequences for handling their child, and the child is given little voice in what will be done. The therapist can ask the youth what change he or she wants and then, if appropriate, negotiate that change with the family or ask the youth what his or her worries about the parents are, indicating that the adolescent's desire to help the parents is known. After normality is established during the ongoing therapy, the child is given the same rights in the family as anyone in his or her hierarchical position (Haley, 1976).

A compulsory court or school referral demands that the therapist concentrate primarily on the parents because they may be angry and require special cour-

tesy (Haley, 1976). With adolescents, it is best to see the family members together as well as separately in order to emphasize that therapy is for all involved members of the family.

When faced with reluctant family members, rather than assume that they are resistant or difficult people, the therapist should believe that they have not fully understood the situation. The therapist is typically defined by the family as an agent of the state, and therefore, he or she must redefine the situation as one in which he or she is on the side of the family to help them prevent such difficulties from happening again (Haley, 1976). A first step is for the therapist to clarify his or her position by stating what is known about the situation and what the goals are. Sometimes it is best to define the situation more positively by saying, "I assume you are all here because you want to do what is best for everyone" (Haley, 1976). To get on the side of the family in their situation, sometimes the therapist can point out that they are *all* there because they have to be, and perhaps it could be helpful to them to make use of their time together to get what they want (Haley, 1976).

The therapist needs to explore who referred the family and why; to ask what they expect from therapy in order to learn whether they are there for some positive reason or are just filling out the required court-ordered time; to inquire who among the family members thought it was a good idea to come; and to discover if the family is in therapy under great duress (Haley, 1976). The therapist should not join with a reluctant member in such a way that the person who can bring the family back to therapy is antagonized. "One goal is to change the therapy to a voluntary one in the sense that the clients realize they can resolve their problems and get out of situations" (Haley, 1976, p. 44).

Crisis Interview

In a crisis situation, as in compulsory court-ordered therapy, it is assumed that whoever is at the top of the hierarchy has not been able to establish or maintain rules for behavior of a family member, and so the community authorities have threatened to act or have already acted by hospitalizing or jailing the person and establishing limits (Haley, 1976). Therefore, a family in crisis requires that the therapist take control. When the crisis has passed, the serious tone of therapy and the directiveness of the therapist can lighten somewhat.

When the identified patient (IP) is sullen and uncommunicative, the therapist needs to be patient and assume there is, to the IP, some good reason for behaving in this manner (Haley, 1976). Sometimes, it is best to see the reluctant patient alone to hear what will not be said in front of the family.

When the crisis involves a threat or attempt of suicide, the therapist needs to focus attention on the parents' concern rather than on establishing rules and consequences for the identified patient. Concern needs to be expressed for why the IP would have taken such a desperate step. The therapist must not leave the session without being assured that a death will not occur, perhaps by suggesting hospitalization (Haley, 1987) or a suicide watch at home in which the family takes responsibility never to leave the IP alone (Bergman, 1985; Haley, 1987). "Whatever is done, the seriousness of the problem is not to be underestimated" (Haley, 1987, p. 50).

In summary, this approach assumes that the therapist will be flexible enough

to alter his or her interventions, if needed. If the plan is not working, the therapist will accept this and develop a different one.

APPLICATION

The First Interview

During the first contact with the family, usually a telephone call inquiring about the possibilities of making an appointment for therapy, the intake worker should obtain the names of all members who live in the household and significant others involved in the presenting problem; ages; addresses; phone numbers; educational levels; employment; previous therapy experience; how and who referred; and one or two sentences about the presenting problem.

An important matter to be decided is who will be coming for the first session. Problems occur in the natural context or group; therefore, whole families should be seen initially. By seeing the entire unit, the therapist is better able to take control of the therapy, to infer family life cycle stage and dysfunctional hierarchy, and to involve all members in the therapy process. Haley (1976) has stated that interviewing less than the natural group in which the problem occurs is to slow down and complicate therapy and risk failure. With the natural group present, the therapist can gather accurate and sufficient data to be able to proceed immediately toward a solution.

Some strategic therapists will see a client alone as long as the problem can be conceptualized as involving at least two or three others and effective intervention in the dysfunctional system can be made through the present member. The present member should be concerned enough to be willing to try something different. If only one member of the family will consent to come to the initial interview, sometimes the therapist may work out an agreement that if improvement does not rapidly occur, the family can be brought in (Haley, 1976). Another alternative is to exclude the identified patient and work solely with the family (Szykula, 1987). With problems concerning a child, the therapist must have control regarding the involvement and interface with other agencies or systems. Everyone involved with the problem—parents, child, grandparents, teachers, and counselors—should be in attendance. Again, Haley (1987) has suggested that since gathering diagnostic information is a part of the therapeutic process, it is usually best to begin with everyone involved.

Introduction. In the first session, information should be completed in three categories: (a) demographic information, such as age, sex, occupation, and religion; (b) family history, such as previous treatment, medical information, physical violence, and sexual functioning, if applicable; and (c) interactional data focusing on family rules, alliances, coalitions, subsystem functioning and dysfunctioning, and sequences of behavior around the presenting problem (Bross & Benjamin, 1983).

In general, the therapist in the first interview should be noting whether one or more of the adults is indicating reluctance in being present; how members deal with the therapist; who attempts to engage the therapist on his or her side; and the relationships between and among the family members. The person who expresses the greatest interest in therapy often does so because he or she is locked into a problem-solving strategy and is preoccupied with failure or because he or she is convinced that all efforts are only making the situation worse (Coyne, 1987).

While there is some flexibility in terms of who should be present and the techniques and directives given, there is *no* flexibility about the importance of the first interview. To have a successful ending, therapy must have a successful beginning (Becvar & Becvar, 1988). The first session must therefore include all of the following five stages: social engagement or joining with the family, definition of the problem, interaction, definition of desired changes, and ending the interview.

Social Stage. This is the "welcome into my house" stage in which the therapist, as host or hostess, attempts to engage the members of the family, to "join" with each member. Joining with each member helps each to feel more relaxed and part of the group. Since the identified patient is the family's reason for initiating therapy, the other members will be confused about why they are present. The joining helps establish the importance of each family member's presence, enable the redefining of the problem as a systemic one, and facilitate the establishment of control.

The family should be invited to seat themselves as they wish because sometimes this can give the therapist an idea of their organization (e.g., IP isolated, IP patient between parents, father at edge of family, mother with children, males together, females together). Behavior and discipline are other indicators of the family's organization.

The therapist should introduce him- or herself, then speak casually with each adult. The therapist should not allow anyone to talk about the presenting problem until a social response from all members has been obtained. The therapist should work at engaging the most distant parent because it may be difficult to involve him or her in the therapeutic process (Haley, 1987). The parents should be asked to introduce the children—a step that observes hierarchical order. Information regarding any missing member should be obtained.

The therapist should note the mood of the family. Matching their mood can sometimes be helpful in gaining their cooperation. The relationship between the adults should be noted (i.e., are they showing disagreement, does one indicate reluctance in being present, or does one try to speak for the other?). The therapist must anticipate a need to keep out of a coalition with any single member.

In observing the family, "the therapist is not necessarily getting the facts from them, but, rather an illustration" (Haley, 1987, p. 16). Information should be gathered, but conclusions should be kept tentative. The therapist should not share observations with the family. In directive therapy, such as strategic therapy, there must be a careful balance between joining the family members and telling them what to do.

Problem Stage. The therapist begins this stage by clearly stating what he or she already knows from the telephone intake so everyone will know what the initiating member has said. If the problem is already known, the therapist should clarify that the whole family needs to be present because each one's opinions and insights are valuable. If a member appears worried about being in therapy, the therapist should state his or her own understanding of the situation, normalizing it by emphasizing that therapy is the normal context for these problems (Haley, 1976).

The therapist moves into the problem

stage by clearly asking why the family is there: what is the problem? If movement from the social engagement to the problem stage is unclear, then the difference between a social situation and the therapy situation will also be blurry. The family may feel that the presenting problem and the identified patient are being minimized by the therapist or that the presenting problem is too awful to even be discussed.

The inquiry has two parts: how it is made and to whom it is addressed. When the therapist asks, "What is your problem?" it defines therapy as the setting where problems will be talked about. This question usually fits the mother's expectations, and she will probably respond at some length. When the therapist asks, "What is it you want from me?" it reduces the possibilities of a family report. The members must think about what the problem is and what the therapist might be able to do about it. This question is thought by Haley (1987) to make the situation less professional and more personal. When the therapist asks, "What changes do you want?" it makes the therapeutic framework one of change instead of defining what is wrong. When the therapist asks, "Why are you here?" it allows the family to focus on the problem or on change. As a rule, the more general and ambiguous the inquiry, the more room there is for the family to display their point of view. The more specific the inquiry, the more the family will focus on one area in their discussion.

In terms of whom is asked the inquiry, usually if the father is present, it is best to address him first. He is considered to be the head of the household (whether he is or not), and he may prove to be difficult if he is not asked for his opinion first. If the therapist is a female and she speaks to the mother first, an implicit coalition may be established against the males. If the mother is not spoken to first, she may feel affronted since she has done the most to bring the family to therapy. However, it is considered best to start with someone other than the mother because she will express herself when it is her turn. It is not a good idea to direct the inquiry to the identified patient because he or she may feel blamed for the family's having to be in therapy. The therapist may begin with the least involved child while making it clear that everyone is going to have a turn. By looking at the floor or ceiling or something in one's hands, the therapist may direct the inquiry to everyone and say, "Can someone tell me what the problem is?" This approach usually draws out the family spokesperson, and it provides information about the father's position. If he responds, then he is more likely to be a willing participant. Whereas the adult least involved with the problem should be addressed first, the person with the most power to bring the family back should be treated with the greatest concern and respect. The therapist needs to respect the hierarchy in the family in order to gain the members' cooperation (Haley, 1987).

In respect to the children, by speaking to the least involved child first, the therapist is modeling that everyone's participation is needed and valued, children as well as adults. To draw out a reluctant child, the therapist should talk to this child last, perhaps bringing a chair up beside the child. If the child is an adolescent, it is often helpful for the therapist to take charge of the reluctance to talk by stating that he or she knows that it must be difficult to talk and therefore the therapist wants the adolescent to be silent. This directive will sometimes

cause a resistant adolescent to talk (Haley, 1987).

"When listening to the report about the child's misbehavior, the therapist should think about what is happening in the total situation of the child that is causing him/her to behave as he/she does" (Haley, 1976, p. 33). The therapist should be concerned about how family members relate to each other and ask only for facts, not feelings. He or she should accept what is said, validating each family member's opinion as important. If something is not clear, it can be asked about, but rephrasing should not reframe for the purpose of insight. Any statement by the therapist about what is wrong should be put in terms of interaction between or among the family members or people involved. By so doing, the problem begins to take on a different view (Haley, 1976). Advice is not to be offered at this stage, even if it is asked for. Instead, the following response is given: "I need to know more about the situation before I can say what might be done." The therapist's attitude should be one of helpful interest. He or she should not be diverted to anything outside the question of why the family is in therapy (Haley, 1976).

Talking should be encouraged and made as easy as possible for family members, but no one person should be allowed to dominate by talking too long. All conversation is directed to the therapist, and discussions between family members are avoided. "If someone interrupts, the therapist should let the interruption happen to observe it briefly and then should intervene and return to the person first talking. The person interrupting can be told he/she will have his/her turn" (Haley, 1976, p. 28). Everyone must have a turn. If the other family members are not listening to the one speaking, the therapist should request everyone to do so.

The therapist needs to observe the defensive tactics of the family members. They will at times attempt to distract the therapist by subtle denials of their allegations of conflict (Haley, 1987). One member may assume the role of spokesperson and consistently comment on or explain the meaning of the family to the therapist. After a statement of the problem from one person, each of the others should be asked what he or she thinks about it. When there are disagreements, an issue should not be made of it; it can be addressed later.

If there is family disagreement about what the problem is, the tendency is generally to emphasize the parental view of it. The therapist can side with the parents, noting that their child has been able to finagle them into disagreeing with each other and thus get his/her own way through a "divide and conquer" strategy.

The more responsive and involved the listeners are, and the more angry and upset at what is said, the more likely it is that the family is in a state of crisis and is therefore unstable. The more calm and detached they are, the more likely it is that the situation is reasonably stable and so may be difficult to change. (Haley, 1987, p. 29)

The therapist should match the family's pace at processing questions and answers and adapt his or her inquiry and position to match the family's educational level. The family should not be in charge of the session, or nothing will change and their "stuckness" will continue. As someone is talking about the problem, the therapist should note the congruence between verbal and nonverbal words and effect. Is the child being talked about like a thing or a person? Is the one speaking worried about what others will think? Does the story about

the problem seem fresh or old? Is hope or hopelessness being expressed? Who is given responsibility for the problem? How do others react to the speaker? Their behaviors will tell the therapist how to speak with each of them (Haley, 1987).

It is particularly important to note how the identified patient responds and what is being said indirectly. Haley (1976) has noted that one can obtain information about the identified patient in advance by listening to the ways the parents talk about him or her. The therapist can think about the data tentatively and check them out later but must keep such information to him- or herself. When a parent is discussing the problem encountered with a child, that parent is giving two types of information: one, about the child; and two, about the spouse and the marriage. It is important, therefore, to assume that a child's problem may reflect or may be a result of a marital or family problem (Haley, 1976).

When the family talks about the problem, the members will usually describe the identified patient by telling what is wrong with him or her. A parent's list of the child's transgressions is an indication that the parent is unable to deal with the child and that nobody else in the family can help in such a way that the family can handle the problem by itself, so they present for therapy (Haley, 1976). They will usually present the child as "sick" or "bad." If they see the child as "sick," usually one parent is more convinced than the other that the child is ill, and the parents do not agree as to how the "illness" should be handled. If they see the child as "bad," there are at least three ways that the parents perceive the child's behavior: open rebellion, disobedient but not defiant, and disobedient but too helpless to be defiant. If the presenting problem is presented as a school problem, there are at least three possibilities for why the problem exists: the problem is with the school; the problem exists in the family and the child reacts at school; and the problem is between the school and parents, and the child is caught in the middle (Haley, 1976).

It is critical that the therapist not confirm the family's perception that the identified patient is the problem and the presenting problem is unchangeable (Stanton, 1981). He or she can request at the end of the interview for a family member to summarize what changes are wanted. The problem the therapist settles on must be a problem the family wants changed and one that the therapist has put in a form that makes it solvable. One of the most important reasons for specifying the problem clearly is so that a therapist can recognize success (Haley, 1987). The symptoms should be countable, observable, and measurable. Otherwise, the therapist and the family will not know when they are successful.

Interaction Stage. In the interaction stage, for diagnostic purposes, the therapist fosters interaction among family members in order to observe how the system functions. At the direction of and under the control of the therapist, the family members discuss the problem among themselves.

In this stage, it cannot be overemphasized how important it is to have the family members interact with each other rather than with the therapist. The therapist remains in charge to the extent that he or she refuses to be pulled into the discussion. If the family members try to continue to talk to the therapist, they must be turned back to each other. It can be helpful to rearrange their chairs so they are facing each other. The therapist

may need to move from his or her chair to break the family's pattern of talking directly to him or her. This move can also communicate to the family how serious the directive is to talk to one another.

Haley (1987) has suggested that when any two persons are talking, the therapist should always be ready to introduce a third person into that conversation. An example of a question to engage a father into a mother-child discussion might be, "They don't seem able to get this straight; could you help them?"

With parent-child presenting problems, the therapist should in this stage try "to bring the action into the room" (Haley, 1976, p. 36). The child should be asked to participate in his or her disobedient behavior or "sick" manner so that the therapist can observe how the family organizes around the behavior. There should be toys in the therapy room for young children to play with so that the parent-child interaction can be observed and assessed via the communication of active play. The therapist can have a parent ask a child to do something at the blackboard, draw a person on a sheet of paper, or do an arithmetic problem. Both the child's ability to perform and the type of family involvement can become evident in such a procedure (Haley, 1976).

The main purpose for having family members interact with each other is so the therapist can observe them and estimate what kind of patterns there are in the family. The therapist should be watchful for indications of dysfunction (e.g., diffuse boundaries, coalitions, triangulation).

Defining Desired Change. It is important that the therapist obtain from the family a reasonably clear statement of what changes everyone, including the identified patient, wants from therapy. This provides goals for the therapy and helps focus on the important issues. The therapist develops suggestions and an in-session summary that are somewhat different in view from those that are held by the family, thereby beginning to reframe the presenting problem.

If the problems and desired changes are left unclear, the family participation and the therapist's judgment of success are more difficult. The contract, written or verbal, should be clear and centered on the presenting problem and identified patient. The goal for the therapy is stated in terms of solving the presenting problem and is specified in behavioral terms—for example, cessation of tantrums (Becvar & Becvar, 1988). Thus the focus is on solving a specific problem and not on more generic goals, such as being less hyperactive or less unhappy.

Ending the Interview. By the end of the first interview, the therapist needs to be joined with the family in such a manner that he or she has made everyone feel at ease and involved during the social engagement, has had everyone contribute ideas about the problem in the problem stage, has involved everyone with one another in the interaction stage, and has included everyone in specifying just what changes are desired from the therapy. Although sometimes more than one interview is necessary to understand the hierarchical dysfunction and family structure and to clarify the issues, usually the therapist can conduct the first interview in a way that provides maximum information and begins a change in the family.

The first interview should end with the setting of the next interview. If a family is somewhat doubtful about coming back, it is sometimes helpful to set a certain number of interviews, or the therapist can say, "Why don't we meet for six times (less or more) and then decide whether more times are necessary?" If the therapist has developed a directive by the end of the session, it can be given as homework for the family to do between sessions. And directives at this time should be simple ones. Such a task can keep the family involved with the therapist and therapy between interviews. It may have become clear in the inteview that a family member who is not present is very important to the therapy. Discussing how to get the person to come to the next session is part of the ending process (Haley, 1987).

Intermediate Interviews

Haley (1976) has stated that a therapist should be able to think in terms of three levels in the hierarchy and three stages in the therapy process.

Once the therapist understands the dysfunctional hierarchy and behavioral sequences, he or she can consider Stage 1 of therapy completed and can begin to move into Stage 2, the intermediate stage in which he or she will develop and implement a plan and intervention strategies. How the therapist proceeds after the first interview will be determined by the particular presenting problem. The simplest strategy to use in this stage would be to draw a hierarchical generation line and prevent coalitions across the generation lines (Haley, 1976, p. 104).

Because it is difficult to move a family from the dysfunctional stage directly to a functional stage, it is helpful to think of Stage 2 as a series of intermediate substeps to be taken between the beginning (dysfunctional) and terminating (functional stages). In other words, faced with a dysfunctioning system, the therapist can lay out a plan of substeps that will transform the initial dysfunctional system into another dysfunctional system that can then be shifted to normal. If the restructuring approach will be one of putting the peripheral parent in charge of the child, there will be a step of forming a coalition among therapist, peripheral parent, and child; then a step of involvement among therapist and adults; and finally a step of the therapist disengaging from the adults. If the approach is through the overinvolved parent and the child, there is a step of intense involvement among that adult, therapist, and child, followed by a disengagement of therapist from both of them (Haley, 1976).

The therapist must also expect that in the following interviews new problems may be presented and new goals may need to be established. The presenting problem is not only what is offered in the first interview but also what is offered as the therapist and family become more involved with each other (Haley, 1987).

Termination Interview

As termination nears, the therapist initiates a disengagement or terminating process, expressing pleasure that the family has done so well and crediting them for the change. Stanton (1981) has commented:

The idea is that the more the IP's *family or parents* feel responsible for helping him/her improve, the greater are the chances that the positive effects of treatment will *last*. If the family or parents feel overly indebted to the therapist, they will see themselves as less competent to cope effectively with new situations or future symptom-provoking events. On the other hand, a sense of accomplishment in having helped and corrected the original problem will prompt them to feel more confident in handling future difficulties. Thus it is tactically wise for the therapist to underscore to them the extent to which their own efforts, ideas, and commitment really "turned things around." If family members terminate a successful treatment feeling that they, rather than the therapist, were responsible for beneficial change, the chances for long-term success are increased. (p. 371–372)

It can be particularly appropriate with some families to express concern about things going *too* well. The therapist warns the parents that the outcome of their success with their child will almost certainly be that the child will become a delight, and then it may become difficult for them to allow him or her to grow up. Therefore, it might be a good idea for them to reinstate the old situation so that they will not be too unhappy when the child leaves home. The therapist asks them to imagine how they might have their first relapse into their old dysfunctional pattern. According to Haley (1976), this predictably only reinforces the change.

An appointment should be set for 2 weeks later to be sure everything is alright. A short amount of time should then be spent shifting from a helping relationship to a social one. In strategic therapy, termination is carried out as soon as possible after positive change in the presenting problem has been achieved. Therefore, therapy is brief. It is therapy of intense involvement and rapid disengagement. Once a family has succeeded in alleviating the presenting problem, therapy is ended in one to four more sessions unless a new contract has been negotiated regarding another problem (Haley, 1987).

TECHNIQUES

The treatment techniques used by strategic therapists include directives and homework tasks, positive interventions, straightforward tasks, and paradoxical interventions.

Directives and Homework Tasks

Directives and homework tasks are the cornerstone of the strategic approach. The strategic therapist is generally quite pragmatic and, according to Haley (1987), views everything done in therapy as directive—facial expressions, body language, reflecting feeling or content, and saying "Tell me more about that," for instance. The therapist uses directives or tasks to break inappropriate sequences of behavior as a way of helping the family change when he or she is not able to do so through ordinary conversation. The strategic therapist tends to be symptom focused and is concerned with techniques that eliminate or substantially reduce the presenting problem or symptom. The approach is essentially a behaviorally oriented one. The clearer the understanding of the dysfunctional hierarchy, the presenting problem, and the goal of the therapy are, the easier it is to design directives.

Haley (1987) lists three reasons for giving directives or homework to family members. First, tasks are one way to get the family to behave differently and have new subjective experiences. Second, directives intensify the client-therapist relationship. If a task or directive is assigned to the family, then the family members must decide whether they are going to comply with the therapist's directive or what they will say to the therapist when they return for the next interview. Third, directives are a way of gathering information about the family by noting their responses to them. If the family does or does not complete the task, the therapist has gleaned useful information. Everyone should be given something to do in the task, even if it is as simple as reminding other family members of the assignment. Emphasis is placed on the family unit, but care must be taken not to confuse the family hierarchy by involving children in adult tasks (Haley, 1987). The task is usually given to be carried out between sessions as a means of using time more fully and generalizing what transpires in the session to the family at home.

There are three distinct components in a strategic technique: task selection, task construction, and task delivery (Bross & Benjamin, 1983). The nature of the family and the therapeutic style of the therapist will determine the task selection and task construction. The therapist must determine whether the family is resistant to change before selecting the task. If the family is not resistant to change, the therapist will choose straightforward, or positive, tasks. If the family is resistant to change, the therapist will design paradoxical directives, or negative cooperative tasks.

The therapist in selecting a task needs to think about the dysfunctional hierarchy and presenting problem in terms of the behavioral sequence in the family and must choose a directive that changes both. The homework task can be a simple one if the primary goal at that stage is to intensify the relationship with the therapist (e.g., have family members make a list of problems, have them observe certain behavior during the week, have them talk together at a set time) (Haley, 1987). However, if the primary goal is to bring about an organizational change, the task to be given requires more thought.

Constructing the task is often determined by therapeutic style. Whatever the directive, it should be appropriate to the family's financial and time situation and simple enough that the family can accomplish it. The task should be consistent with the family's belief system. If the family is logical and orderly, so should be the task. If the family is casual and disorderly, so should be the task. The therapist can discover a family's manner by asking them to do things in the session.

The success of any directive or task is dependent on its proper delivery. Directives should be reasonable and stated in the family's own language. They should be clearly given rather than suggested. Precision in giving directives is important because the therapist wants the task to be done; if the task is not done, the therapist wants to be certain that unclear instructions were not the cause. Often when the therapist is giving a directive, the family members are thinking of talking about ways to get out of doing it. The directive then can be written down for the family, followed by a discussion of ways the family members think they might avoid the task. If the family does not share their thoughts, the therapist can offer some suggestions: "What if somebody forgets?" "Suppose someone gets sick?" How to motivate a family will depend on the nature of the task, the family, and the relationship the therapist has with the family (Haley, 1987).

If the task is successfully accomplished, the family should be congratulated and given a period of time to stabilize while other issues are dealt with in therapy. If the task is not done, the therapist should explore why not. If there is no valid reason, the therapist should not easily excuse them, or the task will seem to have been unimportant.

Positive Interventions

Relabeling or Reframing. The strategic therapist takes the position that all symptoms are highly adaptive for the family and that what they do is for a good reason and is understandable from their frame of reference. Relabeling or reframing, a nonblaming stance on the part of the therapist, ascribes positive motives to the behavior of the family members and in this way seeks to alter their beliefs about the presenting problem, thereby inviting the possibility of change. By relabeling or reframing, the strategic therapist offers a different view of the presenting problem, freeing the participants to think and behave differently in the new context and opening up a new set of action potentials. The family becomes more amenable to change and increases their sense of control (Haley, 1987).

Empowerment. The therapist may help the family see that they have been doing something right or the presenting problem would be worse, that it is only because they have been trying so hard that they feel a failure, and that they have the ability to redefine their coping skills and redirect their efforts. Empowering the family in this manner can let them feel more able to undertake the therapist's directives and to expect reasonable progress. The family members may experience a resurgence of morale and energy (Haley, 1987).

Providing an Illusion of Choices. This is an unobtrusive way of managing resistance. It consists of setting up two choices, neither of which is the real choice—for example, asking the family if they would like an appointment scheduled on Tuesday or Wednesday evening rather than if they want to make another appointment. An elaboration of this approach is called "providing a worst alternative," which consists of setting up two choices, one of which is so dreadful or difficult that the family either comes up with a different but equally effective solution on their own or goes along with the least bad alternative (Hoffman, 1981).

Devil's Pact. With this strategy, the therapist tells the family that he or she has a sure solution to the problem, but the family must agree to do it before it is disclosed (Haley, 1976). The family is given time to decide whether or not they really want to solve the presenting problem. They are told that their decision is very important because the plan they will need to carry out will be very demanding.

Straightforward Directives

In straightforward directives, or positive cooperative tasks, the therapist takes what has been learned about the family members in the session and uses what seems most evident as the basis for persuading them to do the task (Haley, 1987). Less stuck families, those that can use cognitive information, may be dealt with in a relatively straightforward manner (i.e., the pattern the therapist sees may be described so that all the members of the family can see and make their own inferences about how to be different with each other). Some families can use this information and make appropriate changes (Becvar & Becvar, 1988). The straightforward directive or task is presented in expectation of the family members' compliance; whereas with the defiance-based or negative cooperative directive, the therapist anticipates the family's refusal. Straightforward tasks might include advice, explanations or suggestions, or directives to change the interactional sequence in the family (Papp, 1980). They may be construed to help a family become more organized, establish operational boundaries, set

rules, or establish family goals (Madanes, 1981). Madanes has stated:

Straightforward directives are planned with the goal of changing sequences of interaction in the family. The interventions are directed to involve previously disengaged family members, promote agreement and good feeling, increase positive interchanges, provide information, and help a family organize in more functional ways by setting rules, defining generational boundaries, and establishing individual goals and plans to achieve those goals. (p. 24)

It is not unusual for the therapist to have to convince the family that it needs to follow his or her directive. Haley (1976) has offered a number of suggestions to therapists for gaining the family's cooperation with the directive:

1. Ask the family to talk about everything they have tried to do that failed to solve the problem.
2. Ask family members to discuss the negative consequences if the presenting problem continues.
3. Encourage the family to talk about how desperate their situation is.
4. Give a task that is reasonable and easily accomplished.
5. Give a task to fit the ability and performance level of the family members.
6. Use position to get the family to follow the directive or task.
7. Be precise and give clear instructions.
8. Motivate the family to do the task at home by starting them on small tasks during the session.
9. Give everyone something to do in the task.
10. Anticipate what might happen or go wrong.

Metaphorical Tasks. Drawing from the work of Erickson, the strategic therapist is aware that it is not always expedient to make explicit what he or she wants the family members to do to change, that sometimes they will be more willing to follow a directive if they do not have to concede that they have received one (Haley, 1987). The therapist may speak in a metaphor symbolizing the hierarchical dysfunction or presenting problem, thereby planting seeds for possible change. The therapist may have family members engage in a conversation that is not about the problem but, because of the task and the symbolism of the content of the task, may indirectly facilitate change (Becvar & Becvar, 1988). Becvar and Becvar give the example of a metaphorical directive in which the parents are asked to discuss how an orchestra might be conducted successfully with two conductors, each of whom has a slightly different interpretation both of the music and of how the orchestra should perform.

Paradoxical Directives

Paradoxical directives, or negative cooperative tasks, are premised on the idea that some families who come to therapy cannot be dealt with in a straightforward manner because they are resistant to the help offered. It is with these families who appear not to follow instructions easily that paradoxical directives are used. These interventions are in apparent contradiction to the goals of therapy, yet they are actually designed to achieve them. These tasks are defiance based in that they depend for success on the family's defying the therapist's instructions or following them to the point of absurdity and recoiling and thereby changing. "The directives are paradoxical because

the therapist has told the family that he wants to help them change but at the same time he is asking them not to change" (Madanes, 1981, p. 26). They are used when the therapist wants the family to resist so that they will change.

Weeks and L'Abate (1982) suggest five types of family transaction that are appropriate for the use of paradoxical directives or tasks: fighting and bickering; noncooperativeness and failure to complete assignments; continuation of the problem regardless of the intervention; separation and polarization within the family; and disqualifying one another, showing no support, and failing to set limits for the children.

According to Papp (1980), there are three steps in giving a paradoxical directive: (a) define the symptom as the family's way of preserving its stability, and clearly explain the benefits the presenting problem provides to the family; (b) prescribe the symptom by encouraging the family to continue what they have been doing, because to change would result in the loss of benefits to the family; and (c) restrain the family whenever they show signs of improvement or change.

Therapists might employ eight steps when giving paradoxical directives:

1. Define the therapeutic relationship. The therapist joins with the family members to establish a trusting relationship in which change is expected.
2. Define the presenting problem clearly. The problem to be corrected is clearly defined by using the following type of questions: Who is involved in this problem? Where does the problem occur? How frequently does the problem occur? What happens when you

experience this problem? (Brown & Christensen, 1986). What happens next, and what happens after that, and then what (the when-then-then process of obtaining the sequence of behaviors)?

3. Set goals. The goals are clearly stated in concrete terms so everyone will know if and when they have been achieved.

4. Design a plan. The therapist approaches each session with a specific plan and with a directive to be given at the end of the session as homework. The directive should be delivered clearly and authoritatively since the therapist wants the family members to resist. If the therapist wants the family to perform the directive, he or she must encourage the family to complete it.

5. Disqualify the current authority on the problem. The authority is the person who is attempting to solve the problem but in so doing is actually maintaining it; therefore, that person must be disqualified.

6. Give a paradoxical directive. The therapist needs to be very sincere in delivery, thereby increasing the probability of success in helping the family resist the directive.

7. Encourage symptomatic behavior. The therapist should continue observing the response and encourage the usual behavior.

8. Avoid taking credit for the change. Accepting credit means that relapses will be considered the therapist's fault. A way to avoid receiving or accepting credit is to be puzzled by the improvement (Haley, 1987).

Defining the Symptom Positively. The therapist reframes the presenting problem as one needed by the identified patient or the family. In the case in which the family is asked how old the misbehaving child is acting, they will almost always give an age younger than the child's chronological age. The behavior is defined as a way of indicating that either the child or the parents have missed something very important at that earlier age; therefore, the parents must take the child back to that age and he or she must be treated as if he or she is actually that age so that the child can "grow up" appropriately to the present, accurate age.

Positioning. The therapist accepts and exaggerates what the family member is saying, which often highlights the absurdity of the situation.

Prescribing the Symptom. When the problem is very entrenched, the therapist encourages or instructs the identified patient to engage in the presenting problem or specific behavior that is to be eliminated. The wording of the prescription should be brief, concise, and unacceptable in order for the family to recoil at the instruction, but the therapist must appear to be sincere and offer a convincing and reasonable rationale for it (Goldenberg & Goldenberg, 1985). The design of this directive is relatively simple. To use this approach well, the therapist should ask for more extreme behavior than is present in the presenting problem. The therapist observes how the family members deal with each other and directs them to behave more in that way (Haley, 1981). The therapist may offer no explanation for giving this instruction or may provide an elaborate set of reasons or reframes. The prescription may well produce a recoil; family members may announce in the next session that they did not follow it but that their relationship has nevertheless improved (Hoffman, 1981). "The therapist must accept the change when it happens and let the family put him/her down by proving him/her wrong. If he/she wants to ensure that the change will continue, he/she might say to the members that probably the change is only temporary and they will relapse" (Haley, 1987, p. 78). This serves to block a relapse; or, if one occurs, it is under the therapist's direction and the therapist can direct them not to have another relapse.

Restraining. In restraining the family, the therapist may attempt to discourage or even deny the possibility of change. Efforts to change are often accompanied by the therapist's expressing the need for caution regarding the dangers of too-rapid improvement. The therapist might suggest the possibility of only an improvement rather than a total elimination of the presenting problem. This technique suggests that the therapist thinks that the symptom may be useful in some strange way and probably should be maintained, which the family will resist. "This restraining approach can be used as a main therapeutic approach or as a different type of intervention when therapy is not going well. It can also be used when there is competition between a therapist and a parent and directives are not being followed" (Haley, 1987, p. 157).

Pretending. Pretending is the technique used when the therapist prescribes that the identified patient pretend to have his or her symptom, which reclassifies the symptom as voluntary and not real; this can alter the family members' reaction to the symptom. Madanes (1981) has developed a number of paradoxical pretend techniques based on playfulness, humor, and fantasy. She believes these are less confrontational and less likely to invite resistance and defiance, because the identified patient is not expected to resist but rather to cooperate. When asked to pretend to have the problem, the IP is not expected to be unable to pretend. He or she is instead carefully coached and helped to pretend as well as possible, since when acting to have the symptom he or she can't "really" have it, or else he or she would not be pretending. The family members are asked to criticize the performance in order to help the IP perform more realistically. "In this way, the family's behavior, which is an intrinsic part of the symptomatic behavior and which usually consists of benevolently helping the person overcome the symptom, is changed" (p. 92). "When a sequence of interaction is labeled 'This is pretend,' it is difficult for the participants in the sequence to go back to a framework of 'This is real' " (pp. 93–94).

Ordeal Technique. This technique maneuvers the family members into the position where they find it more stressful to maintain the presenting problem than to give it up, thereby abandoning it. The therapist prescribes an ordeal equal to or greater than the distress of the presenting problem itself. The ordeal must be something the family members can do and cannot legitimately object to doing, and it must not harm the family members or any other person. "It is essential to select as the so-called ordeal something that is good for the family or family member, e.g., dieting or exercising" (Becvar & Becvar, 1988, p. 226).

CASE EXAMPLE

A family was seen in therapy whose members consisted of an overwhelmed single-parent mother; a son, age 12, who was refusing to attend school and was failing; and a competent daughter, age

16. The mother presented as uncertain, unsure, and inconsistent in respect to her son's behavior and their family life in general. The daughter related how competent Mom used to be when the daughter was in the fourth grade, the year the father deserted the family. The dysfunctional hierarchy appeared to be the daughter and son in control at the top level of the hierarchy, with the daughter serving as parental child at times with her brother and mother, and Mom in a less powerful, faltering position.

The therapist developed a plan empowering Mom to enable her to get the boy to school. Mom was to contact the truant officer requesting his help when the son refused to go to school in the mornings. She was to direct her daughter to telephone her at work each morning that her brother refused to go to school. The mother would then call the truant officer, who would come after the boy and take him to school. The mother was to check with the school each day to see that the boy was in school if the daughter did not call her.

The therapist formed a temporary coalition with the mother, using the power of the truant officer and empowering the daughter in her parental-child role. This was a temporary and abnormal step between the dysfunctional stage in which the family entered therapy and the functional stage of the mother in control, in which they were to leave therapy. "Often when a therapist wants family members to behave in a certain way, he or she gets them to behave in some other way that resembles the one the therapist wants" (Haley, 1976, p. 73).

The therapist presented the plan to the mother and requested her to think about it until she returned for her next appointment. If she decided she wanted to put this plan into action, she was to contact the truant officer and gain his cooperation. If she decided not to carry out this plan, she was to return for her next appointment because she would be continuing to have more and more difficulty with her son and she would need the therapist's help in handling him.

When the mother returned, she had called the truant officer, who had agreed to come when she needed him and take the son to school. In the session, the therapist first worked with the mother in how she would present the plan to the daughter and son. Then the daughter was brought into the therapy session, and the mother instructed her in the plan. She also told her daughter that she would support her when the daughter called her if her brother complained. Then the son was included in the session, and the mother described to him what would happen should he not go to school any day in the future unless he had a fever over 100°.

When the hierarchical order of the therapist, mother, truant officer, and parental-child sister was activated, the son began to attend school regularly. As the weeks passed and the boy continued to attend school, the need for the daughter's monitoring ceased. However, the mother continued to make it clear to the son that should he not go to school, his sister would call the mother, who in turn would call the truant officer.

In this case, the dysfunctional hierarchy consisted of Mom underfunctioning in the parenting role because she was so stressed and overwhelmed by the desertion of her husband and the need to provide financial support for the family; the daughter trying to function in the parental-child role without 100% support from Mom; and the son in control but out of control. The functional goal of therapy was to empower Mom back into her appropriate parental role with both children, so that the daughter would no longer need to function as a parental child and could be a normal 16-year-old and so that the son would go to school and no longer refuse to do as his mother directed (or as necessary when his sister directed him).

When this functional step was achieved, Stage 3 was entered. The family returned for 4 weeks of therapy during which no further need was expressed regarding the presenting problem. At one of the last sesions, Mom presented a problem of the daughter smoking in the house, which was against house rules. The therapist worked with the mother regarding how she could control what she did not want to have go on in her home, and the mother came up with appropriate consequences to use with her daughter. She then informed her daughter in session of these consequences should there be any more smoking. In the remaining several sessions and in the follow-up sessions, the mother expressed no more difficulty with either her son or her daughter. After several 1-month intervals between appointments and a 6-month follow-up appointment, therapy was terminated.

EVALUATION

Much study and research needs to be done on strategic therapy. Research and evaluation have not been major activities in strategic therapy to date. However, Brown and Christensen (1986) report that investigations in strategic therapy have demonstrated more scientific vigor than is found in other approaches to family therapy. In 1978, Gurman and Kniskern reviewed six studies in strategic therapy that compared families in strategic therapy with families in another type

of therapy. They noted that the investigation of strategic therapy applied more stringent research designs than did other types of family therapy at that time. Stanton, reporting on the quality of research design for strategic and nonstrategic therapies in 1981, found that investigations of strategic therapy were significantly greater in design quality than other types of family therapy studies.

Probably the most pressing problem associated with efforts to undertake research in strategic therapy, as with other therapies, centers on the fact that the requirements of the research design are often not compatible with the scope and function of the therapy approach. Treatment models tend to resist evaluation, not only because of the methodological differences that plague the definition and control of relevant variables, but mainly because of the decisive effect of value judgments in the selection and interpretation of data. Since 1978, the effectiveness of strategic therapy has received mixed reviews. Most articles and books on strategic therapy are nonempirical and anecdotal. Research has not focused on a wide range of presenting problems and sometimes has not employed control groups. Further efforts must be made to investigate the critical components of strategic therapy and their long-term impact. Many questions abound regarding treatment effects beyond improvement of symptoms, such as the use of directives and paradox.

SUMMARY

The development of strategic therapy coincides with the growing popularity of systems theory and the unpopularity of other long-term, highly expensive therapies. Its application of general systems theory offers clients a more effective and efficient mode of therapy. Strategic therapy is considered by Haley (1976) to be "an intervention by an outsider into a tightly structured communication system in which symptoms are a style of behavior adaptive to the ongoing behavior of other people in the system" (p. 105). He has defined strategic therapy as "therapy in which the clinician initiates what happens during treatment and designs a particular approach for each problem" (Gurman & Kniskern, p. 361).

Strategic therapy focuses on levels of organization, with special concern about hierarchical dysfunctions. Emphasis is given to understanding the metaphor expressed by the presenting problem and the sequence of behaviors or cycle of interactions that reinforce it. Problems are defined as involving at least two and usually three or more people.

Therapy is directly geared to changing the complaint. The presenting problem is considered logical to the social context; therefore, it is important to understand the specificity of it—that is, why a particular symptom is chosen. The strategic therapist's procedure for tracking the behaviors around the presenting problem is an invaluable clinical tool, all the more so because it is grounded in the importance of having a clear understanding of the self-perpetuating sequence of behaviors around a symptom.

The main characteristic of this approach is that once the therapist understands the dysfunctional hierarchy and the sequence of behaviors supporting the presenting problem, he or she sets about devising a plan for solving the family's presenting problem. Goals are clearly set, and therapy is carefully planned with step-by-step strategies for helping the family prevent the repetition of destructive behavior. The thrust of the plan is to shift the family organization so that

the presenting problem no longer serves a function. The key to change is the skill with which the strategic therapist reframes the presenting problem so the family's perception can change, thereby making different behaviors possible. Change is seen as occurring not through insight and understanding but through the process of the family's carrying out the directives issued by the therapist.

Strategic therapists attempt to involve each member of the family actively in the therapy. Emphasis is on the present rather than on the past. History is not so relevant because dysfunctional behavior is thought to be maintained by current interactions. Strategic therapists accept the family where it is, as well as its focus on and definition of the problem. They seek to understand the family members as they understand themselves. They assume that the presenting problem characterizes the ways the family members relate to each other, that it is a communicative act with a message between two or more members. The family is viewed as perhaps stuck at a present stage within the family life cycle and as having difficulty making the transition from one stage of the family life cycle to the next.

Strategic therapists give directives or homework for tasks to be completed outside the therapy session. The family goes through new experiences as they follow the therapist's directives. Some of these directives may involve conscious attempts to change. Most assignments are likely to be paradoxical. The therapist's aim is to encourage the identified patient and other family members to develop various ways of defining relationships so that the presenting problem will be abandoned. The therapist, therefore, must take an authoritative stance. Haley (1976) has stated that the therapist must see his or her task as taking responsibility for changing the family organization and resolving the problem that brought the family to see the therapist. The therapist is highly directive, giving the family members precise instructions and insisting that they be followed. The therapist may thus be highly manipulative in his or her procedures.

The strength of strategic therapy is that it has a narrower focus than other therapies. Like the behavior therapists, therefore, strategic therapists have a good chance of achieving what they set out to do. Oddly enough, because of this they also have a better chance of accomplishing more (Hoffman, 1981). They work systemically and hope, if not expect, that a small change in an important family relationship will have a domino effect upon other relationships. Therapy is not growth but change oriented, and the therapist is responsible for successful therapeutic outcomes. Therapy is terminated when the presenting problem has ceased. The contribution of the strategic approach has been to create a parsimonious model for change.

ANNOTATED SUGGESTED READINGS

Haley, J. (1980). *Leaving home.* New York: McGraw-Hill.

A treatment model for severely disturbed young people and their families whose problem revolves around leaving home and becoming competent and individuated.

Haley, J. (1984). *Ordeal therapy.* San Francisco: Jossey-Bass.

How and why ordeals work in therapy. Haley offers many case histories to illustrate how ordeals can be used to help individuals, couples, and families solve a wide range of problems.

Haley, J. (1987). *Problem solving therapy* (2nd ed.). San Francisco: Jossey-Bass.

A must for beginning therapists. Haley presents how to conduct the first interview, give directives, work with hierarchies, sequences, triangles, and coalitions, metaphors, power, and organization.

Madanes, C. (1981). *Strategic family therapy.* San Francisco: Jossey-Bass.

Intervention strategies that therapists can use to correct hierarchical and power dysfunctions and change destructive sequences of behavior among family members.

Madanes, C. (1984). *Behind the one-way mirror: Advances in the practice of strategic therapy.* San Francisco: Jossey-Bass.

A case-report type text. Madanes illustrates how to make creative yet pragmatic interventions in common but complex clinical situations.

REFERENCES

Bateson, G. (1972). *Steps to an ecology of mind.* New York: Ballentine.

Bateson, G., Jackson, D., Haley, J., &

Weakland, J. (1956). Toward a theory of schizophrenia. *Behavorial Science, 1,* 251–264.

Becvar, D. S., & Becvar, R. J. (1988). *Family therapy: A systemtic integration*. Boston: Allyn & Bacon.

Bergman, J. S. (1985). *Fishing for barracuda: Pragmatics of brief systemic therapy*. New York: W. W. Norton.

Bross, A., & Benjamin, M. (1983). *Family therapy: A recursive model of strategic practice*. In A. Bross (Ed.), *Family therapy: Principles of strategic practice*. New York: Guilford Press.

Brown, J. H., & Christensen, D. H. (1986). *Family therapy: Theory and practice*. Monterey, CA: Brooks/Cole.

Coyne, J. (1987). The concept of empowerment in strategic therapy. *Psychotherapy, 24*(35), 539–545.

Erickson, M. H., & Rossi, E. L. (1979). *Hypnotherapy: An exploratory casebook*. New York: Irvington.

Goldenberg, I., & Goldenberg, H. (1985). *Family therapy: An overview*. Monterey, CA: Brooks/Cole.

Gurman, A. S., & Kniskern, D. P. (Eds.). (1981). *Handbook of family therapy*. New York: Brunner/Mazel.

Haley, J. (1963). *Strategies of psychotherapy*. New York: Grune & Stratton.

Haley, J. (1971). *Changing families: A family therapy reader*. Orlando, FL: Grune & Stratton.

Haley, J. (1973). *Uncommon therapy: The psychiatric techniques of Milton H. Erickson, M.D.* New York: W. W. Norton.

Haley, J. (1976). *Problem solving therapy*. San Francisco: Jossey-Bass.

Haley, J. (1980). *Leaving home*. New York: McGraw-Hill.

Haley, J. (1984). *Ordeal therapy*. San Francisco: Jossey-Bass.

Haley, J. (1987). *Problem solving therapy* (2nd ed.). San Francisco: Jossey-Bass.

Hoffman, L. (1981). *Foundation of family therapy*. New York: Basic Books.

L'Abate, L., Ganahl, G., & Hansen, J.C. (1986). *Methods of family therapy*. Englewood Cliffs, NJ: Prentice Hall.

Madanes, C. (1981). *Strategic family therapy*. San Francisco: Jossey-Bass.

Minuchin, S. (1974). *Families and family therapy*. Cambridge, MA: Harvard University Press.

Papp, P. (1980). The Greek chorus and other techniques of family therapy. *Family Process, 19*, 45–47.

Satir, V. M. (1982). The therapist and family therapy: Process model. In A. M. Horne & M. M. Ohlsen (Eds.), *Family counseling and therapy*. Itasca, IL: F. E. Peacock.

Segal, L. (1982). Brief family therapy. In A. M. Horne & M. M. Ohlsen (Eds.), *Family counseling and therapy*. Itasca, IL: F. E. Peacock.

Simon, R. (1986, September–October). The win-win bind. *Family Networker*, 18–29, 64–67.

Stanton, M. D. (1981). Strategic approaches to family therapy. In A. S. Gurman & D. P. Kniskern (Eds.), *Handbook of family therapy*. New York: Brunner/Mazel.

Szykula, S. A. (1987). Child-focused strategic and behavioral therapy processes. *Psychotherapy, 24*(2), 202–211.

Szykula, S. A., & Morris, S. B. (1986). Strategic therapy with children: Single-subject case-study demonstrations. *Psychotherapy, 23*(1), 174–180.

Watzlawick, P., Beavin, J., & Jackson, D. (1967). *Pragmatics of human communication*. New York: W. W. Norton.

Watzlawick, P., Weakland, J., & Fisch, R. (1974). *Change: Principles of problem formation and problem resolution*. New York: W. W. Norton.

Weakland, J., Fisch, R., Watzlawick, P., & Bodin, A. M. (1974). Brief therapy: Focused problem resolution. *Family Process, 13*, 141–168.

Weeks, G. R., & L'Abate, L. (1982). *Paradoxical psychotherapy: Theory and practice with individuals, couples, and families*. New York: Brunner/Mazel.

CHAPTER 7

Brief Family Therapy

LYNN SEGAL

DEFINITION

The idea of "brief therapy" is gaining popularity among mental health professionals, service agencies, third-party providers, and governmental legislators. Stories have always existed about the rapid resolution of human problems, but historically the occurrence of such events was usually understood within the context of traditional mental health wisdom as flukes, wizardry, or, most often, merely symptomatic relief. As newer therapies arrived on the treatment scene—crisis intervention, behavior therapy, strategic family therapy, Ericksonian therapy—brief treatment indirectly became a more legitimate outcome of the therapeutic process.

One group primarily devoted to shortening the length of treatment is the Brief Therapy Project, based at the Mental Research Institute (MRI), Palo Alto, California.* Unlike many brief therapies that derive their theory and techniques from what are essentially long-term traditional models, the work of the Brief Therapy Center represents a radical new way of conceptualizing human problems and has developed a different set of therapeutic techniques based upon this conceptualization. As Watzlawick and Weakland (1977) state, "Its principles are cybernetic, its causality is of a circular,

feedback nature, and with information being its core element, it is concerned with the process of communication in the widest sense—and therefore also with human systems, for example, families, larger organizations and even international relations" (p. xii).

Although this cybernetic explanation sounds complex and abstract, in everyday clinical practice it translates into a down-to-earth, commonsense view about problem formation and problem resolution. The kinds of problems people bring to therapists and the myriad of ways they attempt to deal with them can be viewed as systems of information that feed back on themselves, causing either chronicity or crisis. If new information is fed into such a system, it carries the potential of causing a benevolent change in the interactional pattern. Seen from this vantage point, problems are not resolved or worked through; they simply evaporate!

At the Brief Therapy Center, we believe that having such a model of stability and change is fundamental to doing treatment rapidly. While the model in no way denies past experience as a "cause" of the client's† present attitudes, behaviors, and needs, attention to historical and personality variables almost of ne-

---

*Although this article represents the work of the Brief Therapy Project, Mental Research Institute, Palo Alto, the author is solely responsible for its presentation.

---

†The terms *client, patient, family*, and *customer* are used interchangeably to describe who is seen in treatment. Additionally, these terms are written in the singular, even when referring to more than one person; that is, a family might be referred to as the "client."

cessity make for a longer treatment process and a more pessimistic attitude on the part of the therapist. By contrast, focusing on present interaction with the notion that people are simply "keeping their wheels spinning" increases both the therapist's optimism and the possibilities for intervening.

Although MRI brief therapy is most widely known for its use of paradox and symptom prescription, one can already begin to see that this work is based on a whole new scientific paradigm, sometimes referred to as Batesonian epistemology. As such, every variable of the treatment process is affected in some way. The paradigmatic shift in our work has forced us to rethink many basic issues: What is a problem? What is the nature of change? Who is seen in treatment? What kinds of data are collected? What constitutes therapeutic intervention? What determines success or failure in treatment? Being a model that deals with the self-reflexive nature of communication, what does brief therapy have to say about itself?

This chapter will briefly touch on the aforementioned variables, providing a glimpse of our work and how we view and treat problems. This chapter in no way represents a complete or fully detailed picture, nor does it make any claims of preparing its readers to practice brief therapy with their own patients. Long training experience has shown that although it is easy to grasp the general view, it is no easy matter to put it into practice.

HISTORICAL DEVELOPMENT

Precursors

The seminal ideas underlying brief therapy (BT) were originally introduced into

psychiatric thinking by Ruesch and Bateson (1951). They began sketching the outline of a new epistemology based on the theories of cybernetics, communication, and systems research.

In 1956, the Bateson group—including John Weakland, Jay Haley, and Don Jackson—published the well-known article "Toward a Theory of Schizophrenia." Although this publication is known primarily for the double-bind theory of schizophrenia, it also stands as a landmark for viewing psychiatric problems as communicative behavior, maintained and structured by social interaction, rather than as disease entities residing inside a person.

Don Jackson formed the Mental Research Institute in 1959 for the purpose of exploring how these new interactional insights might be applied to psychiatric treatment. Joined by Haley, Weakland, and other notables in the family therapy movement, including Paul Watzlawick and Virginia Satir, the California Family Therapy Movement got its formal start. Although there were many differences between Institute members, they all agreed on a number of basic assumptions: (a) while one family member exhibits pathology—the identified patient—the problem underlying these symptoms resides in the way the family functions as a group; (b) this group behavior is a rule-governed system exhibiting homeostasis, feedback, redundancy, and other cybernetic principles; and (c) treating the family means changing their interactive behavior, that is, changing their patterns of communication.

Equally important, both as a precursor and as an ever-present influence, is the innovative psychotherapy of the late Dr. Milton H. Erickson of Phoenix, Arizona. Many of the basic themes and specific tactics of Erickson's work were described by Haley (1963, 1967), who worked with the BT project for a few months before relocating in Philadelphia.

Erickson had always been an innovator, departing from the psychiatric establishment. His willingness to take charge of a case, to prioritize what needed to be done in small progressive steps, and then to make directives and prescriptions to accomplish this, provided a model for much of the strategic therapy that is practiced today. Particularly relevant to our project were his use of paradoxical directives or symptom prescriptions, his many ways of using himself via his communication to influence patient behavior indirectly, and his utilization of other family members in treating problems traditionally viewed as individual.

Two members of our project—Weakland and Haley—spent considerable time with Erickson when they were both studying communication as members of the Bateson Project. Bateson already knew Erickson from the time that he and Margaret Mead had consulted him about their work on Balinese trance. Weakland's knowledge of and direct experience with Erickson's work has contributed much to our present theory and practice.

Beginnings

MRI's Brief Therapy Project was started in 1967 for the express purpose of seeing what could be done to alleviate patients' presenting complaints, limiting treatment to ten 1-hour sessions, usually—but not necessarily—spaced 1 week apart. The project met one afternoon a week, with an additional 2-hour meeting later in the week. This format is still followed today and allows for a maximum of three cases to be seen during any given week.

All the members of the project were trained in family therapy, and most were instructed by and worked with Satir. However, the professional backgrounds of project members provided a strange mixture of traditional and unusual areas of expertise that blended well, given the aims of the project. Dr. Richard Fisch, director, was a Freudian psychiatrist. Watzlawick was a Jungian training analyst, spending some time with John Rosen before coming to MRI. His doctoral studies were in communication rather than in psychology. Weakland had prior training in cultural anthropology and chemical engineering. Dr. Arthur Bodin, who left the project in 1974, was trained as a clinical psychologist. Haley, a communication analyst, and Jackson, an analytically trained psychiatrist, spent a fair amount of time with the group, entering into discussions and treating one or two cases. Finally, with formal training in psychiatric casework and behavior therapy, I myself joined the project in 1970.

For the purpose of studying the process of psychiatric treatment as an interactional process, the original research design incorporated many features still in use today.

We work as a team. Using a simple rotational method, one member of the project is the primary therapist for each new case, doing the interviewing and exercising veto power over suggestions from other team members. During the interview, the rest of the team watches from behind a one-way mirror. The treatment and observation rooms are connected by a telephone so that observers may call in corrections and suggestions while treatment is in progress. Team members are also free to enter the treatment room and address either the patient(s) or the therapist. Audio recordings are made for each interview, and one staff member takes process notes keyed to tape footage as part of our record keeping and information retrieval system.

Patients are not screened prior to treatment, and each case is seen for a maximum of 10 sessions. There were no fees charged until 1979. Up to that point, patients were asked to make a contribution for each session, limiting such donations to no more than $30 and no less than $1. Fees per session are now $50.

Time is allotted before and after each interview for discussing what has taken place and for making last-minute adjustments in the planning of the next interview. Cases are then discussed in more detail during our weekly 2-hour meeting. Usually, first interviews are played and studied during this meeting, followed by more involved case planning and general theorizing.

Posttreatment follow-up questions are formulated after the initial data have been collected and prior to case planning. Three and 12 months after the first treatment interview, patients are contacted for follow-up by a project member other than the identified therapist. These results are then scored by the entire project staff (see Research Findings).

Current Status

The Brief Therapy Project is now in its 20th year of operation, and interest in our work continues to grow. We have presented our approach at conferences, workshops, and seminars across the United States, South America, and the major cities of Europe. The Introductory Brief Therapy Workshop, given three times a year at the MRI in Palo Alto, continues to draw an international attendance. In September 1979, the first intensive, 9-month workshop in BT was offered, with approximately 10 partici-

pants who treated their own cases in front of the class as part of their training.

The major written presentation of our theory, *Change: Principles of Problem Formation and Problem Resolution*, has stirred quite an interest in the international psychiatric community and is now published in 10 languages (Watzlawick, Weakland, & Fisch, 1974).

During the past 5 years, most of our attention has been directed to clarifying the tactics and strategies utilized to bring about useful change. Areas such as case management, case planning, patient position, and so forth have been more clearly identified and operationalized. Our work has been guided by a number of general foci: what is minimally needed to resolve a problem; how do we arrive at such conclusions of hypotheses; how can our thinking best be transmitted to others.

In keeping with this end, Fisch, Weakland, and I have written a companion volume to *Change* mentioned above. This text, *The Tactics of Change* (1982), focuses primarily on method and practice, and is illustrated with a number of transcripts from our work.

BT is now used in a wide variety of settings: psychiatric hospitals and clinics, corrections and protective services, social service agencies, and educational and physical health services. It is probably safe to say that one can find BT used in most settings that deal with human problems.

TENETS OF THE MODEL

Basic Concepts

Being pragmatists, we assume that theories are neither truth nor even the approximation of truth. A theory is merely a set of assumptions or working hypotheses that have heuristic value—in this case, to facilitate the solving of human problems. From this perspective, theories are like different human languages. Although most, if not all, do an equally good job as representational systems, some languages are better than others for solving a specific problem. Street language may be better in a hostage negotiation situation, while proper English would be more useful for a scientific presentation. However, it makes no sense to say one language is closer to the truth or reality than another (Weakland, 1976).

Basic to brief therapy is the belief that a person's behavior—"normal" or problematic—is maintained and structured by interaction with other people, including family members, friends, colleagues, and other professional helpers.

People develop problems by mishandling normal life difficulties that are predictable occurrences in the course of a lifetime. Such hardships include accidents, loss of work, natural disasters, disturbances in the usual routine, and transitions in the family life cycle: courtship to marriage; birth of the first child, the children attending school, reaching the teen years, leaving home; and death or divorce of a spouse.

There are three basic ways difficulties are mishandled: (a) by ignoring or denying that anything is wrong and not taking action; (b) by attempting to resolve difficulties that need not or cannot be solved, only endured until they pass; and (c) by taking action but the wrong kind—the most common form of mishandling observed in our clinical practice.

Difficulties are not generally mishandled on purpose or for some unconscious gain. Rather, when individuals or families have a problem, they go about attempting to deal with it in a manner consistent with their frame of reference,

that is, their view of reality and what they believe to be the right way to behave. Their "attempted solutions" are maintained because they are considered logical, necessary, or the only thing to do. When such problem-solving efforts fail, the patient and his or her family are most likely to interpret the failure as confirmation of the problem's severity. This is then followed by "more of the same" solutions, creating a self-perpetuating system of interaction. The patient is like a man caught in quicksand: The more he struggles, the more he sinks; the more he sinks, the more he struggles.

Although there are many different ways people take wrong action to solve a problem, four basic patterns have been repeatedly observed in our clinical practice (Fisch, et al., 1975).

1. *Attempting to Be Spontaneous Deliberately.* This pattern is found in cases involving sleep disorders, sexual difficulties, substance abuse, blocks in creative endeavors, and attempts to force a particular emotion.

It is assumed that most people will occasionally have difficulty with bodily functioning or performance and that feelings wax and wane. If such difficulties are seen as normal life difficulties that self-correct with time, all is well. But once a person sets about deliberate correction, she or he risks the possibility of getting caught in the paradoxical predicament of attempting to force spontaneous behavior. The patient-to-be may try to force her- or himself to sleep, be potent, or cheer up. When such methods as will power, reasoning, or positive thinking fail to bring about the desired response, they are tried yet again, setting the stage for a full-fledged problem.

While this solution sounds like an individual process—what the client says to her- or himself and does to solve the problem—it is also an interpersonal process. That is, one or more members of the client's family or social network may unwittingly be making paradoxical instructions by word or deed that influence the client's behavior. (This interpersonal aspect is true for all the attempted solutions outlined in this chapter.)

For instance, in the following example from a therapist's (T) work at the Center, a woman (P) describes how she and her husband went about deliberately trying to bring about her orgasm and the consequences of such efforts. It may be worth noting that the harder her husband tried to do the right thing (in this case, discuss the problem and be a good lover), the more such behavior carried the implied injunction "you will/should have an orgasm."

P: Before I married, I don't think I...Or I didn't realize I'd never had an orgasm, and I never thought about it. You know, I'd tried sex, and that was fine, and just before I got married I was informed by some friends of mine that I had never had one. Well, we got to talking about it, and I realized I'd never had one. And...

T: I was going to say, they told you...

P: In our discussion it came out...I realized that I'd never had one. And then it became a problem. And sex was just no longer really enjoyable. 'Cause I kept, you know, waiting for this other to happen, or at one point it was so scientific that, you know, it was like there was no pleasure. It was just step by step...to the point where for several months we didn't have any relationship at all.

T: You like or you don't like that sort of thing? So if we could kind of go in sequence, you know, you found out you didn't have orgasms. What have you tried?

P: Then we tried really examining my body and figuring out where everything was. And this was the first stage, and what to manipulate, and discovering the clitoris....And that didn't work. We were both—well, especially I

was preoccupied with having an orgasm and what we were doing, step by step by step. Then it just became a pain. I mean, there was no spontaneity. There was no joy in it at all. It was just a process that we went through. The next thing we did was that we talked to friends. We had another couple that we were very close to. And we talked about the possibilities of things that we were doing wrong, and whatever. And...they...were helpful, really, in telling us about different positions, things that might be easier. My husband's quite a bit bigger than I...things that might make it easier for me to open...and...that helped a little bit. I think things got a little bit better, not as bad as the other thing.

T: What gave you the idea, in talking to them, that you were not having an orgasm?

P: Oh, firecrackers didn't go off, and there wasn't this big...um...When they were talking about it, it was like, after this happened, then you would feel, I don't know, they would talk about this series of peaks, you know, that you would peak and come down, and your body would do something, and...I just knew that never happened. I knew that there was one time, I remember, you know, really...I felt like I had really been very close to it, you know, when I stopped to think back on previous experiences. And that was interrupted...I guess just from what they were describing, I... didn't fit. What I had experienced just didn't fit with what they were describing.

T: OK, so what they were having wasn't what your experience was.

P: Yeah.

T: We know that.

P: Yeah. We do know that.

This example also illustrates nicely how a problem is created. The patient was content with her sexual experience until others told her she was deficient. If one were to speculate on the motivation of her friends, one might assume that their comments were made to help her achieve more sexual satisfaction. But information is causal, and we cannot always predict the effect of a particular communication or act. In this case, the effect was quite negative, setting off the vicious cycle described in the transcript.

2. *Seeking a No-Risk Method Where Some Risk Is Inevitable.* This inappropriate way of solving problems is often found in the areas of work and dating. For instance, the shy single male may try to avoid the risks of rejection or failure when attempting to make new female friends. He becomes so concerned with finding the perfect opening gambit that he never begins a conversation with a woman. Similarly, the single, the salesman, or the job seeker can all run into another variation of this pattern by trying too hard to make a good impression. In doing so, they only turn off the very people they are trying to impress.

Again, while this description focuses primarily on the person who is trying too hard, the actual solution behavior occurs in an interpersonal context where two or more people are in the process of communicating by what they say and do and, strangely enough, by what they *don't* say and do.

The following example comes from a case where the patient (P), self-referred, presented the problem of not being able to get rehired after quitting his last job. He was a high-level manager who, by the time he arrived for treatment, had had more than 18 job interviews without receiving a job offer.

T:...and what may you have done, or what did you do, perhaps most of the time, immediately before, during, and perhaps even after the interview, to maximize your chances of getting accepted?

P: OK, I've done something that probably very few people do, or maybe no one does, and that is I prepare a presentation for the company.

T: Based on your knowledge of...

P: Based on my knowledge. And it's about a 12-page presentation. And it outlines what my approach to management information systems would be at that particular firm. And, so, essentially that's what I do to prepare for the interview process. I had obviously found out a lot about the company...

T: Yes.

P: Now, during the interview process I relate to that...

Here the patient was preparing a 12-page paper on the company, reviewing its present status, weaknesses, and areas of growth. In his mind he was trying to make a good impression, while from our perspective his attempted solution would only alienate those who interviewed him.

3. *Attempting to Reach Interpersonal Accord through Argument.* The popularization of psychology and the human potential movement has led to the erroneous belief that all problems can be solved by discussing and sharing one's feelings. Many families with marital or child-parent problems come to treatment presenting their problem as "we can't communicate." Many of these marital problems arise when one or both partners define the normal fluctuations of closeness or comfort they feel with each other as evidence of a relationship problem. This is then discussed, and their therapeutic chat degenerates into an argument, which is then interpreted as confirmation of their false assumption (i.e., something is wrong with the marriage). This leads to further discussion accompanied by a heightened awareness of the relationship, which makes their interaction even more awkward and uncomfortable. They create the very "reality" they wish to avoid.

Take, for example, the case of a young man who sought treatment because of increasing tension and fighting between himself and his girlfriend. She was dissatisfied with the amount of sexual interest he showed in her and would engage him in long, involved discussions about this problem. These discussions became part of an interactional pattern highlighted by decreasing sexual activity; heightened self-awareness of the man's disinterest in sexual activity (which only perpetuated the problem further); and a weekly Sunday night confrontation that invariably left both of them dissatisfied, frustrated, and no further along the path of finding a real solution to their conflict.

This pattern was perpetuated by the man's taking a "sitting on the fence" position regarding the problem: He did not take a stand about how much sexual contact he wanted, nor did he tell her that her demands and emotional outbursts had the effect of making him more self-conscious and less interested in her. Instead, he took a noncommittal position that allowed him to avoid making any clear statement about what he wanted. He vaguely alluded to the possibility that there might be something wrong with him, that he might be flawed in his sexual responses. Yet he refused to state that his sexual responsiveness was a problem to him. He demonstrated this position in treatment with the therapist and during his conversations about the problem—that is, their attempted solution—with his girlfriend, thereby perpetuating the interactional loop noted above and blocking any real resolution of their conflict.

A number of alternative behaviors were open to them, all within their behavioral repertoires, that would have served the function of interdicting their attempted solution. She might have simply backed off from pressuring him. Or, he might have taken a clear, firm stand about her nagging him to perform. Another alternative for him would have

been to present himself to her as simply a person with low libido, which would have in effect said, "This is the way I am, right or wrong. So make up your mind—take me or leave me." We believe that his taking such a position vis-à-vis his girlfriend could have gone a long way toward solving their problem.

4. *Attracting Attention by Attempting to Be Left Alone.* Many problems traditionally defined as paranoia arise from this solution. A person gets started in this problem when she or he defines some teasing or harassment by others as insidious and indicative of the lack of esteem that others have for her or him. The attempted solution may range from emotional or physical withdrawal to inquiry about the "persecution" or counterattacks. In either case, these solutions are likely to bring on more attention from others. If the person withdraws, others may seek her or him out to find out what is wrong. If the patient retaliates, this just sets off a pattern of escalating hostilities.

This next example illustrates two basic patterns: (a) too much discussion and (b) attention drawn by attempting to be left alone. The therapist (T) is talking with the husband of a patient who had been harassed by his wife since their divorce. Mr. X describes how his wife called him up just prior to his trip to France and insisted on coming with him. Rather than handle the situation simply and directly, he took the following evasive action with somewhat paradoxical consequences.

X:...how come I'm going to France. I said, "What do you mean, how come? I'm not stopping you. No?" And she says, "No, I'd like to go with you!" I said to her, "You can buy your own ticket, and besides, if somebody wants to go, you know, you have to validate your passport, you know." And she keeps insisting, no, she has to go with me. I said, "You cannot go with me." And she kept on insisting. So, does this make sense? I couldn't even reason, so I hung up. She calls me up...

T: Was it...her calling you about going to France?

X: Uh huh.

T: Assuming you didn't want her to go with you...

X: Assuming! I was...made up my mind...

T: You gave her all the reasons why she could go alone....

X: She had the money! She could have done the same thing!

T: Did anything stand in your way of saying, "Look, Anne, I don't *want* you going with me!"

X: Let's say, if she had gone, and by calling someone she would get on the same plane, I wouldn't be able to change, that's it.

T: But did you say to her, at any point, "Look, regardless of whether you could go yourself or not, I don't want you to go with me."

X: I told her, "You know, I'm not stopping you from going, but you're not going to go with me."

T: You're *not* going to go with me.

X: That's what I told her.

T: Did you tell her why...Or, I mean, did you say...

X: No, I didn't....It's not only *why*. I did not want to have any association, anything to do with her. I'm finished.

T: OK, did you say that to her?

X: Yeah, many times.

T: Well, there goes our idea. Let me be picky, 'cause this is a very crucial issue. It has to do with the wording of how you let her know that you didn't want her to go.

X: I did not stop it. I did not say that she cannot *go*.

T: You didn't say that?

X: No.

T: What did you say, not go with *you*?

X: With me? No. No, she insisted she wants to go with me; I said, "You cannot go with me, I already have my ticket...."

T: Ah, you said you *cannot* go with me.

X: Yeah.

T: Did you say...What else did you say, "you *cannot* go with me..."

X: Yeah, under the circumstances. I already had my ticket; I had everything arranged.

T: And those were the reasons you gave her?

X: Yeah, and then I said, "You can go and pick a plane, you know. You can go even with no visa. Just go and buy a ticket and go." OK, I got my ticket, you know, 45 days in advance.

T: Right. So, let me check with you because this is just absolutely central, crucial, to the issue. You said to her, "Look, you can't go with me. I've got my ticket. It took me a long time to set this up. I can't change my plans."

X: I said, even if she would insist, I would not change.

T: Right. OK. At any point in there, did you say to her something to the effect of, "And, even if I could or would change my plans, I don't want to go with you."

X: No, I...

T: You didn't say that?

X: No, I didn't. But I'd like to make a point, you know...

T: When you said, "you *cannot* go with me," would there be anything difficult for you at that time in saying to her, "Anne, I don't want you to go with me, at all, period."

X: Well, you see, I never...First of all, I'd like to make a point. I never made any statements, to her, to aggravate her. I did not want to show resentment. That's not only in this case, in any...under no...Except, you know, when you file for divorce, you know, you can say, "Well, did he..." I don't know what you might call it, if this is resentment or not, but this was my last resort.

T: So this has been kind of your position with her, is to not let her know any resentment, or...

X: I have never...I never expressed any resentment. Never.

In summary, the theory and techniques of brief therapy rest on two major assumptions: "Regardless of their basic origins and etiology—if, indeed, that can ever be reliably determined—the kinds of problems people bring to psychotherapists *persist* only if they are maintained by ongoing current behavior of the patient and others with whom he interacts. Correspondingly, if such problem-maintaining behavior is appropriately changed or eliminated, the problem will be resolved or vanish, regardless of its nature, or origin, or duration" (Weakland, Fisch, Watzlawick, & Bodin, 1974, p. 144).

Before proceeding to how brief therapy is applied, a few more words need to be said about the relationship between brief therapy and family therapy. We take the position that family therapy is a subset within the broader classification of interactional therapy. While the majority of our work has been with families, our approach does not change substantially when we work with other interpersonal groupings such as staff and patients of various treatment facilities, middle managers or their underlings, or an employee having difficulty with peers or superiors at work. The primary unit of focus is the relationship mediated by communication. Even when treating an individual who lives alone and does not work, the unit of focus is the patient-therapist relationship.

Furthermore, the interactional view is a way of thinking about problems and behavior that manifests itself in the interview process. It is quite possible to do individual therapy while having the entire family take part in the interview or to do family therapy with just one person. The primary question has to do with focus: Are the data collected about relationships and interaction, or are they about internal phenomenology? Do the interventions reflect an aim at changing what goes on between people, or at what goes on inside them? One might go so far as to argue that whenever you work with one family member in your office, you are doing family therapy whether you know it or not.

During the course of treatment, we will ask to see different family members as we think needed. We believe that deciding who comes in for a particular interview is a strategic consideration. Although one can see a family interact in the context of a psychotherapy session, one rarely gets them to demonstrate their attempted solutions to the presenting complaint. This usually takes place outside of treatment, which means that one's data are basically self-report. Since the primary task in the initial stages of treatment is data gathering, we choose to see those family members who have the greatest motivation for treatment. Because we want to work rapidly, we will decide who in the family or other social grouping is most amenable to change, the most influenceable. Many times it is the family member who is motivated for treatment, but at times it may be the least motivated member. Our work has a certain judo aspect to it, and we capitalize on the highly resistant, polarized patient to bring about a useful change in family functioning.

APPLICATION

Most Effective Problem Areas

During the past 13 years, brief therapy has been used with a large variety of complaints common to psychiatric practice, including treatment of chronic pain and type-A heart patients and work in correctional institutions.

Fundamentally, brief therapy is a model of change and stability viewed from an interactional, systemic perspective. In this sense, it goes beyond problems to behavior in general, including the behavior of nonhuman systems. Given the nature of this model, it generally makes little sense to talk about which problems brief therapy is best suited for. There are, however, two basic situations that arise in treatment where brief therapy can be particularly useful: (a) when the identified patient refuses to come for treatment and (b) when the identified patient comes in for treatment but is extremely difficult to handle.

There are several typical situations in which the identified patient is not willing to engage in treatment: teenagers with school or behavior problems; young adults exhibiting psychotic behavior; marital difficulties in which one spouse refuses to have anything to do with psychotherapy; and inpatient settings, psychiatric hospitals, and correctional institutions where the staff end up feeling more distressed about the patient's behavior than does the patient.

Brief therapy can circumvent this class of problems by working with those people in the family or social context who are motivated to see things change and who, by their very presence in the system, offer avenues or entry points that the therapist can use for intervening. Since we view the identified patient's problem behavior as part of an interactional loop with significant others, we will aim our interventions at changing the way those others deal with the patient.

For example, Dr. Fritz Hoebel and I studied and treated 10 families in which the husbands had suffered a major heart attack but were still continuing to engage in high-risk behaviors: poor diet, smoking, lack of exercise, and excessive consumption of alcohol. All of these families were referred by cardiologists or by the staff of a cardiac rehabilitation program who had given up on these individuals, fearing they were on a suicide course. In all 10 cases, the identified heart patient would have nothing to do with any further treatment or rehabilitation.

Rather than wasting a lot of time and energy trying to convince the patient to come for treatment, we worked with their spouses. Using a five-session limit, we focused our attention on the way the wives had attempted to reduce their husband's high-risk behavior. Our aim was to change the system, that is, the husband's behavior, by getting the wives to change their attempted solutions. In most cases the wives struggled, argued, and nagged their men to change, so our primary effort was getting the women to back off from such tactics. In one case that worked particularly well, on our instructions the wife returned home and told her husband that she had been doing a lot of thinking about him. She said she had decided that he had a right to live out the rest of his life in his own style, no matter how short that might be. Her primary concern now was herself and the children and how they would be provided for when he died. She then insisted that her husband go over all the life insurance and estate planning, instructing her how to handle things after his death. She also called life insurance agencies and asked whether there was any way her husband's life insurance could be increased. As instructed, she told them to call her back at times she knew she would not be home but her husband would be there to take the calls. Within 2 weeks after she had begun to deal with him this way, the husband had resumed his participation in the cardiac rehabilitation exercise program and was watching his diet. (Another example of working with family members other than the identified patient can be found in the Case Example.)

The second grouping of problems has to do with the patient who comes for treatment but is difficult to manage. This can take many forms: the patient who is vague and gives useless information; the patient who appears motivated for treatment but somehow never carries out suggestions to do something different; the patient who wants to determine the nature of treatment; and the patient who threatens or intimidates the therapist. Most therapists can think of many more ways in which a patient can be difficult.

Obviously, this subject can only be alluded to in the confines of this article; it is such a pervasive factor in treatment that it almost warrants a book of its own. In general, the brief therapist may have an edge over other therapists in dealing with the difficult patient because much of our work has been focused on case management. The brief therapist will not take a position about the nature of treatment until she or he has some hypotheses about what the client expects. Other than stating it is brief, when asked about our treatment we are likely to say it is tailor-made to meet the needs of each individual, thereby maintaining maneuverability. Since the steps to treatment are fairly well outlined and make for a logical progression, the therapist can easily check to see if she or he is moving too fast with a patient or family and then back off if necessary. The therapist might start to make interventions and then realize that there is not enough data to warrant such action. Knowing where you are in treatment allows you to then take strategic action to deal with a particular problem. If the patient is vague, the therapist can communicate the confusion in one-down fashion, pressuring the client to be clearer.

If the patient is resting on her or his "oars," the therapist can sit back or utilize one of our interventions called "dangers of improvement." This is a hypothetical discussion of the possible new problems that would arise if the patient were successful at resolving the problem. This discussion can give the therapist material on which to base and make injunctions about slowing down treatment or warning the client not to change. Within a limited time frame, such "go slow" injunctions usually put a great deal of pressure on clients to get down to business and carry their share of the responsibility for treatment.

Goals of the Therapeutic Process

How goals are formulated in brief therapy is directly related to the therapist's view of problems. As already stated, we believe the presenting complaint is the problem rather than an index or symptom of something more fundamental, such as unconscious psychopathology in the individual or family system. Additionally, it is not the behavior per se that defines the complaint, but the pain or dissatisfaction that one or more family members experience around this behavior. While formulas defining "normal functioning" have their place, in the last analysis it is up to the individual or family to decide what is problematic for them. Some couples fight and define it as the spice of their relationship; others are quite content with little or no sexual activity in their marriage. There seems to be an unending variety of ways couples work out their marital relationships to their mutual satisfaction.

Given this stance, the goal of treatment is relatively simple and straightforward: to bring about change in the behavior and/or the view of the problem that reduces the client's pain sufficiently so that treatment is no longer desired by the client.

Attention is given to pinning down the client as to what would be the smallest change that would indicate that a significant dent had been made in the problem. Although some problems simply vanish when the attempted solution is correctly interdicted, other problems change more slowly only if left alone for a reasonable duration of time. Therefore, it is not necessary for the problem to be completely resolved during treatment but that only a dent be made that is sufficient for the client or family to relax and give up their faulty problem solving.

Defining the goals of treatment in terms of small, concrete, attainable steps has several benefits. If a patient has been feeling hopeless about tackling what seems like a monolithic problem, the goal-setting process breaks it down into something more reasonable and possibly attainable. Additionally, concrete definitions of improvement may work as powerful suggestions. A depressed patient will find it easier to recognize improvement defined as shopping for food and preparing a meal rather than being depression-free. Someone who feels she or he is not living up to potential will find completing a specific task a more attainable indicator of resolving the problem than seeking self-actualization.

During the process of goal formulation a number of considerations guide the therapist's interviewing. First, we believe that goals should be formulated in terms of a positive behavior rather than the absence of the negative condition. For instance, couples seeking marital treatment frequently desire a reduction in their fighting. When asked to state their treatment goals, they may simply say, "We want to stop these god-awful fights!" In keeping with our general notion of accepting what the client brings to treatment, the therapist will accept this and then ask, "When you do reduce your fighting, what might be the smallest thing that would take place, of a positive nature—maybe something that you do together—that would tell both the two of you and me that *you* have made a small but very real improvement in your problem?" One obvious advantage of the positive framing is that the client implicitly shifts the frame of reference from the negative to the positive.

Second, it is important when formulating goals with the client for the therapist to suggest that treatment is not an all-or-nothing proposition that will lead to complete elimination of the problem. Many problems are not simply black and white. Anxiety is a common complaint among psychotherapy patients, yet it is well known that anxiety serves many positive functions in our lives. It can be a warning of impending danger or trouble, and many athletes and performers readily admit that some pregame jitters or stage fright is necessary for a good performance. Thus, it would be important for the therapist to convey the idea that some anxiety is an important and positive feeling for the client to experience. This attitudinal set on the part of the therapist, manifested directly or indirectly during the goal formulation process, can be a powerful intervention in and of itself. Watzlawick (1978, p. 73) refers to this as the "principle of the unresolved remnant"—the therapist never suggests to the client that the problem will be totally resolved, only significantly improved.

Client's Primary Responsibilities

John Weakland, our associate director, has often said that the responsibility for treatment in brief therapy lies 100% with the patient and 100% with the therapist. There are a number of ideas concerning responsibility embedded in this therapeutic homily. First, it is not an easy matter to draw boundaries and decide who is responsible for what takes place during treatment. Second, it points out the fact that patient behavior can be seen as an interactional affair in treatment as well as outside of it. The communicational model gives the therapist the option of viewing all patient behavior as an outcome of the interaction taking place in the psychotherapeutic context. One advantage of this view is that it provides the therapist with options for increasing patient compliance, that is, patient responsibility.

The major patient responsibility in brief therapy is being a "customer"— someone who is motivated for treatment. From time to time, patients will come to treatment who would be better classified as "window shoppers" than customers. This typically includes patients who are under duress from the judicial system, school, or a spouse to get treatment. While these people may act like customers for treatment, in reality they are more like the window shoppers who have stepped into the store to get out of the rain. When approached by a salesperson, they might act as if they are interested in buying something rather than simply stating that they are trying to stay dry. However, as soon as the sun appears, they are on their way.

A good salesperson knows that a lot of time can be wasted with window shoppers. Thus, although he or she might spend some of his or her time checking to see if they can be made into customers, his or her whole approach will be radically different than when dealing with someone who is clearly there to buy something.

Similarly, a good brief therapist will not want to proceed with treatment on finding that she or he is dealing with a window shopper instead of a bona fide customer. In such a situation the therapist has several options. First, she or he may try to renegotiate the contract so that the patient can get down to the business of treatment. (An example of this follows in the next paragraph.) Second, the therapist might ask to see the person who is really upset or unhappy, and who is more likely to be a customer for treatment. This is often the person who pressured the window shopper to seek treatment in the first place. Third, treatment may simply be terminated, with or without some parting intervention geared to increase the window shopper's desire for treatment at a future date.

For example, a man may come to treatment offering his drinking as the presenting complaint. During the course of the first interview, however, the therapist learns that the patient is in fact not bothered by his drinking and doesn't see it as a problem; rather, it is his wife who is extremely upset by it. She might have thrown him out of the house with the ultimatum that he can only return if he begins treatment. Under these circumstances, we feel that it is important to establish directly and explicitly that the drinking is not a problem in the patient's view. If the patient validates this perception, we might redefine and renegotiate the therapy contract by bringing up the issue of his wife's reaction to his drinking, and by asking if this is a problem that he would like some help with. Another option would be to ask his permission to see the wife. The wife may well be the real customer, since she is the one who is upset by the patient's drinking. If she refuses to come in or take part in solving the problem, insisting that it is all up to him, then we would terminate the case accordingly.

Once it is established that the patient is indeed a customer for treatment, the therapist will want to collect information in a form that is most useful for understanding the problem-attempted solution loop and for making suggestions and assignments to be carried out between sessions. Clients may put up roadblocks to this process in any number of ways. For example, they may (a) give vague information, (b) insist on giving information the therapist does not need, or (c) refuse to have other family members interviewed. At a later stage of treatment, clients have the responsibility to carry out our homework assignments, but they may resist by finding excuses for not complying.

In the last analysis, however, the therapist is in charge of treatment and is responsible for getting around resistance strategies such as those mentioned above. The degree to which the therapist takes charge will depend in large part on her or his clinical skills. When compliance problems arise, it is essential that the therapist be flexible enough to employ a different strategy that will overcome the particular difficulty and that will allow treatment to continue. Since brief therapy is not based on an insight model, patient compliance or noncompliance is not discussed and analyzed in treatment. Rather, it is something implicitly utilized and dealt with to effect desired behavioral changes.

Therapist's Role and Function

The therapist is in charge of the case. She or he decides who is to be seen in treatment, the kinds of data to be collected, the interventions to be made, and how and when termination is to take place. More specifically, the therapist needs to determine who is the customer for treatment. (As pointed out, this may be one member of the family, the marital couple, or the entire family.)

During the initial interview, the therapist functions as a data collector, obtaining the kind of information that will allow an assessment of the problem, the attempted solution that is perpetuating it, and the language or position of the client that will provide clues as to how best to present new ideas and suggestions when interventions are made.

Next, the therapist functions as a case planner, spending time outside the interview hour to formulate a plan for interrupting the problem-maintaining solution. (This phase of the work is described in more detail in the next section.)

The next therapeutic function is putting the plan into action, testing the hypothesis derived from case planning. The primary role of the therapist at this stage of treatment is a persuasive one: how to get the client to make a change in behavior and/or frame of reference that will bring about the desired change in the presenting complaint.

Putting the plan into action takes place over many sessions, and the therapist must sort out what has been done, what have been the consequences of such actions, and how best to proceed. In some cases, a patient may have failed to carry out the assignment. The therapist might make a second attempt at getting the patient to do the same task or might decide that a different tack should be taken during the next interview after additional case planning. As in all our work, each interaction determines the therapist's next move—hence the notion of *strategic* psychotherapy.

Finally, the therapist must determine how and when the case shall be terminated. (This is discussed further in the next section.) In short, it its the therapist's role and function to do what is necessary, within the limits of the treatment context, to bring about a positive change in the presenting complaint, reducing the pain around this behavior and therefore eliminating any further need for treatment.

Techniques of Treatment

Given our view of problems and how they persist, the tasks of treatment (techniques and procedures) become clear: (a) obtain a clear definition of the problem and the behavior that maintains it; (b) devise a plan to interdict the attempted solution; (c) implement the treatment plan, revising or proceeding as necessary; and (d) terminate the case. Additionally, the therapist must use a variety of managerial techniques to maintain control over the treatment process.

Case Management. Most therapists would agree that warmth, empathy, trust, and patient involvement are important elements in a good therapeutic relationship. The brief therapist is also concerned with an additional set of relationship issues that permit the best clinical judgment throughout the course of treatment.

More specifically, the therapist needs room to maneuver—the freedom to ask questions and obtain necessary informa-

tion, choose which family members will be interviewed, select interventions, and gain the necessary leverage to see that they are carried out.

Given the limitations of space, it would be impossible to begin explaining how this is carried out. The following list simply outlines some of the main procedures for maximizing therapist maneuverability: obtaining clear, specific information from the patient; using qualifying statements to avoid being pinned down until the therapist decides what is the best position to take vis-à-vis the patient; taking one's time and not being pressured into intervening prematurely because of patient pressure; and using the one-down position, explained later in the Interventions subsection.

Data Collection. Treatment begins by simply asking the patient, "What brought you in today?" Related questions focus on the referral source, why treatment was sought now, and how the problem is getting in the way of the patient's life, that is, what the problem is stopping the patient from doing or making him or her do unwillingly. This last question serves as a useful barometer of patient distress and clarifies the presenting complaint.

Next, an assessment is made of the problem-maintaining behavior. We ask how the patient and others have been dealing with the problem and how they have deliberately attempted to solve it— what exactly do they say and do?

Last, the goal of treatment is determined, emphasizing minimal change on the grounds that there are only 10 sessions with which to work. The therapist might ask, "What, at the very least, would you like to see accomplished as a result of our efforts, and what concrete indicators might serve as signposts to indicate this?"

When collecting data, the brief therapist will phrase questions and remarks with an eye to obtaining descriptions of interaction that resemble the script of a stage play. For instance, if the patient says, "I really let her have it," the therapist will ask, "What exactly did you say? Then what did she say or do?"

Data collection usually takes from one to three interviews. During this period, other family members might be interviewed, alone or with the identified patient, answering the same basic questions. This permits the therapist to assess which family member is a customer for treatment—the one who really wants to get down to the business of problem solving—and what positions the family holds about the problem and its treatment, "positions" denoting their beliefs, opinions, and feelings. Since BT utilizes a systems perspective, we have the option of working with family members other than the identified patient to change the attempted solution (see Case Example).

Case Planning. The first task of planning is determining the logic, rule, or basic thrust of the attempted solutions. By studying the various individual solutions, the therapist seeks to derive their common denominator as seen from the next higher level of abstraction. In this sense, we seek to uncover the "rule" underlying the system of problem solving, for it is here that change usually needs to take place.

For example, a person who becomes anxious when speaking in public may try any or all of the following solutions: practicing in front of a mirror, performing relaxation exercises, making extensive notes and outlines, or taking medication. While each solution is different, they share the common denominator of trying to make a perfect presentation.

The basic solution serves as a guide, telling the therapist what in general might be done to resolve things and, more importantly, what to stay away from: what remarks or directives are the "mine field"—those comments or directives that are simply a variation of the same basic solution. In the case of the anxious public speaker, the mine field would be any intervention that implies it would help make a perfect presentation.

The easiest way to avoid the mine field is to select an intervention 180° out from the basic solution. With the anxious speaker, there are many different behaviors that fulfill this condition. The patient could (a) announce to the audience that he is nervous, (b) make a mistake on purpose, (c) act like he forgot what he was saying and ask the audience for help, or (d) drop his note cards in the middle of his talk. Each of these behaviors represents a 180° shift from the attempted solution.

Obviously, getting the patient to carry out such assignments is not easy. From the patient's perspective, this advice would appear to only make things worse. Therefore, the therapist must frame directives in a way that makes sense to the patient; information for such framing is derived from what has been learned from the patient's positions. Any of the following framings might be suitable for having a patient make a mistake on purpose: (a) as a method of in vivo desensitization, (b) exaggerating a problem as a way of learning how one does it, or (c) as a special exercise designed to stimulate insight. Some patients are simply intrigued with the question "Do you know how to give a really bad presentation?" And with some cases, we might use an intervention called "the devil's pact."

The patient must agree to follow the therapist's assignment without knowing what it is or discussing it once it has been presented. Either the assignment is carried out, or treatment is terminated.

Ideally, the new therapeutic assignment seeks two objectives: to influence the patient to carry out a new solution that is not a variation on the basic solution and, in doing so, to give up solutions that perpetuate the problem. For example, Erickson is reported to have cured an insomniac by convincing him to wax the kitchen floor during bedtime hours. From our perspective, this assignment fulfills both brief therapy objectives: it stops the patient from trying to force himself to sleep by making himself stay up to wax the floor.

Although much time and effort goes into case planning, such a formulation is not treated as sacred or irreversible. The treatment plan is simply a working hypothesis for bringing about change, and it will be pursued, modified, or replaced depending on its usefulness.

Interventions.   It is assumed that the therapist is always influencing the patient as a consequence of the communication process and the context in which it takes place. However, there are points in treatment when the therapist makes a deliberate effort to use her or his influence to reach a particular objective of treatment.

1. *Changing the Patient's View.* Although we don't believe insight is useful in resolving problems, if a patient's view of the problem is changed—not brought into line with reality—trying out a new solution can become easier. Similarly, a different view of the problem can make it *more difficult* for the patient to continue using the same, old solutions that are perpetuating the problem. This technique is called reframing—"to change the conceptual and/or emotional setting or viewpoint in relation to which a situation is experienced and to place it in another frame which fits the 'facts' of the same situation equally well or even better, and thereby changes its entire meaning" (Watzlawick et al., 1974, p. 95).

For instance, if a husband who resorts to physical abuse during marital fights accepts the reframing that he is making a loyal sacrifice for his wife by meeting her unconscious need for punishment, it puts him in a dilemma that is therapeutically useful. Since his abuse is defined as a positive gift, he must find new ways to retaliate. The therapist can capitalize on this by suggesting that he "kill" her with kindness.

Similarly, a salesman who came to treatment because he felt his stuttering impeded his work performance benefitted greatly when his speaking difficulty was reframed as an advantage, distinguishing him in a positive fashion from the stereotype of the fast-, smooth-talking salesman who usually turned off many prospective customers. His acceptance of this new view left him more relaxed about his impediment, resulting in less effort to inhibit it and an improved ability to speak without stuttering. As Shakespeare wrote, "There is nothing either good or bad, but thinking makes it so."

2. *Putting the Patient at Ease.* Patients are more likely to accept new ideas, try out assignments, and give more complete information if the treatment ambience is low-key. At the beginning of the first interview, it will be suggested that everyone use first names. Traditional therapeutic techniques, such as the pregnant pause and requesting that the patient verbalize her or his affect, are rarely used so that the treatment

interview resembles a normal conversation. All of these notions stem from the basic idea of "onedownmanship," with the therapist using a number of tactics to diminish the implied distance between her- or himself and the patient. Rather than coming on like a person with no problems and total understanding, the therapist portrays her- or himself as another human being with unique frailties and limitations.

When collecting information, the one-down position is used for clarification purposes. We are likely to say, "Would you please go over that again? Unfortunately, I am one of those people who have to hear things about five times before I get it. Please bear with me."

In the later stages of treatment, when we present new ideas or directives, we might say they are "not very important" or "just some small thing that might be of some help." At times, one of the most useful therapeutic comments is instructing the patient to "go slow." If the patient returns for a session reporting progress, we will probably comment that while we share her or his satisfaction, it would be wise not to move too rapidly because change always makes waves.

3. *Motivation.* There are many ways of motivating the client to behave differently, depending on her or his opinions, beliefs, and attitudes. The angry and frustrated parent can be given assignments that allow a harmless, therapeutic expression of feelings, while caretakers will be instructed to be even more helpful and sacrificing. Curious, insight-oriented patients can be motivated to try out novel ideas and see what new things they can learn, while resistive patients will be encouraged not to change.

4. *Homework.* Assuming that therapeutic change takes place between sessions, many of our interventions are in the form of homework assignments that instruct the patient to take new action regarding the problem. Directives are in the form of small, concrete, specific tasks to be carried out once or twice before the next session. During the early stages of treatment, the patient's homework might be to formulate a goal of treatment or to decide which problem needs the most attention.

One of the most interesting classes of directives is called the *paradoxical injunction*, more commonly known as *symptom prescriptions*. These are particularly appropriate in cases where the attempted solution takes the form of trying to force spontaneity. In trying to force her or his symptom, the patient must give up all of the solutions used to eliminate it. Fisch, our director, rapidly resolved a patient's complaint of premature ejaculation by instructing the marital couple to return home with a stopwatch; the wife was told to time the speed of her husband's ejaculation so that, ostensibly, Fisch could have the necessary data needed to formulate a diagnosis. (The request for additional information was simply a cover story to make the assignment seem reasonable to the couple.) By attempting to carry out the assignment, the couple dropped all problem-engendering solutions, and, much to their surprise, the husband no longer ejaculated quickly. From the patients' perspective, treatment was over before it really began.

Termination. The brevity of patient contact and emphasis on action rather than insight or expression of feelings make for a relatively simple termination process. In most cases, the subject is not even broached until the last or second-to-last session. Basically, we are looking for three criteria in the patient's report that would indicate that they are ready to terminate: (a) a small but significant dent has been made in the problem, (b) the change appears durable, and (c) the patient implies or states that she or he can handle things on her or his own.

When wrapping up a case, the therapist briefly reviews the course of treatment, giving the patient credit for what has been accomplished. Patients are also cautioned against believing that the problem is solved forever. We predict that very likely they will face this or a similar life difficulty again.

Some patients are hesitant about terminating treatment, and in these cases we are likely to frame termination as a necessary vacation from treatment, giving them time to digest and incorporate the gains made in their daily lives. They are warned that any further change would be counterproductive and that the best thing to do now is to put things on the back burner and let them simmer. In 3 months they will be contacted for a progress report.

Finally, resistive or negative patients will challenge any improvement as inconsequential or temporary, and the therapist will predict that things will probably get worse. As in all our work, every phase of treatment utilizes therapeutic strategy based on the needs of the particular case.

CASE EXAMPLE

Problem

Mr. and Mrs. Jones entered treatment because their 15-year-old daughter, Jan, was misbehaving. She was cutting her classes; staying out late; refusing to do things with the rest of the family (which included three siblings—14, 12, and 11 years old); and constantly demanding money, clothing, and a variety of other things. Both parents emphatically agreed that she "had a knack for breaking you down" with her constant demands, which led to their giving in to her requests.

Attempted Solutions

The parents had dealt with her misbehavior in a variety of ways, primarily by reasoning and by restricting her to the house. They had tried sending Jan to live with her uncle who "was good with kids," but her misbehavior persisted and she was sent home. On one occasion, the father had her picked up by the police and kept in juvenile hall overnight, but this had no positive effect on her behavior.

Interventions

Session 1. Since the parents gave such clear information and seemed quite united about their goals and methods, the therapist felt secure about intervening even more rapidly than usual. He ended the first session by taking the position that they might "give her some of her own medicine" by acting unreasonable themselves when she began nagging them. Not wanting to commit himself fully, he advised they think about this during the next week but *not* put their thinking into action. This assignment subtly suggested that they continue reasoning with her, even though it was identified as unworkable. However, if they were to think about what else they might say in the midst of struggling with her, they could not really deal with her in the same old way. What they did with this directive would also indicate their compliance to therapeutic directives and how such action affected the family system.

Session 2. During the first half of the

second interview, the daughter (the identified patient) was seen with her parents. The therapist concluded his contact with her by explaining that she had an amazing power over her parents by nagging them until they gave in to her wishes. She would be foolish to give this up, even if it meant "walking around in a chronic stage of rage, or taking an occasional trip to juvenile hall. You'll get used to this." She was sent to the waiting room on the note that the only thing left for the therapist to do was to teach her parents to get used to this.

The therapist's statements to Jan simultaneously accomplished three objectives: (a) it aversely suggested that she continue misbehaving no matter what the cost; (b) the manner in which this was said implied that the therapist was in a coalition with the parents, increasing their compliance with treatment; and (c) the message also implied that Jan's main strategy is to break down the parents by nagging, which only works because they try to reason with her unreasonableness and eventually give in to her demands.

The remainder of the session was devoted to working with the parents. The mother still seemed to be operating from a position of power she could not enforce. However, she did report backing off from her usual solution of trying to reason with Jan. Given her positive response to the suggestions made in the first session, we decided to take things a step further.

It was explained to the mother that words were her weakest weapon in dealing with Jan and that much more could be accomplished by teaching her a very important lesson in life—one hand washes the other. To do this, the therapist explained the technique of "benevolent sabotage." Any requests made of

Jan were to be made as follows: "There is something I would like you to do. I can't make you do it, but I wish you would." This would only be said once. If there was no compliance, benevolent sabotage was to be employed. For example, the mother could be late in picking her up for an important appointment or could somehow put her favorite white blouse in with the colored wash. When confronted about any of this, the mother was to apologize and say, "I'm sorry, I don't know what's wrong with me." To make this behavior even more believable, the mother was instructed to tell Jan that in the remaining part of the interview, she learned about some of her own personal problems and was feeling depressed. Her own self-absorption would now implicitly explain some of the mistakes she made that affected Jan's well being.

Benevolent sabotage served two purposes. It harmlessly channeled the mother's anger and frustration into an avenue that did not escalate hostilities, while implicitly steering her away from her usual way of dealing with the problem: reasoning and threats.

Session 3. The parents reported that Jan was "in tears all week because no one would fight with her." Mother had made one request in the prescribed manner, and Jan complied, so there was no need to use benevolent sabotage. However, the assignment had made them realize that they were continuing to make life easy for her on a noncontingent basis.

During this session, they asked for advice concerning Jan's birthday. They could not decide if they should buy her a present, especially the expensive pair of leather boots she had been requesting. Earlier in treatment, the mother had complained that Jan would not wash her bras out by hand, resulting in frequent replacement at considerable cost. After a bit of figuring in the observation room, the following intervention was offered. They were to purchase four bras, have them gift-wrapped, and present them to Jan for her birthday. If she balked at this, they were to apologize and explain they thought she had wanted them.

The mother said that Jan's nagging was on the decline, but at times Jan would attempt to get her back into the same old game of arguing. This was dealt with by instructing the parents in another technique, collusion. The next time Jan attempted to engage her mother in an argument when her father was home, he was to enter the room, pull a nickel out of his pocket, and give it to her. If she asked what the nickel was for, he was simply to say, "I felt like it." Then both parents were to leave the room without saying another word.

Collusion is similar to benevolent sabotage in distracting the parents from their usual verbal responses that are not working, thereby breaking the redundancy of the system. Since the parents complained that "Jan was just too damn sure of herself," the assignment was framed as a way of "injecting her with a healthsome dose of insecurity."

Session 4. The parents continued reporting improvement. The father laughingly told how he gave Jan a nickel and the experience left her bewildered. They also presented the bras to her; when she opened the present, she said in a faint, disappointed voice, "Four bras—that would have been the same price as the boots I wanted." The parents immediately apologized, explaining that they thought she would have liked them be-

cause now she wouldn't have to wash them out by hand. Jan said "thank you" and quietly left the room.

During the last week, they reported that Jan was more relaxed, taking her time eating at the dinner table and watching television with the family. The father told how she had used her allowance to buy her mother some candy and warned the other children not to eat it. The parents couldn't get over the change in her. The therapist warned them (dangers of improvement) that if they continued successfully dealing with her, they would find it difficult to see her leave home in a few years. He suggested that they might want to reverse her progress and directed them to bring about a planned relapse by taking one occasion to deal with her in their old way: reasoning and threats.

Session 5. The parents found it difficult to bring about a relapse (a desired outcome from the fourth session). Jan continued to improve, staying at home more and showing a renewed interest in her sewing. The mother said, "She's a much happier person; I can't believe it."

Three-Month Follow-Up Interview. The parents reported that Jan's behavior was "much better." There was less fighting and arguing, and she complied with simple requests. The parents felt sufficiently confident to take a weekend trip, leaving Jan in charge of the other children. Everything had gone well. The mother reported no need to act helpless or to use benevolent sabotage. There was no further treatment.

Twelve-Month Follow-Up Interview. Jan's behavior continues to improve. She has acted more considerate, giving up her room to visiting relatives. She has shown more concern and respect for her siblings, and, in return, they have done small favors for her. Her school grades have risen from the F–D range to C's and B's. The parents socialize more on their own, and there has been no further treatment.

EVALUATION

In order to assess the impact of our therapeutic work, each case receiving treatment from the Brief Therapy Project is followed up 3 and 12 months after the last interview. It should be noted that this is not a controlled, multidimensional measure of change but a simple follow-up study for in-house purposes.

Family members are asked a number of questions to assess the outcome of treatment. First, specific questions are posed to determine whether any significant improvement has taken place in the presenting complaint. Next, three standard questions are asked of all cases: (a) Have any new problems arisen since stopping treatment? This question is used to assess the issue of symptom substitution in systems; (b) Have any problems in the family that were not addressed in treatment been resolved? This question is designed to find possible spin-off effects when a positive change has occurred in a system; and (c) Has there been any further treatment?

Follow-up questions are a team effort, formulated during the case-planning process. Essentially, the question is asked, "What could this patient or family report that would indicate to us that they are really out of the woods about this problem?" Although it is impossible to formulate exactly what new positive behaviors they might be engaging in if treatment were successful, designing such questions puts us in the general ballpark. As stated earlier in this chapter, our primary aim is to make a small

but significant dent in the problem that is sufficient to reduce significantly or eliminate the anxiety and struggles perpetuating the problem. Another way of describing our general goal orientation is as follows: Patients and families who come to treatment are so caught up with their problems that they are not getting on with the business of living. In keeping with this general notion, we seek criteria that not only indicate that the problem is resolved or improved but that suggest, by other positive action, that they have better things to do than obsess about the problem returning.

If parents whose main complaint had been about the behavior of their teenager, for instance, report improvement in their child's behavior, we might ask if they have done something together without the children. This would indicate to us that they feel the presenting complaint is sufficiently resolved that they can leave their child alone or under the supervision of another, rather than having to stand guard in case the problem surfaces again. On the other hand, if the parents were exhibiting "waiting behavior" (for example, constantly checking up on the daughter or being anxious about the reappearance of the problem), we would feel they were not out of the woods and therefore rate the case as a partial success, even though the presenting complaint was much improved.

Scoring Cases

At our regular weekly, 2-hour meeting, each case follow-up is reviewed by the team and scored on a scale from -2 to $+2$. Negative numbers indicate that treatment has made the problem worse or created new problems; 0 represents no change; $+1$ designates some improvement but not a rave review; $+2$, our highest positive score, signifies that we have reached all our desired ends.

Additionally, for any case to receive a +1 or +2, there must be no further treatment or counseling. Even if the follow-up data show that all our goals have been met, the case is automatically scored as a 0 if further treatment was sought between the last and the follow-up interview. Similarly, any case given a positive score at the 3-month follow-up but a 0 or negative score at 12 months is automatically scored 0. Cases that were negative or 0 at 3 months are not followed up at 12 months; the 3-month score is duplicated at 12 months.

Results

After working one afternoon a week for approximately 13 years, we have treated approximately 148 cases. Our sample includes people from all socioeconomic classes, exhibiting a wide range of complaints covering most of the psychiatric spectrum. Cases were accepted on a first-come, first-served basis and were not screened prior to treatment.

Number of Cases	Sample %	Score
0	0	−2
0	0	−1
57	38	0
38	26	+1
53	36	+2
Total: 148	100%	

Obviously, these data do not represent a controlled, scientific study. Even with every effort to bias the data against ourselves by downgrading the scores whenever possible, these results represent our subjective opinions; there can be no doubt that we are all biased in favor of the model. However, given the facts that we have had no negative scores, that we do follow-up at 3 and 12 months, and that we downgrade our scores whenever

possible, our data do seem to suggest that our way of working can have a positive impact on client systems, sometimes very much so, in a relatively short period of time. Compared to the current state of the art, as reported by such psychotherapy researchers as Hans Strupp, we are certainly doing as well if not better than most treatment modalities.

SUMMARY

The psychotherapy industry is in the midst of a real crisis. Both practitioners and researchers are discouraged by the poor results of psychotherapy outcome studies. Third-party payers are beginning to protest the spiraling cost of mental health services, while the demand for treatment continues to rise. Rumor has it that a national health insurance plan would not be financially feasible if it included psychiatric coverage.

Brief therapy will not solve all of these problems, but the implications and consequences of our work do point in the right direction. Short-term treatment is cost effective, allowing the therapist to treat a greater number of patients within a given time frame. The generic nature of brief therapy permits the therapist to treat a wide variety of problems without devoting time, energy, and money for unnecessary, specialized training—that is, marital therapy, child therapy, and so forth. The nature of the interviewing process and the directive stance make brief therapy highly appropriate for the economically disadvantaged patient who wants to discuss the presenting complaint and expects some concrete, understandable advice.

Finally, brief therapy is more easily and quickly taught to others. It utilizes a minimum of theory, which translates directly into a key number of practice principles and techniques. Supervision also becomes a more efficient enterprise, defined as a professional relationship where the supervisee learns to refine the skills of her or his craft rather than work on personal problems or mental health.

ANNOTATED SUGGESTED READINGS

Fisch, R., Weakland, J., & Segal, L. (1982). *The tactics of change: Doing therapy briefly*. San Francisco: Jossey-Bass.

A comprehensive, detailed manual on how to deal with a wide variety of clinical problems briefly and effectively. It describes, explains, and illustrates the basic elements of brief therapy: maintaining control, setting the stage for treatment, conducting the first interview, assessing patient position, case planning, arranging interventions, and suggesting termination. Three case studies with commentary are also provided. A must for any clinician wanting to use MRI brief therapy.

Haley, J. (1963). *Strategies of psychotherapy*. New York: Grune and Stratton.

Although most of this book was written as a series of articles between 1952 and 1963, when Haley was a member of the Bateson Project, its content is thoroughly up-to-date. Haley describes the interactional process by which the therapist and patient maneuver each other in psychoanalysis, marital and family therapy, and hypnosis. His discussion of schizophrenia as an interpersonal phenomenon gives the reader a look through the communicational lens. Additionally, there are some fine accounts of how the late Dr. Milton H. Erickson worked with hypnosis and techniques of rapid problem resolution.

Segal, L. (1986). *The dream of reality: Heinz von Foerster's constructivism*. New York: Norton.

Heinz von Foerster is a cybernetician, mathematician, physicist, and philosopher who has raised many thought-provoking questions about the nature of reality and how we know the world. He draws our attention to how language unconsciously drives explanations of the world and ourselves. Although the book's subject matter is not clinical, it addresses many issues relevant to the clinician, particularly the brief therapist who must depart from traditional notions of what is real.

Watzlawick, P., Jackson, D., & Beavin, J. (1967). *Pragmatics of human communication*. New York: Norton.

A must for anyone seriously interested in the communication and systems work done on the Bateson Project and utilized at the MRI, and an excellent primer for anyone interested in working with brief treatment. Also discussed are a number of basic axioms of communication and the particular communicational pathologies that can arise around them, paradox, systems theory, and existentialism.

Watzlawick, P., Weakland, J., & Fisch, R. (1974). *Change: Principles of problem formation and problem resolution*. New York: Norton.

The major theoretical presentation of our work at the Brief Therapy Center, with a focus on the subject of change and stability and the interdependence of these two concepts (sometimes referred to as first- and second-order change). Although many examples and illustrations come from psychotherapy and family work (there is also a section on application), the subject matter is taken up in a much more general manner, highlighting the nature of change in both human and nonhuman systems.

REFERENCES

Bateson, G., Jackson, D., Haley, J., & Weakland, J. (1956). Toward a theory of schizophrenia. *Behavioral Science, 1,* 251–264.

Fisch, R., Weakland, J., Watzlawick, P., Segal, L., Hoebel, F., & Deardorff, M. (1975). *Learning brief therapy: An introductory manual.* Unpublished training manual, Mental Research Institute, Palo Alto, CA.

Haley, J. (1963). *Strategies of psychotherapy.* New York: Grune and Stratton.

Haley, J. (Ed.). (1967). *Advanced techniques of hypnosis and therapy: Selected papers of Milton H. Erickson, M.D.* New York: Grune and Stratton.

Ruesch, R., & Bateson, G. (1951). *Communication: The social matrix of psychiatry.* New York: Norton.

Watzlawick, P. (1978). *The language of change.* New York: Basic Books.

Watzlawick, P., & Weakland, J. (Eds.). (1977). *The interactional view.* New York: Norton.

Watzlawick, P., Weakland, J., & Fisch, R. (1974). *Change: Principles of problem formation and problem resolution.* New York: Norton.

Weakland, J. (1976). Communication, theory, and clinical change. In P. Guerin (Ed.), *Family therapy, theory and practice.* New York: Gardner Press.

Weakland, J., Fisch, R., Watzlawick, P., & Bodin, A. (1974). Brief therapy: Focused problem resolution. *Family Process, 13,* 141–168.

CHAPTER 8

Object Relations
Family Therapy

ALLIE C. KILPATRICK AND
EBB G. KILPATRICK, JR.

DEFINITION

A relatively new model of family treatment, object relations theory is considered to be the bridge between psychoanalysis—the study of individuals—and family theory, the study of social relationships. It may be defined as

the psychoanalytic study of the origin and nature of interpersonal relationships, and of the intrapsychic structures which grew out of past relationships and remain to influence present interpersonal relations. The emphasis is on those mental structures that preserve early interpersonal experiences in the form of *self and object-images*. (Nichols, 1984, p. 183)

Object relations theory is an existing general framework in psychoanalysis and psychiatry that provides the means for understanding the earliest developmental phases of childhood. It studies the individual's attachment to and differentiation from others—a process that is of much importance not only for the personality functioning of the individual but also for families and social adaptation. The lack of differentiation of family members has become one of the cornerstones of Bowen's work (1978) in understanding sick families, as well as Stierlin's work (1976) in studying larger social group functioning (Slipp, 1984).

Object relations family therapy is derived from the application of object relations theory to family development and treatment. Object relations theory and its therapeutic approach regard the individual's inner world and external family as components of an open system. It can be used to develop typologies of family interaction and treatment that take into consideration the intrapsychic influences on family patterns, which in turn affect the patient's personality. As Slipp (1984) has stated, psychoanalysis and family therapy can complement each other in a number of ways to enhance the theoretical understanding in both fields and to foster a treatment approach that is dependent not on the theoretical orientation of the therapist but rather on the needs of the patient and his or her significant others.

Object relations theories have not been well integrated. Finkelstein (1987) describes them as generally the result of various individuals writing alone or as parts of different "schools," using different terms and confronting different aspects of relationships with others. Therefore, each writer presents a somewhat different picture of human development and interpersonal relationships. Object relations theories are based primarily on two sources: (a) the psychoanalysis of individual adults and (b) the direct observation of infants and children and their parents. The observation of adult couples has not played a part in the development of psychoanalytic object relations theories, although some practitioners have applied object relations theory in marital therapy.

HISTORICAL DEVELOPMENT

While there is no integrated object relations theory, many theorists have developed their own idiosyncratic object relations perspective that roughly fits Freud's root theory. These theorists have developed new concepts and constructs that build on those of Freud but also add to his theories. For example, Ackerman, Boszormenyi-Nagy, Bowen, Jackson, Lidz, Minuchin, Satir, Whitaker, and other pioneers of the family therapy movement had their training in psychoanalytic theory. Most have retained at least some of these concepts in the development of their own models of family theory. Although they abandoned the depth psychology of individuals and the focus on unconscious vicissitudes of instinctual drives, the early family therapists studied the realities of family and social interactions and built constructs of relationships. Illustrations of this social emphasis are Lidz's "marital schism" and "marital skew" (Lidz, Cornelison, Fleck, & Terry, 1957), Wynne's "pseudomutuality," "pseudohostility," and "rubber fence" (Wynne, Ryckoff, Day, & Hirsch, 1958), and Bowen's "emotional fusion" (Bowen, 1965).

Freud is undisputedly considered the father of psychoanalysis. Psychoanalysis is historically a conservative discipline, and, as described by Nichols (1984), it chooses to modify and refine its basic concepts rather than replace them with new ones. Therefore, it seems appropriate to begin by acknowledging Freud's contribution to the psychoanalytic study of family life and its foundation for object relations family therapy.

Freud

Freud's (1905, 1940) psychology is a study of instinctual drives, which he labels the *id*. He sees the family as the social context where the child develops through the oral, anal, phallic, genital, and later stages and learns to control and channel impulses in socially acceptable ways through the ego and the super-ego (Brill, 1938). Since most of this learning occurs very early in life and since sexual frustration is highly charged with anxiety, many of these crucial interactions are repressed and unconscious. Freud declares that a cure for emotional problems is based on making the unconscious conscious (Breuer & Freud, 1895). He first postulated that the basic drives were sexual and self-preservative. He later dropped the self-preservative drive in favor of the erotic or sexual drive as the major instinctual life force (libido), but then even later he added the aggressive drive as the destructive life force element.

Freud, in his first major presentation of his ideas to his psychiatric colleagues, set forth his seduction theory as the cause of hysterical neurosis. This first theory states that, because of an actual traumatic event—the seduction by an adult or older sibling—the child develops hysterical or obsessional symptoms (Freud, 1940). He later abandoned this theory and turned away from traumatic events in the family—actual interaction—to focus on unconscious fantasy and instinctual drives. Slipp (1984) and others believe that family therapy as a field would likely have been established sooner had Freud not abandoned his initial formulation of the seduction theory, as this was the first psychiatric theory that involved family dynamics and emphasized the pathological influence of one person on another. Freud studied the developmental psychology of children, but he was more concerned with the influence of the family on individual personality development than he was with family dynamics.

Freud's view is really, as Dicks (1967) suggests, a physiological psychology of impulse gratification sufficient to account for the physical base of sexual attraction, perhaps, but short of the human's search for relationships. It should be pointed out, in fairness to Freud, that he does associate the libido concept with object seeking. *Object* in psychoanalytic literature refers to persons or things that are significant in one's psychic life. The phrase *object relations* refers to the individual's attitude and behavior toward such objects. The infant's first contacts with its significant objects (e.g., the mother's breast) are exclusively self-centered and concerned simply with the gratifications the objects afford. When the infant begins to experience need satisfaction through the object, then the object is "cathected," or psychic energy is expended toward the object or the mental representations of the object. Psychoanalysts assume that a continuing relationship with an object develops only gradually to the point where, even in the absence of the object, the child maintains an interest in the object. One of the important characteristics of the experience of early object relations is a high degree of ambivalence. Feelings of love alternate with feelings of hate, the hate resulting from frustrating experiences when gratifications are not experienced. As the child grows, the conscious feelings toward the object tend to be loving, whereas the unconscious bears more of the hateful feelings (Barnard & Corrales, 1979; Brenner, 1973).

Freud influenced many theorists who added to his work and deviated from it. Those who have had a part historically in the early development of object relations theory and therapy have included Ferenczi, Klein, Fairbairn, and others in the British School. Different historians give more credit to various of these contributors for the extent and influence of their contributions. Some of these contributions are briefly presented here as they developed historically.

Ferenczi

One of the most gifted of Freud's pupils, Sandor Ferenczi (1920) is generally considered to be the father of object relations theory. He maintains that Freud's original seduction theory was correct and should never have been abandoned. It is not the distortions of reality caused by the patient's fantasies and instincts that cause psychiatric illness, but actual parental neglect and trauma. Ferenczi's "active" approach to treatment attempts to re-create the early parent-child interaction so that the patient can relive and master the parental deprivations. The therapist's emphatic responsiveness during this regressive reenactment of the parental relationship encourages resumption of the patient's growth and development. Ferenczi believes that a passive and abstinent approach with sicker patients only recapitulates and reinforces the patient's experience of parental neglect and emotional abandonment. He differs from Freud also in his awareness of the interpersonal relationship of the therapist and patient, and his approach avoids a negative transference and a resultant poor therapeutic outcome. Ferenczi thinks that with sicker patients there are always countertransference feelings that cannot and should not be avoided. Emotional interaction between the patient and the analyst does occur and has to be worked with in a controlled fashion. Therapy, therefore, becomes a dyadic system rather than one in which the therapist is a detached, objective observer. Ferenczi was the first to report that patients projected their internal fantasies onto the analyst and others in an attempt to use these persons to fulfill their needs. Such reports were the forerunner of the concept of projective identification. He was also the first to note that a child could act out the unconscious conflicts of a parent (Slipp, 1984).

Klein

Melanie Klein (1948), one of Ferenczi's analysands, brings together many of his insights into a systematic theory. In studying her adult and child patients, she focuses on the earliest years of life and has contributed significantly to our awareness of infant-mother interaction. Klein sees the infant as object oriented from birth. Object relations theory has Klein's work as its basic foundation, especially the subjective dialogue between the self and the projected or introjected object. Through the interplay of projection and introjection, the infant attempts to relate to the mother, who is seen as good and bad, as a part, and later as a whole object.

According to Slipp (1984), Klein's major contribution to the understanding of infantile development is the role played by fantasy. For her, object relations derive from fantasies. Fantasy is the method the infant uses to regulate itself and to become attached to objects. The infant employs fantasy to explore its world and to communicate with the mother. It uses fantasy as the basis for the primitive mental mechanisms, splitting, projective identification, and introjection. *Splitting* is the fantasy that the ego can split itself off from an unwanted aspect of itself as pain, hunger, and so

forth or can split an object into two or more objects as good and bad, pain and comfort, and pleasure and displeasure. *Projective identification* is the result of the projection of parts of the self into an object. It can be viewed as the infant's attempt to control or return to the mothers's body. *Introjection* is when the object is incorporated into the ego, which then identifies with some or all of its characteristics (Segal, 1973). Klein postulates that in the first 6 months of life, the infant organizes experiences by primitive mental processes of splitting, projection, and introjection. At about 8 months, the infant begins to recognize its mother as a whole person about whom ambivalence is felt. As an object, she need no longer be split into separate part-objects.

Klein has been criticized for her failure to take her own observations to their logical conclusions—that object relations are more relevant than instinctual developments for personality development. However, the various theories comprising object relations theory were further developed independently, mainly by Fairbairn, Balint, Winnicott, and Guntrip. These theorists have been called retrospectively the "British object relations theorists" because of their shared basic premises. The Kleinian group, focusing on instincts rather than a need for human attachment, was sometimes called "The English School" and seen as separate from "The British School." The specific contributions of Fairbairn, Balint, Winnicott, and Guntrip are briefly presented next.

Fairbairn

Fairbairn (1954) goes much further than Klein toward object relations and away from instinctual drive psychology. He elaborates on the concepts of Freud and Klein and is said to have evolved the purest, clearest object relations theory. His view provides a viable bridge between intrapsychic dynamics and the interpersonal or systems level. Fairbairn believes that libido is object seeking, not pleasure seeking as Freud had postulated. Pleasure thus is not a goal in itself but a means of forming an attachment. To Fairbairn, the most basic motive of life is a person's need for a satisfying object relationship. He saw the individual's need for others and the desire to feel needed by them as the foundation for social life. Instinct is merely a function of the ego, and aggression is a response to frustration of a person's efforts to find affirmation and satisfaction from the object being sought.

The process of interacting with one's significant others is seen by Fairbairn as a mixture of satisfying and frustrating experiences, love and hate, acceptance and rejection. If, however, the family system is such that the child can test the reality of the parents' responses and can recognize the real person of the mother, father, and siblings, the child can learn a basic sense of trust in self and in one's significant others. He or she can thus develop a tolerance for ambivalent aspects of his or her relationships. Fairbairn equates maturity with the capacity for closeness and intimacy. While he recognizes the importance of individuation, he stresses the importance of tolerance or regression in adult relationships. He also provides us with a model of the personality in which regression and the gratification of childish needs are part of a healthy and intimate marriage. Finkelstein (1987) believes that the power of Fairbairn's theory is that he has evolved an object relations theory that is in total harmony with the marital vows. Applying his theories, marriage appears to be based on our most basic and lifelong need for attachment.

Balint

Balint (1968) notes that some patients must face the awfulness of there being nothing but an emptiness, something missing in their personality. He realizes that this is an early, fundamental flaw that influences the way the ego related to objects thereafter. He calls it "the basic fault," suggesting it arose from a failure of fit between the mother and baby and led to insecurity in future object relations. For Balint, the basis for personality development rests on satisfactory object relations. Therefore, therapists need to offer themselves as objects with whom the patient dares to relate again in order to repair the fault and recover human relatedness (Balint, 1968; Scharff & Scharff, 1987).

Winnicott

Winnicott (1965) has noted a split in the personality resulting from difficulties in early mother-baby interactions. He believes that unempathic mothering can cause the baby to try to mold itself to its mother's needs when its mother cannot respond in a flexible way to her baby. This leads to the baby's suppression of its "true self" and to the development of a "false self," which is typically compliant while the true self diminishes or is nourished secretly inside the self. Winnicott thinks that mothering did not have to be perfect but "good enough" that the infant can feel loved and cared for by her and valued for him- or herself. In this situation of trust and good-enough mothering, the infant's true self will develop without distortion. Winnicott's major contribution to understanding self and otherness is in his concept of *transitional objects*. If the early relationship with its mother is secure and loving, the infant will gradually be able to give her up, meanwhile retaining her loving support in the form of a good internal object. In the process, most little children adopt a transitional object to ease the loss—a stuffed animal or blanket that the child clings to during the time when he or she starts to realize that the mother is a separate object and can go out of sight (Winnicott, 1965).

Guntrip

Guntrip (1961) adds to Fairbairn's view the hypothesis that in severely regressed schizoid states, the libidinal system is further subdivided when part of it is split off as a withdrawn, regressed unconscious self that has no object to which to relate. This withdrawal from reality into the self may become the major part of the psyche in severely pathological states, or it may be a heavily defended, secret part of the self that is not readily discovered. This need for withdrawal he sees as proof of terrifying anxiety about losing the self and disappearing into the void (Guntrip, 1961; Scharff & Scharff, 1987).

Three other early theorists have aided in the development of object relations concepts—one in the area of couple dynamics and marital therapy, another in the area of group behavior, and the third by bringing together four primary theories into a unitary approach.

Dicks

Dicks (1967) applies object relations theory to couple's dynamics in a pioneering psychodynamic method of marital ther-

apy. During selection of a marriage partner, the ego chooses on the basis of finding an ideal object in the spouse. Because the marital relationship is similar to the early mothering experience in that it offers a permanent attachment to a caring figure, it brings out feelings from the infantile experience. In the perceived safety of the marital relationship, the repressed object relationships of the original parenting experiences return to seek expression, both good and bad. Each spouse now sees the other as partly ideal and exciting and partly rejecting of need, as were former objects. In an open, healthy relationship, this offers an opportunity to reintegrate the repressed systems and expand the ego. But in a closed, rigid system, the repressed relationships are repeated and further repressed to preserve the marriage despite impoverishing it. The ego, instead of confirming the separate identity of the object or spouse, then expects the spouse to conform to fit this inner picture. This mutual collusion to repress the troublesome object relationships causes problems for the couple. The tendency is to preserve the marital relationship by projecting the objects or ego onto the children. The child is then seen as a hated part of the self or spouse and bears a resemblance to a hated part of the grandparents. Any one child may be more or less predisposed by birth order, sex, physical likeness, constitution, or circumstance to carry any one projection.

Bion

Bion (1961) applies the projection hypothesis to the functioning of groups. He views the work group as a group beset by behaviors that relate to defenses against anxiety, not to work. Certain members of the group deal with their confusion and helplessness by projecting parts of themselves into other group members who, for their own reasons, become like the projections. Multiple processes of this projective identification cluster around subgroups within the group that express basic defenses against the anxiety of the whole group in relation to the group leader. This group therapy proved to be applicable to families, which can be seen as small, parent-led groups trying to do their work of raising the next generation (Scharff & Scharff, 1987).

Kernberg

Kernberg (1975, 1976) has made a crucial contribution to integrating psychoanalytic theory and practice into a unified approach by bringing together object relations theory, drive theory, structural theory, and ego psychology. He considers biologic and social forces as interactive, not distinct dichotomies; uses general systems theories; and traces the process through developmental stages. His contributions are further elaborated later in this chapter.

CURRENT STATUS

As stated earlier, object relations family therapy has no overall integrated theory. Various theorists have developed their own perspectives over the years, and others have made attempts at integration. In 1974, Foley made the point that the major issue in family therapy at that time seemed to be the relationship of an intrapsychic viewpoint to a system concept. His question was, "Is it possible to reconcile the two, or is there any value in doing this?" (p. 167). He then pointed to Framo and Boszormenyi-Nagy: two theorists who would bring the intrapsychic and the system concepts together by attempting to relate ideas derived mainly from psychoanalysis, such as transference and introjects, to systems theory.

Framo (1972) calls his approach a transactional one that leans heavily on the notion of projective identification as applied to a family system and that presents a new way of viewing transference. He builds on Fairbairn's notion of the fundamental need for a satisfying object relationship. He feels that when a child interprets the parents' behavior as rejection or desertion and cannot give up the external object, it internalizes this loved but hated parent in the inner world of self as an introject or a psychological representation. In the course of time, these split-off object relations become important as the person begins to force close relationships into fitting this internal role model. Framo goes beyond Dicks in that he attempts to widen the dyadic, marital field by including several generations of the family. He sees the introject of the parent as a critical issue in family therapy and one that is much neglected. Framo is trying to put together a basically intrapsychic concept, introjects, with a system concept. In doing so, he draws out the implications in Bowen's formulation of family theory for object relations theory.

Boszormenyi-Nagy (1973) maintains that parents who have been deprived of their own parents through death or separation often see the child as a parental substitute. This is similar to Bowen's concepts of triangulation and the need for a three-generational viewpoint. Unlike Bowen, Boszormenyi-Nagy is concerned about introjects and object relations. He sees family pathology as a specialized multiperson organization of shared fantasies and complementary need gratification patterns that are maintained for the purpose of handling past object loss experience.

Foley (1974) also interviewed Jay Haley, who stated that no compromise is possible between intrapsychic and system concepts since the frames of reference are totally different. Haley sees the introduction of object relations into family therapy as an attempt to placate the psychoanalytic community since the concept belongs to an intrapsychic approach. However, placating or not, therapists and theorists are currently achieving just this integration. Monumental groundbreaking work in this area has been done by Scharff (1982, 1989); Scharff and Scharff (1987), who coined the term *object relations family therapy*; and Slipp (1984, 1988).

For the Scharffs (1987), object relations family therapy derives from the psychoanalytic principles of listening, responding to unconscious material, interpreting, developing insight, and working in the transference and countertransference toward understanding and growth. The family, however, is not related to as a set of individuals but as a system comprising sets of relationships that function in ways unique to that family. The immediate goal is not symptom resolution but progression through the current developmental phase of family life, with improved ability to work as a group and to differentiate among and meet the individual members' needs.

Slipp (1984, 1988) differs from the main thrust of object relations theory of the psychoanalytic study and treatment of borderline and narcissistic personality disorders. His work broadens the focus to include other patient populations and applies its concepts to family studies in order to search for pathogenic factors in the family that influence the identified patient. He studied diverse patient populations and their families to explore the interaction and interdependence of individual dynamics and family system functioning. His ultimate goal is to apply an integrated understanding to family treatment. Some of the major contributions of the Scharffs, Slipp, and others are explicated in the following section on tenets of the object relations model of family therapy. Current therapists have made great strides toward providing an integrated theory and model for object relations family therapy.

TENETS OF THE MODEL

A fundamental tenet of object relations family therapy is that treatment of the individual and treatment of the family are theoretically and therapeutically consistent with each other and are both parts of an open system. The two levels of the intrapersonal and the interpersonal are in a constantly dynamic relationship with each other. An assumption is that resolving problems in relationships in the client's current family necessitates intrapsychic exploration and resolution of those unconscious object relationships that were internalized from early parent-child relationships. A further assumption is that these early influences affect and explain the nature of present interpersonal problems.

The basic tenets of object relations family therapy, though based on psychoanalysis, continue to be modified and refined. The historical development of some of the major concepts as they were developed by primary contributors have already been discussed. Nevertheless, it seems important to look again at specific tenets and concepts as they are currently used in assessment and intervention.

Splitting

Freud (1940) originally mentions *splitting* as a defense mechanism of the ego and defines it as a lifelong coexistence of two contradictory dispositions that do not influence each other. Kernberg (1972) traces the process of splitting through developmental stages. The first stage, from birth to 2 months, is undifferentiated. The second stage, from 2 to 8 months, involves splitting of the "all good" (organized around pleasurable mother-child interactions) and "all bad" (derived from painful and frustrating interactions) self-images, object images, and their affective links. The third stage, from 8 to 36 months, involves the separation of the self from object representations. Splitting into good and bad persists, and this is seen as the fixation point for borderline patients. The fourth stage consists of integrating these opposing good and bad emotional images so that the separate self and object representations are each both good and bad. It is at this point that the ego, super-ego, and id become firmly established as intrapsychic structures and that the defenses of splitting are replaced by repression. Slipp (1984) sees this stage as the fixation point for neurotic pathology. In the last stage, internalized object representations are reshaped through actual current experiences with real people. A goal of object relations family therapy is to assist in the development of this integration and reshaping.

Introjection

Introjection is a crude and global form of taking in, as if those fragments of self-other interactions were swallowed whole. It is the earliest, most primitive form of the internalization of object relations, starting on a relatively crude level and becoming more sophisticated as the child grows (Nichols, 1984). The child reproduces and fixates its interactions with significant others by organiz-ing memory traces that include images of the object, the self interacting with the object, and the associated affect. Good and bad internal objects are included, each with images of the object and the self. For example, if the mother or mothering parent yells, images of a bad parent and an unworthy self are stored.

The infant's first internalized objects are fragmented or experienced as part objects and as either "good" or "bad." Klein (1946) developed two developmental positions that depend on the role of object relations and that replaced Freud's instinctual maturational phases of oral, anal, phallic, and genital. Introjection of bad objects, like an empty breast or angry face, generates fear and anxiety that lead the baby into the paranoid position. Around the time of weaning, the infant begins to experience the mother as one person, with both good and bad qualities. The infant also discovers that he or she has the capacity to hurt loved ones. This leads to the depressive position where the baby is depressed at being ambivalent toward the mother and feels guilty about inflicting pain on her. This position is instrumental in the development of the oedipal conflict beginning in the second year of life (Nichols, 1984). These concepts play crucial roles in the understanding of dynamics and formulation of treatment in object relations family therapy.

Projective Identification

Identification is a higher level of internalization that involves the internalization of a role. Objects and self-images are clearly differentiated. The result of identification is that the child takes on certain roles and behaves the same way parents behave. A child of 2 can be observed imitating parents in many ways. On the other hand, *projective identification* is a defense mechanism that operates unconsciously whereby unwanted aspects of the self are attributed to another person and that person is induced to behave in accordance with these projected attitudes and feelings (Nichols, 1984). Unlike projection, it is truly an interactional process. The concepts of transference (Freud, 1905), scapegoating (Vogel & Bell, 1960), trading of dissociations (Wynne, 1965), merging (Boszormenyi-Nagy, 1967), irrational role assignments (Framo, 1970), symbiosis (Mahler, 1952), and family projective process (Bowen, 1965) are all variants of Klein's (1946) concept of projective identification.

Collusion

An integral part of projective identification is the concept of *collusion*, by which the recipient of the split-off part of the partner does not disown the projection but acts on the conscious or unconscious message (Stewart, Peters, Marsh, & Peters, 1975). Simply stated, a need for a "strong" man to gratify a "weak" woman requires that both partners agree to the assigned roles. Such collusion is often obvious and circumscribed and may be neither problematic nor pathologic. It is when the assigned roles have broken down that the couple experience discomfort or symptom formation. Each spouse's ego identity (which includes both good and bad objects) is preserved by having one or more bad objects split off onto the partner. Thus, each partner disowns his or her bad-object introjects and needs the other to accept the projection of these introjects. Each begins to conform subtly to the inner role model of the other in a collusive manner

(Piercy et al., 1986). Dicks (1963) believes that this collusive process continues because both spouses hope for integration of lost introjects by finding them in each other.

Difficulty within the therapeutic context arises when there is a denial of collusion, an exaggeration of differences, and attempts to obscure clarification of the process. Therapists using object relations theory attempt in various ways to help couples own their introjects and begin seeing their spouses for the people they really are, not projected parts of themselves. Collusion, shared fantasy, and projective identification are not limited to the marital dyad but may also appear in all of an individual's significant relationships, including the one with the therapist.

Ego Identity

Erikson (1956, 1963) theorizes that introjections and identification form the basis of ego identity, which represents the most sophisticated level of the internalization process. Ego identity is the overall organization of synthesized identifications and introjections. It provides a coherent, continuous self-concept and a consolidated world of object representations. It is important to remember that it is not objects that are in the psyche, but fantasies of objects. The internal world of object relations never exactly corresponds to the actual world of real people. It is an approximation strongly influenced by the earliest object images, introjections, and identifications.

This phenomenon corresponds to the concept of *constructivism*, which posits that an organism is never able to recognize, depict, or mirror reality and can only construct a model that fits. These theories are highly relevant in family therapy not only for the world views or realities that various families construct, but also for the picture the therapist forms of a particular family (Simon, Stierlin, & Wynne, 1985).

As the inner world gradually matures and develops, it becomes closer, one hopes, to reality. Kernberg (1976) describes ego identity at its highest level of development:

A harmonious world of internalized object-representations, including not only significant others from the family and immediate friends but also a social group and a cultural identity, constitute an ever growing internal world providing love, reconfirmation, support, and guidance within the object relations system of the ego. Such an internal world, in turn, gives depth to the present interaction with others. In periods of crisis, such as loss, abandonment, separation, failure, and loneliness, the individual can temporarily fall back on his internal world: in this way, the intrapsychic and the interpersonal worlds relate to and reinforce each other. (p. 73)

The Holding Environment

Winnicott (1958) builds on his notion of good-enough mothering to the idea of a "holding environment." If the good-enough mother or primary nurturing person provides a holding environment that is safe, secure, responsive, nurturing, nonretaliating, and supportive of separation-individuation, the child can achieve a firm sense of identity and a lifelong capacity for developing nonsymbiotic object relations.

The Scharffs (1987) develop this concept further in their notions of centered relating, centered holding, and contextual holding. *Centered relating* is facilitated by a mirroring function in which mother or mothering object reflects back to the baby its moods and its ef-

fects on her, while the baby reflects back to the mother its experience of her mothering. Through this experience of relating to each other centrally, at the very core of their selves, the nucleus of the infant's internal object relations is built, and the mother's internal object relations are fundamentally altered as the baby contributes the experience that gives her identity as a mother. *Centered holding* is the mother's ability to provide the space and material for centered relating through her physical handling of and mental preoccupation with her baby. The space in which this centered relating takes place is the distance at which the mother can still feel in communication with her baby. For some working mothers, it may extend to her office and require that she surrender the centered holding to a trusted substitute for a period of time. But it is still the mother who provides the "envelope." The Scharffs call this the *mother's contextual holding*.

There is also the father's (or secondary nurturing person's) role in provision of holding for the baby. Traditionally, the father's direct exchanges with his infant are different and not as central in the ongoing way they are with the mother and baby. In fact, his exchanges with the baby have the purpose of pulling the infant out of the mother's orbit for increasing periods of time, and his need for relating to the mother helps to pave the way for the later separation and individuation of the infant from the mother. Therefore, part of the father's role is to interrupt the mother's centered and contextual holding. Primarily, however, he supports the holding physically, financially, and emotionally; he holds the mother as she holds the baby. The Scharffs call this the *father's contextual holding*. This contextual holding provides an environmental extension of the mother's presence that later extends outward to grandparents and family, neighbors, and others.

These concepts of centered and contextual holding also apply to object relations family therapy. The family therapist needs to offer both aspects in the therapeutic engagement with the family. The contextual holding is provided through the handling of arrangements, competence in interviewing, concern for the family, and seeing the whole family. Centered holding is provided by engaging with the central issues of the family and being caring, interactive, and understanding.

Feminist object relations family therapists have a somewhat different view. Luepnitz (1988) states:

What feminist object-relations theory has to teach therapists who treat families is the overarching importance of creating a new father, a man who will not be the tired nightly visitor, who will be more than a therapist-appointed expert, more than a coach to his irresolute wife, more than her back-up, more than the separator of mothers and children, but an authentic presence, a tender and engaged parent, a knower of children in the way that mothers have been knowers of children. (p. 183)

Luepnitz and others would like to see the father have a more central role with his children because, among other reasons, "many men without loving fathers grow up expecting women to give them all the warmth and limit setting they were denied—and then hating women for not succeeding in what is, after all, an impossible task" (p. 183).

Transference and Countertransference

The Freudian term *transference* is defined as distorted emotional reactions to present relationships (mainly to the analyst) based on unresolved, early family relations (Nichols, 1984). The Scharffs (1987) extend the concept to include the repetition in the therapeutic relationship (transfamilial) of early relationships and even earlier part-object relationships. They think of transference as the living history of ways of relating, influenced by the vicissitudes of infantile dependence and by primitive emotions of a sexual and aggressive nature that arise in pursuit of attachment. They also subscribe to the idea of transference as a universal mental function that may well be the basis for all human relationships. Going further, they say that this sort of transference operates between family members (intrafamilial) where any present relationship is colored by earlier editions of the relationship, based in turn on layered experiences at earlier developmental stages. They are usually transgenerational and could be from parent to child or child to parent. These sorts of transferences in individuals operate as valences to engage with others who have similar or complementary tendencies to relate in certain characteristic ways.

Countertransference is the emotional reaction, usually unconscious and often distorted, on the part of the therapist to a patient or member of a family in treatment (Nichols, 1984). Part of this countertransference is the development of a personal quality of "negative capability." This is a capacity to tolerate not knowing and to suspend the need to know long enough to let the meaning of an experience emerge from inside the experience itself. The Scharffs (1987) say that when we are able to do this successfully, the countertransference experience eventually tells us everything we need to know about our relationship with our patients, with a depth we cannot have if we impose theory as a way of understanding. They see negative capability as an example of object relations being a way of working rather than a theory.

In family treatment where the relationships are seen firsthand and can be worked with directly, the need for developing individual transferences with the therapist is lessened as the intrafamilial transference processes tend to be the most decisive. Countertransference gains an expanded significance and can now be applied to a therapist's attitudes, perceptions, and "blind spots" that hinder his or her attempts to maintain a fair, neutral, and evenly empathic attitude toward the whole family. As a rule, the countertransference problems that therapists have will often be bound up with experiences and unresolved conflicts within their own family of origin (Simon et al., 1985).

Isomorphisms

This is a precise mathematical term borrowed by systems theorists that utilizes object relations concepts. Hofstadter (1979) notes that *isomorphism*

applies when two complex structures can be mapped onto each other in such a way that to each part of the structure there is a corresponding part in the other structure, where "corresponding" means that the two play similar roles in their respective structures. (p. 49)

The copy preserves all the information in the original theme, in the sense that the theme is fully recoverable from any of the copies. Isomorphism, therefore, is an "information-preserving transformation" (p. 9). This concept is most helpful to object relations family therapists as we look for similar structures and con-

nections on various levels that come from splitting, projective identification, collusion, or transference processes. Given that the essential task of family therapists is to understand and influence structures and patterns, therapists must decide to what extent patterns of behavior and communication are isomorphic in a nuclear family, the parents' families of origin, the therapeutic system (family, therapists, supervisors), the treatment team, and the therapists' families of origin (Simon et al., 1985).

Concepts for Marital Therapy

Some theorists have focused specifically on the application of object relations theory to the practice of marital therapy. Meissner (1978) states that the capacity to function successfully as a spouse is largely a consequence of the spouse's childhood relationships to his or her own parents. He further states that

the relative success that the marital partners experience and the manner in which these developmental tasks are approached and accomplished are determined to a large extent by the residues of internalized objects and the organization of introjects which form the core of the sense of self and contribute in significant ways to the integration of their respective identities. The extent to which spouses are unsuccessful in merging these individual identities into a constructive and productive shared marital experience is contaminated by pathogenic introjects they each may bring to it, rather than being organized in terms of a successful differentiated and individuated sense of self and identity. (p. 27)

Finkelstein (1987) utilizes the work of Fairbairn (1954), Kohut (1984), Gilligan (1982), and others to summarize certain object relations principles that have specific applicability to the understanding of marital relationships and marital therapy. This summary serves to pull together many of the concepts previously discussed in this chapter as well as to point out their particular relevance to marriages.

1. Object-seeking and attachment to others can be viewed as a primary motivational force in human beings.
2. Object-seeking is lifelong and attachments can be a source of fulfillment and gratification.
3. Maturity can be measured not only in terms of the development of autonomy but also in terms of the capacity for intimate, mutually interdependent, satisfying relationships, which allow for appropriate regression without loss of respect.
4. Mutually enhancing and satisfying marital relations are based on mutual self-object functioning.
5. Aggression can be seen as due to failure of each partner to provide for the other's dependent or self-object needs; that is, aggression can be seen as frustration aggression. Alternately, aggression results from a break in one's connection to one's spouse.
6. Sexual problems in marriage reflect relational problems as well as individual inhibitions and anxieties.
7. Conflicts resulting from each marital spouse's striving for individuation and separation, as well as his or her striving for attachment and commitment, are an on-going source of tension and conflict in marriage. (pp. 296–297)

These object relations concepts all relate to attachment, connectedness, bonding, caring, love, and responsibility in marriage. They serve to provide an understanding of the deeper reasons for the three most common complaints in marriage: lack of communication, constant arguments, and unmet emotional needs. Such complaints can be seen as the results of the failure of relatedness, of deficiencies in self-object functioning, and of conflicts between relationship goals and individual goals (Finkelstein, 1987).

APPLICATION

Problem Areas for Which the Model Is Especially Effective

Object relations family therapy (ORFT) deals with shared, unconscious, internalized object relations. According to Slipp (1988), it looks for the primitive defenses of splitting and projective identification as the link between intrapsychic and family dynamics. As a result of these defenses and their associated affects, an unconscious collusive system among family members develops that fosters certain behaviors and symptomatology. Therefore, object relations theory can be utilized in order to understand a vast array of behaviors, problem areas, and symptomatology. However, the judgment as to whether or not object relations family therapy is the most effective approach to use in any given situation can be informed by previous studies and experiences. For those cases in which the family seems to play a significant role in aggravating or perpetuating the patient's problems of lack of differentiation, the use of splitting and projective identification, little autonomy, inability to maintain their own sense of self-esteem and identity, and excessive vulnerability to the influence of their families, a family approach does seem indicated. Slipp (1988) states that, although ORFT is appropriate for families who desire and can tolerate intensity and closeness, it is certainly not restricted to only those families. As families develop trust and become closer to the therapist, therapy itself can serve as a model for more open and intimate relationships among family members.

Slipp feels strongly that perhaps the most significant variable in selecting the most suitable type of family therapy is the family's socioeconomic level. Slipp's (1988) study showed that the ORFT approach is particularly fitting for and effective with middle-class families, as well as a blue-collar population. On the basis of his study findings, ORFT with lower socioeconomic families is least effective and not recommended. Clients with overriding poverty and social problems want help that is more immediate and less abstract. Scharff and Scharff (1987), however, caution therapists that it should not be assumed that the poor, or culturally or intellectually disadvantaged, cannot benefit from ORFT. Some such families will fit cultural stereotypes of concrete thinking and dependency on directives and gratification, but others will take to a more reflective approach. Therefore, we can say that ORFT is not for all families but for those that demonstrate an interest in understanding, not just in symptom relief.

Is ethnicity a factor as to whether or not ORFT is indicated? Slipp (1988) observes that in his experience, ethnic differences alone need not dictate the choice of treatment. Although there are differences at the beginning of treatment between ethnic groups, if the therapist is sensitive to these differences and is a skilled clinician, they can be worked through in treatment.

Goals of the Therapeutic Process

The immediate goal of ORFT is not symptom resolution but progression through the current developmental phase of family life, improved ability for work as a group, and better capability to differentiate and to meet the needs of individual members (Scharff & Scharff, 1987). More specifically, the general goals include the following:

1. Recognizing and reworking the defensive projective identifications that have previously been required in the family.
2. Treating the family's capacity to provide contextual holding for its members so that their needs for attachment and conditions for growth can be met.
3. Reinstating or constructing the series of centered holding relationships between each of its members to support their needs for attachment, individuation, and growth sufficient to allow each individual to "take it from there."
4. Returning the family to the overall developmental level appropriate to its tasks as set by its own preferences and by the needs of the family members.
5. Clarifying the remaining individual needs in family members so that they can get them met with as much support as they need from the family. By this, we specifically include individual needs for psychotherapy, as well as more general needs for other growth endeavors. (p. 448)

As Guntrip (1961) puts it, the goal is the "reintegration of the split ego, the restoration of lost wholeness" (p. 94). The concepts of splitting, projective identification, collusion, shared fantasy, and others emphasize the existing need for and use of other family members. An individual family member's need to establish ego boundaries and a sense of identity and to tolerate his or her own ambivalence and conflict (and all aspects of the personality) are parts of the treatment goal (Stewart et al., 1975). Overall goals are as open-ended as the treatment itself because goals change as growth occurs, leading to an expanded vision of future possibilities.

Therapist's Role and Function

The therapeutic environment is established by the therapist's encouragement of open dialogue, respecting confidentiality and setting up the mechanics of treatment (e.g., who to include, time, place, fee, length of time, etc.) in a safe, mutually helpful atmosphere. The therapist generally maintains a neutral stance that supports his or her anonymity and respects each member's autonomy. The therapist avoids assuming a directive approach by not giving advice, reassurance, or instruction, but he or she attends to other material produced in the session as described by Slipp (1988). The past is linked to the present through interpretation of the transference, particularly the ways it is acted out interpersonally in the ongoing family relationships. In order to facilitate the acceptance of these interpretations, the therapist needs to join the family empathically and to create a safe and secure holding environment where space for understanding is provided. Creating such a holding environment has been found to be the most crucial element for change and growth in the psychotherapy research of Sampson and Weiss (1977).

There are also two other essential elements that the ORFT introduces into the process (Slipp, 1988): (a) how the therapist parcels out internalized object relations through projective identification onto family members and (b) how the family similarly evacuates internalized object relations onto the therapist. Therapists use their own empathy as a form of vicarious introspection in order to enter a client's subjective inner world. In addition, therapists allow their own inner world to be entered by the family through their use of projective identifi-cation. Therapists then try to monitor their own countertransference responses that are influenced by and in turn influence the family. The therapist's stance with the family is one that reflects an awareness that he or she affects and is affected by the family.

Slipp (1988) has described the therapist-family relationship as follows:

Object relations family therapy allows for the greatest degree of closeness between the family and the therapist. The therapist, while maintaining autonomy, is able to empathically experience and understand each of the family members. Thus, at a concrete level, object relations family therapy serves as a model to unlearn old distant and controlling interaction, and to learn how to be both an authentic individual as well as an integrated member of the family group. It provides a framework within which individual boundaries and autonomy are respected and confirmed, along with sensitivity to one another in the family. An extreme of either one of these positions leads to either narcissistic distancing or overly close symbiotic relatedness. Object relations family therapy fosters the kind of meaningful shared intimacy with respect for one another's individuality that the philosopher Martin Buber (1958) so aptly described as the "I-Thou Relationship." (p. 24)

Assessment is a vital part of the therapist's role and function. Scharff and Scharff (1987) cite six major tasks in assessment: (a) the provision of therapeutic space; (b) assessment of developmental phase and level; (c) demonstration of defensive functioning; (d) exploration of unconscious assumptions and underlying anxiety; (e) testing of the response to interpretation and assessment format; and (f) making an assessment formulation, recommendation, and treatment plan. Slipp (1984, pp. 204–205) reviews the steps in such an assessment process:

1. *Explore the presenting problem* of patient and its background.
   (a) Does it seem related to overall family functioning, and/or to stress from a family life cycle stage?
   (b) What has been done so far to remedy the problem?
2. *Establish an individual diagnosis* for each family member including a judgment concerning the level of differentiation and the use of primitive or mature defenses.
   (a) Gather data on the client and family development.
   (b) Note any ethnic differences or conflicts.
3. *Evaluate family constancy* to determine if parents can maintain their own narcissistic equilibrium, or if patient is needed to sustain their self-esteem and survival.
   (a) Does a rigid homeostasis or defensive equilibrium exist that binds and prevents the patient from individuating and separating?
   (b) Is there pressure for personality compliance within the family, or social achievement outside the family?
   (c) What affiliative, oppositional, and alienated attitudes exist?
4. *Explore precipitating stress* and its relation to a loss or other traumatic event (negative or positive) or a transitional point in the family life cycle that has disrupted homeostasis.
5. *Define individual boundaries* for members. These may be rigidly too open (a symbiotically close relationship) or too closed (an emotionally divorced and distant relationship).
   (a) Are generational boundaries intact, or are there parent-child coalitions?
   (b) Are the parental coalition, the subsystems, and authority hierarchy intact?
6. *Define the family boundary* to see if it is too open (symbiotic relations persist with family of origin) or too closed (family is isolated from community without social support system).
7. *Determine the ability to negotiate differences and problem solve* through verbal dialogue involving respect for one's own and other's views, opinions, and motivations versus an egocentric controlling viewpoint resulting in coercion and manipulation.
8. *Observe* communication patterns and kinesic regulation for evidence of spontaneous versus rigid stereotyping, distancing, or obfuscating; level of initiative versus passivity; rigidity of family rules; and the power-role structure.
9. *Evaluate the loving and caring feelings* amongst members which allow for separateness (rather than acceptance only by conformity) and provide warmth, support, and comfort.
10. *Define the treatment goals* in terms of difficulties that have been uncovered, and present the frame or boundaries of the treatment process.

In addition to the ethnic differences or conflicts noted by Slipp, attention must also be given to other sociocultural-environmental factors that influence the family.

Primary Treatment Techniques

There are some specific techniques that ORFT uses in the beginning, middle, and last phases of treatment, which Slipp (1988, pp. 199–200) has outlined as a guide for therapists.

During the beginning phase of treatment the techniques are to:
1. Develop a safe holding environment through empathy, evenhandedness, and containment; an environment that facilitates trust, lowers defensiveness, and allows aggression to be worked with constructively.
2. Interpret the circular positive or negative systemic interaction in a sequential non-blaming manner by:
   a. defining its origin

b. defining what was hoped to be gained

c. describing its effects

During the middle phase of treatment, the techniques are to:

1. Interpret projective identification by:
   a. reframing its purpose to give it a positive aim
   b. linking it with a genetic reconstruction
   c. clarifying why an aspect of the self needed to be disowned and projected
   This process diminishes defensiveness, enhances the therapeutic alliance, and facilitates continued work with the reowned projective identification.
2. Use the objective countertransference as a tool to understand the transferences and to provide material for interpreting projective identification.

During the last phase of treatment, the techniques are to:

1. Work through individual conflicts and developmental arrests in the intrapsychic sphere. This process is gradual and may continue in individual therapy after the family treatment terminates.
2. Terminate treatment.

All these techniques are discussed in detail by Slipp (1988) as they are used in the appropriate phase of treatment. As the reader can readily recognize, most of the concepts contained in the outline have been previously discussed in this chapter. However, the added dimensions of when they are to be used in the treatment process and how they fit together are important.

We now turn to the specific treatment techniques that differentiate the object relations approach from other approaches. This will serve to highlight overall techniques used in ORFT as well as to discriminate this approach further. Stewart et al. (1975, pp. 176–177) list six areas of differentiation.

1. While many marital partners may seem quite different, it soon becomes apparent that their psychic structures are very similar. Although they may behaviorally manifest these intrapsychic processes differently through collusion, projective identification, shared fantasy, etc., the similarities should be discussed and made explicit to the couple.
2. The ORFT approach goes beyond countertransference usage in allowing the partner to "put into" the therapist disowned or split-off parts of himself. The more classical analytic approach considers the therapist's reactions as irrational countertransference phenomena. This approach regards such material as a valid, legitimate statement of issues with which the patient is struggling.
3. When therapists split up a couple to see each of them individually, the emotional exchanges between the therapists will be similar to and/or mirror the affective transactions between the partners in the marital dyad.
4. This ORFT approach provides a way of understanding family problems when a child is presented as the identified patient. The child becomes a carrier or container of the split-off, unacceptable impulses of the parent. The child may be idealized just as he may be denigrated.
5. The more classical approach focuses on interpreting the patient's perception in terms of internal processes based on early experiences. This system considers the perception to be based on a need to solve an internal conflict through the use of external objects as carriers. There is an active invitation to other people to fulfill these roles rather than a passive perception of other people.
6. In classical analytical theory, the focus is upon individual psychotherapy and pathological involvement. Behaviorally oriented approaches also emphasize individual functioning. In contrast, object relations theory offers a perspective of the individual as a unit in which even the more pathological traits have a healthy reparative aspect. Consequently, the marital

dyad continues to function in defiance of apparent breakdown and irreconcilable differences and conflicts. Awareness of the reciprocal, pathological, and subtle attempts to carry out ego repair generates a greater understanding in the therapist of the durability and maintenance of the marital dyad.

CASE EXAMPLE

This is a case with which the authors were involved over a period of about 7 years. The setting was a private practice office.

Presenting Problem

Sam and Sally came into treatment with the presenting problem of Sam's anger. He had lost control of his anger and physically assaulted his wife. It seems that they had a disagreement, the disagreement escalated, and Sally made a remark that activated intense rage in Sam. Before he knew what was really happening, he had lunged across the room, physically grabbed his wife, and slammed her against the wall. Her head hit the wall, temporarily dazing her. She sank to the floor and sat there bewildered. At first Sam did not realize how hard he had thrown her or that she was semiconscious. He continued to abuse her verbally. When she failed to respond and then when tears came to her eyes, he began to realize how deeply he had hurt her, physically and emotionally. He immediately began to apologize, assuring her that he did not mean to hurt her and that he was really sorry for what had happened.

This incident was the straw that broke the camel's back, so to speak. Many of the other problems that had surfaced over the first 11 years of their marriage had still not been dealt with. This last in-

cident truly frightened Sally as well as Sam and along with the other unresolved problems motivated them to conclude they needed help. Sam kept wondering where his intense feelings came from and how they could be controlled. This was the first time that treatment had been sought for the problems. There did not seem to be any particular transition stress from a life cycle stage perspective at that time.

History

Sam and Sally perceived themselves, as the community did, as the typical family. He had played high school football, track, basketball, and baseball; Sally had excelled academically and graduated at the top of her class. They had met and fallen in love while in college. Sam was 3 years older than Sally. At the time they were first seen for therapy they had been married 11 years, and their children were 8 and 6 years of age.

Sam and Sally were asked to share their childhood experiences with their parents. Sam said he was born prematurely and there was some concern on the part of the doctors as to whether he would survive or not. His impressions were that the pregnancy was somewhat ill timed and that his mother did not really want the pregnancy at that time. His premature birth and stay in the incubator had likely created considerable anxiety in his mother, which caused her to be overly indulgent at times and somewhat cold and indifferent at other times. Sam felt that she continued to communicate her ambivalence toward him in various ways throughout his childhood.

This experience with his mother had a profound impact on the formulation of Sam's personality. He felt extremely close and loving to his mother at some times;

at other times, he felt quite angry with her and had difficulty controlling his rage. This experience of closeness and distance with his mother was certainly perpetuated in his marriage because he had no other role model and knew no other way to relate to females. Either the marriage was extremely good with a tremendous amount of closeness, love, and sexual compatibility; or there was anger, distance, coldness, aloofness, and some instances of outright punitiveness on his part toward his wife. Sally had a great deal of difficulty handling these unpredictable mood swings.

Sally grew up in somewhat different circumstances. While Sam was the oldest of two sons in his family, Sally was the fourth of five children. Being so far down the line of children, she spent a great deal of time and energy trying to get her parents' attention, especially her father's. She did this by excelling at school, in sports, and at work on the farm, in some ways filling the role of a son. She idolized her father greatly and tried both consciously and unconsciously to win his affirmation and approval.

Sam and Sally were attracted to each other in several areas. Sam came from a family that expressed a wide range of feelings, especially intense anger and negative feelings, while Sally came from a family that did not express strong feelings. Sally was an achiever, especially academically, while Sam was more easygoing and relaxed. They shared a strong sense of humor and a love for sports. No ethnic or cultural conflicts were evidenced.

In this intake material, we see what each individual brought to the marital relationship. Both brought the patterns and processes from their families of origin plus unresolved issues. These unre-

solved issues obviously began to surface in the marital relationship and ultimately led to a considerable amount of pain, turmoil, and conflict. Some personalities are more integrated and differentiated than others; the more integrated and differentiated, the less family of origin material needs to be worked through in the marital relationship. Each individual then can pursue his or her own professions or interests, and less psychic energy is needed in working on the marital relationship. Consequently, treatment is designed to help sort out many of the issues that each individual brings to the marriage. In this case, the underlying processes of splitting, introjection, projective identification, and collusion as they are manifested in Sam and Sally's relationship needed to be addressed within the context of a therapeutic centered holding environment.

Process of Treatment

One of the first issues that needed to be resolved was that of Sam's handling his anger more effectively. Sam always said it was his wife who activated his anger; however, it was actually the unresolved issues of early deprivation and his resulting rage toward his mother that were manifested through the splitting of the good-mother/bad-mother introject. The bad-mother image was projected onto Sally. Her collusion was shown through her withdrawal when he became angry, thus becoming "the depriving mother," and through her constant search for ways not to activate his anger, thus assuming all the responsibility for his wrath. The working-through process was considerably time-consuming and painful as Sam began to relive many of the negative aspects of his relationship with his mother. He felt caught in a terrible bind. On one hand, he loved his mother deeply; on the other, he was extremely angry with her. He hated many aspects of his mother's personality and the way she had dealt with him.

As one reviews these experiences, one becomes quite aware of the multigenerational transmission process. Sam's mother acted out many of the issues that she brought from her own family of origin and projected them onto Sam. Sam in turn carried on the same process in his relationship with his wife. Our challenge was to help him work through that anger and to intervene so that the process would not be projected onto the next generation.

The following incident illustrates the typical splitting, projection, and collusion process in Sam and Sally's relationship. Sally was going to town to buy groceries. On her way out, Sam requested that she pick up some bird seed that he usually purchased from a particular store. It was during the Christmas holidays, and Sally was falling behind in her schedule. Therefore, rather than taking an extra 10 or 15 minutes to go to this particular store, she saw bird seed at a good price in the same store where she was shopping so bought a bag there. When she gave the bird seed to Sam, he immediately saw that it was not the brand he usually bought and became intensely angry. He accused her of purposely buying seed that he did not like in order to upset him. He examined the bag and found many things about the bird seed that he felt were unacceptable. This triggered anger in Sally. In order to preserve peace in the family, she got back in the car and returned to the store to buy the other bird seed, which took up an additional 30 minutes of her time. When this issue was shared in therapy in an effort to try and understand the dynamics,

the projection process was apparent. Sam was dealing with his feelings of being betrayed and deprived by his mother, whom he felt deliberately went out of her way to do things that hurt him. The other dynamic was that Sally fell into the trap of the projection process in which she fulfilled the role of his expectations. He really did not believe she would do what he asked her to anyway. This deprivation-betrayal scenario was obviously played out in many forms. Sam was basically working out his relationship and unfinished business with his mother through his wife. She unwittingly colluded and fulfilled the role of his punitive mother.

During the therapeutic process, Sam was encouraged to obtain more information regarding his family of origin. It seemed appropriate that he spend time with his parents inquiring about some of the issues of his parent's relationship and maybe what went on between his parents and their parents. Sam tried to obtain information from his mother, but she was never very enthusiastic about sharing information regarding her own family of origin. She would only allude to growing up in a very fine family where there was little conflict. Sam turned to his father to ask if he knew very much about his mother's family. His father told him that after having dated for approximately 1 year, he had asked his prospective wife to marry him. She had been ambivalent regarding marrying him and a few days later sent his father a letter in which she shared some very important and pertinent information—namely, that her father had at one time become involved in bootlegging and had been arrested, tried, convicted, and sentenced to the state prison. Sam's mother had never visited her father in prison, although her mother had continued to be very devoted to him. It was so embarrassing to Sam's mother that she never even talked about it. To Sam's knowledge, it was never mentioned again during the whole 50 years of his parent's marriage.

When Sam learned of this, he immediately began to connect childhood incidents when his mother became extremely angry about the resistance he had toward her instructions. When this resistance was acted out, she accused him of being a criminal and predicted that his life would end in the penal system. She would specifically say, "You're going to end up in the chain gang." Therefore, we can see some of the splitting in her own struggles in which she projected the negative images of her father onto Sam and the positive images onto Sam's brother. This whole splitting issue could be easily traced through the multigenerational process where good and bad were divided and in many instances never integrated. The unwitting victim of the projective identification process is either all good or all bad, with very little room for anything in between.

Over a period of 2 years, Sam's anger level diminished. Sam was able to articulate more accurately his anger toward his wife without acting it out. He became much more aware that many of the issues he struggled with were really issues between him and his mother. As Sally became more aware of her extreme need to have Sam's approval, much as she had needed her father's approval, she gradually became less dependent on Sam for validation. She also learned to be less reactive to Sam's anger, to detach from the projective process, and to take responsibility only for her own reactions and behaviors. She concluded that Sam's anger was not related to what she did or did not do but could be imposed on any situation.

Sam seemed to have focused more of his anger on his wife and less on his children. This had not been true with his mother, who had focused considerable anger on her children and less on her companion, which was done in order to maintain the marriage. Sam and Sally's two children were brought into the sessions periodically. They performed well in school and evidenced no problems.

The reliving and working through of such painful material would not have taken place outside the safe, caring holding environment created by the therapists. By utilizing transference and countertransference processes, the therapists linked the past with the present, particularly the ways the past was being acted out interpersonally in ongoing family relationships. After staying in treatment for a period of 2 years and then periodically over the next 5 years, Sam and Sally had come to understand their underlying dynamics, had developed some controls for Sam's anger (which was triggered by feelings of deprivation and betrayal), and were continuing to monitor their own projection and collusion processes.

EVALUATION

Object relations family therapists generally rely on subjective assessment by therapists and clients of the effectiveness of the treatment. Because symptom reduction is not the goal of this model, it cannot serve as the measure of effectiveness. The presence or absence of unconscious conflict, since it is not apparent to family members or outside observers, is difficult to measure. Therefore, assessment of effectiveness depends on the subjective clinical judgment of the therapist and on the family's reactions.

But are these measures sufficient for this generation's focus on scientific evidence and cost-effectiveness? Previous psychoanalytic therapists have answered yes. Clinicians consider the therapist's observations to be entirely valid as a means of evaluating theory and treatment. The Blancks (1972), in regard to Margaret Mahler's methods and model, state, "Clinicians who employ her theories technically question neither the methodology nor the findings, for they can confirm them clinically, a form of validation that meets as closely as possible the experimentalist's insistence upon replication as criterion of the scientific method" (p. 675). Along the same lines, Langs (1982) states that the ultimate test of a therapist's formulation is in his use of these impressions as a basis for intervention. He goes on to state that the patient's reactions, conscious and unconscious, constitute the ultimate litmus test of these interventions and that true validation involves both cognitive and interpersonal responses from the patient.

Eminent object relations family therapists hold similar views. Slipp (1988) states that meeting the goals of treatment is the criterion that both the family and therapist use to consider ending treatment. These general goals, as previously discussed, do not lend themselves to empirical measurement but to subjective assessment by therapists and families. The Scharffs (1987) state that at termination, the family can provide the contextual and centered holding for the members that are so necessary for attachment and growth. The family is able to return to or reach an appropriate developmental level, so that they fit with the individuals' developmental needs for intimacy and autonomy. Slipp (1988) further describes the end result as the restructuring of the internal world of object relations with resultant modification of the family's interpersonal relations.

The self is experienced as separate and less dependent on external objects to sustain self-esteem and identity, and the family will be able to function as a group in a more intimate and adaptive fashion that meets each member's needs.

Typically, outcome reports are primarily uncontrolled case studies. However, Dicks (1967) reported on a survey of the outcome of couples therapy at the Tavistock Clinic. He rated as having been successfully treated 72.8% of a random sample of cases. Others have investigated specific tenets of the ORFT theory. For example, Slipp (1984) conducted a controlled clinical research study of some of the factors involved in the intergenerational transmission of psychopathology. Using 9 children of Nazi Holocaust survivors as subjects, he employed questionnaires, scales, and other standardized inventories plus a structured clinical interview. His findings provide further empirical evidence to attempt to validate the existence of a double bind on achievement in the families of depressives.

SUMMARY

Object relations family therapy bridges the gap between the psychoanalytic study and treatment of individuals, and systems understanding of family development and interactions and family therapy. Most of the pioneers of the family therapy movement had training in psychoanalytic theory and have retained at least some of these concepts in developing their models. While object relations family therapy has had no overall integrated theory, much work has been done toward integration by the Scharffs, Slipp, Stewart, Finkelstein, and others.

Major concepts used in object relations family therapy include splitting, introjection, projective identification, collusion, ego identity, the holding environment, transference, countertransference, and isomorphisms. This model of working with families has been found to be effective with blue-collar as well as middle-class families and others who are interested in understanding and not simply resolving symptoms. It is not recommended for low–socioeconomic class families with problems requiring more immediate help and concrete services.

Object relations family therapy fosters a type of meaningful shared intimacy that respects one another's individuality. The therapist creates a therapeutic holding environment within which change takes place. He or she works with projective identification among family members, on a multigenerational level and within the transference and countertransference phenomena. Goals and readiness for termination as well as effectiveness of outcome are generally determined subjectively by the therapist and family.

ANNOTATED SUGGESTED READINGS

Dicks, H. V. (1963). Object relations theory and marital status. *British Journal of Medical Psychology, 36*, 125–129.

A classic article that extends the object relations theory of Klein, Fairbairn, and Guntrip to the study of marital relationships. Dicks discusses marriage as a mutual process of attribution or projection, with each spouse seen to a degree as an internal object.

Dicks, H. V. (1967). *Marital tensions*. New York: Basic Books.

Dicks applies Fairbairn's object relations concepts to the understanding and treatment of marital dysfunction in this important volume.

Fairbairn, W. R. D. (1952). *An object-relations theory of the personality*. New York: Basic Books.

A seminal work in object relations theory that has had a significant influence on the later work of Dicks, Bowen, Framo, and others. Required reading for those interested in the role of object relations in psychopathology.

Finkelstein, L. (1987). Toward an object-relations approach in psychoanalytic marital therapy. *Journal of Marital and Family Therapy, 13* (3), 287–298.

Describes the features that distinguish psychoanalytic marital therapy from other forms of marital therapy and how object relations theories can be applied to psychoanalytic marital therapy, as well as certain directions for further study.

Scharff, D. E., & Scharff, J. S. (1987). *Object relations family therapy*. Northvale, NJ: Jason Aronson.

Represents the Scharffs' efforts to develop a psychoanalytic object relations approach to families and family therapy. They demonstrate that object relations theory provides the theoretical framework for understanding and the language for working with the dynamics of both the individual and the family system.

Scharff, J. S. (Ed.) (1989). *Foundations of object relations family therapy*. Northvale, NJ: Jason Aronson.

The aim of this book is to reveal the development of object relations from its roots in object relations theory and to indicate its current directions.

Slipp, S. (1984). *Object relations: A dynamic bridge between individual and family treatment*. New York: Jason Aronson.

The pioneer of the clinical application of object relations family therapy in the U.S. develops a typology of family interaction that takes into account the intrapsychic influences on family patterns, which in turn affects the patient's personality. Slipp describes how ob-

ject relations theory can be used to provide an encompassing framework for individual and family treatment and integrates the two fields.

Slipp, S. (1988). *The technique and practice of object relations family therapy*. Northvale, NJ: Jason Aronson.

Extends the clinical application of object relations family therapy that Slipp began in his earlier book. He further develops the application of his family typology to the treatment process with specific attention to techniques and process.

REFERENCES

Balint, M. (1968). *The basic fault: Therapeutic aspects of regression*. London: Tavistock.

Barnard, C. P., & Corrales, R. G. (1979). *The theory and technique of family therapy*. Springfield, IL: Charles C. Thomas.

Bion, W. R. (1961). *Experiences in groups and other papers*. London: Tavistock.

Blanck, G., & Blanck, R. (1972). Toward a psychoanalytic developmental psychology. *Journal of the American Psychoanalytic Association, 20*, 668–710.

Boszormenyi-Nagy, I. (1967). Relational modes and meaning. In G. H. Zuk & I. Boszormenyi-Nagy (Eds.), *Family therapy and disturbed families*. Palo Alto, CA: Science and Behavior Books.

Boszormenyi-Nagy, I., & Spark, G. (1973). *Invisible loyalties*. New York: Harper & Row.

Bowen, M. (1965). Family psychotherapy with schizophrenia in the hospital and in private practice. *Comprehensive Psychiatry, 7*, 345–374.

Bowen, M. (1978). *Family theory in clinical practice*. New York: Jason Aronson.

Brenner, C. (1973). *An elementary textbook of psychoanalysis*. New York: International Universities Press.

Breuer, J. & Freud, S. (1895). Studies on hysteria. In *The standard edition of the complete psychological works of*

Sigmund Freud (Vol. 2, pp. 1–307). London: Hogarth Press [1955].

Brill, A. A. (1938). *The basic writings of Sigmund Freud*. New York: The Modern Library.

Buber, M. (1958). *I and Thou*. New York: Scribner.

Dicks, H. V. (1963). Object relations theory and marital studies. *British Journal of Medical Psychology, 36*, 125–129.

Dicks, H. V. (1967). *Marital tensions*. New York: Basic Books.

Erikson, E. H. (1963). *Childhood and society*. New York: Norton.

Erikson, E. H. (1956). The problem of ego identity. *Journal of the American Psychoanalytic Association, 4*, 56–121.

Fairbairn, W. (1954). *An object-relations theory of personality*. New York: Basic Books.

Ferenczi, S. (1920). The further development of an active therapy in psychoanalysis. In *Further contributions to the theory and technique of psychoanalysis*. London: Hogarth Press.

Finkelstein, L. (1987). Toward an object-relations approach in psychoanalytic marital therapy. *Journal of Marital and Family Therapy, 13*(3), 287–298.

Foley, V. D. (1974). *An introduction to family therapy*. New York: Grune & Stratton.

Framo, J. L. (1970). Symptoms from a family

transactional viewpoint. In N. W. Ackerman (Ed.), *Family therapy in transition.* Boston: Little, Brown.

Framo, J. L. (1972). Symptoms from a family transactional viewpoint. In N. W. Ackerman, N. Lielg, & J. Pearce (Eds.), *Family therapy in transition.* New York: Springer.

Freud, S. (1905). Fragment of an analysis of a case of hysteria. In *Collected papers.* New York: Basic Books.

Freud, S. (1940). An outline of psychoanalysis. In *The standard edition of the complete psychological works of Sigmund Freud* (Vol. 23, pp. 139–171). London: Hogarth Press.

Gilligan, C. (1982). *In a different voice.* Cambridge, MA: Harvard University Press.

Guntrip, H. (1961). *Personality structure and human interaction: The developing synthesis of psychodynamic theory.* London: Hogarth Press and the Institute of Psychoanalysis.

Hofstadter, D. R. (1979). *Godel, Escher, Bach: An eternal golden braid.* New York: Basic Books.

Kernberg, O. F. (1975). *Borderline conditions and pathological narcissism.* New York: Jason Aronson.

Kernberg, O. F. (1976). *Object relations theory and clinical psychoanalysis.* New York: Jason Aronson.

Kernberg, O. F. (1972). Early ego integration and object relations. *Annals of the New York Academy of Science, 193,* 233–247.

Klein, M. (1946). Notes on some schizoid mechanisms. *International Journal of Psycho-Analysis, 27,* 99–110.

Klein, M. (1948). *Contributions to psychoanalysis, 1921–1945.* London: Hogarth Press and the Institute of Psychoanalysis.

Kohut, H. (1984). *How does analysis cure?* Chicago: University of Chicago Press.

Langs, R. (1982). *Psychotherapy: A basic text.* New York: Jason Aronson.

Lidz, T., Cornelison, A., Fleck, S. & Terry, D. (1957). The intrafamilial environment of schizophrenic patients; II: Marital schism and marital skew. *American Journal of Psychiatry, 114,* 241–248.

Luepnitz, D. A. (1988). *The family interpreted: Feminist theory in clinical practice.* New York: Basic Books.

Mahler, M. S. (1952). On child psychosis and schizophrenia: Autistic and symbiotic infantile psychoses. In *Psychoanalytic study of the child,* Vol. 7, pp. 286–305. New Haven, CT: Yale University Press.

Meissner, W. W. (1978). The conceptualization of marriage and family dynamics from a psychoanalytic perspective. In T. J. Paolino & B. S. McCrady, *Marriage and marital therapy.* New York: Brunner/Mazel.

Nichols, M. (1984). *Family therapy: Concepts and methods.* New York: Gardner Press.

Piercy, F. P., Sprenkle, D. H., et al. (1986). *Family therapy sourcebook.* New York: Guilford Press.

Sampson, H. & Weiss, J. (1977). Research on the psychoanalytic process: An overview. *The Psychotherapy Research Group,* Bulletin No. 2 (March), Department of Psychiatry, Mt. Zion Hospital and Medical Center.

Scharff, D. E. (1982). *The sexual relationship: An object relations view of sex and the family.* Boston: Routledge & Kegan Paul.

Scharff, D. E., & Scharff, J. S. (1987). *Object relations family therapy.* Northvale, NJ: Jason Aronson.

Scharff, J. S. (Ed.) (1989). *Foundations of object relations family therapy.* Northvale, NJ: Jason Aronson.

Segal, H. (1973). *Introduction to the work of Melanie Klein.* New enlarged edition. London: Hogarth Press.

Simon, F. B., Stierlin, H., & Wynne, L. C. (1985). *The language of family therapy: A systemic vocabulary and sourcebook.* New York: Family Process Press.

Slipp, S. (1984). *Object relations: A dynamic bridge between individual and family treatment.* New York: Jason Aronson.

Slipp, S. (1988). *The technique and practice*

of object relations family therapy. Northvale, NJ: Jason Aronson.

Stewart, R. H., Peters, T. C., Marsh, S., & Peters, M. J. (1975, June). An object-relations approach to psychotherapy with marital couples, families and children. *Family Process, 14(2)*, 161–178.

Stierlin, H. (1976). The dynamics of owning and disowning: Psychoanalytic and family perspectives. *Family Process, 15(3)*, 277–288.

Vogel, E. F., & Bell, N. W. (1960). The emotionally disturbed as the family scapegoat. In N. W. Bell & E. F. Vogel (Eds.), *The family*. Glencoe, IL: Free Press.

Winnicott, D. W. (1958). *Collected papers: Through pediatrics to psycho-analysis*. London: Hogarth Press.

Winnicott, D. W. (1965). *The maturational processes and the facilitation of environment*. London: Hogarth Press.

Wynne, L. C. (1965). Some indications and contraindications for exploratory family therapy. In I. Boszormenyi-Nagy & J. L. Franco (Eds.), *Intensive family therapy*. New York: Hoeber.

Wynne, L., Ryckoff, I., Day, J., & Hirsch, S. (1958). Pseudomutuality in the family relations of schizophrenics. *Psychiatry, 21*, 205–220.

CHAPTER 9

Evolving Milan Approaches to Family Therapy

REECE CHANEY

DEFINITION

The "Milan" approach to family therapy has become synonymous with Mara Selvini Palazzoli, Luigi Boscolo, Gianfranco Cecchin, and Giuiana Prata. These individuals were longtime partners and formed the original team of collaborators who pioneered systems approaches to family therapy research. Their approach to family therapy has been an evolving process that started in the 1960s and continues today.

This group of partners were scientist-practitioners who specialized in research in the area of discovering new techniques that were appropriate for treating mentally ill patients and their families. Although they did discover many techniques that were workable, they were not satisfied until their research results supported them. Many techniques and approaches were tried and later abandoned for lack of support.

The ability to change, to abandon previously held beliefs, and to look for new methods has been a hallmark of the Milan teams.

The original group of collaborators split into two teams in 1979. Their approaches continue to be very similar in many ways; however, each team has pursued a somewhat different direction. Selvini Palazzoli and Prata worked together at refining the earlier approaches and developing and researching new ideas. In 1985, Selvini Palazzoli began working with a new team, including Stefano Cirillo, Matteo Selvini (her son), and Anna Maria Sorrentino. Boscolo and Cecchin have worked together devoting most of their energies to training teams located in Europe and America.

HISTORICAL DEVELOPMENT

Selvini Palazzoli was the founder and organizer of the Milan team. Like many of the modern founders of family therapy, Selvini Palazzoli was trained in psychoanalysis. She received her early training in internal medicine, where the encounters with anorectic patients convinced her to reconsider her career goals and thus to become a psychiatrist (Selvini, 1988). As a psychiatrist, she delved into the treatment of anorexia with great interest, a fascination lasting throughout her career. One important article that reflected her early work was "Anoressia Mentale," published in 1963. Although Selvini Palazzoli reported that she was very competent in the treatment of these patients during her early years, she soon developed an uneasiness about the number of sessions that were necessary (often 400–600) and the duration of treatment (as many as 5–7 years) in relation to the very meager success rate (most patients had a quick relapse even though they had been thought to be cured). Furthermore, her research failed to support the effectiveness of her approach.

Selvini Palazzoli proved to be an eager learner whose search for innovative ways to understand and improve her work was influenced by several new ideas emerging in the United States and Europe during the 1960s. Object relations theory focused attention on transference and countertransference and a dyadic relational interpretation over the previous preference of a theory based on intrapsychic dynamics. Phenomenologists (such as Buber, known for "I" and "Thou"), whose interest in existential analysis stressed the importance of remaining in the present, appeared to be of central importance to Selvini Palazzoli's studies in human communication. New developments emerging in the profession and a strong dissatisfaction with many of the individual theories led her to abandon her original approach in favor of an experimental style to conjoint family therapy.

The Communication Era

Selvini Palazzoli founded the Center for Family Studies in 1967, which organized the base from which decades of research and study would result. Boscolo, Cecchin, Prata, and three other psychiatrists trained in psychoanalysis joined with Selvini Palazzoli to start the Center. The team attempted to use psychoanalytic principles with the new communicationalists ideas. The new communicationalists were advocating that styles of communication were central to many problems. Wynne and Singer (1963) described the style and method of communication used by families that had a schizophrenic member. Bateson, a British anthropologist and pioneer of the application of cybernetics to human sciences, investigated the general nature of communication in terms of logical levels. He maintained that paradoxes generated in the layered structure of human communication threaten the foundations of

human behavior, thus causing it to become pathological (Bateson, 1972). Mental disturbance was viewed as the result of confusion, ambiguity, dissimulation, misinterpretation, contradiction, and paradoxical elements in family communication (Selvini, 1988). For quite some time, communications theory was viewed as a means to understand the etiology of the identified patient.

The central element in the communicationalist approach is the belief that correct communication can be taught. The therapist is viewed as a teacher in a very special sense. After a few years the attempt at the communicationlist approach was abandoned in favor of a nonanalytic approach. Several of the team members disagreed with this decision and departed, leaving Selvini Palazzoli, Boscolo, Cecchin, and Prata to carry out the new approach.

This new team made a profound commitment to abandon most of their previous training and devoted themselves to finding a better method on their own. They ignored other family therapists, deciding that their own research results would guide their approach. They made a commitment to devote 2 days a week to the Center with no financial compensation. They avoided all training activities because they believed that it was detrimental to their research goals. For years they worked in isolation reading, studying, and conducting their research with the families that came to the Center for therapy.

Systemic Beginnings

The team came across what was to be a most significant book in shaping their thinking, *Pragmatics of Human Communication* by Watzlawick, Beavin, and Jackson (1967). These authors, along with Bateson and Jay Haley, were involved in studies at the Mental Research Institute (MRI) in Palo Alto, California. The discovery of Bateson's ideas proved to be one of the most significant contributions. Various members of the team have often said that Bateson's' influence was the single most important factor in shaping their efforts (Boscolo, Cecchin, Hoffman, & Penn, 1987). Bateson's (1972) book, *Steps to an Ecology of Mind*, led the team to adopt a systemic way of thinking. They undertook a difficult task—not only to understand the systemic way of thinking but also to apply it and to invent systemic interventions, systemic rituals, systemic comments, and other related strategies (Barrows, 1982).

The MRI ideas were appealing to the team because they were congruent with their own views. In particular, they agreed that the notion of the "identified patient" as the family member with the pathology was a rather limited perspective. The Milan group presented the argument that the relationship context in which the problem behaviors took place was the more important point of focus. If the family interactional patterns could change, the problem behavior could also change.

Paradox and Counterparadox

For a time, between 1972 and 1975, the team operated from the theory that pathology was derived essentially from Bateson's double-bind communication theory (i.e., self-contradictory messages from parent to child: "stay away closer"). A *double-bind* is a situation in which no matter what a person does, he can't win (Bateson, Jackson, Haley, & Weakland, 1956). Bateson and his coauthors provided a very good example of a double-bind: A mother visited her schizophrenic son in the hospital, and when he reached to hug her she stiffened. At this, he backed away. His mother asked, "Don't you love me anymore?" When his face turned red, she said, "You should not get embarrassed so easily."

The team took some of the methods pioneered by the MRI and expanded them. They incorporated the therapeutic double-bind, calling it *counterparadox*. The publication of *Paradox and Counterparadox* (Selvini Palazzoli, Boscolo, Cecchin, & Prata, 1978) was a culmination of years of research and study of this method.

Adopting an MRI procedure, the group utilized an observing team behind a one-way mirror. Initially, a male-female therapist team conducted the interview while a male-female observer team watched from behind the screen. The therapists were called out when deemed appropriate, and a discussion ensued around the observations of both groups. This was particularly important at this point because a great deal of time and energy was taken up trying to figure out how to keep the family from rendering the team powerless.

While the family seemed especially adept at confusing and confounding the therapist, the team was equally determined to figure out how to avoid the traps and snares of the family. The "paradoxical prescription," a strategy popularized by Haley, was chosen because, as he maintained, there was no way a family could resist a therapist who told them to continue with those behaviors they were already engaged in unless, of course, they were to give up those behaviors. It was thought that families entered treatment with a double-level paradoxical message: "Please change us"/"Don't you dare try to change us." The paradoxical message from the therapist was "Don't change whatever you do!"

During this particular era (which appeared to favor more strategic styles), the team provided the family with a paradoxical prescription at the end of the session. The family might be told to continue with the symptom because it was helpful to the whole family; this is termed *positive connotation*. For example, in a family where Diane is refusing to eat and the parents have tried everything possible to convince her to eat, the family may be told to stop their efforts because the daughter is expressing something very important. The family needs to have this problem at this time. Further, the family should view this problem as something that needs no changing. They may be prescribed a ritual where each family member would be directed to thank the identified patient at dinner each evening for having this problem because of its benefit to the speaker. As Selvini Palazzoli et al. (1978) described the logic in the use of the counterparadox, "...our research has shown how the family in schizophrenic transaction sustains its game through an intricacy of paradoxes which can only be undone by counterparadoxes in the contest of therapy" (p. 8).

Positive connotation was another significant invention of the Milan team. According to Selvini Palazzoli et al. (1978), positive connotation was inspired by the need not to contradict themselves when giving a paradoxical prescription. The practice of positively connotating negative behavior to a positive purpose often resulted in the family becoming angry and leaving therapy. To tell a couple that their child had taken up sickness as a means of protecting the marital couple was met with considerable anger. In the

end, the team decided to connote positively not only the behavior of the identified patient but also the symptomatic behavior of the other family members. In so doing, the therapists were dealing with the entire system on an equal basis. They explained to the family that even the most simple problematic symptom was in the service of the family's well-being. Blame was not placed on any member so that assuming fault could be avoided.

The practice of maintaining neutrality became an essential element in the therapist's behavior. To remain neutral, the therapist behaves in such a way so individuals do not feel as if the therapist has taken sides but is impartial in treating the family members. The principle of neutrality is one factor in the redefinition of positive connotation. A redefinition of a "sacrificial" behavior of one member to a more family-oriented statement of the problem eliminated the possibility of placement of individual guilt.

In *Steps to the Ecology of the Mind* (Bateson 1972), the Milan group was intrigued by the notion of cybernetic circularity as a model for living systems. From this concept the team developed another very effective strategy, "circularity" or circular questioning. Circular questions are based on the premise that living systems are characterized by loop formations rather than by linear sequences of cause and effect (Boscolo et al., 1987).

Hypothesizing, Circularity, and Neutrality

Bateson's ideas helped the team develop a set of procedures that revolutionized their methods. Translating Bateson's cybernetic circularity into the day-to-day work of consulting with families resulted in a significant article, "Hypothesizing-Circularity-Neutrality: Three Guidelines for the Conductor of the Session" (Selvini Palazzoli, Boscolo, Cecchin, & Prata, 1980). Hypothesizing translated the concept into an assessment process; circular questioning translated it into an interviewing technique; and neutrality translated it into a basic therapeutic stance (Boscolo et al, 1987).

The previous strategy, outlined in *Paradox and Counterparadox* (Selvini Palazzoli et al., 1978), had placed the family and the team as adversaries, as though they were involved in guerilla warfare. The team had to strip the family of all their secrets. In some ways the team seemed to have been involved in a rather peculiar game with the family, each making moves and countermoves designed to keep the other at bay. In the end, there was little research evidence to support counterparadox as an effective and viable strategy.

Hypothesizing. Since the Milan center was a small, private clinic, their clients were usually referred by other physicians. From the referrals the group possessed a certain amount of information that was combined with additional data provided by telephone contact. It was the habit of the team to meet prior to the session and review the case at hand. In their review of information, they discussed the various aspects of the case and presented ideas freely among themselves. Eventually they would arrive at a hypothesis about the family pathology.

Just as is the case in other fields of science, a hypothesis for the team represented a supposition to be tested as a basis for further investigation. By definition a hypothesis, however stated, would never imply truth; it acts as a means of collecting information. Hypotheses are developed based on information the team has on hand about the family, coupled with the knowledge of families gathered over years of research, study, and observation. The establishment of hypotheses provides the basis for testing suppositions about the family and gathering additional information from which further hypotheses might result.

When the family arrived for the session, the team was already prepared to begin the process of testing their hypotheses. If the hypotheses proved false, the team would have gathered significant new information. It was not important if the initial hypothesis was supported because a new hypothesis would be possible given new information provided in the testing of the previous hypothesis. New hypotheses were formulated and tested until they had finally verified the hypothesis that accounted for the family situation.

The functional value of the hypothesis in the family interview is substantially that of guaranteeing the activity of the therapist, which consists in the tracking of relational patterns. It is quite probable that such patterns are provoked and brought into the open by the active behavior of the therapist....The hypothesis of the therapist...introduces the powerful input of the unexpected and the improbable into the family system and for this reason acts to avoid derailment and disorder. (Selvini Palazzoli et al., p. 5)

The hypothesis provides the therapist the opportunity to test out suppositions. Furthermore, it allows the therapist to unbalance the system with unexpected information the therapist was able to provide the family.

The team is consistent in their belief that the hypothesis must be systemic if it is to be useful. A systemic hypothesis requires that the team be particularly sensitive to the deeper levels of family involvement. The more effectively the hypothesis is formulated with regard to deeper systemic issues-games, the more potential exists for the family to change.

Circularity. Based on Bateson's (1972) concept regarding differences, the Milan team developed their views of circularity:

That which we call circularity is therefore our consciousness, or better yet, our conviction of being able to obtain from the family authentic information only if we work with the following fundamentals:
1. Information is a difference.
2. Difference is a relationship (or a change in a relationship). (Selvini Palazzoli et al., 1980, p. 8)

They further elaborated: "By circularity we mean the capacity to conduct his investigation on the basis of feedback from the family in response to the information he solicits about relationships and, therefore, about difference and change" (p. 8).

Every member of the family is invited to explain how he or she sees a particular relationship. For example, a daughter is asked to talk (metacommunicate) about the relationship between her father and brother. It is far less threatening than asking the father or brother directly. The daughter or others that are asked often provide information that is instructive, both to the therapist and to the father or the rest of the family. This new information provides the basis for additional circular questions in the same manner. The therapist is never at a loss for information because the circular questions provide a continual flow of new information about relationships.

Selvini Palazzoli et al. (1980) express the advantages of circular questions:

What is perhaps less obvious is the extreme efficiency of this technique in initiating a vortex of responses in the family that greatly illuminate the various triadic relationships. In fact, by formally inviting one member of the family to metacommunicate about the relationship of two others, in their presence, we are not only breaking one of the ubiquitous rules of dysfunctional families, but we are also conforming to the first axiom of the pragmatics of human communication: In a situation of interaction, the various participants, try as they might, cannot avoid communicating. (p. 8)

The team developed five practical methods that have proven to be very valuable in soliciting information (Boscolo et al., 1987):

1. Specific interactive behaviors in specific circumstances. Example:
    (*T*) When Mary refuses to get out of bed what does your mother do? How does your mother react to what he does?
2. Differences in behavior and not in terms of predicates supposedly intrinsic to the person. Example:
    (*C*) When my sister comes home she is a real pain.
    (*T*) What does your sister do that makes her a pain?
    (*C*) She manipulates my parents.
    (*T*) Who does she manipulate the most, your mother or your father?
    (*C*) Well, Mother of course.
    (*T*) Who gets most upset when your sister manipulates your mother, your father or your mother?
    (*C*) My father. He seems to have this thing with my sister.
3. Ranking by various members of the family of a specific behavior or a specific interaction. Example:
    (*T*) Your mother seems to be depressed a great deal. Ranking your family from most

to least, how helpful is each family member in cheering Mother up?

4. Change in the relationship before or after a precise event. Example:

   (*T*) Did your brother and sister fight more before or after your grandfather moved into the house?

5. Differences in respect to hypothetical circumstances. Example:

   (*T*) If one of the children were to have to take care of you, should you both become incapacitated, who would be best for Mother? Who would be best for Father?

The use of these methods in circular questioning allows the therapist to avoid the inevitable quagmire resulting when the therapist allows the family members to present their story, one member at a time. Instead, the therapist avoids all such pitfalls by directing the session toward relationships. Each member reacts to a symptom, and each of the other members thus provide their reaction to previous reactions. By developing a broad perspective of family interactions, the therapist is able to enlarge the field of relationships and to discover an increasingly sharper image of the family pathology.

Neutrality. By neutrality the team suggests that the therapist assumes a therapeutic posture that puts him or her in direct contact or interaction with every member of the family. At one point, the therapists may appear to be aligned with one family member while that member is being addressed; but as soon as the emphasis shifts to another, the alignment also varies. The example used by the team is that if a family were

to be asked to state whom the therapist had sided with or supported, the family would remain puzzled or uncertain (Selvini Palazzoli et al., 1980). Neutrality is enhanced by the use of circular questioning because the focus is constantly changing and the information under consideration was introduced directly or indirectly by the family. The therapist wants to obtain information and solicit feedback. There is no interest in directing the family to take certain actions except those related to their openings, which they provide in their responses.

The goal of these strategies is to assist the therapist to obtain sufficient information about the family relational modality so that the therapist, and team, can develop interventions, comments, simple prescriptions, ritualized prescriptions, or family rituals (Selvini Palazzoli et al., 1980).

The Original Team Separates

By the time the team had published "Hypothesizing-Circularity-Neutrality" (Selvini Palazzoli et al., 1980), they had ended an era that spanned 10 years of research and study. For the most part they had been relatively isolated because they chose not to become involved in training. By the mid-70s, Boscolo and Cecchin had been somewhat more active in training activities and ended their relationship with the team a few years later to pursue training on a widespread basis. Selvini Palazzoli and Prata transferred to a new center in 1982, the New Center for Family Studies, and continued to work together until 1985 in much the same way as the original team had done; they continued to pursue research with mentally ill families as their primary objective. Boscolo and Cecchin, now calling themselves the Milan Associates, have continued as trainers and consultants to numerous groups throughout the world. Their research and therapy activities have been limited for the most part to the association with trainees with whom they work.

The Milan Associates: Boscolo and Cecchin. The approach to therapy-consultation for the Milan Associates remains very close to the work published by the team in 1980. The major changes in their approach have been instigated by their association with their trainees. Much of what had worked so well with the team in Milan proved to be most inappropriate when practiced by trainees, whose work settings were not necessarily sympathetic to working with families in the traditional Milan way. As a result of failures and considerable discouragement in applying their methods in these training situations, the Milan Associates were forced to alter their views and methods. They became more concerned with the problem of the larger systems, the systems in which the trainees were employed. They began to apply their principles of family systems therapy to the larger systems or the "significant system" (i.e., community, institutions, agencies, etc.) that interact with and impact on the family system.

Second-Order Cybernetics. A continuing interest in recent advances in cybernetic thinking in other systems led Boscolo and Cecchin to develop ideas that have been described as "second-order cybernetics" (Boscolo et al., 1987). From first-order cybernetics, the family system in trouble is seen as a homeostatic machine—the system plays an important part in maintaining the homeostasis of the family. Second-order cybernetics incorporates the idea of an observing team with the observer and the observed becoming one system. In other words, as soon as the therapist becomes involved with the family system, he or she also becomes a part of it, and as such the therapist and the observing team become part of the problem.

Actions taken on behalf of the family system are necessarily pejorative, since the therapist is now part of the system. Actions here are thought of as strategic moves on the part of the therapist to get the family to take a particular action to solve a particular problem. This becomes difficult since the therapist has decided, or has unwittingly determined with the family, what the problem might be. These kinds of actions will only lead to negative consequences such as resistance, or, worse, the therapist may have fallen into the trap of the family by working on the identified problem, which may be an effort to derail the therapy or to render the therapist impotent. Second-order cybernetics has led the Milan Associates to be conscious of their impact on the family system. Likewise, it has led them to enlarge their neutrality stance in order to avoid such problems.

Boscolo and Cecchin expanded the ideas related to hypothesizing, circularity, and neutrality (Boscolo et al., 1987; Cecchin, 1987). One particularly significant addition was the concept of curiosity. The idea was to instill curiosity in the mind of the therapist so as to allow exploration and invention of alternative views and moves, and different moves and views (Cecchin, 1987).

Based again on Bateson's (1972) premise, linear explanations have the effect of terminating dialogue and conversation. Linear explanations are concerned with cause and effect and lead the therapist into simplistic thinking, such as believing that he or she understands the basis of a problem rather than continuing to seek new meanings or relationships. Remaining neutral and curious about patterns of ideas, people, events, and behaviors allows the therapist to perturb the system in ways that are different from hindrances based on attempts to discover a correct explanation (Cecchin, 1987).

The therapist has the responsibility to help systems appear logical to the family, which implies unconditional acceptance of the family system and a constant awareness created through curiosity about family interactional patterns. While hypothesizing is dependent on information, curiosity is a means of providing even more information. Also, curiosity nurtures circularity. If a therapist is curious, he or she naturally is inclined to look for differences or relational patterns or to question premises—both those of the family as well as those of the therapist him- or herself.

Technique of Questioning. Questioning has been refined to maximize the therapist's effectiveness. Boscolo and Cecchin use circular questioning to reveal patterns and to highlight differences for the therapist as well as for the family. Different types of questions further aid the therapist in the continuing efforts to focus on differences. Some examples of questions follow:

1. Questions concerning the future— "what if" or "suppose": If your sister were to get married, who would miss her the most?
2. Hypothetical questions: Since John and Mother seem to fight on the weekends, what would happen if John were to stay at school and not come home?
3. Comparative, classification, or dif-

ferences questions: Who is the biggest pain in the neck, your brother or your sister?
4. Mind-reading questions: If I ask your father, will he agree with your sister or your mother?
5. Existential questions: Do you think it would have been better if Jane had not been born?
6. Survival questions: If your daughter leaves for college, do you think your husband will improve or be more depressed?
7. Explanatory questions: John, what do you think has kept your mother from hearing your complaints?

Such questions serve several purposes. The focus is on all family members; no one is singled out. Explanations and opinions are offered by family members and not by the therapist. Openings are provided by family members; that is, they invite the therapist to talk about certain topics or themes. Since the therapist does not ask value or moral questions or make suggestions, he or she is nonjudgmental, nonthreatening, and neutral.

The impact of this type of questioning has lessened the need for prescriptions or rituals. Circular questioning in this way has proven to provide adequate resources to the family to facilitate change.

Selvini Palazzoli and Prata. Selvini Palazzoli and Prata developed what was to be known as the "invariant prescription" in the early 1980s. It was used with virtually every family that came into therapy and is still used in many cases. For every problem presented (most with anoretic or schizophrenic patients), the parental couple was instructed to take secret vacations, starting at first with a few hours and gradually extending to weekends or weeks at a time. The vacations were unannounced and unexplained. This "prescription" proved to be very powerful, producing dramatic results even after the first attempt, and became the central focus of study for a long period.

The Invariant Prescription. Each parental couple was delivered the invariant prescription in the following manner:

Keep everything about the session absolutely secret at home. Every now and then, start going out in the evenings before dinner. Nobody must be forewarned. Just leave a written note saying, "We won't be home tonight." If, when you come back, one of your children inquires where you've been, just answer calmly, "These things concern only the two of us." Moreover, each of you will keep a notebook, carefully hidden and out of the children's reach. In these notebooks each of you, separately, will register the date and describe the verbal and nonverbal behavior of each child, or other family member, which seems to be connected with the prescription you have followed. We recommend diligence in keeping these records because it's extremely important that nothing be forgotten or omitted. Next time you will again come alone, with your notebooks, and read aloud what has happened in the meantime. (Simon 1987, p. 24)

Information obtained from the responses of family members was very telling. Often parents proclaimed their utter inability to carry it out, whereas some were able to do part but not all. Those that were able to follow through as prescribed showed a very high rate of success. The resultant information was the key to understanding the family dynamics. In addition, the invariant prescription provided a constant as a research device. All families' patterns and data could be compared based on a controlled clinical stimulus.

The basic rationale behind the prescription was based on the experiences of the team in working with mentally ill patients and their families. They had noticed an overwhelming tendency for these patients to be involved with their parents, meddling into their lives and tending to pit them against each other. Further, the blurring—or worse, the effacement—of generational dividing lines is a constant in families with severe patients (Selvini Palazzoli, Cirillo, Selvini, & Sorrentino, 1989).

After Prata separated from Selvini Palazzoli in 1985, Selvini Palazzoli joined another team that had been utilizing the same techniques. She was joined by Stefano Cirillo, Matteo Selvini, and Anna Maria Sorrentino. Their current thinking and direction is outlined in *Family games: General models of psychotic processes in the family* (Selvini Palazzoli et al., 1989).

During the work with the invariant prescription, Selvini Palazzoli et al. (1989) made this realization:

Family members who have hitherto been ignored or considered insignificant suddenly burst onto the scene with telling bits of behavior that hint at the part they may be playing in the family game. As for the game itself, pieces of the intricate puzzle will begin to take shape, even though they are still disconnected. (p. 37)

Imbroglio. Selvini Palazzoli and her new team became increasingly aware of the games that families are inevitably involved in that seemed to be significantly related to pathology. The phenomenon they called *imbroglio* was the first to emerge from their research (Selvini Palazzoli et al., 1989). Imbroglio was defined initially as a specific dyadic phenomenon, namely the deceit and betrayal the identified patient senses have been perpetrated by the most loved and trusted parent. Further study of the phenomenon, however, led them to a different definition:

Imbroglio, then is a complex interactive process that appears to arise and develop around the specific behavior tactics one of the parents brings into play. It consists of bestowing a semblance of privilege and preference upon a dyadic transgenerational (parent offspring) relationship, when, in reality, this professed rapport is a sham: It is not grounded in genuine affection and is nothing but a strategic device used against someone else—generally the other parent. (p. 68)

For tactics to work, there must be collusion. Collusion invites reactive behavior of all other family members who are actively involved in achieving his or her own objectives. Family members exchange behaviors, which influence each other. All momentous exchanges take place at an analogical (unconscious or unverbal) level where, paradoxically, there is the greatest danger of misunderstanding, denial, and disproof (Selvini Palazzoli et al., 1989).

Bateson (1972) had provided part of the understanding of the complexity of analogical communication. Unverbal and unconscious processes are at work in the processes described above and make it difficult for the therapist to understand what is going on or to find a way to intervene. Interventions, Bateson reasoned, should be carried out that were relatively unconscious and only imperfectly subject to voluntary control.

Instigation. A second phenomenon in mentally ill families discovered by the team was labeled instigation; that is, someone is instigating someone else against a third party as part of an ongoing interactional process. It implies that all members of the interaction are active

participants. This phenomenon is not limited to the nuclear family and may involve members of the extended family as well. In fact, the team checks out the possibility of instigation by members of the extended family with every family they treat. Selvini Palazzoli et al. (1989) describe the circular elements involved in instigation:

Thus, in order to tie in all the circular elements of the sequential segments that make up the phenomenon we have come to call instigation, we have had to go all the way back to the patient. To get there, we have had to blend into a single person two aspects only seemingly in contrast—namely the instigation's victim and its perpetrator. This fusion of opposites was something we became aware of once we discovered the very potent and refined means the patient would resort to in order to implement instigation. We have classified these stratagems under the loose heading of seduction. Seduction, here, applies to a vast repertoire of sophisticated bits of behavior, all of which are basically a maneuver to ingratiate oneself to someone who wants to set up against someone else. (pp. 125–126)

The Game Metaphor. Selvini Palazzoli has been quick to point out that she does not have a game theory. "Game" is used as a metaphor for an ongoing process of interactions that leads to mental illness. Games imply individual moves and countermoves. It implies individual involvement in relation to other family members. Rules of conduct and order are implied in games.

To some extent these notions go somewhat against the systemic notion. Selvini Palazzoli et al. (1989) have reemphasized their devotion to systems principles, but they seem to have moved beyond it in some ways. Their experience has convinced them that individual actions, in addition to systemic principles, must be considered as significant contributors to family dysfunction. Families come in for therapy, and games within the family can be observed. The individual move in the family game defies systemic interpretation. Individual moves are selected to promote the interests of one family member against another or others.

Parental Stalemate. A game identified by Selvini Palazzoli and her team involves rather complex interactions within the parental couple:

Our research has taught us that the disturbance with a morbid outcome is, in every case, the special game we have called the spouses' stalemate—and that game alone. In a stalemate game the two opponents, like two chess players, seem doomed to go on challenging each other endlessly. There is no way out of the deadlock. No acute crises take place in the couple's rapport, no furious cathartic scenes clear the air, no temporary separations offer respite. (Selvini Palazzoli et al., 1989, p. 164)

The couple is bound to continue the game of provoking each other, but at the same time each makes sure that nothing happens to change a thing. Moves are met with countermoves designed to prevent any real change from occurring. The homeostases of the system maintain and guarantee the continuation of this game.

Selvini Palazzoli used the term "dirty games" to describe a particularly nasty set of maneuvers that family members use to hide their coalitions and strategies for the purpose of manipulating and controlling each other. It is the responsibility of the therapist to identify and confront this game. The team is valuable in that the therapist alone would have great difficulty identifying such a perverse and well-concealed set of behaviors.

The Psychotic Process. Based on their study and observation, Selvini Palazzoli et al. (1989) proposed a six-stage psychotic process:

- *Stage 1*: The Parent Couples Stalemate.
  The existence of a game, as described above, has been put into place by the couple.
- *Stage 2*: The Son/Daughter's Involvement in the Game.
  The patient is seduced into the parents' game and unwittingly takes sides only to be betrayed by that parent.
- *Stage 3*: The Son/Daughter's Usual Behavior.
  Having "lost" in their effort to gain from the parents' stalemate the child will revert to previous behavior.
- *Stage 4*: The Trusted Ally Does a "Volte-Face."
  Often the parent sided with originally will turn on the child when the usual behavior becomes problematic. The child again is faced with "losing" and being betrayed at the same time.
- *Stage 5*: Psychosis Erupts.
  The child feels forsaken by everyone, withdraws into depression or rage.
- *Stage 6*: Symptom-Based Strategies.
  Family responses to psychotic episodes vary a great deal. What has been found is that the stalemate game has become chronic and when this happens, therapy is very difficult. Three or more individuals are always involved in the process described above, the parents and one or more children. It is described as a diachronic model—a coordinated succession of interactive behaviors involving a time factor, i.e., the time

of onset of symptoms is difficult to explain.

Early in their work, the team behaved like explorers in a new continent having no map or model to follow as a guide. It was as if a different separate hypothesis had to be developed for each family. Selvini Palazzoli now maintains that she has a general model which she applies with every family:

Now I have a general model of the game which I have to embody in the specific variables of each family. So I know that in an anorectic's family, the child thinks, "My father is such a clever man, so honest and important. My mother is such a mean woman. But he is incapable of defending himself against her. So I have to humiliate my mother because my father cannot handle her." (Simon, 1987, p. 28)

Selvini Palazzoli suggested that the model described briefly above may be her most important contribution to family therapy. At last she seems to have found a model that has proved to be satisfactory for treating mentally ill patients and their families. If history is any indication, new developments will undoubtedly be forthcoming from this dedicated researcher.

TENETS OF THE MODEL

The interest of the Milan teams has been to develop a more effective way to treat families with mentally ill patients. While the single largest group of patients has been anorexics, a wide range of mental disorders has been represented among their many patients.

Pathology that develops in an individual is viewed as a manifestation of the family system and also of a "significant system" (Boscolo et al., 1987). The significant, or larger, system includes the family, community, institutions, and organizations that impact on the family.

Pathology is a choice, a decision made in the process of interacting, interpreting, and responding to the ongoing family game. The purpose of the symptom does not achieve its goal. Instead, it further exacerbates the family situation and escalates the problem. The therapist reinforces the reality of the choice and exploits the myth inherent in maintaining the symptom.

The Milan premise is largely in line with Framo's (1965) assertion that whenever there are disturbed children there is a disturbed marriage, although all disturbed marriages do not create disturbed children.

Understanding the System

Systems, according to Bateson (1979), involve language, relationships, and interactions. Relationships are the product of interactions and differences. Limitations of our language have led us to accept linear causality. Mental processes require a more elaborate, complex, or circular chain of determination. Likewise, cybernetic explanations require much more than linear causality. Behaviors defy linear explanations and thus therapists must look for more complex explanations involving differences.

For many students of family therapy, one of the more difficult concepts to understand involves linear versus multidimensional thinking. Since our language is very linear in its structure, the information we send to our brain is determined by our language. The brain is not necessarily limited to linear processing, however. Much like the software we use in powerful computers, if the software is limited in its presentation, the computer can do little more than the software allows. Our language, with its linguistic limitations, is the software to our brain. With a more appropriate way of conceptualizing human systems and problems, we can increase the value of the software and thus allow ourselves to understand systems from a multidimensional perspective. In addition, behaviors, interactions, and patterns that we observe in family systems are generally organized in a linear fashion in our thinking; consequently, the observer is subject to the errors inherent in this limited perspective.

Bateson (1979) presented the idea that there are different levels of meanings in behavior and utilized Korzybski's dictum that "the map is not the territory" and the behavior we observe can be usefully conceptualized as information about some system of organization. All systems have ways to organize themselves. Any observable behavior is a part of a larger pattern of interactions. Thus, all behavior is information that provides clues at some level about the nature and functioning of the system.

Each family presents the therapist with conflicting sets of information. Systemic approaches commonly hold that family systems have homeostatic tendencies and are highly resistant to any form of change, whereas the Milan approach maintains that family systems are evolutionary rather than static. They are recursive in that they are constantly shifting and changing; and they are highly resistant to change from outside. Family systems are rather adept at sending out confusing, misleading messages designed to unbalance any intruder.

Much of family interaction takes place at nonverbal and unconscious levels. To expect that family members can adequately verbalize the interactions within the family is inappropriate. Verbal therapy with the development of insight as a major focus provides little help since so many interactions are not verbal or were experienced at an unconscious level. Boscolo et al. (1987) were in agreement with biologist Humberto Maturana when they wrote:

there can be no "instructive interaction," only a perturbation of a system that will then react in terms of its own structure. For this reason, interventions, whether in the form of rituals, final comments, or the interviewing process itself, are not directed toward any particular outcome but act to jog the system toward unpredictable outcomes. (p. 18)

The intent of therapy is to disrupt the homeostatic tendencies of the system by confronting them with rituals, behaviors, prescriptions, or insights that capture levels of deeper meanings within the family structure. Like the irritant to an oyster, the intruder invokes an immediate response; without the external disruption, there would be no need to develop a different response and thus no pearl. Actually, what seems to happen to many therapists is that they become assimilated by the family much as the irritant to the oyster. The team did not wish to suffer the same fate as the pearl, that is, to become neutralized. Families are very adept at taking in a therapist into their system and making him or her an accomplice to their games, even though they appear to be "good" clients in therapy.

Therapists must be constantly on their guard to avoid this trap. When a therapist agrees to conduct therapy with a patient, he or she has already become a part of that system and becomes even more involved as therapy progresses. The Milan team guarded against this by constantly monitoring the therapists in the session and by examining the ongoing relationship between the family and the therapists.

Role of Therapist

The role of the therapist is to gain an appreciation of the family system in order to come to understand the purposes of the behaviors that are observed and the various levels of communication transpiring. "The therapist tries to open up possibilities in a certain area, to disturb the thinking pattern of the system, to suggest different connections, different punctuations, and then leaves the system in that area and changes the subject completely" (Boscolo et al., 1987, p. 299). Selvini Palazzoli et al. (1989) have suggested that the goal of therapy is to instill circular epistemology into the family's dysfunctional pattern in place of their long-standing pathogenic linear epistemology. Circular epistemology introduces the family to broader relational issues and patterns that are related to the problem instead of the simple linear explanation they have developed (e.g., Carl is sick because he is weak).

Change occurs in the family system when the therapist is able to grasp and communicate, often at a metacommunication level, some significant disconfirming information relative to the family pattern, premise, or game. Family games are identified through careful observation and checking out the hypotheses made possible through observation and interaction. Selvini Palazzoli et al. (1989) have adopted a model of family games that presupposes a certain set of interactions (games) that are in operation before a family comes in for treatment:

Suppose, for example that we are starting therapy with a family whose daughter has been anorectic for several months. In line with our model, we will assume the symptom has exploded in the wake of some specific conduct of the mother's (that has aroused the girl's fury or caused her acute distress) and

that it has been strongly enhanced by an inadequate behavioral response to the mother's behavior by the girl's father. Although we obviously take into account the family's special characteristics and life events, our inquiry will head in this direction. (pp. 212–213)

Armed with the model, the therapist sets out to confront the game by revealing their secret moves and the manner in which the games are played in the relationship.

The Milan teams have always believed that families come in with "maps" of what is going on. It is the responsibility of the therapist to identify these maps and to challenge or shift them. Also, they look for a premise or myth that seemingly holds the behaviors attached to a problem in place and try to enunciate this premise or myth in their messages to the family (Boscolo et al., 1987).

Change takes place first at the individual level and then at the family level (Boscolo et al., 1987). Families change only after individuals change. This logic goes somewhat counter to systems theory, which considers change as an issue at the family system level rather than at the individual level.

Unlike other systems theories—such as the strategic, which often sets out to devise specific strategies that will lead to changes in structure of family relationships—Milan therapists maintain a posture of neutrality. They neither select goals for families, nor do they attempt to change specific behaviors of family members.

The Referring Professional

Very frequently patients were referred to the Milan team from other professionals who had been unsuccessful in treating them. The team soon learned that the referring professional was an important ingredient in the process of therapy, and they are invited to come with the family. Often the professional is in the room with the family; at other times, he or she may observe with the team behind the window. The professional receives a positive acknowledgment about his or her work with the family, being complimented, for example, on good judgment in referring the family and also in coming to the session. This is important for the professional and for the family. The belief is that the family-therapist relationship system will benefit from treatment. While the team works primarily with the family, the professional does not miss this metacommunication.

Termination

Therapy is terminated when the family has made some positive change or move. In many cases, the family makes the decision to end therapy by not returning. These decisions are not questioned in any way. When families insist that they are not ready for termination, this protestation is treated like other information. The team looks at it from the perspective of the system and treats it within that context. A family may be told that if in 6 months they still feel the same, then they might contact the center, but not before. Families are told that they have improved and that their problem no longer requires therapy—it is no longer a psychiatric problem. Therapy has been compared to unblocking a congested river: the purpose of therapy is to unclog the stream, not to follow the stream all the way to the ocean.

APPLICATION

Clients are referred to the Milan center by other professionals and sometimes by former clients. The families that are appropriate for treatment are interviewed

by phone with a rather elaborate plan for obtaining as much relevant information as possible for the team to consider before the family arrives. It has been the practice of the team to discuss the family at length and to develop hypotheses about the family functioning and the elements that seem significant in the symptomatic behavior.

The ability of the team to develop hypotheses quickly to test during therapy is related to (a) years of experience with similar families, (b) the results of studies they have conducted, and (c) the theoretical orientation they are following. Hypotheses are important since they give direction to the therapy. Once tested, they can lead to further action or be discarded in favor of a new one.

The team concept allows more than one person to be involved in the ongoing therapy process. Consultation before, during, and after the session allows for a consideration of the family from the therapist's perspective as well as that of the observing team. The observing team often is able to "see" and "hear" significant material that the therapist may have missed (e.g., the mother looks away and the son covers his ears each time the father addresses the daughter). Such information, when shared by the team, could be crucial in arriving at an understanding of the family dynamics. Thus, the observing team would call out the therapist and discuss the transactions they have observed. A new procedure might be devised, or another hypothesis might be formulated and a plan set forth to test it.

Boscolo and Cecchin's first session highlights the principles of hypothesizing, circularity, neutrality, and curiosity. Boscolo et al. (1987) use the following questions as a means of getting the interview started:

- "What is the problem now?"

- "How did you arrive at that definition?"
- "How did you decide that?"
- "Who decided that you should have a problem?"
- "Do you agree?"
- "When did you decide that you shouldn't eat?"
- "When did you decide to commit suicide?"

The purpose of these questions is to demonstrate an atmosphere of neutrality through curiosity and circular questions. This method changes the family's thinking about the symptom because it is classified as a choice both for the family and for the individual. It also suggests something about therapy: the therapist is suggesting that the family can change this symptom since they decided it was a problem, the family will not be told what to do or how they should do it, only the material the family presents will be used, and the therapist waits for openings before launching into a new area. Boscolo et al. (1987) believed that families will provide all the openings early in the session.

Openings provided by the family give permission for the therapist to proceed into new territory. They also provide important clues about family functioning that are necessary if the therapist is to gain further understanding of the problem. The first session sets the stage for the remainder of therapy. If the therapist is successful early in the session, he or she may be in a position to give the family an intervention before they are sent home. Boscolo and Cecchin prefer a ritual for the family that might go something like this: "On odd days Mother will only take care of Alice. Sally and John will not bother her on these days. Instead they will wait until another day,

or they can take their concerns to Father. On even days, Sally and John will have Mother, and Alice will not interfere in the manner we described." This type of ritual has been very successful with some cases that involve pathology growing out of games within the family that are rather difficult to deal with verbally. By interfering with the game, if the family follows the rules of the ritual, the therapist is directing a deeper communication to the family.

Subsequent sessions are often handled in a similar manner as the first depending on the nature of the family symptom, the willingness of the family to cooperate, and the ability of the therapist to understand the symptomatic behavior and to intervene or provide the family with disconfirming information. More recently, Boscolo and Cecchin have relied heavily on their stance of curiosity, neutrality, and circularity as the intervention. There is less reason to give families rituals or prescriptions (even though they continue to be important components of therapy) since their stance works so effectively.

Selvini Palazzoli and her present colleagues go a bit further than this in their treatment of families. Now the general model of the psychotic process has become the guide for conducting the therapy. According to Selvini Palazzoli et al. (1989), the team now follows a preeminently cognitive strategy in their hypothesizing. In earlier times, the Milan team appeared to be more interested in disturbing the system or trying something in order to observe the outcome. Now they have a specific, conscious model that they subscribe to in their hypothesizing about a family problem (described earlier under Psychotic Processes).

Like the Milan Associates, the telephone contacts are extremely important for collecting information. Unlike them, Selvini Palazzoli and her colleagues are very interested in the chronology of events leading to the onset, evolution, and possible flaring-up of the symptom (Selvini Palazzoli et al., 1989). If all the information about this is not available, it is obtained immediately during the first session.

The style of the recent Milan team is to arouse a highly intense emotional atmosphere in the therapy session. The therapist is directive in that he or she maintains responsibility for keeping the session on task, believing that most family explanations and verbalizations are the family's way to divert the therapist. Following their theory about family pathology, the therapist focuses the family on material and relationships that aid in testing the hypothesis.

When formulating a hypothesis, Selvini Palazzoli et al. (1989) considers six general areas from which to draw information:

1. How each parent's relationship to each of the children has developed over time.
2. Individual reactions to important life events.
3. How each member's relationship to his/her extended family has changed over the years.
4. How strongly each of the parents is still tied to her/his family of origin and what position this parent held in the past, as well as the present implications of having played such a role.
5. Problems hinging on the parental couple's marital rapport.
6. The symptom's pragmatic effects: one needs to find out who, in the family, is most deeply affected by the symptom. (p. 209)

The first part of the therapy is devoted to collecting information and checking hypotheses. Soon the therapist will have

assembled the necessary information and will deliver an intervention by the use of "openings." Opening, in this case, refers to the opportunity taken by the therapist to offer his or her own expert point of view to the family regarding the symptom. In so doing, the therapist provides an interpretation of the symptomatic behavior and the game being played by each of the members and raises questions about why such behaviors are taking place. All this is done in a rather rapid-fire order with great energy and unsettling statements, which often leaves the family shaken. The purpose of this is to reveal the family game. "The therapeutic process, then, starts with the interventions aimed at unmasking the game and then tackles the family's reactions to this revelation, whereupon it uses the prescription to obtain concrete evidence of change" (Selvini Palazzoli et al., 1989, p. 221).

While this strategy has worked very effectively, it has not been without its difficulties. It has placed the therapist in somewhat of an adversarial role. Selvini Palazzoli and her colleagues are researching ways to become less adversarial and much more collaborative in their relationship with families.

CASE EXAMPLE

The case that follows was modified with the intention of presenting a descriptive and detailed approach to Milan family therapy. It demonstrates that these methods can be applied in settings that are dissimilar to the Milan center.

Carl was a 20-year-old patient who had been hospitalized after he had made some vague suicide threats. Carl, the youngest, had two brothers: Bill, 24, a successful engineer, and Don, 22, in college and living at home. Carl's parents were Henry, 44, a successful engineer; and Rita, 43, a nursing supervisor. Five years earlier his parents had separated for a 4-month period, shortly before Carl's first hospitalization. Family therapy was recommended by the unit psychologist, who suggested that the family help Carl before he returned home to stay.

Information available to the therapist indicated that Carl's grandparents had passed away within the last 7 years. He had been his paternal grandfather's favorite grandchild. Carl's grandfather had been a professional man who had overcome considerable odds in attaining his position.

Hypothesizing about the Problem

Having only this limited information, the team developed a tentative hypothesis. The son's previous hospitalization had been a signal that problems existed within the marriage, which was also true for the present hospitalization. Several questions were raised by the team: What had precipitated the suicide threats? With which parent is Carl siding? Was this an effort to protect his mother? The specific hypothesis to be tested was that Carl had meddled in the affairs of his mother and father, and he was miserably renounced; the hospitalization was the result of narcissistic injuries he suffered from their battle. It should be pointed out that experience in working with this model as well as working with families of this type have led the Milan teams to certain assumptions that are likely to be true. Often they are not true, but even so, the data obtained as a result of the testing are very valuable because a new hypothesis will eventually be formulated. The plan for the first session was to at-

tempt to identify what was transpiring in the family and to test the tentative hypothesis.

Curiosity, Circularity, and Neutrality

Therapist: Let's start by telling me what has brought you here.

Father: Carl will be getting out of the hospital soon, and we want to make sure that he adjusts well at home.

Therapist: Who decided that Carl was ill and needed to be hospitalized?

Father: The doctors did.

Therapist: No, I mean in the family.

Mother: His dad, of course.

Therapist: On what basis did your husband decide that?

Mother: Well, Carl said some pretty nasty things to him, and that really worried us.

Therapist (to Bill): Who was most worried about your brother, your mother or your father?

Bill: Mother worries about all of us.

Therapist (to Don): Tell me, in rank order, who does your mother worry about, from the most to the least.

Don: She has always worried the most about Carl, then maybe me, and then Bill.

Therapist: Has it always been this way?

Father: She started worrying after my father got sick several years ago. Carl was pretty upset when that happened.

Therapist: Carl, you have been pretty quiet so far. Do you agree with your father that you were ill? And do you agree that your mother worries most about you?

Carl: Yeah, I think that they both are right.

Therapist: Who else in this family worries a lot?

Bill: Nobody has ever admitted it, but I think Carl does. He has always been very sensitive somehow.

During this part of the interview, the family has talked freely and has provided several openings—the mother worries but so does Carl. Carl is very sensitive, even though the family has never admitted it. The therapist introduced the ideas that the family had made the decision that Carl was sick and that Carl's illness was a choice. If choices are made in favor of illness, they can also be made toward wellness. Some aspects of the hypothesis have been validated, although new information will likely change this. The therapist has maintained a neutrality stance and used the curiosity-circularity framework in his questioning. By neutrality, we mean that the therapist is equally open to each member of the family, involves all family members throughout the session, avoids any suggestion that the family has a problem, and does not suggest in any way what the family ought to do to solve their problem. The curiosity stance is reflected in the circular questions. He is interested in how relationships are connected and how individuals view information about the family. The circular questioning suggests that the therapist involves all members of the family. Also, information provides the basis for further questions, which in turn provides the basis for more, and so forth.

Therapist: Rating all the members of the family from most to least, who is most sensitive.

Dad: I think Carl first, then Mother, then Don, Bill, and me. In my family at home, it was always my father though.

Therapist: And so you think Carl was a lot like your father in that way.

Dad: Yes, but my dad was tough too; he made it up from the bottom.

Therapist: What other ways was Carl like his grandfather?

Dad: My father really loved Carl, but he was not like Carl in any other way. He knew how to work and get things done. He worked and got his life together.

At this point the father seems to be expressing some anger toward Carl. But why the anger at this sensitive young man? This raised a question about Carl's position in the family. The mother worries about him. Everyone agrees that he is sensitive. He was grandfather's favorite. Could it be that Dad was somehow threatened by this fragile young man? What role does Carl play?

Therapist: Who in this family knows how to work hard and to get things done?

Mother: Bill has always been like that. He was a good student and a dependable worker. He was like Grandfather in that way.

Therapist: If Grandfather were still living, how might things be different?

Carl: Granddad always spent time with me and took me places. I stayed with him alot.

Mother: Carl was much happier when he was alive.

Therapist: Who else misses Grandfather?

Don: Dad does; he and Granddad had a lot of arguments.

Therapist: Who argues the most with Dad now?

Don: Mom and Bill.

Therapist: Of these two, who is apt to get most upset with Dad?

Carl: Mom, but she usually doesn't win.

Therapist: When does Mom win?

Bill: The only way Mom wins, maybe, is when she gets involved with her friends and leaves the house. She does that a lot.

Revising the Hypothesis

At this point several pieces of information have emerged: Carl's relationship with his grandfather was important to Carl and somehow to his father, maybe in a negative sense. The relationship between the mother and father appears to be strained—she usually does not win against him.

Later in the session when the team had a conference, the following ideas were exchanged. Carl's illness may be related to the parental difficulty as was originally hypothesized. He may be secretly siding with one parent who he perceives to be the underdog and has suffered severely from that coalition by being cast aside by that parent. The second hypothesis was accepted as the most probable. The next step was to test it out with the family. The decision to connote the problem positively provided the opportunity to gather further information about the family process before testing the hypothesis. The team decided to share some disconfirming information about Carl's relationship with the family and give them some time to adjust to its impact. It was decided that it would be better to test the hypothesis later in the therapy process.

Positive Connotation

Therapist: I have been consulting with my team, and we have several ideas that we would like to share with you. First, we have been very impressed by your willingness to be open and discuss this problem with us. We have also been impressed with another thing in this family, and it seems to be a long tradition. People in this family have very high standards—they expect a great deal from themselves and from each other. In fact, the expectations are extremely high. It seems that Grandfather set high standards, so high that he and Father argued about them. Father has attained a prominent status in his profession. The same is true for Mother; after all, she is a supervisor. Bill is a success. Don seems to be headed on his way now. What we don't understand is Carl's place in all of this. He was successful with Grandfather but not with the other family members. We are not sure why this family needs to have this problem. This family that has been so successful in so many areas has found one thing that you have not been able to solve, and that is this problem we have been talking about. One thought we had—and it was just a thought—Carl is so sensitive that it may be that he has sensed some danger to this family and he has been very successful by using himself to try to protect the family from it. After all, people in this family show a lot of willingness to get involved with each other even to the point of getting angry and yelling at each other. It takes a lot of concern and caring to do something like that. Maybe this is the way that Carl has been a success. Well, that is what we thought. With that we will end the session for this week. Good-bye.

A comment about the last intervention: The family has viewed Carl as the problem up to now. The therapist has remained neutral on this issue by not introducing the problem or suggesting a solution. The positive connotation of Carl's behavior and also the positive aspects of the family's nature (i.e., caring, high standards, hard work, etc.) enables the family to think about itself differently. It also serves to provide a connection between the part of the family that has been described as bad with the good in the family; the bad has many good parts previously unnoticed. Through positive connotation, the bad is diminished and the good is highlighted through strengths, assets, and the like. This kind of intervention is particularly useful because it expands the family's perspective on the problem, but more importantly it challenges the basic underlying assumptions operating in the family—their way of thinking about this problem. It raises a very disconcerting question: Is it also possible that there are assumptions being used that are wrong? Are we making other mistakes like this one?

Boscolo and Cecchin argue that this type of intervention may be enough to allow the system to change. They maintain that the system has the capacity to change in positive directions—a self-healing property. If the therapist provides the family with appropriate information or stimulus and then gets out of the way, the system will do the rest. What usually happens is that interventions such as the above are provided regularly to the family until they show evidence of change at the system level.

The second session was held 2 weeks after the first. In preparation for the upcoming session, the team reviewed their notes from the previous session and discussed the hypothesis agreed upon earlier. Would the family be different? Was the intervention appropriate? What additional information is needed to test the hypothesis?

Therapist (to the family): Where shall we begin?

Father: It is still alarming because we only have a few more days before Carl comes home.

Therapist: Who in the family is concerned about Carl coming home?

Father: We are all concerned of course.

Carl (to father): Why is everyone alarmed; there is no reason to be alarmed. I am just coming home.

Therapist: Some are concerned. Who in the family will be relieved when Carl comes home?

Bill: I think Mother will be relieved. She visits the hospital often. Most of the time she gets home too late to prepare dinner.

Therapist: Who suffers most when Mother is visiting the hospital?

Bill: Father—he often has to fix his own dinner.

Father: If no one is here I go down to the restaurant; my wife is gone much of the time anyway. She is president of this and secretary of that. Since she got important she is not around too often.

Therapist: Who else in the family feels left out of things once in a while?

Father: I don't feel left out; I have things to do.

Carl: It is hard when you don't get dinner. When a person is too busy to take care of her husband, it's a problem. (To mother:) Why

do you belong to all those clubs and who are those people?

Father: Well, I do just fine; it's not a problem.

Carl: Women do this and women do that. My friend's wife is never at home. She even goes out with other men.

The Final Hypothesis

At this point, the observer behind the one-way window signals the therapist to come out for consultation. The observer has noticed the father's annoyance with the mother, even though he attempted to mask it. More importantly, she noticed that Carl is suddenly alive and full of talk about his mother and women in general. With the new information, the team decided to revise their present hypothesis. Not only has Carl been interfering in his parents' affairs, he has apparently taken the father's side against the mother. This addition was triggered by the behavior of the father. He was involved in a game with the mother. Carl was unhappy with his mother's position against the father (i.e., he resented her independence and new status).

The Prescription

The therapist returned to the room with the following statement:

Therapist: My colleague and I have been discussing this case, and we have arrived at a decision. We are of the opinion that Carl is indeed a sensitive and caring young man. We think that he has fallen prey to a complicated game operating between Mom and Dad. Mom has been a successful climber lately in the social circles and has left Dad behind. Carl observed all this and decided that Dad was getting the short end of the stick. He decided to take Mother down a notch or two in order to help Father keep control of his wife. In doing all this he has gotten involved in a game whereby he can only get hurt. It doesn't take too long to get very depressed because of such treatment. He chose to be sick rather than deal with this game.

For next time, we want only Mother and Father to come to the session. We thank you three sons for helping us understand your family. It was important that you be here, but now that will no longer be necessary. Goodbye.

At this point in the therapy, the team is satisfied that they have isolated the significant elements in the family system. Carl's talk helped the team realize the role he had attempted to play in the couples game. This is a situation that the Milan teams have studied for many years. The attention was focused on the parental couple for the duration of therapy. Therapy often ends without further intervention. However, in this case, a version of the invariant prescription was prescribed. The parents were able to follow it, and the change in Carl was immediate. He was able to leave the hospital on time without further incident. The therapy sessions with the parents continued for three sessions.

Therapy does not always go as smoothly as those described in a textbook. These sessions were edited somewhat to allow for a more effective and abbreviated presentation here; however, the editing did not distort the actual case itself.

Comment

The case presentation would most likely be considered closer to the Milan Associates' approach than to that of Selvini Palazzoli and her colleagues. Their approach would perhaps have been somewhat more direct in the confrontation of the games or moves being made by the various family members. They might be more inclined to exploit their understandings more vigorously, asking pointed questions, making observations, and calling attention to particular strategies and moves. This is a difference worth noting; however, it does not suggest a completely different approach. It simply points out that each of the teams is currently focusing on somewhat different but generally closely related issues.

EVALUATION

Research conducted by the Milan teams has focused on families with mentally ill patients. The objective was to identify methods and techniques that would prove effective for treating pathological families. Not only was the Milan team interested in approaches that assisted in change, they were also interested in approaches that brought about lasting change.

Hundreds of families have been treated by the various Milan teams. However, each time the team changed their ideas or strategies, the research methodology also changed, resulting in several studies with relatively small populations. It appears that the studies were based on information collected during the therapy process and also on telephone follow-ups conducted months or even years later.

Selvini Palazzoli and her colleagues have been criticized concerning their particular methodology. Much of this criticism has been related to an absence of the normal controls required in experimental design studies. The most severe opinion has been related to an unwarranted set of conclusions drawn from a very small sample of subjects with a wide range of diagnostic classifications (Anderson, 1986).

Selvini Palazzoli (1986) reported on the results of 19 families that were treated using the invariable prescription. Each identified patient had a very severe disorder, ranging from anorexia to schizophrenia. Ten families followed the prescriptions exactly with excellent results; four followed it only partially with poor results; three followed it exactly with initial good results but later suffered a relapse. It was concluded that "the therapeutic power of the invariable prescription, when obeyed, had now been confirmed beyond all doubt" (p. 343).

Prata, during a personal communication with Speed (1985), reported that of the 15 families written about in *Paradox and Counterparadox* (Selvini Palazzoli et al., 1978), 13 showed significant changes. In a personal communication with Tomm (1984), Cecchin said that the Milan team had an improvement rate of about 68%. If these data are true, the improvements from the Milan therapy are very good considering the difficult families with whom they worked. There can be little doubt that the research conducted by the Milan teams has made an important contribution to the field of family therapy. It would be nice if all their results were available for closer scrutiny; it will have to be enough that all of us have profited from it through their writings and lectures.

SUMMARY

The Milan approaches have evolved over several decades, resulting in at least two relatively similar approaches with each possessing certain distinct and unique qualities. Boscolo and Cecchin have relied heavily on the earlier work with hypothesizing, circularity, and neutrality. The addition of curiosity seems to have provided a rather straightforward approach that therapists can utilize with their clients without extensive training. The learnings from second-order cybernetics (the observing team phenomenon) and the impact of the small groups of trainees (which led to a realization that larger systems must be included when studying family systems) has further refined the approach of the Milan Associates.

Selvini Palazzoli and her colleagues of the past 10 years have adopted a model focusing on family games. Relational interactions, the point at which games clearly come into focus, has become an important arena again for study. However, the awareness about individual involvement and contribution to family pathology has led Selvini Palazzoli to reconsider the systemic explanation of family pathology and explore a new model that may lead to a individual-systemic conceptualization of family therapy. This may be the new thinking for the future.

ANNOTATED SUGGESTED READINGS

Boscolo, L., Cecchin, G., Hoffman, L., & Penn, P. (1987). *Milan systemic family therapy: Conversations in therapy and practice*. New York: Basic Books.

Several transcripts of therapy sessions conducted by the Milan team, plus discussions among the authors about these particular cases and also the methods, strategies, and thinking behind the therapy of the Milan Associates.

Campbell, D., & Draper, R. (Eds.). (1985). *Applications of systemic family therapy: The Milan approach*. New York: Grune & Stratton.

Applications of the Milan approach on both sides of the Atlantic. Several practitioners from diverse workplaces and backgrounds describe their unique version of the Milan therapy.

Selvini Palazzoli, M., Cirillo, S., Selvini, M., & Sorrentino, A. M. (1989). *Family games: General models of psychotic processes in the family*. New York: W. W. Norton.

The most recent presentation of the work of Selvini Palazzoli and her associates. The new model of psychotic processes in pathological families is discussed with case material illustrating the new thinking and methods. The "game metaphor," which has been useful in identifying the processes that lead to psychotic behavior, is described.

Selvini, M. (Ed.). (1988). *The work of Mara Selvini Palazzoli*. Northvale, NJ: Jason Aronson.

The son and now colleague of Selvini Palazzoli has assembled her papers chronologically up to 1980, providing an intimate look at the person, her ideas, and her struggle to develop and research new strategies for working with families of mentally ill patients.

REFERENCES

Anderson, C. M. (1986). The all-too-short trip from positive to negative connotation. *Journal of Marital and Family Therapy, 12*(4), 351–354.

Barrows, S. E. (1982). Interview with Mara Selvini Palazzoli and Giuliana Prata. *American Journal of Family Therapy, 10*(3), 60–69.

Bateson, G. (1972). *Steps to an ecology of the mind*. New York: Ballantine Books.

Bateson, G. (1979). *Mind and nature: A necessary unity*. New York: Dutton Books.

Bateson, G., Jackson, D. D., Haley, Jr., & Weakland, J. (1956). Toward a theory of schizophrenia. *Behavioral Science, 1*, 251–264.

Boscolo, L., Cecchin, G., Hoffman, L., & Penn, P. (1987). *Milan systemic family therapy: Conversations in theory and practice*. New York: Basic Books.

Cecchin, G. (1987). Hypothesizing, circularity, and neutrality revisited: An invitation to curiosity. *Family Process, 26*(4), 405–413.

Framo, J., (1965). Rationale and techniques of intensive family therapy. In I. Boszormeni-Nagy & J. Framo (Eds.), *Intensive family therapy*. New York: Harper & Row.

Selvini, M. (Ed.). (1988). *The work of Mara Selvini Palazzoli*. Northvale, NJ: Jason Aronson.

Selvini Palazzoli, M. (1986). Towards a general model of psychotic family games. *Journal of Marital and Family Therapy, 12*(4), 339–349.

Selvini Palazzoli, M., Boscolo, L., Cecchin, F. G., & Prata, G. (1978). *Paradox and counterparadox*. New York: Jason Aronson.

Selvini Palazzoli, M., Boscolo, L., Cecchin, G., & Prata, G. (1980). Hypothesizing-circulatory-neutrality: Three guidelines for the conductor of the session. *Family Process, 19*(1), 3–12.

Selvini Palazzoli, M., Cirillo, S., Selvini, M., & Sorrentino, A. M. (1989). *Family games: General models of psychotic processes in the family*. New York: W. W. Norton.

Simon, R. (1987). Palazzoli and the family game. *The Family Therapy Networker, 12*(5), 17–26.

Speed, B. (1985). Evaluating the Milan approach. In D. Campbell & R. Draper (Eds.), *Applications of systemic family therapy: The Milan approach.* New York: Grune and Stratton.

Tomm, K. (1984). One perspective on the Milan systemic approach: Part II. Description of session format, interviewing style and interventions. *Journal of Marital and Family Therapy, 10,* 253–271.

Watzlawick, P., Beavin, J. H., & Jackson, D. D. (1967). *Pragmatics of human communication.* New York: Norton.

Wynne, L. C., & Singer, A. T. (1963). Thoughts, disorders, and the family relations of schizophrenics. *Archives of General Psychiatry, 9,* 191–206.

CHAPTER 10

Gestalt Family Therapy

WALTER KEMPLER

DEFINITION

Gestalt family therapy is a generic approach to the treatment of families in distress. This model focuses attention on the immediate—what people say, how they say it, what happens when it is said, and how it corresponds with what they are doing and what they are attempting to achieve. Regardless of whether discord is found within an individual or between two or more persons, treatment consists of bringing discordant elements into mutual self-disclosing confrontation. The conversational anchor point is the current conflict of the day and what can be done to resolve it in place of a more analytical or understanding (seeking why) orientation.

The therapist is a welcoming host who counsels through exemplary behavior and excerpts from his or her own life as well as with directions, suggestions, and advice. Though a guide, the therapist remains vulnerable as others are expected to do.

Since this model concerns itself with change through the personal intervention of the therapist on current issues and does not prescribe how the therapist should behave (e.g., advising, cajoling, role playing, "parenting") or what theories to follow, the approach is considered generic, that is, useful to all family therapists regardless of their orientation. Moreover, the principles of Gestalt family therapy are also applicable to groups and individuals.

Gestalt family therapy is predicated on the Gestalt preclinical premises of how we develop awareness and perspective for the world around us and on Gestalt clinical psychology as demonstrated by the life of Fritz Perls, which calls for the creation of experiences to influence our awareness and subsequent behavior. The goal of Gestalt family therapy is the restoration of the family as the primary resource for the succor and development of its members.

HISTORICAL DEVELOPMENT

Precursors

Nothing in Gestalt family therapy can be considered original; all its theoretical considerations can be found throughout humankind's written history. Furthermore, there is nothing in its activity that has not been done by someone, somewhere, sometime. The most that can be said for it is that it represents an updated language and pertinent recommendations for the effective application of that which people have known and sporadically applied throughout history.

The prehistory of Gestalt therapy begins in the Garden of Eden. Genesis 3:7 tells us that when Adam and Eve ate the apple, "The eyes of both of them were opened, and they knew that they were naked." It is not too difficult to interpret from this description that the knowledge gamed from the tempting morsel was self-awareness. Today, the philosophy behind Gestalt family therapy urges people to taste from a modern tree of knowledge in order to gain further insight, while the therapy itself is concerned with correcting defects in that self-awareness through new experiences.

Further Genesis 3:22 quotes God as saying, "Behold, the man is become as one of us, to know good and evil." Again, this lends itself readily to the interpretation that simultaneously people also learned polarization—the world of opposites—and this knowledge made them more than just other creatures in God's playground. Today, Gestalt family therapy postulates that coming to "know" one's own psychological polarizations is the first step toward psychological integration and consequently a higher state of awareness.

Preceding Christianity was the Sankhya Philosophy of India, which inspired Patanjali (Vivekananda, 1899) to create his 10 monumental pages of wisdom. Included in those pages is the belief that experience on this earth is the key that reawakens all the knowledge of the universe that is locked in each of us, waiting to be released. The philosophy of contemporary Gestalt family therapy holds that direct, interpersonal experience is the key to the cultivation and restoration of mental health and perhaps also a path to the knowledge Patanjali describes.

Between those early records of humankind and now, many people have tried to describe people's existence in terms of awareness, the polarization that makes awareness possible, and the limits to awareness imposed by the very polarization that makes awareness possible. They endorsed the concept that people's experiences must be the foundation on which they build their awareness and to which their awareness must be faithful.

The philosophical attitude that underlies Gestalt family therapy and that develops spontaneously during one's personal development is seen in the writings of many, even though these writers themselves seem often unaware of their unique position. Such writers as Thornton Wilder in *Bridge of San Luis Rey*, Cervantes in *Don Quixote*, and Pierre Teilhard de Chardin in *Phenomenon of Man*, for example, all sensed this awareness.

Beginnings

In the middle of the 19th century in an advanced sector of mankind's social evolution, a popular philosophy emerged that urged man to consider his immediate existence, to reconsider how he views his immediate existence, and to examine the possibility that he may be the exclusive force that influences that existence.

This philosophy, existentialism, crystallizes a particular attitude of man about himself, an attitude that finds expression in many institutions of 20th-century man. One of these institutions—psychology—became a particularly fertile place for the further development of existential thought and for its application to the mundane dilemmas of daily living. One of the psychological plants to emerge from the garden of existential thought is the model for Gestalt therapy.

The use of the term *Gestalt* in clinical psychology is intimately tied to Frederick Perls, MD, PhD. In actuality, the reverse may be more accurate: Fritz Perls, the man, was known as Gestalt therapy in his working clothes. *Gestalt* was perhaps chosen too casually and prematurely to be a descriptive contraction for what he did professionally; nevertheless, the use of the term in clinical circles has come to be identified with Perls. The term is not totally irrelevant. Perls came from a professional background in psychoanalysis; through his contact with Kurt Goldstein and concepts found in preclinical Gestalt psychology, he found his way out of the net of psychoanalysis and into the world of existential psychology.

Perls was an unusual man whose professional behavior attracted many people. His skill consisted of a remarkable ability to perceive and influence behavior. His own behavior was provocative, evocative, and inspiring. To meet him and come away feeling more complete in oneself was not at all unusual. This skill, this talent, this man wandered about the earth for many years claiming no special professional title other than his nickname Fritz, although he was both an accredited psychiatrist and psychologist. He did not like to be labeled. In his later years, colleagues who had been touched by Perls wanted to bottle him. When his colleagues searched for a suitable title, Perls suggested Gestalt.

Gestalt psychology, when brought to the clinical arena, quite naturally fell into the existential frame. Existentialism concerns itself with how one *experiences* immediate existence, whereas preclinical Gestalt psychology concerns itself with how one *perceives* immediate existence. From the Gestalt psychological position, Perls began urging his patients to alter their perspective or awareness as a means of changing their behavior. So for Perls, altered awareness or changing the current Gestalt was the inauguration of new behavior, which meant new experiences for the patient. Thus, discussing historical factors—that is, why persons developed their self-limiting Gestalts in the first place—was ignored. Clinical Gestalt psychology was thereby comfortably placed within the framework of existential philosophy.

In the mid-1960s, Perls, a self-acknowledged prototype of the Wandering Jew, thought he had at last found a home near Big Sur, California. This was a vanguard cultural and educational center, where people met to experience and experiment with new trends in human relating. With Perls staying in one place for a while, the widespread interest in him had a chance to crystallize. And although earlier there were small clusters of Perls-influenced professional people scattered over many parts of the United States, Big Sur was where the movement called Gestalt therapy took on a visible shape.

The first West Coast summer-long Gestalt therapy workshop took place there in 1963. It was led by Perls, James Simkin, and Walter Kempler. The formation of a Gestalt Institute was discussed but did not become a reality at that time for many reasons. One obvious and cogent one was a procedural difference leading to discord between Perls and Kempler.

"I and Thou" and "The Here and Now" were popular phrases that characterized the theoretical essence of the day. The difference between Perls and Kempler was over the issue of "I and Thou." In theory everyone was in full accord; in practice it was another matter. Perls came from a psychoanalytic background, which contributed in no small measure to his developing the "hot seat" pattern of working. This consisted in the subject voluntarily submitting to Perls's adept guidance. It was this "You're the patient, I'm not" pattern that gained for Perls the friendly but frustration-inspired title of "top dog" and popularized his needed "hot seat" format.

In no way could Perls's behavior be called "I." He was the puppeteer, the manipulator, the director, and that was how it had to be. Any remark inviting

Perls to look at his own behavior met with the invitation for the subject to look at *his* own motives in making the suggestion. There is no doubt that Perls did his job well, but there was always something missing. And it was the personal Perls.

Kempler objected.* He came from a background as a general practitioner and was basically a street fighter. He wasn't happy unless everyone was in. Although he and Perls respected one another and were in philosophical and theoretical accord, they functioned differently. They split over this issue, Kempler concluding that he could not call himself a pure Gestaltist as long as Perls persisted with his "hot seat" working model. Kempler chose to describe his model as Gestalt-experiential to show his preference for a more personally interactive working experience in preference to the "hot seat–top dog" model used by Perls. Kempler then moved to the periphery of the Gestalt movement and applied the Gestalt-experiential model in treating the family, which was his particular interest.

Perls remained in Big Sur for several years, then, a short time before his death in 1970, he moved to Canada where he started a Gestalt Training Center and Community. Near the end of his life, Perls became acutely aware of the problems created by people trying to imitate his way of working. He was disturbed by the frequent attempts of Gestalt protégés to learn techniques instead of letting their work be a natural consequence of who they were. As a result, he emphasized the importance of keeping the I-ness of the therapist as an active part of the working model. This restored Kemp-

ler's feeling of identity with Fritz and the Gestalt movement once again.

Kempler continued working and teaching in the Los Angeles area. In 1961, the Kempler Institute for the Development of the Family was begun, inaugurating the idea of Gestalt therapy as a clinically viable basis for the treatment of families. During the late sixties and the seventies, Kempler began traveling throughout the United States and northern Europe, living for some years in Scandinavia. In 1973, he wrote *Principles of Gestalt Family Therapy*, a brief outline of the principles of clinical Gestalt family therapy thoroughly saturated with examples and dialogues of the principles in action.

Current Status

Gestalt family therapy, along with the many other models of family therapy burgeoning in current psychotherapy, is enjoying the familiar popularity of the "new idea" of family therapy. In the particular world of Gestalt therapy, it is now recognized and is found in the curriculum of established training programs of various Gestalt institutes. The Kempler Institute, in addition, has 3-year training programs in Gestalt family therapy in the Netherlands and in Scandinavia.

TENETS OF THE MODEL

General Comments

Gestalt family therapy asserts that in the dynamic sense there is no such thing as an "individual," that we exist only as part of a relatedness, without which we do not survive. Ascetics survive in relatedness with God, hermits animate their surroundings, isolates vivify to the point of delusion in order to stay alive. To survive, everyone has family—real or imagined.

---

*In this chapter the writer (Kempler) will refer to himself in the third person even though this distancing is inimical both to his own lifestyle and to the fundamental premise of Gestalt.

To thrive is another matter. To grow and develop, which means to do more than survive or merely accumulate information, requires the passing through, the being witnessed by a particular other. To grow and develop does not require the other to be perfect, always available, kind, thrifty, brave, clean, or reverent. It only requires a tangible physical presence that is neither always threatening nor always unconditionally accepting. Thus, although imaged family is useful for survival, a more realistic engagement is required for thriving.

Family then by definition becomes at least two persons whose lives are concerned with each other. Contrary to popular terminology, children do not create a family; they merely enlarge it.

Gestalt family therapy is predicated on the assumption that each family contains the essential ingredient that makes it possible for all members within that family to thrive without persistent symptoms. That is the challenge for the therapist: to awaken and guide the dormant or misguided assets toward more beneficial influences. The therapist functions as a guide, an inspiration, and at times an exemplary adversary.

Gestalt family therapy is predicated on the premises that the desire to cooperate and to be pleasing to each other is the deepest motivation in all human beings; that it is the unwitting obstruction of this deepest desire that produces all disturbed or disturbing behavior; that anger and sadness are the natural reactions and first signs of this obstruction; that all symptoms are merely signals expressing both (a) a longing to return to a state of mutual cooperation and (b) the frustration of not being there; that the therapist can better mobilize the available unspoiled assets in each family member than focus on the signals of distress such as anger, sadness, bodily symptoms, or distressed behavior.

The following material concerning basic tenets of clinical Gestalt psychology is as applicable to families as it is to individuals and premises of therapy, family or other.

Since Gestalt family therapy is a phenomenological approach, it is extremely difficult to theorize about it. Any theoretical formulation places restrictions, definitions, and boundaries that are inevitably both artificial and somewhat erroneous. At best, words can only approximate experience; theory can only conceptualize experience. The optimal achievement for a writer of a section on the theory of Gestalt therapy would be for the reader to come away from it with an emotionally shaken experience rather than a head full of theoretical understanding.

The alternative is to suggest a framework that is broad enough to encompass the infinity of possibilities inherent in human behavior and, simultaneously, that avoids hazards of judgment and provincial values. To achieve this, the model must be portable. It cannot be anchored in absolutes. Through it, we must be able to peer at any human interaction (or intraaction) without imposing on it. Although that task is admittedly impossible, the phenomenon of man and the theory of Gestalt psychotherapy may be profitably viewed through the conceptual eye of processes.

Basic Concepts

Man may be seen as a momentary precipitation at the vortex of a transient eddy of energy, in the enormous and incomprehensible sea of energy we call the universe. Man is a unique materialization (a matter-realization) of that energy.

Could man order his energy like gravity, magnetic flow, or the laser phenomenon, we might expect him to disappear from tangible view and exist exclusively as the powerful force that is now only his inherent potential. Matter integrated becomes energy; energy distracted materializes.

In terms of processes, man's lifetime can be described as an actively evolving process with energy and matter representing the poles. To recognize man as a process is a beginning. To see him as a composite of processes in an endless universe of processes is to define him.

Gestalt family therapy operates in a smaller circle within the larger circle. It does not concern itself directly with the energy-matter process of man, but within that context it focuses on the discordant psychological processes. In other words, it does not directly concern itself with the fact of man's birth but rather with the discordances that arise within and about him as a consequence of living that birth.

Theoretically, at least, a completely successful course of treatment could result in the total physical disappearance of both patient and therapist. In actuality, both the patient and therapist usually do change as the result of reciprocal influences on each other; however, the usual results are admittedly somewhat less spectacular than theory would allow. The consequences of successful therapy are usually symptom amelioration for the patient and further development of the therapist, which leads to new ways of working and living.

Processes in General

For the purpose of trying to comprehend his universe, man breaks down the universal continuum into thinkable bits and pieces. He separates and labels everything he can, then treats each piece as though it were an entity unto itself. This permits him to play with it, to think about it. One of the things he does as he toys with his bits and pieces is to see if he can now find new ways to fit them together. When he finds a phenomenological relationship between two pieces, he yells, "Eureka, I've discovered a process!" A process is two points happening.

Since thinking begins with the identification of separate objects, it is not difficult to recognize the two points in a process. My head hurts me, you attract me, I am repelled by noise, I am not a cow; head-me, you-me, I-noise, I-cow. Two-point discrimination is simple. Discovering processes, however, is more challenging. For instance, what is the relationship between the head pain and the me? Appreciating the relatedness between the two points, then, is the beginning of the comprehension of processes.

There are two ever-present characteristics of the relatedness between the two points in any process—a simultaneous attraction and repulsion; a tendency to merge with, and an urge to remain differentiated from, each other. In the broadest sense, this is always the happening.

In all processes, the forces moving in both directions maintain an undulating activity that gradually influences and alters the relationship of the two points. Sometimes the pulsation is so slight and our vision so crude that we suspect there is nothing happening. This is especially true, for example, in matters of frustrated love. But between any two points in a process, there is always undulation, a flow to and fro, a movement toward and away from—be they frustrated lovers, the sun and the moon, or contented lovers.

Although sometimes appearing rather stable, all processes are moving toward extinction. We also know that the end of any process is the creation of new processes. To the best of our knowledge there are no beginnings or ends to the universal whole. There are only beginning and ends of our arbitrary designated segments.

The process of loving tells us more about the fate of processes than it tells us about the psychology of love. Two people meet and are attracted. A process is begun as they move into each other's orbit. Although the character of their negotiation is always somewhat different from any other pair, their struggle is the same: an attracting–longing to merge (integrate, unite) and a repelling urge to retain differentiation and separateness. An individual typically identifies with only one of the forces within herself and might say, "I want to be one with you but it is impossible" rather than simply recognizing the process that says, "I want to be one with you. I want to be separate from you. Sometimes both forces are so intense it is painful."

Both lovers search for a position of comfort. The intensity clearly reveals the singularity of mind and body. Movement changes from random to irregular to intensely rhythmic. The to-and-fro increases in every possible way. As the lovers near the climax, individuality is lost in activity that involves their entire being, even as the awareness of feeling self and other begins to blur into pure sensation. Each movement, appearing the same as the last, is different; there is progression. The peak is drowned in a sea of changes.

All the issues of separateness versus union disappear along with the disappearance of movement. The process is completely joined and disappears. All that remains is the dawn of new processes in an aimless reverie of calm. Changes are occurring in both of them, changes that will cause alterations in the overall process called their relationship. They must wait for this experience to register its impact on a multitude of other processes in each of them, whether it be reverie, sleep, or spontaneous meditation. The beginning of a child is an appropriate and symbolic testimony of the creative fate of processes.

Whether describing cosmic processes, mental processes, symptomatic processes, or treatment processes, the principles governing processes generally are applicable specifically.

PSYCHOTHERAPY

Theory of Psychotherapy

Gestalt family therapy is a generic approach to treating families in distress. It calls for the awakening and restoration of the family to their rightful place as the primary promoter of personal potentials for all members, parents and children alike.

The therapist is a temporary catalyst who uses whatever talents are available to revitalize the family. At a given moment a Gestalt family therapist may be seen drawing a picture of a family dynamic on a blackboard and in another moment challenging one member's position. Any behavior that suits a therapist's personality, thereby making it possible for that therapist to lean effectively on a family or on an individual to bring forth more successful behavior, is Gestalt family therapy. Gestalt family therapy is concerned with effective influence first and always, theory or premises second if at all.

When patient and therapist meet in a

situation called psychotherapy, the therapist is like a composing maestro facing an accomplished musician. Both are skilled, and both are familiar with world-famous melodies. The maestro expects that between them new and beautiful tunes will be created, while the musician comes sometimes for a creative jam session but more often with only the desire to learn to play her old tunes with fewer mistakes. Together they are a creative process and the goal is the concerted behavior of each.

The maestro operates, initially at least, with the idea that any notes he can think of, the musician can play. Also, if he is able to make use of the musician's talent, they will create their new songs more quickly. The musician comes with the best of intentions. She wants to respond, for she too likes the excitement of new consonance, but she is afraid. She knows she has frailties and incompetencies; that is why she came. Despite the fact that both she and the maestro already know this, she still fears its discovery. Her attempt to obscure her frailties will slow the process.

Less well publicized but also prevalent are the maestro's frailties and his wish to hide them. However, it is his ability to discover, reveal, and respond with them that is his creative genius. Sometimes he believes and his musicians usually think that his creative ability lies in his almost faultless familiarity and cleverness with chords and discords.

Each time patient and therapist meet, their starting point will be the same, but they themselves will each be different. Their growing familiarity intensifies the challenges to be met between them. Their expectations of one another change, as do the sounds they produce. In this situation, familiarity breeds continually increasing self-disclosure with admissions, confessions, revelations. As the veneer of each drops away and the hidden frailties are exposed and acknowledged, each person is validated, and the frailties somehow wane in the process. The maestro and the musician discover a greater range to the music they create together, and they feel growing satisfaction and a significance in their activity. This discovery is a mixture of joy and sadness, for they both realize that in creation there is loss—the outgrowing of interest in familiar tunes, the approaching end to their creative venture. But now they can create music together that expresses the joy and sadness, and that is almost enough. The experience of the musician tells her that she can also be her own maestro and search for other maestro-musicians to play with and further her fulfillment. For the maestro, there is the taste of a new experience, an added skillfulness to his ability to create music with others, and, most exciting to both, a growing appreciation of the music that each is.

Restating this in terms of processes, psychotherapy can be described as a process created for the purpose of influencing symptomatic psychological processes.

In Gestalt therapy, all symptoms are seen as signals of a distressed process, that is, a process that is not evolving suitably according to one of the points or participants in the process.

The task of the Gestalt psychotherapist is to bring both principals into juxtaposition so that the attracting and repelling forces of each can exert their full influence. The fate of the process is left to the experiences created by these full-blown forces.

The two polarized, discordant elements in a symptomatic process may be described within one individual or between two persons, or one element may be projected abroad to the infinity of nameable and unnameable objects from "time" to "uncertainty."

The forces of attraction and repulsion, like and dislike, are not fixed or permanent. Self-disclosure, the full expression of both positive and negative feelings and thoughts, releases the individual from the bondage created by blocked expression. In the wake of such expression, the more pure, simple, and fundamental interest in one another emerges and determines the fate of the relationship for that moment.

The principles used to achieve these ends include focusing on current interaction as the pivotal point for all therapeutic activity, and the full personal participation of the therapist who recognizes that he or she is always one pole in the large context of the psychotherapeutic process.

Gestalt therapy does not use diagnostic labels. Diagnoses are considered an escape from participating in the patient-therapist process, an admission that the therapist cannot participate fully in it. A therapist's frustration with the patient should properly bring him or her first inward to taste the depth and character of frustration and then outward again to reveal that frustration to the other person. Personal frustration is to be revealed and not to be stopped at the center point of the figure eight of knowing with only a diagnosis or description of the distal point of the outer ring.

The psychological processes within an individual are infinite, making the possibility for interactions with others infinite. However, rarely do people tap the potentials within themselves or between themselves and another. Usually, awareness is directed to a few areas that are consistent with a person's sense of iden-

tity about him- or herself, and all experience is funneled through that self-concept. Should two people, for instance, communicate with each other from remote parts of the earth without benefit of telephone, telegraph, or post, it would immediately be called remarkable, labeled as extrasensory perception or telepathy, and carefully filed away since it is not consistent with the image most people have of themselves. Limited self-concepts constrict awareness and inhibit such experiences or, if impossible to avoid, simply exclaim and classify them. It is difficult to allow uncategorical freedom to one's awareness. Gestalt family therapy seeks to create experiences that increase the range of awareness, which in turn spur new experiences on their undulating way into new processes.

Process of Psychotherapy

The process of psychotherapy, like all other processes, begins with two points. Point 1, initiating the process, is the symptom. Point 2 is a special person, selected for the purpose of engaging the symptom, called the therapist. The goal is the goal of all processes: the end of the process with the disappearance of the symptom, the therapist, and their relationship; and the consequent creation of new and, in this instance, more satisfying processes.

Family therapy may be viewed profitably as two primarily intertwined processes: the relationship between the family and the therapist, and the process within the family that aroused the need for assistance. There are, of course, an infinite number of processes operating every moment. In family therapy, however, all the others are subordinate to these two.

Activation of the therapeutic process can begin on any topic but usually it begins in the neighborhood of the symptom. "I want relief from..." is the patient's basic message. If not forthcoming spontaneously, it is invited by the therapist, who is usually more comfortable and wants to get the therapeutic process started.

The symptom is always presented as a discordant polarization, for example, "My head hurts me," "My child has trouble in school," "My husband abuses me," "I can't stop drinking," "My probation officer insists I come here," "My mind doesn't work right," "Anxiety plagues me," "Feelings overwhelm me." Whatever the symptom, personal or interpersonal in description, it has several clear characteristics. There are always two parts, always in disagreement: one is always presented as the victim of the other, and, most important of all, the patient invariably identifies him- or herself as the victim and never as the oppressor. This is essentially the gross character of the symptom process that the patient brings to the patient-therapist process.

The therapist initially appears as an integrated process, all sweetness and help, ready to engage the patient's process seemingly without reservation. For the sake of descriptive simplicity, we shall begin there, although in actual practice the therapist often is not at that tranquil starting position.

Having no need to attend to anything personal (his or her own processes being in good working order), the therapist's full attention goes to the patient's unhappy process, and he or she picks up the discordant poles (the victim versus the oppressor) and tries to create a dialogue between them. The immediate objective is always the same: to assist all uncomfortable (symptomatic) processes toward an ultimate union and consequent extinction. The therapist watches carefully, always moving to the particular process considered the largest obstacle and to which all the other recognized discordant processes fit, regardless of the initial symptom or starting point. While working at a process regarded as the crucial one, the therapist uses all his or her personal and therapeutic skills to bring the parts to a balanced confrontation until the two elements merge or disappear into a new realization.

Symptoms are created and maintained by one part refusing to accept another part. Cure comes only when the two parts recognize and come to appreciate one another to the point that they have absolutely no conflict or dissatisfaction with each other. Only then do they lose their significance to each other, thereby ending their painful interactive process.

As long as the therapist has no internal discord and his or her own processes flow smoothly, he or she has only to persuade the patients to confront their own discordant elements. Knowing what are polar opposites is an important skill for the therapist to learn and the second factor in this therapeutic skillfullness. The first factor, mentioned above, is being able to recognize the largest discordant premise at any one time. The third factor is skill at keeping discordant elements actively engaged in this vis-à-vis posture.

Persuading the patient to face him- or herself or whoever is identified as the oppressor (sometimes a parent, sometimes a lover, sometimes an institution, sometimes the therapist) requires all the personal and professional skill the therapist can muster. It is the force of the therapist's total person that is his or her contribution to the movement in therapy. This force has been called sincerity, confidence, basic trust, inspiration, and many other things. It corresponds with the patient's hope for change.

Discovering the polarity in the presentation of the symptom is relatively simple, as already indicated. Sometimes, however, the initial complaint is vague; then it is necessary to pursue it to specificity. Two working rules in this approach are always to gravitate (a) from the general to the specific and (b) from the past or future to the present.

Initial polarity is always between therapist and one family member who speaks first. During the course of therapy the therapist engages different members much as the various members engage one another. A task of the therapist is to see that each engagement between any two persons present is the relevant one that serves all other processes. For instance, if a parent and child bicker uselessly, the therapist will likely interrupt that process by inviting the other parent to start a new and hopefully more fruitful process with a remark such as, "Can you help them discuss more clearly what really bothers them?" In a single-parent family, the therapist would function as the other parent and suggest a better track.

Initial formulations vary. Some families identify their difficulty as personal or individual ("I've had anxiety for years and now it's getting worse"), physical, social, or interpersonal ("I'm having trouble with my boss"). Regardless of their initial description, all problems can be viewed as familial. It is to say that within one's immediate family it is desirable, appropriate, and likely that we can find and activate factors needed to improve an individual's way of living in the world. Our current personal attachments have this enormous capability.

To better demonstrate how an indivi-

dually oriented presentation can be guided into family therapy, let us suppose a husband in a family defines a problem individually as suggester earlier, saying "I've been nervous most of my life." The dialogue presented below illustrates this point.

Therapist: I'd be interested in knowing what prompted your call at this point in your life.

Husband: I don't know. Perhaps it has something to do with my job.

The extensiveness both in time and description make it impossible to work; it is necessary to bring them into current focus. Obviously, something motivates the consultation at this time, and a good place to begin would be to search for that situation. The answer must be a conflict situation that somehow aggravates the lifetime anxiety currently. The patient is not likely to respond with "I have nothing pressing me just now so I thought I'd look into this lifelong problem."

The context in which something is said is an important and integral part of the worded message. Nonverbal motor behavior is watched for and the phrases surrounding the message are attended. What would be confronted immediately is left to the therapist's judgment as to whether calling attention to it is disrupting or propelling the ongoing process.

His reply is bathed in doubt. It could be significant or not, but it is noticed and recorded as the therapist pursues the search for specific opponents. His job is inanimate, and conflicts are initially always between people. The therapist pokes around in search of a live opponent at the job.

Therapist: Someone upsetting you at work?

Husband: Well, yes, my boss. He is so demanding and exacting. I don't think I can tolerate it. He makes me crazy.

Current interpersonal situations take precedence over therapeutic operations whenever possible. Rather than explore the matter psychologically first, it is explored practically.

Therapist: Have you discussed this with him?
Husband: No.
Therapist: Could you?
Husband: Of course not!
Therapist: What stops you?
Husband: He'd fire me.

Had he said he could try to discuss it with his boss, the therapy would be essentially concluded with the recommendation that he do that and come back perhaps with his boss if he is unable to resolve his differences with him. Some exploration and a few words of encouragement or instructions, such as "Tell your boss what frightens you and how difficult it is to discuss it with him," might be included.

But he has said otherwise. He is the victim; the demanding oppressor will annihilate him if he dares say anything. The therapist can surmise this is a projection, but it is where the patient locates his conflict that is the starting point.

Therapist: If you were assured there would be no repercussions, what do you imagine you would say?

The use of fantasy is a valuable distancing mechanism to permit a person to look at something that seems overwhelming. Fantasy-inspiring tactics are suggestions such as "If you had a magic wand and could do (or create or say) anything you wish, what would you...?" Or the therapist could use positive transference feelings and say, "Suppose I were with you...?"

The more practical the discussion, the better it is. By the same token, the closer the fantasy is to the real situation and the simpler the construction of it, the shorter is the distance back.

Husband: I'd tell him he scares me with his curt attitude and gruff voice.
Therapist: For saying that, you think he'd fire you?

Keeping any experiment sensible even though predicted on an experimental fantasy is essential.

Husband: Well, no, but he might.

He returns to the security of uncertainty once again. Is this a serious problem in his personality, or is he just using it as a braking device to prevent getting too rapidly into something frightening? One way it could be healthy, in another way not. His first oppressor was his nervousness; the second was his boss. Is his doubt also an oppressor, or is it the therapist whom he experiences as the oppressor while identifying himself as doubt? The therapist moves to this area to investigate.

Therapist: What do you mean, "he might?"
Husband: I can't know he won't.
Therapist: You seriously think it's possible?
Husband: Yes.
Therapist: It sounds absurd to me. I don't believe that you take it seriously either.
Husband: Maybe you're right, but I'd still be too frightened to say it.

Back to doubt again. The new polarization now is between his living the part of uncertainty and the therapist. The therapist considers this the larger context, since his doubtful attitude relieves him of responsibility for his behavior and simultaneously from facing the therapist. The therapist presses.

Therapist: What do you mean, "maybe I'm right"?

Husband: Alright, you are right. But I still couldn't say it.

Doubt gives way to certainty, and a new discordance is evident. His boss was identified as the oppressor. Now he says that the boss is not, but he will still treat the boss as if he were. It is necessary to see if he realizes what he says and what he does with that. The discrepancy is the new and larger discordant process so far uncovered in the search for the as yet unrevealed oppressor.

The therapist waits, subscribing to the premise that self-help is to be preferred to therapist help whenever possible.

But the husband becomes restless in his chair. He smiles blankly, picks at the cushion with one hand, and taps the arm rest with the other, saying nothing. Is he intentionally avoiding? Is he in doubt about what to do? Is he regressing into the state of nervousness he spoke about initially? The therapist takes his uncertainty to the patient with "You are getting restless. I'd like to know what it is saying."

As long as the central polarization is not reached, the therapist relentlessly, seriously, humorously, playfully pursues this objective. He or she would deflect attempts by the patient, conscious or unwitting, to avoid finding the largest recognizable conflict and to set into motion its reconciliation. All the patient's words and actions are weighed in terms of this goal. Innocence, undue seriousness, crying, whatever—the behavior will be judged by the therapist in terms of whether it enhances progress or inhibits it. The therapist does not take a behavior seriously merely because it is serious, just as he or she will not ignore a joke because of its levity. All behavior in ther-apy is considered in the context of the evolving process.

So far, only the husband's half of the intertwining processes called psychotherapy has been discussed. When does the therapist's process become something more than that of a simple process chaser? The answer was touched earlier when, in response to the husband's view that he could be fired for a rather casual comment, the husband is challenged by the personal opinion of the therapist. A therapist has many personal opinions. When they conflict seriously with the client's activity, there is an obligation to introduce them. Distress in the process belongs actively in the larger patient-therapist process.

That is the first and simplest introduction of the therapist's own personality into the patient-therapist process. For therapy to reflect the principles of the Gestalt experiential model fully, much more participation than that is required. Whenever the therapist bogs down during the process of guiding a patient to the working point, this must, in some fashion, become a part of the larger patient-therapist process. In other words, the therapist's own conflicted process is an active part of the therapy and not just dispassionate and clear contributions. This brings a host of other activities to the therapy besides cool questions, friendly suggestions, or erudite interpretations from the therapist.

Had the therapist introduced the wife to the therapeutic process, it may have proceeded differently. What has been described thus far is Gestalt therapy directed toward an individual in which the two folds were (a) a man and his anxiety and (b) a man and his boss. Had the therapist involved the wife early, the therapy may have proceeded differently, as follows:

Therapist (to wife): What do you think?

Wife: It's an old story.

Therapist: Meaning?

Wife: That's why he is on a new job. It's always been the same thing.

Therapist: What's always been the same?

Wife: He never gets along with his boss.

The therapist wants to encourage them to talk together to discover where they can be more helpful and supporting to each other but must wait until either the husband spontaneously reacts to the wife's perspective or until the wife says something that belongs to the husband and might serve to ignite their conversation.

Husband: That's not true.

Wife: (silent)

Therapist (to wife): Is it or is it not true?

Wife: He knows.

Therapist: Apparently not. You don't help him to know by falling silent.

Wife: What's the point—he won't listen.

Therapist: I think you do better to talk to him about that [which is likely the same problem as on the job but here, because of their dedication to each other she will not likely fire, i.e., abandon, him. The issue becomes more one of how she can help him more effectively than by merely falling silent].

Wife (to husband): It's really hard to talk to you.

Husband: I don't know what you mean. I'm listening.

Wife: When I tell you something you just tell me I'm wrong.

Husband: Well, in this case you are. Am I supposed to pretend you aren't?

Wife: (falls silent again)

The wife has been knocked out twice now in the first few minutes. The therapist may now choose to come in as a principal to meet the husband, may suggest how the wife might be more effective, or may offer the husband a chance to alter his way of meeting her. These issues depend on the thrust that the therapist chooses to take at that moment, based on his or her personality and professional perspective.

The purpose of this example is to suggest how the therapist can shift the arena from individual to familial. By doing so the patient's distress pattern becomes living, not talked about. He talked about fear of a firing boss. He functions in his family as firing boss. It matters now on which end of the polarization we find him. But more important, the pattern is up for reconstruction in an area that contains more incentive from both his side and the other side (his wife would likely be more interested to find a good solution than an employer). Furthermore, if he solves it at home, he is more likely to generalize and retain his improved capacity to meet the world than if he resolves it with one employer or with a therapist.

One minute a therapist may be calmly suggesting and shaking a finger at a family member exasperatingly the next. Another time the therapist may shout and cry and still another time talk soberly, for instance, exploring his or her embarrassment about not knowing how to proceed. No behavior is the exclusive property of the patient alone. If the patient-therapist process is to be kept alive, it depends as much on the full participation of the therapist as it does on demand for the patient's full commitment.

Telling a patient what you think of him or her in a fit of pique is as important as recognizing a polarized conflict in the patient; admitting your fear of telling the patient off, even more important. The track between patient and therapist must be kept open. This is achieved by the therapist's own openness, more so than by the patient's. After all, the patient has come to the therapist to learn how to live with people without strangulating them or mutilating him- or herself. The exemplary path is full personal expression.

Full personal expression does not mean increased volume or anger. It means whole messages, saying, for instance, "There is something about you that I can't stand, and it's difficult for me to tell you because I'm afraid of your reaction." And then listening to the patient's response to know if you can try to go on. It means saying, "In spite of your reassurance, I am unable to do it," and then going on to reveal what it is that gets in the way. It is this sensitive revealing of oneself that is the growing edge of mental health. The therapist's responsibility is to live it and not merely to preach it by interpreting the other person's behavior.

Nor does full personal expression mean saying everything that comes into the therapist's mind. Full personal expression is not without judgment. *The therapist is urged to say everything on his or her mind that is expected to be of value or that would diminish his or her ability to participate if he or she withheld it.* Too often the therapist's full participation is withheld with the justification that it would be damaging to the patient. Before that sentence is passed, the patient should be offered a fair trial to determine whether it is the patient's or the therapist's self-image that would suffer.

When we are trying to find the poles of a patient's process and assist the patient to reconcile these polarities to mutual extinction, full personal expression of both poles is what we are striving for. The context, the atmosphere most likely to inspire the patient risking it, is created by the therapist's own example.

MECHANISMS OF PSYCHOTHERAPY

"Round and round she goes; and where she stops nobody knows."

Whether the wheel of fortune, the cycle of life, the circulating proton or the stellar swirls, round is undoubtedly "the way she goes." And, of course, the reason nobody knows where she stops is that she doesn't.

Psychotherapy fits this pattern. It is a process, and like all other processes its shape is round. The mechanism of psychotherapy is the process of circulating one human being through another.

Circular theorizing is not new to psychology. Starting the life cycle with *im*pressions, one theory claims that man moves away from integrated wholeness by a collection of *re*pressions and finds the way back again by the proper *ex*pressions. Another starts with a chemical *de*ficiency and seeks a distal point in the cycle called medicated *su*fficiency in hope of restoring a state of organismic *ef*ficiency.

Regardless of the frame of reference, the generic psychological cycle requires one in need at the starting point who at the apogee of one's circle must pass through another person in some fashion before one can return to oneself, if not fulfilled, at least one loop closer. Although the precise nutrient obtained during the passage defies clear, simple description, its existence is undeniable. Though intangible to the familiar senses, the consequences of its absence or presence are abundantly evident. This process applies to the healthy child who needs another to maintain his growing process as it does to the person who has lost her integratedness and needs restoration.

Symptomatic behavior tells us that a person has a stuck process somewhere inside that obstructs integrated flowing, that the undulating flow of some process has congealed and the two poles are deadlocked. Translating that into psychological terms, we say that the person has parts of him- or herself that are not acceptable to other parts, that in certain locales the person doesn't want to have anything to do with him- or herself. In order for the process to flow again, these two estranged components must meet and find mutual acceptance.

This acceptance is not to be construed as an end point. A person morally conflicted with a policeman and a thief within does not end the struggle with each part mutually endorsing the other's activity. Processes joined are processes extinguished, and the end of their meeting and reconciling is a disappearance of both policeman and thief. The resultant union produces a new process, a newly oriented individual—a psychotherapist, a fine photographer, or perhaps a probation officer. Although the original two disappear, the new creation will, of course, bear testimony of its history.

Regardless of the name used to describe how the person arrived at the conflicted state—shame, guilt, repression, denial—the recovery path is the same: reintegration by circulation through another.

To begin with, there are always forces within the symptomatic patient that desire reintegration regardless of the patient's conscious attitude and, at times, the therapist's frustrated opinion: processes need to flow and evolve. It is these forces that the therapist allies him- or herself with in work, forces without which he or she would be powerless to intervene.

Splitting a personality is created by the substitution of approval and disapproval in place of the child's need for simple acknowledgment and response. Reintegration requires, then, the restoration of acknowledgment to its rightful place and the elimination of the approval-disapproval operation. To achieve full integration, the therapist must frustrate both approving and disapproving. However, since the patient's processes get stuck with the disapproving side of the coin facing up, this is often the place therapy must begin. Then, as the disapproving element is eliminated, the approving counterpart loses its significance, and acknowledgment finds its way back as the needed factor in nutritious relating.

The precise steps, often taken simultaneously, are as follows: The patient must find someone who will be granted the power to judge the patient, that is, someone in whom he or she can place the confidence required to reexamine him- or herself—since the patient lives with the fear that further reexamination will risk further disapproval.

Confidence is inspired by a therapist who is revealed as a person also in need of acknowledgment. The familiar posture of the kind, approving therapist plays into the patient's fantasy that disapproval is dangerous and reveals the therapist's own residual wishes for approval. Many patients having lived most of their lives in an approval-disapproval-tinted context may not be prepared for a more forthright meeting and initially must be weaned by judicious but uncompromising and persistent challenge of their wish for approval.

With a fairly sturdy patient, a vexed therapist may reveal with great exasperation, "I can't stand the way you just sit there and say nothing. Sometimes I regret ever becoming a therapist. You are impossible." And when the patient wanly responds with "I'm sorry," the therapist's volume may increase as she proclaims, "There it is. Sorry! Always sorry. How do you expect me to survive on sorrow? I need a hell of a lot more than that in return for my efforts." Following this discharge, the therapist, feeling better, says, "There, now I feel OK. How do you feel?"

Patient: I feel terrible. I didn't like what you said.
Therapist: As I said, I feel good.

Confidence is inspired by the therapist's own need for expressiveness, and simultaneously he or she demonstrates a way out of the approval-disapproval maze by risking the patient's disapproval.

Then, with the skillful encouragement of the therapist, the patient must reveal him- or herself, must circulate hidden, unacceptable elements through the therapist's acknowledgment. In this atmosphere, the approval-disapproval struggles are reactivated and renegotiation begins. Symptoms wane the moment activation begins. They may likely return if the process is not pursued to completion with the patient's own self-acknowledgment replacing the old approval-disapproval operation. Without completion there is always the danger that the patient will use the therapist's acknowledgment as an approval operation—a phenomenon watched for and frustrated by an alert therapist when he or she does not need to play the game of approving and disapproving.

Renegotiation is the mechanism for ending approval-disapproval operations. Under the sensitive guidance of the therapist, the two elements in an approval-disapproval operation meet and reveal

themselves to each other—their frustrations with one another and their longings for reconciliation. Also every other most petty and insignificant detail must be expressed and negotiated to extinction.

The therapeutic mechanism in treatment has been called the process of validation. It is not quite that. Nor is it a process of acknowledgment, although the therapeutic mechanism has both elements, and it is perhaps these mechanisms that, more than anything else, empower the therapy. The fundamental mechanism is the creation of a context in which a person can be revealed to another in order to be able to find him- or herself.

The optimal parent is a transparent, a person through which a child can pass, obtaining acknowledgment while growing without too much impedance by parental approval and disapproval operations. The optimal therapist is the one who also has, or has restored, acknowledgment of him- or herself in areas that correspond to areas where the patient needs to exchange old disapprovals for new self-appreciations. In family therapy family members are always encouraged to become that responsive, expressive other that then serves as a cornerstone to the restoration of the family as the primary personal resource for all of its members.

APPLICATION

The application of any model is the applied, sensitive, competence of the therapist. During treatment no "model" is present, and "application" is fantasy. Present are only people manifesting their entire histories. The so-called model applicability depends exclusively on the therapist's ability to share his or her history in integrated word and deed. In the final analysis, Gestalt family therapy (or any other model, for that matter) is most effective when the therapist is presented in a way that touches, inspires, guides a family toward a more satisfying and rewarding life together.

Example: One basic tenet of Gestalt family therapy states that when a child is identified as the problem, all the children are to be included in the therapy. One Gestalt family therapist had serious doubt about the possibility of effectively influencing a family when one of three adolescent daughters, a central figure in the family conflict, refused to attend the sessions despite vigorous attempts by her mother and the therapist.

The question is not one of model applicability. The question is, How can one be of most value to this family? By visiting the daughter at home to see what I can do to engage her? By seeing whoever is willing to attend the sessions? By offering to see the daughter alone once? By refusing to see the family without her, thereby forcing the family to choose between two ultimata, mine and hers?

Though the basic premise calls for everyone to be present, the challenge is the therapist's, not the model's. Should only one member attend sessions, and the therapist decides to accept that starting point, the therapist is still doing Gestalt family therapy—and it is applicable.

Problems

An artist sees through artist's eyes. Likewise, a therapist aware of the psychophysical processes inherent in all human behavior, inevitably views any peopled activity through this perspective and consequently sees evidence that indicates that his or her work might be useful. Quite naturally, he or she would like to

think his or her lifework has the broadest possible use, since the greater its range, the more the therapist and his or her premises are validated. Of course, information to the contrary is also valuable. Since Gestalt family therapy is quite young and since it is founded in the field of psychology, its usefulness in fields afar such as the political arena has not been explored and therefore can be discussed only as the author's fancy. And that fancy begins with the premise that the tenets of Gestalt family therapy could be beneficially applied to any interpeopled situation, disturbed or not. Admittedly, there are some reservations that will be discussed shortly.

Gestalt family therapy, although formally presented as a specific type of psychotherapy, is based on principles considered to be a sound way of life. In other words, it is first a philosophy, a way of being, and superimposed on that are ways of applying that knowledge so that others may benefit from it. Gestalt family therapy is the service organization of the Gestalt philosophy. Hopefully, the Gestalt therapist is identified more by who he or she is than by what he or she is or does. The presumption, then, is that the fundamental premises underlying this psychotherapeutic model are as applicable at home as they are at the office, to a healthy child as to a disturbed child, at a party as at a seminar, to a teacher as to a student, to a supervisor as to a subordinate.

One person can personally live these experiential premises, but a therapist requires collaboration. The superstructure, the therapeutic amplification of a Gestalt philosophy depends on some willingness, some cooperation, some readiness to persevere in the negotiations from the recipient before suitability as a therapeutic influence can be determined. A unilateral view of suitability is a fantasy that requires experiential confirmation.

This does not mean to say that a patient must come to therapy highly motivated. A patient can come with little motivation but must come; somehow the patient must also be prepared to stay for a while, at least. If the patient is sent, for instance by law as a condition for probation, even against his or her own will, he or she has arrived and can be considered suitable. Now, of course, the suitability of the therapist becomes the crucial issue that determines whether they can establish a therapeutic process together.

The therapist's interest first, then skillfulness determine what problems or symptoms are suitable to treat. A talented and sensitive Gestalt therapist may work well with passive, withdrawn, hospitalized individuals and be quite unable to cope with addicts, while another Gestaltist may be able to influence addicts. It is the therapist, not the therapy, that determines suitability. It is the character of the process that can be created between therapist and patient that decides the suitability of the method that the therapist is (or is said to represent).

The same principle applies to areas beyond the ordinary psychotherapeutic arena. Hospitals, industrial organizations, political bodies from the UN to a local two-person post office in a remote community can benefit from the application of Gestalt therapy to its interpersonal problems. But again it would require some interest from the therapist and some motivation—even if it is only an injunction from above—from the recipients. There is nothing in Gestalt family therapy itself to block its applicability.

Organizations not specifically created for the purpose of psychotherapy present certain special characteristic problems, regardless of size and composition. In psychotherapy, the participants have nothing to gain but themselves. There is little room for debate on that issue. However, in situations like divorce, business, and politics, where bookends, budgets, and markets are at stake, the task is at once admittedly more complex.

It could be argued that when the goal includes the division of spoils between strangers or estrangers, there comes a time when the psychotherapeutic process is no longer appropriate, when the issue is no longer one of feelings but rather one of facts: the psychotherapeutic process is ended, and each party is resolute in an unequivocal and opposing viewpoint. After all, psychotherapy is preparation for concerted action and not offered as a substitute for action.

It is also reasonable to postulate that given enough time, the most material-infested discord could eventually reach a point where all parties concerned are sufficiently interested in mutual survival that material matters take a secondary place. While undoubtedly true, the time schedule is often beyond the therapist's influence.

Frustration is an inevitable by-product of any organized activity that can seriously impede man's singular or cooperative movement. By encouraging integrated and immediate responsiveness, Gestalt therapy offers an alternative that diminishes such impairment from back-logged frustration. It also offers ways of relating that can reduce the incidence of frustrating experiences. Therefore, in spite of the differences between psychotherapeutic groups and other types of organizations, there are things to be tried and benefits to be gained by the use of Gestalt family therapy in organizations not specifically established for psychotherapeutic benefit, regardless of their size, composition, or central purpose.

Goal Definition and Diagnosis

The goals of the therapeutic process are to mobilize the assets and talents within a family and to guide their appropriate application in the concerns of daily living. In the final position, we can say the goal of the therapeutic process is the restoration of the family as the core resource for the personal growth and welfare of its members; these are achieved by awakening the dormant capabilities of its members to perceive, negotiate, and act.

The tradition of the medical model from which psychology, psychotherapy, and consequently family therapy take form has been predicated on first establishing a proper diagnosis, the cure of which becomes the goal of the therapeutic process. Symptom relief like getting rid of a cough, whether caused by cancer or the common cold, is considered a side issue for the patients' convenience. The model yet prevails in Western medicine and in the more traditional areas of psychology where individual diagnosis is still considered necessary. A growing segment of the psychological world, including Gestalt clinical psychology and Gestalt family therapy, realizes that the concept of diagnosis is obsolete.

Diagnostic labels are dangerous. They may influence the patient adversely and they can astigmatize the vision of the next therapist who sees the chart before the patient. And worst of all, they impair the vision of the therapist who makes them.

Diagnostic labels carry implications. A therapist who applies a label gets tainted with those implications, most of which were not the therapist's to begin with. He or she then wastes precious time thinking about whether the patient is a classic case or an atypical one. It also influences therapeutic judgment and skill. This patient must be treated carefully, that one must be considered for electroshock therapy, since treatment modalities often are appended to diagnostic labels.

Individual diagnoses, if used, should take their rightful place as a description of the describer—his or her frustrations, concepts, and processes in reaction to the frustrations. Better still they should be resolutely abandoned, sent to the archives of psychotherapy along with history taking and individual therapy.

It is easier to knock something down than it is to create something else to replace it. There is no good substitute available to be used in the place of individual diagnoses. The more important question—the one at least that must be answered first—is whether replacement is necessary at all. The only reason for diagnostic labels is to treat the anxiety of the therapist. A therapist wants to walk in and meet a patient with some structure, and diagnostic categories provide that wall of pigeonholes that can be used to locate the patient and thereby locate the therapist in relation to that person. The therapist has not been encouraged to experience creatively his or her own relatedness to another and simply pursue it.

If a diagnosis is necessary, we must find one that stays fluid, one that flows off as easily as it goes on, one that sensitively changes from moment to moment as processes are altered.

Every family is considered unique, each therapist's participation in a family only adding another dimension of uniqueness. To attempt a categorization for families that is useful or applicable to families of unique individuals in unique relationships in different cultures is manifestly absurd. Constellations such as "single-parent families" can be said to exist, but their commonality is limited more to their particular culture than to similarities from one single-parent family to another.

The goals of the therapeutic process in Gestalt family therapy then rest on the heads of the therapists in association with the desires of the immediate family with whom they are working. Families usually begin with the goal of symptom relief; the therapist helps remove the pattern that led to the creation of the signal or symptom. Short-term immediate goals such as motivating the father to join the sessions, getting a kid back in school, stopping a brutal father, bringing a runaway back into the family scene by giving them hope are often initial goals replaced as quickly as possible by the goal of facing difficult family issues in each session and trying to get them redirected without damaging residual—and, before the session ends, enabling each session to be a completed step in the treatment program.

Clients' Responsibilities

The family has only one primary responsibility: to come once with as many members as possible to the therapeutic interview. After that, their motivation is in the therapist's responsible hands.

Though this may sound harsh, biased, or grandiose, it is my experience that all individuals and families want a better life, a better situation if possible. It is, therefore, the challenge of the therapist (a) to provide hope to a family—particularly for those who have the greatest influence to decide whether the family comes to treatment—and (b) to demonstrate (and not merely describe or

promise) the relation between the signal and its cause, thereby making self-evident the value of family therapy.

Therapist's Role and Function

Sometimes a guide, sometimes a principal, but always present, the Gestalt family therapist offers guidance; perspective; advice; examples from personal experiences; suggestions to look inward, outward, toward each other; to listen, not to listen; to obey; to question; to refuse. The therapist encourages, discourages, praises, and appreciates.

The therapist listens to him- or herself, sometimes honestly shares doubts, sometimes, when bankrupt, intentionally fakes it. The therapist does the best possible with what he or she is.

Treatment

The subject of selecting appropriate treatment models is a discussion of contexts, ways of constructing the working field, and contacts—matching specific actions to specific askings. It is too simple to say individual therapy for individual problems, family therapy for family problems, and group therapy for patients who need sheltered socialization experiences or therapists who simply prefer to work with groups. Then we have modalities with such names as "milieu therapy" for people caught in milieus and "industrial therapy" for those caged in industries. The various titles create unnecessary confusion by mixing contexts and contacts, that is, the location of the processes and the specific character of the process itself. Selecting the context is best decided after the contact points are established. The contact point to be considered first is the nontherapist point or the specific asking.

This "other" contact point, the request, is not always a symptom. There are many ways of asking for therapeutic contact. Improving hospital morale, facilitating industrial operations, therapists applying for sensitivity training to develop themselves are examples of asymptomatic askings. Of course, the numbers involved in asking will influence the later determination of the context. But before that point is reached, the contact point called the therapist must be considered. This reduces itself largely to the skill and area of interest of the therapist, as has already been mentioned.

Once the two points have been joined, we are ready to consider the model most suitable, the context in which their processes may be best manifested. The fundamental principles of the Gestalt approach prevail, regardless of the nature of the two contact points and regardless of the context or model selected. In other words, whether we discuss individual, family, or group therapy, or sensitivity training, all therapeutic activity seeks the ground level of the immediate and encourages everyone's most forthright and personal expression and interest in that immediate.

For working purposes, there can be no more than two people at the most advanced working edge regardless of group size or composition. Although four people may be talking at once, the lead point will reduce itself to the behavior of two. Though one may be the obvious leader at a given moment, the lead point still involves two people—the leader and his or her counterpart. This is not to say that the others do not have influence on the situation or that the two lead people are oblivious to the presence of the others. But the foremost working point is always characterized by a phenomenon between two points, both usually individuals.

There are exceptions. One point, however, is always one individual in the process. For brief moments that person may stand against the entire group, but if that exists there will be an unspoken hierarchy forming among the noisy or silent others until one of them clearly prevails as their spokesperson. So, though there are always influences that can be seen and sensed from the size and configuration of a group, the focal point of the group's evolution, the working edge, is always the behavior of two individuals. The therapist may be one of them; or, in an introspective period, be both of them; or when also integrated, be only a guide or observer at the periphery of two other focal points of the evolving group.

Some group therapists strive for active verbal participation of as many members as possible, as much of the time as possible, and describe success in terms of voluble numbers. This tends to create a social atmosphere where the weakest link, so to speak, determines the allowable pressure on the chain. This may be valuable in the field of mechanics but serves more as an impedance than an insurance when applied to psychotherapy. In group processes, verbal participation of everyone at one time or another is desirable and can be rewarding for the individual speaking as well as the group. But to adhere doggedly to that premise reduces intensity and the rate of group process. The intensity of the psychotherapeutic process depends on the depth of experience two people create together, not on the breadth of the membership's voluble contributions. If silent members are a concern in a group, then specific one-to-one conversation, for example, between the most verbal and the most silent member of the group is one way of encouraging a meaningful one-to-one working point. Attention to silent members can be achieved also by focusing on that topic, encouraging personal opinions and attitudes directed to specific persons. Soon, a two-point working edge will emerge.

In family therapy the same premises prevail. Conversations about children are reshaped into personal requests, opinions, or statements directed to a specific child. In families, of course, every behavior of one member naturally is related to and influences in some way every other person present, and thereby facilitates the work. However, regardless of this fact, the premise of the two-people working point prevails.

The premise of the two-person working point does not mean that others are to be excluded. Perls developed the "hot seat" format, well known to those who worked with him, in which he worked exclusively with one or another person, while the rest of the group observed. This was most comfortable for him. However, Perls often stated and agreed that individual therapy is history. Working with one individual in a group is not individual therapy. While working with one individual at any given moment, the therapist influences and welcomes participation from others. However, he or she will try to deter it if it is disruptive. It is challenging to stay at the working edge between two persons and still encourage others to jump in as the spirit moves them. The therapist must qualify third-party comments: Does it enhance the working edge? Is it a distraction? Is it a valuable modification away from a dying working point to a fresh topic?

When the intensity of a working edge dwindles and the therapist is uncertain how to proceed, he or she can appropriately invite comment whether doing individual, family, group, or sensitivity work. The therapist is following an underlying philosophical premise: when you don't know what to do, ask for help.

Although the Gestalt model is described through the two-point, one-to-one, nose-to-nose experience, the family context is considered the most profitable working context. A person's family is the power behind the throne of all members, adult and child alike. When the family ceases to be that, a person is deprived and deserves better. The family should either be restored as the primary source and resource for emotional succoring or be replaced. Additionally, the family is the most influential force that encourages, sustains, or discourages symptomatic behavior of members. It is not possible for a person to live in a family and not be contaminated by their vibrations—their processes—for better or for worse. The Gestalt therapeutic model of psychotherapy applied within the context of the family is considered the optimal treatment modality.

Criminal recidivism rates have been correlated to availability of family and found consistently lower among offenders with families. The gang and the prison have been identified as family surrogates, important in the continuance of criminal and prison-seeking behavior. Now, we also know that alcoholics require alcohol-endorsing partners. We are gradually discovering what we knew all along: people require people to conduct the business of behaving; people alone are an incomplete process and therefore cannot sustain. Much symptomatology would disappear immediately if all family members were obliged to share the hospital and prison fate of their symptomatic members.

When family exists, family therapy is the therapeutic modality of choice. Institutions, wards, and organizations can profit by being treated as family units also. As with group therapy, any group outside the family lacks the cohesive pressure that is so valuable to the therapeutic process with families. Coworkers don't have to get along, and distance is an alternative to negotiation. This is also true for group psychotherapy, making it a second choice to family therapy. As suggested earlier, individual therapy is not a recommended modality per se.

Management

The Setting. The optimal setting for working can be described in a word—comfortable. Whether in office, home, retreat, or conference center, the setting that provides the greatest opportunity for people to experience themselves in relation to one another is a setting that is not distracting. The physical requirements should be consonant with an informal, unpretentious atmosphere. Familiarity of setting (seeing families in their homes, e.g.) is a fine idea but is generally impractical. The pressures of time and cost make a central setting, created and selected by the therapist, the most feasible model.

I sometimes film my work to provide students who cannot see what I do first-hand with the next best thing—an audiovisual experience. I prefer to teach by direct demonstration. I do not use films of a family to show back to that family as a therapeutic activity. I try to avoid pounding patients with pills and paraphernalia. The personal experience in the moment is preferred to a review of yesterday's moment, however good it might seem; and today's relationship is preferred to tomorrow's drug effect.

Language. No special language as such is encouraged, although psychological jargon is discouraged. Patients are encouraged to use their usual and familiar language. However, expressions that veil communication are challenged. For instance, a person who customarily surrounds statements with amenities and courtesies is challenged to verify them. A frequent "I'm sorry" or "Forgive me for saying so but..." type of speech is challenged. Forthright expression is always encouraged. The vernacular and the profane are enjoyed but only when they are on the crest of personal expressions and beyond calculation. When such remarks become a tradition or style to create an image, they are confronted. An "Oh, damn!" or "Oh, shit!" when a person is overwhelmed with sudden frustration is of no concern, while a style that uses such language continually is a character style that is challenged much the same as the refuge of social amenity. Language is for expression, not impression.

Initial Interviews. Psychological testing, like medication and other equipment, is considered diversionary. I prefer to look at the person in front of me, and I do not try to see him through any interpreting device beyond my intuitiveness and ordinary senses.

Physical Symptoms. I believe we create our own physical disease processes as a part of our disturbed adaptation. Therefore, I treat all physical symptoms as I would psychological complaints with one exception: Physical examinations are recommended for all physical symptoms so that the patient can know his or her medical status and take full responsibility for what is done about it. I will not participate, however, in the medical aspects of the diagnosis or treatment, though my background is a medical one. If a patient has treatable, physical pathology, I would likely recommend considering the necessary medical or surgical care. After all, just because we cause our own pathology psychologically is no reason to proclaim that we must therefore banish it in the same way. I do not ask my patient to subscribe to my views about physical illness. It is not necessary for my work, and I prefer that a patient pursue his or her own views.

Role Playing. The concept of role playing, in its broadest sense, is anathema to me. Since one of the underlying premises is that patients become symptomatic by living or growing in states of duplicity, the corollary that follows naturally says that any deviation from genuine self-disclosure is contraindicated. The patient and I find each other by virtue of our correlated roles initially, but once work begins our identities must depend on who we are and not on what we are or who we are supposed to be. I do not play the role of doctor.

Sometimes I play a role. For instance, once I recall playing a colleague's father. It seemed to fit for me, and I did not feel false. As he described his relationship with his father, I felt that I really knew what his father wanted to say, and I invited myself to be his father's mute interior—the voice this colleague had never heard. Our experience together was a memorable one.

I prefer, whenever possible, to reveal myself. This is the most difficult part of my work, partly because I am always changing. Self-disclosure leads to new self-awareness, so what I say today I usually cannot say tomorrow. It is difficult to keep up with who I am, but when I can, I enjoy sharing myself. Sometimes, however, it is most difficult for me to disclose myself.

Resistance. There is no such thing as patient resistance. There is only *my* lack

of development or lack of familiarity with what I meet in another. Experimenting with the patient's and my relationship is one way to work when I don't know what to do. Or I will ask my patient for help. The concept of patient resistance is a terrible thing for the patient but a worse thing for the therapist. It tempts the therapist to rest when a personal invitation to develop has been given.

Dislike. Accurately expressed disliking usually fades. If it doesn't and I find nothing else to say about it, I move on to something else and will review it again only if it gets in my way. Should it persist, I will refer the family to another therapist.

Problems. For me there are no such things as "patient problems." The patient may have what he calls his problems, I have mine.

My problems keep changing. I am always becoming aware of new ones and surprised when old ones don't reappear. It's tempting to discuss them as professional issues (e.g., the crying patient, the threatening patient, the suicidal patient, etc.). But "they" are not my problem.

The problems I have in therapy occur when someone is presented and I am unable to meet him or her with concerted behavior. Even then it is not a problem per se as long as I am able squarely to acknowledge and present my disconcerted behavior. I am only a problem when, on occasion, I am discordant and unable to disclose it. Then I begin to act like a therapist and hope some professional success will justify my personal absence.

Results or Outcomes. People have asked, "How do you know your therapy works?" And I answer seriously, "Because I am changing." I think process and believe the only way to recognize changes in a process is by the recognition of movement inside oneself. But this creates many uncomfortable "problematic" moments in my work. As I change, I cannot use yesterday's successful tactics since it is no longer me. I feel obliged to meet a person with who I am today. Today I may be less certain than yesterday, though the situation or presenting other is similar. I feel that I am losing my competence at times, and in a sense that is true. But in the middle of the changing I sometimes lose perspective and forget that a new process will result. I have faith that new competence will eventually follow as long as I do not deceive myself or try to deceive others in the process, as when I switch to playing therapist.

As a consequence, one day a suicidal patient may ignite a problem in me and on another day, not. One particular suicidal patient may arouse conflict in me, while another may not. It is difficult to say one type of patient or one kind of behavior consistently creates conflict in me and therefore could be labeled as a standard problem.

I have tended to be more familiar, and more comfortable, with my own assertive and aggressive expression. Recently I am recognizing tender feelings I had previously transformed into aggressive expression. As a consequence of this, I feel frightened sometimes when someone else is aggressive—a feeling I had rarely known before. Somehow for me to be tender has meant to be vulnerable. I have heard people repeat that sentiment for years, but I never trusted it. Now I know I was right. I don't trust it in myself either, for I have also now tasted tenderness without feeling vulnerable or weak. They need not be joined. How I will re-

spond to aggressiveness these days depends on the condition of my evolving tenderness and feeling of vulnerability.

Patient problems are a misnomer and an unfortunate one. The idea of patient problems is part of the heritage of objective psychology and should be sent to the archives. It urges therapists to take "their" problems to colleagues and cheats the therapist of a chance to grow. Simultaneously, it creates an artificial distance between the therapist and patient as it also deprives the patient of the chance to witness growing in action.

CASE EXAMPLE

The therapy consisted of three 1.5-hour interviews for 3 consecutive weeks, with follow-up 6 months and 2 years later at the request of the therapist.

This condensation of one family's therapy is selected for several reasons. First, the symptom precipitating therapy was decisive and dramatic; second, there was a cohesion in this family that simplified the dynamics—that is, everyone's behavior related clearly and directly to everyone else's. In many families the relationships are less sharply defined and do not lend themselves so readily to description. Finally, this family was chosen because follow-up was possible and the results clearly positive.

Background

This is an ahistoric approach. When the mother called for the appointment, the only question was about the nature of the problem as seen by the mother, to determine whether it was necessary to see the entire family or only the parents. Stan, 12, the youngest of three boys, was setting fires, small ones at first, but the most recent one required the fire department and brought other local authorities into the picture. Stan had been playing with matches for a long time, and the family had been unable to stop him. I requested that the mother bring her husband and all three boys with her. Families fit together like a picture puzzle. In the same way, an individual's personality creates a unique but always complete composite even though there may be conflict and discord within the frame. The mother hastened to assure me that the oldest boy, 16, was fine and "besides, he is visiting relatives for the summer in another part of the country and couldn't possibly come." The treatment ensemble consisted, then, of the therapist; the mother; the father; David, 14; and the identified patient, Stan, 12, who sets fires.

Further background information was not sought. Parents' employment, ages of family members (provided here since the reader cannot see the family members), family income, marital status, and whatever else amuses data collectors have no meaning alone. Anything pertinent emerges relevantly during the course of treatment, which focuses on the essence of current relationships. If a historical fact becomes pertinent, it will become part of the treatment in a timely and useful way. For instance, one parent's reluctance to participate in the discipline of the children may be related to the historical fact that the parent is not a natural parent and has only recently joined the family. When, during the interview, discipline is called for and it becomes obvious and problematic that one parent is not participating appropriately in this family, the historical information will emerge in a timely and meaningful way. It is not necessary to accumulate such data in advance. In fact, history taking blunts the therapist's chances of

seeing precisely how historical facts may be used to excuse current effective participation.

The same applies to individual therapy where the focus of the therapist's attention is on how the person presents him- or herself and what the person does in the allotted time rather than on the facts explaining his or her behavior.

The Problem and the Treatment

In this ahistoric process, the problem and the treatment are inseparable. There is no preamble consisting of a search for a problem to be followed at some later time by some therapeutic maneuvers. The identified problem, the presenting complaint, is not the problem. It merely signals the problem. The problem is always the defective manner in which people function together, and the concomitant treatment is a process of challenging the unsatisfactory functioning as it is revealed.

The family is invited into my office and encouraged to sit down wherever they wish. My office looks like a living room with many stuffed chairs, all with armrests and most of them rockers. I sit down in one of the remaining chairs and look the family over.

I am aware of the mother's leadership. She called. She competently guided her family into the office but wasn't pushy about where people sat. She introduced herself, the 14-year-old, the 12-year-old, and her husband, who came in last, slowly and a bit delayed. I think to myself that he is her oldest son and a reluctant dragon. I listen for other reverberations inside me. How do I like them? Is there anything unusual? Are they tense? Talkative? Supportive toward each other? Whom do I like the best? Anything frightening or unpleasant for me?

I don't consciously think these things, but I have learned that they are some of the things my sensing apparatus is attending. I suppose this is my form of history taking. I prefer my current fantasies to their historical facts as a starting point. I prefer our current experience to their past experience as the working point.

Aside from the initial phone call, fire setting was mentioned only one time at the beginning of the first interview. As the mother was reiterating the reason for seeking therapy, she identified Stan as the problem and reported, solicitously, that he had been setting fires and, as she put it, "telling things that weren't true and taking things sometimes that did not belong to him." Fire setting, lying, and stealing were not discussed at that time, nor were they ever mentioned again. The symptom or identified problem had served its purpose; it called attention to an unsatisfactory family operation, and it was no longer needed. We were now ready to get down to work.

In order to see how people negotiate improperly, it is necessary to start a conversation. Almost anything will do, preferably something serious enough to hold everyone's attention and not so overwhelming that it will paralyze. I can't know what that would be without poking around a bit. The topic must also be interesting for me.

I noticed that the mother visually checks out each of her wards and settles her attention on me. The kids look around the room frequently glancing at mother. The father alternates glances between the floor and his wife. I'm wondering what I would like to say when the mother asks, "Where would you like us to begin?"

I think a moment. I feel no pressing need of my own, so I respond with a friendly comment that in effect says I would like to know what they want from me. If not too artificial, I try to make statements rather than ask questions. I urge the same from them as part of creating an atmosphere of self-disclosure.

The mother responded, as expected, with a speech about Stan, concluding, "We don't know what to do now. What we have tried obviously doesn't work."

When I have nothing inside pressing me—if I did that would get my attention first—I try to get a conversation started among the family members. I do this by moving from general remarks to immediate and pertinent ones in search of a specific statement one person can make to another, either revealing something they want from that person or something they are getting currently that they don't like. If I were working exclusively with one person, I would be the partner for the conversation and follow the same principle. What the individual wants from me and how he or she goes about trying to get it is of central importance.

Although verbalizing is the medium for our working, I am more concerned with process than with verbal content. I am sensing and observing how cooperative and responsive the person tries to be. I am noticing the way her mind flows, the associations she makes. Is she sensitive? Does she have and use good common sense? Is her behavior congruent with her words? Is her thinking process simple or complex? Is she thoughtful or shallow? Is she methodical and logical in her thinking or chaotic? How the person's mind works is important since it is a door we must pass through to reach one another.

While we are searching for the starting point for a family conversation, I notice the mother's mounting exasperation that is quickly covered with a distorted and incongruent face. Her brow wrinkles into a frown, and her mouth smiles. The martyred smiling-through face, I think to myself as I call attention to her inappropriate smile.

When pointing out something I choose a way that will be evocative. I don't want to be ignored; I don't want to be taken lightly; I don't want to overwhelm. I want my remarks to be penetrating. With this woman as I listen and watch her, I sense that she is sturdy and capable of being direct, so I offer her the smile without attenuation and say, "You smile inappropriately as you talk about painful matters."

This initiates a dialogue between us that further confirms her sturdiness. Her immediate response is "I don't see anything wrong with smiling. I think it helps to be cheerful."

"Good," I think to myself. She doesn't swallow me whole. She has a mind of her own, and her reasoning is direct and uncomplicated.

"I don't think it helps to pretend to be cheerful when you are not. Save your smile for happy times," I answered decisively. Now I am not afraid that she will be overwhelmed, so I am emphatic.

"I'm not sure that I agree with you, but I'll think about it," she answers.

I am now finished with that topic, satisfied that she will think twice before she again dissociates her thoughts and feelings in this manner. This is the first step to making this discordance ego-alien, as we used to say, but it is not central at this moment. In group therapy I might continue on this path, but here I am more interested in igniting, studying, and treating the family interactive pattern.

"OK, so what do you have to say to whom?" I say, guiding her back to the search for a point to begin a family conversation.

The starting point for the mother turns out to be a long, apologetic, plaintive appeal to Stan in which she points out how patient and reasonable she and his father have been and concludes with a pitiful "We just don't know what to do anymore to help you."

Stan squirms, smiles at her sheepishly, is obviously uncomfortable, and says nothing. No one else speaks. The father is immobile but glances from the mother to Stan and back again. The mother has a sickly sweet patronizing look of suffering mankind, which she offers to the therapist when it fails to produce anything from Stan.

The field is now loaded with possibilities—starting points for creating significant dialogues. I could respond to the mother, pointing out any number of things, such as her burdening Stan with her martyrdom or perhaps mentioning the difference in the way she decisively responded to me a moment earlier as compared to the indecisive, pathetic way she appeals to her son. I might turn to Stan and pick up his imitating the mother by smiling when he is uncomfortable; I could turn to the father and point up his lack of participation. I might say to all of them that the mother turns to a child for help instead of to a spouse, which would be more appropriate. I could point out the father's apparent lack of awareness about his wife's martyred posture. I might similarly ask the father to help.

To know where to go, I turn not to what I might or could do but rather to what I am experiencing. I am acutely aware of Stan's discomfort. My feelings are with him and not against the mother or father, as they might be on some other occasion. I want to help him reduce the pressure that has been put on him, in a way that does not put more pressure on

Stan. Yet, at the same time, I do not want to bypass him by simply fighting his battle for him. I turn to Stan, inviting his participation with questions that require simple answers and not too much thinking, questions that can lead us back toward a family discussion.

Therapist: That speech of your mother's is a hard one to respond to, isn't it?

Stan (still smiling weakly): Yeah.

Therapist: If I were in your shoes, I wouldn't know what to say either. Would you like some help?

Stan: Yes.

Therapist: Well, perhaps we could start with where you are and say to both of your parents, "Hey, this is a tough spot to be in, I don't know what to say. Could you guys help me out? After all that's what parents are for." Does that sound like that speech could do for you right now, Stan?

Stan smiles and nods and looks a bit less tense but still says nothing. I wait. The mother picks up what I said and responds, "I don't mean to put pressure on Stan. We've had so many family talks already I just don't know what else to do. The only thing that I can think of is that we should be more understanding."

Finally, the father speaks. His expression is impassive, his voice cold and unmodulated. "Nothing works. He just doesn't care. He won't do anything he is told." And then to his wife: "You know we've tried everything."

Wife: Yes, but I still think we are a bit hard on him. I mean you are very intolerant of him and I think you discipline him harder than the others.

Husband: He earns it. He knows what his chores are and he rarely does them. He's much worse than the others, who are bad enough.

The verbal content, the conversation, is the vehicle for transporting relationships. But it is the process, that is, what is going on, that is the high-octane fuel for the vehicle. Pouring process knowledge into the vehicle of content (the conversation) is what propels the therapeutic conversation. By paying attention to my own internal processes, I am able to bring impetus to the situation and sustain my own interest. A valuable dialogue has begun between the mother and father. I am interested in observing how they negotiate to solve discord.

Wife: I don't think you are being fair. After all, he's younger than the others and you know very good and well that he is always on the short end when anything happens among the children. His life is a more difficult one. (The husband is silent.)

Therapist (to the husband): I'd like to know what you are thinking.

Husband: What can I say? She always defends the kids. I think all we need is for these kids to develop more of a sense of responsibility. But she always stops me and defends the kids. Especially Stan.

I am aware of the father's pattern of sullen withdrawal when he becomes frustrated. At the same time, I notice David, the 14-year-old, squirming in his chair. I know what's going on with the father, but I don't know what David's restlessness is saying. I'm curious.

Therapist (to David): I'd like to know what you think about all this, David?

Tears come to David's eyes, and he has difficulty speaking. No one moves toward him. I wish someone in the family would. I can sense that the mother would like to but doesn't want to give proof to the husband's charge of partiality, and the father is too estranged to respond in a friendly way to David. It could be valuable to discuss these thoughts, but I prefer to follow my feelings toward David and know more about his discomfort. I invite him to sit in a chair alongside of me. He slowly comes over and sits down. I put my arm around him and tell him that I'd like to know what about all this makes him feel so sad. Sobbing, he tells me that he feels many demands and does not feel recognized or appreciated by his father. David has never revealed his distress before and was identified originally by the mother as a "no-problem child."

Attempting to restart further family talk, I suggest to the father that he assume David was speaking directly to him and encourage the father to respond.

Father: I find this a little startling. I see things quite differently. I see us doing much for you kids, demanding almost nothing and getting very little. Perhaps if you did more I'd find more to appreciate.

Opposites. Apposing opposites. Bringing opposing views into clear focus, not for the purpose of creating a battle but to have these differences out in the open alongside each other for all to see, taste, experience, know, is a primary characteristic of this approach. Where many other therapeutic models advocate support, love, rapport, trust, and other moralities as the cornerstone of therapy, the Gestalt experiential approach, although agreeing with the virtue and value of all of those items, prefers the clear, clean apposition of opposing forces as the number one ground rule for negotiating interpersonal or intrapsychic dilemmas.

An important first step has been taken in the restoration of this family. The father and son have exposed and confronted each other with their differences. Now I want to guide them as far as possible to further reveal and define themselves to each other in this critical area. I return to the process and wait to hear if and how David will answer. I expect the

child in a parent-child discourse to need more encouragement, but that is not always true. I must first wait and see.

David doesn't answer.

Therapist (to David): What do you think about your father's remark?

Sometimes it's easier for someone to begin by talking about rather than to someone. But David just shakes his head and continues to look at the floor. I think to myself that David is behaving like his father, using a kind of sulking posture, while Stan seems more identified with his mother with the smiling approach. But these seem irrelevant at the moment. So the observation is filed away.

Therapist (to David and his father): Can either of you think of an example?

Moving from the general to the specific by calling for examples is a good way to keep a conversation vital.

David: In the Scouts, for instance.

Father: There are things you wanted to do in the Scouts and if you wanted these things I thought you should work toward them.

David: You wanted me to do so much more than I was able to do.

Father: No. I thought you were able to do those things. I'm thinking of some of the merit badges you could have earned a year or two ago when you did everything except pass the final review on them. You earned your hiking merit badge, your cooking merit badge, and you didn't go ahead and finish them up. I think you were perfectly capable of finishing it up. The other boys who were at the camp on the camp-out did finish them up, and they were not more capable than you.

David: I think you should have been with me a little more instead of just telling me and urging me to do those things.

Father: The merit badges are something you are supposed to earn yourself and not have me earning them for you. I'm not supposed to be helping you.

David is silent. I sensed that I knew what David was saying, but, first, it was a bit sophisticated for a 14-year-old to express; second, the father was not making it easier; and third, I felt David was really trying. So I sat in David's chair and spoke for him. It felt comfortable for me.

Therapist: But, Dad, you don't understand. If I could have done those things I would have. The fact was that I couldn't achieve it, and I wasn't appreciated for what I could do. If I had a little more friendship with you, a little more encouragement from you—appreciation—then maybe I would have more confidence in myself to do some of those things.
Father: But he could have done them.
Therapist: If he could have done them, he would have done them (emphatically). You're doing it again.
Father: I think it was just procrastination.
Therapist (as David): I wish you could know me and like me. I can't always carry through the way you would like me to. I wish I could have but I couldn't.
Father: I still think it was procrastination.
David (taking heart from my support): You always just criticize me.
Father: I don't ask anything from you that I wouldn't ask of myself in the same situation.
David: But I'm not you, Dad. Can't you see that?

The father does not answer. There is a long silence, a working silence that I do not want interrupted. David penetrated. Some minutes later:

Father: I guess I was disappointed for you. I knew how important it was for you to have finished...maybe, like you say, it was important for me that you finish.

The father has just taken two large steps. He has seen that his resentment toward David was really disappointment he himself did not want to feel; and second, he begins to separate David from himself. The interview time is nearly gone. This feels like a good place to stop. I would prefer that the father's internal reorganization not be imposed on by drawing his attention outward just now.

We sit silently together the remaining few minutes until the father says, "Well, that's enough to think about for a while. When do we come back?"

Resolution. In the second interview, the father's cold, sullen reactions were challenged, as was the mother's martyrdom. Once these behaviors were disrupted, they began to confront each other with personal frustrations they had each accumulated. When the smoke cleared, they were no longer talking as martyred mother and downcast father. They were talking as man and wife.

On the third interview, the atmosphere in the family was palpably different. The father ushered his family into my office. The feelings of oppression and depression were gone. The children moved about more loosely in their chairs, and the conversation was spontaneous. Still no mention was made of fire setting, but some time was spent in friendly animated discussions about the management and responsibility of a newly acquired family pet. The subject matter and the atmosphere suggested that further visits at this time were not indicated. The goal is not guaranteed: eternal mental health for all family members. The family was working together and had learned something of how they blocked working together previously. I could see no one in the family being inadvertently excluded or purposely denied at this time.

With the way this family was now functioning, I felt confident that Stan would not need to set fires to get warmth. Because of the work that was done, I also felt confident that the gains made were not flights into health or other casual changes but rather that this family was strong on course with a good sense of how to keep going, though there was not specific discussion or instruction. Seriously defective ways of relating were challenged, battles were fought, and changes were made that could not readily be reversed. Besides, beneath the estrangement, there was a great affection among them, now evident in their behavior toward one another.

I felt useless and that was my signal to suggest my withdrawal. It was discussed and the family agreed with the understanding that they could return whenever necessary.

Follow-up. Follow-up of any kind is, at best, a poor system for interpreting the results of therapy since so many powerful intervening life circumstances continue to bombard a family or an individual in the period between the end of formal therapeutic interviews and the follow-up contact. Nonetheless, it is a familiar system and is what many people use for validating, instead of testing by immediate personal experience.

On the first follow-up visit about 6 months after the therapy concluded, the father still ushered his family into the office. The character of the interview was shaped by active participation of all members with jovial yet serious leadership provided by the father. This visit included the 16-year-old son for the first time, who spontaneously remarked about how much better the family was since therapy. The father was obviously an active member of his family; the mother, though not without differences with her husband, was meeting him with direct comments instead of her martyred posture seen in the initial visits; Stan and his brother were both active, struggling

for a comfortable place in the family as kids. David was now more like a boy. He was not trying to be the serious father-substitute that was so noticeable in the first interview.

There were still issues, still discordances. Had there not been, I would have had to investigate further. But they were there. The family was alive. The way issues were being met drew my attention—the forthrightness of each member presenting himself with the expectation a satisfactory solution was possible and that discord was acceptable. These were the notable ingredients that had been missing when they began.

Four years after treatment ended, Stan, 16 and in high school, had not to anyone's knowledge set another fire, nor has any other child in the family called for help. It is impossible to proclaim and to prove that our three sessions cured his fire setting, lying, and stealing. But I know that helping these parents out of their deadlock and consequently freeing up their ability to enjoy each other and their children once again, removed, at that time, any need for Stan to continue sending up smoke signals of impending personal disaster.

Evaluation. Evaluation cannot be objectified. Results come over a lifetime and beyond. To establish objective criteria is to limit the time for results and to select particular gross objectives such as symptom relief or certain changes. Such studies are worse than useless—they can be misleading.

Subjective results are better but also problematic as they reflect, when requested, more the mood of the moment than a reliable appraisal. It also depends on who asks and who is asked.

Furthermore, so many vivid living phenomena intervene between treatment and evaluation when one allows for needed time to cook results, that evaluation itself becomes nonsense. In one attempt made to evaluate a group of families 2 years after treatment, besides such issues as families moving and becoming impossible to trace, serious disturbances occurred: a death in the family, a tragic accident, a divorce, the moving in of a widowed mother, cancer. How is it possible to say, for instance, whether therapy relieved a symptom and was not a contribution to the cancer or accident.

Life is difficult to cut up into segments in order to evaluate change with any scientific validity. Family therapy—a moment in the lives of families—is even more difficult.

The real evaluation of a treatment cannot be measured by any arbitrary instruments. Whether Gestalt family therapy will sustain as a valued contribution to family life will depend on the quality of the applied human sensitivity contained in its treatment—not on the defined goals of its therapeutic process, the intended role of its therapists, or the particular techniques used by them.

As I subjectively consider my career as a family therapist, which began officially about 20 years ago, I first realize that my criteria today are different from 1 year ago, quite different from 10 years ago, and totally different from my first days as a family therapist when I was focused largely on speedy symptom relief so that I could feel more adequate in what I was attempting to do. Today speed is of no interest, and symptom relief is only one of many criteria that I use to judge the value of what I do. Today I no longer choose victory over a symptom, salvation of a child's life over seemingly brutal parents. I can no longer see individual victims though I see individual bruises; today I see symptoms as

faithful signals, not enemies to be extirpated. They will depart when no longer needed. Were I to evaluate myself today as a family therapist constructed out of feedback, lack of feedback, personal observations, and memories, I can only smile at myself and feel grateful that I am past the point where today's wisdom looks back and cringes at yesterday's work and that, for the most part, I sleep well after a day's work.

SUMMARY

The Gestalt style of psychotherapy is one of many names exploding on the psychotherapeutic horizon in an age of ferment. In a social context where man is revamping his concepts of social orders, in a world where the individual family— the hub of civilizations throughout history—is being challenged as man experiments with communal and uncommitted living in search of new forms, the concepts of psychotherapy must face radical revisions. The hope for further development of the Gestalt approach will depend on its ability to stay close to universal principles and at the same time modify its manifestations in keeping with the social changes. The value of any system must be tested by its timely applicability. At present, with the core of the Gestalt approach rooted in the immediate experiences of people, the approach is in a sound position to develop and to contribute in a turbulent, changing world.

Regardless of the social changes, man will always meet frustration in his need for unity and yet separateness with others. New social forms have come and gone, and new forms will continue to come and go; but it is not likely, at least in the foreseeable future, that man can create such wisdom in each individual that interpersonal relating will not produce frustration, or create a social order where the wisdom of relating is not needed. Until then we will need experts to guide those less experienced, those who have spent their lives with their attention elsewhere, until a personal crisis occurs, those who get persistently stuck for whatever reason.

The Gestalt experiential model, by focusing its attention on the most personal aspects of immediate relationships, lives at the hub of the wheel of changing times and therefore is not readily thrown off by centrifugal force as the wheel of change turns momentarily faster or in different directions.

Many of the currently emerging systems sound alike. They often sound like the same lyrics set to a slightly different tune. But when one observes performance—the therapist in action—the differences become quickly apparent. Intimacy, here and now, existential, confluence, awareness, and a host of other terms are the psychological high camp of the day. And it is far easier to talk, lecture, and write about the words and ideas than it is to develop oneself to live up to all those fine ideas. It is the approach that keeps the faith with performance that will provide the greatest psychotherapeutic contribution tomorrow. The path that joins highflows, sensible ideas with the ordinary and often distressing daily lives of people is a difficult one for a therapist to walk. It is easier to fall off to one side and become either a capable theorist or a well-loved neighborhood success. To accept both invitations is not easy, yet it is only by living both that the psychotherapist keeps the faith.

To keep the faith, the Gestalt family therapy approach urges a constant vigil on the therapist by the therapist in addition to the task of keeping a careful watch on what goes on in the immediate peopled environment.

SUGGESTED READINGS

Gestalt family psychotherapy is relatively new and the active people in this field are more concerned with doing than writing; therefore, the literature is scant. You are urged to seek your own experiences rather than read about someone else's. However, below is a limited list of publications and films to help anyone learn more about this movement.

Akhilananda, S. *Hindu psychology*. (1948). London: Routledge & Kegan Paul.

Fagan, J., & Shepherd, I. L. (1970). *Gestalt therapy now*. Palo Alto, CA: Science and Behavior Books.

Goldstein, K. *The organism*. (1939). New York: American Book Co.

Jones, A. (Ed.). (1966). *The Jerusalem Bible*. New York: Doubleday.

Kempler, W. (1965). Experiential family therapy. *International Journal of Group Psychotherapy, 15*, 57–71.

Kempler, W. (1968). Experiential psychotherapy with families. *Family Process, 7*, 88–99.

Kempler, W. (1981). *Experiential psychotherapy within families*. New York: Brunner/Mazel.

Kempler, W. (1967). The experiential therapeutic encounter. *Psychotherapy, 4*, 166–172.

Kempler, W. (1966). The moving finger writes. *Voices, 2*, 107–111.

Kempler, W. (1974). *Principles of Gestalt family therapy*. Costa Mesa, CA: The Kempler Institute.

Kempler, W. (1969). The therapist's merchandise. *Voices, 5*, 57–60.

Levinas, E. (1969). *Totality and infinity*. Pittsburgh: Duquesne University Press.

Perls, F., Hefferline, R. F., & Goodman, P. (1958). *Gestalt therapy*. New York: Julian Press.

Pursglove, P. D. (1971). *Recognition in Gestalt therapy*. New York: Harper & Row.

Vivekananda, S. (1899). *Vedanta philosophy lectures with Patanjali's Yoga aphorisms and commentaries*. New York: Baker & Taylor.

FILMS

Sessions in Gestalt experiential family therapy with Walt Kempler. The Kempler Institute, PO Box 1692, Costa Mesa, CA 92626.

CHAPTER 11

Toward a Person-Centered Approach to Family Therapy

LOUIS THAYER

DEFINITION

The founder of the person-centered approach is Carl R. Rogers (1902–1987). Although others have contributed, he has been the key developer. The more formal beginnings of the approach started with the publication of *Counseling and Psychotherapy* (Rogers, 1942). Since that time, the movement has had a number of name changes—from nondirective counseling in the 1940s, to client-centered therapy in the 1950s and 1960s, to the person-centered approach in the mid-1970s and 1980s. The most recent label for the movement characterizes its expanded application into new areas of human behavior. Labels have also been attached to specific areas within the movement to indicate a particular theme—student-centered teaching, group-centered leadership, and, more recently, family-centered therapy.

What is the primary focus? One key emphasis in this approach is on people and their tremendous potential for growth and change. There is an inherent tendency in people to actualize their full capacities for maintenance and enhancement of the self. This basic respect for the dignity and integrity of individuals and their forward momentum is based on research and much clinical experience in therapy. A second key building block of this approach is the formative tendency, a universal trend in all things toward increased order and interrelated complexity; it is the creative, constructive force in the universe.

What are the conditions for change? When a therapist is genuine and integrated in the therapy situation, holds a positive and unconditional regard for persons, and seeks to experience an empathic understanding of the persons' realities, then a relationship can develop in which the persons can discover within themselves the capacities to use the relationship for growth and change. The facilitative climate tends to help release the potential within individuals and families for self-awareness, self-worth, and self-direction in resolving concerns. People have a basically positive directional process. The process reflects the individuals' and families' forward movement of actualizing inner potentials. Based on research and experiences in therapy, the movement is away from the "oughts" and "shoulds" dictated by elements outside the self and family toward a direction based more on persons' and families' inner awareness and potentials and their own phenomenological views of the world.

The person-centered approach continues to be one of the most human approaches. It has an emergent quality about it that is exemplified by its expanding nature and new characteristics coming forth. The approach has an openness to change, continually taking root in new areas such as family therapy. The person-centered philosophy is becoming a way of living for many people who started exploring concepts in helping.

HISTORICAL DEVELOPMENT

Precursors

What has prepared the groundwork and fertile soil for a rich theory of this nature to take root and grow? Many of Rogers's views were first formulated from his experiences in clinical work and subsequent research. Later, his ideas and writings were confirmed and compared to the ideas of significant historical thinkers as the writings of these people came to his attention.

The concepts of the person-centered approach can be linked to Oriental writings such as the *Lao Tzu/Tao Teh Ching* (Wu & Sih, 1961). There are many passages in the *Tao* that describe the quiet, persistent, inward journey that a person makes who becomes at peace with human nature, living creatures, and life. Rogers (1961a) says that he, too, has learned that "what is most personal is most general" (p. 26). The following passage from the *Tao* speaks of the views that Rogers, a sage in his own right, has learned through his experiences in helping others.

You govern a kingdom by normal rules;
You fight a war by exceptional moves;
But you win the world by letting alone.
How do I know that this is so?
By what is within me!

The more taboos and inhibitions there are in
the world,
The poorer the people become.
The sharper the weapons the people possess,
The greater confusion reigns in the realm.
The more clever and crafty the men,
The oftener strange things happen.
The more articulate the laws and ordinances,
The more robbers and thieves arise.

Therefore, the Sage says:
I do not make any fuss, and the people
transform themselves.
I love quietude, and the people settle
down in their regular grooves.
I do not engage myself in anything, and
the people grow rich.
I have no desires, and the people
return to Simplicity.
(Wu & Sih, 1961, pp. 81–83)

In an interview (Thayer, 1987, 1989), Rogers was asked about his view and response to this passage. He indicated that it held a great deal of meaning for him, then he stopped the interview to get his wallet from another room. He offered the following excerpt from a different translation of the *Tao*, adding that this passage, his talisman, was the only thing of this nature that he carried in his wallet.

A leader is best
when people barely know he exists,
Not so good
when people obey and acclaim him,
worse when they despise him...
But of a good leader, who talks little,
When his work is done, his aim fulfilled,
They will say, "We did this ourselves."
(Bynner, 1962, pp. 34–35)

Rogers (1980c) enjoyed the teachings of Lao Tzu and learned some Taoist principles. Lao Tzu's *Tao Teh Ching* has been adapted for the leader of a group and may be especially helpful to the family therapist (Heider, 1985). Thayer and Harrigan (1990) have compared and contrasted key principles of the person-centered approach with basic principles of Taoist thinking and the physical representation of Taoism in Tai Chi Chuan.

Throughout history, individuals have emerged in their own right, individuals who turned inward for the long journey of becoming the most creative human beings that their inner potential and relative places in time would allow. These men and women are the real precursors to person-centered theory.

Rogers found many of his person-centered ideas confirmed in the existential thought of Soren Kierkegaard and Martin Buber, and he was especially fond of Ralph W. Emerson's views. Like Rogers, these philosophers seem to have valued and trusted that which was within themselves as a guide to their lives and creativeness.

The traditions of different approaches to awareness and life such as Buddhism, Zen, and Sufism seem to be in accord with some of Rogers's views. There are additional elements for comparison with Rogers's thinking in the Nag Hammadi texts discovered in 1945 in Upper Egypt. *The Gnostic Gospels* (Pagels, 1979) investigates the origins of early Christianity where, in certain gnostic groups, self-knowledge was equated with knowledge of a God, the way to salvation. The divine was within the human. These newly discovered gospels shed light on the struggles of early Christians who sought to develop inner potentials, know a God, and deal with politics of organizations. Rogers is most sensitive to the development of self-knowledge and to the politics involved in organizations and the impact of politics on the person.

Sufi teaching stories (Shah, 1972) have been used to help individuals gain a more holistic view of consciousness (Ornstein, 1977) by developing the "right-brain" potentials. And Joseph Campbell (Campbell & Moyers, 1988), in his many works, has helped us to understand our commonalities and our more universal experiences as he considers myth and its power. Rogers's approach in therapy aids persons in discovering the more mysterious, intuitive parts of themselves and in trusting these elements of their personality. Rogers (1961a) com-

ments that his "total organismic sensing of a situation" is more trustworthy than his intellect (p. 22).

Not surprisingly, a person-centered theory has had its formative stage in the United States. While this system of democracy and its valuing of the person has fostered individualism, self-reliance, and personal creativeness, the fundamentals of democracy in action have offered the rich soil for the development of a whole theory of the person. The openness of the system and its acceptance of individual creativity has facilitated Rogers's work in really understanding how people develop their inner self and trust their own experiences. Rogers's criticisms of institutions and organizations are an effort to maintain and enhance the openness and acceptance of individuals in the system in order to allow them to develop their full capacities in humanness and creativeness.

Most of all, Rogers and his colleagues set a path for themselves. The path is one that has "heart," one in which they looked to their experiences and to themselves for key questions and tentative directional conclusions. Their experiences in therapeutic sessions helped them to formulate the questions that would set a process in motion that continues to evolve as a major theoretical approach to helping, humanness, and living.

Person-centered therapy is a precursor in itself. It offers the basis for a *wave of the future*—an existential view of ways for people "being" together in all forms of relationships in life. These relationships range from love, work, and play to friends, families, organizations, educational institutions, religious groups, and nations. Glimpses of this wave appear in persons, families, organizations, political and governmental groups, and directions of a nation that are "emerging" with new ways of relating and being in this complex world (Rogers, 1977a).

Beginnings

A highly perceptive and beautiful statement on Rogers's life was written by Eugene T. Gendlin (1988). Rogers carried the main responsibility for the theoretical formulations of the person-centered theory. He grew up in a highly conservative Protestant family that valued hard work. When he was 12, his family moved to a farm. Rogers's reading and work with feeds and feeding, soils, animal husbandry, and the farm activities instilled in him a respect for the scientific method for solving problems. His fondness for the physical and biological sciences continued in his early years of college.

As Rogers moved away from his family's view of religion, he chose to spend 2 years at Union Theological Seminary, which was committed to freedom of philosophical thought, regardless of whether the thought led to or away from religion. Because of his changing views on religion, he moved to the Teachers' College, Columbia University, from 1924 to 1928 where he received a thorough exposure to statistics and objectivity. It was at the Teachers' College that Rogers was thoroughly exposed to the writings of John Dewey through the teachings of William H. Kilpatrick. Rogers, like Dewey, came to hold his own "experience" as the highest authority (Rogers, 1961a, p. 23). Also, Leta Hollingworth was a warm, friendly person with whom Rogers studied clinical psychology. The major contrast with the Teachers' College view came in 1927–28 when Rogers spent a year of internship at the Institute of Child Guidance. The Institute was strictly psychoanalytic. The first step in working with a child was to take a long case history from all members in the family. Then a case conference was held to determine what the treatment should be. The psychiatrist conducted treatment interviews with the child, the psychologist did tutoring or other needed activities, and the social worker dealt with the parents. Rogers bought into that analytic way of thinking for a time, because he distinctly remembered Alfred Adler's saying that some conclusions could be drawn from talking with the child. According to some professionals at the time, Adler's view was different and, perhaps, naive.

Next, Rogers went to Rochester, New York, for 12 years where he worked first in a Child Study Department of the Society for Prevention of Cruelty to Children and then served as director for the Rochester Guidance Center. The staff took a case history from the parents and from the child, gave lots of tests, interviewed the child, then held a case conference to decide on the treatment of the child. Rogers felt that these conferences were the best in the country. The staff worked with the teacher, the parents, the social agency involved, the school social worker, the court (probation officer), or any agency that was concerned with the situation. Together, they decided on a plan of treatment for the child, and they saw to it that the plan was put into effect. The staff had a lot of power over the child, and they used it.

Rogers said that he began to change during those years in Rochester, primarily because of his listening experiences. He told a story about his learning to listen:

One of our staff members was working with a child in play therapy—a very cantankerous, difficult boy. I was seeing the mother to help in the treatment process. In those days, we called them treatment interviews, not therapy, not counseling. And as I worked with the mother, we had already decided in case conference that the basic problem was the mother's rejection of the boy. So, I endeavored to very gently and persuasively get that across to her, that she was really the problem and that it was her attitude that was causing the difficulties with the boy. I look back on that now with a certain amount of horror, but anyway that was what I was doing. Strangely enough, she did not seem to accept what I was saying. We worked very hard on this. I was very conscientious. After a number of interviews, I realized that we were not getting anywhere. And I told her that I thought we had both worked hard on the situation. We weren't getting anywhere. I thought we should probably call it quits. She agreed that she didn't think it was helping either. So, she got up to leave the office. As she got to the door, she turned around and said, "Do you ever take adults for counseling here?" And I said, "Yes." So, she came back to the same chair that she left and began to pour out her own problems as she saw them from her point of view. And it was so different from the nice orderly case history that we had gotten that I couldn't believe that this was the same woman talking. As she poured out her own problems with her husband and so on, very little about the boy, it began to be what I would now say was a real therapy relationship. I didn't know what to do. I was quite nonplussed by this whole situation, so I primarily listened. We worked together then for quite a number of interviews. Her marital situation improved. The boy's behavior changed. And I realized that possibly if I wanted to be the real expert, I would go about it in the same way that I always had. If I wanted to be of help to people, possibly it was better to listen. I began to pay much more attention to focusing on the person who came in rather than on my thoughts about that person. (Rogers, 1980b)

Then Rogers came into brief contact with Otto Rank and some of Rank's social work students and psychiatrists from the Philadelphia School of Social Work. Rogers liked Rank's (1936) ideas on

"will" therapy with the client taking responsibility. These ideas began to influence Rogers's thinking. Later, a social worker who had studied with Rank came to work at the Clinic. Rogers learned a great deal from her about paying attention to the feelings behind words and responding to those feelings rather than to the content of the words. Rogers suspects that the idea of "reflecting feelings" in the therapy interview is something that he picked up from her.

Another influence about that time was Jessie Taft's book on *The Dynamics of Therapy* (1933). The book contained a story of therapy with a child. It was clear that the relationship was what counted with the therapist depending on the child to take positive steps. The book had a great impact on Rogers. He realized that his views were changing from his making an expert's diagnosis to one of relying on the initiative and self-directive authority of the client.

As a result of his experience at Rochester, Rogers wrote *The Clinical Treatment of the Problem Child* (1939). In 1940, he moved to Ohio State University. He found that his new methods for helping others were different from the approaches used by other therapists. In 1942, his classic book *Counseling and Psychotherapy* was published. The book began to lay the foundation of his new approach. The second chapter of his book, given to the Minnesota chapter of Psi Chi in December 1940, was the first major attempt to present his new views on helping. The 5 years at Ohio State University and the subsequent 12 years at the Counseling Center of the University of Chicago put Rogers in touch with critical-minded graduate students who were creative, eager to experience new methods, and willing to contribute to theory, research, and knowledge in this new approach. During the 1940s, the "nondirective" counseling-therapy label was attached to Rogers's approach because the direction for the process came from the person, not the therapist. But in the early 1950s, the name of the approach was changed to that of "client-centered therapy." This name seemed to fit a bit better because it indicated more explicitly where the keys to the potential for therapeutic movement rested— totally within the client.

Client-Centered Therapy was published by Rogers in 1951. This book opened the way for major advances in the theory and research during the 1950s. *Psychotherapy and Personality Change* (1954) presented studies of change factors in therapy. Also, four remarkable papers were published that had much impact on training programs, research, and education: "The Necessary and Sufficient Conditions for Therapeutic Personality Change" (1957a), "Personal Thoughts on Teaching and Learning" (1957b), "A Theory of Therapy, Personality, and Interpersonal Relationships, As Developed in the Client-Centered Framework" (1959), and "A Process Conception of Psychotherapy" (1961b). The third paper stands as a major statement of the theory.

Rogers moved to the University of Wisconsin in 1957 to teach and do research. His research and colleagues' focused on working with hospitalized schizophrenics and trying to test the question of "the necessary and sufficient conditions" for therapeutic change. What is amazing about Rogers is that from 1928 to 1958, he spent 15 to 20 hours a week, except on vacations, working therapeutically with individuals. From these helping experiences, he has drawn many of his insights into therapy and questions for research.

In 1961, Rogers's classic *On Becoming a Person* was published. Today, this book serves as an inspiration to those in the helping professions. After a 1-year stay at the Center for Advanced Study in the Behavioral Sciences in Stanford (1962–63), Rogers left the University of Wisconsin and in 1964 went to work at the Western Behavioral Sciences Institute (WBSI) in LaJolla, California. In 1968, after several years of writing and research there, Rogers and several colleagues severed their relationship with WBSI and created the Center for Studies of the Person (CSP) in LaJolla, a nonprofit, "nonorganization" organization. The Center has been fertile soil for the flourishing of creative projects for helping persons grow and change. Rogers also completed work on several other books: *The Therapeutic Relationship and Its Impact: A Study of Psychotherapy with Schizophrenics* with E. T. Gendlin, P. J. Kiesler, and C. Truax (1967b); *Person to Person: The Problem of Being Human* with B. Stevens (1967c); and *Man and the Science of Man* with W. Coulson (1968).

Current Status

What has contributed to the current direction of the person-centered approach? From about 1964, Rogers had been spending increasing amounts of time in small encounter groups and larger community learning groups as well as continuing to write and to give presentations. The groundwork for the expansion of his theoretical formulations outside the therapeutic interview (Rogers, 1959) had been laid, as described in the following books: *Freedom to Learn: A View of What Education Might Become* (1969), *Carl Rogers on Encounter Groups* (1970), and *On Be-*

coming Partners: Marriage and Its Alternatives (1972). In the late 1960s, the 17-day LaJolla Program (a CSP project), directed by W. Coulson, D. Land, and Bruce Meador, was established. It received attention for its creation of a healthy and supportive psychological climate (Coulson, Land, & Meador, 1977). Rogers, a consultant to the project, contributed greatly with his philosophy on how persons grow. The project was an experiment in providing a climate for personal growth and in developing community with person-centered group leadership—"a view which emphasizes that there is maximum growth for both group and facilitator where the facilitator participates as a whole person rather than as a technical expert" (LaJolla Program brochure). The major emphasis is on directly experiencing the kind of group that Rogers described:

[The group] usually consists of ten to fifteen persons and a facilitator or leader. It is relatively unstructured, providing a climate of maximum freedom for personal expression, exploration of feelings, and interpersonal communication. Emphasis is upon the interactions among group members, in an atmosphere which encourages each to drop his (her) defenses and facades and thus enables him (her) to relate directly and openly to other members of the group—the "basic encounter." Individuals come to know themselves and each other more fully than is possible in the usual social or working relationships; the climate of openness, risk-taking, and honesty generates trust, which enables the person to recognize and change self-defeating attitudes, test out and adapt more innovative and constructive behaviors, and subsequently to relate more adequately and effectively to others in his (her) everyday life situation. (Rogers, 1967a, p. 718)

As Rogers began to examine the incredible learning that took place in the small groups and in the larger commu-

nity, a renewed optimism, potential, and energy in his approach surfaced. In 1974, he and several colleagues experimented with two 3-week workshops on community building and his approach. As the approach moved from the realm of the therapeutic milieu, the term *person* seemed more fitting with the focus: the person and his or her inner potential. The term *person-centered approach* was thus adopted for the 1975 workshop.

This key paragraph came from the person-centered workshop brochure:

The aim will be to build a workshop around an approach to human relations which recognizes that the potential to learn and the power to act lie within the person—rather than in an expert dealing with him or her, or in a system controlling him or her. The workshop will provide a place where people who believe in the dignity of the individual and in each person's capacity for self-direction can come together to create a community. The community will, we hope, provide for a sharing of our professional worlds, our personal questions, problems, and satisfaction, our creativity, and our innovations. (Rogers 1977b, p. 61)

Rogers (1977b) found that the group proceeds at its own pace, resists manipulation or pushing, and takes risks leading to interpersonal trust. "Power resides definitely in the individual" (p. 62). He found that "the conviction I held about the significance of discovering one truth about a relationship between two individuals also applied to groups. If we can find even one partial truth about the process by which 136 people can live together without destroying one another, can live together in a caring concern for the full development of each person, can live together in the richness of diversity instead of the sterility of conformity, then we may have found a truth with many implications" (p. 94).

At about the same time, other projects with a definitely person-centered flavor were making inroads into medicine (Human Dimensions in Medical Education: A CSP project directed by Orienne E. Strode), government (Self-Determination: A Personal-Political Network in California with John Vasconcellos as one of the leaders), education (Louisville, Kentucky Schools Project [Foster & Back, 1974] and the Immaculate Heart College Project [Rogers, 1974]), and others.

In 1977, Rogers published *Carl Rogers on Personal Power*, which focused on the politics of a person-centered approach and development of the power of the person. Rogers was writing about his new experiences in large groups that were developing a sense of community and of related social and political implications. Rogers continued to spend time in large group workshops and seminars and had speaking engagements throughout the world.

In the fall of 1979, Rogers invited a group of colleagues to his LaJolla home to discuss the establishment of a more intense person-centered learning program. Prior to this time, he had resisted attempts at a "Rogerian Institute" of sorts. After a number of planning meetings, he selected 12 associates who aided him in developing a long-range learning program. The program was called "Carl Rogers & Associates: Person-Centered Programs" and was connected with the CSP. The program was more cognitive than experiential in nature and sought "to enlarge that repository with new formulations appropriate to an expanded consciousness for the 21st century: it will seek to be generative rather than reactive, helping to create new conditions, new concepts, new methods of research; it will endeavor to explore the areas in which science and mysticism, the prag-

matic and the transcendent, are coming together. An overall aim will be to blend the demonstrated efficacy of person-centered approaches into a disciplined effort" (Rogers, 1980a). The new learning program began formally with a 2-week workshop in the summer of 1980. Eighty participants attended from the United States and other countries. The ongoing learning program commenced in September 1980 with coursework being offered at CSP offices. Currently, Norman Chambers directs the Carl Rogers Institute of Psychotherapy, Training, and Supervision, which provides extensive training and supervision in client-centered psychotherapy through the CSP.

Rogers's book *A Way of Being* (1980c) provides additional insights into his approach as well as an opportunity to examine some of his thinking as he grew older and yet remained a learner. In 1983, he published *Freedom to Learn for the 80's*.

In 1981, David J. Cain founded the Association for the Development of the Person-Centered Approach. The Association has a newsletter, *Renaissance,* and Cain serves as editor of ADPCA's journal, *Person-Centered Review*. The first issue of the *Person-Centered Review* was published in February 1986.

As Rogers continued his professional journey, his efforts turned toward peace (Rogers, 1986a, 1986b, 1987), and he worked to help factions within countries and between countries try to resolve conflicts. Perhaps, Rogers's most significant initiatives are those that focus on peace. He and his colleagues offered a way of being for individuals, groups, and countries; his message carried hope. In approximately 1984, he initiated the Carl Rogers Peace Project. Today, Gay Leah Swenson directs the Carl Rogers Institute for Peace at the CSP. John Whitely

(1987) guest edited a special journal issue that focused on Rogers's Person-Centered Approach to Peace. In an interview (Thayer, 1987, 1989), Rogers spoke of his efforts to seek peaceful solutions to human conflict and the use of person-centered principles to foster peace. At the time of his death in 1987, he was scheduled to make another trip to South Africa for workshops and a trip to the Soviet Union for workshops.

Since 1982, there have been four international forums (Oaxtepec, Mexico; Norwich, England; LaJolla, California; and Rio de Janeiro, Brazil) on the person-centered approach. People from many countries have come together to learn from each other about their work and the implications and applications of the person-centered approach.

TENETS OF THE MODEL

The tenets on which the person-centered model is based have come from the work of several people. While the theoretical constructs of the theory are necessarily abstractions from experience, the process for their development has included several steps: "clinical observation, initial conceptualization, initial crude research to test some of the hypotheses involved, further clinical observation, more rigorous formulation of the construct and its functional relationships, more refined operational definitions of the construct, more conclusive research" (Rogers, 1959, p. 203). The refinement process continues as well as the openness to experience and the development of new theoretical constructs.

The first 40 brief definitions provided here are excerpts from Rogers's (1959, pp. 194–212) chapter on "Therapy, Personality and Interpersonal Relationships," which offers an extended discussion of these constructs.

1. *Actualizing tendency.* "This is the inherent tendency of the organism to develop all its capacities in ways which serve to maintain or enhance the organism." The movement is toward more autonomy and away from control by others. The construct includes other concepts of motivation such as need reduction, tension reduction, and drive reduction.

2. *Tendency toward self-actualization.* "Following the development of the self-structure, this general tendency toward actualization expresses itself also in the actualization of that portion of the experience of the organism which is symbolized in the self."

3. *Experience* (noun). This concept includes "all that is going on within the envelope of the organism at any given moment which is potentially available to awareness." The concept is a psychological one, not a physiological definition, that "includes events of which the individual is unaware, as well as all the phenomena which are in consciousness." Other terms Rogers has used to convey the total quality of the concept are "sensory and visceral experiences," "organic experiences," "experiential field," or Combs and Snygg's (1959) term of "phenomenal field."

4. *Experience* (verb). "To experience means simply to receive in the organism the impact of the sensory or physiological events which are happening at the moment.... 'To experience in awareness' means to symbolize in some accurate form at the conscious level the above sensory or visceral events."

5. *Feeling, experiencing a feeling.* This concept means "an emotionally tinged experience, together with its personal meaning." The "cognitive content of the meaning of that emotion in its experiential context" is also included in the concept. "Experiencing a feeling fully" is

denoted when the individual is "congruent in his experience (of the feeling), his awareness (of it), and his expression (of it)."

6. *Awareness, symbolization, consciousness.* The three synonymous terms are seen as "the symbolic representation (not necessarily in verbal terms) of some portion of our experience."

7. *Availability to awareness.* "When an experience can be symbolized freely, without defensive denial and distortion, then it is available to awareness."

8. *Accurate symbolization.* This means that "hypotheses implicit in awareness will be borne out if tested by acting on them."

9. *Perceive, perception.* It is noted that "a perception is a hypothesis or prognosis for action which comes into being in awareness when stimuli impinge on the organism." Perception and awareness are synonymous terms; however, perception emphasizes the stimulus in the process, whereas awareness is the "symbolizations and meanings which arise from such purely internal stimuli as memory traces, visceral changes, and the like, as well as from external stimuli."

10. *Subceive, subception.* This construct, developed by McCleary and Lazarus (1949), signifies discrimination without awareness. Rogers believes that the individuals can "discriminate an experience as threatening, without symbolization in awareness of this threat."

11. *Self-experience.* Standal (1954) uses this term to denote "any event or entity in the phenomenal field discriminated by the individual which is also discriminated as 'self,' 'me,' 'I,' or related thereto. In general self-experiences are the raw material of which the organized self-concept is formed."

12. *Self, concept of self, self-structure.* "These terms refer to the organized, consistent conceptual gestalt composed of perceptions of the characteristics of the 'I' or 'me' and the perceptions of the relationships of the 'I' or 'me' to others and to various aspects of life, together with the values attached to these perceptions." It is a gestalt that has changing and fluid process.

13. *Ideal self.* This is "the self-concept which the individual would most like to possess, upon which he places the highest value for himself."

14. *Incongruence between self and experience.* Here "a discrepancy frequently develops between the self as perceived, and the actual experience of the organism. Thus the individual may perceive himself as having characteristics a, b, and c, and experiencing feelings x, y, and z. An accurate symbolization of his experience would, however, indicate characteristics c, d, and e, feelings v, w, x. When such a discrepancy exists, the state is one of incongruence between self and experience."

15. *Vulnerability.* This word refers to the "state of incongruence between self and experience, when it is desired to emphasize the potentialities of this state for creating psychological disorganization. When incongruence exists, and the individual is unaware of it, then he is potentially vulnerable to anxiety, threat, and disorganization."

16. *Anxiety.* "Anxiety is phenomenologically a state of uneasiness or tension whose cause is unknown."

17. *Threat.* "Threat is the state which exists when an experience is perceived or anticipated (subceived) as incongruent with the structure of the self."

18. *Psychological maladjustment.* "Psychological maladjustment exists when the organism denies to awareness, or distorts in awareness, significant experiences, which consequently are not accurately symbolized and organized into the gestalt of the self-structure, thus

creating an incongruence between self and experience."

19. *Defense, defensiveness.* "Defense is the behavioral response of the organism to threat, the goal of which is the maintenance of the current structure of the self. This goal is achieved by the perceptual distortion of the experience in awareness, in such a way as to reduce the incongruity between the experience and the structure of the self, or by the denial to awareness of an experience, thus denying any threat to the self."

20. *Distortion in awareness, denial to awareness.* "It is an observed phenomenon that material which is significantly inconsistent with the concept of self cannot be directly and freely admitted to awareness. . . . When an experience is dimly perceived (or subceived is perhaps the better term) as being incongruent with the self-structure, the organism appears to react with a distortion of the meaning of the experience (making it consistent with the self) or with a denial of the existence of the experience, in order to preserve the self-structure from threat."

21. *Intensionality.* The person tends "to see experience in absolute and unconditional terms, to overgeneralize, to be dominated by concept or belief, to fail to anchor his reactions in space and time, to confuse fact and evaluation, to rely upon abstractions rather than upon reality-testing." This term is from general semantics and includes the concept of rigidity.

22. *Congruence, congruence of self and experience.* Here "the individual appears to be revising his concept of self to bring it into congruence with his experience, accurately symbolized." Synonymous terms are *integrated, whole,* and *genuine.*

23. *Openness to experience.* "When

the individual is in no way threatened, then he is open to his experience. To be open to experience is the polar opposite of defensiveness. . . . It signifies that every stimulus, whether originating within the organism or in the environment, is freely relayed through the nervous system without being distorted or channeled off by any defensive mechanism."

24. *Psychological adjustment.* "Optimal psychological adjustment exists when the concept of the self is such that all experiences are or may be assimilated on a symbolic level into the gestalt of the self-structure. Optimal psychological adjustment is thus synonymous with complete congruence of self and experience, or complete openness to experience."

25. *Extensionality.* The person "tends to see experience in limited, differentiated terms, to be aware of the space-time anchorage of facts, to be dominated by facts, not by concepts, to evaluate in multiple ways, to be aware of different levels of abstraction, to test his inferences and abstractions against reality." This term comes from general semantics.

26. *Mature, maturity.* "The individual exhibits mature behavior when he perceives realistically and in an extensional manner, is not defensive, accepts the responsibility of being different from others, accepts responsibility for his own behavior, evaluates experience in terms of the evidence coming from his own senses, changes his evaluation of experience only on the basis of new evidence, accepts others as unique individuals different from himself, prizes himself, and prizes others."

The following constructs (27 through 35) have been influenced by Standal (1954) to replace less rigorously defined ones.

27. *Contact.* "Two persons are in psy-

chological contact, or have the minimum essential of a relationship, when each makes a perceived or subceived difference in the experiential field of the other."

28. *Positive regard.* "If the perception by me of some self-experience in another makes a positive difference in my experiential field, then I am experiencing positive regard for that individual. In general, positive regard is defined as including such attitudes as warmth, liking, respect, sympathy, acceptance."

29. *Need for positive regard.* Standal postulates that "a basic need for positive regard, as defined above (28), is a secondary or learned need, commonly developed in early infancy."

30. *Unconditional positive regard.* This is a key construct in the theory. "If the self-experiences of another are perceived by me in such a way that no self-experience can be discriminated as more or less worthy of positive regard than any other, then I am experiencing unconditional positive regard for this individual." Rogers likes John Dewey's use of *prize* to express this caring for another. It means "to value a person, irrespective of the differential values which one might place on his specific behaviors." Another term used is *acceptance.*

31. *Regard complex.* It consists of "all those self-experiences, together with their interrelationships, which the individual discriminates as being related to the positive regard of a particular social other."

32. *Positive self-regard.* It is "a positive regard satisfaction which has become associated with a particular self-experience or a group of self-experiences, in which the satisfaction is independent of positive regard transactions with social others."

33. *Need for self-regard.* "It is postulated that a need for positive self-regard is a secondary or learned need, related to the satisfaction of the need for positive regard by others."

34. *Unconditional self-regard.* "When the individual perceives himself in such a way that no self-experience can be discriminated as more or less worthy of positive regard than any other, then he is experiencing unconditional positive self-regard."

35. *Conditions of worth.* "The self-structure is characterized by a condition of worth when a self-experience or set of related self-experiences is either avoided or sought solely because the individual discriminates it as being less or more worthy of self-regard."

36. *Locus of evaluation.* "This term is used to indicate the source of evidence as to values. Thus the internal locus of evaluation, within the individual himself, means that he is the center of the valuing process, the evidence being supplied by his own senses. When the locus of evaluation resides in others, their judgment as to the value of an object or experience becomes the criterion of value for the individual."

37. *Organismic valuing process.* "This concept describes an ongoing process in which values are never fixed or rigid, but experiences are being accurately symbolized and continually and freshly valued in terms of the satisfactions organismically experienced; the organism experiences satisfaction of those stimuli or behaviors which maintain and enhance the organism and the self, both in the immediate present and in the long range."

38. *Internal frame of reference.* "This is all of the realm of experience which is available to the awareness of the individual at a given moment." This subjective world includes the "full range of sensa-

tions, perceptions, meanings, and memories, which are available to consciousness."

39. *Empathy.* This is "to perceive the internal frame of reference of another with accuracy, and with the emotional components and meanings which pertain thereto, as if one were the other person, but without ever losing the 'as if' condition. . . . If this 'as if' quality is lost, then the state is one of identification."

40. *External frame of reference.* "To perceive solely from one's own subjective internal frame of reference without empathizing with the observed person or object, is to perceive from an external frame of reference."

A more recent theoretical construct that, along with the actualizing tendency, serves as a foundation block of the person-centered approach is the *formative tendency.* This construct, broader and more universal in nature, is the opposite of entropy. It represents the creative, building energy present in the universe rather than the deterioration process. Rogers's hypothesis is stated this way:

There is a formative directional tendency in the universe, which can be traced and observed in stellar space, in crystals, in microorganisms, in more complex organic life, and in human beings. This is an evolutionary tendency toward greater order, greater complexity, greater interrelatedness. In humankind, this tendency exhibits itself as the individual moves from a single-cell origin to complex functioning, to knowing and sensing below the level of consciousness, to a conscious awareness of the organism and the external world, to a transcendent awareness of the harmony and unity of the cosmic system, including humankind. (Rogers, 1980c, p. 133)

Other Systems: Therapist-Centered or Family-Centered?

Perhaps a way to approach a discussion about other systems is to formulate a set of questions to use in reviewing theories in family therapy. In a sense, the divergences and convergences in family therapy may be placed on a continuum, with the therapist as director-expert on one end and the family members as the directors-experts on the other end.

What are the key values inherent in the person-centered approach (PCA) to family therapy, and where do the differences exist with other approaches? To what extent do family therapists foster independence and responsibility, or do they, through their expertise and articulateness, subtly reinforce dependence on them and their prescriptive directions? What attention is given by therapists to the development of the inner organismic valuing process of each member of the family? Of high value in the PCA is the person and a respect for the integrity and dignity of each person in the family, regardless of age or role. The family's potential is exemplified and extolled in each individual member. The PCA recognizes the rights of family members to express their feelings and participate in an open, free, and increasingly self-directed process.

What are the therapists' views about the nature of the person? Do therapists generally perceive people as rational or irrational, as innately bad (must be socialized by and for society) or innately good (having a positive direction in growth), or not viewed on a good-bad dimension at all? What fosters healthy development of children and enhances the continuing mature growth of adults? In another sense, to what extent are therapists working for the system, the society, and the norm; or to what extent are therapists helping each family member develop and reach for a healthy personality and a healthy family? Normative behavior may not be healthy for each individual (Jourard, 1959). The PCA views people in a positive way. If the right psychological conditions are offered, then persons and families will develop their potentials as well as maintain and enhance themselves.

How does the behavior develop in the context of a family? Is a conditioning process present where a child or person "operates on" an environment and, subsequently, behaviors are extinguished or reinforced by external events? Or is there an inner actualizing tendency in the organism motivating the person to maintain and enhance the self? As the person symbolizes experiences in awareness, the person perceives what is experienced, desired, or rejected. Therapists' views about how behavior and attitudes develop will most certainly affect their methods of helping families with issues.

What is the therapist's role in helping others grow and change? Is the therapist the expert on families who understands most nuances of family development and individual psychological development? To what extent does the expert family therapist determine who will be seen in therapy, diagnose the family problems, probe for causes of problems, prescribe remedial family actions, reinforce and challenge selected behaviors of family members to bring about resolutions to conflict, and generally direct the total therapy process? What are the goals of the therapist in therapy—to alter family or individual behaviors by the use of behavioral learning principles, reinforcement, extinguishing procedures, or manipulation? The PCA strives to understand the inner worlds of the family members, with all their feelings, and to help the family move in a direction that they choose. O'Leary (1989) suggests that person-centered family therapists need to address the objective reality

of the family as well as respond to the personal meanings of the individual.

What are the psychological conditions of therapy that are necessary for therapeutic change in families? Is it enough to say that a positive therapeutic relationship between a therapist and a family is a crucial factor in family change? What are the key ingredients of a facilitative therapeutic climate? To what extent do most therapy approaches give attention to the conditions necessary for change, or to what extent do they focus their energies on the diagnosis of the family's concern and decide on treatment techniques to affect behavioral change? Is the focus on the conditions and the process (means), or are outcomes (ends) the primary target? The PCA seeks to establish facilitative conditions for a family developmental process. If the core conditions are present to a certain minimal degree, then a relationship and a forward moving process with exploration, growth, and change takes place. A therapist focuses on the conditions and the process because the results are inherent in the process. A family will move in positive, healthy psychological directions and seek resolutions to concerns consistent with the family dynamics. When trusted, a family will do what is best for itself; the family *can* be trusted.

How does the family therapy process unfold? To what extent does the focus center on the past (there and then), the present (here and now), or the future? If the climate and a trusting relationship are present for the family, will the process inevitably occur? Does the therapist use a previously developed psychological model to diagnose the family problems and then prescribe directions or procedures in therapy? Or to what extent do the family members, under positive therapeutic conditions, serve as the key diagnosticians and determine the therapeutic directions based on their own views? Does the family lead or the therapist lead? Who is the expert? What are the areas of expertise for the family and for the therapist?

What are the differences and similarities in techniques that help the process evolve? To what extent does the therapist analyze and interpret the meanings of the family's communications, or does the therapist help the family discover the meanings of their own experiences? To what extent does the therapist manipulate and frustrate the family members into discovery of their main problems? What meanings do transference and countertransference hold in the therapy process? The PCA sees the therapist's helping behaviors as reflections of inner attitudes toward the family. The PCA is not a bagful of tricks and techniques. The PCA therapist is not going to interpret the meanings of family experiences to the family. The PCA attempts to help clients explore feelings and express inner thoughts as well as discover the meanings of their feelings and how these feelings motivate the daily interactional, living behaviors of family members.

What are the most visible outcomes in different approaches? Is the goal of therapy to change behavior or to alter self-concept and family esteem? To what extent is the goal to change specific situational behavior or to recognize inner potentials for dealing effectively with situational events? Is the therapeutic movement away from "non-response-ability" toward "response-ability" in handling life situations, away from a more behavioral view of events toward construing events in a more phenomenological-perceptual view? Is the new locus of evaluation resting within the family or with significant other persons? Is the di-

rection of change toward more self-responsibility and self-direction by the family? As Barrett-Leonard (1984) discusses a person-centered systems view of family relationships, his key point is that "the membership structure of a family has direct and profound bearing on the relationships that are possible and likely to be experienced and, therefore, on the learning-developmental potentialities of each member" (p. 222). Individual family members are also viewed in diverse and multiple family interactions and relationships. Levant (1984b) compares a psychodynamic perspective of the family as a system with the emerging client-centered view of the family as a system and the basic assumptions underlying client-centered family therapy.

To what extent is the therapy process therapist centered or family centered?

APPLICATION

Family Issues for Which the PCA Is Applicable

Because of the evolving nature of the person-centered approach through practice and research, it has special meaning for most family issues that involve interpersonal relationships (Rogers, 1959). And the family group is probably the closest of all interpersonal circles and has high emotional intensity.

Issues vary, and families are different. That is why the therapist may work with many different family configurations in therapy situations. The family members in attendance vary, depending on who in the family will make a commitment to the therapy process. In one situation, all family members may participate, while in another only two members attend and initially are seen separately. In another situation, the father may not attend therapy, yet three of the other four members begin therapy. The father joins later. Sometimes there is only one parent along with the children. Occasionally, grandparents or close relatives may be part of the therapy process.

The following family issues are not in any way intended to cause a therapist to develop preconceived notions about what to look for in a family therapy situation. These family issues are ones that have often surfaced in therapy situations. The general family issues for which the person-centered approach can be of particular help are (a) realness in family relationships, (b) the expression of feelings in the family, (c) acceptance of family members as individuals, (d) listening and two-way communication, (e) a process for family development and problem solving, and (f) clarity of societal effects on the family group.

Realness in Family Relationships

What hampers persons within the family from being themselves and from establishing real contact with other family members? Often, clients believe that they become more vulnerable in the family when they express their true thoughts and feelings about family dynamics. In a sense, there is a fear of loss—loss of love or of place in the family.

There is the question of trusting family members: "Can I trust other members with my real self?" "Can I bring my thoughts and feelings out into the open?" In essence, the family situation cannot be lived on a real basis because the clients perceive the need to be defensive and shield their inner selves. When defensiveness is present, there is an incongruence *within* some individual members, which is reflected *between* members of the family in interpersonal relationships.

Expression of Feelings in the Family

The expression of innermost feelings is essentially part of being genuine in family relationships. What can family members do with intense feelings of shame, anger, desperation, annoyance, tenderness, joy, jealousy, resentment, love, fearfulness, and sensitivity? Must these feelings be hidden from family view? What are their fears? What will be the cost of hiding feelings? How can family members learn to accept their own feelings as well as accept the feelings of their family members if there is the constant question of whether other family members will accept the persons and their feelings? Expressing positive feelings of love and affection can be just as much of a problem as expressing negative feelings. When feelings are suppressed, family members may decrease their trust in their own experiencing. Often, family members have denied their feelings for so long that they are not fully aware of their feelings toward people and events in the family. Family members may live family relationships according to what someone else believes is right rather than what they think is right. If members pay attention, the family's nonverbal communication carries a heavy load of feelings being expressed. With feelings as key motivators of behavior, what is the place of feelings in family politics?

Family Members as Individuals

Family members believe at times that they are not viewed as unique, with their own ideas and potential. They are not regarded by others in the family as separate persons. Consequently, they are not perceived as individuals so much as a family group. The notion that each individual has a set of potentials and abilities to give direction to his or her life is subsumed under the family plan for the future. The family, or certain persons in it, may describe what reality or the real world is like and indoctrinate the family with their views. There is "a" prescribed reality for the family, and each member is not viewed as having his or her own separate reality (Rogers, 1978). Therefore, forced identification with family doctrines does hurt individuals, and the inner realities of each individual member affect the family.

Family expectations of its members can be an issue for members—wives, husbands, children, and others. "If you want me to love you, then you must have the same feelings I do. If I feel your behavior is bad, you must feel so too. If I feel a certain goal is desirable, you must feel so too" (Rogers, 1961c, p. 325). The roles and role expectations of the family are often not the same expectations as those of the individual. Occasionally, parents and close relatives try to mold children and others in their own images. They try to shape the children and others with their expectations, goals, enthusiasms, unfulfilled wishes, and unexplored dreams. It is a vicarious experience of sorts. Who will follow in their footsteps? Ellinwood (1989) stresses that children in the family therapy process need to be heard, understood, and offered the conditions of empathic understanding, unconditional positive regard, and genuineness as well as the adults.

Can family members learn to listen to their own inner feelings while in the family unit? Do family members have a right to share their expectations with the family? Can members listen to others in the family and still maintain a sense of self-identity? Some family members ask, "Am I needed in the family? Am I worthwhile in this family?" "What is my self-worth and my worth to the family?" Practically always, each individual is a needed part and resource for the family.

The perceived lack of support by members is another aspect of this issue. Is the family devoted to helping members develop their full potentials? Many family members seek to identify with the family, a tight-knit support group, and still maintain individuality and separateness. Another aspect that creeps into families is the "Me First" issue of selfishness (Coulson, 1979, p. 12).

Listening and Two-Way Communication

When there is a breakdown in communication, members perceive that they are not listened to and certainly not understood. They believe that other members do not understand their experiences in the family and in the world. The process of communication may be only a one-way avenue with one family member giving out orders, decisions, values to follow, and guidelines for living. Power over others is used to resolve conflicts. Some individuals are not allowed to maintain much personal power in the family. Since there is little mutual listening, there is less acceptance of the views of others. Members' views are not respected, and authority may reside in one person.

Lack of communication and understanding can put undue and divisive pressures on the family group. If members are not communicating, they may be working at cross purposes and not be mutually consulted and involved. They lack each other's support and resources.

Communication issues have another devastating effect on a family. The real expression of affection between family members is decreased proportionately to the lack of communication. Love, caring, and acceptance within a family are crucial to the survival of its members and the family group. The process of relating to each other breaks down when there is a lack of communication.

A Process for Family Development and Problem Solving

Another cause of family problems stems from the lack of a method or process through which the family can resolve issues and problems as they arise. Too often, no process for handling developmental issues and problem solving exists, and problems are either left to one person to resolve or are ignored as if they never existed. Without a process to handle family problems and issues, change and positive, healthy family development are hindered. Families often have no mechanism to deal with crisis situations of death, grief from loss or separation, accidents, or other traumatic events.

Each adult partner in a family brings with him or her a definition or concept of "family" (van der Veen & Olson, 1983). This definition may include rules for living, roles to be assumed by various family members, and expectations for various roles. Sometimes these deep inner views are not communicated until one partner violates the unwritten rules or there are children in the family. This whole definitional or conceptual set may not even be in the partners' awareness, yet it certainly affects the family dynamics, growth, and new developing family concept. Family therapy offers partners an opportunity to clarify these definitions, synthesize them with their partners, and establish new avenues of communications for the family.

There may be no process for discussing values and living. How does a family member gain values and a sense of clarity about these values? Should it be up to a religious group to teach values to the family? The individual may feel like a receptacle for the values of others and see no opportunity for a search and clarification of personal values.

There may be no process for decision making in the family. Are the decisions handed down by one or two persons in the group? How do family members learn about making decisions if they are not involved in some democratic process of deciding issues or selecting issues?

There may be no process in which the family members can integrate their experiences. "Is there provision for the periodic meeting of the minds?" (Coulson, 1979, p. 3). How do the family members bring together their experiences and their lives?

Clarity of Societal Effects on the Family Group

The family competes with many societal influences for the attention and development of its members. The demands of careers, education, peers, television, wars, and world events may sap the very energies of the family. Families may fail to realize the effects of a culture and establish their unique or conflicting priorities as a group. Does the family become the first priority, or do external interests take over? Does the locus of evaluation for the family rest outside the family group? Is there a family process for "thinking the priorities"? Does the family become a dumping ground for displaced anger and intense feelings toward external events? Does the family serve as a support group as its members become accountable in the world outside the family? When can the family members be "fully present" to devote energies to the family equation? Can a family set its own pace of life and not let the pace be set by society?

Goals for the Counseling Process

Perhaps it would be helpful to review several points that describe what the person-centered approach does *not* advocate. First, the therapist does not enter therapy with a preconceived model of how families interact and how problems are generated by specific interactions in components of that model. Nor does the therapist begin therapy with a model of exactly how a family should believe, change, and live or state whether it is always in the members' best interests to remain together as a family. Patterson (1968) says that the therapy process is not one of "influencing attitudes, beliefs or behavior or means of persuading, leading, or convincing no matter how indirectly, subtly or painlessly. It is not the process of getting someone to think or behave in ways (in) which we want him to think or behave, or in ways we think best for him" (p. 1).

The therapist does not begin therapy with a preconceived idea of who should be seen in counseling, in what order and under what circumstances, or whether all attending members will be seen together. The therapist does not perceive that he or she will be the expert, skilled diagnostician who single-handedly pinpoints the family's problems and prescribes a treatment plan. Heider (1985) offers a passage from the *Tao of Leadership* that says, "The wise leader does not impose a personal agenda or value sys-

tem on the group." The family therapist would be open and attentive to whatever emerges. He says that "openness is simply more potent than any system of judgments ever devised" (p. 97).

Each family is viewed as a group of unique individuals with unique interactional patterns and issues. They are also seen as possessing many potentials of their own for maintaining and enhancing themselves as well as the family. The members are perceived as ones who can actualize their potentials to resolve family problems of an internal or external nature. They are capable of shaping their own growth both as individuals and as a family. In essence, the family members are their own architects. The therapist shows a tremendous respect for the family's potential to be actualizing and self-determining. The family even decides who will be present for therapy. The therapist recognizes that the family or some part of the family seeks therapy because of their own state of incongruence or conflict in the family group, or with one or more members of the family. Although there may be similarities among families, the therapist remains open to the specialness and the nuances of each and every family and its members. The therapist may not even think about the similarities in families until his or her involvement with the family has ended.

What then are the goals of a person-centered process? The therapist strives to establish a healthy psychological climate (Rogers, 1957a, 1970) that the family members can use to establish realness in family relationships, express true feelings, remain separate and yet identify with the family, develop effective two-way communication, start a healthy process for family development and problem solving, and clarify societal effects on the family as well as determine conflicts, seek solutions, explore values, make decisions, experiment with new behaviors, and develop a family model-direction unique to its needs and wants. The family experiences a climate in which they are not judged or evaluated. They have the opportunity to explore their difficulties in a nonthreatening environment when they are with the therapist, who nurtures a sense of caring, honesty, and understanding. A mutual, close, trusting relationship often develops between the therapist and family members.

The six conditions that Rogers (1957a) postulates from the individual therapeutic process are as follows.

1. Two persons are in psychological contact.
2. The first, whom we shall term the client, is in a state of incongruence, being vulnerable or anxious.
3. The second person, whom we shall term the therapist, is congruent or integrated in the relationship.
4. The therapist experiences unconditional positive regard for the client.
5. The therapist experiences an empathic understanding of the client's frame of reference and endeavors to communicate this experience to the client.
6. The communication to the client of the therapist's empathic understanding and unconditional positive regard is to a minimal degree achieved. (p. 96)

These conditions are necessary and sufficient for a process of constructive personality change to occur. Gaylin (1989) has reviewed the six conditions in view of the family therapeutic process and has found them "to be a good foundation for the refining and clarifying occurring within the family therapy hour" (p. 275). He elaborates on these conditions for family therapy and how they are viewed in the context of family helping. He indicates that family therapists need a basic knowledge of child development, and on a needed occasion they will shift to doing child guidance. He informs his clients of this shift from family therapy. Gaylin especially likes the notion of the "family actualization" process. Bozarth and Shanks (1989) also support the actualizing process in the family as well as the formative tendency in the family as an organismic unit moving toward health and wellness.

Additional discussions of person-centered views for individuals (Mearns & Thorne, 1988; Patterson, 1985), for a perceptual-experiential theory of therapy (Combs, 1989), for person-centered therapy (Raskin & Rogers, 1989), and for an overview of family therapies including a person-centered view (Levant, 1984a) are well worth examining.

What are the traits of this healthy psychological climate? The first component is that of the therapist's genuineness with the family members. Genuineness involves an attempt to be real with them as family members and as persons. Congruence also describes this quality. What a therapist experiences inside is present in his or her awareness and is part of his or her communication. The therapist who is genuine strives to be whole and fully present in the therapy situation, totally aware of and refusing to deny or suppress his or her thoughts and feelings. Such a therapist shows his or her true inner feelings—irritation as well as enjoyment—and seeks to be congruent and to avoid presenting a facade. In another sense, the therapist is quite transparent in the therapy experience. He or she is open and expresses feelings and thoughts as they arise in the here-and-now family therapy session. Although therapist's responsibilities may differ somewhat from those of the members, he or she is, like each of them, a person with feelings, thoughts, and ideas. The effective family therapist has a clear sense of being and is down-to-earth (Heider, 1985).

When family members perceive a realness on the therapist's part, they become more genuine and honest in their interactions not only with the therapist but also with each other. The members strive to be more in touch with their own thoughts and feelings as these emerge into awareness and become present in members' communications. The members have become somewhat more integrated. When the therapist places more trust in the members, they come to trust themselves more and to feel themselves worthy of trust. As the therapist is more genuine in the relationship, the family members also become more honest and real in the therapy process, in the family interaction, and outside the therapy setting.

A second component is that of the therapist's ability to care for the members and to prize them. The therapist experiences an unconditional positive regard for the members and for the family as a group. The members are accepted as persons, even though all behaviors of the members may not be likable. The dignity and integrity of each person in the family is respected as well as the whole family group.

If the family members perceive that the therapist prizes them and cares about them, they will come to value themselves more. They will believe in themselves and see themselves as more worthwhile. In other words, their self-concepts will begin to change and affect family relationships and their view of the family. Perhaps there is no other place where the potential for unconditional positive regard is greater than in the family. Heider

(1985) proposes that the wise leader (family therapist) is like water: "water cleanses and refreshes all creatures without distinction and without judgment; water freely and fearlessly goes beneath the surface of things; water is fluid and responsive" (p. 15). He says the leader is yielding.

A third component is the therapist's willingness to listen carefully to what family members have to share. An effective therapist hears and understands family members' needs, wants, conflicts, fears, joys, loves, goals, values, hates, disappointments, dreams, sorrows, and their worlds or realities. Family members' realities are often described from their vivid imagery with rich metaphors and stories that when understood can add significantly to the therapy process. The therapist also senses how metaphors and stories are used to teach children lessons on life and living. The therapist does not try to interpret to the family members the meanings of their realities. Members are encouraged and helped to explore, clarify, and understand their own meanings and how these relate to the family milieu. The therapist tries to understand each family member's view of the family problem(s) as well as any emerging family themes. Then the therapist's understanding is communicated to the family members. This communication helps the therapist stay in touch with the direction taken by the members in the counseling process. Heider (1985) says "to know what is happening, push less, open out and be aware. See without staring. Listen quietly rather than listening hard. Use intuition and reflection rather than trying to figure things out" (p. 27).

If members find that the therapist listens and attempts to understand their issues, feelings, and hopes, they will work toward understanding themselves better and in turn will work at understanding other family members and the family as a group. They will work at not making assumptions about what other members mean to communicate. The members tend to develop an ability to be empathic with each other. When members perceive that they are understood by the therapist and other family members, they feel a part of the process and the family problem-solving group. They see themselves as needed resources within the group. Members identify with the family, and family esteem begins to change in positive directions.

The three components are essential to a good counseling process. When the therapist attempts to experience unconditional positive regard for family members, to be integrated and genuine in the therapy situation, and to show empathic understanding by listening to members, the members also demonstrate these qualities with other family members as well as with the therapist. *They learn what they are experiencing.* If the conditions of empathic understanding and unconditional positive regard are perceived to a minimal degree by the family, they begin to work together to create and define their separate and shared visions of the family. A trusting relationship develops (psychological contact), and a creative process unfolds. When family members also become facilitative in the process, this speeds up the process of therapy. Some family members pick up very fast on how the therapist is facilitating in the situation (Ohlsen, 1979). At this point in the therapy process, constructive and positive conditions for a healthy psychological environment have emerged within the family group. Then family members can proceed to tackle family problems in a caring environment

characterized by a growing mutual trust between members, a lack of threat, more risk taking by members, feedback between members, real behaviors, and family members' growth. The therapist's commitment to the process also includes an *intent* to be fully present by focusing on the family's potentials and growth resources. The family and its members remain the focus, the center of the process.

The task of the therapist is to facilitate each member's discovery of the inherent potentials of the family members to solve their own problems and to be more the persons that they wish to be as individuals and as a family. The therapist must be constantly aware of the therapy process and of the members' feelings, fears, and hopes. Finally, the family learns a process for family development and problem solving. The family therapy situation may be one place where family members can experience support, acceptance, and encouragement to develop their potentials as separate individuals and as family members. This holds true for children as well as mothers, fathers, and others.

Primary Responsibilities of Family Members in Therapy

The responsibilities taken by the family members have an emergent quality about them; that is, the family accepts more responsibility for the process and their part in it as therapy progresses. Often, in the beginning, the members look to the therapist for direction and advice on problem solutions. When they do not receive advice and solutions to their problems, the members can become dismayed. Occasionally, family members have not liked this responsibility. They have wanted the therapist, as an expert, to tell them what to do and to take responsibility for the outcomes. Yet the therapist seeks to help them reach solutions by listening, caring, and being real in the therapeutic relationship. If the therapist is able to offer a facilitative climate, then a therapeutic process of growth and change will inevitably occur. The therapist believes in the members and respects their own strengths, abilities, and potentials to use the therapy process, to clarify issues, and to resolve problems, regardless of their ages. They can assume the initiative for their own growth and contribution to the family problem-solving process. Family members can accept the responsibility for actions and consequences. They are the agents of change. Ultimately, the locus of evaluation for family actions and results resides in the family members as a group.

The movement in therapy is from dependence and lack of "response-ability" on the part of the family toward more independence and use of their abilities to be responsive to family problems. The movement is toward responsibility, direction, determination, decision making, and assessment by family members.

The readiness and commitment to the therapy process are up to the family members. They have the freedom to choose the participants, extent, and pattern of participation. The members often try to answer this question: What will be most productive and comfortable for individual members and the family group? The process is open to all members if they choose it to be.

As well as determining who will participate, the members fully explore and identify the problem on which therapy is to be focused. In this sense, the members are very much a part of diagnosing what the problem is, what appear to be the current determinants of the problem, and what steps should be taken inside

and outside of therapy. In the therapy process, the family group weighs its members' values and often comes in touch with a *family-valuing* approach. This weighing of values is closely followed by a *family decision-making* segment, with all members in the therapy group taking part in the decision. With the therapist's help, the family members contribute significantly to the treatment plans as well as in the assessment of the effectiveness of those plans for the family. As a result of assessment, new directions and plans are determined by the members.

All of these responsibilities are assumed by the family members over the course of therapy. Complete ownership of the problem is accepted by the family group. The risks for change belong to the family members, and so do the consequences, satisfactions, and disappointments. It is the family members' responsibility to explore the meanings of their actions and the family therapy experience, to initiate actions for change, and to terminate the sessions when all members perceive it to be appropriate to do so.

Functions of a Therapist

As the family therapist begins to enter a counseling relationship, several questions may serve as helpful checks. These come from a passage (Heider, 1985) on unbiased leadership: "Can you mediate emotional issues without taking sides or picking favorites? Can you breathe freely and remain relaxed even in the presence of passionate fears and desires? Are your own conflicts clarified? Is your own house clean? Can you be gentle with all factions and lead the group without dominating? Can you remain open and receptive, no matter what issues arise? Can you know what is emerging, yet keep your peace while others discover for themselves?" (p. 19). Combs (1989) views the therapist's self as a most crucial instrument in the therapy process.

In helping family members move toward responsible, independent problem solving, the therapist attempts to offer the conditions that create a positive climate for therapy. These human qualities of the therapist were described earlier: a willingness to understand the perceptions and realities of family members (empathic understanding), a desire to be genuine in the therapy situation (congruence), and a prizing of the family members as persons (unconditional positive regard). *These human qualities, the more significant aspects of therapy, are reflected in the therapist's helping behavior.* In this chapter, these reflections will be called *skills.* The importance of reflecting these qualities cannot be stressed too much because of the numerous person-to-person interactions in family therapy situations. Therapist-family interactions call for much communicative skill in understanding the wants, needs, and feelings of family members. Warner (1989) indicates that when the risks of open communication are perceived as too great, some families develop patterns of meeting needs through indirect or strategic communication. The therapist must be aware of the surface meaning and the strategic meaning and have empathy for the emotional reality underlying the interaction. Guerney and Guerney (1989) and Gaylin (1989) believe strongly that, at times, the family therapist needs to offer educational guidance and to teach selected parenting-relationship skills. The family members also learn the skills of helping by watching and experiencing the therapist. Thayer (1977) has described an experiential approach to learning helping skills.

The following skills are some of the basic ones that contribute to the expression of the therapist's human qualities (Thayer, 1981). These skills do not represent all of the "particulars" of helping family members.

Being Attentive. The therapist signals an intent or willingness to engage in communication with family members. Attentiveness communicates that the therapist is ready to focus on the members and what they are saying and feeling—in essence, on all that the individuals are experiencing and communicating. The therapist's physical posture is turned toward the person who is speaking to show interest in what is being communicated. Furthermore, the therapist generally encourages the family members to select the topical content and process direction. Communication is facilitated by helping the members talk about the subjects they have chosen. The focus is on the family members. Rather than directing the discussion, the therapist follows the members' expressions of thoughts, feelings, and meanings on the family situation.

Being relaxed. To aid in attentiveness to the members and to the process, the therapist appears comfortable with families. The muscles of the therapist's body are relaxed. Taking several deep breaths helps in becoming more relaxed. Tensing the body muscles several times for 5 to 7 seconds and then releasing the tightness also aids in relaxing the muscles. In contrast, tenseness suggests that other conditions or events, such as uneasiness about the current situation or personal concerns, are distracting the therapist and might impair the therapy process.

Sensing and Communicating an Understanding of Thought (Verbal Mes-

sages). The therapist is able to hear the members' messages and state in his or her own words what they are saying. Such statements communicate to the family what is heard and allows for an accuracy check by the members. The therapist's communication helps to assure the group members that someone is really trying to understand their ways of viewing life in the family situation. The therapist is sensitive to misunderstandings between family members. The *intent* is to follow the members' leads in order to understand the members and then, in turn, to communicate this understanding to the group. Questions are used infrequently since they often represent the therapist's curiosity and desire to direct the process. Instead, the therapist encourages the members to direct the flow of communication because they know what the concerns are.

Sensing and Communicating an Understanding of Feelings and Meanings.

The therapist tries to grasp the members' entire communication, both verbal and nonverbal, and then expresses what is understood of their feelings in relation to family events and experiences. The therapist listens carefully for "feeling" words and observes the simultaneous nonverbal messages in the family's voices and physical expressions. Responding to feelings and meanings is a key skill that can communicate to the family members the therapist's understanding of their worlds. The therapist must be particularly sensitive to the nonverbal messages of family members, because these messages are not always the same as the verbal messages. As much as 65% of the feelings and meanings of messages are communicated nonverbally; thus, it's important for the therapist to be aware of facial expressions,

voice tones, eye contact, hand gestures, body movements, and other nonverbal components. A difference between verbal and nonverbal messages may signal that members are not completely aware of their own experiencing. The member(s) may be in a state of incongruence.

Being Aware of Personal Experiencing and Expressing the Related Thoughts and Feelings.

The therapist is in touch with his or her own opinions concerning the current moment of experiencing in the family therapy situation. In other words, the therapist tries to pay attention to his or her own inner self and internal dialogue. He or she focuses inward to be aware of feelings and thoughts and then expresses these feelings and thoughts appropriately in "I" messages. Using "I" indicates that the therapist owns these messages and is responsible for them. Expressing inner feelings and thoughts helps the therapist become more honest and direct in interactions with the family, more integrated as a person in the therapeutic relationship.

Experiencing Positive Regard and Appreciation for Family Members as Persons and Showing Respect for Them and for Oneself.

The therapist reflects a caring attitude, taking time to consider the feelings of the family members as well as his or her own rights as a person in the therapy situation. In essence, the therapist tries to demonstrate to the members "I prize you as persons and as members of this family."

Trusting and Expressing Intuitive Hunches.

Often instincts are more valuable to the therapy process than logic and intellect. The therapist who remains open with all senses will, at some points, experience a real "gut," visceral sensation about family members, the therapy process, and what the members are experiencing. This hunch, often perceived only minimally by the therapist, can become a very accurate indicative perception and a useful tool in the therapy process. A therapist needs to test out the viability of these hunches in safe situations outside of therapy, learn to trust their usefulness, and then incorporate them into his or her helping style.

Three additional skills are noted for use by the family therapist (Thayer, 1984).

Recognizing and Responding to that Personal Material that Is Most Conspicuous by Its Absence. Occasionally, family members will communicate information that reveals some component of feelings, thoughts, or information that is conspicuously absent. With sensitivity, the therapist may choose to respond depending on what the missing component might be. Take, for example, a teenager who talked of sports, school, his mother, siblings, grades, and teachers. The component that seemed obviously missing was talk of his father. Responding to the absent information, the therapist learned that the boy's father had died several months earlier and that it was difficult for the boy to accept his father's death. In this case, the situation was sensitive. The therapist had to respond with care. But much can be learned by understanding what family members or a family group is speaking about and what is conspicuously absent in the themes of communication.

Paying Attention to Personal (Facilitator) Mental Images. Images based on stimulus statements and communication from the family provide a rich source of data for understanding the world of the family members. At times, concurrent feelings and thoughts will be generated in the therapist that bring him or her closer to the visual-perceptual world of a family member or family. In addition to understanding the member, the therapist can help the member to develop imaginative ideas, explore fears and blocks to learning, project risks and consequences of desired actions, and others. Paralleling the visualizations from the eye of the member's mind can make for greater empathic understanding and personal relevancy of therapy. It is a doorway to unlock the creative process of family therapy.

Recognizing Polarities and Helping Family Members Balance These Apparent Differences. Frequently in family situations, polar differences are dealt with separately when they might be seen as part of the same unit. Too often family members have been caused to deny feelings and their relationship to the total process of family. The therapist has an exciting adventure ahead if he or she can help members accept the polarities that exist, balance the different aspects of family, stop denying the affective part, and recognize that the result will be a whole, fuller process of therapy, greater than the sum of the two parts.

Process of Family Therapy

The focus in this section is on what is occurring "within" the individuals and "between" family members in the process of family therapy. Both components of change and development occur in therapy.

Rogers (1961b) has a view of how the process of therapy affects personality change, taking a more "naturalist's observational, descriptive approach" to the events in therapy (p. 128). From these observations, he has made "low-level inferences" about the most basic events in the process. Although the process to be discussed describes the individual in therapy, the stages are also indicative of what happens within individuals in family therapy. The potential for the family being a healthy, creative, complex whole lies within each family member.

Heider (1985) reminds the therapist that "you are facilitating another person's process. It is not your process. Do not intrude. Do not control. Do not force your own needs and insights into the foreground. If you do not trust a person's process, that person will not trust you" (p. 33). In many ways, this statement applies to the therapy process for family members.

Of special note in Rogers's study of the therapeutic process is the importance of feelings, coming closer to experiencing the feelings of the moment, accurately symbolizing this experiencing of feelings for better communication, and "moments of movement" in therapy. Anderson (1989b) believes that the therapist's empathic responses to the personal and subjective narrative self stories of the individuals can be expanded or shifted to include shared, collective experiences of the family. Rigid views about what happens or should happen in therapy just won't hold in reality.

If the optimal conditions described earlier are present and perceived by the individual family members, then a therapeutic process emerges. Rogers's view of an emerging continuum is "from fixity to changingness, from rigid structure to flow, from stasis to process" (Rogers, 1961b, p. 131). But the process is "not forced." Given the appropriate conditions, the therapy process will flow. The family sets a pace. The clients' expressions would be indicators of where they stood on this process continuum.

Although seven stages are noted in the process conception, Rogers maintains that the process is a continuum. The clients are likely at *approximately* one stage in their development and do not necessarily show characteristics of several other stages. The stages of the process follow (Rogers, 1961b, pp. 132–154):

[Stage 1] There is an unwillingness to communicate self. Communication is only about externals. . . . Feelings and personal meanings are neither recognized nor owned. Personal constructs are extremely rigid. Close and communicative relationships are construed as dangerous. No problems are recognized or perceived at this stage. There is no desire to change. . . . There is much blockage of internal communication.

[Stage 2] Expression begins to flow in regard to non-self topics. . . . Problems are perceived as external to self. . . . There is no sense of personal responsibility in problems. . . . Feelings are described as unowned, or sometimes as past objects. . . . Feelings may be exhibited, but are not recognized as such or owned. Experience is bound by the structure of the past. . . . Personal constructs are rigid, and unrecognized as being constructs, but are thought of as facts. . . . Differentiation of personal meanings and feelings is very limited and global. . . . Contradictions may be expressed, but with little recognition of them as contradictions.

[Stage 3] There is a freer flow of expressions about the self as an object. . . . There is also expression about self-related experiences as objects. . . . There is also expression about the self as a reflected object existing primarily in others. . . . There is much expression about or description of feelings and personal meanings not now present. . . . There is very little acceptance of feelings. For the most part, feelings are revealed as something shameful, bad, or abnormal, or unacceptable in other ways. Feelings are exhibited, and then sometimes recognized as feelings. Experiencing is described as in the past, or as somewhat remote from the self....Personal constructs are rigid, but may be recognized as constructs, not external facts....Differentiation of feelings and meanings is slightly sharper, less global, than in previous stages....There is recognition of contradictions in experience ....Personal choices are often seen as ineffective.

[Stage 4] The client describes more intense feelings of the "not-now-present" variety.... Feelings are described as objects in the present....Occasionally feelings are expressed as in the present, sometimes breaking through almost against the client's wishes ....There is a tendency toward experiencing feelings in the immediate present, and there is distrust and fear of this possibility....There is little open acceptance of feelings, though some acceptance is exhibited....Experiencing is less bound by the structure of the past, is less remote, and may occasionally occur with little postponement....There is a loosening of the way experience is construed. There are some discoveries of personal constructs; there is the definite recognition of these as constructs; and there is beginning questioning of their validity....There is an increased differentiation of feelings, constructs, personal meanings, with some tendency toward seeking exactness of symbolization....There is a realization of concern about contradictions and incongruences between experience and self....There are feelings of self-responsibility in problems, though such feelings vacillate. Though a close relationship still seems dangerous, the client risks himself, relating to some small extent on a feeling basis.

[Stage 5] Feelings are expressed freely as in the present....Feelings are very close to being fully experienced. They "bubble up," "seep through," in spite of the fear and distrust which the client feels at experiencing them with fullness and immediacy....There is a beginning tendency to realize that experi-

encing a feeling involves a direct referent.... There is surprise and fright, rarely pleasure, at the feelings which "bubble through."... There is an increasing ownership of self feelings, and a desire to be these, to be the "real me."...Experiencing is loosened, no longer remote, and frequently occurs with little postponement....The ways in which experience is construed are much loosened. There are many fresh discoveries of personal constructs as constructs, and a critical examination and questioning of these....There is a strong and evident tendency toward exactness in differentiation of feelings and meanings.... There is an increasingly clear facing of contradiction and incongruences in experience....There is an increasing quality of acceptance of self-responsibility for the problems being faced, and a concern as to how he has contributed. There are increasingly freer dialogues within the self, an improvement in and reduced blockage of internal communication.

[Stage 6] A feeling which has previously been "stuck," has been inhibited in its process quality, is experienced with immediacy now. A feeling flows to its full result. A present feeling is directly experienced with immediacy and richness. This immediacy of experiencing, and the feeling which constitutes its contents, are accepted. This is something which is, not something to be denied, feared, struggled against....There is a quality of living subjectively in the experience, not feeling about it....Self as an object tends to disappear....Experiencing, at this stage, takes on a real process quality....Another characteristic of this stage of process is the physiological loosening which accompanies it....In this stage, internal communication is free and relatively unblocked....The incongruence between experience and awareness is vividly experienced as it disappears into congruence. The relevant personal construct is dissolved in this experiencing moment, and the client feels cut loose from his previously stabilized framework....The moment of full experiencing becomes a clear and definite referent. Differentiation of experiencing is sharp and basic.... In this stage, there are no longer "problems," external or internal. The client is living, subjectively, a phase of his problem. It is not an object.

[Stage 7] New feelings are experienced with immediacy and richness of detail, both in the therapeutic relationship and outside. The experiencing of such feelings is used as a clear referent.... There is a growing and continuing sense of acceptant ownership of these changing feelings, a basic trust in his own process.... Experiencing has lost almost completely its structure bound aspects and becomes process experiencing—that is, the situation is experienced and interpreted in its newness, not as the past.... The self becomes increasingly simply the subjective and reflexive awareness of experiencing. The self is much less frequently a perceived object, and much more frequently something confidently felt in process.... Personal constructs are tentatively reformulated, to be validated against further experience, but even then, to be held loosely.... Internal communication is clear, with feelings and symbols well matched, and fresh terms for new feelings. There is the experiencing of effective choice of new ways of being.

This process is one that is set in motion when clients are fully accepted. An approach stressing the cognitive rather than emotional aspects may set in motion entirely different processes from the one described here. Generally, "the process moves from a point of fixity, where all the elements and threads described above are separately discernible and separately understandable, to the flowing peak moments of therapy in which all these threads become inseparably woven together" (Rogers, 1961b, p. 158).

Family therapy process emphasizes not only what happens within individual members but also what occurs between family members in their interpersonal relationships. The challenge for the family therapist is to be congruent in the relationship, to prize the family, and to understand empathically each member's subjective meaning while understanding and responding to the interpersonal, intersubjective meaning in the context of the family (Anderson, 1989a). This distinguishes family therapy from individual therapy. The therapy situation offers the family an opportunity to interact in an increasingly nonthreatening environment where they are respected as individuals and not labeled in any way by the therapist. Since the members often hold deep, intense emotions about family events, another aspect of family therapy appears very much like the process in an encounter group experience.

Rogers (1970, ch. 2) has described the observable events in encounter groups, and these are similar in some respects to the events that have been observed in family therapy; yet more study needs to be conducted on person-centered family therapy. Rogers (1970, ch. 3) focuses on the question "Can I be a facilitative person in a group?" He covers issues related to philosophy and attitudes, climate-setting functions, acceptance of a group, acceptance of the individual, empathic understanding, operating in terms of feelings, confrontation and feedback, expression of problems, avoidance of interpretive or process comments, and other related facilitator functions. A key difference in family therapy and encounter groups is that after a family leaves a therapy session, they may go home together or see each other a great deal before the subsequent session. The family staying together has its advantages and certainly adds to the complexities of therapy.

Families do not always start in the first stage of a therapy process because some parts of a helping process may have already been worked through. Here is a brief overview of the stages based on work with encounter groups (Rogers, 1970, ch. 2).

1. *Milling around.* Family members are uncertain what their responsibilities will be in setting the structure of therapy. Some frustration and confusion is natural. The members will attempt to answer "What is our purpose for being here?"

2. *Resistance to personal expression or exploration.* Members may tend not to reveal their thoughts and feelings about family events or about themselves. There is often a subtle testing of the therapist and other family members. "How safe is it to express views here?" Members may fear revealing themselves and may lack a trust in the family group.

3. *Description of past feelings.* The expression of feelings consumes more of the therapy time, but the feelings are about past events or ones external to the therapy situation. The feelings essentially exist in the "then and there."

4. *Expression of negative feelings.* A hint of the first real here-and-now feelings are negative in nature. They may be directed at other members, the therapist, or the therapy situation in general. These negative feelings may be a way to test the trustworthiness of the members and the freedom of the therapy situation. Is this a place where individuals can truly be themselves, regardless of the nature of their feelings?

5. *Expression and exploration of personally meaningful material.* A member of the family may take the risk of revealing him- or herself to the other family members. Individuals are beginning to perceive that they can help to shape what the family is and can be. Although there is a risk in expressing oneself, a climate of trust is building.

6. *The expression of immediate interpersonal feelings in the group.* Members

are beginning to express their moment-to-moment feelings toward one another. These feelings may be positive or negative and often are explored considerably by the members. The members may begin to understand intuitively that something in the family is changing.

7. *The development of a healing capacity in the group.* The family begins to unleash its tremendous potential for helping members deal with their pain and suffering. Some family members can intuitively sense what others are experiencing and, in a climate of trust and freedom, can respond with acceptance and understanding. Individual members are helped to be aware of and deal with their present experiencing.

8. *Self-acceptance and the beginning of change.* As family members come to accept themselves as they are, this acceptance of self signals the starting of change. Resistance to change subsides as members begin to accept themselves as they are in the family. This acceptance generates more self-exploration and initial acceptance of others. More genuineness is evident from members. As members are more in touch with their own feelings, they are moving away from being so rigidly organized. They seem more open to "flowingness" and change. The acceptance of one's own experiencing is a significant event.

9. *The cracking of facades.* As the process continues, family members are less patient with defenses. The members are moving toward a more basic congruence within the family. Members demand realness of others in terms of current feelings and thoughts. This component can be hurtful, at times, but the other members respond with sensitivity and caring for the family member and help to heal the hurting person.

10. *The individual receives feedback.*

Individual members receive data on how they appear to others in the family. With caring and openness, feedback is often quite constructive, regardless of its positive or negative tone. The feedback can trigger more self-exploration and sharing between family members. When a member "receives" feedback, that is a major indicator that more openness is occurring. Members are learning to request, accept, and use feedback (Ohlsen, Horne, & Lawe, 1988).

11. *Confrontation.* Constructive feedback is occasionally too mild a word to describe the intense interaction between family members. Confrontation can be positive but is often decidedly negative.

12. *The helping relationship outside the group sessions.* Family members take advantage of the numerous opportunities outside of therapy to offer support and understanding to other individual members. This is one of the significant signs of changes occurring in interpersonal relationships between family members. They are exhibiting their abilities to be accepting, caring, supportive, and helping.

13. *The basic encounter.* As the trusting climate has developed, family members are coming in closer and more direct contact than is customary. The intense experiencing appears to release the potentials of the members to be genuine in the family and to work together to solve issues confronting the family. It is a time of change. The family is becoming connected. A change in one member affects all other events and members in the family dynamics; it is an interrelating bond.

14. *The expression of positive feelings and closeness.* As sessions proceed, an increasing amount of feelings of warmth, family spirit, and trust is developed. More feelings are shared and accepted by the family members. There is significant realness in the family's inter-personal relationships. Members can work toward the resolution of issues because there is a feeling of acceptance among members and a feeling of worthwhileness by individuals. There is a sharing and acceptance of responsibility for resolving family problems.

15. *Behavior changes in the family group.* Of special significance is the way family members relate to each other. Their interactions are based on real feelings without the normal amount of defensiveness. There is more sensitivity and helpfulness among individuals. Individuals are permitted their separateness, yet they may be closer to family members. Family members listen to each other with more understanding, and two-way communication is better. The family members have proceeded in learning a process in which they can continue to explore and clarify values, examine and make decisions, and challenge the issues that may come before the family. It is a special process. The family becomes a "mutual happening."

When they are at home, there is a need for family members to maintain the level of openness that they reached in therapy. They need to continue the work of providing support for members, making acceptance of each other "real" in the interpersonal relationships. Members need to continue to work at the goal of living in the family on a real basis. There also may be times when a member of a family will need to continue in therapy alone because of additional need for support. The family can be a support system for this person.

While there continually seems to be an emergent, fluid quality in the family therapy process, several family directions seem to stand out. The family seems to move *away from facades* and *toward genuineness* and increased openness in family interpersonal relationships. They move away from meeting the "oughts" and expectations of others and toward greater self-direction as a family. And as the family experiences more prizing, accepting of its members and listening more carefully to its own members' feelings, thoughts, and meanings, then the family moves toward greater acceptance of the family as a group and understanding of the dynamic, actualizing group. The family is more aware of its own fluid, flexible process (Rogers, 1961c). The self-esteem of individual members as well as the general value of the family as a group is enhanced. The family recognizes its own tremendous potential for development and positive, healthy psychological change. A family's beliefs about itself change to a more positive, hopeful stance.

CASE EXAMPLE

The example included here is one variation of the person-centered approach taken by one family. In this example, the mother and two young daughters from a family of five came for therapy. The father and youngest daughter were not involved in the therapy process.

At the start of therapy, all three family members began in individual therapy. Mary, a 7th-grader, sought help because of low achievement in her classwork. Susie, a 5th-grader, was anxious about going to school and would get physically sick each morning. Their mother entered therapy to learn how to deal with these problems. One therapist saw Mrs. Milson and Susie separately while a second therapist worked with Mary. Eight individual sessions were held with each of the family members. During these individual sessions, a trust developed so that sharing and exploring processes were developed. As they learned that their therapists were accepting, em-

pathic, and genuine, the family members began to express and explore their internal feelings of anger and disappointment over their interpersonal relationships with each other. As a result of these processes, key problem areas became more clearly identified. Of special concern to each of the three family members was the lack of good interpersonal relationships between them at home. The members, separately, talked about their own wants and needs. They wanted to meet in a group situation to share feelings and concerns and work out more positive relationships between them at home. The two therapists were encouraged to make arrangements for a family meeting between the three family members, the two therapists, and an additional facilitator-therapist who had not been involved with the individual therapy.

In the final two sessions of individual therapy, the family members prepared to discuss their feelings and concerns in the group and to decide what they hoped to gain from the family therapy sessions. Because the family members had prepared for the family meeting, they initially specified the areas on which they wished to focus. Mrs. Milson wanted to discuss cooperation between the three of them. Mary didn't like being bothered by noise from her sister, Susie, when she was on the telephone. Susie hoped for more quiet time when she was doing her homework.

Here are several excerpts that show some of the communication exchanges and part of the process from the first family therapy meeting.

Excerpt 1
Susie: Like if Mary is mad or something and I'm like in her way, sometimes she'll go, "You wanna fight?" You do say that, Mary.
Mary: Uh uh.
Susie: Yes, you do.
Facilitator-Therapist (F-T): Just hang on.

Try to hear what Susie is saying, Mary. So you're saying, Susie, that she really says to you, "You wanna fight?" (Long pause.) Shall I ask Mary to respond? OK, Mary.

Mary: Well, it's like in my classroom, like if somebody does something to me, I get so angry when I come home and then I get...I take my coat off and put my books down. Then, when I'm angry and she tries to get it double for me, like when I come in and I'm angry and I'm really disappointed 'cause somebody had done something at school.

F-T: Your anger is from something that happened at school.

Mary: Yeah. And...I tell Mom what happened and then when I'm walking out or something, Susie tries to make it bigger and bigger...huge...like a snowball or something.

F-T: So Susie sees that you're angry, and she just makes it worse.

Mary: Yeah.

F-T: Makes it worse! And what you're angry about is really something that happened at school.

Mary: Yeah.

F-T: And that starts it?

Mary: Uh huh.

Excerpt 2

F-T: You have to yell above them and then you have to separate everybody and Susie has to go to her room and Mary to her room and you to another place.

Mother: Yes.

F-T: So all three of you are apart.

Mother: Yes, definitely. Because there's no reasoning at that moment. There is none whatsoever.

F-T: You are saying that from the girls there is no reasoning and you're including yourself?

Mother: Uh, when I reach that point, I am just extremely angry.

F-T: Just really angry!

Mother: And if someone would logically, um, explain what was happening, I'd say horsefeathers, because it has just completely gotten out of control.

F-T: Uh huh.

Mother: And to try and reason with Mary ...she is a very strong little person. (To Mary:) Don't get angry with me.

Mary: I'm not.

Mother: This is the moment of truth.

Mary: I know.

Mother: And there is no reasoning when she gets going full blast. And so to try and sit down and say, now the reason I am feeling this way...you are um...

F-T: It just doesn't seem to work.

Mother: There's nothing—no right, wrong, indifferent—nothing. It's, um, just anger and "I am going to get what I want" so...

F-T: That's how you're seeing it! Mary, can you come in? Do you want to respond to your mom?

Excerpt 3

Mother: There is always this friction. I think there always will be.

F-T: Uh huh.

Mother: I really don't...I really, uh, can't foresee a solution right now.

F-T: You don't think anything can be helped. It can't be helped in any way?

Mother: Um...

F-T: Between Susie and you and Mary...

Mother: Maybe it's just my frame of mind tonight, but, uh, between these two, then I step in which I wish I didn't have to. I wish they could resolve it themselves, but I don't think that can be...at least not right now. Uh, when they both meet at home after school, it's an automatic negative situation, almost physical, and, uh, one aggravates the other and it's deliberate. And I, uh, immediately come on extremely strong with Mary. Being she's the oldest, I feel she should know a little bit better.

F-T: So you're harder...you change the word...you're harder on Mary than Susie in a sense. You're saying, because she's older, that's the reason you're harder on her.

Mother: Uh huh, 'cause I feel that Mary should, um, or I wish she would understand or see the situation and not allow herself to, um, come on so strongly. I mean if Susie deliberately went out and punched her in the stomach, I could see where, you know, this would set off a natural defense mechanism. But this little stuff that really, we have no business even, um, bothering with because it's so nothing. I mean, this accidentally knocking on her on purpose...

Mary: You mean the time in the kitchen?

Mother: Oh, I don't care. It's kitchen, living room, basement, or...

F-T: It happens, you're saying...

Mother: Out in the middle of a field. I can put you girls into a 2,000-square-foot house, and it is still not large enough. Tonight was a perfect episode. I'm sorry. I'm getting...

F-T: Go ahead.

Mother: Um, you're upset about the pen. The reason I got upset about it was I felt you had lost it...that no one took it...you had lost it.

Mary: Well...

Mother: I'm sorry. That's my mistrust.

Mary: Yeah.

Mother: Then you get it on with Susie.

Mary: Wait, um, and sometimes you blame it on me.

Mother: Mary, I am not sitting here and saying it is your fault. I am not blaming you ...don't. (Mary begins to cry.) I am just trying to find a solution or something. Now this pen business...I will go to K-Mart. I will get you another pen. This was the whole thing tonight. I mean, "You have to go and get me that pen, Mommy or I will go into a tantrum." Now, isn't that it?

Mary: Huh?

Mother: You have not sat and told me, "If you don't do this, I will get angry"?

F-T: What is it, Mary? Can you tell her?

Mary: That's not...Susie...She starts it and every single time...when I try to do something, she starts it and I'm sick and tired of all the homework and everything. (To Susie:) Like when I'm on the phone or something, then you start in. I just wanna know why do you do that? I'm feeling so angry...I wanna know why do you do this to me, Susie. When I'm on the phone with my friends, you start in. I wanna know why, Susie. I'm fed up with it to here.

F-T: So you feel like you have just had enough of it.

The facilitator-therapist tried to understand the family members' feelings and perceptions as well as encourage the members to listen to each other's feelings and perceptions and encounter each other. Each member had an opportunity to express her views and feelings about the conflicts between them. Because of the preparation phase in the individual sessions and the support of their individual therapists who were present at this session, the family members were more honest and quite expressive in the new therapeutic atmosphere. The climate was tested and seemed accepting, so real conflicts were discussed.

Here is a segment in which the family members' individual therapists participated. Although the individual members' therapists spoke infrequently during this first session, they were facilitative by supporting their members' desires to be completely honest, empathic, and involved.

Excerpt 4

(Mary is crying throughout this segment.)

Mary (to Susie): Are you jealous of me or something?

Susie: No, Mary. I'm trying to say I want us to be sisters.

Mary: I know, but why do you, like when I'm on the phone or something, you try something. Like I wanna know why you do it. I just want an answer from you.

Susie: Because I'm tired and I do cause trouble.

(Silence for 2 or 3 minutes.)

Therapist 2: Sounds like you're blaming yourself for something.

F-T: Can you talk about it a little bit?

Therapist 3: Sounds almost like you don't like to get into these fights either.

Susie: I wanna be born to love my sister.

F-T (to Susie): One thing you really want is to be more sisterly. More of a sister with Mary.

Mary: I just wanna point out why and...

Therapist 2 (to Mary): Maybe this is your question, maybe...why if she wants to be sisterly so you can love each other, why does she do these things to you?

Mary: I don't know.

Therapist 2: Is that your question?

Mary: Yeah, I just wanna find out why, you know, she just gave one answer that she's tired and she caused trouble and I just wanna find out a few weeks ago why—(To Susie:) I tried to talk to you, um, last week but you, you started nagging me and stuff. I wanna talk to you, why? You never did. Why, Susie? I just wanna ask you why do you sometimes, like last Friday, and I wanted to talk to you about it and you said no. You started calling me names and stuff and you said no and then, um, I just didn't do nothing. I just wanna ask you why, why do you do this to me?

Susie: 'Cause sometimes I get mad at you for nothing and I just blame it on you.

Therapist 2: You need someone to blame it on, and Mary is there so you blame her. It's hard to have something you are upset about and not know what to do with it.

Therapist 3: Susie, I really hear you saying a lot that you, and Mary, too, that you really, neither of you are very happy with the way you have been treating one another. And Susie, I hear you saying that sometimes you're at fault. And Mary, I hear you saying sometimes that you start it, and it appears to me that neither one of you, um, really deep down inside is very happy with the way you've been treating one another.

Mary: No, 'cause I wanna talk to you, Susie, but you never give me a chance to.

These segments represent some of the exchanges in the family therapy process. As the process continued, it appeared that Mrs. Milson and Mary had a number of issues to work out while other issues existed between Mary and Susie. Near the end of the session, the family members made one request of each other for the upcoming week. The plans for homework that the members established were related to very specific situations

that caused friction in their interpersonal relationships. At this point, it was agreed that the therapy process would continue.

Of special note are several points that were brought out in this example. First, the family members began in individual therapy. They talked about their concerns, developed a trusting relationship with a therapist, examined issues relating to interpersonal relationships in the family, decided to enter into a family therapy situation, and then prepared for the family therapy process. Entering into a family therapy process was something the three members wanted. Each of the three was committed to the process and willing to work on concerns in therapy and to work on specific situational issues at home. There was a great respect for the members' abilities to work out their problems. The members participated in ways that were comfortable to them yet growth producing. The facilitator-therapist and the other two therapists felt at ease in expressing themselves in the situation. They left the topics for discussion and the direction of therapy to the family members. The members could be trusted to take the responsibility of working on resolutions to their conflicts. The final decision on the meaning and extent of therapy remained with the family members.

Development of Family Meetings

The person-centered view may also be applied in families who are not in therapy. It can be a way for families to grow and to develop together (Coulson, 1973, 1979).

Rogers (1977a, pp. 34–37) tells of Ben and Claire with their unique situation as they searched for new ways of living in family relationships.

What happens when parents regard their children as unique persons in an ever changing communicative relationship? The story of Ben and Claire illustrates the dynamics of this process. Claire had raised her children along authoritarian lines until her divorce and remarriage to a man who was committed to the person-centered approach. Each partner brought to this marriage children by previous marriages, and there were many new relationships with varying degrees of trust and communication. Claire found herself changing.

In trying to resolve some of the new issues, Ben and Claire decided to have meetings in which every member of the family, no matter how young or old, was free to express his (or her) feelings—the complaints, satisfactions, or reactions—to the others.

The father of Walter, Claire's oldest son, had disappeared from Walter's life with little warning. Otherwise Claire's statement is self-explanatory. I simply asked her how their family group meetings had started.

Claire: We scheduled them. We picked a time. It turned out that it was every Tuesday. And nothing interfered with Tuesday—not a business meeting or a movie or entertaining, or if somebody came over we had to ask them to leave and come over another day. The children learned to count on that. There were a lot of adjustments to be made between me and Ben, between Ben and my children, and me and his children, and between the children. And Ben had been involved in group work before and wanted this kind of experience—the closeness and sharing and expression of feelings—to be a natural part of the family unit. He called a meeting following dinner. We all stayed at the table—the children wondering what was going to happen. He started it by trying to teach them how to express feelings and get away from accusations, you know—"You are a bully," or "You pick on me." I was picked to be the first one to start going around the circle. There were eight of us at the table and I had seven people to cover and to tell them how I felt about them, each one. And not only the posi-

tive but some of the negative things, some of my concerns and worries that were very different with each child. And it was really the first time I had talked about negative things in a constructive way in front of everybody else. That usually is a private thing. I could say to one of the boys how proud I felt of his scholastic accomplishments but at the same time how worried I was about what I perceived as selfishness—that I didn't really understand where it came from and I wanted to talk to him more about it so that we could resolve it or I could understand it better. It was the first time I hadn't just shouted at him and said, "Share this with your sister, what's the matter with you?" And he could *hear* me. The children were restless and embarrassed at first. And then Ben, my husband, was next and he was a lot more skilled than I and topped off what I had said from his point of view. By that time the children had settled down and one of them was first and went around the circle—they really did a darned good job. I was surprised and very pleased. And they were proud and surprised and pleased with themselves.

And then an important thing happened. My oldest son, Walter, had had the hardest time with my divorce. He was the one who was chewing his fingernails and having nightmares. And not doing very well in school. He adored Ben. He was so happy to have Ben for his father—his stepfather. When he went around in the circle he said a lot of things about all of us, but when he got to Ben he just said, "And of course I love you," and passed right on. And we were all aware of something missing there. But as soon as Walter finished, Ben was the first one to say, "Gee, Walter, I feel cheated. Everyone seemed to get so much more from you, and I love hearing that you love me but there must be more and I really want some of that." And Walter in kind of a cool way said, "Well, ah ...I don't want to give you any more. I don't want to love you too much or get too close to you because I am afraid you are going to leave me." Wow! Tears started all around the table. We never would have heard that coming from Walter, would never even have known that was a part of him if we hadn't had this kind of structured scene to get in touch with this sort of thing. It gave Ben an opportunity to let Walter know he understood him, like, I know how you loved your father and trusted him to be with you always and he left you and then your mother has had two other men she was seriously interested in who claimed to love you and they left. And now here I am and I claim to love you and you don't have any guarantees about me. And then he said, "But I'll tell you something: I want you to know that I am going to love you just as long as I live and you can trust me to be available to you and never leave you for as long as you want me." And Walter looked at him and started to cry and got up and walked around the table and just threw himself in Ben's arms and they sobbed. And everybody did. And the children at the table... got up and touched Walter. It was just a natural thing for them to do. At any rate, you can imagine it was something.

Rogers (1977a) discusses what he sees as some of the significant contrasts with the traditional family relationship—a family that is communicating as psychological equals:

1) The focus on relationships between the members of the family had higher priority than any other engagement of any kind. 2) The effort was made to focus on owned feelings, not accusations or judgments of another. 3) This shift was fully as hard for the parents as for the children. For Claire to change from "Share that with your sister!" to "I don't understand your selfishness" (as it appears to me) is an enormous change. 4) The new approach is not initially trusted. Everyone is uneasy, a bit suspicious, except possibly Ben. 5) The respect for the children is highly rewarded, because they turn out to be worthy of respect. 6) The openness which develops leads to a totally unexpected self-revelation, and a deep communication. 7) The relationship between all members of the family as separate but interdependent persons is much strengthened. (p. 37)

EVALUATION

Cain (1989) poses a number of questions about the adequacy of a therapy model based on work with individuals rather than with families. He supports the need for more research and dialogue on family therapy practices and theory. Formulations of family therapy need to be made so that specific hypotheses can be tested to determine the effects and effectiveness of the person-centered approach. Rogers and his colleagues have undertaken research and have opened up therapy sessions for examination with the use of recording equipment. Studies (Aspy & Roebuck, 1974; Barrett-Leonard, 1962; Meador, 1971; Raskin, 1952 [ch. 6]; Rogers et al., 1967b; Rogers & Dymond, 1954; Shlien & Zimring, 1970; Standal, 1954; Stephenson, 1953; Tomlinson & Hart, 1962; Walker, Rablen, & Rogers, 1960) have looked at the therapeutic conditions, process, and other aspects of person-centered theory. These results suggest that the core conditions of congruence, empathic understanding, and unconditional positive regard are effective in facilitating learning, development, and positive therapeutic change. The results are supportive of the person-centered theory and its effectiveness.

In terms of family therapy, an additional construct has been formulated. The construct, *family concept,* is the family member's view of his or her family (van der Veen, Huebner, Jorgens, & Neja, Jr., 1964). "The *family concept* consists essentially of the feelings, attitudes, and expectations each of us has regarding his or her family life.... The family concept is assumed to have several characteristics: it influences behavior; it can be referred to and talked about by the individual; and it can change as a result of new experience and understanding" (Raskin & van der Veen, 1970, p. 389).

An instrument called the *Family Concept Q Sort* has ben developed by van der Veen to measure change in the family concept associated with family therapy. The *Q Sort* contains 80 family items relating to psychological functioning and to clinical interaction. "The items concern the entire family unit, not individual relationships within the family. Thus the test provides a description of the most salient aspects of a person's family experience, regardless of the specific relationships involved. It also enables exact comparison between the views of different family members, and with other persons, such as a therapist or friend. Also possible are comparisons across generations, between child, parent, and grandparent" (Raskin & van der Veen, 1970, pp. 400–401).

Here are four of the measures that the *Family Concept Q Sort* provides: The *Family Effectiveness Score* is "the degree of agreement between a person's family concept and a professional concept of the ideal family. . . . The *Family Satisfaction Score* gives an estimate of the similarity between a person's family concept as it now is and his (her) concept of the family as he (she) would ideally like it to be. The *Real Family Congruence Score* provides an index of agreement between the real family concepts of the family members. The *Ideal Family Congruence Score* measures the correspondence between the ideal family concepts of the family members" (Raskin & van der Veen, 1970, p. 401). Additional research and practice has enlarged the number of assessment scores available. Over 50 research studies have been completed using this instrument (van der Veen & Olson, 1983). Van der Veen and Olson (1983)

have prepared a manual on the use of this family concept assessment method. The manual and annotated bibliography of related research studies is available from van der Veen (see References).

Other professionals have also adapted the person-centered approach to family-related training seminars and experiments. Gordon (1970a, 1970b), has developed a person-centered training program for parents called PET (Parent Effectiveness Training). This program highlights many person-centered principles as a means of preparing parents for healthier interpersonal relationships with their children. More recently, Gordon has developed a program similar to PET for young people, Youth Effectiveness (YET). The new YET program provides young people with interpersonal relationship skills and helps build their self-esteem. Guerney and Guerney (1989) developed child relationship enhancement (CRE) family therapy to teach parents the skills and behaviors of the child-centered play therapist and the Parent Skills Training Program (PSTP) to teach parents to use empathy in daily interactions with their children. Snyder (1989) describes the relationship enhancement approach that was designed by Guerney (1977). She shows how he has brought together Rogers's philosophy and Gregory Bateson's family systems view.

Coulson has had a unique experience with his wife and family as they have attempted to bring a person-centered view as well as other organizational principles into their family life. The "glue" for their family has been a family jazz band, which has had tremendous effects on their togetherness and family priorities. The Coulson family has also used family meetings as a way of resolving family issues. Their family practices are most interesting and are worthy of careful review for ideas on the psychology of family success (Coulson, 1972, 1973, 1978, & 1979). Their book (and record) *Banding* is the story of the Coulson's musical adventures and family togetherness (Coulson, 1978).

SUMMARY

The proponents of the person-centered approach believe that families have much potential to resolve many of their own problems. The actualizing tendency in each family member is a driving force to alter events for a more positive experience. Given the optimal psychological conditions, energies and inner potentials of family members will be released to solve family issues.

If family members perceive these optimal conditions of congruence in the relationship on the part of the therapist, an unconditional prizing of the family members by the therapist, and an accurate empathic understanding of the members' worlds by the therapist, then they will experience a process of family therapy with a forward direction.

When these psychological conditions exist, the family's forward directions reflect certain characteristics.

1. Family members become more in touch with their own experiencing of the family. Because of a greater awareness of their own inner feelings and increased mutual trust in family members, individuals express more of their real feelings. In essence, there is a greater genuineness within individual members and more honesty between family members. The family members can live in the family on a real basis.

2. Family members begin being themselves, with a reality of his or her own, in the family relationships. Each family member is viewed as a unique and separate person who is not to be molded in some way by the family.

3. There is greater movement toward listening to each other in the family. Members work at trying to hear and understand what other family members are communicating while also having the opportunity to have their own views heard. Communication and understanding aid tremendously in the process of solving family problems.

4. As a result of experiencing person-centered therapy, a family also learns a process of sharing and experiencing that can be continued at home for the purpose of solving problems, clarifying values, and making decisions. The new process is one involving all members of the family and encourages family development.

5. The therapy process also aids the family in helping it to establish priorities related to the external community and demands of the larger society. The process facilitates the family's accountability and response to the world outside the home. Healthy individual and family actualizing processes unfold.

There is a formative tendency in family development. When all members of the family cooperate, they tend to reorganize it into a new form—more coherent, more ordered, more complex, more psychologically healthy, and moving in the direction of wellness. The family creates itself and its directions. Sudden and creative changes can occur. The family has the option of creating harmony in a person-centered climate. Together, they build new interpersonal relationships.

The person-centered approach is a wave of the future that is applicable outside of therapy situations as well. It can already be seen in the movement of some families toward a more democratic process involving all family members—the emerging family. The new emerging family will not have its power concentrated in one authority figure but will have a family process with far greater resources and power to heal, to resolve family issues, and to provide positive experiences for growth and recreation. The new family is truly a support group for the person as he or she seeks a path with "heart" for living.

ANNOTATED SUGGESTED READINGS

Rogers, C. R. (1959). A theory of therapy, personality, and interpersonal relationships, as developed in the client-centered framework. In S. Koch (Ed.), *Psychology: A study of a science, Vol. 3. Formulations of the person and the social context* (pp. 184–256). New York: McGraw-Hill.

A chapter rich in ideas for research and clinical practice. It lays the theoretical framework for the person-centered approach and shows how it has application in other fields of human experience that involve interpersonal relationships and personality-behavior change. It has a small theoretical section on family life.

Rogers, C. R. (1980). *A way of being*. Boston: Houghton Mifflin.

The most recent of Rogers's writings, representing his thinking in the 1970s. It presents his changing views of the person-centered approach and its relationship to living—"a way of being." Of special interest are the chapters on the changes during the last 46 years of his life.

Rogers, C. R. (1970). *Carl Rogers on encounter groups*. New York: Harper & Row.

Family therapy groups often have a flavor of encounter groups. This book provides a good discussion of the process of encounter groups and what it takes to be facilitative in an encounter group.

Rogers, C. R. (1977). *Carl Rogers on personal power: Inner strength and its revolutionary impact*. New York: Delacorte Press.

Empowering the person and the impact of the person-centered approach are major themes of this book. Three chapters on family therapy focus on the new family, on a person-centered community-building workshop, and on the emerging person. The book has far-reaching implications for the person-centered approach in many aspects of living: marriage and partnerships, education, administration, intercultural tensions, and the political base of the person-centered approach. It is a book about power.

Rogers, C. R. (1961), *On becoming a person*. Boston: Houghton Mifflin.

A very special book about how people grow. It has touched many people and aided them in developing their own inner potentials. Three chapters are related to family therapy—the characteristics of a helping relationship, a process conception of psychotherapy, and the implications of client-centered therapy for family life. This book provides a personal yet professional statement on the philosophy of a person-centered approach.

Rogers, C. R. (1972). *On becoming partners: Marriage and its alternatives*. New York: Delacorte Press.

An inner view of several intimate man-woman relationships with all their complexities and growth-producing events. Good-bad judgments are not made about the relationships.

Kirschenbaum, H. (1979). *On becoming Carl Rogers.* New York: Delacorte Press.

A good resource book for information and insights on Rogers's personal and professional life. The reader will also learn more about Helen Rogers, a caring person who had a key role in Rogers's life.

Levant, R. F., & Shlien, J. M. (Eds.). (1984). *Client-centered therapy and the person-centered approach: New directions in theory, research, and practice.* New York: Praeger.

An excellent resource for examining the continuing evolvement of client-centered therapy and the person-centered approach. Sections focus on the facilitative conditions, focusing, self-concept, individual psychotherapy, family therapy and enhancement, clinical supervision, large groups, and other applications of this theoretical view.

Association for the Development of the Person-Centered Approach.

ADPCA was founded in 1981 by David J. Cain. For additional information on the Association and its newsletter, journal, annual conference, and purposes, please write to Person-Centered Association, 2831 Cedarwood Way, Carlsbad, CA 92008. The journal carries information on person-centered activities, workshops, and learning programs (e.g., The Carl Rogers Institute for Psychotherapy, Training, and Supervision, directed by Norman Chambers, La Jolla, CA; Center for Interpersonal Growth, directed by Peggy Natiello and Curtis Graf, Port Jefferson, NY; Training in Focusing, directed by Eugene Gendlin, Chicago; Living Now Institute, di-

rected by Gay Swenson; La Jolla Program, directed by Bruce Meador, La Jolla, CA; Person-Centered Expressive Therapy Institute, directed by Natalie Rogers, Santa Rosa, CA; the International Forums for the Person-Centered Approach; and the learning activities of the Center for Studies of the Person, 1125 Torrey Pines Road, La Jolla, CA 92037).

Counseling and Values, 1987, *32*(1).

The journal of the Association for Religious and Values Issues in Counseling provided a special issue on Carl R. Rogers and the Person-Centered Approach to Peace, guest edited by John M. Whitely. Many of the articles are by Carl Rogers. They focus on his experiences in South Africa and the Soviet Union as well as his views on tension reduction and the underlying theory in working toward peaceful solutions to human conflict. Single copies may be purchased for $6.00 a copy from AACD Press, 5999 Stevenson Avenue, Alexandria, VA 22304.

Person-Centered Review, 1989, *4*(3).

This issue of the journal of the ADPCA focuses on "Person-Centered Approaches with Families." David Cain, editor, and two editorial board members, Wayne Anderson and Charlotte Ellinwood, collaborated on this issue. Topics focus on various components of person-centered family theory and practice with young children, couples, families, and other theoretical aspects of Rogers's concepts as related to family work. Single copies are available at $10.00 for individuals from Sage Publications, 211 West Hillcrest Drive, Newbury Park, CA 91320.

REFERENCES

Anderson, W. J. (1989a). Client/person-centered approaches to couple and family therapy: Expanding theory and practice. *Person-Centered Review, 4*(3), 245–247.

Anderson, W. J. (1989b). Family therapy in the client-centered tradition: A legacy in

the narrative mode. *Person-Centered Review, 4*(3), 295–307.

Aspy, D. N., & Roebuck, F. M. (1974). From humane ideas to human technology and back again many times. *Education, 95*(2), 163–171.

Barrett-Leonard, G. (1962). Dimensions of

therapist response as causal factors in therapeutic change. *Psychological Monographs, 76,* Whole No. 562.

Barrett-Leonard, G. T. (1984). The world of family relationships: A person-centered systems view. In R. F. Levant & J. M. Shlien (Eds.), *Client-centered therapy and the person-centered approach: New directions in theory, research, and practice* (pp. 222–242). New York: Praeger Publishers.

Bozarth, J. D., & Shanks, A. (1989). Person-centered family therapy with couples. *Person-Centered Review, 4*(3), 280–294.

Bynner, W. (1962). *The way of life according to Lao Tzu.* New York: Capricorn Books.

Cain, D. J. (1989). From the individual to the family. *Person-Centered Review, 4*(3), 248–255.

Campbell, J., & Moyers, B. (1988). *The power of myth.* New York: Doubleday.

Combs, A. W. (1989). *A theory of therapy: Guidelines for counseling practice.* Newbury Park, CA: Sage Publications.

Combs, A. W., & Snygg, D. (1959). *Individual behavior: A perceptual approach to behavior* (rev. ed.). New York: Harper & Row.

Coulson, W. R. (1972). *Groups, gimmicks, and instant gurus: An examination of encounter groups and their distortions.* New York: Harper & Row.

Coulson, W. R. (1973). *A sense of community.* Columbus, OH: Charles E. Merrill.

Coulson, W. R. (1978). *Banding: The psychology of family success.* LaJolla, CA: Helicon House.

Coulson, W. R. (1979). *The strength test: Leadership manual.* LaJolla, CA: Helicon House.

Coulson, W. R., Land, D., & Meador, B. (1977). *The LaJolla experiment: Eight personal views.* LaJolla, CA: The La-Jolla Program, Center for Studies of the Person (1125 Torrey Pines Road).

Coulson, W. R., & Rogers, C. R. (1968). *Man and the science of man.* Columbus, OH: Charles E. Merrill.

Ellinwood, C. (1989). The young child in person-centered family therapy. *Person-Centered Review, 4*(3), 256–262.

Foster, C. F., & Back, J. (1974). A neighborhood school board: Its infancy, its crises, its growth. *Education, 95*(2), 145–162.

Gaylin, N. L. (1989). The necessary and sufficient conditions for change: Individual versus family therapy. *Person-Centered Review, 4*(3), 263–279.

Gendlin, E. T. (1988). Carl Rogers (1902–1987). *American Psychologist, 43*(2), 127–128.

Gordon, T. (1970a). *Parent effectiveness training: The "no-lose" program for raising responsible children.* New York: Peter H. Wyden.

Gordon, T. (1970b). A theory of healthy relationships and a program of parent effectiveness training. In J. T. Hart & T. M. Tomlinson (Eds.), *New directions in client-centered therapy.* Boston: Houghton Mifflin.

Guerney, B. G., Jr. (1977). *Relationship enhancement: Skill-training programs for therapy, problem prevention, and enrichment.* San Francisco: Jossey-Bass.

Guerney, L., & Guerney, B., Jr. (1989). Child relationship enhancement: Family therapy and parent education. *Person-Centered Review, 4*(3), 344–357.

Heider, J. (1985). *The Tao of leadership:Lao Tzu's Tao Teh Ching adapted for a new age.* Atlanta, GA: Humanics Limited.

Jourard, S. M. (1959). Healthy personality and self-disclosure. *Mental Hygiene, 43,* 499–507.

Levant, R. G. (1984a). *Family therapy: A comprehensive overview.* Englewood Cliffs, NJ: Prentice-Hall.

Levant, R. G. (1984b). From person to system: Two perspectives. In R. F. Levant & J. M. Shlien (Eds.), *Client-centered therapy and the person-centered approach: New directions in theory, research, and practice* (pp. 243–260). New York: Praeger.

McCleary, R. A., & Lazarus, R. S. (1949). Autonomic discrimination without awareness. *Journal of Personality, 18,* 171–179.

Meador, B. D. (1971). Individual process in a basic encounter group. *Journal of Counseling Psychology, 18,* 70–76.

Mearns, D., & Thorne, B. (1988). *Person-centered counseling in action.* Beverly Hills, CA: Sage.

Ohlsen, M. M. (1979). *Marriage counseling in groups.* Champaign, IL: Research Press.

Ohlsen, M. M., Horne, A. M., & Lawe, C. F. (1988). *Group counseling* (3rd ed.). New York: Holt, Rinehart and Winston.

O'Leary, C. J. (1989). The person-centered approach and family therapy: A dialogue between two traditions. *Person-Centered Review, 4*(3), 308–323.

Ornstein, R. E. (1977). *The psychology of consciousness* (2nd ed.). New York: Harcourt Brace Jovanovich.

Pagels, E. (1979). *The gnostic gospels.* New York: Random House.

Patterson, C. H. (1968). The nature of counseling: Some basic principles. *Michigan College Personnel Association Journal, 5,* 1–11.

Patterson, C. H. (1985). *The therapeutic relationship: foundations for an eclectic psychotherapy.* Monterey, CA: Brooks/Cole.

Rank, O. (1936). *Will therapy.* New York: Alfred A. Knopf.

Raskin, N. J. (1952). An objective study of the locus-of-evaluation factor in psychotherapy. In W. Wolff & J. A. Precker (Eds.), *Success in psychotherapy.* New York: Grune & Stratton.

Raskin, N. J., & Rogers, C. R. (1989). Person-centered therapy. In R. J. Corsini & D. Wedding (Eds.), *Current psychotherapies* (4th ed.). Itasca, IL: Peacock Publishers

Raskin, N. J., & van der Veen, F. (1970). Client-centered family therapy: Some clinical and research perspectives. In J. T. Hart & T. M. Tomlinson (Eds.), *New directions in client-centered therapy.* Boston: Houghton Mifflin.

Rogers, C. R. (1939). *The clinical treatment of the problem child.* Boston: Houghton Mifflin.

Rogers, C. R. (1942). *Counseling and psychotherapy.* Boston: Houghton Mifflin.

Rogers, C. R. (1951). *Client-centered therapy.* Boston: Houghton Mifflin.

Rogers, C. R. & Dymond, R. F. (Eds.). (1954). *Psychotherapy and personality change.* Chicago: University of Chicago Press.

Rogers, C. R. (1957a). The necessary and sufficient conditions of therapeutic personality change. *Journal of Counseling Psychology, 21*(2), 95–103.

Rogers, C. R. (1957b). Personal thoughts on teaching and learning. *Merrill-Palmer Quarterly, 3,* 241–243.

Rogers, C. R. (1959). A theory of therapy, personality, and interpersonal relationships, as developed in the client-centered framework. In S. Koch (Ed.), *Psychology: A study of a science. Vol. 3. Formulations of the person and the social context.* New York: McGraw-Hill.

Rogers, C. R. (1961a). *On becoming a person.* Boston: Houghton Mifflin.

Rogers, C. R. (1961b). A process conception of psychotherapy. In C. R. Rogers, *On becoming a person.* Boston: Houghton Mifflin.

Rogers, C. R. (1961c). "To be that self which one truly is": A therapist's view of personal goals. In C. R. Rogers, *On becoming a person.* Boston: Houghton Mifflin.

Rogers, C. R. (1967a). A plan for self-directed change in an educational system. *Educational Leadership, 24*(8), 717–731.

Rogers, C. R., Gendlin, E. T., Kiesler, P. J., & Truax, C. (Eds.). (1967b). *The therapeutic relationship and its impact: A study of psychotherapy with schizophrenics.* Madison: University of Wisconsin Press.

Rogers, C. R., & Stevens, B. (1967c). *Person to person: The problem of being human.* Moab, UT: Real People Press.

Rogers, C. R. (1969). *Freedom to learn: A*

view of what education might become. Columbus, OH: Charles E. Merrill.

Rogers, C. R. (1970). *Carl Rogers on encounter groups.* New York: Harper & Row.

Rogers, C. R. (1972). *On becoming partners: Marriage and its alternatives.* New York: Dell Publishing.

Rogers, C. R. (1974). The project at Immaculate Heart: An experiment in self-directed change. Parts I, II, & III. *Education, 95*(2), 172–189.

Rogers, C. R. (1977a). *Carl Rogers on personal power: Inner strength and its revolutionary impact.* New York: Delacorte Press.

Rogers, C. R. (1977b). Personal power at work. *Psychology Today, 10*(11), 60–62, 93–94.

Rogers, C. R. (1978, Winter). Do we need "a" reality? *Dawnpoint,* 6–9.

Rogers, C. R. (1980a, Winter). A letter from Carl Rogers on person-centered learning programs.

Roger, C. R. (1980b, August). [A presentation by C. Rogers on the development of PCA.] Presented at the Person-Centered Two-Week Workshop, San Diego, CA.

Rogers, C. R. (1980c). *A way of being.* Boston: Houghton Mifflin.

Rogers, C. R. (1983). *Freedom to learn for the 80's.* Columbus, OH: Merrill.

Rogers, C. R. (1986a). The dilemmas of a South African white. *Person-Centered Review, 1*(1), 15–35.

Rogers, C. R. (1986b). The Rust workshop: A personal overview. *Journal of Humanistic Psychology, 26,* 23–45.

Rogers, C. R. (1987). Inside the world of the Soviet professional. *Counseling and Values, 32*(1), 47–66.

Shah, I. (1972). *The exploits of the incomparable Mulla Nasrudin.* New York: E. Dutton.

Shlien, J. M., & Zimring, F. M. (1970). Research directives and methods in client-centered therapy. In J. T. Hart & T. M. Tomlinson (Eds.), *New directions in client-centered therapy.* Boston: Houghton Mifflin.

Snyder, M. (1989). The relationship enhancement model of couple therapy: An integration of Rogers and Bateson. *Person-Centered Review, 4*(3), 358–383.

Standal, S. (1954). *The need for positive regard: A contribution to client-centered theory.* Unpublished doctoral dissertation, University of Chicago.

Stephenson, W. (1953). *The study of behavior: Q-techniques and its methodology.* Chicago: University of Chicago Press.

Taft, J. (1933). *The dynamics of therapy.* New York: Macmillan.

Thayer, L. (1977). An experiential approach to learning skills. *The Humanist Educator, 15*(3), 132–139.

Thayer, L. (1981). Toward experiential learning with a person-centered approach. In L. Thayer (Ed.), *50 strategies for experiential learning: Book 2.* Ypsilanti, MI: LT Resources.

Thayer, L. (1984). On person-centered experiential learning and affective development. In G. L. Jennings (Ed.), *Affective learning in industrial arts. The American Council on Industrial Arts Teacher Education 33rd Yearbook* (pp. 52–103). Bloomington, IL: McKnight.

Thayer, L. (1987). An interview with Carl R. Rogers: Toward peaceful solutions to human conflict. Part I. *Michigan Journal of Counseling and Development, 18*(1), 58–63.

Thayer, L. (1989). An interview with Carl R. Rogers: Toward peaceful solutions to human conflict. Part II. *Michigan Journal of Counseling and Development, 19*(2), 2–7.

Thayer, L., & Harrigan, S. (1990, March). *PCA and Taoism: Comparing facets from each.* A presentation at the Annual Convention of the American Association for Counseling and Development (AACD), Cincinnati, OH.

Tomlinson, T. M., & Hart, J. T., Jr. (1962). A validation study of the process scale. *Journal of Consulting Psychology, 26,* 74–78.

van der Veen, F., Huebner, B., Jorgens, B., &

Neja, P., Jr. (1964). Relationships between the parent's concept of the family and family adjustment. *American Journal of Orthopsychiatry, 34,* 45–55.

van der Veen, F., & Olson, R. E. (1983). *Manual and handbook for the family assessment method.* Encinitas, CA: Author.

Walker, A. M., Rablen, R. A., & Rogers, C. R. (1960). Development of a scale to measure process changes in psychotherapy. *Journal of Clinical Psychology, 16,* 79–85.

Warner, M. S. (1989). Empathy and strategy in the family system. *Person-Centered Review, 43*(3), 324–343.

Whitely, J. M. (1987). Carl R. Rogers and the person-centered approach to peace. Special Issue. *Association for Religious and Values Issues in Counseling, 32*(1).

Wu, J. C. H., & Sih, P. K. T. (Eds.). (1961). *Lao Tzu/Tao Teh Ching.* New York: St. John's University Press.

CHAPTER 12

Neurolinguistic Programming and Family Therapy

PETER A. D. SHERRARD

DEFINITION

Neurolinguistic programming (NLP) names the discipline that models the structure of subjective experience. It was created by Richard Bandler and John Grinder in the mid-1970s. Bandler and Grinder (1975b) describe themselves as modelers and their approach as a modeling of human experience. By this they mean that NLP provides the means to construct a pattern or copy of the structure of experience that, when mapped, affords the modeler an opportunity to imitate and re-create that portion of experience so mapped. NLP practitioners believe that outcomes achieved by one person can be achieved by others *when* they map or model the first person's experience and imitate it.

In NLP, a model is a representation of experience in the same way a map is a representation of a geographic territory or a model car is a representation of a full-sized automobile. The models generated by NLP procedures are blueprints for moving from unwanted to wanted experience. Cameron-Bandler (1985) claims that NLP models of change satisfy four conditions:

(1) they work to produce the results they were designed for, (2) they are described in a step-by-step manner, so they are learnable and reproducible, (3) they are elegant, i.e., they use the least number of steps necessary to achieve the outcome, and (4) they are independent of content and deal with the *form* of the process, and therefore have universal applicability. (p. 10)

Bandler and Grinder (Dilts, Grinder, Bandler, Cameron-Bandler, & DeLozier, 1980) make no commitment to theory but rather claim that NLP is merely a model—"a set of procedures whose *usefulness not truthfulness* is to be the measure of its worth" (p. x).

Consider, for example, the impact that Henry Ford's assembly line had on the automobile industry. By studying *what* elements and *which* sequences were necessary to build cars, Ford constructed a model that could be imitated by anyone who wanted to mass produce automobiles (Lankton, 1980). Ford demystified the automobile industry and made cars affordable. Like Ford, Bandler, Grinder, and associates studied what elements and which sequences constitute successful human performance; they demystified success and made it possible to replicate successful models of human experience.

The secret to their craft is in the name, neurolinguistic programming. As Dilts et al. (1980) state:

"Neuro" stands for the fundamental tenet that all behavior is the result of neurological processes. "Linguistic" indicates that neural processes are represented, ordered and sequenced into models and strategies through language and communication systems. "Programming" refers to the process of organizing the components of a system to achieve a specific outcome. (p. 2)

NLP is an outcome-oriented procedure that utilizes sensory sensitivity and interpersonal influence (Laborde, 1984).

When using NLP in couples and family therapy, the therapist helps each person to behave toward others in the family in ways that elicit the most desirable responses and to respond to difficulties as if they were opportunities for collective enrichment (Cameron-Bandler, 1985).

This chapter will review the basic propositions and procedures utilized by NLP to create greater behavioral flexibility and goal attainment among its adherents.

HISTORICAL DEVELOPMENT

NLP has its roots in cybernetics, linguistics, personality theory, and behavior modification. After a tour of duty in military intelligence in the Far East, John Grinder earned a doctorate in linguistics and taught at the University of California at Santa Cruz in the early 1970s where he coauthored a *Guide to Transformational Grammar* (Grinder & Elgin, 1973). Grinder and Elgin assert that transformational grammar best addresses the dilemma of human experience identified by Aldous Huxley (1954):

The suggestion is that the function of the brain and nervous system and sense organs is in the main *eliminative* and not productive. Each person is at each moment capable of remembering all that has ever happened to him and of perceiving everything that is happening everywhere in the universe. The function of the brain and nervous system is to protect us from being overwhelmed and confused by this mass of largely useless and irrelevant knowledge, by shutting out most of what we should otherwise perceive or remember at any moment, and leaving only that very small and special selection which is likely to be practically useful. According to such a theory, each one of us is potentially Mind at Large.... To make biological survival possible, Mind at Large has to be funneled through the reducing valve of the brain and

nervous system. What comes out the other end is a measly trickle of the kind of consciousness which will help us to stay alive on the surface of this particular planet. To formulate and express the contents of this reduced awareness, man has invented and endlessly elaborated those symbol-systems and implicit philosophies which we call languages. Every individual is at once the beneficiary and the victim of the linguistic tradition into which he has been born—the beneficiary inasmuch as language gives access to the accumulated record of other people's experience, the victim in so far as it confirms him in the belief that reduced awareness is the only awareness and as it bedevils his sense of reality, he is all too apt to take his concepts for data, his words for actual things. (pp. 22–23)

Grinder and Elgin (1973) assert that the grammar of each person's "linguistic tradition" becomes part of that person's nervous system, an internal representation of that external set of rules, categories, and forms that govern language use. This internal representation operates unconsciously so that we fail to see the distortions it induces. These distortions are created in two ways:

T1. What is to be described apparently has to be described within a particular natural language system that consists of a series of rules, categories, and other elements whose effect is to force one to express experiences in a form sometimes unintentionally ambiguous, and to use words that presuppose or imply more or less than was actually intended by the speaker. (p. 3)

T2. It has been claimed that these same sets of rules, this same set of categories, that structure your native language themselves structure perception as well. Specifically, these categories, or rather the distinctions presupposed by them, operate on the information being carried in the nervous system at the preconscious level, performing a transformation on this material, grouping, summarizing, deleting, and in effect introducing distortions, prior to the nervous system's presenting the resultant impoverished picture of the "world out there" to the conscious mind. (p. 4)

The grammar that structures our language system organizes the data of sensory experience in a form that is "unintentionally ambiguous" even before it enters consciousness. The result is an impoverished model of experience that prevents us from recognizing or noticing the intricacies, richness, and variety in our life. Grinder and Elgin (1973) assert that an antidote to this impoverishment is making the unconscious (i.e., the grammar wired into our nervous system) conscious:

In the attempt to construct an explicit set of formal statements that reflect the structure of the language being analyzed, one becomes aware of the categories and distinctions inextricably interwoven in the fabric of the language system itself. This awareness or bringing to consciousness of the systematic distortion induced by one's language system gives one the opportunity to escape from the unconscious or preperceptual distortion mentioned above. (p. 8)

The task, then, is to create a grammar of grammars. Richard Bandler, a mathematician with a master's degree in information sciences, joined Grinder in this task. Together, they formulated the "meta-model," which they published as *The Structure of Magic I* (Bandler & Grinder, 1975b). The meta-model utilized the tools of transformational grammar to model the work of Fritz Perls and Virginia Satir, who were seen as exquisite communicators. *The Structure of Magic II* (Grinder & Bandler, 1976) extended this work by developing concepts (such as representational systems) that provided users with a grammar of sensory experience. Next, Bandler and Grinder

modeled the linguistic and behavioral patterns of Milton H. Erickson, one of the foremost practitioners of medical hypnosis in the world. Their work became *The Patterns of the Hypnotic Techniques of Milton H. Erickson, M.D., Vol. 1* (Bandler & Grinder, 1975a) and Volume 2 (Grinder, DeLozier, & Bandler, 1977).

They joined Satir in coauthoring a book applying the meta-model to family therapy (Bandler, Grinder, & Satir, 1976) and joined Robert Dilts, Leslie Cameron-Bandler, and Judith DeLozier in establishing specific procedures that were published in *Neuro-Linguistic Programming, Vol. 1* (Dilts et al., 1980). After completing these efforts, Bandler and Grinder went their separate ways. Each has continued to write, lead workshops, and train. They and their students have created the Society of Neuro-Linguistic Programming, a partnership made up of Not Ltd. and Unlimited Ltd. The Society grants trainees three levels of certification: practitioner, master practitioner, and trainer. Those interested in securing information about training may contact Not Ltd., Division of Training and Research (Dotar), 517 Mission Street, Santa Cruz, CA 95060.

TENETS OF THE MODEL

NLP offers its practitioners a meta-map (i.e., a map about maps) or meta-model that is useful for thinking about and conducting family therapy. NLP assumes that we humans are engaged in a continuous and universal modeling process designed to help us achieve our desired ends. The fruits of our labor are the maps we create that we use to guide our negotiations in the world. According to Bandler et al. (1976), these models or maps are not to be judged as true or false, accurate or inaccurate, but rather *useful or not useful* for the purposes for which they are intended. NLP practitioners serve as consultants to psychological map-makers; they provide observational and linguistic tools that people can use to fill in the missing pieces of their experience. Their goal is to expand and enrich experience, not replace it, and to expand the possibilities and choices that enhance self-efficacy.

Learning to use NLP requires both precision and flexibility. The approach consists of specific steps to be taken in eliciting, utilizing, designing, and installing efficacious strategies. The approach also requires creativity and daring in engaging clients and generating solutions. The foundation of the approach rests on 15 treatment principles that provide clarity and direction.

1. *People operate out of their internal maps and not out of sensory experience* (Lankton & Lankton, 1983). Each of us creates maps or representations of our experience that reflect the idiosyncrasies of our representational process. Our maps are derived from both sensory and linguistic processing strategies. Grinder and Bandler (1976) propose that our senses serve as input channels through which we contact the world. These input channels constitute the perceptual systems through which we operate on the "world out there": *vision* (sight), *audition* (hearing), *kinesthesis* (body sensations), and *olfaction/gustation* (smell/taste). Dilts et al. (1980) claim that all of the distinctions we as human beings make concerning our environment (internal and external) and our behavior can be usefully represented in terms of these four systems, known in NLP as the *four-tuple* (see Figure 1). Each of these systems forms a sensory-motor complex that becomes "response-able" for behav-

ior. These sensory-motor complexes are called *representational systems* in NLP.

Each representational system forms a three-part network as illustrated in Figure 2: input (sensory stimuli), thruput (representation/processing), and output (external behavior). Dilts et al. (1980) suggest:

The first stage, *input*, involves gathering information and getting feedback from the environment (both internal and external). *Representation/processing* includes that mapping of the environment and the establishment of behavioral strategies such as learning, decision-making, information storage, etc. *Output* is the casual transform of the representational mapping process. (p. 19)

Sometimes, persons will use one representational system to input; this is their *lead* representational system. Then they process information and express themselves using a different representational system; the latter is their *preferred* representational system.

The significance of representational systems can be demonstrated in the following exercise (Grinder & Bandler, 1976):

We may choose to close our eyes and create a visual image of a red square shifting to green and then to blue, or a spiral wheel of silver and black slowly revolving counterclockwise, or the image of some person we know well. Or, we may choose to close our eyes (or not) and to create a kinesthetic representation (a body sensation, a feeling), placing our hands against a wall and pushing as hard as we can, feeling the tightening of the muscles in our arms and shoulders, becoming aware of the texture of the floor beneath our feet. Or, we may choose to become aware of the prickling sensation of the heat of the flames of a fire burning, or of sensing the pressure of several light blankets covering our sighing bodies as we sink softly into our beds. Or we may choose to close our eyes (or not) and create an auditory (sound) representation—

Figure 1. Representational systems: The four-tuple.

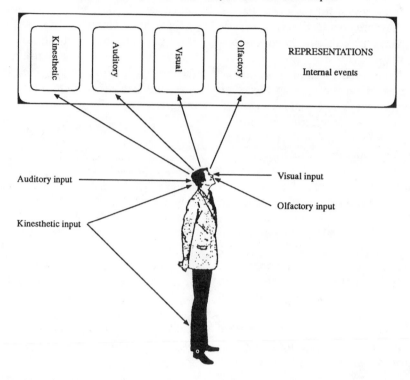

Excerpted from *Practical Magic* (p. 40) by S. Lankton, 1980, Cupertino, CA: Meta Publications.

the patter of tinkling raindrops, the crack of distant thunder and its following roll through the once-silent hills, the squeal of singing tires on a quiet country road, or the blast of a taxi horn through the deafening roars of a noisy city. Or we may close our eyes and create a gustatory (taste) representation of the sour flavor of a lemon, or the sweetness of honey, or the saltiness of a stale potato chip. Or we may choose to close our eyes (or not) and create an olfactory (smell) representation of a fragrant rose, or rancid milk, or the pungent aroma of cheap perfume. (p. 6)

While reading through the descriptions of the preceding paragraph, you may have experienced *seeing* a particular color or movement, *feeling* hardness or warmth, *hearing* a specific sound, or recalling certain *tastes* or *smells*. The reader may have experienced all or only a few of these sensations. Those who had a sharp, clear picture have a highly developed *visual* representational system; those who developed a strong feeling have a highly developed *kinesthetic* representational system; those who heard, smelled, or tasted in response to the suggestions have a highly developed *auditory and/or olfactory-gustatory* representational system.

Most of us rely on one or two sensory representational systems rather than all four. For example, it is likely that different family members may represent their

Figure 2. NLP systems model.

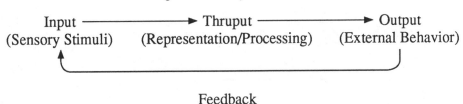

Feedback

experience of being loved in different preferred systems. One may say, "I know I'm loved when Mother *tells* me so." Another may say, "I know I'm loved when I *see* Father smiling at me." And another may say, "I know I'm loved when Mother *hugs* me." The auditory predicate "tells," the visual verb "see," and the kinesthetic term "hugs" all express a preferred representational system that reflects an internal neurological pattern (Dilts et al., 1980). By mapping and restructuring that pattern, NLP practitioners generate strategies for change.

2. *The map is not the territory* (Korzybski, 1941). Maps are so much a part of our everyday lives that we may think of them as being more real than the "real world" itself. Consider Huck Finn and Tom Sawyer's conversation while soaring high above the Midwest in a hot air balloon (Makower, 1986):

> Estimating their location, Huck claims they're still over Illinois; Tom thinks they are above Indiana.
> "I know by the color," says Huck. "And you can see for yourself that Indiana ain't in sight."
> "What's color got to do with it?" asks Tom.
> "It's got everything to do with it," explains Huck. "Illinois is green, Indiana is pink. You show me any pink down here, if you can."
> "Indiana pink? Why, what a lie?"
> "It ain't no lie; I've seen it on the map and its pink." (p. 8)

Maps often get confused with the territory mapped, but maps and maps about maps are only representations of the territory, *not* the territory itself. We have access to the world only through our maps; we can never know the world as it "really" is. We construct (map) reality by drawing on internal sensory and linguistic representations of external stimuli. We use language to represent our sensory representations or, as Grinder and Bandler (1976) suggest, to make maps about maps. In NLP, language is referred to as *secondary* experience because it is even farther from the world out there than sensory experience (which constitutes our *primary* representational system).

Much of the map-making process occurs outside of conscious awareness in the other "zones of awareness" (i.e., preconscious and unconscious awareness) depicted in Figure 3. The important differentiation shown is between surface structure and deep structure, a distinction drawn from transformational grammar (Grinder & Elgin, 1973). Surface structure refers to public, verbal descriptions of experience that have been subject to the three universal modeling processes: deletion, distortion, and generalization (Bandler & Grinder, 1975b). Surface structure is a representation of the full linguistic representation from which it is derived, namely, the deep structure, which in turn is derived from a

Figure 3. Three zones of awareness.

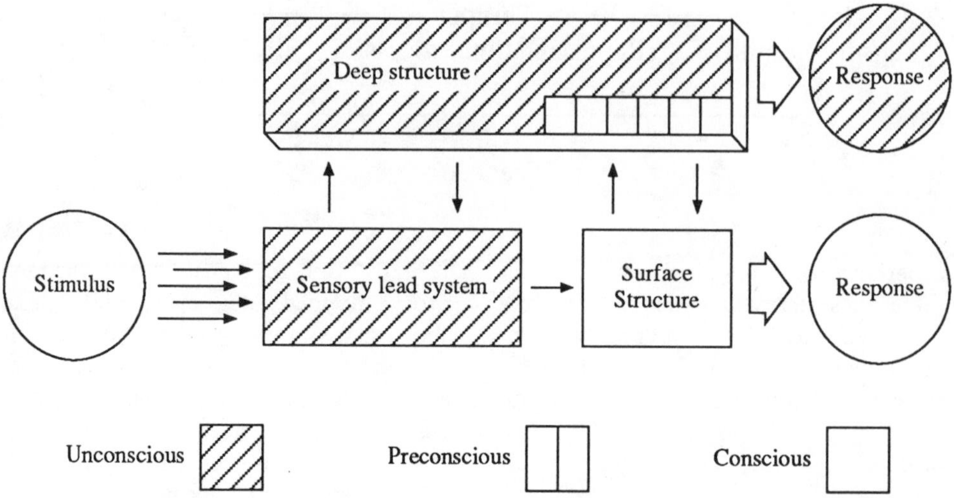

fuller, richer source—the sum total of sensory experiences.

In summary, sensory input stimulates sensory representations (maps) that are transformed into linguistic representations (maps about maps), which are further streamlined (through the processes of deletion, distortion, and generalization) on their way to conscious awareness. Our behavioral output is influenced by both conscious (surface structure) and unconscious (deep structure) processes, as is demonstrated in Figure 4. Grinder and Bandler (1976) developed the meta-model to help people recover from deep structure the pieces of their experience missing in surface structure. The meta-model serves as a map of the maps about maps. NLP strategies are designed to access the deep structure and representational system formulations inherent in our experience (i.e., our internal processing) so that we can transcend the limits imposed by our impoverished surface structures. In this sense, NLP helps people by making the unconscious conscious.

3. *The explanation, theory, or metaphor used to relate facts and observations about a person is not the person* (Lankton & Lankton, 1983). Again, the map is not the territory. NLP offers a set of concepts and procedures that map sensory data, but these concepts and procedures are abstractions; they are not "raw" experience itself. Rather, we live in a world of constructed approximations that constitute but never exhaust our experience (i.e., the whole is greater than the sum of its parts). Verbal (digital) and paraverbal (analogical) expressions are merely the surface structure of the complex deep structure of fully formed human experience, which is a map of yet another territory.

4. *Respect all messages from each family member* (Lankton & Lankton, 1983). NLP provides a language about language, both verbal and paraverbal. Using this language requires clean, active, open sensory channels that enable us to monitor all the responses we are eliciting at every moment (Lankton, 1980). Only then can we perceive the im-

Figure 4. NLP expanded systems model.

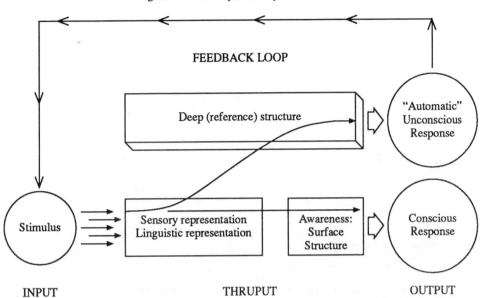

pact that our behavior is having on others. This is particularly relevant to family therapy. Often individuals in a family system respond to their memories or projections regarding each other rather then the "here and now" of each encounter. Similarly, family members limit their behavior around others in the family because of expectations and experiences drawn from long ago that have never been questioned. These memories and projections direct the "calibrated communication cycles" that characterize conflicted communication in the family. The distortions, generalizations, and deletions inherent in these cycles can be addressed when we take each message seriously and restore it to its fully formed representation by using the meta-model to create "feedback communication cycles" (Bandler et al., 1976).

The advantage of feedback communication cycles over "calibrated communication cycles" is that learning replaces habit. When we respect all messages from each family member, we create an opportunity for learning rather than an instance of repetition. The shift is analogous to the benefit gained from two eyes over one: the two-eyed method of seeing is an act of comparison that produces the news of difference called depth; learning refers to the corrective processes activated by the perception of error or incongruity, which in turn is a benefit of the act of comparison. Bateson (1979) refers to this two-eyed method of seeing as the "method of double or multiple comparison" (p. 87). "It is correct (and a great improvement) to begin to think of the two (or more) parties to the interaction as two eyes, each giving a monocular view of what goes on and together, giving a binocular view in depth" (Bateson, 1979, p. 133). The combination of two or more fully formed descriptions produces a depth of vision of the patterns that link family members that is impossible with one description alone, let alone an impoverished one. Thus, the

Figure 5. Visual accessing cues.

VISUAL ACCESSING CUES FOR "NORMALLY ORGANIZED" RIGHT-HANDED PERSON

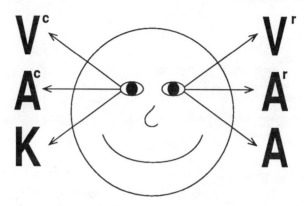

V^c Visual constructed images	V^r Visual remembered (eidetic) images

(Eyes defocused and unmoving also indicates visual accessing.)

A^c Auditory constructed sounds or words	A^r Auditory remembered sounds or words
K Kinesthetic feelings (also smell and taste)	A Auditory sounds or words

Excerpted from *Frongsonto Princes* (p. 26) by R. Bandler and J. Grinder, 1979, Moab, VT: Real People Press.

multiple comparisons that emerge when each person is listened to produces such depth of understanding and breadth of possibility that new solutions emerge, as if by magic.

5. *Meet family members at each member's map or model of the world* (Lankton & Lankton, 1983). This imperative begins in the initial encounter when we identify eye-scanning cues and match representational system predicates as a means of developing rapport (Brooks, 1989; Richardson & Margulis, 1981; Sharpley, 1984). Eye-scanning patterns provide clues to representational system usage (Grinder et al., 1977). As the dia-

gram in Figure 5 suggests, a father may look up and to the right (V^r) to remember the look on his child's face when receiving a gift. He might look up and to the right (V^c) to construct an image of his child as an adult and down to the left to talk (A) to himself about either picture. He may access a memory of his child telling him "I love you" by looking straight and level to the left (A^r) and rehearse his reply by looking straight and level to the right (A^c). He may look down and to the right (K) to access his feelings about his child.

Such eye movements have been the subject of considerable scrutiny by re-

Figure 6. Predicates expressing sensory-based representations.

Visual	Auditory	Kinesthetic	Olfactory/Gustatory
See	Hear	Feel	Taste
Picture	Tone	Touch	Smells
Bright	Loud	Warm	Fresh
Clear	Tune	Smooth	Fragrant
Vague	Amplify	Soft	Stale
Focus	Harmonize	Handle	Sweet
Flash	Screech	Grasp	Pungent
Perspective	Shout	Tight	Sour
Dark	Scream	Rough	Bitter
Colorful	Ringing	Hard	Salty

Excerpted from *Solutions* (p. 41) by L. Cameron-Bandler, 1985, San Rafael, CA: Future Pace, Inc.

searchers (Beck & Beck, 1984; Dorn, Atwater, Jereb, & Russell, 1980; Ellickson, 1983; Thomason, Arbuckle, & Cady, 1980). Buckner, Meara, Reese, and Reese (1987) report support for the notion that experienced observers who are trained in NLP can agree on what types of eye movement are being exhibited by persons whom they are observing. They also cite support for the notion that visual and auditory components in a person's thought can be identified by observing that person's eye movements; their results do not support the NLP notion that eye movement reveals kinesthetic components in thought. This latter finding may be a function of the confusion associated with cross-over mapping or synesthesia where, for example, behavior may be initiated by the feeling of the sound (Dilts et al, 1980).

In addition to eye movements, we can identify representational usage and nurture rapport when we mirror paraverbal behaviors. Breathing depth, skin color changes, speech tone and tempo, gestures, body postures and movement, and facial expression are all considered consistently dependable indicators of representational preference and rapport (Lankton, 1980). When we mirror the nonverbal behavior of others, we offer them not only visible and subconscious images of themselves but also images that are delivered without our meanings attached to them (Brooks, 1989).

Finally, we can identify representational preference and nurture rapport by attending to predicate usage as suggested in Figure 6 (Cameron-Bandler, 1985); by matching predicate usage, we further generate the magic of rapport and establish the foundation for change. Matching prepares the way for translating: for

Figure 7. Predicate translation table.

Meaning	Kinesthetic	Visual	Auditory
I (don't) understand you.	What you are saying feels (doesn't feel) right to me.	I see (don't see) what you are saying.	I hear (don't hear) you clearly.
I want to communicate something to you.	I want you to be in touch with something.	I want to show you something (a picture of something).	I want you to listen carefully to what I say to you.
Describe more of your present experience to me.	Put me in touch with what you are feeling at this point in time.	Show me a clear picture of what you see at this point in time.	Tell me in more detail what you are saying at this point in time.
I like my experience of you and me at this point in time.	This feels really good to me. I feel really good about what we are doing.	This looks really bright and clear to me.	This sounds really good to me.
Do you understand what I am saying?	Does what I am putting you in touch with feel right to you?	Do you see what I am showing you?	Does what I am saying to you sound right to you?

Excerpted from *The Structure of Magic II* (p. 15) by J. Grinder and R. Bandler, 1976, Palo Alto, CA: Science and Behavior Books.

example, the kinesthetic predicates of a son can be translated into the visual predicates of his father. Figure 7 (Grinder & Bandler, 1976) offers examples of this translation process.

6. *People choose the best alternative available at any given moment* (Cameron-Bandler, 1985). As the limitations of consciousness make clear (Grinder & Elgin, 1973; Miller, 1956), the surface structure constructions that constitute ordinary consciousness are impoverished representations of experience. Unless challenged, we live within the limitations of our surface structure. Often these limitations enable us to negotiate life efficiently without being overwhelmed by "overchoice" (Toffler, 1970). However, these limitations con-

strain us to deciding among only those courses of action available within the frame of reference we use. Given these limitations, a "problem" behavior or feeling may be the best choice a person has. For example, if a person can be confident when playing the piano alone but not when performing in front of a group, then it is not because the person is resistant or prefers failure; rather, the person has not learned to access the resources of confidence in a new setting.

7. *Teach choice; encourage people to generate options that give them room to move and never attempt to take choice away* (Cameron-Bandler, Gordon, & Lebeau, 1985; Lankton & Lankton, 1983). When utilizing NLP in family therapy, therapists seek to create situations

wherein family members willingly change their thinking and behavior. Attention is focused on expanding each family member's map or limiting frame of reference to include behaviors, thoughts, and feelings that may have been previously unavailable. NLP practitioners do not eliminate experience; they instead expand awareness of experience so that people can choose among alternatives.

8. *People have all the resources they need to achieve their desired outcome* (Dilts et al., 1980). Each person has a repertoire of skills and behaviors, memories and experiences that provide a vast resource of untapped potential. In addition, family members can elicit resources from one another. The therapist's job is to help clients access these resources from contexts in which they operate and connect them to new contexts.

One way family members lose access to resources is when these resources become frozen in language, as when verbs become nouns. For example, family members often say that they want more attention, love, respect, support, care; these words are nominalizations (Bandler & Grinder, 1975b). Nominalizations reveal a shift in consciousness from process to product; experiences that evolve over time are frozen into event-structure that has distinct boundaries. Attention, love, respect, support, and care become objects like watches and cars; to say you lost your partner's love is like saying you've lost your watch. This transposition changes an ongoing process, action, or relationship into an object or thing. When this object becomes a process again, the lost is often found, and frozen assets are again available.

9. *The person with the broadest repertoire of behaviors and choices will be the controlling element in the system*

(Lankton & Lankton, 1983). This principle is based on Ashby's (1956) law of requisite variety and reminds us of the efficacy inherent in flexibility and variety. This principle suggests that if we do not elicit the responses we want, we should keep changing our behavior until we do get the response we want. The principle is evident in "problem" families who are controlled by an "incorrigible" child who behaves in ways no one else can match.

10. *A person cannot not communicate* (Watzlawick, Beavin, & Jackson, 1967). Behavior has no opposite; one cannot not behave. Therefore we are always communicating because we are always behaving; the analogical-paraverbal components of self-expression are visible whether or not that behavior is intentional, conscious, or successful (i.e., when mutual understanding occurs). We behave even when we do not speak. And we continuously search for meaning in the subtle messages we receive from others. This search is a major source of confusion and conflict in couples and families.

11. *The meaning of any communication is the response it elicits, independent of the intentions of the communicator* (Bandler & Grinder, 1979). Effective communicators have the sensory experience and behavioral flexibility to elicit the response they intend to elicit. When they don't, they have to deal with the message(s) received independent of the message(s) sent. Failure to do so produces conflict, confusion, and misunderstanding, as often happens in families. Parents may not realize the impact their advice may have on their children; an offer to help can become an unintended expression of lack of confidence in the receiver, for example. Message delivery is complex because the simultane-

ous presence of verbal and paraverbal components can express multiple possibilities to the receiver. Detecting and differentiating among these multiple messages is an important activity for the family therapist.

12. *Resistance is a comment about the inflexibility of the communicator* (Bandler & Grinder, 1979). Communication is complex and multifaceted. When family therapists are confronted by family members who have misunderstood them, it does no good to be defensive and claim it was not meant as received. Rather, it is important for the *therapist* to be flexible and change behavior so as to utilize the misunderstanding for therapeutic gain.

13. *Outcomes are determined at the unconscious level in conflicted communication* (Lankton & Lankton, 1983). As indicated above, communication is multifaceted and multilayered. When there is conflict or incongruence between the secondary experience system (language) and the primary experience system (sensory representational system), the primary system (which usually operates outside awareness) will determine the outcome. NLP practitioners utilize this principle when they behave congruently when clients behave congruently and behave incongruently when clients behave incongruently; programmers mirror the congruence or incongruence of their clients. They do this because the messages that have greatest impact in the midst of confusion are the incongruent paraverbal messages (whether or not they are related to the verbal message); therefore, they mirror the incongruence rather than call attention to it verbally.

14. *Individual skills and behavior are controlled by internal processing strate-* *gies* (Cameron-Bandler, 1985; Cameron-Bandler et al., 1985b; Dilts et al., 1980). The key to learning any skill or enhancing any talent is breaking the required performance down into its neural system representations—sight, sounds, feelings, smells, and tastes—and organizing these components in a relevant sequence. Then the resulting strategy can be taught as a model that the performer imitates, whether the strategy involves kissing your partner, throwing a baseball, spelling a word, or driving a car.

For example, Dilts et al. (1980) diagrammed the steps used by effective visual spellers (see Figure 8). Beginning with the sound of an externally pronounced word (A^e), the speller constructs an image (V^i_c) and compares it with the remembered (V^i_r) image. If it feels right (congruence: K^i), then the speller can exit (i.e., spell the word). But if the comparison doesn't feel right (incongruence: $\bar{K}^i$), the speller pronounces the word again (A^i) in order to generate a new constructed image (V^i_r). This process is repeated until it feels right and the word is spelled. The speller's success is dependent on following the sequence of representations in the spelling strategy. NLP practitioners use a calculus for notating this sequencing of representational systems (i.e., strategy); using the notation system, the visual speller's strategy is presented in Figure 9.

15. *Perception operates only on difference* (Bateson, 1979; Grinder et al., 1977). What each of us as human beings detects with our sensory channels is news of difference. To produce news of difference, we must draw a distinction creating two entities that can be compared; differences between them are computed as news. We then judge the significance of the news—whether the

Figure 8. Visual spelling TOTE

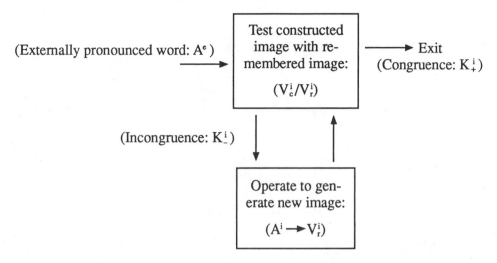

(Externally pronounced word: A^e) → | Test constructed image with remembered image: (V_c^i/V_r^i) | → Exit (Congruence: K_+^i)

(Incongruence: K_-^i)

Operate to generate new image: $(A^i \longrightarrow V_r^i)$

Excerpted from *Neuro-linguistic Programming*, Vol. 1 (p. 36) by R. Dilts et al., 1980, Cupertino, CA: Meta Publications.

difference is a difference that makes a difference. "Differences that are too slight or too slowly presented are not perceivable. They are not food for perception" (Bateson, 1979, p. 29).

By contrast, habituation refers to a lack of difference; when there is no difference to detect, there is no need consciously to represent "it." Without distinction, each "thing" is—for the mind and for perception—a nonentity, a non-

being, an unknowable, a sound of one hand clapping. Habituation, then, describes the process of sensing and responding unconsciously to the portion of our experience that is constant. Calibrated communication cycles are examples of habituation. Typically, it is only when the unconscious pattern in our behavior (e.g., playing our part in a calibrated communication cycle) fails to yield the unconsciously anticipated

Figure 9. Visual spelling strategy using notation system calculus.

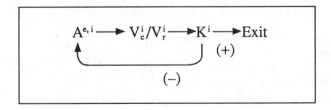

$$A^{e,i} \longrightarrow V_c^i/V_r^i \longrightarrow K^i \longrightarrow Exit$$
$$(+)$$
$$(-)$$

Excerpted from *Neuro-linguistic Programming*, Vol. 1 (p. 39) by R. Dilts et al., 1980, Cupertino, CA: Meta Publications.

Figure 10. The TOTE and the three tasks of therapy.

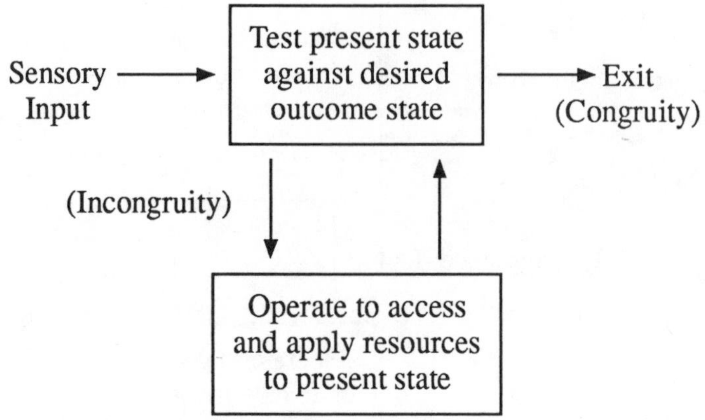

```
                    ┌─────────────────────┐
                    │  Test present state │
Sensory ──────────► │  against desired    │ ──────► Exit
Input               │  outcome state      │         (Congruity)
                    └─────────────────────┘
                         │        ▲
(Incongruity)            │        │
                         ▼        │
                    ┌─────────────────────┐
                    │  Operate to access  │
                    │  and apply resources│
                    │  to present state   │
                    └─────────────────────┘
```

Excerpted from *Neuro-linguistic Programming*, Vol. 1 (p. 29) by R. Dilts et al., 1980, Cupertino, CA: Meta Publications.

result of perpetuating the cycle that we become aware of any portion of that pattern. Again, consciousness is limited (Miller, 1956) to news of a difference.

APPLICATION

Goals

The neurolinguistic programmer's role in marriage and family therapy consists of three tasks (Cameron-Bandler, 1985):

1. Establishing rapport and gathering information concerning the client's present state and desired state: Find out where clients want to go and where they are now.
2. Evolving the client from their present to their desired state: Pick a method of getting to that desired state and use it.
3. Integrating the desired state experience into their ongoing behavior (i.e., future pacing): Notice whether the desired destination has been reached. If it has, take measures to insure that it can be reached in the future without you. If the desired destination has not been reached, then pick another method and use it. (p. 27)

The three tasks can be organized by the TOTE (test-operate-test-exit) format advanced by Miller, Galanter, and Pribram (1960) and depicted in Figure 10.

The TOTE

A TOTE consists of operations in our sensory representational system that are chunked together and sequenced to form a functional unit of behavior (as in the visual spelling strategy noted earlier) that operates at an unconscious level (Dilts et al., 1980; Grinder et al., 1977). The TOTE operationalizes the notion of "images and plans" that mediate stimulus and response; it describes how actions are controlled by an organism's internal representation of its universe (Miller et al. 1960).

The TOTE sequence is presented visually in Figure 11. The *test* represents the conditions that have to be met before a response to sensory stimulus will occur. If the conditions of the *test* phase (which compares present state and desired state)

Figure 11. The TOTE sequence.

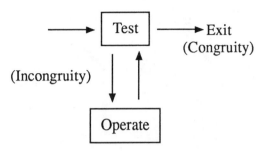

Excerpted from *Neuro-linguistic Programming*, Vol. 1 (p. 28) by R. Dilts et al., 1980, Cupertino, CA: Meta Publications.

are met, the action stimulated by the stimulus *exits* to the next step in the chain of behavior. If the conditions are not met, the feedback loop elicits *operations* to change some aspect of either the stimulus or the organism's state in an attempt to satisfy the test (Dilts et al., 1980). According to Miller et al. (1960):

> ...the response of the effector depends upon the outcome of the test and is most conveniently conceived as an effort to modify the outcome of the test. The action is initiated by an "incongruity" between the state of the organism and the state that is being tested for, and the action persists until the incongruity ...is removed....Thus, there is "feedback" from the result of the action to the testing phase, and we are confronted by a recursive loop. (pp. 25–26)

Feedback transforms linear process into circular process. Feedback loops enable a system to talk to itself and to benefit from the conversation. Feedback facilitates learning because it makes self-correcting comparisons possible. Through feedback we gain news of differences that may make a difference. When the difference is significant, as in the case of incongruity, operations are activated to resolve the incongruity.

When the difference is insignificant, as in the case of congruity, no operations are required and action proceeds as expected (e.g., habituation).

The existence of a TOTE indicates that an organizing, coordinating sequence of behavior has been established, that a plan of action is available.

> The TOTE represents the basic pattern in which our plans are cast, the test phase of the TOTE involves the specification of whatever knowledge is necessary for the comparison that is to be made, and the operational phase represents what the organism does about it— and what the organism does may often involve overt, observable actions. (Miller et al., 1960, p. 31)

These overt, observable actions consist of such activities as eye-scanning patterns, eye movements, paraverbal behaviors, and predicate usage, which were discussed previously.

TOTEs can be nested within one another; that is, the operational components of TOTE units may themselves be TOTE units. Each TOTE is isomorphic with the others, whether at the level of plans (instructions regarding the construction and use of strategies and tactics), strategies (sequences of representa-

Figure 12. Four phases of the NLP interview.

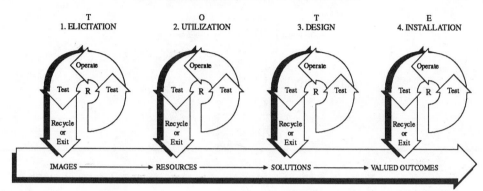

tional system utilization), or tactics (preferred representational system). The TOTE pattern can be used to describe all relevant processes.

TOTEs and the Helping Interview

The TOTE offers a format for planning the therapy sequence and testing its outcomes at each point of transition. In NLP, the TOTE coincides with the four-phase outline used by Dilts et al. (1980): elicitation (test), utilization (operate), design (test), installation (exit). Phase 1 addresses Cameron-Bandler's first task; Phases 2 and 3, the second task; and Phase 4, the third task. *Elicitation* refers to the procedure the programmer uses to make explicit the ordered sequence of current representational activity that constitutes a particular strategy. *Utilization* describes the process of applying an existing strategy to achieve a desired outcome. When the strategy is adequate and the outcome congruent with desire, resolution is achieved and the TOTE is exited; when the strategy is inadequate, the incongruities persist. *Design* signifies the process of devising a new plan or strategy to achieve a desired outcome. Design

operations are evoked when utilization efforts are unable to resolve incongruities. *Installation* refers to the process of integrating the desired state experience into ongoing behavior. Installation processes must respect the fragile relation between behavior and environments and attend to the ecological significance of solution possibilities.

These four activities constitute the four phases of the interview and are depicted in Figure 12.*

1. *Elicitation* (Test): Eliciting the desired scenario or desired state and comparing it to the present scenario or present state, noting congruities and incongruities; and satisfying well-formedness conditions.
2. *Utilization* (operate): Scanning the well-formed representations of desired state and present state, accessing relevant resources to resolve the incongruities between desired state and present state, and identifying the limitations of these resources.
3. *Design* (Test): Generating solution possibilities when old strategies

---

I am indebted to Steve Lord for the design of Figures 12 through 16.

Figure 13. Phase 1 of the NLP interview.

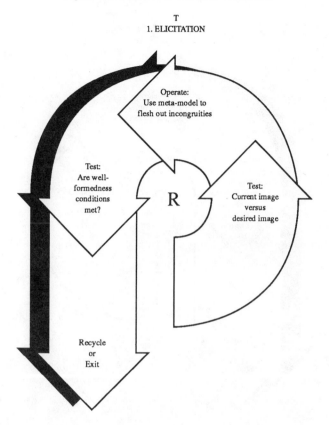

T
1. ELICITATION

Operate:
Use meta-model to
flesh out incongruities

Test:
Are well-
formedness
conditions
met?

R

Test:
Current image
versus
desired image

Recycle
or
Exit

don't work, deciding among them, and formulating a plan of action;

4. *Installation* (exit): Identifying contexts relevant to solution application, future-pacing, and evaluating efficacy.

In addition to the four-phase TOTE, the operations *within* each phase also follow the TOTE format. The activities of Phase 1 are depicted in Figure 13 and those of Phase 2 in Figure 14. (The meta-model will be discussed in detail in the Primary Techniques section of this chapter.) Figure 15 illustrates Phase 3 of the NLP process; Figure 16 designates Phase 4. Each figure presents the letter *R* at its center to remind us of the necessity for

maintaining *rapport* throughout the helping relationship. Further, the exit function represents a choice point: unless the test function generates the outcome appropriate to that working phase, the interview does not proceed to the next phase; rather, work recycles between operate and test until the expected outcome is achieved.

Client's Role and Therapist's Role

All that is required of clients who use neurolinguistic programming is that they have an outcome that they would like to achieve. Clients do not have to have a

Figure 14. Phase 2 of the NLP interview.

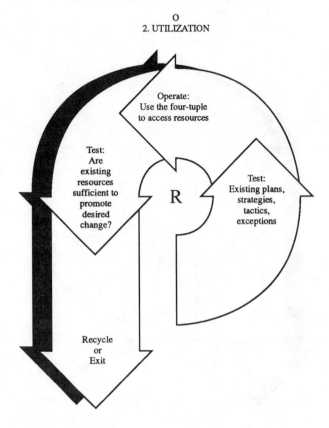

O
2. UTILIZATION

Operate:
Use the four-tuple
to access resources

Test:
Are
existing
resources
sufficient to
promote
desired
change?

R

Test:
Existing plans,
strategies,
tactics,
exceptions

Recycle
or
Exit

problem or be termed "dysfunctional." Rather, all they have to do is identify something that they want to change in their lives and agree to try something new in order to make it happen. NLP expands the breadth and depth of human experience; it does not take experience away.

The therapist's role is to establish rapport with clients, accommodate to each client's model of the world, and invite clients to use the language of NLP to articulate their experience and desired outcomes.

Therapists elicit surface structure descriptions or demonstrations of desired outcomes and present states, and they attend carefully to congruity and incon-

gruity in client reports. Questions such as the following are useful in obtaining present state descriptions:

1. What are you experiencing now?
2. In what contexts do you experience this?
3. With whom do you experience this?
4. Is there ever a time when you do not experience this (exception)?
5. What positive benefits, if any, are associated with this experience?

For example, suppose Pete says, "I love them; I love them a lot" when asked about his feelings for his children. His voice tempo is very fast, his volume is uncharacteristically loud, his lips are drawn tight, his body is rigid, and his

Figure 15. Phase 3 of the NLP interview.

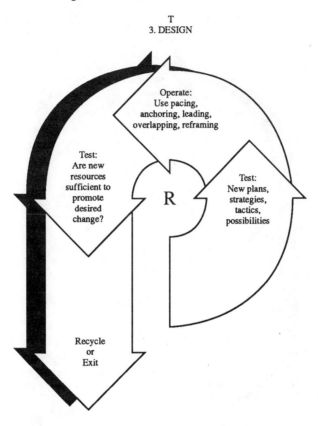

fists are clenched. Pete's paraverbal messages are not congruent with his verbal report. While we can see and hear the absence of verbal-paraverbal alignment in his communication, we do not yet know what it means. NLP therapists will use the meta-model and the four-tuple to access the deep structure representations of Pete's experience in order to generate a well-formed description of his present state.

Attention is given then to establishing well-formed outcome statements that are connected to sensory experience. The following questions help the client explain his or her desired state:

1. What, specifically, do you want?

2. What does it look, feel, and sound like?
3. In what contexts do you want it?
4. Are there any contexts in which you don't want it (exception)?
5. Has there ever been a time when you had it? What did it look, feel, and sound like then? How did you know you had it?
6. How will you know when you have it now?
7. What stops you from getting it?
8. What will happen when you get it?

There are five conditions that must be met for an outcome to be well formed (Cameron-Bandler, 1985). First, the outcome must be stated positively; find out

Figure 16. Phase 4 of the NLP interview.

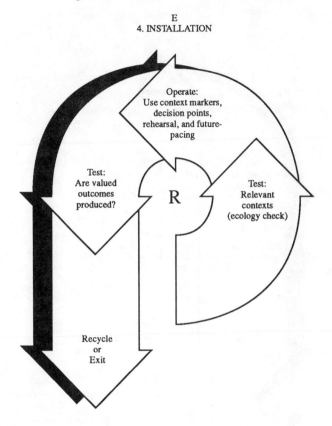

E
4. INSTALLATION

Operate:
Use context markers,
decision points,
rehearsal, and future-
pacing

Test:
Are valued
outcomes
produced?

R

Test:
Relevant
contexts
(ecology check)

Recycle
or
Exit

what each client *does want,* not what is unwanted. If a family member says, "I want to get rid of anger" or "anxiety" or "depression" and we accept this outcome statement, then all attention and energy is directed toward the problem. Concentrate on what a person will do when the problem is no longer a problem.

Second, the outcome must be specific as to behavior and context; find out precisely what clients want to do and when, where, and with whom they want to do it. If clients want to be assertive, establish what assertiveness means behaviorally and explore when, where, and with whom assertiveness is useful and when, where, and with whom it is not. By ap-

propriately contextualizing the requested change, the client's well-being will be protected.

Third, the outcome must be demonstrable in sensory experience; learn what sights, sounds, and feelings clients want to experience. Sensory-based data peel away the superfluous meanings until we get to the core of what this outcome means to each client (Laborde, 1984). A conscious, sensory-based outcome helps clients persist in pursuing what they want while ignoring distractors.

Fourth, the outcome must be initiated and maintained by clients themselves; identify what resources clients have to sustain them through change. The therapist's job is to assist clients in creating options, choosing among them, and developing a plan for implementing their choices.

Fifth, the outcome must preserve the positive by-products, if any, inherent in the present state; discover what benefits are gained in the present state. For example, when a spouse wants to give up smoking, determine when, where, and with whom smoking occurs; if she always smokes at the kitchen table while talking casually with her partner, make sure the talking continues when the smoking stops.

PRIMARY TECHNIQUES

Neurolinguistic programming offers the family therapist a wide variety of techniques designed to enhance therapist-client rapport and to equip the therapist with interventions that help clients establish closer contact with full-bodied sensory experience (e.g., the four-tuple); generate well-formed linguistic representations of experience (e.g., the meta-model); create well-formed, sensory-based outcome statements; and design strategies that promote efficacy. The number of strategies and techniques currently available exceed the scope of this chapter, so the reader is encouraged to pursue outside reading (see References). What is presented here is an overview of the model together with a sampling of techniques. Some of these have already been briefly discussed earlier in the chapter.

1. Differentiating the elements of sensory experience into the four representational systems summarized by the *four-tuple*.
2. Distinguishing between *primary* (sensory-based) and *secondary*

(linguistic) representations of experience.
3. Identifying internal processing modes such as the *lead* system, the *preferred* system, the *output* system, and *synesthesia* (which is evidenced when one of the above systems is different from the others, as when behavior-output is initiated by the feeling/preferred of the sound/lead).
4. Establishing *rapport* by *matching* predicates, *mirroring* paraverbal behaviors, and *translating* from one representational system to another.
5. Using mirroring to accommodate to the client's sense of timing or *pacing* so that the therapist does not move too quickly. Once an effective pace has been established (e.g., mirroring the client's breathing rate), the therapist can gracefully begin to *lead* the client into new experience (i.e., an altered breathing rate).
6. Making synesthesia deliberate by guiding conscious awareness from the representational system in which it is operating to awareness in another channel; this is called *overlapping*.
7. Using pacing, leading, and overlapping to interrupt *calibrated communication cycles* so as to create *feedback communication* cycles.
8. Identifying and differentiating among multiple (often incongruent) messages so that family members can more accurately perceive and evaluate the impact their behavior has on others in the family.
9. Observing and using *sensory-accessing cues* (e.g., eye movement

patterns) and sensory-specific language to pace the client's internal process and lead the client into expanded representational possibilities.

10. Expanding impoverished verbal maps into higher quality, well-formed descriptions of sensory experience that produce behavioral demonstrations of desired states.

11. Cooperating with whatever responses are elicited from clients by creatively incorporating these responses into plans that nurture client movement toward their desired outcome.

12. Concentrating on differences that make a difference and ignoring the rest.

13. Recognizing and using existing plans, strategies, and tactics to the client's benefit while creating additional alternatives that assist clients in achieving their desired outcomes.

14. Using the TOTE format to organize and evaluate interventions.

In addition to these techniques, the meta-model, the expanded four-tuple, anchoring, and future-pacing are elaborated next.

The Meta-Model

As clients tell their story, they simplify, simplify, simplify. They use the three universal modeling processes—deletion, distortion, and generalization—consciously and unconsciously to screen out what they consider unnecessary and to shape the story so that it has the impact they wish. These surface structure expressions are impoverished representations of the deep structures from which

they are derived. The meta-model was established by Grinder and Bandler (1976) to restore these expressions to their fully formed state. The meta-model consists of an explicit set of linguistic information—gathering tools designed to reconnect a person's language to the experience it represents.

As we learn language in childhood, we attach specific four-tuples or sets of four-tuples to specific words (Lankton, 1980). But just as our sensory representations of reality (the map) are not reality itself (the territory), so our linguistic representations (the map of maps) only approximate our inner and outer experience. For example, suppose a client says, "I'm hurt; I'm really hurt." The client's statement hides as much as it reveals. She has deleted both the source of the hurt and what it specifically feels, sounds, smells, and looks like to hurt. By asking, "What are you hurt about?" and "What specifically hurt you?" the therapist helps the client retrieve a fuller representation of the experience, thereby taking the first step toward changing it.

The meta-model rests on the premise that words only have meaning when they are connected to fully formed internal representations of sensory experience. Meta-model questions are designed to bridge the gap between language and sensory experience by fully developing the four-tuples attached to their verbal expression. Meta-model questions specifically reverse the eliminative function of the three universal modeling processes: deletion, generalization, and distortion.

Deletion. The process by which selected portions of our experience are excluded from the representation created is called *deletion*. More simply, it is the process by which we selectively pay attention to certain aspects of our experience and exclude others. An example of the benefits of deletion occurs every time we attempt to read a book while people around us are talking, or the TV is on, or the radio is playing; we're able to concentrate by screening out all of the distractions so that we're not overwhelmed by them. This process works well for us until we screen out something that merits attention, as, for example, the painful cry of our child.

Generalization. *Generalization* occurs when components or pieces of a person's representation of experience become detached from its original form; the detached representation comes to symbolize the entire category of which the original experience was but an example. We learn to function efficiently in the world by generalizing from one experience to another. For example, sons and daughters follow house rules when dining as a family and often assume that the same rules apply when eating at a friend's house or at an awards banquet; they may be shocked when this generalization breaks down and they are accused of having no manners. Therefore, whether or not a generalization is useful must always be evaluated with regard to the particular context within which we are operating.

Distortion. We call on *distortion* whenever we transform sensory data from one thing to another by reorganizing the relationships that hold among elements of our experience or by exaggerating their importance or significance. Distortion works well for us when we begin to generate a vision of what does not now exist. Envisioning the future, initiating new relationships, and dreaming about faraway places are all examples.

Distortion serves us poorly, however, when we begin to exaggerate criticism or danger.

These three universal modeling processes are the tools we use to organize our representations of reality so that we are not overwhelmed. Nonetheless, at times these modeling procedures serve to create models of the world that are far too limiting. This is most evident when people come to therapy expressing pain and dissatisfaction: the limitations that they experience are typically in the representation of their experience and *not* in the experience itself.

As stated earlier, the meta-model reverses the limiting effects of deletion, distortion, and generalization by eliciting a well-formed statement of the surface structure expression. These statements can then assist our clients to expand the portions of their representations that impoverish and limit them, thereby expanding their behavioral options.

The meta-model asks *what, how,* and *who* type questions to elicit from the interviewee's deep structure a fuller representation of his or her experience. Meta-model questions are designed to restore deletions by gathering information, to challenge generalizations by identifying the limits of the speaker's model, and to confront distortions by addressing statements that are semantically ill formed. The questions allow the interviewer to focus on external sensory experience so as to get sensory-based information from the client rather than from internal imagining. By requiring the interviewee to be clear, the interviewer does not have to invent the missing pieces.

The meta-model distinctions fall into three groups: (a) semantic ill-formedness, (b) limits of the speaker's model, and (c) gathering information

(Cameron-Bandler, 1985; Grinder & Bandler, 1981). These groups and the distinctions associated with each are listed below together with illustrative speaker statements that are challenged by meta-model questions.

A. The interviewer's aim is to confront statements that are so *semantically ill formed* that portions of the statement are distorted in some way.

   A1. *Distortions:* statements that misrepresent the data and twist things out of shape.

   A2. *Causal Modeling:* statements that link two or more situations in cause-effect fashion.

Expression	*Meta-model Question*
"You frustrate me."	How do I frustrate you?
"My family makes me mad."	How? Who, specifically?

   A3. *Mind Reading:* statements that infer that one person can know what someone else is thinking and feeling without direct communication with that person.

Expression	*Meta-model question*
"I know what's best for you."	How, specifically, do you know?
"You can see how I feel."	How can I *see* what you *feel?*

   A4. *Presuppositions:* statements in which the truth of some claim is required for the statement to make sense.

Expression	*Assumption*
"If Sue has to be so possessive, then I'd rather not be involved with her."	Sue is possessive.

B. The interviewer's purpose is to identify the *limits of the speaker's model.*

   B1. *Generalizations:* statements that project the same meaning or value to a whole class of experience.

Expression	*Meta-model Question*
"I hate American cars!"	What do you hate about American cars, specifically?
"I'm afraid of women."	Who are you afraid of, specifically?

   B2. *Lost Performative:* generalizations (usually judgments) that delete the authority behind the statement.

Expression	*Meta-model question*
"This is the right way to do it."	For whom?
"People should know better."	Who should know better?

   B3. *Model Operators of Necessity:* words that indicate a lack of choice.

Expression	*Meta-model question*
"I can't do it."	What stops you?
"I have to finish by Tuesday."	What will happen if you don't?
"I can't think."	What prevents you?

   Note: A second meta-model strategy is to change the modal operators of necessity into modal operators of possibility (e.g., words like *can, will,* etc.).

B4. *Universal Quantifiers:* words that exaggerate.

Expression	*Meta-model question*
"I never do anything right."	You absolutely never do anything right?

B5. *Complex Equivalence:* meanings that are attached to behaviors.

Expression	*Meta-model question*
"My husband never appreciates me...my husband never smiles at me."	Does your husband's not smiling at you always mean that he doesn't appreciate you?

C. The interviewer's goal is to gain an accurate and full description of the content being presented by gathering information.

C1. *Deletions:* information has been left out of the sentence.

Expression	*Meta-model Question*
"I'm inadequate."	To do what?
"I'm not able to cope."	With what? With whom?
"I'm scared!"	Of what? Of whom?

C2. *Referential Index Deletion:* a person, place, or thing is introduced in the sentence but not specified.

Expression	*Meta-model question*
"Things get me down."	What things?
"People get me down."	Who specifically?
"Something should be done."	What should be done about what?

C3. *Unspecified verbs:* the verb is introduced but not specified.

Expression	*Meta-model question*
"She rejected me."	How, specifically?
"I'm blocked."	How are you blocked? By what?
"They ignored me."	Who? How, specifically?

C4. *Nominalizations:* words have been transformed from verbs to nouns.

Expression	*Mega-model question*
"I don't get any recognition."	How would you like to be recognized?
"I regret my decision."	How about deciding again?
"Pay attention."	To what do you want me to attend?

Robbins (1986) offers an easy way to remember the essence of the meta-model; he has simplified it and named it "the precision model" (see Figure 17). Each finger on the right hand represents categories of the meta-model; each finger on the left hand represents questions relevant to the categories on the right. For example, start with the little finger: the category reminder "Universals" tags the right finger and the meta-model questions relevant to that category (all? every? never?) are on the left finger. Similarly, model operators of necessity (should, shouldn't, must, can't) tag the ring finger on the right and are countered by relevant questions associated with the comparable finger on the left (what would happen if you did?).

The meta-model is organized in hierarchical fashion (Lankton, 1980), so that categories of a higher logical type oper-

Figure 17. Precision model.

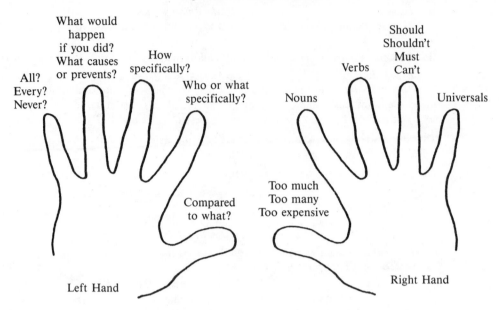

What would
happen
if you did?
What causes
How
or prevents?
specifically?

All?
Every?
Never?

Who or what
specifically?

Nouns

Should
Shouldn't
Must
Can't

Verbs

Universals

Too much
Too many
Too expensive

Compared
to what?

Left Hand

Right Hand

Excerpted from *Unlimited Power* (p. 201) by A. Robbins, 1986, New York: Simon and Schuster.

ate on those below (see Figure 18). Lankton (1980) offers the following illustration to demonstrate the hierarchy at work:

"I can't find what I need to get love from any of these angry wombats and its just making me crazy." Now, the speaker is in a spot. First, he presupposes that wombats exist, then that they are angry (Mind Reading), and worse, that they are making him crazy (Causal Modeling). The bleak set of assumptions on this highest logical level leads to further complications: at the next level we find that there are not any (Universal Quantifier) wombats that are other than angry and that the speaker can't (Modal Operator) find what he needs to stop them. All of the wombats are the same, too (Generalization). At the more mundane level, the statement implies that the speaker is having a rough time trying to find (Unspecified Verb) what the "something" is that he needs to get love (Nominalization). All in all it is a real tough jam.

In helping this person we would best begin gathering some information by questioning at the highest logical level. If we ask him what he means by "love" or how specifically he is trying to get it, we are wasting our time. If we ask him what prevents him from finding what he needs, we might be on greener turf. We might also challenge the Universal Quantifier "any" or the generalizations about the nature of the wombats. But this would really be like trying to remove a door by chopping it down with a hatchet. By directing our questions first to logical level one—the Presuppositions, the Causal Modeling, and the Mind Reading—we begin to remove the hinge pins upon which the entire dilemma revolves. (pp. 54-55)

Expanding Four-Tuple Notation

An additional approach to restoring impoverished surface structure expressions to their well-formed state involves gener-

Figure 18. Meta-model hierarchy of categories.

A. Semantic Ill-Formedness
Distortions
Causal modeling
Mind reading
Presuppositions

Operates on

B. Limits of the Speaker's Model
Generalizations
Modal operators
Universal quantifiers
Complex equivalence
Lost performatives

Operates on

C. Information Gathering
Deletions
Referential index deletion
Unspecified verbs
Nominalization

Adapted from *Practical Magic* (p. 54) by S. Lankton, 1980, Cupertino, CA: Meta Publications.

ating full representational experience. The four-tuple (recall Figure 1) can be expanded to include more precise distinctions (Dilts et al., 1980). In addition to the four basic representational systems (auditory, visual, kinesthetic, and olfactory-gustatory), a distinction can be drawn as to whether the system in use is oriented toward internally generated experience (indicated with a superscript i) or toward experience that is imploding from external sources (indicated by a superscript e). Furthermore, internally generated experience can be distinguished as either constructed (c) or remembered (r). Another distinction is the difference between digital (verbal) representations in the auditory representational system and tonal and tempo (paraverbal) qualities; since digital (d) distinctions refer to secondary experience while tonal and temporal (t) distinc-

tions are more primary, the auditory-digital designation is placed outside the four-tuple (as shown in Figure 19).

Dilts et al. (1980) consider the four-tuple a key to unlocking the internal neurological processes that drive behavior. The goal of gathering information about lead, preferred, and sequential representational usage is "to decode the overt transforms of the neurological strategies, which are generally not available to the consciousness of those in whom they operate, in order to gain understanding of how the representational components are organized with respect to one another" (pp. 77–78).

Discovering how representational components are organized can lead to discovering regularities between an individual's internal processes and her or his observable behavior. These regularities can in turn generate recognition of re-

Figure 19. Expanded four-tuple formula.

$$A_d^{e,i(r,c)} \left\langle A_t^{e,i(r,c)}, V^{e,i(r,c)}, K^{e,i(r,c)}, O^{e,i(r,c)} \right\rangle$$

Excerpted from *Neuro-linguistic Programming*, Vol. 1 (p. 75) by R. Dilts et al., 1980, Cupertino, CA: Meta Publications.

dundancy or patterning that often leads to predictive efficacy (Bateson, 1972): "When an observer perceives only certain parts of a sequence or configuration of phenomena, he is in many cases able to guess, with better than random success, at the parts which he cannot immediately perceive" (p. 420). By connecting the four-tuple to neurological functioning, Dilts et al. (1980) have formulated a powerful tool for understanding stability and change, as will be evident in the next section.

Anchoring

Anchoring uses the natural associative processes common to memory recall. For example, the aroma of baking cookies can conjure up childhood memories of my grandmother baking in the kitchen, sneaking in behind her to snatch warm cookies from the counter while she pretended not to notice, and so forth. These "spontaneously" elicited memories are the product of the olfactory anchor that, when triggered, ushers in the memories associated with the aroma. By bringing up this memory, I reexperience many of the same feelings that occurred when this memory was formed.

Anchoring converts this spontaneous process into a planned one by deliberately associating a stimulus to a specific experience (Cameron-Bandler, 1985). By

deliberately inserting a discrete new stimulus while a person is fully in contact with a vivid experience, we can elicit that experience again in all its vividness by invoking the new stimulus now associated with the experience. The new stimulus can be a sound, a touch, a specific image, a smell, or a taste; it is called the *anchor*. When the association is firm, the anchor can be used to trigger the associated experience again and again.

In order to anchor a response successfully, we should follow the following procedures (Cameron-Bandler, 1985):

1. Have the client access the desired experience (or elicit it) as powerfully and fully as possible.
2. Insert your stimulus at the moment of fullest expression or greatest intensity. Timing is crucial.
3. Be sure your stimulus can be reproduced exactly. Repeating the stimulus will bring back the internal state *only* if it is repeated exactly as originally introduced.
4. Test the anchor by letting the client change mental states; then trigger the anchor and observe if the response is the state desired.

Anchoring is a useful technique with couples because much of their interaction is influenced by the anchors of past experiences. For example, a man and a woman who have lived together for 15 or

20 years do not always have to spell things out. When he comes home after a day at work, he knows from the way she moves and her tone of voice what kind of day she had; she may not have to say a word. Her movement and tone of voice may suggest an amorous evening or one in which each keeps distant from the other. Thus, her movement and tone of voice are anchors for his behavior. These anchors may have to be changed to trigger new behavior if their old behaviors become problematic.

Anchoring is the key to understanding calibrated communication cycles in couples and families. When a wife's tone of voice or facial expression results in an angry response from her husband, which in turn elicits an angry response from the wife, and so forth, a calibrated loop has been initiated by the anchor of the wife's vocal tone or facial expression. One way to interrupt the "vicious" cycle is to insert an anchor that prompts a new response from the husband to the wife's tone or expression.

Future-Pacing

Future-pacing is the process of ensuring that changes accomplished during therapy become generalized and available in other relevant contexts. The primary method of future-pacing new behavior is anchoring the new behavior to a sensory stimulus that naturally occurs in the applicable context (Cameron-Bandler, 1985). First, ask the client, "What is the first thing you will see, hear, or feel that will indicate you need this resource?" When the specific experience or circumstance is identified, have the client generate it internally and then anchor the appropriate resource to that experience. Then when the anticipated stimulus occurs in the relevant context, it can natu-

rally and unconsciously trigger access to the desired resources.

For instance, anchoring feelings of passion (the resource) to the smell of a favorite perfume, or to the feeling of smooth clean sheets, or to the sound of a partner's voice, or to the sight of a lit candle, all demonstrate future-pacing the resource of passionate feelings to specific externally occurring stimuli. When future-pacing, it is important to be situationally specific so that the desired resources are activated at the appropriate time, in the appropriate place, and with the appropriate people.

This completes a sampling of techniques developed and utilized in neuro-linguistic programming. Additional techniques include reframing (Cameron-Bandler, 1985), hypnotic language patterning (Grinder & Bandler, 1976), therapeutic metaphors (Gordon, 1978), eliciting strategies (Dilts et al., 1980), changing personal history (Cameron-Bandler, 1985), defusing phobias (Bandler & Grinder, 1982), restructuring emotions (Cameron-Bandler & Lebeau, 1986), patterning mental aptitudes (Cameron-Bandler et al., 1985a), breaking habits (Cameron-Bandler, Gordon, & Lebeau, 1985b), restoring sexual desire (Cameron-Bandler, 1985), and exerting influence in business (Laborde, 1984).

CASE EXAMPLE

A newly married couple spent a total of nine sessions with me in marital therapy. The couple had been married for a little over 2 years, he for the second time and she for the first.

The first session began with the establishment of rapport by matching predicates and subtly mirroring paraverbal behaviors with each person. It became apparent that the wife's lead and preferred representational system was kinesthetic; the husband's lead and preferred system was visual. Both persons were well educated and highly articulate—she readily talked about her feelings; he talked about what he saw.

Their initial complaint was that they fought "all the time." It later became clear that they fought in the evening when specific topics were raised by either one of them. They wanted to talk together in relaxed fashion so that they could solve the problems they faced. Clear, well-formed outcomes were developed and contrasted with their present state.

In the early stages of the third session, a turning point arrived. Ann and Fred (as I shall call them) were sitting in my office side by side with their arms entwined facing me. In response to a question, Ann began to describe her situation using lots of hand gestures (which meant that she let go of Fred's arm). While listening, Fred slid his chair away from Ann's chair and turned it so that he faced her right side; he sat looking at her while she talked with me. Almost without warning (I had noticed her neck had begun to flush, but Fred didn't appear to notice), Ann turned to him and began speaking angrily. He was at first startled, then sat with a glazed expression saying nothing.

After observing this scene for a few minutes, I interrupted and asked Fred what had happened; he said he didn't know. I then turned to Ann and asked her; she knew she was angry but didn't know why. Since I had been videotaping the session, I invited them to review the tape with me. When Ann saw Fred move his chair on the replay, she said, "That's why." She went on to say she *felt* abandoned when he moved away from her. By contrast, Fred indicated that he enjoyed looking at Ann and had moved his

chair so that he could *see* her better.

When I asked if this outburst was typical of the arguments they were having, they said yes. Usually, they would be sitting at the kitchen table talking casually when a serious topic was introduced. The topic elicited paraverbal cues of displeasure, and Fred would get up and move away from the table to the sink. The conversation would escalate until they just shouted at each other until one of them (usually Ann) left the room. When questioned, they indicated that she spoke with lots of animation, but he spoke calmly (until he blew his cool, shouted, and then withdrew). They often remembered harsh phrases spoken, but not the details of the argument. They appeared to be locked in a calibrated communication cycle.

Clearly, Ann and Fred used different representational systems. During the third session Fred changed his seating position so that he could watch (visual) Ann; when he looked at her, he felt close to her. Ann preferred physical contact (remember, their arms were entwined) and felt abandoned (kinesthetic) when Fred moved his chair away from her or left the kitchen table at home; by contrast when she held hands with Fred or made physical contact with him, she felt close to him.

We explored together this difference that made a difference. I paced, led, and overlapped their internal experience and then translated each person's experience from one preferred representational system (kinesthetic) to the other (visual) and back again until they could translate for themselves. I also suggested that they do something different at home to break the calibrated communication cycle in which they were trapped. The pained expression on Ann's face when controversial topics were raised was anchored to a new response from Fred: rather than

Figure 20. Therapist's intervention.

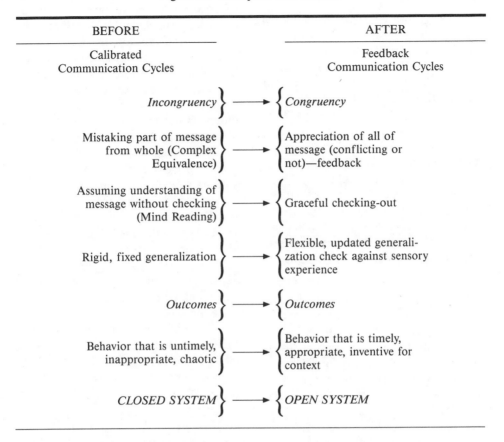

BEFORE	AFTER
Calibrated Communication Cycles	Feedback Communication Cycles

Incongruency } ⟶ { *Congruency*

Mistaking part of message from whole (Complex Equivalence) } ⟶ { Appreciation of all of message (conflicting or not)—feedback

Assuming understanding of message without checking (Mind Reading) } ⟶ { Graceful checking-out

Rigid, fixed generalization } ⟶ { Flexible, updated generalization check against sensory experience

Outcomes } ⟶ { *Outcomes*

Behavior that is untimely, inappropriate, chaotic } ⟶ { Behavior that is timely, appropriate, inventive for context

CLOSED SYSTEM } ⟶ { *OPEN SYSTEM*

Adapted from *Changing with Families* (p. 118) by R. Bandler, J. Grinder, and V. Satir, 1976, Palo Alto, CA: Science and Behavior Books.

withdraw, Fred turned to face her (so he could see her clearly) and reached for her hands. They found when they did this that they were able to talk through topics without anger that had previously fired them up. In addition, Ann's feeling of abandonment was replaced by feelings of warmth when she saw Fred looking into her eyes; she realized that she was demonstrative and attractive and that Fred loved looking at her.

These new understandings and behavior emerged from the shift from calibra-tion to feedback, as suggested by Bandler et al. (1976) and depicted in Figure 20. By recognizing preferred representational systems and translating from one to the other, incongruency was transformed into congruency, complex equivalence was replaced by feedback, mind reading was replaced by perception checks, and rigid generalizations were replaced by sensory-specific representations. This is the essence of NLP's approach to marital and family therapy.

EVALUATION

Sharpley (1984) reviewed 15 empirical studies that investigated the use of the "preferred representational system (PRS)" in NLP and concluded that there is little supportive evidence for the use of PRS in NLP and "no data to show that NLP can help clients change" (p. 247). Sharpley's conclusions were strongly challenged by Einspruch and Forman (1985) and by Buckner et al. (1987), whose results were cited earlier.

Einspruch and Forman (1985) reviewed 39 empirical studies of NLP documented through April 1984. Their article identifies six categories of design and methodological errors contained in the 39 studies:

1. Lack of understanding of the concepts of pattern recognition and inadequate control of context (p. 590)
2. Failure to understand NLP as an approach to therapy (p. 591)
3. Failure to understand the meta-model of linguistic communication (p. 592)
4. Failure to consider stimulus-response associations (p. 593)
5. Inadequate interviewer training for understanding the nature of rapport in the counseling relationship (p. 593)
6. Logical mistakes (p. 593)

Einspruch and Forman consider NLP an extraordinarily complex model of human cognition and behavior that re-quires sensitive, disciplined inquiry. They suggest that researchers should be trained by competent NLP practitioners, that research procedures should be applied at the individual level and calibrated to each person's personal characteristics, that treatment studies should be performed only by therapists with demonstrated mastery of the model and its techniques, and that outcome measures should be behavioral in nature.

On the basis of the research that has appeared in the literature, it is not yet possible to determine the validity of either NLP concepts or NLP-based procedures. The model has earned a considerable following among practitioners, however, because of its usefulness for generating choice and change. Only when well-designed empirical investigations are executed will we be assured of NLP's validity as a model of therapy. Meanwhile, to summarize the promise of NLP, I cite once again, Bandler et al. (1976):

When I can see and hear what is here now,
    feel what I feel now;
Say what I feel, think, hear, see now;
When I can reach out for what I want now;
And can take risks in my own behalf now;
When I can communicate all of this con-
    gruently now;
And can get feedback creatively now;
Then I am in a position to cope inventively
    with the situation outside of myself and the
    life inside of me successfully—NOW.

pp. 5–6

ANNOTATED SUGGESTED READINGS

Bandler, R., & Grinder, J. (1979). *Frogs into princes*. Moab, UT: Real People Press.

Edited transcripts from a 2-day workshop conducted by Bandler and Grinder in January 1978, providing a very readable introduction to NLP.

Bandler, R., & Grinder, J. (1975). *The structure of magic I*. Palo Alto, CA: Science and Behavior Books.

Therapy addressed from the vantage point of transformational grammar. It presents the meta-model in great detail.

Bandler, R., Grinder, J., & Satir, V. (1976). *Changing with families*. Palo Alto, CA: Science and Behavior Books.

The application of NLP to family therapy, modeling Virginia Satir's approach. My favorite.

Cameron-Bandler, L. (1985). *Solutions*. San Rafael, CA: Future Pace.

NLP techniques applied to couple and sex therapy in clear, step-by-step fashion.

Dilts, R., Grinder, J., Bandler, R., Cameron-Bandler, L., & DeLozier, J. (1980). *Neuro-linguistic programming. Vol. 1*. Cupertino, CA: Meta Publications.

The cognitive processes that underlie all behavioral strategies presented in great detail. An important work for a serious NLP practitioner.

Grinder, J., DeLozier, J., & Bandler, R. (1977). *Patterns of the hypnotic techniques of Milton H. Erickson, M.D. Vol. 2*. Cupertino, CA: Meta Publications.

How the meta-model informs therapeutic interventions in a detailed analysis of two of Milton H. Erickson's therapy sessions.

Lankton, S. (1980). *Practical magic*. Cupertino, CA: Meta.

An excellent introduction to NLP.

REFERENCES

Ashby, W. R. (1956). *An introduction to cybernetics*. London: Methuen.

Bandler, R., & Grinder, J. (1975a). *Patterns of the hypnotic techniques of Milton H. Erickson, M.D. Vol. 1*. Cupertino, CA: Meta Publications.

Bandler, R., & Grinder, J. (1975b). *The structure of magic I*. Palo Alto, CA: Science and Behavior Books.

Bandler, R., & Grinder, J. (1979). *Frogs into princes*. Moab, UT: Real People Press.

Bandler, R., & Grinder, J. (1982). *Reframing*. Moab, UT: Real People Press.

Bandler, R., Grinder, J., & Satir, V. (1976). *Changing with families*. Palo Alto, CA: Science and Behavior Books.

Bateson, G. (1972). *Steps to an ecology of mind*. San Francisco: Chandler.

Bateson, G. (1979). *Mind and nature*. New York: E. P. Dutton.

Beck, C., & Beck, E. (1984). Test of the eye-movement hypothesis of Neuro Linguistic Programming: A rebuttal of conclusions. *Perceptual and Motor Skills, 58*, 175–176.

Brooks, M. (1989). *Instant rapport*. New York: Warner.

Buckner, M., Meara, N. M., Reese, E. J., & Reese, M. (1987). Eye movement as an indicator of sensory components in thought. *Journal of Counseling Psychology, 34*, 283–287.

Cameron-Bandler, L. (1985). *Solutions*. San Rafael, CA: Future Pace.

Cameron-Bandler, L., Gordon, D., & Lebeau, M. (1985a). *The emprint method*. San Rafael, CA: Future Pace.

Cameron-Bandler, L., Gordon, D., & Lebeau, M. (1985b). *Know how*. San Rafael, CA: Future Pace.

Cameron-Bandler, L., & Lebeau, M. (1986). *The emotional hostage*. San Rafael, CA: Future Pace.

Dilts, R., Grinder, J., Bandler, R., Cameron-Bandler, L., & DeLozier, J. (1980). *Neuro-Linguistic Programming. Vol. I*. Cupertino, CA: Meta Publications.

Dorn, F., Atwater, M., Jereb, R., & Russell, R. (1983). Determining the reliability of the NLP eye-movement procedure. *American Mental Health Counselors Journal, 5*, 105–110.

Einspruch, E. L., & Forman, B. D. (1985). Observations concerning research literature on neuro-linguistic programming. *Journal of Counseling Psychology, 32,* 589–596.

Ellickson, J. L. (1983). Representational systems and eye movements in an interview. *Journal of Counseling Psychology, 30,* 339–345.

Gordon, D. (1978). *Therapeutic metaphors.* Cupertino, CA: Meta Publications.

Grinder, J., & Bandler, R. (1976). *The structure of magic II.* Palo Alto, CA: Science and Behavior Books.

Grinder, J., & Bandler, R. (1981). *Tranceformations.* Moab, UT: Real People Press.

Grinder, J., DeLozier, J., & Bandler, R. (1977). *Patterns of the hypnotic techniques of Milton H. Erickson, M.D. Vol. 2.* Cupertino, CA: Meta Publications.

Grinder, J. T., & Elgin, S. H. (1973). *Guide to transformational grammar.* New York: Holt, Rinehart & Winston.

Huxley, A. (1954). *The doors of perception.* New York: Harper & Row.

Korzybski, A. (1941). *Science and sanity: An introduction to non-Aristotelian systems and general semantics* (2nd ed.). New York: Science Press.

Laborde, G. Z. (1984). *Influencing with integrity.* Palo Alto, CA: Syntony.

Lankton, S. (1980). *Practical magic.* Cupertino, CA: Meta.

Lankton, S. R., & Lankton, C. H. (1983). *The answer within: A clinical framework of Ericksonian hypnotherapy.* New York: Brunner/Mazel.

Makower, J. (Ed.). (1986). *The map catalogue.* New York: Vintage.

Miller, G. A. (1956). The magical number seven, plus or minus two. *Psychological Review, 63,* 81–97.

Miller, G. A., Galanter, E., & Pribram, K. H. (1960). *Plans and the structure of behavior.* New York: Henry Holt.

Richardson, J., & Margulis, J. (1981). *The magic of rapport.* San Francisco: Harbor.

Sharpley, C. (1984). Predicate matching in NLP: A review of research on the preferred representational system. *Journal of Counseling Psychology, 31,* 238–248.

Thomason, T. C., Arbuckle, T., & Cady, D. (1980). Test of the eye movement hypothesis of neurolinguistic programming. *Perceptual and Motor Skills, 51,* 230.

Toffler, A. (1970). *Future shock.* New York: Random House.

Watzlawick, P., Beavin, J., & Jackson, D. (1967). *Pragmatics of human communication.* New York: Norton.

CHAPTER 13

Adlerian
Family Therapy

DON DINKMEYER, JR. AND
DON DINKMEYER, SR.

DEFINITION

Adlerian family therapy is a specific intervention strategy that gives therapists concrete procedures for understanding the family. Emphasis on identifying and understanding patterns, goals, and movements within the family is productive. Therapists are leaders, formulating questions and giving suggestions that first identify and then reframe the family system.

The Adlerian approach draws from a wide range of specific assessment techniques and therapeutic suggestions. Adlerians have a strong resource in family education, which is often used as a facilitative adjunct to therapy. The therapy encourages changing the system and individual functioning within the new system.

HISTORICAL DEVELOPMENT

Evidence of predecessors to the Adlerian approach to families is minimal. Clinics established by Alfred Adler were among the first professional models for couple and family counseling. While this chapter's focus is therapy, not counseling, we wish to point out that the historical antecedent for family therapy is clearly from the same psychology. There has been a progression from family counseling and education to family therapy.

An appropriate contrast is shown by Sherman and Dinkmeyer (1987):

Adler's concerns, ideas and methods cut across what today are called structural, strategic, communications, experimental, behavioral, cognitive, multigenerational, and ego psychology approaches to the family. He called his theory Individual Psychology, referring to the essential unity of the person and of all persons within the social system. (p. xi)

Adlerian family therapy follows the principles and practices of Adler and Rudolf Dreikurs, and several of their students have also made significant contributions to Adlerian theory. The work of Harry Stack Sullivan, Karen Horney, and the rational-emotive and reality therapists are examples of contemporary therapies influenced by individual psychology.

Adler organized the first of 31 child guidance centers in and around Vienna in 1922. Counseling was done in public, open to both professionals and families and became quite popular. Family counseling conducted in these centers was the precursor of Adlerian family therapy. These centers were an important part of Adler's early work in Vienna and remained open until 1934, when events leading to World War II forced their closing.

Adlerian family counseling was done before an audience. The counselor worked with the parents at the start of the session, then talked with the child or children individually. Finally, the therapist again worked with the parents. This contrasts with Adlerian family therapy, in which all members of the family are seen simultaneously.

Dreikurs, a student of Adler, came to Chicago in 1937. He established a child guidance center at Abraham Lincoln Center and other centers across the Chicago area and trained counselors in many other parts of the world, encouraging the creation of family education centers (FECs). Centers were created in more than 20 cities throughout the United States, Canada, and in many other countries. Many of these FECs continue to operate, and new ones have been established since Dreikurs's death. In many communities, the FEC is a referral source for Adlerian family therapy. Dreikurs had a profound commitment to making Adlerian psychology available to the public. While in Chicago, he founded the North American Society of Adlerian Psychology (NASAP) and the Alfred Adler Institute of Chicago, institutions that continue to serve individual psychology throughout North America.

Dreikurs was an excellent teacher and an exemplary model of the process of public family counseling. He developed a system for identifying the purposive nature of behavior in children with four goals of behavior: (a) getting attention, (b) seeking power, (c) getting revenge and (d) displaying disability.

Dreikurs was the most dominant influence on the Adlerian family approach in the United States. *Adlerian Family Counseling: A Manual for Counseling Centers* (Dreikurs, Lowe, Sonstegard, & Corsini, 1959) became the bible of Adlerian family counseling, and it included all of the basic information necessary for establishing and running an Adlerian family counseling center. Coauthors Raymond Corsini, Raymond Lowe, and Manford Sonstegard continue their work in Adlerian family education and therapy.

Current Status

The Adlerian tradition of open-forum family counseling continues throughout North America and other strongholds developed by Dreikurs and others. This counseling often occurs as part of a family education center's service to the community. A recent issue of the NASAP *Newsletter* indicates family counseling demonstrations and training occurred in such diverse locations as Silver Springs, Maryland; Orlando, Florida; Chicago and surrounding suburbs; and Vancouver, British Columbia.

Adlerian therapists attend annual conventions of the NASAP organization, held each May in a different city of North America. The number of therapists practicing Adlerian techniques is difficult to estimate; however, it is clear that therapy continues as a major emphasis of NASAP. Two of the four annual issues of *Individual Psychology* are devoted to practice and application. Within the NASAP structure, the Clinician Interest, Adlerian Counseling and Therapy, and the Theory and Research sections all attend to issues concerning family therapy.

Influence on Other Approaches

Adlerian psychology has had a strong impact on many therapists and theories, including the schools led by Harry Stack Sullivan and Karen Horney, Albert Ellis's rational-emotive therapy, and William Glasser's reality therapy.

The influence of Adler's work cannot be minimized. A widely used textbook puts individual psychology in this perspective:

Alfred Adler was far ahead of his time, and most of the contemporary therapies have incorporated at least some of his ideas.... The Adlerian viewpoint is applicable to a wide range of human relations, including but not limited to individual and group counseling, marital and family therapy, and the alleviation of social problems. (Corey, 1986, p. 65)

Corey continues by listing contributions of Adlerian theory to the existential, person-centered, transactional analysis, behavioral, rational-emotive, and reality therapies.

TENETS OF THE MODEL

Adler was a member of Freud's Psychoanalytic Society and served as its first president. However, the Freud-Adler relationship became strained over basic differences in the emerging conceptualizations of human nature:

Adler
Social beings motivated to belong; indivisible, total personality.

Freud
Biological beings motivated by instincts; personality divided into id, ego, superego.

Adlerian theory speaks directly to family therapy. Each person is embedded in an interacting, social system. All behavior has social meaning. Change can be facilitated by working within the system of interactors. New behaviors by family members can be suggested by therapists.

Adler was the first to acknowledge the importance of the family atmosphere and the family constellation. Relationships between the parents and within the children are the family atmosphere. This includes the family system's position on such common issues as money, educa-

tion, and religion. For example, even if the family has little money, is that a major emphasis, or is their attention focused on other areas?

Family constellation is a concept applied to both the birth order and psychological order of the children; for example, constellation positions include oldest, only, middle, and youngest child. This concept is further illustrated in the Case Example later in the chapter.

Adler also believed that all behavior has a purpose and is goal directed. This goal direction is socioteleological (in a social direction). The goals are created by the individual. The therapist observes the goals to understand the direction and purpose of all transactions. Within the family, change can be created once goals are understood.

Sherman and Dinkmeyer (1987) have presented the most extensive discussion of Adlerian family therapy concepts. Within the scope of this chapter, we shall summarize their work.

It is useful to see each family member with the following characteristics: (a) indivisible, (b) social, (c) creative, (d) decision making, and (3) goal-directed beliefs and behaviors. This view implies a holistic approach that looks for patterns, unity, and consistency. These major principles can be separated in our descriptions, but the reader is reminded of the unity and whole of both theory and person.

Behavior's Social Meaning

The social context of behavior is a resource for understanding the individual. A child's poor schoolwork makes sense when another sibling's excellence in school discourages this child. The father's refusal to do any housework affects not only the mother but also all children who see noncooperation as an acceptable male value. Effective interpersonal relationships are based in socially meaningful behaviors. When behavior is appropriate, the therapist seeks to understand its meaning.

Our view of social meaning includes "social interest," the give-and-take and positive contributions between family members. The concept relates to cooperation outside families and is referred to by the German origin word, *Gemeinschaftsgefühl*. We seek to belong and make efforts to do so positively. When these fail, or we believe they do, our efforts to belong and strivings for significance continue. Misbehavior is an expression of mistaken beliefs about how to fit into the family.

The Purpose of Behavior

Simply stated, all behavior has a goal. The movement toward a goal is revealed in a person's behaviors.

For example, a 15-year-old moves with his family to an overseas post when his father receives a military transfer. He becomes sullen, his grades in the new school drop, and he becomes argumentative with his parents and siblings. One night this boy throws a brick through the base commander's front window and waits to be apprehended. What are the unifying belief and goals behind these behaviors? He wants to return to his old home. His goal is getting his family returned stateside. In his subjective belief system, all behaviors leading to this goal were justified. Because goals are created by the individual but affect others, the understanding of purposive behavior is a crucial concept for relationships. Once understood, goals can be redirected into more helpful directions.

Sometimes this concept can be made clearer by considering the alternatives.

Why do people misbehave? The most accurate and helpful explanation may be simple. However, some simple explanations about misbehavior are frequently expressed by clients and do not prove helpful to the therapist.

Four common explanations for misbehavior are (a) heredity, (b) environment, (c) ages and stages, and (d) sex-role stereotyping. If, in fact, mishbehavior *is* caused by one or more of these factors, both therapist and family are left with impractical or impotent avenues for corrections. This causal orientation is not effective. We believe the goal itself is the final cause.

Four effective explanations of goals are (a) attention, (b) power, (c) revenge, and (d) display of inadequacy. The reader is encouraged to become familiar with these goals, to know how to recognize them and how to interpret them to the families. Although presented in an educational context, the family therapist can learn about the goals and related Adlerian concepts in books by Dinkmeyer and McKay (1973, 1982, 1989); Dinkmeyer and Carlson (1984); Dinkmeyer, McKay, Dinkmeyer, Dinkmeyer, and Carlson (1985); and Dinkmeyer, McKay, and Dinkmeyer (1980).

Sherman and Dinkmeyer (1987) explain the role of simple concepts such as goal-directed behavior:

The family therapist can become aware of goals by examining her feelings or by having the members involved in the transactions examine their actions and reactions. For example, in a parent-child conflict, the parents feels annoyed and the parent devotes much time to the child. It may be the child is attempting to seek the parent's attention. However, if the parent feels challenged and would like to prove that the child cannot do that, it is likely that a power struggle will ensue. And if the parent feels hurt, the child's desire to get even will be apparent. Feeling utter frustration or the need to rescue, the parent will know that although the child is capable, he is displaying inadequacy in order to cause the parent to give in and do for him. (p. 6)

The therapeutic intervention using this basic concept is discussed later in this chapter in the Tentative Hypotheses section. The educational applications of these ideas are numerous.

Striving for Significance

All behavior attempts to overcome feelings of inferiority. We seek superiority in part because our earliest experiences surrounded us with superiors. Adults and siblings have more abilities and control. This striving for superiority mixes with feelings of inferiority as we realize our insignificance in the broadest perspective. While we are, in fact, "insignificant," many individuals have exaggerated feelings of inferiority. This leads us to the next concept, subjective perception.

Subjective Perceptions

The point of view of each family member is a fertile ground for the therapist:

It is essential that the therapist understand the perception of the family members. Each person develops and is responsible for his or her subjective view of life. People give all of their experiences meaning. This process has been described as follows: Each person writes the script, produces, directs, and acts out the roles. We are creative beings deciding our perceptions, not merely reacting. We actually often elicit responses which help us to maintain our self-perceptions, including negative ones. (Sherman & Dinkmeyer, 1987, p. 8)

Techniques for understanding the subjective perception of family members are described later in this chapter.

Adlerian Family Therapy System

Adlerian family therapy is an interactional, or systemic, treatment model. It is not an individual approach that has been adapted to family therapy.

Adlerian psychology has always emphasized work with families. Adler's earliest work included the family constellation, the family atmosphere, sibling relationships, the methods of parental training, and communication within the family. Adler's work in Vienna was with families. This work frequently was in public demonstrations of family counseling.

What happens *between* family members is crucial to the Adlerian therapist. The basic principles focus on the social meaning of behavior and purposiveness and the line of movement that reveals the meaning in transactions and interactions.

In our systems approach, we identify the following principles:

1. Each person seeks significance by *belonging* within a social system. The original social system is the family.

2. Problems brought to therapy reflect alienation or lack of worth and acceptance from others in the family.

3. The move to power or control comes from the desire of the individual and the family to protect themselves through a line of movement that is aligned with their idiosyncratic beliefs. This line of movement reflects the methods each person in the family uses to achieve their goals. The therapist is aware of how these lines of movement direct transactions. The goals of each individual as well as the family are revealed in these movements.

4. Social interest is at the core of our view of family systems. The family is di-

rected to be more concerned with the give-and-take and the concern about relationships within the family than with individual goals.

Social interest helps to move the family toward constructive, positive, useful goals for both the individual and the family. Examples of therapeutic social interest are given later in the Application and Case Example sections.

When the family has underdeveloped social interest or an antisocial feeling, they tend to direct the power against each other. The therapist helps the family become aware of their mutual interdependence. The necessity of becoming concerned with each other and learning to cooperate and work together is emphasized.

Family therapy focuses on developing social interest through interactions and overcoming alienation (lack of interest). The family is a dynamic entity created by the interaction among family members.

5. One's personality actually unfolds and is defined in the group and to the group interaction. This leads to the development of both the individual and the family lifestyle. This lifestyle, which includes beliefs and goals, is used by the therapist to help the family understand and evaluate the individual.

Understanding the family means working with the family as a group. Family interactions are guided by the goals, lifestyles, and private logic of each member as well as the group goal, lifestyle, private logic, and family atmosphere.

There are biological and assumed roles in the family. The biological place is the individual's birth-order position and gender. The assumed roles can be given names such as the good child, the initiator, the peacemaker, the victim, or the controller. These assumed roles are created by each person, based on subjective perceptions. The person tries to elicit behavior in others that confirm his or her perceptions and goals.

The family also assigns roles to members based on how the family deals with certain issues. Cooperation, conflict, and negotiation are examples of issues for which roles are assigned. Each family system is a continuous process. The family's characteristic private logic, lifestyles, goals, and methods of striving toward their unique goals and lines of movement contribute to the process.

The family is understood as a holistic system. Each member contributes as part of the whole. When one person gives more, or differently than the system requires, the system is then disrupted and must reorganize. The therapist helps the family reorganize. Each person donates to the whole in a meaningful way just as the family contributes to the development of each member.

The family interacts around nine dynamic qualities (Sherman & Dinkmeyer, 1987):

- power and decision making
- boundaries and intimacy
- coalitions
- roles
- rules
- similarities
- complementarities and differences
- myths
- patterns and styles of communication

Behavior always makes sense when viewed within the private logic of the family. How it appears to the objective observer is not as important as how it makes sense within the family's logic. For example, a family's desire for control may manifest itself in daily meetings concerning what is worn, who sees what friends, and what is done together. To the therapist, these behaviors may seem restrictive. To the family, they are logical demonstrations of their priorities.

In the Adlerian family therapy system, treatment is based on helping clients observe their behavior. Counterproductive goals are explored, then new options for behavior are identified and tested. The therapist creates a new system organized around egalitarian or democratic principles, and the therapist is the initial leader of the group. Therapeutic change takes place in the system as a result of developing new subjective perceptions, goals, information, skills, improved communication, and the reorganization of places and roles in the system.

APPLICATION

Adlerian family therapy is especially effective because it allows therapists several entry levels into the family system.

Many families present issues related to power. This therapy works because it has a specific understanding of power misbehaviors and ways to restructure the goal. For families in which power is "the" issue, this therapy can be effective. Some families can be seen as lacking adequate social interest or cooperation with each other. The Adlerian concept of social interest is particularly valuable to these families.

Finally, when clients have lack of progress, this therapy has an effective set of concepts for the therapists. There is an immediate goal or purpose to the resistance, and the family can be viewed as discouraged.

Goals of the Therapeutic Process

Therapists often see families who frame the therapeutic relationship in answers, who believe the therapist has all the solutions to their problems.

One method of examining the goals of the therapeutic process is to equip the therapist with a set of questions. Your responses to these queries will help to frame the goals of the therapeutic process (Sherman and Dinkmeyer, 1987).

1. What does each person want to happen in the family relationship?
2. What does each family member see as the main challenge or issue faced by the family?
3. Are family members aware that the purpose of the sessions is to focus on change, not merely to complain?
4. What does it feel like for each person to be a member of this family and live in this family?
5. What do the family members believe and think about each other?
6. Identify the family atmosphere. Is the family atmosphere autocratic, democratic, permissive, friendly, or hostile?
7. What are the lifestyles, games, and patterns that are revealed in the transactions between people?
8. Identify family constellation information. As you identify the parents' positions and you observe the position of siblings in the family, note whether family members often conflict with children who are in the same position. For example, if the father was an oldest child, is he having problems with the oldest child in the family?
9. Identify where the family stands on developing family cohesiveness, cooperation, community, and satisfaction. This can be accomplished through questions like the following:

a. What is the level of self-esteem? Does each family member have a sense of worth? Does each feel valuable, capable, loved, accepted?

b. What is the level of social intent? Does each family member have a sense of belonging, a feeling that they are part of the group? What is the commitment to cooperation, involvement, and sharing?

c. What is the sense of humor that exists in the family? Can family members see themselves in perspective? Can they make jokes about themselves, accept their mistakes, have the courage to be imperfect, avoid nagging supervision and defensiveness?

10. What roles do various members play in the family? Are they functioning in a variety of tasks, or does each family member have certain restricted roles to play in the family?

11. Identify the rules that govern family relationships. What are the interpersonal relationship agreements that have been established? How are they limiting the range of behaviors?

12. What are the boundaries that have been set up? How confined do members feel? How restricted are they? How much inclusion or exclusion is felt within the family? How well are individual members differentiated from the others? What kinds of coalitions are formed?

13. Who is for or resistant to change? It is important to understand who is seeking change. Are they willing to change themselves? What is the type of change they want in the family, in individuals, and in themselves? It is equally important to analyze and identify who it is that is resisting change. Clarify the purpose of the resistance and what the person gets for that resistance.

14. It is traditional to become involved in the diagnosis of family faults, weaknesses, and psychopathology. Even more important is the diagnosis of the *assets* of the family. What are the general assets of the family as unit? What are the assets of each family member? How do they blend into the family system? What resources are available in the extended family and community?

Client's Primary Responsibility

Clients are asked to change, but they cannot do this without the therapist's support. Change in the family can include (Sherman and Dinkmeyer, 1987):

- redirected uses of power;
- new understanding and insight;
- new or refined goals;
- new skill knowledge or options, particularly in communication, problem solving, and conflict resolution;
- increased courage and optimism, a sense of empowerment;
- heightened social interest;
- new roles within the family system; or
- commitment to growth and change.

Techniques Used in Treatment

Our discussion of techniques is general; therapists always adapt techniques to the family in treatment.

Influence Psychological Movement. The therapist attends to the pattern of relationships that exist in the family. This pattern consists of purposive, goal-oriented behavior. Goals may be expressed verbally and nonverbally. Observation of movement between the family members is essential. A basic Adlerian premise—"Trust only movement"—is helpful. Movement might be expressed in goals to be superior, to be excused, to be powerful, to get even, or to please.

Work with the Family Communication System. Understand how family members communicate with each other. For example, observe how family members respond to a general topic. Examples of subjects include what family members would like different in their family, what is "right" or "wrong" with a particular member or the family as a whole, and how they can cooperate. Communication patterns in response to therapist-assigned homework reveal the current state of the family's communication pattern.

The therapist determines whether communication is as equals or whether it is from a superior to an inferior. Patterns of miscommunication, misperception, or the withholding of information are also detected.

Simple communication rules can be established in the counseling relationship. They are basic to improving communication and relationships (Sherman & Dinkmeyer, 1987):

1. Speak for yourself. Don't suggest what somebody else means or thinks.
2. Speak directly to each other, not to the therapist or some other family member.
3. Do not scapegoat or blame.
4. Listen and be empathic.

5. Build the communication skills in the family.

Problems within the family may be due to the lack of communication skills. A therapist teaches these skills by modeling effective communication skills. When communication is poor, it is often necessary to intervene between members of the family and teach skills directly. Listening to feelings, being empathic, and using "I" messages are examples of communication skills. Therapists also model communication skills in their relationships with family members. In each of the five guidelines is a value or belief about effective communication.

Work on Communication Skills. Families often lack basic communication skills. These are taught through modeling and specific referrals to information and education. Feelings, emotions, beliefs, and values of the family members are affected when ineffectively communicated. For example, the father may feel used and unappreciated. The daughter may be angry. The son feels neglected. Unless they share their perceptions, feelings, and beliefs, it is impossible to work on solutions to the problems in the relationship.

Family members learn to identify what they feel. They are taught to communicate understanding of feelings and responsibility for their emotions and actions. There may have been "gunny sacking"—the feeling of holding back and not sharing. Typical responses such as "It's alright, it doesn't bother me" indicate an inability to express feelings.

The therapist's job is to help individuals identify and express what they are experiencing and feeling. Then they are taught to express anger, hostility, disappointment, or any other emotion. I messages can indicate these feelings: for example, "When you attack me, I feel very upset." Improved communication decreases the hostility and distance between family members.

I messages are one of the most effective expressions of feelings. These statements are not attacks. The I message focuses on your feelings about the other person's behavior, not the person. As you complete the statement "When...," it indicates how you are disturbed with the *behavior*. This is very different from being disturbed with the person. The description of how you feel communicates the consequence to you and lets the other person know how their actions have influenced you.

This simple process teaches family members to describe a behavior rather than blame a person. For example, "When I see you coming in late again...," (state the feeling) "I feel angry and hurt..." (state the reason or consequence)..."because then I will have to do additional work."

Another important communication skill is the ability to process feedback to each other. Processing feedback to a family member helps them understand what they are experiencing but makes no demand for change. Family members focus primarily on mutual awareness. Feedback can be either positive or negative. Either way, the challenge is to make the feedback neither critical nor blaming. Instead, feedback directly shares how the person is being experienced. The goal of feedback is to make the communication process more open, more honest, more congruent.

Feedback has become closely identified with negative or unpleasant feelings. This is only half the possible feelings and misses an important Adlerian interpretation of feedback, namely that feedback can be equated with consequences, either positive or negative. The results of a

behavior are consequences, the communication about a behavior part of the feedback. The terms "positive feedback loop" and "negative feedback loop" describe typical or desired behavior patterns.

A simple negative feedback loop is as follows: A mother and father complain that an 11-year-old only child acts immature. They frequently scold him for leaving a messy room, throwing temper tantrums, and refusing to do household chores. The goal of the boy's behavior appears to be to engage adults in power struggles. Parents spend a great deal of time fighting the boy's decisions. The consequences of these interactions are that the boy does not feel powerful or accepted by his parents and that he is discouraged over any ways to exert his influence. In this sense, the negative feedback between the parents and child repeats itself in an endless loop, awaiting therapist intervention. It needs to be done tentatively. For example, "When you are not getting the work accomplished, it seems you don't care about helping the family."

The family learns to encourage and affirm each other, to increase each other's self-esteem. The therapist and family recognize each family member's strengths and what is positive about them, then communicate acceptance. Each positive statement provides feedback and builds self-esteem, affirming that each member is valued.

Affirming is an indication of valuing the family member: "I appreciated your taking time to help me with the cleaning. It helps to know I can count on you" or "I enjoyed watching your basketball game." In this way, positive feedback loops are initiated.

Focus on the Real Issue. It is often challenging to determine which of the family symptoms are most important. Adlerian therapists observe the symptoms for the purpose of determining the family members' goals, beliefs, and priorities. Once discovered, it is important to identify how these goals, beliefs, or priorities are used. Symptoms become consistent in their movement toward a goal or purpose.

For example, on the surface a conflict in the family may indicate: members don't get in on time—Dad is always late; the daughter breaks curfew; the 7-year-old doesn't come in when called for dinner. This family does not have to be screened for a neurological inability to tell time. The real issue may be power or deciding for oneself.

Another surface issue may be children getting their homework done when the real issue is being in charge or making certain people do things your way. Therapists may mistakenly focus on the symptom, not the issue. Other therapies may take symptoms and use them as the basic foothold for intervention. It is more useful to see symptoms as symbols, not solutions.

When the therapist helps the family work on the real or underlying issue, it is possible to solve subsequent problems efficiently. Instead of solving a continuing series of smaller problems, the real issue of control, decision making, or power is discussed. Often, more than one real issue is involved. Continue to identify real issues and do not become sidetracked by symptoms.

Encouragement. Encouragement focuses on increasing self-esteem and the feelings of worth of the family members. Empathy is also an example of therapist encouragement. The therapist demonstrates this by identifying assets and strengths instead of focusing primarily on problems and weaknesses.

The therapist redefines the reported symptoms or problems into positive terms. An apparently negative trait can be turned into a positive one. For example, when one family member complains about passiveness, it can be redefined as the person being relaxed. A stubborn person can be seen as determined, a more positive perception. This approach does not deny the negative expressions of the characteristic. It does understand that for all negative movement, there is a potential for a positive expression of that same goal. This is a profoundly enlightening perception, once the therapist understands and utilizes the perceptual alternatives.

Many families are discouraged when they seek family therapy. The family is in conflict and has few solutions to these challenges. Encouragement increases the therapist's leverage into the family system. This concept can be broken into simple and direct components. Adlerian family therapy is encouraging through the following characteristics (Sherman & Dinkmeyer, 1987):

1. Each person in the family feels he or she is listened to.
2. Members of the family are empathic and understanding. They not only hear feelings, but they indicate that they hear feelings.
3. There is a focus on strengths, assets, and resources. An emphasis is on identifying strengths that can be used to foster family and individual growth.
4. Development of perceptual alternatives is fostered first by the therapist and then by family members. Members learn to recognize that there are positive ways to look at any situation.
5. A sense of humor helps the family see themselves in perspective. It en-

ables them to laugh at some of their mistakes, foibles, and attempts to overpower each other.

6. Families are encouraged to focus on efforts, contributions, and any attempt to move in a positive direction.

Paradoxical Intention. Paradoxical intention encourages the person to produce the symptom, even though it is an undesirable behavior. The person is encouraged to become even more symptomatic. This reframing of the symptom changes the meaning given to a situation. The family member comes to learn the capacity to start or to stop that symptom.

This technique could be introduced by saying, "I have an idea that would help you. Would you be willing to try something that might seem very different but might be helpful?" Then the therapist suggests that the person practice some symptom they are complaining about. For example, if it is fighting with another family member, ask them to argue at a specific time, for exactly 2 minutes.

Role Reversal. Family members may not understand how behavior is perceived by others. By using role reversal, each person acts as if he or she was the person with whom they are in conflict. They are asked to express as clearly and honestly as possible how they believe that person sees the relationship. The persons who are reversing roles then have the opportunity to react. From their perception, accurate or inaccurate statements are reviewed. Through role reversal, they learn to experience what it feels like to be in the other person's shoes.

A simple example of role reversal is to ask an adult to reverse positions with one of the children or teenagers. This permits each family member to give their perception of the "real" role that the family member provides to the system. In addition, it allows each person in the reversal to express their subjective perception of the other's role. Role reversal can be a powerful, active therapeutic technique.

Structure and Promote Direct Interaction. Family therapy provides an opportunity to apply the group process. Family members in therapy learn to interact directly with each other. For example, a father will make complaints about his son to the therapist. The therapist must be certain to avoid the role of "translator." The therapist only needs to say, "Please tell your son directly." This basic change in the interaction will be useful in all relationships, not just father and son. It teaches family members to process feedback directly, the most effective way to stimulate change.

Family members need specific skills such as family meetings and encouragement meetings. Family meetings provide an opportunity for all members of the family to participate in decision making. The meeting is an opportunity for each family member:

- to be heard;
- to express positive feelings;
- to give encouragement;
- to agree on a fair distribution of chores;
- to express concerns, feelings, and complaints;
- to help settle conflicts and deal with issues; and
- to participate in planning family leisure activities.

Guidelines for family meetings include the following points (Dinkmeyer & McKay, 1989):

1. Establish a specific weekly meeting time.
2. Rotate the office of the chairperson.
3. Establish and maintain time limits.
4. Be sure all members have a chance to offer ideas.
5. Encourage everyone to bring up issues.
6. Don't permit meetings to become simply gripe sessions.
7. Distribute the family work fairly.
8. Plan some family fun.
9. Use encouragement and communication.

Resistance and Goal Alignment. Resistance in family therapy is a lack of a common goal between the therapist and family members. When the goals move toward a common purpose, change is likely. Family therapy becomes complicated and ineffective when, for example, the mother is concerned about the child's academic achievement, the father is pushing music, and the son and daughter are interested in bigger allowances. In this set of apparently confused purposes, the therapist helps the family to find areas of agreement and compromise.

The purpose of resistance must be identified. Although family members may have different resistant behaviors, it is likely the family agrees on the purpose of its resistance. Although family dynamics can be complicated, it is helpful to see if resistance has a simple explanation. For this purpose, the previously discussed goals of misbehavior are helpful.

Tentative Hypotheses. The therapist makes tentative hypotheses concerning the purpose of a family member's behavior. They are tentative in the sense that the therapist indicates "Could it be...?"

or "Is it possible...?" The person never feels accused or diagnosed. The hypothesis helps investigate what is happening at the moment in order to create insight into behavior. Disclosure through these tentative hypotheses is not concerned with the cause of the behavior but only with the *purpose* of the behavior.

Tentative hypotheses are often offered with the therapist's diagnosis of goal-directed misbehavior. If incorrect, the tentative framing of the diagnosis reduces conflict or misperception.

Setting Tasks and Obtaining Commitments. Progress in therapy can be measured by behavior changes. Therapists can help families define tasks and elicit commitments. This begins with the first meeting. Each member states their goals and what they would like to change. The more specific the task is, the more readily the task can be accomplished. Members then are requested to make specific contracts and to share progress reports at the next meeting. The cycle of tasks and commitments becomes a method of moving toward their goals.

Conflict Resolution. All conflicts are interpersonal, and problems in families are always relationship problems. The family therapist needs a specific conflict resolution process for conflicts. We believe that the most effective process for resolving conflicts is Dreikurs's (1971) four-step process:

1. *Show mutual respect by neither fighting nor giving in.* The principle is that you neither overpower nor give in. Instead, conflict is resolved on the basis of understanding and respect for each other's point of view.
2. *Pinpoint the issues.* This means identify the issue behind the com-

plaint. The issue may be a threat to one's status or prestige or the feeling that you are being treated unfairly. Deal with what appears to be the real issue.

3. *Seek areas of agreement.* Instead of looking to another member of the family, concentrate on what you are willing to do. Do not demand that your partner change. Agree to cooperate.

4. *Mutually participate in decisions.*

Summarizing. Summarizing focuses on perceptions and themes and can occur during or at the end of the session. Summaries can be an indicator of the family's progress on issues. If each family member is asked to complete the sentence "I learned...," the summary gives equal time to all. It is a two-way communication. The therapist learns what is important to each person, and each has a chance to verbalize their learning.

The therapist may decide to have a summary at the close of the session and ask family members to describe what they have been learning. The therapist also recapitulates and perhaps clarifies the commitments made that are to be carried out by the next meeting.

CASE EXAMPLE

The following brief case example illustrates some of the dynamics and techniques of family therapy from the Adlerian perspective.

Mr. and Mrs. W are in their late 30s. They present in therapy with acting-out children and marital concerns. They have three children: two boys from Mrs. W's previous marriage (L, 14, and J, 6) and a daughter, S, age 2. They have been married for 3 years after a 2-year courtship. Mr. W had not been married previously, and Mrs. W's first marriage ended after 12 years, 3 years prior to beginning their present marriage.

Mr. and Mrs. W report little peace at home, frequent arguments about disciplining J, and concerns about S's temper tantrums. Both agree they would like a more peaceful climate in their home.

Initial Interview

The family came to the first interview after a telephone call by the mother. She reported on the intake form that she wanted "anything to help us with J" and that "we need to be less argumentative between the adults" and "concerned about S's temper tantrums and don't want her to grow up that way."

Excerpts from the initial interview:

Therapist: How can I help you?
Mrs. W: Well, I don't know where to start. There's a lot of things.... We seem to be less happy than before... but we love each other and there are too many fights....
Mr. W (interrupts): She and I fight about how to discipline J. He doesn't act his age and I am trying to make him grow up. Sometimes he is less mature than S!
(L laughs, J hits L.)
Therapist: J, what do you think about all this?
(J says nothing; L interrupts the silence.)
L: He's usually pretty good, but sometimes he doesn't pay attention to when Mom or A [Mr. W's first name] tells him to do something. He doesn't obey.
Mrs. W: Don't speak for him, that's part of the problem.
Therapist: J, what do you think about this?
(J again says nothing.)
Therapist: OK, what else is going on?
Mrs. W: S has major temper tantrums. She's real moody and doesn't seem to cooperate as much as she did 2 months ago. I think ...well, I'm not sure I should say this in front of him, but I think that J's bad habits are rubbing off on her.

Later in the initial session, the therapist asks each person what they would like to see happen in the therapy.

Mrs. W: The boys should stop their fighting, and S should have less temper tantrums. We [Mr. and Mrs. W] should be calmer and have fewer arguments, and we should have more fun as a family.

Mr. W: Things should be different. Whatever it takes, I'm interested in making it different. This is no good.

L: J shouldn't get into as much trouble at home, and we shouldn't argue so that S doesn't have bad examples.

(J doesn't respond.)

The Assessment Process

Family constellation information revealed that both parents were first-born children. Mrs. W is the oldest of three, with a sister 3 years younger and a brother 5 years younger. She was raised in the South, was the first in her family to graduate college, married immediately thereafter, and moved to the Midwest, where she has lived in the same town where her husband was raised. Paradoxically, he did not have close ties to his family, and she frequently complained about his not being close to her family or his unwillingness to accept or visit her family. For Mrs. W, family is important and family harmony is paramount.

Mr. W is the older of three, with a brother 3 years younger and a sister 9 years younger. He was raised in the Midwest and completed an advanced degree. He had not married until his mid-30s. Family interactions were normal but not particularly close.

The W family moved to this community within the last 6 months as the result of a job transfer for Mr. W. Although Mrs. W has worked in the past, she is currently not working by choice and spending days home with her daughter.

The family appears to be struggling to establish a routine. The day begins early with the boys preparing for school, but the bus is never on time. This allows J to justify his delay of dressing, watching television, not eating breakfast, and refusing to go for the bus if he has not finished breakfast. On numerous occasions, Mrs. W has had to drive him to school after missing the bus. L then complains this is unfair and embarrassing.

Sometimes Mr. W participates in these scenes by trying to control with orders, threats, and later demands toward his wife. However, his job often takes him out of town, making it Mrs. W's responsibility to handle these situations. When asked how many times out of the last 10 school days have been bad when preparing to go to school, Mrs. W reported seven.

S then becomes Mrs. W's challenge for the daytime. She constantly demands attention from Mrs. W, whines, and is easily frustrated when playing with toys. There are no other children her age in the immediate neighborhood, and the family has been unable to place her in any daycare setting.

When Mr. W returns from business trips, he and Mrs. W wait until the children go to bed before arguing over the family situation.

Therapist Explanation

The family system is being controlled by J through his goals of attention and power. He gets his way both by actively challenging any attempts to gain his cooperation and by passively refusing to participate in the family therapy.

J has succeeded in creating some conflict between his parents. Mrs. W feels tension because J's behavior is unacceptable, but she feels sorry for him because of the changes in his family life. Mr. W has done all he can to establish some boundaries with J, but he is cautious because he realizes his actions and suggestions are seen as a personal criticism of Mrs. W.

L becomes the cooperative one, and J's behavior is to L's advantage because it makes him look good. Thus, there is a benefit for L in J continuing the bad behavior. L is relatively uninvolved in S's life because of the 12-year age difference.

The Change Process

The focus was on helping Mr. and Mrs. W restore the relationship that brought them to the marriage. They need to do things together when he is home. While there has been an emphasis on building togetherness in the family, there now needs to be a focus on the marital relationship. When this has been strengthened, the Ws will be in a better position to work on the problems with the children.

The therapist provided some simple but powerful exercises to strengthen the marital relationship. These included regular dialogue and encouragement meetings. Mr. and Mrs. W need to develop a common set of parenting principles. They were referred to a parent education course that helped to make them more aware of their children's behavior. The therapist spent time in the early sessions showing how the ideas could be directly applied to the children. The therapist also suggested he would like to see the family begin family meetings, as soon as they were comfortable with the principles and understood the family meeting process.

The family therapy sessions focused on helping build cohesiveness and cooperation. As Mr. and Mrs. W developed a

more effective marital system through the dialogue and encouragement meetings—as well as by spending more quality time together, apart from the children—they felt more united and positive in their approach to the children and the family atmosphere.

The therapist also observed any non-verbal behavior between the boys and used tentative hypotheses—"Could it be you are doing that to...?" (alluding to power or attention getting). The therapist also helped the boys explore more active and constructive ways to get attention and power.

As the family meetings began, there were more opportunities for the family to explore how to increase cooperation and satisfaction. Through the combination of family therapy and regular family meetings, a noticeable improvement in cooperation and responsibility developed.

EVALUATION

A unique comparison between Adlerian family therapy and five other major family therapies is presented in Sherman and Dinkmeyer's *Systems of Family Therapy* (1987). Five contributing Adlerian authors who were trained in five other theories compared and contrasted that theory with Adlerian psychology. The theories are Satir, rational-emotive therapy (RET), structural family therapy, strategic family therapy, and MRI. (The MRI Interactional View is based on a systemic circular process derived from cybernetic theory which focuses on the processes of communication within human systems.) Authors were asked to evaluate 66 items for the degree of emphasis of that item within the theory. Items were in three major areas: major concepts, change, and techniques. Within these 66 items, there was general agreement on 74.3% of the items between Adlerian and the other five theories.

We now present areas in which there was *not* a significant degree of general agreement and share the Adlerian perspective on these points. For example, there was not a high level of agreement on the role of insight in these six therapies. Adlerian and RET strongly stress insight; Satir puts a moderate emphasis on this concept; and MRI, strategic, and structural give no significance to this concept. Insight and cognitive change are important to Adlerian therapists. Whenever possible, therapy should develop insight so that the family sees the situation from the new perspective.

Another area in which there appears to be disagreement between these six therapies is the role of growth as a primary objective of therapy. Both Adlerian and Satir place a high level of theoretical importance on this concept. Strategic and RET place a low level of emphasis on growth: MRI and structural, no emphasis. As clearly outlined in this chapter, education and growth are basic concepts in Adlerian family therapy.

There were 22 techniques within these six family therapies. Of these, only 2 seem to have a different priority within Adlerian family therapy. The role of interpretation and confrontation is important for Adlerian family therapy as well as for RET. For the other therapies, it appears to have less importance.

Finally, the role of touching as a therapeutic technique has a low emphasis within Adlerian and MRI, while it has no apparent role in strategic, structural, and RET. In Satir's approach, however, it has a high level of significance.

This analysis of the similarities between the six family therapies showed that Adlerian theory was in general agreement with 92.4% of the five other theories and their constructs. From this statistic, one might conclude that Adlerian family therapy has a high degree of correlation with other therapeutic interventions.

SUMMARY

The family therapy field has a wide number of theories and substantive models for the therapist. Adlerian psychology has a long tradition and established presence in both education and therapy. It is the substantive predecessor for many other theories and is distinctly similar to major family therapy approaches. Within this chapter, we have given the reader a basic structure for future investigation and application of Adlerian family therapy.

ANNOTATED SUGGESTED READINGS

Dinkmeyer, D., Dinkmeyer, D., Jr., & Sperry, L. (1987). *Adlerian counseling and psychotherapy* (2nd ed.). Columbus, OH: Merrill Publishing.

A thorough treatment of the theoretical stages of Adlerian counseling. A new integration of Adlerian psychopathology and the DSM-III-R is included, as are phases of the counseling process. Special chapters describe counseling in these areas: children and adolescents, health care, group, family, and marriage.

Dreikurs, R., Lowe, R., Sonstegard, M., & Corsini, R. J. (Eds.). *Adlerian family counseling: A manual for counseling centers.* Eugene: University of Oregon Press.

The original American publication focusing entirely on Adlerian family counseling. It sets forth details for the development of a family counseling center.

Manaster, G. J., & Corsini, R. J. (1982). *Individual psychology: Theory & practice.* Itasca, IL: F. E. Peacock.

The basic Adlerian theory as it relates to the development and maintenance of personality. A theory of therapy and the counseling process are included with some attention to family and group counseling and therapy.

Sherman, R., & Dinkmeyer, D. (1987). *Systems of family therapy: An Adlerian integration.* New York: Brunner/Mazel.

The only major definitive text on the Adlerian system of family therapy, covering family dynamics, the structure of the therapy, and the basics for change. It also includes a set of chapters describing the relationship between various schools of thought and the Adlerian system. These schools of thought include: Satir, MRI, strategic family therapy, structural family therapy, and Ellis's rational-emotive therapy.

Sweeney, T. (1989). *Adlerian counseling: A practical approach for a new decade* (3rd ed.). Muncie, IN: Accelerated Development.

The basic Adlerian constructs, plus detailed information on both natural and logical consequences, encouragement, goals of disruptive behavior, some goals of adolescence, and family counseling and consultation.

REFERENCES

Corey, G. (1986). *Theory and practice of counseling and psychotherapy* (3rd ed.). Monterey, CA: Brooks/Cole.

Dinkmeyer, D., & Carlson, J. (1984). *Time for a better marriage.* Circle Pines, MN: American Guidance Service.

Dinkmeyer, D., & McKay, G. D. (1989). *The parent's handbook* (rev. ed.). Circle Pines, MN: American Guidance Service.

Dinkmeyer, D., McKay, G. D., Dinkmeyer, D., Jr., Dinkmeyer, J., and Carlson, J. (1985). *PREP for effective family living.* Circle Pines, MN: American Guidance Service.

Dinkmeyer, D., & McKay, G. D. (1973). *Raising a responsible child.* New York: Simon & Schuster.

Dinkmeyer, D., & McKay, G. D. (1982). *STEP/teen parent's guide.* Circle Pines, MN: American Guidance Service.

Dinkmeyer, D., McKay, G. D., & Dinkmeyer, D., Jr. (1980). *Systematic training for effective teaching.* Circle Pines, MN: American Guidance Service.

Dreikurs, R., Lowe, R., Sonstegard, M., & Corsini, R. J. (Eds.). (1959). *Adlerian family counseling: A manual for counseling centers.* Eugene: University of Oregon Press.

Dreikurs, R. (1971). *Social equality: The challenge of today.* Chicago: Henry Regnery Company.

Sherman, R., & Dinkmeyer, D. (1987). *Systems of family therapy: An Adlerian integration.* New York: Brunner/Mazel.

CHAPTER 14

Rational-Emotive
Family Therapy

ALBERT ELLIS

DEFINITION

Rational-emotive family therapy follows the principles and practice of rational-emotive therapy (RET), a theory of personality and a method of psychotherapy developed by Albert Ellis, a clinical psychologist, in the 1950s. RET holds that when family members become emotionally disturbed or upset (e.g., anxious, depressed, hostile, self-pitying, or behaviorally dysfunctional) at Point C (emotional and behavioral consequence) following a significant activating experience or activating event (Point A), A may significantly contribute to but actually does not "cause" C. Instead, disturbed consequences (in individuals and in families) are largely (though not exclusively) created by B—the family members' belief system. When undesirable or disruptive consequences (C) occur, these can largely or mainly be traced to people's irrational beliefs (iB's)—absolutistic or *must*urbatory or unrealistic demands, commands, or expectations on themselves, others, and/or world conditions. When these irrational beliefs (iB's) are effectively disputed (at Point D) by challenging them logically, empirically, and rationally, the disturbed consequences are minimized or disappear and seldom recur (Ellis, 1957, 1962, 1988, 1989a, 1989b; Ellis & Dryden, 1987; Ellis & Harper, 1961, 1975).

Ellis is the father of RET and the grandfather of cognitive-behavioral therapy (CBT). More than 10 years after he started practicing, speaking, and writing about RET in 1955, several other cognitive-behavioral therapists began practicing and writing about various kinds of CBT—especially Albert Bandura; Aaron T. Beck; Marvin Goldfried and Gerald Davison; Neil Jacobson; Arnold Lazarus; Michael Mahoney; Maxie Maultsby, Jr.; Donald Meichenbaum; and Victor Raimy. General RET and CBT are similar, but preferential RET differs from CBT in that it is more forceful, more emotive, more multimodal, and more philosophic than CBT (Ellis & Dryden, 1987).

HISTORICAL DEVELOPMENT

Precursors

The philosophic origins of RET partly go back to Stoic philosophers, particularly Epictetus and Marcus Aurelius. Although most of the early Stoic writings, such as those of Zeno of Citium, have been lost, their main gist comes through Epictetus, who in the first century AD wrote in *The Enciridion* (or *Manual*), "People are disturbed not by things, but by the view which they take of them" (1890, p. 13). His disciple, the Roman emperor Marcus Aurelius, advanced Stoicism in his famous *Meditations*; and various philosophers such as Spinoza and Bertrand Russell endorsed some of its principles in the Western world. Shakespeare beautifully rephrased Epictetus in *Hamlet*: "There is nothing either good or bad, but thinking makes it so." Several ancient Taoist and Buddhist thinkers also emphasized two of its main points: Human emotions are basically ideogenic in their origin; and to control or change even intense feelings, one had better change one's ideas. Sigmund Freud, in his first work with Joseph Breur (Freud, 1965) noted that "a great number of hysterical phenomena, probably more than we suspect today, are ideogenic" (p. 10). Unfortunately, in his later writings he often talked about emotional processes vaguely and implied that they exist in their own right, divorced from thinking.

The main modern psychotherapist who antedated RET theory and practice was Alfred Adler, who wrote, "I am convinced that *a person's behavior springs from his ideas*" and "The individual. . . does not relate himself to the outside world in a predetermined manner, as is often assumed. He relates himself always according to his own interpretation of himself and of his present problem. . . .It is his attitude toward life which determines his relationship to the outside world" (Adler, 1964, p. 19). Adler (1931) put the ABC or stimulus-organism-response theory of human disturbance quite neatly:

No experience is a cause of success or failure. We do not suffer from the shock of our experience—the so-called *trauma*—but we make out of them just what suits our purposes. We are *self-determined* by the meaning we give to our experiences; and there is probably something of a mistake always involved when we take particular experiences as the basis of our future life. Meanings are not determined by situations, but we determine ourselves by the meanings we give to situations. (p. 24)

In his first book on individual psychology, Adler's motto was *omnia ex opinione suspensa sunt* (everything depends on opinion) (Adler, 1964, p. 19). It would be hard to state the essential tenets of RET more succinctly and accurately.

Other important precursors of the rational-emotive approach were Paul Dubois, Jules Dejerine, and Ernest Gaukler, who used persuasive psychotherapy with their clients in the first decade of the 20th century. Alexander Herzberg, a renegade psychoanalyst, was one of the inventors of homework assignments. Hippolyte Bernheim, Andrew Salter, and many other therapists employed hypnosis and suggestion in a highly active-directive manner. Frederick Thorne created what he once called directive therapy. Karen Horney, Wilhelm Stekel, Franz Alexander, Thomas French, John Dollard, Neal Miller, Viktor Frankl, Erich Fromm, and Lewis Wolberg all practiced forms of psychoanalytically oriented psychotherapy that diverged so far in practice from the mainstream of Freudian theory that they more properly can be classified in the active-directive therapy column and can in many ways be identified with RET.

In addition, a number of therapists during the early 1950s, when RET was first being formulated, independently began to arrive at theories and methodologies that significantly overlap with the methods outlined by Ellis (1957, 1962, 1971, 1973, 1988; Ellis & Abrahms, 1978; Ellis & Dryden, 1987; Ellis & Grieger, 1977; Ellis & Whiteley, 1979). These include Eric Berne, Rogelio Diaz-Guerrera, Jerome Frank, George Kelly, Abraham Low, E. Lakin Phillips, Julian Rotter, and Joseph Wolpe.

Beginnings

Ellis started to develop marriage and family therapy during the late 1940s and to create RET in the early 1950s, after he practiced classical psychoanalysis and analytically oriented psychotherapy, which he found ineffective for treating individuals, couples, and families. He found that no matter how much insight his clients gained or how well they understood the events of their early childhood and saw how these "caused" their present disturbances, they only improved partly or inelegantly and still retained strong tendencies to create new symptoms. He realized that this was because they were not merely indoctrinated with irrational ideas about how perfect they should be and how ideal the world must be but that they actively *invented, accepted,* and *kept reindoctrinating* themselves with these childish notions.

Ellis also discovered that as he pressed his clients to acknowledge and surrender their basic irrational philosophies, they often resisted doing so—not because, as the Freudians hypothesized, they hated the therapist or were still resisting their parents but because they *naturally* tended to musturbate: to demand absolutistically (a) that they do well and win others' approval; (b) that other people act considerately and fairly; and (c) that environmental conditions be unfrustrating and gratifying. Ellis concluded that humans, just because they are human (and not because they are reared in specific family-centered ways) tend to have strong, irrational, empirically unvalidatable ideas; that they are self-talking, self-evaluating, and self-sustaining creatures; and that for biological as well as social reasons, they often take simple preferences (such as desires for love, approval, success, and pleasure) and foolishly define them as "needs" or "necessities." They especially tend to do this when they live intimately, in marital or family groups; therefore, their "neu-

rotic" interactions are partially intrinsic to family living but are also part and parcel of the biologically based premises that they almost always bring to intimate relationships (Ellis, 1976a, 1988; Ellis & Dryden, 1987; Ellis, Sichel, Yeager, Di-Mattia, & DiGiuseppe, 1989).

By experimenting with different therapeutic procedures during his analytic and postanalytic years, Ellis also discovered that deep-seated human irrationality is rarely unblocked by most therapeutic techniques. Because individuals and family members are so habituated to their crooked thinking and dysfunctional behavior (and so prone to invent new prejudices and illogicalities), weak methods are unlikely to budge them. Passive, nondirective methodologies (such as reflection of feeling and free association) rarely help them change. Warmth and support often enable clients to live more "happily" with unrealistic notions. Suggestion and "positive thinking" sometimes encourage them to cover up and live more "successfully" with underlying self-devaluations but seldom help them eliminate these notions. Abreaction and catharsis frequently enable them to feel better but tend to reinforce rather than decrease their unrealistic demands. Classic desensitizing sometimes relieves clients of anxieties but does not elegantly undermine their anxiety-arousing basic philosophies (Ellis, 1972, 1988; Ellis & Yeager, 1989).

What works more effectively, Ellis found in the early days of RET, is an active-directive, cognitive-emotive-behavioristic uprooting of clients' major self-defeating value systems—an attack not directed against clients but against their *irrational beliefs.* The essence of psychotherapy—in group, family, and individual settings—is full tolerance of people as *individuals* combined with a strong, persistent campaign against their self-defeating ideas, traits, and performances.

When still using psychoanalysis, Ellis began to do conjoint marital counseling and family therapy but found these techniques to be much more efficient and less time-consuming as he replaced analytic with rational-emotive methods. For RET family therapy, as will be shown, not only gets to the fundamental philosophic premises that underlie people's disillusionment with themselves and their marital arrangements, but it also uses cognitive, emotive, and behavioral methods of teaching them communication, sexual, relating, and other skills that will help them enhance their family relationships.

Current Status

The Institute for Rational-Emotive Therapy, a nonprofit scientific and educational organization, was founded in 1959 to teach the principles of rational living and to train therapists. With headquarters in New York City and branches in several cities in the United States as well as in England, Italy, Holland, Germany, India, Canada, Mexico, Australia, and other countries, the Institute conducts activities to disseminate the rational-emotive approach, including (a) adult education courses; (b) postgraduate training programs for professionals; (c) moderate-cost clinics for individual, group, and marital therapy; (d) special workshops, seminars, practica, intensives, and marathons for professionals and the public given regularly in various parts of the world; and (e) the publication and distributions of books, monographs, pamphlets, recordings, and the *Journal of Rational-Emotive and Cognitive-Behavior Therapy*.

The Institute has a register of hundreds of psychotherapists who have received training certificates in RET, including in RET family therapy. In addition, hundreds of other therapists mainly follow RET principles, and a still greater number use some of the major aspects of RET in their individual, group, and family work. Cognitive restructuring, employed by almost all cognitive-behavioral therapists (and many other therapists) today, mainly consists of RET.

Research Studies. Many articles and books evidence the effectiveness of RET and related cognitive-behavioral therapies with all kinds of neurotic, borderline, and even psychotic individuals. Clinical case studies and anecdotal testimonials, however, have a minor place in the scientific evaluation of a school of psychotherapy. Fortunately, although RET is one of the newer major therapeutic systems, it already has led to the publication of over several hundred outcome studies, most of which have shown that it seems to help various kinds of clients improve significantly more than other modes of therapies or no-therapy control groups. Another large group of related studies also show that rationality scales derived from Ellis's (1962) basic irrational ideas have acceptable reliability and validity (Baisden, 1980; DiGiuseppe, Miller, & Trexler, 1979; Ellis & Whiteley, 1979; Engels & Diekstra, 1986, Haaga & Davison, 1989; Jorm, 1987; McGovern & Silverman, 1984; Miller & Berman, 1983; Smith & Glass, 1977).

In addition, literally hundreds of controlled experiments have been done that lend support to the main theoretical principles of RET as well as to its most important clinical hypotheses (Ellis & Whiteley, 1979). Following Ellis's lead, several closely related cognitive-behavioral therapies have been devised, and hundreds of studies confirming their effectiveness have now been published (Haaga & Davison, 1989).

Although cognitive-behavioral therapy is no panacea and has a large number of theories and practices that have by no means been firmly validated, it has the advantage of having its main tenets stated in a fairly easily definable and testable manner. Consequently, it has recently sparked more research studies by far than any other form of treatment except its close ally, behavioral therapy.

The use of controlled studies applied to validating the rational-emotive and cognitive-behavioral approach to family therapy has also produced some findings that tend to show that RET and CBT can be used effectively in helping couples and families with emotional problems. Outcome studies that support the RET and CBT hypotheses include papers by Eisenberg and Zingle (1975); Elliott (1979); Freeman (1983); Glass, Gottman, and Shmurak (1976); Gottman (1979); Jacobson (1979); Jacobson and Margolin (1979); Margolin and Weiss (1978); McClellan and Stieper (1971); Saxon (1980); Steed (1971); and Tsoi-Hoshmand (1976).

The first major books applying the principles of RET to marriage and family problems were *How to Live with a "Neurotic"* (Ellis, 1957) and *A Guide to Successful Marriage* (Ellis & Harper, 1961). Subsequently, many articles have been published that demonstrate how RET can be efficiently applied to marriage and family therapy and to parenting problems (Ellis, 1978a, 1978b) and a number of books on RET and marital and family issues have appeared, including those by Ard and Ard (1976); Blazier (1975); Hauck (1967); Ellis, Wolfe, and Moseley (1966); and Ellis et al. (1989).

In the specialized area of sex therapy, which is an integral part of marriage and family therapy, RET has been one of the prime influences in sparking the modern revolution in sex, love, and marital attitudes and in the treatment of sexual problems. Although William Masters and Virginia Johnson, with much good reason, receive most of the credit for modern sex therapy, the cognitive-behavioral approach to sex problems was largely pioneered by Ellis in the 1950s and 1960s in such books as *Sex without Guilt* (1958), *The Art and Science of Love* (1960), *Sex and the Liberated Man* (1976c; original edition, 1963); and *The Intelligent Woman's Guide to Dating and Mating* (1979; original edition, 1963). As the 20th century draws to a close, the rational-emotive and cognitive-behavioral multimodal approach to the treatment of sex problems has preempted the narrower psychodynamic behavioral approaches. It has led to the outstanding work in sex therapy of Arnold Lazarus, Joseph LoPiccolo, Lonnie Barbach, Janet L. Wolfe, Jack S. Annon, Bernie Zilbergeld, and other authorities.

TENETS OF THE MODEL

Basic Concepts

Although regular RET and RET-oriented family therapy are, as far as the use of multimodal techniques is concerned, exceptionally integrative, they are based on a set of philosophical and clinical premises that guide the therapist in selecting which of a large number of possible methods will be used with most clients and with the specific family members who are now being treated. The basic theory of RET consequently includes the following hypotheses about human nature and how it leads to individual and family disturbance and to potential personality and social change.

Biological and Social Interactionism. Humans are born with strong biological predispositions, including the powerful tendency to be gregarious and to have sex-love relationships and to live in some kind of family groups. One of the strongest of their innate tendencies is to be teachable or suggestible and to easily pick up, from their early childhood onward, the customs and traditions of significant others with whom they live, especially the members of their original families. Once they learn certain "correct" social standards and preferences (e.g., to eat, dress, and relate in "proper" ways in the family and group in which they are reared), they almost all have strong inherent tendencies to convince themselves not only that it is preferable or desirable for them to follow these ways but also to raise these into absolutist, perfectionistic demands and musts. They are easily influenced to accept the *must*urbatory thinking of others; but they also have their own creative and inventive proclivities to overgeneralize and absolutize. How they finally behave, in self-helping or self-defeating ways, is a product of their inherited biological predispositions and their (also partly innate) susceptibility to early and later environmental influences.

Vulnerability to Disturbance. Virtually all people, for biological as well as sociological reasons, are easily disturbable. This means that they frequently think, emote, and behave in ways that are against their own chosen interest and that sabotage the social groups in which they choose to live. Their main goals or values, which they are innately and environmentally prone to adopt (consciously or unconsciously) are:

- to stay alive;
- to enjoy themselves when they are alone;
- to live in a social group and to get along amicably and successfully with others;
- to engage in satisfactory intimate and often sustained affectionate, sex-love relationships with a selected few members of the other or their own sex;
- to work productively at some absorbing endeavor(s) that will enable them to survive and enjoy some degree of comfortable living; and
- to participate in recreational, esthetic, physical, creative, and other pursuits that will add to their pleasure and satisfaction.

They frequently, however, sabotage some or all of these major goals by their own grandiose, unrealistic, absolutist thinking and by the inappropriate feelings and self-sabotaging behavior that is an almost invariant concomitant of this kind of thinking.

Cognitive-Emotive-Behavioral Interactionism. Humans very rarely, if ever, have pure thoughts, emotions, or behaviors that do not interact or transact with each other. What we call their "thinking" is profoundly related to and influenced by their desiring (e.g., to stay alive and to feel happy) and their behaving (eating, living with others, and working). What we call their "emoting" is strongly influenced by their cognitions (evaluating the way others treat them as "good" or "bad," as "right" or "wrong") and by their actions (eating certain foods and exercising or not exercising). What we call their "behavior" is importantly pervaded by their thoughts ("I think that I am doing the wrong thing and that is horrible!") and by their emotions (feelings of love or hatred for a person or an event). When we therefore label the members of a family (or entire family) "emotionally disturbed," we really mean that they have disordered self- and society-defeating feelings, thoughts, and actions.

Choice in Disturbance and in Personality Change. In spite of the fact that all human behavior is partly "caused" or "determined" by innate factors (hereditary predispositions) and by external conditions (environmental influences) that are beyond anyone's full control, people seem to be born with a good degree of potential self-determination, choice, or will. Whether they are aware of it or not, they to some extent choose to listen to and be influenced by early environmental situations. As they grow older, they develop even greater abilities to select the kinds of thoughts, feelings, and behaviors that they prefer and to avoid or minimize the kinds they decide to change (Ellis, 1962, 1973, 1988). Because of their innate and acquired tendencies to change themselves and to choose new behaviors, psychotherapy is highly feasible for them. One of the main goals of family therapy is to help people see that they can change their dysfunctional reactions to themselves and to other family members and that they had often better choose to do so. Rational-emotive family therapy strives to show them how to maximize their "free will" and their inherent ability to achieve self-actualization.

Definition of Rationality. In RET-oriented family therapy, rationality is by no means defined as 18th-century rationalists might define it: as behavior that is compulsively logical, unimpassioned, unemotional, or detached. Rational, in-stead, refers to people's setting up or choosing for themselves certain basic values, purposes, goals, or ideals and then using efficient, flexible, scientific, logico-empirical ways of attempting to achieve these values and goals and avoiding contradictory or self-defeating results (Ellis, 1962, 1973, 1989a; Ellis & Whiteley, 1979; Maultsby, 1975). RET therapists do *not* select clients' values and purposes or show them what their basic aims and choices should be. They discover what these fundamental goals are; how family members think, feel, and behave in ways that interfere with such goals; and how they can rationally—that is, more efficiently and less rigidly—get more of what they want and less of what they don't want out of life.

Importance of Cognition in Personality Change. Although, as noted, RET takes an interactional approach and stresses that cognition, emotion, and feeling invariably influence each other, and although it points out that a significant change in people's feelings or actions often brings about important philosophic change, it particularly emphasizes that a major change in their philosophy can help bring about profound changes in their emotions and behaviors. This is because humans are uniquely thinking or symbolizing animals. Unlike other members of the animal kingdom, they not only think in complex ways but also have the unique ability to think about their thinking—and at times to think about thinking about their thinking. Consequently, RET—more so than any of the other schools of family therapy—employs a large number of cognitive methods (which will be outlined later). It is a highly depth-centered and philosophically oriented system of personality change and, particularly in its preferential form, tries to help all the individual family members, as well as the family itself, make far-reaching changes in their basic attitudes (Ellis, 1962, 1971, 1973, 1988).

Although RET does not focus on deeply repressed thoughts and feelings, as does psychoanalysis, it holds that people's basic disturbance-creating philosophies are often tacitly held, just below the surface of consciousness, and that they can be fairly easily revealed and disputed by several RET techniques (Ellis, 1989a; 1989b Ellis et al., 1989).

The ABCs of Emotional Disturbance.
RET hypothesizes that whenever family members get upset about anything or behave dysfunctionally at Point C (emotional or behavioral consequence), C is usually preceded by A (an activating experience or event), such as this family member failing at some important task or being rejected by another member whose love he or she seeks. RET holds that when A occurs and seemingly "causes" C, it actually does *not* directly cause or create C, although it may indirectly contribute to it. Instead, B (the family member's belief system about what is occurring at A) more directly "creates" or "causes" C.

More specifically, RET hypothesizes that if, say, a husband gets upset about almost anything at Point C (consequence), he has both rational beliefs (rB's) and irrational beliefs (iB's) about what the other family members are doing (or supposedly doing) to frustrate or bother him at Point A (activating experience). His rational beliefs at B take the form of wishes, wants, and preferences—for example, "I would like to be a good husband and have my wife

love me. I don't like failing as a father or provider and having her despise me." These rational beliefs (rB's) almost invariably lead him to feel appropriate consequences, such as sorrow, regret, or annoyance, when he fails and gets rejected at A.

If this husband stayed rigorously with his rational beliefs, RET contends, he wouldn't feel and act in a disturbed and self-defeating manner when the activating experiences (A's) of his family life were obnoxious. He would rationally tell himself, at Point B, something like "Too bad! I have not yet succeeded in being a good husband and having my wife love me. Tough! I'll try harder to succeed in these ways and thereby feel better about my family life. But if I can't, I can't. That's unfortunate, but hardly the end of the world! I can still be a happy, though not quite so happy, person."

Sadly enough, however, this husband usually adds to his rational beliefs (rB's) a set of highly irrational beliefs (iB's), along these lines: "I *must* be a good husband and have my wife love me! How *awful* if I don't succeed in these respects. I *can't stand* failing and being rejected by my family! What a *rotten* person I am for doing so badly!" As a result of these irrational beliefs (iB's) and *not* as a result of his failing and being rejected at Point A, this husband tends to feel the consequent (C) horror, low-frustration tolerance, and self-downing, and he thereby becomes what we usually call "emotionally disturbed." Also, at C, he may resort to dysfunctional behavior, such as abusing his wife and children, becoming an alcoholic, staying away from home, or requesting a hasty divorce.

The ABC theory of RET, then, states that the basic or main "cause" of disturbed emotional consequences (C) in family life (or in any other kind of human activity) does not rest in the activating experiences that happen in the family at A but in the spouses' and children's irrational beliefs (iB's) with regard to these A's. Although people can theoretically have a large number of irrational beliefs, about 12 of these are exceptionally common (Ellis, 1962). These, in turn, can be reduced to three major absolutistic musts, each of which includes several important subcategories (Ellis & Grieger, 1977; Ellis & Harper, 1975; Ellis & Whiteley, 1979):

1. "I *must* (or should or ought) perform well and/or be approved by significant others. It is *awful* (or horrible and terrible) if I don't! I *can't stand it!* I am a pretty rotten person when I fail in these respects!"
2. "You *must* treat me considerately and fairly. It is *horrible* if you don't! When you fail me, you are a *bad* individual, and I *can't bear* you and your crummy behavior!"
3. "Conditions *must* be the way I want them to be, and it is *terrible* when they are not! I *can't stand* living in such an awful world! It is an utterly *abominable* place!"

If family members subscribe to one or more of these three basic musts and their various derivatives, several forms of emotional disturbance and dysfunctional behavior will almost inevitably follow. If they clearly see these absolutist and unrealistic commands on themselves, on others, and on the universe and work hard at surrendering them and replacing them with strong preferences, they will rarely disturb themselves about almost anything—although they will still often have strong appropriate feelings of displeasure, frustration, disappointment, and sorrow (Ellis, 1988).

Insight and RET. While RET places great emphasis on cognition, it does not hold that psychoanalytic or psychodynamic insight leads to significant personality change but that, instead, this kind of insight is usually wasteful and sidetracking. Instead, it stresses a number of rational-emotive insights, especially those described here.

Family problems also often uniquely lead to interactional ABCs. Thus, a husband may criticize his wife at Point A; she may believe, at Point B, "He *must* not do this to me and is a louse if he does what he absolutely *should* not do!"; and thereby create the consequence (C) of rage. But he then may take her rage (C), make it into his own activating event (A), then tell himself at B, "I *must* not make her angry! What a worm I am for doing what I *must* not do!" He may thereby make himself guilty and depressed at C (consequence).

Then the wife may take her husband's consequence (C), make it into her own activating event (A), tell herself, "He *must* not be depressed! I can't stand it" at Point B and thereby bring about her own consequence (C) of self-pity and low frustration tolerance.

So in all close relationships, one person's C's may easily be used or interpreted to produce another's A's. That is why in RET family therapy much effort is exerted to help reduce the emotional and behavioral disturbances (C's) of *all* the interrelated individuals (Ellis & Dryden, 1987; Ellis et al., 1989). There are three kinds of insight and awareness that clients had better achieve:

Insight 1: The "causes" of the practical problems of family members may lie in environmental situations, but the "causes" of their emotional problems (or their problems *about* the practical problems) mainly lie in their irrational beliefs (iB's) about the activating experiences that the family undergoes.

Insight 2: Regardless of how family members originally became (or made themselves) disturbed, they feel upset today because they are *still* indoctrinating themselves with the same kinds of iB's that originated in the past. Even if they learned some of these iB's from their parents and other early socializing agents, they keep repeating and retaining them today. Therefore, their *self*-conditioning is more important than their early external conditioning.

Insight 3: If family members achieve Insights 1 and 2 and thereby fully realize that they have created and keep carrying on their own disturbed feelings, these two insights will not automatically make them change their irrational beliefs. Only if they constantly work and practice, in the present as well as in the future, to think, feel, and act *against* these iB's are they likely to change them and make themselves significantly less disturbed (Ellis, 1962, 1988).

Humanistic Outlook. RET takes the humanistic and existentialist position that family members largely create their own world by the phenomenological view they take of what happens to them. It also accepts the philosophy that people had better define their own freedom and cultivate a good measure of individuality but at the same time, especially if they are to live successfully in family ways, adopt an attitude of caring, sharing, and social interest (Ellis, 1977). In accordance with its humanistic outlook, RET especially emphasizes what Carl Rogers calls "unconditional positive regard" and what rational-emotive practi-

tioners call "full acceptance of oneself and others" (Ellis, 1962, 1973, 1988; Ellis & Harper, 1975). As a consequence, RET takes the unusual stand that we'd better not rate ourselves, our essence, or our being but only our deeds, acts, and performances. We can choose to do this limited kind of rating not in order to *prove* ourselves—that is, to strengthen our ego and self-esteem—but in order to *be* ourselves and *enjoy* ourselves (Ellis et al., 1989).

Behavioral Outlook. Because RET holds that family members are easily disturbable and that, even when they have persuaded themselves to give up irrational beliefs, they easily fall back into self-defeating pathways, and because it sees people as being biologically prone to habituating themselves to dysfunctional behaviors and resisting giving up these activities, it employs a great deal of behavior modification or retraining experiences. In fact, RET practitioners often use more operant conditioning and in vivo desensitization procedures than do many classical behavior therapists. Along with the usual behavioral therapy methods, however, RET almost always employs many cognitive and emotive approaches. Therefore, it is intrinsically a form of what Lazarus (1981) calls "broad-spectrum" or "multimodal behavior therapy." While highly cognitive and philosophic, RET is at the same time a truly pioneering unique form of cognitive-behavioral therapy (Ellis & Dryden, 1987).

Disturbance about Disturbance. RET has always emphasized the self-talking or self-indoctrinating aspect of human disturbance and family malfunctioning. In addition, it particularly stresses that individuals and family members almost always tend to have secondary as well as primary symptoms of disturbance. Thus, a wife may, at Point A, experience criticism from her husband; tell herself, at Point B, "I must not be criticized so severely! I am sure that there is something very wrong with what I am doing. That means I am a bad wife and a worthless person!" At Point C (emotional consequence) she then feels depressed. But, being human and having innate self-downing tendencies, she then makes C into another A and notes to herself, at her secondary B, "I see that I am depressed. I must not be depressed! It's stupid of me to depress myself! I'm a stupid worthless individual for being depressed!" She then is depressed about her depression, and her secondary symptom may be more intense and prolonged than her primary one.

Rational-Emotive Family Therapy and Other Family Therapy Systems

There are almost innumerable schools of family therapy today, but the main (or at least most popular) ones seem to be the psychoanalytic, systems, and behavioral models (Paolino & McGrady, 1978). The following is a brief attempt to show how RET family therapy overlaps with and differs from these systems.

RET and Psychoanalytic Family Therapy. RET differs considerably and radically from what might be called "pure" or "genuine" psychoanalytic therapy as originally presented by Freud (1965) and his close followers. Fortunately (or unfortunately), psychoanalysts and psychoanalytically oriented therapists rarely stick to Freudian theories or techniques these days; and what has been termed neo-Freudian therapy—

such as that of Karen Horney, Erich Fromm, Franz Alexander and Thomas French, and Harry Stack Sullivan—is actually much more neo-Adlerian than neo-Freudian. Thus, what Paul Wachtel (1977) calls "psychoanalysis" really emphasizes clients understanding and changing their current interpersonal relationships (rather than mulling around endlessly in their past lives) plus what might be called low-level or mild RET—that is, showing them how to acknowledge and dispute their unrealistic and irrational beliefs about themselves, others, and the world.

Classical Freudian psychoanalysis includes several basic assumptions that psychoanalytic family therapists such as Nathan Ackerman (1958) partially adopt:

1. Current family problems largely stem from people's past experiences in their own original families, which they then transfer to their present mates and family members.
2. Deep-seated family difficulties stem largely from the fairly severe emotional disturbances of the individual family members.
3. Only by understanding the early origins of their own disturbances and working through these in prolonged psychoanalytic therapy will people really overcome their current family upsets.
4. The main therapeutic tool is the transference relationship between therapists and clients, and only by the therapist arranging for the client(s) to experience a transference neurosis during treatment and by using his or her personal relationship with the client(s) is this neurosis, as well as the original neurosis,

of each family member to be truly resolved.

5. At bottom, virtually all disturbed individuals, including family members, have unresolved oedipal complexes, castration fears, and repressed hostilities toward their parents and siblings; the understanding of and working through these complexes and hostilities largely comprises cure.

6. All serious family disturbances result from people's deeply unconscious or repressed thoughts and feelings; when they are made fully aware of these, they no longer act or feel disturbed.

7. Severe emotional disturbance, such as schizophrenia, is largely caused by the treatment of children during their early childhood life and also by generations of poor family conditions.

8. Intellectual and emotional insight leads to behavioral change, and behavioral solutions in themselves are almost useless and do not lead to intellectual and emotional changes.

9. Resistance to therapeutic change largely results from early family-inculcated disturbances and from unconscious resistances to childhood-imbibed feelings and to transferring these feelings to the therapist.

All of these basic psychoanalytic theories of personality formation of psychotherapy, except the second one listed above, are strongly opposed by the theory and practice of RET. The RET view is that these theories are mostly false, are based on fictional "evidence," are not backed by research, and almost always lead to more therapeutic harm than good (Ellis, 1968, 1988). RET—even

though it agrees with the analytic view that family members are usually disturbed in their own right and that elegant therapeutic resolution involves their overcoming their intrapersonal (as well as their interpersonal) disturbances—has few other agreements with classical psychoanalysis. I would hold, in fact, that the closer therapists stick to "pure" or "real" psychoanalysis, the more ineffective and the more iatrogenic they tend to be. When they significantly deviate from psychoanalytic theory and practice mildly analytically oriented psychotherapy, they then are much more helpful to individual and family clients. (Ellis, 1962, 1988).

RET and Systems Family Therapy.
RET largely goes along with a great deal of the "systems theory" perspective, including its endorsement of the following propositions that tend to be held by different kinds of systems therapists, such as Gregory Bateson, Don Jackson, Paul Watzlawick, Jay Haley, Salvadore Minuchin, and Murray Bowen:

1. In studying families and family therapy, we had better pay attention not only to interpretation of individual thoughts, feelings, and behaviors but also to wholeness, organization, and relationship among family members.

2. We had better also seriously consider general (as well as reductionist) principles that might be used to explain biological processes that lead to increasing complexity of organization (for the organism).

3. We had better concentrate on patterned rather than merely linear relationships and on a consideration of events in the context in which they are occurring rather than in

isolation of them from their environmental context.

4. The study of communication among family members shows how they often become disturbed and what they can do to ameliorate their disturbances.

While agreeing with these basic views of systems theory-oriented family therapy, RET would offer a few caveats as follows:

1. Focusing on wholeness, organization, and relationship among family members is important but can be overdone. Families become disturbed not merely because of their organization and disorganization but because of the serious personal problems of the family members. Unless, therefore, these are considered and dealt with, too, any changes that are likely to occur through changing the family system are likely to be superficial and unlasting, and family therapy will tend to be wasteful.

2. Family systems therapy tends to require an active-directive therapist who makes clear-cut interventions and who engages in a great deal of problem solving. RET is highly similar in these respects. But most family system therapists tend to ignore the phenomenological and self-disturbing aspects of family members' problems and mainly or only deal with the system-creating aspects (Ellis, 1978a; Ellis et al., 1989). In RET terms, they often focus on solving A-type (activating events–type) family problems and not on the more important B-type (belief system–type) problems. RET first tends to show family members how they philosophically disturb themselves about what is happening to them at Point A and how, at B, *they* basically create their own disturbances. It then also shows them how to change their family and personal situations at A. Its

approach is double-barreled rather than single-barreled in this respect (Ellis, 1985; Ellis & Dryden, 1987).

3. Because they focus largely on family situations and interpersonal communications and problems, family therapists, for all of their cleverness and use of many cognitive methods, often miss the main reasons behind most people's emotional and behavioral problems: namely, their absolutist *must*s and *should*s and their other irrational beliefs. In this respect, systems family therapy is partially effective but still may be superficial (Ellis et al., 1989; Huber & Baruth, 1989).

Systems therapy, as Bowen (1978) has indicated, covers many widely differing "systems," many of which significantly contradict each other and had better be given specific names. Some of them, like Bowen's and Haley's (1989), are quite cognitive-behavioral and significantly overlap with, and may easily be integrated with, RET (Allen, 1988; Ellis et al., 1989; Huber & Baruth, 1989).

Sampson (1989), following a number of other psychological and sociological thinkers, has recently made a good case for the point that what we call human "personality" is part and parcel of the global environment in which just about all humans live and is by no means as individualistic as Rogers (1961), Ellis (1962), and others have often made it out to be. This is an important observation, particularly in regard to family therapy. RET, while acknowledging this reality and seeing the great importance of humans' accepting the fact that their "individuality" is partly a function of their sociality, stresses the point that a family system (or any system that includes humans) consists of *both* the system (or sociality) *and* the genetically differing individuals who comprise it. RET therefore deals, in its family therapy, with the family system *and* individuals within it; it tries to help the latter significantly change within the system but also tries to help them notably change the system (Ellis et al., 1989).

RET and Behavioral Family Therapy. RET subscribes to virtually all the main principles of behavior-oriented family therapy, since it is a form of cognitive-behavioral therapy itself and invariably uses (as noted earlier) many behavioral theories and methods. However, it uses behavioral techniques mainly to help family members change their basic philosophic assumptions and to make an "elegant" change in their thinking, feeling, and acting, rather than the symptomatic change that some of the "pure" behavioral therapists, such as Joseph Wolpe, aim for (Wolpe, 1982). RET recognizes that some behavioral methods of individual and family change—such as social reinforcement and gradual desensitization of fears—not only have distinct limitations but have profound philosophic implications that may lead to antitherapeutic results. Thus, if therapists reinforce family members' changes by giving them social approval, these clients may become overdependent on the therapist and may increase rather than decrease their dire needs for approval, which are often one of the main sources of their disturbances (Ellis, 1985).

APPLICATION

Clients for Whom RET Is Especially Effective

All forms of therapy seem to be especially effective with clients who are young, intelligent, verbal, and not too seriously disturbed (Garfield & Bergin, 1978); RET, too, works best with family clients who are in this range. However, it is one of the few forms of treatment that also is effective with what I call DC's (difficult customers)—that is, individuals who are in the psychotic, borderline, organic, or mental-deficient category. Naturally, it does not work as well with these DC's as it does with less disturbed clients. But it particularly helps such clients to accept themselves with their disturbances, to stop downing themselves for being emotionally inadequate. Then, because it is realistic and can easily accept the concept of limited gains for some individuals, RET helps borderline and psychotic family members to train themselves to be less seriously aberrated, although it does not pretend to "cure" them (Ellis, 1973, 1985, 1989b).

Moreover, rational-emotive family therapy is particularly effective at helping less seriously disturbed family members fully accept and nicely put up with more aberrated members. If children are, as they often are, dyslexic, overimpulsive, antisocial, or psychotic, RET shows their parents that although they may have significantly contributed to these children's disturbances, they usually did not directly *cause* them. It teaches such parents that there are almost inevitably strong biological factors in their children's over- or underresponsiveness and that they, the parents, are hardly to blame for such factors. It also shows parents how to accept fully their emotionally or physically handicapped offspring and how to try to help them to be less (though not necessarily non-) disabled (Ellis, 1978b).

At the same time, RET frequently shows children, such as older children and adolescents, how to accept their alcoholic, psychopathic, borderline, and psychotic parents with *their* handicaps; and how to stop roundly criticizing and excoriating them from being the way that they currently are. Thus, in the case of 14- and 12-year-old sons who are extremely incensed about their alcoholic father's irresponsibility and their mother's neglecting them for a lover who was only a few years older than themselves, they were able to see, after only a few sessions of RET family therapy, both that their parents were acting in a highly irresponsible manner—since they had some choice about drinking and about neglecting their children and were choosing to in reprehensible ways—and also that they, like all humans, had a *right to be wrong*. They were fallible, disturbed individuals who decided to act the way they did but who could be accepted and forgiven in spite of their antifamily behaviors. Once these two youngsters learned, in family therapy, to accept their parents *with* their irresponsible behaviors, they were able to maintain reasonably good and loving relationships with these parents and to focus on what they, the children, were going to do to get along better in this poor family environment. Their schoolwork and their relations with their own friends then considerably improved, and they were even, to some degree, able to help their parents face their problems and to act somewhat more responsibly. This is what frequently happens in rational-emotive family therapy: by only rating the poor *behaviors* of other family members and not damning their *selves*, parents or children are then able to help these others improve their behavior.

Goals of the Therapeutic Process

Rational-emotive family therapy usually strives to accomplish the following goals:

1. To help all the family members, or at least as many as possible, to see that they largely disturb themselves by taking the actions of the other members too seriously; and that they invariably have the choice, no matter how these others behave, of not seriously upsetting themselves about their behavior.

2. To help the members continue to keep, and even augment, their desires, wishes, and preferences (including their desires for family love, amity, and responsibility) but to be keenly aware of and to largely surrender their musts, demands, and commands that others in the family act the way they would prefer them to act.

3. To encourage parents and children to feel strongly sad, regretful, frustrated, annoyed, and determined to change things when they are not getting what they want or are getting what they don't want in and out of the family setting. But to clearly demonstrate how to differentiate these appropriate negative feelings from feelings of severe anxiety, depression, hostility, self-pity, and low frustration tolerance; and to minimize the latter while acknowledging, feeling, and at times even augmenting the former.

4. To pinpoint and be closely in touch with their irrational beliefs—their absolutist shoulds, oughts, and musts—that usually underlie their neurotic feelings and dysfunctional behaviors; and to keep disputing and challenging these ideas and replace them with logico-empirical, scientifically based, rational, flexible philosophies of living.

5. To learn a variety of cognitive,

emotive, and behavioral techniques that will combat their irrationalities and encourage them to think, feel, and behave more appropriately and self-enhancingly.

6. As they change their basic disturbance-creating attitudes and philosophies, to investigate more effective problem-solving ways of changing the practical issues—the real frustrations and annoyances—that are preventing them and other family members from being as happy and effective as they would like to be. In RET terms, as they particularly work on their B's (irrational beliefs) also, simultaneously, to work on changing their A's (activating events or activating experiences) that accompany and contribute to these B's and that also contribute to their C's (disturbed and dysfunctional consequences).

7. Not only to learn to deal effectively with the present crises in their families and stubbornly to refuse to upset themselves about these crises, but also (and even more importantly) to realize that, no matter what occurs to them and their close relatives in the future, they can develop a rational-emotive way of accepting these exigencies, again refusing to upset themselves about what occurs, striving to achieve both practical and emotional solutions to their family (and other) problems and trying for self- and family actualization.

Client's Primary Responsibilities

RET teaches clients that, in the course of therapy as in the course of the rest of their lives, their primary responsibilities usually had better be to themselves—not to the therapist, the therapeutic situation, even other family members. They are shown that therapy can be a most helpful procedure but that there is no reason why they *must* undergo it or follow its rules or teachings. As in everything else, it is highly preferable that they do so but not *necessary!*

At the same time, all family members (or those old enough to understand) are shown that if they really want to be responsible to themselves and to other family members, they had better fully accept the decision to do this; and that such acceptance only truly exists when they decide, and act on their decision, to *work* and *practice* at helping to change themselves and others. They are continually shown that there is no free lunch and that the most desirable behaviors, on their own and others' part, do not automatically come into existence but almost always result from strong determination and hard work to change.

In RET family therapy, therefore, each family member is pretty much made responsible for his or her inner changing and for trying to modify the practical aspects of family problems. As in the family counseling methods of Dreikurs (1974), it is recommended that children be given a chance to set family policies, along with their parents and other adults, but that they also take responsibility for their actions and try not to cop out by blaming others for what they do. Adult family members, too, are shown how to acknowledge their own activities and take responsibility for them—even when other individuals in the family are acting badly and are contributing to difficulties. It is continually emphasized that one family member has little ability to change others (though he or she can encourage such changes) and that changing oneself largely depends on one's own attitudes and efforts, not on the manner in which one is treated.

Clients are held to be responsible for their attendance at family therapy sessions and for doing their homework assignments. If they do not like what is happening during the therapy, they are encouraged to speak up about their feelings and to object to what is going on. They should also express their feelings about other family members and voice clearly what they would and would not like to see accomplished within the family system.

Clients are held fully responsible for their own change, since no therapist can really change them. They can only modify their own behavior (or refuse to do so), and they are never blamed for choosing not to change. They are consistently shown that they are in control of their own emotional destiny and that they distinctly have the power to alter their own thinking, emotion, and behavior. But if they stubbornly persist at self-defeating actions, they are undamningly shown that this is their way and that they are fully entitled to keep it but that they still have strong options to change.

Therapist's Role and Function

RET is one of the most active-directive forms of therapies, and this applies to RET family therapy. The therapist is presumably a highly trained individual who understands how people needlessly upset themselves and what they can usually do to stop doing so and to actualize themselves in (and outside of) the family setting. RET therapists, therefore, are authoritative without being authoritarian; bring up discussions of basic values without foisting their own personal values on to clients; and push, coach, persuade, and encourage (but never command!) clients to think and act against their own self-sabotaging tendencies.

Some of the specific skills that RET practitioners display in family therapy are the following (Ellis 1988, 1989a; Ellis & Dryden, 1987; Ellis et al., 1989; Wessler & Ellis, 1983):

1. They empathize with clients' thinking and feeling and *also* with their basic disturbance-creating philosophies.
2. They monitor clients' reactions to other family members and to the therapist and show them how to become highly involved but not overinvolved and dependent on others (including the therapist).
3. They show clients how they are relating well and poorly and teach them communication skills.
4. They teach the general principles of nondisturbance and self-help and instruct clients specifically how to apply these to themselves and to other family members.
5. They confront clients with their avoidance, defensive, and resistant behavior; show them the irrational beliefs behind this kind of behavior; and persuade them to change these beliefs and to become much less defensive.
6. They at times are intrusive, questioning, forceful, and action encouraging just as a successful teacher of children or adults would be.
7. They reveal their own feelings and ideas and show clients how they are not afraid to express themselves during therapy sessions and to take risks in the therapeutic process.
8. They unhesitatingly teach a variety of sex, love, marital, relating, and

other skills as these seem appropriate for different clients; but at the same time, as noted above, they do not overdo practical skill training as opposed to teaching the specific RET-disputing skills.

9. They specifically focus on teaching themselves and clients several unique RET-oriented skills, such as

   a. actively listening, probing, and evoking clients' statements of what they are telling themselves: their rational and irrational beliefs;

   b. showing clients the connections between thinking and emoting—between B (their belief system) and C (the emotional and behavioral consequences) of this thinking;

   c. disputing (D) and challenging irrational beliefs (iB's) and giving follow-through homework assignments to aid the achievement and maintenance of the corrected misperceptions.

Primary Techniques Used in RET Family Therapy

Cognitive Techniques. In RET family therapy, clients are shown what they do to create largely their own disturbances; how they have irrational (as well as rational) beliefs; and how they demand that they *must* do well and be approved, that others (especially, family members) must treat them fairly and lovingly, and that conditions must be nice and easy. They are especially shown how to use the logico-empirical methods of science to *dispute* and *surrender* these irrational beliefs. On a lower or less elegant level of disputing, they are shown how to give themselves rational or coping statements to replace their irrational beliefs: including such statements as "I am a fallible human who doesn't *have* to behave competently!" "Others will do what *they* want and not necessarily what is right or what *I* want!" "I do not *need* what I want and can still be a reasonably happy human when frustrated or deprived!" They are taught to use some of the principles of general semantics, promulgated by Alfred Korzybski (1933) and to interrupt their all-or-none thinking when they make such statements as "I *always* fail," "I *can't* change," and "I'll *never* get what I want." They are given several different forms of cognitive homework to do: look for their absolutist shoulds and musts; fill out the *RET Self-help Report Form* (Sichel & Ellis, 1984) published by the Institute for Rational-Emotive Therapy. They are shown special cognitive methods, such as disputing irrational beliefs (DIBs) (Ellis, 1974), which they can use on their own. They are helped to figure out several choices and actions that are better alternatives to the ones that they are now utilizing. They are taught rational philosophies, such as "Nothing is awful—only inconvenient!" "There's no gain without pain!" and the philosophies of tolerance, flexibility, humanism, and unconditional acceptance of themselves and others. They are vigorously and consistently shown some of the present and evil consequences of their self-defeating behaviors and how they will inevitably suffer more from their low frustration, short-range hedonism, and insistence on trying to get away with things. They are taught imaging techniques that will help them in their marital and sex lives. They are shown how to use methods of cognitive distraction, such as Edmund Jacobsen's (1938) relaxation technique or the sensate focus, to divert them from their anxiety and depression (Ellis, 1988; Ellis & Grieger, 1977, 1986).

Emotive Techniques. RET family therapy employs a good many emotive, evocative, and dramatic techniques of therapy that are also designed to show people how they feel and think and to get them to make profound philosophic changes. Thus, RET therapists use rational emotive imagery (Maultsby, 1975; Maultsby & Ellis, 1974) to help clients get in touch with their worst feelings (horror, despair, and rage) and to change them to appropriate feelings (disappointment, sorrow, and annoyance). They use role-playing methods to get clients to express and work through some of their feelings and self-sabotaging behavior. They employ shame-attacking exercises (Ellis, 1972; Ellis & Abrahms, 1978) to induce clients deliberately to bring on and then surrender their feelings of intense shame and self-downing. They resort to dramatic and evocative confrontation, especially with clients who refuse to acknowledge or work through some of their feelings. They often use forceful language to help loosen people up and get them to face some of their "unfaceable" problems and emotions. They get clients to repeat vigorously and powerfully to themselves, in a highly emotive manner, sensible statements, such as "I do NOT need what I want!" "I never HAVE to succeed, no matter how DESIRABLE it may be to do so!" "People SHOULD sometimes treat me badly! That's the way they naturally behave!" They often use humor and paradoxical intention to strongly attack some of their clients' irrational beliefs and to show how silly they are (Ellis, 1977). They give clients unconditional acceptance and thereby show them that they *can* accept themselves, even when their behaviors are abominable.

Behavioral Techniques. RET has always been exceptionally behavioral as well as cognitive, more so in some ways than the behavioral therapies of some of the main behavioral therapists, such as Joseph Wolpe. One such behavioral technique it frequently utilizes is activity homework assignments, most of them to be done in vivo rather than merely in the clients' imagination. Frequently, these assignments consist of clients staying in an unpleasant marital or family situation until they make themselves unupset about it and then perhaps leaving it. RET also makes use of a good deal of operant conditioning and contracting methods: helping family members contract with other members to do one thing (such as communicate more often) if the other will also do something else (such as be more tidy around the house). Parents are also frequently shown how to use operant techniques to help their children change their undisciplined or other self-defeating behaviors. Skill training—such as assertion training—is often taught, cognitively and behaviorally. Other deconditioning and reconditioning methods are also used in RET family therapy, including covert desensitization, emotional training, sexual resensitization, and flooding (Ellis, 1978a). In regard to the latter technique, in vivo implosion or flooding is recommended for some family clients, since it has been found to be one of the most effective means to help them overcome longstanding phobias, compulsions, and obsessions that seriously interfere with their marital and family lives.

CASE EXAMPLE

The following is a typescript of part of the initial family treatment session with a mother, father, and their 15-year-old daughter. The mother is 45, a housewife who has done a little professional dancing during the last few years. The father is also 45 and runs his own business in the garment center. They also have 21- and 17-year-old sons, both of whom are doing well in school and not having any serious difficulties. They are both very upset about their daughter because she has always shown herself to be quite bright (she has an IQ of 140 on regular intelligence tests and can think very clearly in certain respects), but she doesn't do her schoolwork, refuses to cooperate in regard to family chores, doesn't get herself a job when she promises to do so for the summer or after school, fights with her brothers, steals from her family and from the neighbors, and is quite disruptive in several ways. She acknowledges some of these behaviors but makes innumerable excuses for or denies the other things that her family members accuse her of doing.

At the beginning of the first family therapy session, she admits that she is a "kleptomaniac" and that she uncontrollably steals, but she only partially admits that she steals in order to have money for alcohol and pot and that she uses them steadily. She and her parents agree that she had 2 good years, in the 7th and 8th grades, when she was in a strict Catholic school, but since that time she has lost her purpose in life—which was to be a lawyer in order to be a politician and that she now feels purposeless and hopeless and has no incentive to work at school or anything else. Early in the session she noted that she had a purpose during the 2 years she did well: "I knew I wanted to be a lawyer."

Therapist: Yes?
Debbie: And I worked on that process.
Therapist: But you've now given that up?
Debbie: Yeah.
Therapist: Why did you give that up?

Debbie: Because I really wanted to become a politician.
Therapist: And you don't want to become a politician any more?
Debbie: No. They have bad practices and stuff.
Therapist: So that's out of the window?
Debbie: Yes, I have no goal.
Therapist: You're right. If you had a goal in life, that would probably help you be happier and keep out of the trouble you're getting in. But if you no longer want to be a politician, what stops you from picking some other profession and working toward achieving that?
Debbie: Well, I usually only pick on one goal and don't think of other things.
Therapist: Well, you could still choose to be a lawyer, even if not a politician. And there are lots of other things that you could pick that you are capable of doing. Do you think you're capable of doing what you really want to do?
Debbie: For the most part, yes.
Therapist: You had really better give some more thought to that. When bright people like you screw up and give up on goals, they frequently feel that they're incapable of succeeding at those goals. So perhaps you are in that category, too.
Debbie: Maybe.

The therapist's main hypotheses, which he would hold on theoretical grounds in most cases like Debbie's are (a) she has low frustration tolerance and refuses to do things, such as disciplining herself, which are hard and uncomfortable; and (b) she has severe feelings of inadequacy, which prevent her from trying too hard to achieve anything and encourage her to cop out at school and at other tasks at which she perfectionistically thinks that she might not do well enough. He tries to get her to bring out information to back these hypotheses and only partly succeeds in doing so. But the manner in which she answers his questions and responds to the statements of her parents, who are present during the entire session, lead him to believe that there is considerable evidence to back his hypotheses.

Therapist: Do you want to keep getting into the kind of trouble that you're in, with your parents, with the school, and with your brothers?

Debbie: No.

Therapist: Why do you think you steal?

Debbie: 'Cause I can't control myself.

Therapist: That's a nutty hypothesis! Horeshit! You have *difficulty* in controlling yourself. But that doesn't mean that you *can't*. Suppose that every time you stole, the authorities cut off one of your toes. How long do you think you'd continue to steal?

Debbie (mumbles): Many times.

Therapist: Many times? Well, that's a strong belief you have—but it's not true. You most probably wouldn't. You would then have a powerful *impulse* to steal; but you don't have to give in to your impulses. For 2 years you weren't doing many self-defeating things and did well at school and at home, and didn't steal. Doesn't that show that you're *able* to control your impulses?

Debbie: Yes, to some extent.

Therapist: Yes, for 2 whole years you were apparently OK. You were obviously able to control yourself to some degree.

Debbie: Because I was allowing myself to have a purpose. And I was working on that purpose.

Therapist: Yeah. And that was fine. If you have a purpose, you'll use your energies in that direction, and then you won't be using them in the other, self-defeating directions.

Although it is quite early in the first session, the therapist wants to try to show Debbie and her parents that, in RET terms, activating events (A) do not mainly cause or create emotional consequences (C) but, instead, beliefs (B) do. So he tries to get Debbie to see that just before she gives in to her urge to steal she is telling herself something and that this set of beliefs (B) is the main cause or contributing factor to her dysfunctional consequences (C).

Debbie: I want it.

Therapist: You mean, "I want the money I take"?

Mother: I think the main thing she wants is to buy liquor or dope with the money.

Therapist: That may be. But let's go along with Debbie's views. You're saying that you want the money. Right?

Debbie: Yes.

Therapist: But if you only stuck to that belief—"I want the money"—You probably wouldn't steal. Do you know why?

Debbie: Because I'd see that I often get caught and wouldn't want to get caught stealing it.

Therapist: Right! Whenever we have a want or a wish, we tend to see the consequences of having it, and we often reject it. So you're probably saying something much stronger than "I want the money" when you steal. Do you know what that stronger belief probably is?

Debbie: No. Uh, maybe: "I need it."

Therapist: Correct! "I need the money that I want! I MUST have it because I want it!" And that *need* and that *must* will often drive you to steal, even when you know you may get caught and suffer the consequences. But is that need or must true? *Must* you have the money? Or *must* you have what you get with the money—alcohol, pot, or anything else?

Debbie: No.

Therapist: That's right: No! But if you keep insisting that you *must* have the money (or anything else), you're going to feel not only uncomfortable but horrible, off the wall, when you don't have what you think you *must*. Then, when you feel exceptionally uncomfortable, you may well go on to another must: "I *must* not feel uncomfortable. I *can't stand* this discomfort of not having what I *must* have!" Is that what you're saying, too?

Debbie: Yes. I *can't* stand it. I *can't*!

Therapist: Stop a minute, now! *Can't* you really stand it? *Can* you stand the discomfort of being frustrated and not getting exactly what you want at this very moment that you want it?

Debbie: I don't like it.

Therapist: Right. But you're not merely sticking to "I don't like it." That would be fine, if you did. I hear you saying, "*Because* I don't like it, I *can't stand* it! It's *awful* if I don't have it!"

Debbie: But I really want it!

Therapist: Yes, of course. But your want is not what drives you to stealing. Your basic attitude, "I *must* have what I want!" is what does so. And we call that attitude low frustration tolerance. You're apparently telling yourself, "I want, and *must have*, what I want right now! I can't bear frustration and deprivation." Isn't that what's really going on in your head?

Debbie: Yes, I *can't* stand it!

Therapist: Well, as long as you have that basic philosophy—"I absolutely *need* what I want, and I *can't stand* not having it!" you'll be driven, driven by those ideas, to steal, fight with your family, break things, goof at school, and do the other things that tend to get and keep you in trouble. But you could have, instead, the philosophy "I want what I want and am determined to try to get it. But if I don't get it right now, tough! So I don't! I do not *need* everything I immediately want!" But you are saying to yourself, as far as I can see, "I *do* need it!"

Debbie: Well, perhaps I'm doing it because I'm escaping.

Therapist: Escaping from what? What are you escaping from? Feelings of inadequacy, you mean? The feeling that you haven't the ability to get some of the things that you want or think you need?

Debbie: That could be one.

Therapist: Let's talk about those inadequacy feelings for a moment. What are they? Are you willing to talk about them in front of your parents?

Debbie: It doesn't matter.

Therapist: Well, what do you feel inferior about?

Debbie: I'm confused. I haven't figured out what's the purpose of it all. I don't see how to react to certain problems.

Therapist: Such as?

Debbie: Well, some domestic problems. And I just don't get along with people. I like them, but I don't understand them.

Therapist: And you think that you *should*, you *must* understand them?

Debbie: Yes. And that's why I often try to get high.

Therapist: And do you blame yourself, then, for getting high?

Debbie: Yes, sometimes.

Therapist: Well, let's assume that getting high won't solve things and make you understand people better, and it's therefore something of a mistake. And let's suppose you're not yet very good at understanding and getting along with people. Why do you put yourself down for these errors or deficiencies?

Debbie: Because I know that it's not right.

Therapist: Yes, well, let's assume that. Suppose what you're doing is wrong. How does that make you a worm, that wrong behavior?

Debbie: (Silence)

Therapist: Suppose your mother and father do something wrong. Are they shits for doing that wrong thing?

Debbie: No.

Therapist: Then why are you?

Debbie: Because then I'm a wrong person.

Therapist: But you're *not* a wrong person! That's your nutty thinking! That's what we call an overgeneralization. If we can get you to give up that kind of irrational thinking and get you to completely accept yourself, even when you are doing the wrong thing, then you can usually go back and correct your error. But if you put *yourself* down and define yourself as a shit for acting shittily, there's no good solution to the problem! For how can a shit be dishittified? (Debbie and her parents all laugh fairly heartily at this statement.) And feelings of inadequacy don't come from doing the wrong thing. They come from *condemning yourself* for doing it—putting yourself into hell. Then that makes things worse.

Debbie: Yes, it does.

Therapist: But do you really see all of what's going on here? You first do badly—or think that you will do badly at something. Then you put yourself down, *make yourself* feel inadequate as a person. Then you tend to do something like drink or take pot, to make yourself relax temporarily and feel a little better. But then you get into more trouble, because of the alcohol or pot or the stealing that you did to get the money for it, and then you blame yourself more and go around and around in a vicious self-damning circle.

Debbie: I guess I do. I keep thinking that I'm really no good. And then things get worse.

Therapist: Right!

Debbie: But how can I stop that?

Therapist: The best solution is to see very clearly what I said before: that some of your acts are poor or self-defeating but that *you* are not a worm for doing them. If we could get you to fully accept *yourself*, your *being*, your *totality*, even when you are screwing up and acting stupidly or badly, then we could get you to go back and work on improving your screwups. And you could change most of them, which you are quite capable of doing—if you weren't wasting your time and energy and making things worse by your self-blaming. That isn't going to work.

Debbie: It doesn't. I just feel worse. And then I think that I have to keep repeating this, uh, inadequate behavior.

Therapist: Right! The more you condemn yourself for your poor behavior, the more you lose confidence in your ability to correct that behavior.

Debbie (smiling): A shit can't be deshittified!

Therapist: Exactly! If you are, to your core, a thorough turd, how can you change your turdiness? No way!

Debbie: But how do I stop blaming myself?

Therapist: By getting rid of your fundamental musts. For, at bottom, you seem to be saying, "I *must*, I *have to* do well." Not "I'd *like* or *prefer* to do well." And you're also saying to yourself, and very strongly, "I *must* not suffer inconveniences. It's *awful* if I do." Not "I'd *like* to avoid inconveniences. But if I don't, I don't! I can still abide them—and still be a happy human!"

Debbie: I see what you mean. But how am I going to keep seeing that and believing it?

Therapist: By damned hard work! By continuing to *think* about what you say to yourself and do. And by changing your perfectionistic, demanding thinking into preferences and desires.

The therapist, without knowing too much about Debbie and her parents, takes the main information he does have—that she demands that she does well and that the universe treat her kindly—and quickly and forthrightly attacks these unrealistic, irrational beliefs and tries to show her that she can do this herself and can give them up. As he talks to her, he interrupts from time to time to show the parents that they, too, have musts about Debbie and that they are unrealistically demanding that she act well and are condemning her and upsetting themselves when she doesn't. So he lets them listen to his disputing of her irrational beliefs, but he also indicates that they are often doing the same thing as she is and that they are irrational, too—and do not have to continue to be. Toward the end of the session the therapist speaks to Debbie and then to her parents.

Therapist: If I can help you to keep your desires and to give up your musts, you'll get somewhere in feeling better and acting better. By so doing, you'll most probably get more of what you desire and less of what you don't want. But you won't get *everything* you desire. (To Debbie's parents:) She has normal desires, but then she tells herself, "I *must*, I *must* fulfill them!" And "I *must* get what I want *immediately*!" Now, if I can get all of you, including her, to look for the *should*, look for the *must*, which you are all bright enough to do, and if I can persuade you to tackle these absolutes and give them up, you will be able to stop upsetting yourselves and usually solve the original problem of getting along together and living happily in this world. (To Debbie, again:) If I can help you do *that*, then you'll get along with your parents and siblings and live more successfully. But what you tend to do is to give up your desires because of your musts. "I *must* do this and *must* be that! But maybe I won't. And that would be *terrible!*" Then you feel depressed and anxious and start goofing. Then you blame yourself for the goofing and feel more anxious and depressed. A very vicious circle! Have you read any of my writings on this?

The therapist closes the session by assigning all three of them, Debbie and her parents, to read a group of pamphlets on RET that the Institute for Rational-Emotive Therapy gives to all clients at its clinic in New York and also to read *A New Guide to Rational Living* by Ellis and Harper (1975), which most clients are assigned to read. They are to make another appointment, next week; in between to make a note of all the times they feel upset during the week, especially about each other, and what is happening in the family; to look for the shoulds and musts that lead to these feelings; and to find them or fail to find them and to bring them up during the next session, so that they and the therapist can look for them and find them.

Following this first session, Debbie and her parents were seen once a week for a total of 16 weeks. Debbie was largely seen for individual sessions by herself, but usually one or both parents were also seen with her for a half hour, while she was seen by herself for a half hour. On a few occasions, her parents were also seen by themselves to deal with their anger and other upset feelings about her "rotten" behavior and about their own problems with each other and with outsiders (especially her father's problems with his business associates and her mother's problems with her women friends).

It would have been preferable as a part of the rational-emotive family ther-

apy that was done with Debbie and her parents to see her two brothers too during some of the sessions. But the parents insisted that the brothers had no problems and might be harmed by participating in the therapy. The brothers themselves also resisted coming, since they thought that their sister had a serious emotional problem but that they did not. Under more usual conditions, the brothers would have been seen along with the other members of the family in RET family therapy. The main RET family therapy techniques that were used with Debbie and her parents during these sessions are discussed next.

Cognitive Methods

Whenever Debbie or her parents showed any feelings of anxiety, depression, anger, and self-pity (which they frequently did) or when Debbie continued her antisocial and antifamily behavior and failed to go for job interviews or to work at the jobs she temporarily obtained, they were shown the ABCs of RET: That their C's (emotional consequences) did not stem from their A's (activating experiences) but largely from their own iB's (irrational beliefs) *about* these A's. They were shown their absolutistic shoulds and musts and how to dispute these (using the logico-empirical method of questioning and challenging these musts). They were given the cognitive homework of doing the rational self-help report form published by the Institute for Rational-Emotive Therapy (Sichel & Ellis, 1984), and these were gone over with them and corrected by the therapist. They were given, as noted, bibliotherapeutic materials on RET to read and discuss with the therapist—particularly *A New Guide to Rational Living* (Ellis & Harper, 1975), *How to*

Live with a "Neurotic" (Ellis, 1957), and *Overcoming Procrastination* (Ellis & Knaus, 1977). They were also encouraged to listen to some of the cassette recordings distributed by the Institute, such as *How to Stubbornly Refuse to Be Ashamed of Anything* (Ellis, 1972) and *Conquering Low Frustration Tolerance* (Ellis, 1976b). They also participated in some of the 4-hour workshops on parent-child relationships and overcoming depression that the Institute held.

Cognitively, too, the members of this family, especially Debbie, were given practical advice and suggestions on how to solve certain practical problems that arose (such as how Debbie could get and keep a job, in spite of her poor reputation in the community and her poor record of holding a job up to that time). They were shown how to write down and focus on the real disadvantages of their avoidant behaviors. They were taught some of the principles of general semantics dealing with overgeneralization and allness. They were made aware of their wrongly attributing motives and intentions to others (e.g., Debbie continually thought that her parents were against her when they were merely trying to get her to become more self-disciplined) and how to challenge these misattributions. They were shown how to use cognitive distraction methods, such as Edmund Jacobsen's muscular relaxation methods, when they wanted to temporarily calm themselves down or overcome insomnia. The therapist sometimes used humor and paradoxical intention with them; for example, he tried to get Debbie deliberately to fail at certain tasks to prove to herself that the world did not come to an end when she did, and he tried to get her to see the humorous side of her taking things too seriously and blaming herself for her poor behavior.

And they were continually taught how to accept themselves fully and to stop condemning themselves for anything, even when they indubitably screwed up and made stupid mistakes.

Emotive Methods

Even though I pulled no punches in showing Debbie how she was being irresponsible to herself and others and did not let her get off the hook with her clever rationalizations in this respect, she could always see that I fully accepted her, as a human, with her failings and that I had confidence that she definitely could—if she would—change. I also helped her, as homework assignments, to do rational-emotive imagery: to imagine that she really did very badly, at work or socially, and that others despised her for her poor behavior, and to make herself feel only sorry and disappointed rather than depressed and self-downing. I did role playing, with her and her parents, and let her confess to them some of the things she hadn't yet told them, let herself feel very ashamed, and then persist at the confessions and work through the shame and be able to handle their responses. I gave her out-of-session homework assignments deliberately to do "foolish" or "shameful" things—such as wear very "loud" clothing—and to work at not making herself feel embarrassed or humiliated when she did this. I helped her to write out some rational self-statements—such as, "I do not need immediate gratification, no matter how much I really want it!"—and to repeat these to herself very vigorously 10 or 20 times a day. I deliberately used "obscene" language with her parents, who were very prim and rigid in this respect, to help loosen them up and to show them that they could even use this kind of language themselves. I used George Kelly's (1955) dramatic enactment method with both Debbie and her parents, having them write scripts about the kind of people they would like to be and then enact these scripts for a week, until they became used to acting in that unfamiliar way.

Behavioral Methods

With Debbie in particular I used several behavioral methods and taught her parents how to use them with her. Whenever she spent at least 2 hours a week looking for a part-time job, she was permitted to socialize with her friends or do other things she enjoyed. And whenever she lied or stole, she was confined to her room for several hours at a time. Whenever her parents criticized her in an angry, damning manner, they were also to refrain from socializing with their friends, in person or over the phone, for that day. These reinforcements and penalties worked fairly well—as long as they were enforced. But her parents had to keep after Debbie, and she, to some extent, had to keep after them to enforce their reinforcements and penalties.

Debbie was given several different kinds of activity homework assignments including looking for a job, doing various family chores, and behaving in a cooperative instead of disruptive manner with her parents and her siblings. Some of these she quickly carried out, and she got a great deal of benefit from the fact that she saw that she was able to do them and was not totally out of control, as she often said she was. Other assignments, such as the chores, she did sporadically but still seemed to derive some benefit from doing them.

At the end of 16 weeks of rational-emotive family therapy, Debbie was do-

ing her schoolwork regularly, had ceased stealing, and was getting along much better with her family members. Even more than this, she was accepting herself much more than before, even when she goofed and failed to do something up to her own standards. Her mother and father were considerably less angry at her, even when she fell back into her old disruptive behavior. Though the emphasis of the family therapy was not very much on the parents' relations with each other, they voluntarily used some of the rational ideas we were all discussing and began to be much less angry at one another and to behave more cooperatively. Their sex life also improved considerably, though there was little discussion of this during the therapy sessions. They especially understood Debbie much better and were able to take her with her failings. The father returned for several therapy sessions a year and a half later, because he was avoiding some of his office work and was putting himself down for this. At that time, it was ascertained that Debbie was still acting remarkably better and that a great degree of family harmony existed.

EVALUATION

As noted in the section on research studies, RET has an unusually detailed and good record as far as research into its basic personality hypotheses and its claims for clinical effectiveness are concerned (DiGiuseppe et al., 1979; Ellis, 1971; Ellis & Whiteley, 1979). In the field of marriage and family therapy in particular, several outcome studies favorable to it have been published, but research in this area is still in the formative stage. Clinically, RET appears to work very well, whether clients are seen separately or conjointly; and it works in premarital, marital, and divorce cases (Ellis, 1962, 1978c). Case studies and anecdotal reports of the effectiveness of any form of therapy, especially family therapy, are highly suspect, however. In the final analysis, rational-emotive family therapy will show proven effectiveness only when a considerable number of controlled experiments have been performed showing that it brings better results than other schools of family therapy, than no therapy, and than placebo therapy.

SUMMARY

Rational-emotive family therapy is a special form of RET and follows the general principles and practice of individual and group rational-emotive therapy. It overlaps with noncognitive behavior therapy and with systems therapy in many of the techniques that it uses, but it is a form of cognitive-behavioral therapy (CBT) that includes the following unique features:

1. It importantly stresses the cognitive or philosophic "causes" of emotional disturbance and of family disruption.
2. It teaches most family clients that they largely disturb themselves and that they can effectively refuse to continue to do so.
3. It almost always employs a number of cognitive, emotive, and behavioral techniques but employs them not merely to achieve symptomatic change but to help family clients achieve a profound philosophic reconstruction that will hopefully lead to elegant and permanent change.
4. It clearly acknowledges the biological as well as the sociological bases of individual and family disturbance and therefore stresses vigorous and forceful, active-directive methods that will impinge on and help alter the strongly held disturbances that family members frequently experience.
5. It holds to a rigorously scientific and yet highly humanistic outlook in both its theory and its practice.
6. It stresses a phenomenological, intraindividual, and depth-centered approach to understanding and tackling human disturbance but at the same time uses practical problem-solving and skill-training methods of changing family situations and interactions.

ANNOTATED SUGGESTED READINGS

Ellis, A. (1975). *How to live with a "neurotic"* (rev. ed.). New York: Crown.

The first book published on RET showing how almost anyone can use it to cope with and to help disturbed individuals, and especially instructing married and mated individuals in how they can live successfully with disturbed partners.

Ellis, A. (1962). *Reason and emotion in psychotherapy*. Secaucus, NJ: Lyle Stuart and Citadel Press.

The first book presenting RET in textbook form, mainly written for therapists and counselors but also widely used by those who want to help themselves overcome their emotional problems.

Ellis, A. (1971). *Growth through reason: Verbatim cases in rational-emotive therapy.* Palo Alto, CA: Science and Behavior Books.

Verbatim dialogues between rational-emotive therapists and their clients, with Ellis stopping the tape, so to speak, at frequent intervals to explain what is happening, what techniques of RET the therapist is using and what growth is taking place.

Ellis, A., & Grieger, R. (1977, Vol. 1 and 1986, Vol. 2). *Handbook of rational-emotive therapy.* New York: Springer.

A sourcebook of some of the most salient and classic writings on RET, with sections on the theoretical and conceptional foundations of RET, the dynamics of emotional disturbance, primary techniques and basic processes of rational-emotive therapy, and the use of RET with children.

Ellis, A., & Dryden, W. (1987). *The practice of rational-emotive therapy.* New York: Springer.

Brings RET theory and practice up-to-date and specifically shows how it is practiced in different kinds of settings, including individual, group, couples, and family therapy settings.

Ellis, A., McInerney, J. F., DiGiuseppe, R., & Yeager, R. J. (1988). *Rational-emotive therapy with alcoholics and substance abusers.* New York: Pergamon.

Applies RET to individuals and families who are involved in alcoholism and substance abuse.

Ellis, A., Sichel, J., Yeager, R., DiMattia, D., & DiGiuseppe, R. (1989). *Rational-emotive couples therapy.* New York: Pergamon.

Details the RET theory and practice of couples and family therapy.

REFERENCES

Ackerman, N. W. (1958). *The psychodynamics of family life.* New York: Basic Books.

Adler, A. (1931). *What life should mean to you.* New York: Blue Ribbon Books.

Adler, A. (1964). *Social interest: A challenge to mankind.* New York: Capricorn.

Allen, D. M. (1988). *Unifying individual and family therapies.* San Francisco: Jossey-Bass.

Ard, B. N., Jr., & Ard, C. (Eds.). (1976). *Handbook of marriage counseling.* Palo Alto, CA: Science and Behavior Books.

Baisden, H. E. (1980). *Irrational beliefs: A construct validation study.* Unpublished doctoral dissertation. University of Minnesota, Minneapolis.

Blazier, D. (1975). *Poor me, poor marriage.* New York: Vantage.

Bowen, M. (1978). *Family therapy in clinical practice.* New York: Aronson.

DiGiuseppe, R. A., Miller, N. J., & Trexler, L. D. (1979). A review of rational-emotive psychotherapy outcome studies. In A. Ellis & J. M. Whiteley (Eds.), *Theoretical and empirical foundations of rational-emotive therapy* (pp. 218–235). Monterey, CA: Brooks/Cole.

Dreikurs, R. (1974). *Psychodynamics, psychotherapy and counseling* (rev. ed.). Chicago: Alfred Adler Institute.

Eisenberg, J. M., & Zingle, H. W. (1975). Marital adjustment and irrational ideas. *Journal of Marriage and Family Counseling, 1,* 81–91.

Elliott, S. S. (1979). *Desired behavior change irrationality and anger arousal related to marital stress.* Unpublished doctoral dissertation, Virginia Polytechnic Institute, Blacksburg.

Ellis, A. (1957). *How to live with a neurotic: At home and at work.* New York: Crown. (Rev. ed. 1975)

Ellis, A. (1958). *Sex without guilt*. New York: Lyle Stuart. (Rev. ed. 1965)

Ellis, A. (1960) *The art and science of love*. Secaucus, NJ: Lyle Stuart.

Ellis, A. (1962). *Reason and emotion in psychotherapy*. Secaucus, NJ: Citadel.

Ellis, A. (1968). Is psychoanalysis harmful? *Psychiatric Opinion, 5*(1), 16–25. (Reprinted: New York: Institute for Rational-Emotive Therapy)

Ellis, A. (1971). *Growth through reason*. North Hollywood, CA: Wilshire Books.

Ellis, A. (Speaker). (1972). *How to stubbornly refuse to be ashamed of anything* (Cassette recording). New York: Institute for Rational-Emotive Therapy.

Ellis, A. (1973). *Humanistic psychotherapy: The rational-emotive approach*. New York: McGraw-Hill.

Ellis, A. (1974). *Technique of disputing irrational beliefs (DIBS)*. New York: Institute for Rational-Emotive Therapy.

Ellis, A. (1976a). The biological basis of human irrationality. *Journal of Individual Psychology, 32,* 145–168. (Reprinted: New York: Institute for Rational-Emotive Therapy)

Ellis, A. (Speaker). (1976b). *Conquering low frustration tolerance* (Cassette recording). New York: Institute for Rational-Emotive Therapy.

Ellis, A. (1976c). *Sex and the liberated man* (rev. ed.). Secaucus, NJ: Lyle Stuart.

Ellis, A. (1977). Fun as psychotherapy. *Rational Living, 12*(1), 2–6. (Also: Cassette recording. New York: Institute for Rational-Emotive Therapy)

Ellis, A. (1978a). Family therapy: A phenomenological *and* active-directive approach. *Journal of Marriage and Family Counseling, 4*(2), 43–50. (Reprinted: New York: Institute for Rational-Emotive Therapy.

Ellis, A. (1978b). Rational-emotive guidance. In L. E. Arnold (Ed.), *Helping parents help their children* (pp. 91–101). New York: Brunner/Mazel.

Ellis, A. (1978c). A rational approach to divorce problems. In S. M. Goetz (Ed.), *Breaking asunder* (pp. 27–33). Green-

vale, NY: Post Center, Long Island University.

Ellis, A. (1979). *The intelligent woman's guide to dating and mating* (rev. ed.). Secaucus, NJ: Lyle Stuart.

Ellis, A. (1985). *Overcoming resistance*. New York: Springer.

Ellis, A. (1988). *How to stubbornly refuse to make yourself miserable about anything—yes, anything!* Secaucus, NJ: Lyle Stuart.

Ellis, A. (1989a). Rational-emotive therapy. In R. J. Corsini & D. Wedding (Eds.), *Current psychotherapies* (4th ed., pp. 198–240). Itasca, IL: Peacock.

Ellis, A. (1989b). *The treatment of psychotic and borderline individuals with RET*. New York: Institute for Rational-Emotive Therapy.

Ellis, A., & Abrahms, E. (1978). *Brief psychotherapy in medical and health practice*. New York: Springer.

Ellis, A., & Dryden, W. (1987). *The practice of rational-emotive therapy*. New York: Springer.

Ellis, A., & Grieger, R. (Eds.). (1977). *Handbook of rational-emotive therapy. Vol. 1.* New York: Springer.

Ellis, A., & Grieger, R. (Eds.). (1986). *Handbook of rational-emotive therapy. Vol. 2.* New York: Springer.

Ellis, A., & Harper, R. A. (1961). *A guide to successful marriage*. North Hollywood, CA: Wilshire Books.

Ellis, A., & Harper, R. A. (1975). *A new guide to rational living*. North Hollywood, CA: Wilshire Books.

Ellis, A., & Knaus, W. (1977). *Overcoming procrastination*. New York: New American Library.

Ellis, A., Sichel, J., Yeager, R., DiMattia, D., & DiGiuseppe, R. (1989). *Rational-emotive couples therapy*. New York: Pergamon.

Ellis, A., & Whiteley, J. M. (Eds.). (1979). *Theoretical and empirical foundations of rational-emotive therapy*. Monterey, CA: Brooks/Cole.

Ellis, A., Wolfe, J. L., & Moseley, S. (1966). *How to raise an emotionally healthy, happy child*. North Hollywood, CA: Wilshire Books.

Ellis, A., & Yeager, R. (1989). *Why some therapies don't work: The dangers of transpersonal psychology*. Buffalo, NY: Prometheus.

Engels, G. I., & Diekstra, R. E. W. (1986). Meta-analysis of rational-emotive therapy. In P. Eelan & O. Fontaine (Eds.), *Behavior therapy: Beyond the conditioning* framework (p. 121–140). Hillsdale, NJ: Erlbaum.

Epictetus (1890). *The collected works of Epictetus*. Boston: Little, Brown.

Freeman, A. (Ed.) (1983). *Cognitive therapy with couples and groups*. New York: Plenum Press.

Freud, S. (1965). *Standard edition of the complete psychological works of Sigmund Freud*. New York: Basic Books.

Garfield, S., & Bergin, A. E. (Eds.). (1978). *Handbook of psychotherapy and behavior change* (2nd ed.). New York: Wiley.

Glass R., Gottman, M., & Shmurak, H. (1976). Response acquisition and cognitive self-statement modification approaches to dating-skills training. *Journal of Counseling Psychology, 23,* 520–526.

Gottman, J. M. (1979). *Marital interaction: Experimental investigations*. New York: Academic Press.

Haaga, D. A., & Davison, G. C. (1989). Outcome studies of rational-emotive therapy. In M. E. Bernard & R. DiGiuseppe (Eds.), *Inside rational-emotive therapy* (pp. 155–197). San Diego, CA: Academic Press.

Haley, J. (1989). *Problem-solving therapy* (rev. ed.). San Francisco: Jossey-Bass.

Hauck, P. A. (1967). *The rational management of children*. New York: Libra.

Huber, C., & Baruth, L. G. (1989). *Integrating rational-emotive and systems family therapy*. New York: Springer.

Jacobsen, E. (1938). *You must relax*. New York: McGraw-Hill.

Jacobson, N. (1979). Increasing positive behavior in severely distressed marital relationships: The effects of problem solv-

ing training. *Behavior Therapy, 10,* 311–326.

Jacobson, N., & Margolin, G. (1979). *Marital therapy*. New York: Brunner/Mazel.

Jorm, A. P. (1987). *Modifiability of a personality trait which is a risk factor for neurosis*. Paper presented at World Psychiatric Association, Symposium on Epidemiology and the Prevention of Mental Disorder, Reykjavik.

Kelly, G. (1955). *The psychology of personal constructs*. New York: Norton.

Korzybski, A. (1933). *Science and sanity*. San Francisco: International Society of General Semantics.

Lazarus, A. A. (1981). *The practice of multimodal therapy*. New York: McGraw-Hill.

Margolin, G., & Weiss, R. L. (1978). Comparative evaluation of therapeutic components associated with behavioral marital treatments. *Journal of Consulting and Clinical Psychology, 46,* 1475–1486.

Maultsby, M. C., Jr. (1975). *Help your self to happiness: Through rational self-counseling*. New York: Institute for Rational-Emotive Therapy.

Maultsby, M. C., Jr., & Ellis, A. (1974). *Technique for using rational-emotive imagery*. New York: Institute for Rational-Emotive Therapy.

McClellan, T. A., & Stieper, D. R. (1971). A structured approach to group marriage counseling. *Rational Living, 8*(2), 12–18.

McGovern, T. E., & Silverman, M. S. (1984). A review of outcome studies of rational-emotive therapy from 1977 to 1982. *Journal of Rational-Emotive Therapy, 2*(1), 7–18.

Miller, R. C., & Berman, J. S. (1983). The efficacy of cognitive behavior therapy: A quantitative review of the research evidence. *Psychological Bulletin, 94,* 39–53.

Paolino, T. J., Jr., & McGrady, B. S. (1978). *Marriage and marital therapy*. New York: Brunner/Mazel.

Rogers, C. R. (1961). *On becoming a person*. Boston: Houghton-Mifflin.

Sampson, E. E. (1989). The challenge of social change in psychology. Globalization and psychology's theory of the person. *American Psychologist, 44,* 914–921.

Saxon, W. (1980). *The use of rational therapy with emotionally upset parents of handicapped children.* Hattiesburg: School of Social Work, University of Southern Mississippi Press.

Sichel, J., & Ellis, A. (1984). *RET self-help report form.* New York: Institute for Rational-Emotive Therapy.

Smith, M. L., & Glass, G. V. (1977). Meta analysis of psychotherapy outcome studies. *American Psychologist, 32,* 752–760.

Steed, S. P. (1971). *The influence of Adlerian counseling on familial adjustment.* EdD dissertation, University of Arizona, Tucson.

Tsoi-Hoshmand, L. (1976). Marital therapy: An integrative behavioral learning model. *Journal of Marriage & Family Counseling, 2,* 179–192.

Wachtel, P. L. (1977). *Psychoanalysis and behavior therapy: Toward an integration.* New York: Basic Books.

Wessler, R. L., & Ellis, A. (1983). Supervision in counseling: Rational-emotive therapy. *Counseling Psychologist, 11,* 43–49.

Wolpe, J. (1982). *The practice of behavior therapy* (3rd ed.). New York: Pergamon.

CHAPTER 15

Reality Therapy

ROBERT E. WUBBOLDING

DEFINITION

Since the publication of *Reality Therapy* by William Glasser, MD, in 1965, there has been a steady increase in interest and application of the principles of reality therapy. It is now used by counselors, therapists, teachers, nurses, youth workers, geriatric workers, clergy, lawyers, supervisors, foremen, and company managers as well as parents. Although mastering the skills requires study, practice, and supervision, the techniques can be used even after brief exposure to them. For example, many parents use the suggestions with their children after hearing about some aspects of the system. The principles of reality therapy are sometimes described as "down-to-earth," "easy to understand," and "jargon-free." The user of the ideas takes a positive approach, stresses present and future behavior, and refrains from blaming or criticizing.

Nevertheless, to become proficient in learning and practicing the principles requires the development of detailed skills. The Institute for Reality Therapy has developed an 18-month training program of certification by which a person is recognized as being skilled in the application of the principles. To learn the skills thoroughly takes time, practice, and supervision.

The theory underlying reality therapy and the method itself have evolved significantly over the years and have developed far beyond the original publication by Glasser. Reality therapy has become more simplified in some ways and far more detailed and complicated in other ways. Nevertheless, throughout its history, those formulating the principles of reality therapy have sought to use language that can be clearly understood by most people. An explicit effort has been made to avoid a vocabulary unique to reality therapy. Thus, words like *belonging, power, needs, wants, plans,* and *consequences* are used to explain the concepts. These are words easily understood by most people.

The use of this Anglo-Saxon terminology has a twofold effect. The theory and method are easy to understand. But like the rules of a sport that are simple to comprehend, the implementation of the method, like playing the sport, is more difficult.

There is often discussion at training workshops about where reality therapy fits among the various schools of thought: behavioral, humanistic, cognitive. Some have mistakenly stated that reality therapy is a system of behavior modification. In my opinion, the system belongs in the cognitive school of thought, for it is based on a theory of brain functioning called "control system theory" or "control theory," which is explained later in detail. While the method of reality therapy contains action plans as a significant component, they are preceded by evaluation of one's life direction, specific behaviors, and attainability of goals. In short, a considerable amount of cognitive change is included in changing a behavior.

Finally, Wubbolding (1990b) provides a summary definition of reality therapy:

It is a method of helping people take better control of their lives. It helps people to identify and to clarify what they want and what they need and then to evaluate whether they can realistically attain what they want. It helps them to examine their own behaviors and to evaluate them with clear criteria. This is followed by positive planning designed to help control their own lives as well as fulfill their realistic wants and their needs. The result is added strength, more self-confidence, better human relations, and a personal plan for a more effective life. It, thus, provides people with a self-help tool to use daily to cope with adversity, to grow personally, and to get more effective control of their lives.

Reality Therapy is based on several principles, such as:

1. People are responsible for their own behavior—not society, not heredity, not past history.
2. People can change and live more effective lives.
3. People behave for a purpose—to mold their environment as a sculptor molds clay, to match their own inner pictures of what they want.

The intended results described are achievable through continuous effort and hard work. (p. 173)

HISTORICAL DEVELOPMENT

"Reality Therapy is one of the newest of man's formal attempts to explain mankind, to set rules for behavior, and to map out how one person can help another to achieve happiness and success; but at the same time, paradoxically, it represents one of the oldest sets of maxims referring to human conduct" (Glasser & Zunin, 1973, p. 287).

The contribution of reality therapy is that it has enshrined in the practice of counseling and psychotherapy some of the most fundamental, intercultural, and philosophical principles of human conduct that are universally accepted and lived by millions of people. Central to these underlying principles is that human beings are responsible for their behavior. They cannot blame past history, the environment, or their unconscious drives.

Precursors

The principles of personal responsibility for our behavior were not discovered in the 19th or 20th centuries. In the 2nd century AD, Marcus Aurelius wrote, "If anything is within the powers and province of man, believe that it is within your own compass also" and "Men's actions cannot agitate us, but our own views regarding them." Similarly, "The agitations that beset you are superfluous and depend wholly on judgments that are your own" (Antoninus, 1944, p. 21).

Glasser and Zunin (1973) cite Paul Dubois, a Swiss physician, as a direct spiritual ancestor. Dubois helped his patients substitute healthful thoughts for disease-laden thoughts. The assumption is that the patients can have at least some control over their health.

William James is often quoted as saying that one of the greatest discoveries in history is that we can alter the circumstances of our lives by altering our attitudes. He stated, "we do not sing because we are happy. We are happy because we sing."

A more direct influence in the development of reality therapy was Helmuth Kaiser. Kaiser was a training analyst at the Menninger Foundation where G. L. Harrington, later to be Glasser's teacher, worked for 10 years. Though Kaiser stated that it is the responsibility of the analyst to cure the patient (a principle not incorporated into reality therapy), he stated that "it is the analyst's task to make the patient feel responsible for his own words and his own actions" (Kaiser, 1965, p. 4).

He also influenced Harrington to approach the therapeutic relationship from a more egalitarian perspective and to view labeling the relationship "patient-therapist" as less than crucial. Glasser and Zunin (1973) add, "He also, and perhaps inadvertently, illustrated that a basic assumption for therapy is that the therapist be healthier than the patient and that, if he is not, he must at least be healthier in the area of the patient's illness (p. 289).

The most important precursor to the development of reality therapy as it is known today was Dr. G. L. Harrington himself. It was due to his influence and inspiration that Glasser began and continued to develop the principles of reality therapy.

Beginnings

Reality therapy began when Glasser became dissatisfied with the Freudian methodology that he learned during his residence at the UCLA Medical Center. Harrington, whom Glasser still calls "my teacher," provided a sympathetic ear because of his own similar beliefs. Ford (1982) states, "This encouragement from his supervisor plus his own determination to seek a more practical way of helping people gave Glasser the impetus to develop his ideas further" (p. 389). Within a few years Glasser and Harrington introduced the seminal notions of reality therapy to the most disturbed patients at the Veterans Administration Hospital in Los Angeles. There seemed

to be a tacit acceptance of the fact that the patients were there to stay and that they should remain "peacefully psychotic." As Glasser and Zunin (1973) state, "Harrington began to shatter this contract when he took over the ward" (p. 289). The new program had astonishing results. In a unit of 210 patients whose average stay had been 17 years, 90 left the hospital in 3 years, 85 left in 2 years, and 45 left in 1 year (Glasser & Zunin, 1973).

In our society we separate people from the mainstream who break either the written laws or the unwritten laws. When the patients described above could abide by the unwritten laws (i.e., could act normal and sane), they were returned to society. There is no written law that says a person should not hear voices. But there seems to be an unwritten law that states that no one should allow imaginary voices to interfere with work or family life. When such interference is judged excessive, the person in question is taken to the mental hospital. On the other hand, there are written laws that we are required to respect. When people break these laws, they are ushered off to jail.

Glasser further developed the background ideas in a correctional institution, the Ventura School, which was a school for delinquent girls near Los Angeles where he served as a consultant in the late 1950s. He laid the groundwork for his yet to be named theory in *Mental Health or Mental Illness?* (Glasser, 1961). But when his work at the Ventura School became so successful, he labeled his method "reality psychiatry" and presented it to the 1962 meeting of the National Association of Youth Training Schools. He said that the response was "phenomenal," adding, "Evidently many people doubted the effectiveness of any therapy that did not ask people to accept responsibility for what they chose to do with their lives" (Glasser, 1984, p. 327).

The term *reality therapy* was initially used in the book by the same name that was first published in 1965. In this landmark work, Glasser speaks of his work in mental health and in corrections. He also began to develop the basic theory, especially the importance of human needs as motivators of behaviors, love, and self-worth. He stressed the importance of responsibility, which he defined as "the ability to fulfill one's needs, and to do so in a way that does not deprive others of their ability to fulfill their needs" (Glasser, 1965, p. xi).

While acceptance of the concepts was less than universal among therapists, the principles elucidated in *Reality Therapy* struck a responsive chord among educators. Since the institution in which people break both the written and unwritten laws early in life is the school, it seemed only logical to apply the same successful principles to schools. Thus, out of his experience in the schools of Palo Alto and in the Los Angeles area, Glasser wrote *School without Failure* (1968), which described a program designed to eliminate failure from schools. Concerning the application to schools, O'Donnell (1987) says, "Glasser's book *Schools without Failure,* published in 1968, turned out to be one of the biggest sellers in education since the John Dewey books" (p. 4). When counselors, teachers, and correctional workers used reality therapy, they found that it was effective for building inner responsibility in students and clients who had little experience with such a notion.

Still, it was not clear as to why it was effective. Then when Glasser happened to read a statement by Marshall McLuhan that students are searching for a role, not a goal (Glasser, 1972), it became clear that reality therapy helped people to find out who they were by providing them with tools to fulfill their psychological needs. It seemed that, as Ford (1982) said, people were becoming more interested in their identity needs, "sociability and personal worth, and less concerned with...survival and security" (p. 390). Glasser pointed out that in the '60s we witnessed not just rebellion, but a cultural revolution. He observed that people became interested in identity needs for three reasons: increased affluence because of which the survival needs of most people were insured, laws that ensured equality among groups of people, and increased communication because of the efficiency of the instant media. Even if affluence and equality were not experienced by large segments of our society, still people realized that it was possible to achieve it and in fact became more frustrated at not being able to fulfill their psychological needs as fully as others could.

Another significant thread in the development of reality therapy was the additional idea that there could be a shortcut from a failure identity to a success identity. This could be achieved not in an *easy* way but rather through the performance of effortful behaviors that were carried out for 6 to 12 months for relatively brief daily time intervals. These activities do not engage the person's concentration but rather allow the mind "to float" and to wander in a productive and positive manner. *Positive Addiction* (Glasser, 1976) reflected this idea and provided another tool for the reality therapist to use in helping clients gain a success identity, added inner responsibility, increased self-esteem, and more effective control over their lives.

It is at this point that another thread

of history becomes evident. As with many therapies, reality therapy as a method developed first, followed by a formulation of the theory. The sociological theory had been sculpted in *The Identity Society,* but a psychological theory of brain functioning was lacking. This was formulated by Glasser in *Stations of the Mind* (1981), in which he explained the principles of control system theory or control theory in the context of psychotherapy. Describing the human brain as a psycho-social, biological negative feedback input control system is not new with reality therapy. Weiner (1948) described the human brain as a cybernetic loop that seeks input from the world around it. He spoke of the role of feedback in engineering and in biology. He later warned of possible excesses in the use of feedback machines (Weiner, 1950).

The immediate predecessor of Glasser's contribution to control theory is the work of William Powers, *Behavior, the Control of Perception* (1973). In this book as in other works by control theorists, Powers states that the brain seeks input from the world around it. Human beings are driven by forces inside them; therefore, we are not merely conditioned by external stimuli as the behaviorists teach. Glasser (1981) has applied and extended control theory by incorporating the human needs belonging, power, fun, and freedom as the genetic instructions or forces that drive human beings.

The fact that human output (behavior) has a purpose and is a choice is emphasized in Glasser's most significant work, *Control Theory* (1985). That we choose our behavior is a central element in the control theory as taught by Glasser.

And so reality therapy, along with its companion and theoretical base, control

theory, should be seen as ideas that have evolved over many years. Their current status consists of applications to nearly every type of personal and professional interaction.

Current Status

The Institute for Reality Therapy has developed an 18-month training program for people seeking certification in the practice of reality therapy. It begins with attendance at a Basic Intensive Week. During this 5-day program, the participants learn both the theory and methodology as well as practice specific skills in small groups under the supervision of an approved instructor. This is followed by a period of at least 6 months during which the candidate takes a practicum with an approved practicum supervisor. Then follows an Advanced Intensive Week and an advanced practicum. These are at least the same length as the Basic Week and practicum. However, a higher level of skill is required at this stage of the training. The final phase of the certification process is another 5-day session in which the candidates prove to a faculty member that they have adequate knowledge and are skilled in reality therapy.

The philosophy underlying this program is that of inclusion. Every effort is made to spread the concepts of reality therapy rather than restrict them to a few professionals. Thus the program is designed to appeal to people who have full-time employment and cannot leave work to do lengthy and costly internships. The Center for Reality Therapy in Cincinnati, Ohio, in conjunction with the Institute conducts such workshops Friday through Tuesday so that participants will miss 2 or 3 days of work instead of 5. Since the inception of the certification process in 1975, nearly 3,000 people have been certified by the Institute. At present, over 200 are certified each year.

Currently, reality therapy is widely used in drug and alcohol programs. In 1974, over 90% of 200 drug and alcohol programs for the U.S. military used reality therapy as their preferred modality for treatment (Glasser, 1984). Moreover, hundreds of thousands of teachers have been trained to use the Schools without Failure (SWF) program, which includes the 10-step disciplinary system and class meetings.

Applications to schools not only include the SWF program but have been extended to substance abuse education. The *CHOICE Program* (Glasser, 1988) is a drug prevention program that emphasizes the application of control theory to Grades 7 through 9. It can be incorporated into the school curriculum through the use of lesson plans and includes a major component involving parents. The most recent advancement in the application to schools consists of the mingling of Glasserian thought with that of Deming (1982) within the school context. Through the application of reality therapy in the "Quality School," students are led to higher achievement and better relationships without coercion and with involvement (Glasser, 1990).

Reality therapy has also been used successfully in group homes, marriage relationships, suicide prevention, psychosis, adolescent counseling, geriatrics, and other contexts (Glasser, N., 1980, 1989).

The application of reality therapy in counseling and psychotherapy continues to be further delineated and extended. In this book *Using Reality Therapy*, Wubbolding (1988) describes a reality therapy model of counseling applied to marriage and family. He also has incorporated

paradoxical techniques as ways to deal with resistance, and his application of reality therapy as a "cycle of counseling" (Wubbolding, 1989a) will be explained later.

Relationship counseling within the context of reality therapy has been developed by Ford, who stresses the importance of common need-fulfilling behaviors, time spent together, and changing perceptions toward the other person (Ford, 1974, 1983; Ford & Englund, 1979).

The parent-child relationship has received special attention by reality therapists. Ford (1977) describes effective ways to show love, build discipline, and develop an abiding faith or belief in something outside themselves. Similarly, Bluestein and Collins (1985) describe ways for parents to fulfill their needs, to negotiate, and to impose consequences.

In the world of work, the principles of reality therapy are called "reality management" or "reality performance management." The goal of these applications is to train supervisors nad managers to create an environment that is need fulfilling for workers as well as to help them develop coaching skills that they can use to help employees increase responsible behavior (Glasser, W., 1980; Wubbolding, 1985b, 1989b, 1990b).

The principles of reality therapy have been applied to nearly every genus of human interaction, and the field of self-help has not been neglected. Since the ideas can be expressed in language understandable to most people, clients are often asked to be on a reading program so that they can take better control of their lives. They are asked to spend time writing about goals, plans, and perceptions (Wubbolding, 1985a, 1990a). They can be encouraged to examine their behaviors relative to their needs and to take direct action on their own regarding their problems (Good, 1987). Specific applications to problems that many people seek help for are categorized as burnout. Reality therapy offers a rationale for this phenomenon as well as specific ways to address such upsetting feelings (Edelwich, 1980; Wubbolding, 1979).

The phrase "reality therapy" was coined because the world in which we live is organized on certain principles; people decide what they want, evaluate their behavior, and plan to achieve it. In the daily conduct of our lives, they don't examine unconscious and unresolved conflicts. The principles of reality therapy have universal application because they have been derived from commonsense observation of how healthy people live their lives.

TENETS OF THE MODEL

In order to grasp the principles of reality therapy, it is first necessary to understand control theory as developed and applied by William Glasser (1981, 1985). A control system acts on its environment so that it can get the input it has sought by its behavior. Wubbolding (1990c) describes a sculptor molding and shaping clay so that it matches his images of how he wants it to appear. We are all sculptors who mold the world around us to make it congruent with our perceptions of what we want.

The human brain as a control system is best understood through the analogy of a thermostat. This mechanism is designed to control its environment, to get a "perception" of its own impact on the world around it. If the "control" on the thermostat is set at 72°, the thermostat sends a signal to the furnace or air conditioner to generate specific and purposeful actions. They are designed to fulfill a "desire" within the mechanism

—to keep the room at the level of 72°. The thermostat "perceives" the effectiveness of its behaviors through its thermometer. In other words, the thermometer tells the control how it is doing or whether its behavior is effective.

An interesting and important sidelight is that the system can be fooled. If a match is held under the thermometer, it will read and report the room temperature inaccurately. All the control can know is what it perceives. Through its "perceptual system," the thermometer, it believes the room is much hotter than it really is. As a consequence, it relentlessly drives the air conditioner harder and harder. It will continue to drive the machinery until it can get another perception (temperature reading) or until the air conditioner ceases to function.

So, too, it is with the human brain. It seeks to get what it wants from the world around it. Through its perceptual system, it gets feedback on how effective its behavior has been. But the feedback can be very misleading. Alcohol and drugs, for example, provide the illusion that behavior is more effective than it really is. Family members who are drug free perceive the alcoholic's behavior quite differently. They see even the chemically dependent person's behavior as very destructive.

Human Needs

Unlike a thermostat, the human control system—the brain—is driven by what Glasser has termed "genetic instructions." These are human needs or internal forces that are the root causes of all human behavior. Throughout our entire lives we seek, by means of our behaviors, to meet one or more of the innate needs. Sometimes the behavior is effective, sometimes not effective, and sometimes even counterproductive. But whether it is effective or not, all human endeavor is purposeful. It is an attempt to gain belonging, or involvement with people, power or achievement, enjoyment or fun, and freedom or independence, and survival.

Belonging. All human beings are born with a need to relate to others. In family counseling this need is of paramount importance, because the family is the natural environment in which belonging is met. Family members are taught that demeaning each other within the counseling or at home is always harmful. Ventilating anger at each other is discouraged. The person releasing a pent-up feeling might feel better for the moment, but a sense of belonging is not enhanced.

Rather, the family is encouraged to spend time together so that pleasant perceptions of each other as need fulfilling can be increased and stored for further use at a later time. These positive memories, valuable in themselves, also serve as a foundation for future plan making and compromise. This concept of "quality time" will be explained in detail later.

Power, Achievement. The word *power* has come to imply dominance, exploitation, and even ruthlessness. It is, however, used here to denote the meaning from the French *pouvoir* and the Spanish *poder,* "to be capable," "to be able." It is a broad concept and a strong need that is paramount for many people. In the initial stages of relationships the need for belonging is more pronounced. After the heat and enthusiasm of the initial stages of a relationship have cooled, there often emerges a struggle related to power. The new baby fulfills a yearning for more belonging for the parents. Yet, before long, the baby seeks constant attention (power) at all hours of the day,

sometimes resulting in parental frustration at having to give so much attention to the new family member. When children grow to the teen years, they seek ways to achieve power that often conflict with the need fulfillment of the parents and other family members. Such struggles surround the use of a car, homework, grades, sexual behavior, and a myriad of other family problems.

Another aspect of this need is that we all seek a sense of competence and adequacy. Parents want to see themselves as having done a good, if not superior, job of parenting. Children seek the same fulfillment at their level. When family members feel inadequate in the family, they often resort to illusory ways to gain a sense of importance—through drugs, antisocial behavior, withdrawl, depression, or even psychosis. These negative symptoms are often signs of inadequate power-need fulfillment.

Enjoyment, Fun. Aristotle said that people are human because we are "risible"; that is, we can laugh. A fundamental human desire is to escape boredom and at least maintain a sense of interest in our world, our behavior. A quality that separates us from the animal kingdom is our ability to see humor and play. Playing seems natural to children, and through it they grow intellectually and fulfill their needs. Often times, when a family seeks counseling, the enjoyment they experience is sought outside family relationships. On the other hand, fun is sometimes the result of behaviors that are hurtful to the other members of the family. A prank becomes teasing; teasing becomes vicious; vicious becomes violence. Sometimes such families voluntarily seek or are court ordered to attend family counseling sessions. The counselor's goal is to help the family learn enjoyment-directed behaviors that lead to more intimate relationships and closeness within the family.

Freedom, Independence. This need is sometimes seen as similar to power. It means that we all need to have choices and to stand on our own. We wish to make our own schedule, live in places we opt for, have friends we select for ourselves, and act in many other autonomous ways.

In families, a choice of one member often interferes with the choice of another family member. The range of choices surrounding chemical dependency, for instance, often infringes on the choices of the other family members. When the failure to fulfill this need adequately is linked to out-of-control behaviors, there is often a clash of choices related to all four needs.

It should be understood that the needs are general. They can be likened to empty bowls that we seek to fill by means of a variety of behaviors. They are not specific. We have a need for belonging, but we have a specific want for relationships with specific people. These particular wants are related to each need and are changeable. We can change what we want, but we cannot change what we need. Likewise, the needs are universal. Everyone has them. They seem to be present in people from all cultures.

Survival. Finally, we all have a need to live, to maintain health, to breath air. In fact when our survival is threatened, we frequently take radical action to preserve it.

Human Wants

While the needs are the fundamental driving forces of human behavior, the specific wants are the more proximate energizers for what we do, think, and feel. It is useful to think of the spectrum of wants as analogous to a picture album. Glasser (1990) has also referred to this picture album as the "quality world," with each picture in the album or quality world representing a want. We have pictures or wants related to each need. Some are more important than others, some are blurred. The counselor using reality therapy explores this picture album with the family members by asking them what they want from the family relative to each need. Family members are asked to define what they want that they are getting and not getting from the family members, their friends, their jobs, their schools, and even the counselor.

In exploring the wants of the family members, it is crucial to help family members determine their level of commitment. Wubbolding (1988) has described five levels of commitment that clients exhibit:

1. "We don't want to be here. You can't help us." This is the lowest level of commitment and must change if amelioration of family problems is to occur. Families coerced into counseling frequently display this level in the beginning sessions. By utilizing the principles described as "environment" and "procedures," the reality therapist can help the client move to a higher level of commitment.

2. "We'd like the pleasure of the outcome but not the effort required to achieve it." Such a level is seen in the family that has some desire to change and work out problems. They know they are troubled and even desire a better life for them-

selves, but they have not yet made the commitment to take action, to do anything differently, or to change their direction.

3. "We'll try; we might; we could." This level of commitment is higher than the first two. Here the family is motivated to change. They feel the pain of not getting what they want from their family life, but they are not yet to the point where they are totally committed to changing behaviors. An escape hatch to failure has been preserved. They subsequently can say "We *tried,* but we simply couldn't work out the family problems."

4. "We'll do our best." This level represents a very high level to work toward harmony. They are willing to evaluate their behavior, to make plans to follow through if they don't have to "change too much." The counselor builds on this level and helps them to attain an even higher level of commitment.

5. "We'll do whatever it takes." The highest level of commitment is expressed by this statement. The family is willing to put 100% effort into the achievement of the counseling goals.

It is important to help the family members individually to commit themselves to work toward the resolution of problems. They can be asked about their level of commitment occasionally when resistance is encountered. Also, commitment is developmental (i.e., a low level can evolve to a higher one). In fact, a major task of the reality therapist in the first several sessions is to help them increase their commitment to a more effective level.

Behavior

Another component of the human control system is behavior. Behavior is given a slightly different definition than in other systems of therapy. Behavior is here seen has having four components: (a) acting or doing, (b) thinking or cognition, (c) feeling or emotion, and (d) physiology. All behavior contains these four elements. The "acting" component receives most but by no means all of the emphasis in the counseling sessions, for two reasons. First, human beings have more control over the doing or acting aspect of their behavior. A mother, father, or child can rarely change their feelings of anger or resentment by a simple fiat. They can, however, change more easily what they say to each other. They can *choose* to spend time together. They can choose to remain silent, though often with much difficulty, when they *feel* like exploding in anger or resentment. Second, human beings are less aware of their "acting" than they are of their thoughts, feelings, and physiology. People are generally aware of how they feel at a given moment: awake, tired, hungry, upset, angry, guilty, and so forth. Though they are often unable to attach a clinical label to their feeling, they generally know if they feel good or bad. But it takes reflection to attend to the acting. While I write these words I am aware of thirst, hunger, feeling good about what is written, but I am less aware of how I'm sitting—arm on table, feet on floor or on rung of chair. In families, the members are aware of their upset feeling but less aware of how they spend their time, what they say to each other, and how they treat the other family members.

Thus, in reality therapy the counselor pays attention to the feelings, talks about them, and allows the family to acknowledge and discuss them. The therapist, however, makes a concerted effort to connect the feelings with the doing because feelings are like the lights on the dashboard of the automobile. When they light up, the driver knows when something is wrong as well as when something is right. Then, action is planned and taken to resolve the problem.

Perception

The next component of the human control system consists of how the person views the world. Perception functions through two filters, high and low. Through the high filter the person puts a value on incoming perceptions and images. Thus, when parents see a child hitting another family member, they disapprove or see the behavior from a high negative level. If the child hits a punching bag in order to stay in good physical condition, the parents might see this behavior from a positive level, thereby giving approval. Seeing one's circumstances from a low level of perception means simply recognizing the environment without making a judgment. Most events in families are seen from a low level of perception. For example, when people walk into a room, they observe the room without explicitly approving or disapproving of the furniture, the carpeting, or the atmosphere. They often relate later that they don't even remember the physical setting they were in. They have no strong pleasant or unpleasant memories of it because they saw the circumstances from a low level of perception.

The Outside World

The last element is not a part of the human control system, but it requires explanation relative to the control system. The world outside us impinges on us in many ways, and through our behavior we seek to change it to match what we want. In a family, the individual members often want the "world"—the other family members to change. Consider a couple that hopes the other person will change. If this were to occur, they insist, the world would be a better place for each of them. Yet it is difficult, indeed impossible, to change another person directly. What can be hoped for and held out to the family is that if each one can commit to even a slight change, the others might also choose to change.

In summary, the human person is seen as a control system seeking to get what it wants from the world around it. It generates behaviors designed to mold the world as a sculptor molds clay. In families, the sculptors often conflict with each other. Their choices are to change what they want, to vary their behavior, or to alter their perceptions. These three elements are interconnected so that a change in one results in a change of the other two. The most easily changed part of the system is the "doing" component of the behavioral system.

APPLICATION

Clients for Whom Reality Family Therapy Is Effective

Reality therapy was first developed in institutions in which mildly, moderately, and severely disturbed people were treated—a mental hospital and a correctional school for young women. It has since been applied to virtually every kind of client(s). It is used with families who have major or minor problems, including those that are verbal or nonverbal, from upper or lower socioeconomic levels, and from a wide spectrum of cultures including many Oriental groups. It has been used to remediate severe family problems such as alcoholism and abuse as well as to develop family growth and closeness. The application to problems has been more widespread because families more often seek counseling to solve problems than to enhance family growth or closeness.

Goals of the Therapeutic Process

The general aim of reality family therapy is to help the family gain a sense of inner control. When a family enters counseling, they often feel even more out of control than before they made the decision to seek help. They believe that they not only have a problem, but now it has reached a level so serious that they must involve an "outsider" in their personal family business. Thus, it is important that the family therapist gain a sense of relief or inner control. More specific goals include the following:

Gain at Least a Modicum of Need-Fulfillment. Each person must feel some sense of belonging or involvement with the family or at least with one other member. If the counseling is to be successful, each one must feel some degree of power. If they are at least listened to and appreciated during the session, some feeling of power and competence is felt by the family members. Also, all members need to feel enjoyment or fun. The counseling sessions themselves should occasionally contain *some* fun. Even if this is not possible at every meeting, the counselor helps the family to have fun together outside on their own. The final psychological need, freedom, is experienced when all family members make individual choices as well as

choices to spend time together or to relinquish ineffective behaviors.

Change Levels of Perception. The members of the family are also assisted in altering their levels of perception toward the problems and toward each other. For example, if they see each other's behavior from a high emotional level of disapproval, they are taught to lower their perception so that their behavior is less impassioned. On the other hand, if a perception of the family or a family member is low, the counselor might help them raise it. Thus, when the chemically dependent member or perpetrator of abuse does not perceive such behavior as a problem, the counselor assists the family member(s) to raise the level of perception so that judgments are made regarding such behavior. It's been said that this specific skill is "comforting the afflicted" and "afflicting the comfortable."

Use Quality Time. One of the most important outcomes of reality family therapy is quality time. This is the foundation of any change. It includes time spent together in a noncritical manner, and it will be explained later as one of the cornerstones of reality family therapy as well as a prerequisite for fulfillment of the following goal.

Change Behavior. A more measurable, tangible goal of counseling is to help the family change behavior, more specifically, to change how they act toward one another. This means changing how they talk to each other in and out of the sessions as well as how they treat each other. If they are able to spend time together and build up a bank of positive memories about each other, they will be more likely to be able to communicate in a mutually need-fulfilling manner as well as to negotiate effective compromises.

Clients' Primary Responsibilities

Reality therapy is based on the beliefs that people are accountable for their behaviors and can choose more effective actions, that any choice is generated with the aim of shaping the external world in a way that matches internal wants (Wubbolding, 1988).

And so, it is the clients' responsibility to realize that changes come from within. Behavior is *chosen* and not caused by outside forces. Yet it is the conventional wisdom that external stimuli, or the environment, is responsible for our behavior. Among the indications of this kind of thinking among family members are statements such as "You *make* me angry"; "You *cause* me such great pain"; "I had an anxiety *attack*"; "A fit of depression *came over* me." Others see their *locus of control* as existing somewhere in their past history. Their own childhood abuse or parents' chemical dependence is the cause for their present abuse of their children or their alcoholism.

Another client responsibility is to want to *do* something to change. There is a major distinction between wanting *a* change and wanting *to* change. When the family members want *a* change in the family, they at least have some motivation for improvement. They are probably at the second level of commitment: "We'd like the pleasure of the outcome but not the effort required to achieve it." Nevertheless, better control and more effective need fulfillment require a higher level of commitment—at least "We'll try."

Beyond the verbal commitment to change is the willingness to follow through on action plans. They make plans to incorporate quality time, to negotiate family boundaries, to communicate in more empathic ways, and so forth. Reality therapy requires that they are willing to try new behaviors, that they rearrange priorities, that they examine and evaluate their expectations of themselves and each other. Because this sometimes requires, especially in the early sessions, that they follow the suggestions and prescriptions of the therapist, they need to trust the therapist.

It is important to note that these "responsibilities" cannot be separated from those of the counselor. Though therapists cannot *force* the family to accept these responsibilities, they can set an atmosphere and utilize procedures that make it possible and need fulfilling for the family members to make more responsible choices and to accept these responsibilities.

Therapist's Role and Function

The general work of the therapist is to create an atmosphere conducive to change. Glasser (1986) states, "The counselor should attempt to create a supportive environment within which clients can begin to make changes in their lives." Wubbolding (1988, 1989a) has described in detail how a reality therapist sets an environment for change. Positive suggestions include assuming an attitude that "we will work things out." This is in no way a guarantee, but it is an attempt to communicate a feeling of hope to the family. The client doing the unexpected, especially reframing, is a paradoxical technique that is used extensively and can be employed in the very beginning of the counseling relationship. The suggestion of Weeks and L'Abate

(1982) is quite helpful: when the family first arrives for counseling, they are congratulated for having taken a first step to improve. They have already begun to take action. This is an effort to help them abandon their feeling of weakness and powerlessness and to recognize that they have begun the healing process—another positive suggestion.

Like any therapist, the reality family therapist utilizes good listening and empathy skills. Especially useful is the ability to hear and use metaphors spoken by the family members and to provide added ones. When the mother of a family said, "I feel like we're in a plane that's on automatic pilot, and I don't know if we're headed up or down," the counselor helped the family members define their own roles on the plane—copilot, navigator, passenger, or terrorist—as well as how they could get better control of the plane. When the family describes their perceptions of family life, the counselor encourages them to *focus* on themselves rather than on the others. They are gently encouraged to describe "WDEP" as it applies to them, that is, their own *w*ants, what they *d*o, the *e*valuations of their own behavior, and their own *p*lans. The skilled reality therapist combines directness, empathy, and confrontation in a manner that allows openness, frankness, and responsible communication by the family members.

As a result of practicing the above skills, the reality therapist avoids several negative situations. For instance, he or she does not request or become embroiled in excuses when the family members describe their locus of control as being outside themselves. The therapist quickly brings the focus back to the speaker and his or her own behavior. Lengthy arguing among family members is also skirted. It is helpful to listen to the family's story and to assess how the family communicates, at what levels they perceive each other, and how realistic their goals are, but it is fruitless to allow ongoing arguing, blaming, or criticizing. Belittling statements, demeaning remarks, and the wanton expression of anger are not regarded as helpful and therefore are likewise discouraged. Since animosity is seen as counterproductive, the therapist intervenes to stop its expression by skillfully using the procedures described in the next section.

Primary Techniques

The most basic skill and overriding technique used in reality family therapy is that of asking relevant questions. In some counseling theories, questions are discouraged and reflective listening is encouraged. But the skilled practitioner of reality therapy asks many questions pertaining to the human control system. He or she questions family members in order to help them identify and clarify their wants and perceptions; to describe the various components of their total behavior; to evaluate their wants, behaviors, and perceptions; and to make individual and common plans to gain control and fulfill their needs.

Determination of Wants, Perception, Level of Commitment (W). The family members are asked what they want to derive from the counseling process. They are asked to define what they want from the family, from each other, and from need-fulfilling behaviors outside the family. They are helped to express how they view these categories, without criticism of each other. When an inevitable attack begins, the counselor intervenes by directing the conversation to less judgmental descriptions. Practitioners of reality therapy also share their wants and perceptions by describing what they expect from the family and how they see the progress of family growth.

Description of Four Components of Behavior with Emphasis on Doing or Acting (D). Family members are asked to describe how they spend their time together and individually. The counselor acts as a TV camera viewing exactly what happened on a specific day at a precise time. This narration serves as a self-diagnosis by the family and is a prelude to evaluation and planning.

Frequently individuals fail to have skills or activities that they perform alone that are effectively need fulfilling. They can be counseled individually or within the family sessions to develop behaviors performed alone that increase their self-esteem. When their self-esteem is elevated, they will benefit more quickly from family counseling.

The heart of this component is the use of quality time (QT), which is introduced early in therapy. This is built on effective behaviors but is strengthened simultaneously with self-esteem-enhancing behaviors that are performed alone by each family member. In other words, the counselor does not work with individuals in the family session *before* dealing with QT. To be called truly QT, the common behavior must have several characteristics:

- Requires effort. Passive behaviors such as watching TV do not build close relationships.
- Includes value. The behavior must be seen as important to each person.
- Involves awareness. The participants need *at least* to be aware of the other person. Preferably, they *need* the other person, such as when a game is played.

- Is planned for a limited amount of time. It is best to begin with a plan to perform the activity for 10 to 15 minutes a day. If the people involved plan for a lengthy amount of time, they are less likely to follow through.
- Is done repetitively. If the QT is to have a lasting effect, it must be done repeatedly.
- Shuns criticism. This and the following characteristics are the most significant. During this time there should be no put-downs or attacks on the other person. To sustain the behavior, each individual should see the behavior as pleasurable and need fulfilling, not as painful.
- Avoids discussions of past misery. During these precious moments, each person pledges not to bring up past conflicts, past failures, or past pain.
- Discourages complaining. Griping about other people creates an inner dissatisfaction and a feeling of smugness that is counterproductive to the goals of the reality therapist.
- Discuss present or past successes. The conversation need not be phoney or shallow. Nevertheless, the dialogue might be artificial at first, for families who are suffering often find it difficult to converse in ways that healthier families find easy.
- Converse about WDE. (Avoid the P.) Family members can be taught how to talk to each other using the procedures of reality therapy. Over a period of time, they can learn to ask one another about wants or about how they spend their time. When they become skilled at this, they can then utilize the evaluation procedure explained in the next section. Wubbolding (1990c) describes a conversation with a niece in which she re-

lated to him that she had to read *Beowulf* over the weekend but was not going to do this painful homework assignment. In a lengthy discussion, he asked her what she wanted to do when she graduated and whether or not reading *Beowulf* would help her get where she wanted to go. No attempt was made to push her for a plan. The next evening they spoke again briefly. Before he could say a word to her, she blurted out, "You'll be happy to know I read all my *Beowulf.*" It is not always necessary to push for a plan. But it is necessary to remain nonjudgmental and accepting of the other person.

The marriage therapist helps the family increase their quality time so that they can build a storehouse of pleasant memories and perceptions. These eventually will outbalance the painful ones, creating a basis for communicating effectively, solving problems, compromising, dealing with the daily stresses of life, and getting through the inevitable crisis faced by every family.

Development of Skill in Evaluation (E). The therapist uses six forms of evaluation with a family (Wubbolding, 1990a, 1990c). It should be noted that many family members have much difficulty with this procedure. Although the evaluation must ultimately be made and internalized by the family members, it is often futile merely to ask them evaluative questions. Chemically dependent or abusive families, for example, often are unable to make self-evaluations without the direct intervention of the counselor. The evaluations concern the following:

1. Attainability of wants. An adolescent family member may want total freedom: "I want my parents to leave me alone." The counselor helps the person ask him- or herself if this is realistic.

2. Helpfulness of perceptions. When asked how they see the child, parents might say that they see a lazy, rebellious, unkempt, unmanageable child. The therapist helps them examine if this viewpoint is really and truly helping them work out their family problems.

3. Effectiveness of behaviors. There seems to be a trait common to human beings of all cultures. Many people live by the maxim "If it is not helping, keep doing it." Thus, parents shout at their children, a behavior that rarely works for any length of time. If such behavior helped to solve problems, parents could scream once and never again need to repeat the screaming. The very reason parents yell at children is that it does not work. The practitioner of reality therapy acts as a mirror by asking the family to describe their behavior and by asking them, "Is this getting you what you want?"

4. Consequences of overall direction. This is done quickly and is not always distinguishable from 3 above. It is more general and includes such questioning as "Is the direction and destination of this family a plus or a minus?" "Are you headed in a direction that is beneficial or destructive?"

5. Level of commitment. The counselor helps each family member evaluate whether their respective levels of commitment to the family and to a positive direction are weak or strong. An effort is made to find a common level of commitment among family members.

6. Efficacy of plans. The goal of the

counseling process is to help the family make plans that result in harmonious family living. These plans should be evaluated either explicitly or implicitly. The characteristics of a plan (described next) serve as a basis of this evaluation.

Formulation of Plans (P). The culmination of the process is the formulation and more importantly the successful execution of need-fulfilling plans. Plans should be simple, realistic, precise, and firm. They should not be vague or overwhelming to the family members.

Importance of the WDEP System

The WDEP system appears to be simple, and it is indeed easy to understand because it uses clear, down-to-earth terminology. (In other words, the paucity of arcane phraseology has been based on intentionality!) Most of the jargon-free explanations are quite comprehensible to both the layperson and the professional and involve only a few Latin and Greek derivatives. But like the skills required in a sport, these understandable skills are much more difficult to carry out in practice. The first-year student of chemistry might understand the principles of how various paints interact to form color, but only a skilled painter can then create an artistic work. And very few reach the level of Picasso, Matisse, or Warhol.

Second, the most important aspect of using the WDEP system is not the specifics of each component but rather the concomitant learning that occurs. Families learn indirectly and as a side effect that their wants are important, that their opinions and viewpoints are worth listening to, that their behaviors are changeable, that they are not immutably destined for failure and unhappiness,

that they have *the power and the responsibility to change for the better.* These positive, hopeful lessons are learned less by the direct statements of the therapist and more in an indirect, experiential manner. They are the result of skillful questioning by the counselor and the inner evaluations of the family members.

CASE EXAMPLE

The following section represents part of the initial session of a family of five. Mrs. L called to set up an appointment because of tension in the family. After she made the appointment, Leon, 11, was struck by a car while walking with his brother, Bart, 13. Leon remains in critical condition in the hospital. The four remaining family members are present for the first session: mother Wendy, 38; father Hal, 37; daughter Ginny, 14; and son Bart, 13.

The segment described here took place after the professional and ethical details were discussed: informed consent, fees, professional disclosure, limitations of confidentiality, and so forth.

Therapist: Mother, you called saying there is a lot to talk about. You said there was a great deal of turmoil in the family, and in the second call you gave me a summary of the accident and the upset that has resulted. Since you, Mother, made the call, I'd like to ask you first, Dad, what do you think about being here?

Hal: I don't really think it's necessary. We're upset, but I think we just have to handle it.

Wendy: But I made the original call for other reasons. One of them is your apathy toward the rest of us.

Hal: I don't feel that I'm apathetic.

Therapist: Ginny, what do you think about being here today talking with this "outsider" to your family?

Ginny: It's OK, I guess. But I'm afraid.

Therapist: Bart, how about you?

Bart: It was all my fault. If I'd been paying more attention, my brother would be OK.

Hal: I've told those kids 1,000 times to be careful.

Therapist: Before we go any further, I'd like to ask each of you what you would like to get out of these discussions and especially what you want to get from today's session.

Wendy: I think we better talk about the accident.

Therapist: How about you, Bart.

Bart: Yeah, it was my fault.

Therapist: Ginny, what would you like to have happen here today?

Ginny: I don't know. I'm afraid, but I'd like them to leave me alone at school.

Therapist: So far, each of you has expressed some intense feeling—fear, guilt, hesitancy—about being here. We'll come back to how you feel, but first I want to ask you, Dad, do you want to discuss this upsetness in your family today?

Hal: I'm not sure.

Therapist: Let's put it this way. Will your 1,001st lecture help solve this current crisis?

Hal: Well, I guess not!

Therapist: Can you be more definite than that? What's your judgment on it?

Hal: No, it won't help us.

Therapist: In other words, now is the time to try something different?

Hal: Yes.

Therapist: Mom, could you repeat your thoughts about being here?

Wendy: I was so upset about the fighting and bickering in the family. Hal either argues with the kids or ignores them completely and now this accident...I don't know how I can take much more.

Therapist: Do you think that this counseling can relieve some of your burden?

Wendy: I certainly hope so.

Therapist: I hope so, too, because it is evident that you are all hurting in your own ways. Dad, do you feel any pain about this?

Hal: Yes, I sure do. It's hard to admit it, however.

Therapist: I admire you for your honesty. I want to ask you, all of you, a question. Do you want to discuss the tension and problems you had as a family previous to the accident or do you want to talk about the accident and how it has affected you?

All: The accident.

Therapist: That's exactly what I thought. But I wanted to have you define what you wanted to talk about today. We can talk again about the other problems later, OK?

All: (Nod in agreement.)

Therapist: Mother, would you describe what happened, please?

Wendy: (Explains in detail how Leon and Bart were in the shopping center and left to come home, crossed the street, and how Leon was hit by a car.)

Therapist: Bart, can you add any details?

Bart: (Describes a few more details.) It was all my fault. If I had stopped him, he would not be in the hospital.

Therapist: I've noticed one thing. No one has been blaming you, Bart. When you just now started to cry, your mother put her hand on your shoulder. Your dad wants all of his kids to be careful, but I didn't hear him saying it was your fault.

Hal: You didn't cause it, Bart.

Bart: It's all my fault!

Therapist: I know you feel that way, Bart, but did you hear what your dad said?

Bart: What?

Therapist: Dad, say it again, please.

Hal: Bart, no one is blaming you. It's not your fault.

Therapist: Bart, you will feel guilty for a while. It's only natural. I just want you to hear what your dad said. I noticed that your mother nodded in agreement. Do you understand what they said even though you don't agree with it?

Bart: Yes.

Therapist: When you hear them say what they just said, do you feel any better?

Bart: Not much.

Therapist: Do you feel any better at all, even a tiny bit?

Bart: A little bit.

Therapist: So, when they give you assurance you feel a little better even now. I'm surprised it has such a good result so quickly. I wonder if anyone else needs a little encouragement once in a while.

Wendy: We all could use it.

Therapist: Could you use it?

Wendy: Yes, I'm really upset. I told them to go to the shopping center. If I hadn't told them to go there, this wouldn't have happened.

Therapist: Dad, do you blame Wendy?

Hal: No, it's not her fault.

Therapist: Dad, would you put her hands in yours as you tell her?

Hal: Wendy, you're not to blame. If anyone is to blame, it's me, for not being home enough.

Therapist: So far everyone said they are to blame except you, Ginny. Do you want to join the group?

Ginny: It's his own fault for not watching what he was doing!

Therapist: You sound angry about it.

Ginny: Yeah.

Therapist: Are you also angry, Mom, Dad, Bart?

Hal: You're damned right I am.

Wendy: I'm so upset I can't stand it.

Therapist: How about you, Bart?

Bart: Yeah. I'm plenty mad, mostly at myself.

Therapist: So, there is something that now unites this family. You're all angry, and there is some guilt among most of you about the accident. I want to ask you all a question. I have a hunch that you've been stewing about this. It's been on your mind—the self-recrimination, self-criticism, self-blame has been impossible to get away from. Is that an accurate description?

Wendy: It's been on my mind day and night.

Therapist: You lie awake at night thinking about it?

Wendy: Constantly.

Therapist: How about you, Dad. Does it prey on your mind?

Hal: I'm very distracted at work.

Therapist: Bart, how about you?

Bart: I was too sick to go to school.

Wendy: He's been vomiting and has had diarrhea.

Therapist: So, it's affected you physically. That does not surprise me.

Bart: So that's normal?

Therapist: It doesn't surprise me in the least. You witnessed the whole thing. If you weren't physically sick for a few days, I'd be amazed. Gimny, how about you?

Ginny: The other kids keep asking me questions. The teachers want to know what happened. I wish they'd leave me alone. I don't want to talk about it.

Therapist: You want to keep it inside?

Ginny: I wish it would just go away.

Therapist: Do you think this problem is simply going to vanish?

Ginny: I want it to go away.

Therapist: Has that happened?

Ginny: No, it's worse than ever.

Therapist: Ginny, have you told anyone at school the entire story as you know it?

Ginny: No. I don't want to talk about it.

Therapist: I don't blame you. It's so painful to have everyone pushing their "help" on you.

Ginny: You're right.

Therapist: On the other hand, has it helped you to keep all this bottled up in you? Has refusing to talk about it at school made the problem go away?

Ginny: I guess not.

Therapist: So there's another thing you all have in common. This accident is constantly on your minds. You think about it day and night, at work, at school. It's even affected you physically.

Wendy: We seem to have pain as a common bond.

Hal (nodding): Yes, we finally have something we agree on.

Therapist: Since you have pain in common as well as anger, guilt, or whatever you want to call it, would you like to lessen the pain a little bit? How about you, Ginny, do you want to feel a little better?

Ginny: Yes...if they would only leave me alone, I'd feel better.

Therapist: Would you be interested in figuring out how to get them to leave you alone?

Ginny: Yes, I would. Can you help me do that?

Therapist: I bet I could. How about you, Bart. Would you want to leave a little piece of your guilt here, not all of it, just a part of it?

Bart: How could I do that?

Therapist: We'll try to figure that out, too. Right now, I'm wondering if you *want* to leave a little pain here when you leave.

Bart: Yes, I sure would!

Therapist: Mom, Dad, would you like to get away from the upsetness for a few minutes each day or several times each day? You are all going to be miserable for a while. It's quite normal to be upset at a time like this. I'm only asking if you *want* to get away from it for a while?

Hal: It's like carrying a 100-pound weight around with me. I can't set it down, and I can't get away from it.

Therapist: I like how you describe it. Does it seem that way to the rest of you?

Wendy: That's a good way to describe how I feel, too.

Bart: That's it. Maybe more for me.

Therapist: Ginny, how about you? Does it feel like a weight you're carrying around?

Ginny: Yeah. It sure does.

Therapist: It feels like more to you, Bart? I want you to come back to that later. But I still need to ask you, Mother. Do you want to lessen your pain slightly?

Wendy: I sure do. If I could only set the weight down for a while...

Therapist: Is that something you would all like? To set the weight down for a while?

Hal: Does this mean this shouldn't bother us?

Therapist: No. No. No. You will always feel concern, and the weight of pain will be there for a long time. I'm merely asking if you want *some temporary* relief from the agonizing burden for a *short* and *realistic* amount of time.

Hal: I'd love to have that.

Therapist: How about you, Bart? Would you like to feel better for a while each day?

Bart: Sure!

Wendy: Me, too. That would be great. Ginny, how about you?

Ginny: Yes, Mom, I'd like to go back to the way it was.

Therapist: Now we have several common bonds in this family. The accident is on your minds day and night, you are in pain about it, and each of you would like to lessen the hurt inside if you could figure out a way, and you agree on the fact that it feels like a 100-pound weight. How much have you felt you had in common up to the last week when Leon was hit by the car?

Wendy: I felt we were not a family anymore.

Hal: Was it that bad?

Therapist: It sounded pretty bad to me. But today you seem to be at a fork in the road in your family life. You can make a decision to work together to help each other to handle this crisis, or you can allow this tragedy to tear your family apart by not working together to help each other. Which will it be?

Hal: Work together.

Wendy: I want to save the family and help Leon.

Ginny: I want to make our family a happy family like some of my friends have.

Bart: Me, too.

Therapist: I believe you can leave some of your pain here. I also believe you can work together to confront this problem and feel better and help each other through it. It will, however, be necessary to take action and to do some things differently than what you have been doing. Are you willing to commit yourselves to working together with me to go down the road of less pain?

All: Yes, we are.

Therapist: How committed are you? Do you really want to accomplish those goals?

Ginny: I do.

Hal: It's OK with me. When I first came here, I thought you were going to blame me for all the family problems. I was determined you weren't going to point the finger at me.

Therapist: Would that have gotten us anywhere?

Hal: No!

Therapist: I try to avoid doing harmful things or things that prevent progress. Besides, I don't see the problem as being caused by any one person. I see the solutions in such a way that you all could *help* work on them. I don't want to talk forever about the problems. I'd rather stress action aimed at reducing the pain and the stress. So, Dad, how committed are you to taking the road of less pain?

Hal: Since you put it that way, I'd sure like to do it.

Therapist: Let me help you clarify your want for this important commitment. Is it a "maybe," a "weak whim," or an "I'm going to bust my chops to do it"?

Hal: I'm firmly committed.

Therapist: Bart?

Bart: Yes, I want to work on it.

Therapist: Ginny?

Ginny: Yes, if the kids and teachers...

Therapist (interrupting): Let's not worry about them right now. Do you want to work hard at feeling better, regardless of anyone else at school?

Ginny: Sure.

Therapist: Wendy, how about you?

Wendy: I don't know if anything will work very well.

Therapist: Let's put it this way—I'll make an unconditional guarantee.

Hal (interrupting): I thought you told us it was unethical to make a guarantee.

Therapist: It is. But this is a different kind of a guarantee. If you work hard, do some things I suggest, make plans, and carry them out and if you don't feel any better, I promise I'll refund all your misery, pain, and guilt.

Hal & Wendy (smiling): Sounds like a deal.

Therapist: When you smiled just then, did you feel a tiny bit better?

Hal & Wendy: Yes.

Therapist: We need to work on ways to stretch that microsecond into a minute and then into 15 minutes. I'd like to ask you, Ginny, is there anything you've stopped doing at home that was enjoyable since the accident?

Ginny: Not at home. But I am on the girls' basketball team, and I have not gone to practice since the accident.

Therapist: Do you feel better now that you've stopped going?

Ginny: Well, I guess I don't.

Therapist: I see. So, giving up basketball hasn't helped you drop part of the 100-pound burden?

Ginny (hesitantly): No, it hasn't.

Therapist: Bart, what do you think would help Ginny drop part of the weight?

Bart: She needs to get out to practice.

Therapist: You don't think she should stay at home, get sick, and feel guilty?

Bart: No.

Therapist: Would you tell that to her directly?

Bart: Why don't you go to practice? It would do you good.

Hal: I don't think it will help you, Bart, to stay home either—unless, of course, you feel physically sick. How'd you feel today?

Bart: Better. I can go to school tomorrow.

Therapist: Mom, don't you think Bart should stay at home and feel as bad and as guilty as he could?

Wendy: No. Bart, you're not guilty. You're entitled to your own life at school and your music.

Therapist: You play music?

Bart: I'm in the school orchestra.

Therapist: Have you played anything since the accident last week?

Bart: No.

Therapist: Mom, in your opinion, what effect is this choice not to play having on Bart?

Wendy: It's making him feel worse.

Therapist: Ginny, what do you think?

Ginny: It's making him feel worse.

Therapist: Bart, do you agree?

Bart: I guess so.

Therapist: Ginny, would you like to hear him play his instrument?

Ginny: Yes, sometimes I like it.

Therapist: Would you ask him to play?

Ginny: Bart, play your instrument. You don't have to give it up.

Bart: I could play for a while.

Therapist: Bart, don't overdo it. Could you play just 10 minutes?

Bart: I usually play a lot more.

Therapist: But for now could you play 10 minutes? Mom, Dad, what do you think about this?

Wendy & Hal: It would be good to hear you play again.

Therapist: Ginny, if you don't go to practice, what will happen?

Ginny: I'll get kicked off the team.

Therapist: Will that help you feel better or worse?

Ginny: Much worse.

Therapist: Dad, what do you think would help her in this situation?

Hal: There is *no* doubt about it. I think she should return to practice.

Therapist: Would you tell her?

Hal: Ginny, could you handle going to practice?

Ginny: Yes, I can.

Hal: I could come to watch your game. I haven't been to one. But this would do me good, too.

Therapist: Wow, you're volunteering to make a good plan. That's terrific. Maybe you could put some of your hurt and guilt aside for a couple of hours during the game.

Hal: I never thought of it that way.

Therapist: Would you think of it now? It's a good way to set aside the upsetness for a while. You can always come back to the 100-pound weight after the game.

Ginny: Maybe I could drop the burden for a while, too.

Therapist: It's worth a try! Now, Mom, how about you? Do you want to leave some of it aside for a while?

Wendy: You betcha I do!

Therapist: How could you do it?

Wendy: I haven't the slightest idea.

Therapist: Let me ask you some questions. How much time have you been spending at the hospital?

Wendy: When he was in the Intensive Care Unit, I was there 'round the clock. Now I go home to sleep.

Therapist: What effect has that had on you?

Wendy: I'm pretty exhausted. I've even neglected my aerobics.

Hal: That's unusual for you.

Wendy: These are unusual circumstances.

Therapist: Ginny and Bart, what do you think? Should your mother feel guilty if she comes home long enough to do her exercises and maybe a few other things for herself?

Bart: Who'll be there with Leon?

Therapist: About 10 nurses and doctors.

Ginny: I think you're going to get sick if you don't take care of yourself. That's what you always tell Dad and us.

Bart: Yeah, Mom, if you get sick, you'll be in bed like I was.

Therapist: Mom, are these words of wisdom for you? They even sound like your own words of wisdom coming back at you.

Wendy: Yes, I've said them many times.

Therapist: So will it help or hurt if you come home from the hospital for a few more hours?

Hal: The kids and I need you, too.

Wendy: I can't really do much at the hospital. I can get away for a while.

Therapist: This is very interesting. I hear you all wanting to help each other, telling each other to get away from the pain for a while. It sounds like you truly want to be a family and to show your love for each other.

Hal: It's hard for me to admit it, but yes, that's true.

Therapist: Is that how you look at it, Bart?

Bart: Yeah.

Therapist: Ginny?

Ginny: Uh huh.

Therapist: Mother?

Wendy (crying): Yes. We need each other, and we need to show it.

Therapist: So you've developed some ways to set aside the 100-pound weight for a short while. I'd like to ask you if you want to leave a small part of it here and go home a little less burdened? What do each of you think about this possibility?

Hal: How would we do this?

Therapist: First, do each of you want to do it if it could be arranged?

Wendy: Yes.

Hal: I would.

Ginny: I'd love to feel better.

Bart: Uh huh.

Therapist: I like to use symbols when I counsel, and I encourage clients to do the same. I have here four pieces of paper. (Holds up four $8\frac{1}{2} \times 11''$ sheets of paper.) Each sheet represents your pain, 100 pounds of it. Would each of you take a sheet and describe how much of the pain you'll leave here. Tear off whatever portion you'll leave with me. Keep in mind I don't want to have all of it left here. Try to be realistic. Keep your share and take it with you, and bring it back next time. Let's start with you, Bart. How much would you like to leave here?

Bart: I'd like to let you have all of it.

Therapist: No, you'll need it for a while. Just give me some.

Bart: How about half?

Therapist: Is that realistic? Can you get rid of half your pain that easily?

Bart: I guess not.

Therapist: How much can you leave here?

Bart: I'll leave 20%. (Tears off $^1/_5$ page.)

Therapist: Sounds good. I'll keep it in the file. What about you, Dad?

Hal: Here's 25%. (Tears off $^1/_4$ page.)

Therapist: Ginny?

Ginny: I'll get rid of 10%. (Tears off $^1/_{10}$ page.)

Therapist: And you, Mother?

Wendy: I'm going to give you 40%. That will still leave me with plenty to bear.

Therapist: OK. I'll keep these in your file. If you want them back, we'll have to discuss in detail your reasons. Remember you still have pain. It is natural and healthy. But now you have just a little less. Also there is one more topic I would like to talk about with you. It is a way to relieve some distress. But as a side effect, it addresses the underlying tension due to the strained relationships—the original reason you scheduled an appointment. Would you be willing to do something together as a family? Something that helps you get away from the strain and pain? (There follows a long discussion of what they could do together. Each person presents his or her ideas. After a while they negotiate to take a 10-minute walk each night after dinner before returning to the hospital.)

Therapist: There are several guidelines that will make this time truly quality time. The most important one is that for these few moments you refrain from talking about the hospital or about any problems...*no* discussion of any past misery, *no* criticism and *no* lectures.

Hal: What will we discuss?

Wendy: This could be a challenge.

Ginny: We could talk about my team.

Therapist: You've got the right idea—light conversation. No controversy. What would you like to talk about, Bart?

Bart: I could talk about school, homework, or music.

Therapist: That's it. Mom and Dad, for the first few nights could you listen and ask questions?

Hal: What good will this do?

Therapist: Tell me. Maybe you already have an idea about it.

Hal: Well, it might help us get away from our usual arguments.

Therapist: Exactly. It will help you build up pleasant memories and perceptions of each other. It will take time. And when you feel like stopping this QT, what do you need to think about?

Wendy: The tension we *used to have.*

Therapist: Yes! Are each of you willing to follow through on this plan?

All: Yes.

Therapist: Let's review what you're going to do and what you did.

Bart: I left some of my pain here today.

Therapist: You sure did!

Wendy: We're going to talk.

Hal: And we're going to listen to the kids without griping.

Therapist: And each of you has an individual plan. Do you all remember it?

All: Yes.

Therapist: We need to work on several areas in the future. I see them as (a) the pain, guilt, and anger because of the accident; (b) the tension in the family which was there before the accident. So, let's get together in 1 week or sooner, if there is a pressing need on your part.

All: Sounds good.

Discussion of First Session

In the first session, a distilled summary, the counselor used various aspects of the WDEP system. He helped each family member identify what he or she wanted from the counseling. He helped them talk about their feelings about the accident but did not discuss these in isolation from their actions. He attempted to tie their feelings to their actions because people have more direct control over what they do than how they feel. The family members were led to make their own evaluations of the effectiveness of their own behaviors and of their attainability. Plans included individual steps to gain a better sense of inner control as well as a family strategy for helping them to function more satisfactorily as a unit.

Subsequent Sessions

There is definitely a wealth of unfinished business for the family as a unit and for each individual. In the remaining sessions, the counselor would help the family accept the uncontrollable elements of the crisis. He or she would emphasize the use of family QT as a way to lessen pain and increase favorable perceptions by serving as a basis for solving problems and compromising. Each person would be encouraged to develop plans for QT with each member of the family on a one-to-one basis. They would be encouraged to define what they want from each other and how they see one another. The counselor would teach directly by explanations and teach indirectly by skillful questions that more effective communication can occur when they clearly converse by saying "I want...."; "This is how I look at the situation..."; "Does this behavior help?"; "Let's make a plan."

They would thus have alternatives to lectures, criticism, belittling, arguing, attacking, and withdrawing from each other. In summary, the reality therapist uses the WDEP system with the family and teaches them to use it.

EVALUATION

Reality therapy is based on the principle that people are responsible for their behavior and that most behaviors are chosen. Some have therefore mistakenly seen this theory as superficial. The reverse is more accurate. Choice and degree of responsibility are never simple, and it would be a mistake to say that "choice" has exactly the same meaning for all behaviors. The theory and practice of reality therapy is an evolving system with new insights continuously emerging. For instance, in years to come I hope to develop a more detailed taxonomy for levels of freedom subsumed under the phenomenon of human choice.

The practice of reality therapy has spread from its origin in corrections and a mental hospital to schools. Glasser (1968, 1988, 1990) has formulated ways to use it in classrooms for drug abuse prevention and for restructuring school itself.

Wubbolding (1989b, 1990b) has applied it to management and supervision as well as to self-help and probation. The ideas are universally applicable and have been taught in North America, Europe, and Asia. They aid in crossing cultures and with skillful adjustments can be used not only with the so-called "direct" cultures of the West but are also adaptable to the "indirect" cultures of the East.

To become skillful in the use of the principles, the practitioner must recognize that endless discussion of feelings is not equivalent to dealing effectively with them. Rather, they are treated successfully when clients change what they do. Also, the practitioner emphasizes present behavior rather than personal history, which is often interesting but beyond the current control of the family. Questioning skills are important and are appropriately used not to interrogate but indirectly to teach and help clients develop an in-control, responsible, and need-fulfilling lifestyle in which they live harmoniously with others. To achieve this end, the 18-month training program described earlier has been developed by the Institute for Reality Therapy. You can obtain more information on these and other training programs by writing me at the Center for Reality Therapy, 7777 Montgomery Road, Cincinnati, OH 45236 (phone [513] 561-1911); or the Institute for Reality Therapy, 7301 Medical Center Drive, Suite 407, Canoga Park, CA 91307 (phone [818] 888-0688).

SUMMARY

The proponents of reality therapy accept control system theory as a basis for the practice of reality therapy. This theory has not been discussed to any great extent in the educational, counseling, or psychological literature; its origins are more rooted in the engineering and computer tradition. Norbert Wiener, author of *Cybernetics* (1948), was a mathematician. William Powers, a computer consultant, wrote *Behavior, the Control of Perception* (1973), which has served as the basis for William Glasser's efforts to ground the practice of reality therapy in solid theory.

Control system theory teaches that human behavior is generated by inner drives that move us forward to gain what we want. We seek to mold the external world around us to match what we perceive as want and need fulfilling. The human needs are belonging, power or achievement, fun or enjoyment, freedom or independence, and survival.

Although these needs are general and universal, the wants related to them are specific and unique to each individual.

In order to gain the perception of having needs met, human beings generate behaviors—acting, thinking, feeling, and physiological sensations.

Consequently, behavior is *not* the result of external stimuli received from the environment, nor is it an attempt to resolve unconscious conflicts. Rather, each choice is quite purposeful and has the aim of want and need fulfillment. Thus the practitioner of reality therapy sees acting-out, depression, and even psychosis and psychosomatic pain as an ineffectual attempt to meet needs. These negative symptoms are a person's and a family's best attempt to fulfill wants and needs at a given moment. The counselor's work is designed to help them identify the underlying unmet wants and needs and, with appropriate questions to formulate strategies for more efficient want and need attainment.

The delivery system, called the cycle of counseling, is made up of two general activities: (a) establishing a friendly and firm environment and (b) utilizing the procedures summarized in the WDEP system. The latter consists in helping the family members identify what they want as individuals and as a family, what they are getting, what they are not getting, how they perceive their locus of control, and how committed they are to the process of change. Family counselors using reality therapy also share their own wants and perceptions with the family in noncritical ways.

Families are helped to examine what they are doing. Thus, behavioral symptoms comprised of the acting component, the thinking aspect, the emotional or feeling side of behavior, and even physiological symptoms are discussed in detail, depending on each case. Individuals and families are then helped to evaluate their lives in general and in detail—

the attainability of wants, effectiveness of behavior, and so forth. Finally, specific plans are built on these crucial evaluations.

As a result, families learn that they can change, that there is hope, and that they are not imprisoned in past misery. These lessons, learned by means of questioning, are most effectively taught if the therapist does not focus on direct teaching. Reality therapy is practical, easily understood, but hard to do. Nevertheless, its principles can be learned by families and used to resolve current and future problems.

ANNOTATED SUGGESTED READINGS

Glasser, W. (1965). *Reality therapy.* New York: Harper & Row.

The first significant book on reality therapy. The applications of the method in a mental hospital and in a correctional institution are discussed, stressing that change in human behavior occurs when people are held responsible and treated humanely.

Glasser, W. (1986). *Control theory.* New York: Harper & Row.

A book summarizing the brain as an input control system and how this system relates to clinical practice.

Ford, E., & Englund, S. (1979). *Permanent love: Practical steps to a lasting relationship.* Minneapolis, MN: Winston.

A book written on building relationships between couples, but the ideas are also applicable to parent-child and friend-friend interactions.

Ford, E. (1983). *Choosing to love.* Minneapolis, MN: Winston.

The importance of perceptions in relationships and how they can be changed are discussed. Includes rationale for avoiding criticism and conflict in marriage.

Wubbolding, R. (1988). *Using reality therapy.* New York: Harper & Row.

A thorough, practical book on how to use reality therapy containing specific questions on how to apply the principles and how to integrate paradoxical techniques into the practice of reality therapy.

Wubbolding, R. (1990). *Understanding reality therapy.* New York: Harper & Row.

An explanation of control theory and reality therapy through the use of metaphors. It includes a discussion of the WDEP system with specific applications.

REFERENCES

Antoninus, Marcus [Aurelius]. (1944). In A. Farquharson (Ed.). *The meditations of Marcus Antoninus.* London: Oxford University Press.

Bluestein, J., & Collins, L. (1985). *Parents in a pressure cooker.* Albuquerque, NM: I.S.S.

Deming, W. (1982). *Out of the crisis.* Cambridge, MA: MIT Center for Advanced Engineering Study.

Edelwich, J. (1980). *Burn-out.* New York: Herman Scievers.

Ford, E. (1974). *Why marriage.* Niles, IL: Argus.

Ford, E. (1977). *For the love of children.* New York: Doubleday.

Ford, E. (1982). Reality therapy. In A. Horne (Ed.), *Family counseling and therapy.* Itasca, IL: Peacock.

Ford, E. (1983). *Choosing to love.* Minneapolis, MN: Winston.

Ford, E., & Englund, S. (1979). *Permanent love: Practical steps to a lasting relationship.* Minneapolis, MN: Winston.

Good, P. (1987). *In pursuit of happiness.* Chapel Hill, NC: New View.

Glasser, N. (Ed.). (1980). *What are you doing?* New York: Harper & Row.

Glasser, N. (Ed.). (1989). *Control theory in the practice of reality therapy.* New York: Harper & Row.

Glasser, W. (1961). *Mental health or mental illness?* New York: Harper & Row.

Glasser, W. (1965). *Reality therapy.* New York: Harper & Row.

Glasser, W. (1968). *Schools without failure.* New York: Harper & Row.

Glasser, W. (1972). *Identity society.* New York: Harper & Row.

Glasser, W. (1976). *Positive addiction.* New York: Harper & Row.

Glasser, W. (1980). *Both-win management.* Los Angeles: Institute for Reality Therapy.

Glasser, W. (1981). *Stations of the mind.* New York: Harper & Row.

Glasser, W. (1984). Reality therapy. In R. Corsini (Ed.), *Current psychotherapies.* Itasca, IL: Peacock.

Glasser, W. (1985). *Control theory.* New York: Harper & Row.

Glasser, W. (1986). *The basic concepts of reality therapy.* Los Angeles: Institute for Reality Therapy.

Glasser, W. (1988). *Choice drug prevention programs.* Los Angeles: IRT.

Glasser, W. (1990). *The quality school.* New York: Harper & Row.

Glasser, W., & Zunin, L. (1973). Reality therapy. In R. Corsini (Ed.), *Current psychotherapies,* 2nd ed. Itasca, IL: Peacock.

Kaiser, H. (1965). The problems of responsibility in psychotherapy. *Psychiatry, 18,* 205–211.

O'Donnell, D. (1987). History of the growth of the Institute for Reality Therapy. *Journal of Reality Therapy, 2,* 2–8.

Powers, W. (1973). *Behavior, the control of perception.* New York: Aldine.

Weeks, G., & L'Abate, L. (1982). *Paradoxical psychotherapy.* New York: Brunner/Mazel.

Wiener, N. (1948). *Cybernetics.* New York: John T. Wiley.

Wiener, N. (1950). *The human uses of human beings, cybernetics & society.* Boston: Houghton, Mifflin.

Wubbolding, R. (1979). Reality therapy as an antidote to burnout. *American Mental Health Counselors Association Journal, I,* 39–43.

Wubbolding, R. (1985a). *Changing your life for the better.* Johnson City, TN: Institute for Science & Arts.

Wubbolding, R. (1985b). Reality management: Getting results. *Landmark, 11,* 6–7.

Wubbolding, R. (1988). *Using reality therapy.* New York: Harper & Row.

Wubbolding, R. (1989a). *The cycle of counseling.* Cincinnati, OH: Real World.

Wubbolding, R. (1989b). *Improving your management conferences.* Cincinnati, OH: Real World.

Wubbolding, R. (1990a). *Effective management.* Cincinnati, OH: Real World.

Wubbolding, R. (1990b). *Understanding reality therapy.* New York: Harper & Row.

Wubbolding, R. (1990c). *Evaluation.* Cincinnati, OH: Real World.

CHAPTER 16

Social Learning Family Therapy

ARTHUR M. HORNE

DEFINITION

Social learning is a result of the process of people teaching people how to relate interpersonally. It refers to learning that takes place within a social environment as one person observes, reacts to, and interacts with other people; in short, social learning is an education in human relations. People do not develop in isolation, but rather they are born into a social system—be it a nuclear family traditionally identified as being a typical family or some other system of significant others. No one is exempt from the learning experience. Within such a social matrix, children learn ways of behaving—behavior patterns—by receiving support for some actions and punishment for others, by imitating behavior they see supported and avoiding activities they see discouraged. The result of this selective social reinforcement is the behavior that we characteristically exhibit: our personality. A corollary can also be stated: Without the opportunity of learning to perform in a particular manner, the individual will not develop social skills in a specific area. A social learning treatment approach, then, attempts to provide an environment in which effective learning may occur. Behavioral alternatives are expanded and new options presented, so that families and couples may remedy deficits and develop new skills for dealing with the problems of living in close human relationships. This learning occurs in a systematic teaching-modeling program that emphasizes learning procedures derived from psychology and related behavioral sciences.

Social learning theory began with the clinical application of principles derived from behaviorally oriented learning theories in psychology. Since its beginnings, it has expanded to include elements from experimental, cognitive, and social psychology. Whereas behavior therapy in general and social learning in particular started as an application of techniques derived from learning theory to the modification of discrete behavioral problems of individuals, its evolution as a treatment discipline has developed it into becoming a more general set of principles applicable to a wide variety of human problems. Rather than a series of techniques, behavior therapy generally and social learning family therapy specifically have become a method of inquiry for analyzing problems, designing intervention strategies, and evaluating effectiveness that transcends specific techniques. In its broadest sense, then, social learning family therapy is not simply a series of techniques for treating families but is a systematic method of assessing family interactions, developing intervention strategies, and evaluating change. As illustrated in Figures 1 and 2, it is a process of conceptualizing family interactions that identifies functional and dysfunctional patterns based on learning principles that explain how interactions are established, maintained, and changed.

Figure 1. Mutual impacting family interaction.

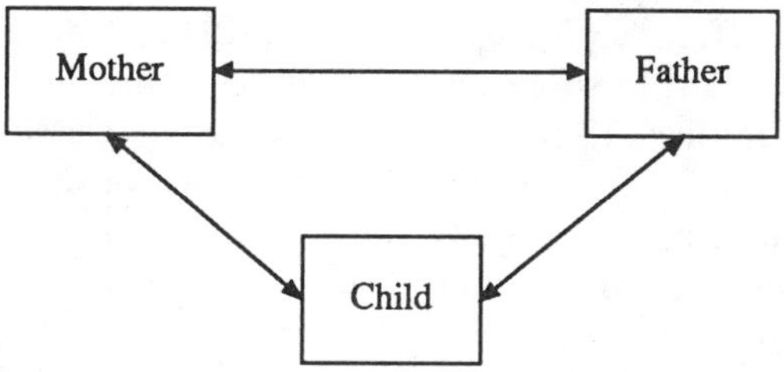

Mother ←→ Father

Child

Figure 1 illustrates that interactions occur among the members of a family, with each person having an impact on and being impacted by the others. What the father does influences the child, but the child also influences the father. This sphere of influence spreads so that all members of the family are impacted. Figure 2 illustrates that within the individual there are differential influences occurring: the behavior of the person affects the environment, and the environment affects the person. The personal factors (cognitions, beliefs, values, affective response) have an impact on the individual's environment, and the environment influences the personal factors. Self-efficacy—the level of personal belief that a person can accomplish a particular task, for example—influences how much a person will work at accomplishing a task, but the nature of the task will influence the person's self-efficacy (Bandura, 1986; Colpe, 1990).

HISTORICAL DEVELOPMENT

Behavior theory preceded behavioral practice, unlike most theories, which often follow practice to explain what occurred. In social learning approaches to working with families, behavioral tenets were not specifically developed for treating families, but since extensive work on a theoretical base for behavioral approaches had been done, they were adapted to marriage and family treatment. Behaviorism has been such an integral component of psychology that it is referred to as the second force in psychology, with psychoanalytic theory being the first force and humanistic psychology being the third force. While behavioral approaches and social learning have been studied as a major theory within psychology for decades, applications to working with couples and families is fairly recent, developing primarily since the 1960s. This increased interest in

Figure 2. Differential influences within the individual.

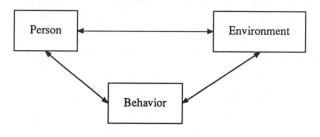

Person ←→ Environment

Behavior

family applications resulted in part from studies that demonstrated a social learning approach may be effective with a variety of populations and diversified settings, including families (Bandura, 1969).

Unlike many approaches to family therapy, social learning family therapy does not have a single name or persona associated with the development of the approach. Patterson (1988), for example, has indicated that the early years of behavioral approaches to family therapy were

...characterized by a strange mix of characters working together to develop a technology that could be applied to the task of helping families change themselves. The group was comprised of turncoat traditional clinicians ..., academics who knew much about pigeons and laboratories but nothing about the inside of outpatient clinics, and rogue entrepreneurs who knew a parade when they saw one. (p. vii)

Clinicians and researchers from a variety of approaches began adapting behavioral interventions based on their knowledge of behavioral approaches and the clientele available to them in their practices. Instead of a single leader, a number of contributors provided the groundwork for the development of social learning family therapy. The major areas of early development were in working with families with disruptive or dysfunctional children, marital relationships, and sexual dysfunctions. Currently, this has been expanded to many more areas, and applications to other areas of dysfunction are rapidly arising.

Working with Families with Aggressive Children

The treatment of children with dysfunctional behavior goes back to the beginnings of behavioral interventions. As early as 1920, Watson (Watson & Raynor, 1920) demonstrated that phobias in children could be experimentally produced using classical conditioning. A student of Watson, Mary Cover Jones, successfully removed phobias in children using similar methods (Jones, 1924). A stronger focus more recently has been on disruptive children. During the 1950s, it became apparent that aiding families with child rearing and family relationship concerns within the community context is important: nearly one-third of all referrals by teachers and parents for mental health services were for children identified as out of control or unmanageable within the school and home (Roach, 1958).

The necessity of formulating more effective treatment methods for family relationship problems was made evident by Bahm, Chandler, and Eisenberg (1961), who found only a small fraction of the children referred for services actually received an offer of services. Levitt (1971) reported that of those who did go to mental health services and were accepted for treatment, the treatment offered typically was individual, traditional therapy that did little to help socially aggressive children. Treatment of the individual child by traditional methods left much to be desired in terms of effecting lasting change of inappropriate behaviors of children in the home and school (Meltzoff & Kornreich, 1970; Teuber & Powers, 1953). Children with conduct problems tended not to change for the better if not treated (Beach & Laird, 1968; Morris, 1956; Patterson, 1982; Robins, 1966).

The more traditional family or individual therapies also apparently had little to offer children and families with acting-out, aggressive behaviors. Traditional therapies for the most part were based on verbal expressive modes that sought to unbind the inexpressive, emotionally repressed individual. It was, in fact, this very type of child and family structure that was first the focus of family-oriented treatments. Family therapists cut their teeth by treating the emotionally repressed child, and they did develop several techniques to liberate the overly bound-down family, to help in the experience of expression of genuine emotion. They did not, however, come up with methods to deal with individuals and families who were already very expressive, who were without bounds. This has been regarded as one of the major shortcomings of traditional family therapy.

Early intervention procedures from a social learning approach involved having family members help elicit change in their children. Williams (1959), for example, in treating nighttime temper tantrums, had the parents provide the treatment (affectionately put the child to bed, close the door, and ignore tantrums, extinguishing the volatile behavior). Boardman (1962) trained parents to treat the aggressive behavior of their child, and Lovibond (1963) taught parents to implement a bell-and-pad apparatus for treating their enuretic children. Risley and Wolf (1967) used parents to work with autistic children to develop speech.

Since 1965, families with child management and family relationship problems have been studied by therapists interested in examining effective change for the families from a social learning orientation. The predominant group for this work has been the Oregon Social Learning Center under the direction of Gerald Patterson and John Reid. The project in Oregon initially pursued a series of case studies for the purpose of developing a treatment methodology based on social learning principles, including training parents and others in the child's environment to act as agents of change. Early treatments included the use of buzzer boxes and M&M's candy but quickly moved toward using basic point systems, modeling, time-out, and contingent attention (Patterson & Brodsky, 1966; Patterson, Jones, Whittier, & Wright, 1965; Patterson, McNeal, Hawkins & Phelps, 1967). In the course of the project's growth, a definite shift was made from the psychology lab to the natural environment in order to observe family patterns in a more realistic setting.

Initial work with families provided encouraging results, so the project was expanded to provide treatment to additional families with parent-child conflicts. Patterson and his associates recognized that observing family members in a natural environment (the home, school, or neighborhood) was far superior to laboratory or clinical settings for understanding family dysfunctioning. Consequently, they developed a family observational coding system that was utilized by trained observers who went into the home to see the family interact. All family members were expected to be present, and certain restraints were placed on the family (e.g., no visitors, no television) while the observers were present. From the observations, family patterns surfaced demonstrating that children's dysfunctional behavior was more than simply an example of poor learning or skill development; what became apparent was the interactional effect of family members. Rather than being linear (Billy wanted a toy Chuck had, so he took it and now Chuck is crying), it became clear that problems were interactional in nature (Billy and Chuck interact in such a way that Chuck teases Billy, who takes a toy away from Chuck. Chuck cries and gets Mother involved; she spanks Billy, and Billy later hits Chuck for revenge. Chuck tattles on Billy to Father, who fusses with Billy but then plays ball with him to show he isn't too angry. Chuck gets jealous of Billy's time with Father and teases Billy...). These interactions were understandable and observable in the natural environment but not in clinical settings. Also, behavior patterns could be identified as well as the contingencies maintaining the behavior. In social learning family therapy, the problems are defined by the family, and the observations yield data to determine the frequency and conditions for the behavior before attempting to change it, thus providing a baseline measure of behavior before intervention strategies are implemented.

Initial work involved training parents in the principles of social learning theory, using programmed text materials developed specifically for working with families (e.g., Patterson & Gaullion's *Living with Children* [1971] and Patterson's *Families* [1975]). The therapist would work as the expert, teaching parents the skills to manage the intervention used with the children. Patterson recognized from the beginning that changing only the parents' behavior in response to a child's deviant behavior would be insufficient:

To produce a change it seemed necessary to change several aspects of this social system, simultaneously. Therefore, the initial programmes were designed to fulfill four functions: (1) train the mother to use positive reinforcers, (2) train her to initiate more social contacts, and (3) at the same time train Earl to function as a more effective social reinforcer for the behavior of the parent, and (4) initiate more social contacts to his parents. (Patterson et al., 1967, p. 187)

The early work of Patterson resulted in substantial improvements in children's behavior, with a 60 to 75% reduction of inappropriate behavior from baseline to termination, with an average of 22.8 hours of professional time required per family (Patterson, Cobb, & Ray, 1973).

In-school behavior was often a problem (Patterson & Brodsky, 1966; Patterson et al., 1965), so classroom procedures were developed based on social learning theory using peers and teachers as change agents. This involved instructing teachers in the use of points and time-out and providing peers with additional recess time when the identified child behaved more appropriately in class. Resultant changes in the child were achieved with little cost to the teacher and persisted through follow-up (Patterson, Shaw, & Ebner, 1969).

Encouraged by these results, the Oregon group initiated a new study with extremely aggressive, out-of-control boys in 1968. The children were from lower socioeconomic classes, eight from father-absent homes, and five being treated with medication and having diagnoses of minimal brain damage. Details of the procedures used were first presented by Patterson et al. (1973, pp. 139–224) and later elaborated in a manual aimed at the working clinician, *A Social Learning Approach to Family Intervention* (Patterson, Reid, Jones, & Conger, 1975). During this time, the treatment procedures were redefined and became more standardized. Programmed materials were given to parents who were then tested on the materials. Before moving on to advanced-level work, parents were required to demonstrate mastery of the material presented at each level.

In previous work, therapists had attempted to alter only one or two behaviors; but in the next phase of treatment, they began to work with a large number of parent and child conflicts. Treatment generally encompassed all the child's inappropriate behaviors that were of concern to the parents and referring agent. An average of 31.5 professional hours was required to produce changes in home-observed problem behaviors, and approximately two-thirds of the treated boys evidenced reductions of at least 30% in their output of aggressive behavior as measured by home observations. In addition, parents provided daily reports on the occurrence of symptoms of primary concern to them. These data also showed significant reductions from a level of 63% reported at baseline to 33% reported at termination. One year of follow-up data showed persistence of the effects along both measurement dimensions. In many cases, however, brief booster treatments involving additional counseling were necessary.

Significant decreases were observed in undesirable behavior by termination. These improvements endured through 1 year of follow-up and were also found for the siblings of the identified child (Arnold, Levine, & Patterson, 1975). Improvement in the siblings' behavior was evident whether or not the therapists extended treatment directly to them, which seems to substantiate the notion that treatment provides the parents with skills to generalize to other family members.

Classroom intervention was required for 14 of the 27 families. The classroom procedures included using feedback mechanisms so that children would be able to identify when they were engaging in appropriate classroom behaviors. These were later replaced by less conspicuous work cards to record points earned for appropriate behaviors. These programs were initially developed and conducted by therapists involved in research projects but were later turned over to the teachers for implementation and maintenance. It was found that, with practice, teachers needed only a few minutes each day to carry out treatment effectively. In families where learning deficits were quite extensive, parents were taught to work as remedial teachers for their children (Patterson et al., 1975).

In this initial work, the client population did not suffer from the 56 to 70% attrition rates experienced with more traditional treatment of the time (Eideson, 1968; Hunt, 1961; Overall & Aronson, 1963). Eight of 35 referrals (23%) dropped out during the intake-baseline, and 6 others left treatment prior to therapist recommendations. However, these latter 6 cases who were seen by a therapist were counted as treated (i.e., counted in the sample). Given demographic and clinical characteristics of the sample, the treatment's lower attrition and higher effectiveness were particularly encouraging. In terms of referral categories, behavior-problem and out-of-control youngsters are typically less successful than their withdrawn or neurotic peers (Levitt, 1958; Levitt, 1971; Robins, 1966). Regarding client socioeconomic status, low socioeconomic status families are the most likely to drop out of more traditional types of treatment shortly after intake (Overall & Aronson, 1963). Family socioeconomic status and single parenthood did have an impact on treatment for the study of 27 families (Patterson, 1974a, 1974b), and replication (Fleischman, 1976) showed that single mothers and impoverished families are more difficult to treat, require longer treatment times, and comprise a greater proportion of the failures. Generally, however, the data suggested that such families are amenable to a social learning treatment approach.

In reviewing the phases of work completed through 1975, Patterson et al. (1975) found the social learning family therapy to be effective for reducing problem behaviors of the child identified as the problem in the family, and treatment also had generalized to other family members, including siblings. Further, parents began to see their child's behavior as more positive, and parents became more effective at providing rewards for appropriate behavior and punishments for acting-out behavior. Overall, mothers seemed more satisfied with their children and rated the family as happier, and fathers developed a more influential role in the family by controlling coercive actions of the child.

In the years since, Patterson has continued to examine treating families with dysfunctional children, including examining specific treatment conditions. He has conducted carefully controlled studies to examine the effects of treatment versus control group outcome (Wiltz & Patterson, 1974), treatment versus placebo controls (Walter & Gilmore, 1973), working with families with stealers (Reid & Patterson, 1976), and with other forms of deviant behavior (Patterson, 1982). In addition, other researchers have carried out programs to replicate his research with equally positive results (Fleischman & Horne, 1979; Sayger, 1987; Sayger, Horne, Passmore, & Walker, 1988; Walker, 1984), and some have extended his work by addressing additional components of treatment and evaluation (Fleischman, Horne, & Arthur, 1983; Horne & Sayger, 1990). Other major contributors in the area of treating families in a social learning family therapy model have included Anthony Graziano, Rex Forehand, Daniel and Susan O'Leary, Robert Wahler, Elaine Blechman, and Ron Prinz.

Other Early Contributors to Social Learning Family Therapy

A second area of development in social learning family therapy has been in the field of marriage and couples work. Treatment of marital issues in the early stages of development for social learning family therapy had the therapist treating individuals in an attempt to develop more effective marital relationships. Goldiamond (1965), for example, worked with only one spouse, with the assumption that improvement in marital satisfaction would increase through such activities as teaching reinforcement, punishment, and extinction principles to the wife in order to alter the marital dyad (Goldstein, 1971). Larzarus (1968), an early contributor to treatment of marital conflict from a behavioral perspective, taught wives assertiveness skills and provided them with desensitization to help balance the marital relationship.

Another early contributor in this field was Robert Liberman (1970), who identified ways of applying operant learning conditions, in combination with modeling concepts from Bandura (Bandura & Walters, 1963), to the treatment of four adults. Liberman interviewed family members to determine desired changes, but then he developed the behavioral goals and intervention strategy to be used. He maintained assessment of the problem throughout treatment to note the level of change occurring, and throughout he remained the expert rather than allowing the family to assume that role. The treatment emphasis was on restructuring family interactions in such a manner that reciprocal rewards would be developed and maladaptive interactions would be reduced.

A cause of marital dissatisfaction is inadequate reinforcers in the relationship. In research examining functional and dysfunctional relationships, for example, it was discovered that both types of couples have disagreements and conflict at about an even amount but that functional couples had significantly more positive exchanges in their relationships (Gottman, Markman, & Notarius, 1977; Gottman, Notarius, Gonso, & Markman, 1976; Jacobson & Margolin, 1979; Stuart, 1980). Also, all couples engage in conflict, but functional families develop effective problem-solving skills to handle such trouble (Weiss, 1978). In early studies of marital conflict, the relationship of positive interactions to negative ones was seen as highly predictive of marital satisfaction. Those relationships experiencing marital discord had individuals reporting that they received too little reinforcement from the relationship, felt little satisfaction, did not have new activities reinforced, gave more than they received, had a routine of marriage interfering with outside activities, and believed that aversive control dominated the relationship (Azrin, Naster, & Jones, 1973).

Stuart was an early contributor to marriage and couples treatment who used the concepts of marital communication and satisfaction to develop marital therapy in which the marriage was the focus with both members of the relationship involved. He emphasized understanding the interpersonal environment that existed between wife and husband. He accepted the exchange theory of Thibault and Kelley (1959): Each member of a relationship behaves in a manner to provide the greatest satisfaction and avoid the greatest discomfort possible, and the interactions are not accidental but planned and purposeful.

Stuart (1969) applied behavioral principles to couples in order to increase their satisfaction with the relationship. His initial reinforcement program asked each individual to list the behavior he or she desired from the other, record the frequency with which the partner demonstrated such behavior, and specify what he or she was willing to give for the desired positive actions. At first Stuart used tokens that members of the couple exchanged, but later he employed social reinforcers, which proved to be more powerful and often were the behaviors sought from the partner.

As Stuart (1980) further refined his model, he identified specific steps that members of a couple must take to bring about change. These included:

- a mutual agreement that change was wanted and needed;
- an understanding that each member would initiate changes first;
- a method of assessing change on a daily basis; and
- an agreement on exchanges for desired behaviors.

Since his early contributions, other researchers have provided additional refinement for social learning approaches to working with couples, including Jacobson and Margolin (1979).

Current Status

Social learning family therapy continues to be fine-tuned and applied to ever-increasing types of problem areas, with increased success and validation of the approach. An example of continued development is Falloon's (1988) *Handbook of Behavioral Family Therapy*, which expands on the more traditional units of treatment (families with aggressive children, couples, sexual dysfunctioning) as well as areas not previously addressed. These topics include enhanced diagnosis and assessment, managing resistance, working with families with developmentally disabled members, treating anxiety disorders and obsessive-compulsive patients from a family perspective, treating depression from a marital therapy approach, using family interventions in inpatient settings, preventing morbidity in schizophrenia, social learning family approaches for treating alcoholism, senile dementia, and uses in primary healthcare centers. Other authors have identified ways of expanding social learning applications from the family alone to treating the family in relation to other systems (Henggeler & Borduin, 1990).

The initial orientation of social learning family therapists was to use simple paradigms of learning theory (linear) to attempt to change families. Today the process is much more involved, incorporating systemic theory and looking at more involved interactional (circular) explanations for behavior change. In reviewing the current status of social learning family therapy, Nichols (1984) states:

The first professional journal in this field, *Behavior Research and Therapy,* in 1963, elicited a flood of outcome and process studies demonstrating dramatic and impressive change. One question that arose in those early days was, how permanent were the behavior changes? Yes, it was clear that behavior therapists could shape new sequences of behavior; but would these changes last? In learning theory terms, this is a problem of generalization, a problem which remains crucial to any form of psychotherapy. It is better to consider this question a problem to be solved, rather than something to be debated. Behavior therapists have been able to generalize their results by using naturalistic reinforcers, using family members as therapists, and by fading (gradually decreasing) external contingencies. Generalization is now programmed rather than expected or lamented. (p. 298)

While social learning family therapy was not recognized as part of the "family therapy family of theories" early in its development, it is now recognized as a primary model of intervention. The American Association for Marriage and Family Therapy (AAMFT) honored Gerald Patterson in 1988 with the Distinguished Contributions to Marriage and Family Therapy Award, and social learning family therapists are regular presenters at the AAMFT national convention.

TENETS OF THE MODEL

Almost all family therapy begins with concern about one family member who is identified by the family or some community agency as disruptive, delinquent, deviant, disturbed, or the like. Therapy, therefore, generally begins with the one targeted individual as the focus of attention, but very quickly a more complex situation is uncovered as the therapist begins to investigate the role of the identified patient within the family. The counselor discovers that other members are unknowingly encouraging or even reinforcing these undesirable behaviors. This is held to be true for all approaches to family therapy.

Early nonbehavioral writers in family therapy such as Bateson, Jackson, Haley, and Weakland (1956) argue that the individual cannot be considered apart from the social system of which he or she is a member; the family is a system of interbehaving people. Therefore, the deviant child is seen as an individual responding to the behaviors of others within the system. Others' actions within the family contribute to the deviancy of the patient, and the problem behavior in turn supports their behaviors. Within this view, deviant behavior of the identified patient is not seen as dysfunctional;

rather, it is seen as an appropriate response to contingencies of the system, and there is in fact a continuous reciprocal interaction between cognitive, behavioral, and environmental determinants. People and their environments are reciprocal determinants of each other (Bandura, 1977, 1986).

The model presented by Bateson and his colleagues is very similar to a social learning conception of the family because most behaviorally oriented family therapists are guided by social learning theory, which purports that family members behave in an interdependent manner (Horne & Sayger, 1990; Wahler, 1976). In a social learning orientation, family members' interdependencies are described as reinforcing the discriminative stimuli provided by various family members. Wahler (1976) states:

Thus, the child's problem behavior is seen as controlled by reinforcers and discriminitive stimuli dispensed by the child's caretakers and siblings. However, the question of who is controlling whom is not this simple. One could also attempt an analysis of factors that determine the behaviors of the latter stimulus dispensers. From this perspective the child's problem behaviors could be conceptualized as stimulus events that partially control the actions of his caretakers and siblings. Here, the "loop" is completed and the assignment of responsibility or blame to any one family member requires an arbitrary decision. (p. 517)

This interactional process has been illustrated in Figure 1. The mother presents cues and reinforcers to the child that determine how the child will behave toward her. At the same time, the child is emitting cues and reinforcers to the mother that influence her interaction with the child. The father interacts with the mother and child, also dispensing cues and reinforcers for particular actions. Thus, each member of the family has an impact on and is impacted by the other members. According to this illustration, the child's behavior, both normal and deviant, is a function of interchanges with the mother and father.

If the child should become identified as a problem child and the family interaction pattern becomes unsatisfactory (as may be the case if the child begins to perform poorly at school, argues with his family about doing chores, or lies or steals), it is still indicative of the family interaction pattern presented in the diagram. The child's behavior in this case still serves some function, for the child's behaviors—both positive and negative—are maintained through cues and reinforcers available within the family structure, and the other family members' behaviors are maintained in large part through interactions with the child. Each individual's behavior is affected by and affects that of other members. Thus, it is important to understand the discriminative and reinforcing stimuli of family members and to recognize that change for one person will require change for the entire family. Counseling, therefore, should address the interactional patterns by involving all family members in the treatment process.

One way that individuals learn inappropriate behavior is through the *positive reinforcement trap* (Patterson, 1982; Wahler, 1976). In this situation, family members may find a particular class of behaviors appealing and therefore encourage that behavior. A 2-year-old who clowns around and has to be the center of attention, for example, may be a nuisance when she acts the same way at age 6. Or a parent who enjoys helping a child get dressed as a preschooler may be providing considerable reinforcement for dependent behavior and be reinforced for engaging in that activity. When the child enters school, though, problems are likely to develop that could affect the whole family. Likewise, a husband who reinforces homemaking and domestic skills for his spouse early in the marriage may find those same behaviors less appealing after several years when he has completed graduate school or been advanced through the company. If the wife still behaves in ways that were earlier reinforcing to the husband, the potential for conflict is high.

A second and much more common way of learning inappropriate behavior is through the *negative reinforcement trap* (Patterson, 1982; Wahler, 1976). Negative reinforcement involves stopping some stimulus, which then leads to an increase in the frequency of that preceding behavior. A parent may learn, for example, that the most effortless way to escape a temper tantrum is to provide candy or some other reinforcer. The child in the department store who engages in crying and whining for a toy may usually be quieted by giving him the toy. When this happens, the noxious behavior stops (temporarily), and the parent has thus been reinforced for giving the child what was wanted. Unfortunately, the child has just been reinforced for behaving in the very way the parents wish to stop, for the child has learned that crying can lead to positive results. Therefore, the child is likely to cry again in that situation, and because the parent has learned that giving in will end the noise, he or she will likely give the reward again in the future. This accidental learning is quite powerful and, once acquired, difficult to change. The same process, of course, works for adults. A wife who whines and then receives encouragement to purchase new clothes has taught the spouse to reward her for

complaining behavior; the husband who pouts when he doesn't get his way but becomes very pleasant when the wife accedes to his demands is being taught to be an expert sulker.

Accidental learning occurs frequently within families. *Accidental learning* refers to any behaviors developed through unintentional reinforcement or unintentional punishment; there are numerous examples. Overeating habits are taught by rewarding a child for cleaning her plate (even when there were more calories than necessary) and by acting hurt when the child leaves some food (even if the child is satiated). Aggression is taught when a child fights and the father tells him that he shouldn't fight but if he has to, always to hurt the other kid because then he'll be "just like his old man." Accidental learning occurs when a child shows off and her parents laugh and say she'll grow up to be a movie star; they are only encouraging more of the same behavior. If a child comes home from school and complains about how bad school is and if the mother listens compassionately, she may be reinforcing complaining behavior. When a child shows the mother a good school paper and the mother criticizes the child's appearance, she may be teaching the child to avoid seeing her after school.

A core concept of social learning family therapy is that individuals strive to maximize rewards while minimizing costs. The concept, presented by Thibaut and Kelly (1959) as an exchange theory model of social psychological interaction, indicates that social behavior is maintained in a given relationship by a high ratio of rewards to costs and by the perception that other possible relationships have more costs and/or fewer rewards. Conflict develops under this model when optimal behavior-maintaining contingencies do not exist (a child demands more than he gives; a wife finds another person more appealing than her husband) or when efforts to change behavior fail.

Two social reinforcement mechanisms are in operation in social learning theory: reciprocity and coercion (Patterson & Hops, 1972). *Reciprocity* refers to a social interaction exchange in which two people reinforce each other at an equitable rate, both maintaining the relationship through positive reinforcement. In a reciprocal relationship, the probability of a reward (positive event) from the partner is more likely following the delivery of a reward (pleasant experience) in both distressed and nondistressed couples. *Coercion,* on the other hand, describes an interaction in which both persons provide aversive stimuli (reactions) that control the behavior of the person, and negative reinforcement results from terminating the aversiveness. Coercion in relationships leads to a reciprocal use of coercion by the other person—or as Lederer and Jackson (1968) say, "nastiness begets nastiness" (p. 269). Research in family therapy has clearly indicated that this phenomenon holds. The family member who behaves the most aversely also receives the most aversive actions from other family members (Patterson, 1982; Reid, 1967). A fairly clear way of differentiating distressed from nondistressed families, in fact, is to examine the rates at which family members exchange aversive stimuli, for distressed families provide lower rates of pleasing behaviors and higher rates of punishing behaviors than nondistressed families (Birchler, Weiss, & Vincent, 1975; Gottman, Notarius, Markman, et al., 1976). If inadequate positive consequences are available to family members, if there is a scarcity of

positive outcomes, a distressed relationship occurs (Jacobson & Margolin, 1979; Stuart, 1969, 1980). Even if positive exchanges continue, difficulties can arise as a result of increased punishing interactions, for rewarding and punishing interchanges have been found to be independent in intimate relationships (Wills, Weiss, & Patterson, 1975). The probability of a punisher is more likely following the delivery of a punisher from the partner, particularly in distressed couples (Jacobson & Margolin, 1979).

Marital and family therapy research has carefully examined the reciprocity and coercion processes and has found that for nondistressed families companionship with other family members is reinforcing, resulting in people enjoying being together and engaging in activities that bring them closer; whereas companionship is nonreinforcing in distressed families, resulting in people attempting to avoid one another (Jacobson, 1978; Jacobson & Margolin, 1979).

Gottman, Notarius, Markman, et al. (1976) describe the reciprocal interactions of family members as a "bank account" model of social exchange in which individuals have "investments" and "withdrawals" in terms of relationships with others in their family. They suggest that nondistressed families receive a relatively high rate of exchange and that occasional inequitable exchanges are more acceptable since there is a long-term history of positive equal exchanges. This situation is not true for distressed families, in which considerably more attention is paid regularly to "balancing the books" to assure one member does not receive an unfair share of available rewards. Reciprocity in functional, nondistressed families places greater emphasis on long-term clusters of behavior that provide rewarding experiences, whereas distressed families attend more to short-term equity within single dyadic interactions.

Developmental Stages

The understanding of reciprocity in reinforcement and punishment is very important in studying the developmental phases of families, particularly when attempting to determine the source of a distressed family situation. The developmental processes of a family require flexibility and an ability to adapt to change. Families experience the meeting of two individuals, courtship, marriage, children, moving geographically, changing jobs, children learning, changes in social and political climate, retirement, plus many other situations that might arise to shake the equilibrium of the family (affairs, deaths, in-laws moving in, illness, children leaving home, etc).

Initially when two people meet and begin courting, there is a high rate of positive exchanges flowing from a positive attraction and pleasing novelty in the relationship. Early in the relationship, couples tend to see only the positive aspects of each other and ignore the negative; at the same time, each person attempts to present her- or himself as attractive and so goes to extremes to be reinforcing. During the "honeymoon" phase, individuals entertain only positive thoughts about each other and the future of the relationship, focusing generally on happy predictions that the future will be just like the present.

The honeymoon ends at some point, however. When this happens, the couple may develop realistic expectations of each other and the relationship and foster open, clear communication. Couples realize now that not all aspects of the relationship will be pleasing but that by communicating early on in a straightforward way about conflict, it is possible to settle disagreements satisfactorily. On the other hand, the couple may maintain unrealistic expectations of each other and the relationship, leading to dissatisfaction with the partner and distress in the relationship. "Catastrophizing" cognitions ("I'm not in love because he isn't ideally suited to my concept of the perfect spouse. If he was then he would have been more considerate. He probably doesn't love me anyway.") and coercive behavior via punishment may even result.

Beyond the difficulties possibly encountered in the initial stages of the relationship, each phase of the family's developmental process may bring additional challenges to the positive exchanges already developed. Over time, for example, the novelty of the relationship typically lessens and, as it does, each partner's potential for reinforcement is also diminished, a result of habituation to each other. Habituation requires expanding repertoires of reinforcing behaviors in order to prevent satiation. The more widely varied the reinforcing behaviors are, the less dependent the couple is on a limited menu of reinforcers and the less likely reinforcement erosion will occur. As sexual encounters become more commonplace, for example, couples may expand their sexual behaviors to include new ways of being together. Couples who interact in the same unchanging routine are likely to find the relationship boring and less rewarding, leading to distress.

Beyond reinforcement erosion, discord may also result from deficient family skills of the couple. Family life requires many skills—some that the couple may have been exposed to and mastered, others that may be new and perplexing. The couple must master the skills for which they are untrained, and this requires an openness and acceptance of each other as a human being (as opposed to a superperson) and the opportunity to learn, including an appropriate model. Rarely do people learn behaviors they have never seen performed by others (Bandura, 1977, 1986). Behavioral family skills include the ability of spouses to communicate clearly, to solve problems creatively, to provide support and understanding, to maintain a viable sex life, to support a household, to rear children, to wash dishes, to manage finances, and to change with a changing world. The importance of each skill will vary from stage to stage in the development of the relationship, and in functional couples the skills may be learned as needed.

In addition to skills deficits that may lead to distress for couples, changes in the external environment may also contribute to the difficulties. If alternatives outside of marriage, for example, develop more reinforcement value than is available within, conflict will likely result. Each individual examines the costs and benefits of a relationship and compares those costs and benefits with outside alternatives. Outside alternatives may include a third party entering the scene (an affair) or career opportunities that provide increasing rewards (as the marriage may be becoming stale or commonplace, the worker may become a "workaholic"). People may perceive more options as societal changes provide greater choices (divorce is easier, women have increased opportunities in the business sector, midlife career changes have become more common). All of these factors may lead to distress within the relationship.

Role of the Therapist

The definition presented of the social learning approach to therapy with families emphasized that it is a method of helping that involves analyzing problems, designing intervention strategies, and assessing change. This places responsibility on the therapist to have the skills and training to do so. The following skills are necessary:

1. Establish a therapeutic relationship
2. Define concerns
3. Develop expectancies
4. Implement change strategies
5. Follow through on implementation
6. Assess progress
7. Generalize results

The therapist is responsible for having the basic interpersonal relationship skills to establish a therapeutic environment in which the family members will feel safe and comfortable discussing their concerns. Families come for counseling in the midst of great discomfort. Attitudes about seeking help have changed for the better in recent years, but most families still see the need for outside assistance as a sign of weakness or inadequacy. In addition, families that come for help have genuine pains (somatic as well as psychological); a dysfunctional family life is very painful. It may be expected that anger is operating at some level also, for family members that hurt one another badly enough to force the family to receive help (voluntarily or, even more maddening for some families, involuntarily) give and receive pain and experience significant anger. Anger may exist as a result of an outside party, such as the school or a court demanding that the family come for counseling against their wishes. Fear generally is operating at a high level also, and it is unknown what the family members will do if therapy is not effective.

It is imperative, therefore, that the therapist have the relationship skills necessary to understand the state of the family, to demonstrate that understanding, and to develop a sense of confidence that change is possible. This relationship is essential from the beginning and should be maintained throughout. Family members must experience the therapist as empathic, warm, genuine, caring, and supportive; to do so, the therapist must actually have these characteristics.

The attitudes and beliefs of the therapist will play a large part in developing the therapeutic relationship. Each member of the family is doing his or her best given the circumstances and previous learning experiences. It is important to maintain that belief; otherwise, therapists may find themselves pulling back and becoming evaluative and nonaccepting. When working with child abuse cases coming for counseling as a result of court orders, the therapist must remember that even these parents are doing the best, and only, thing they know how to do under the circumstances. But that is what therapy is all about—to change the circumstances by teaching people more effective methods of interacting, more satisfying ways of being with others. It is crucial that we don't "blame the victim for being the victim." Neither should we condone or accept the behavior—we cannot accept child abuse. But by understanding the family's situation and by offering to provide them with alternative, more facilitative ways of living in families, we demonstrate caring and respect that can foster a rewarding relationship. It is the therapist's responsibility to accomplish this task.

The major purpose of the initial contact with the family is to set the stage for helping by developing a supportive relationship and by building positive expectancies on the part of the family members. During the initial session, the therapist should aim to alleviate the sense of hopelessness and isolation often experienced by families. If these goals are not accomplished, then it is unlikely the family will continue treatment. Building positive expectancies involves establishing credibility of the treatment program. This is an important though often neglected step in the process. Therapist statements such as "We have worked with many families experiencing similar concerns and have had good success with most"; "We've worked with many families that were experiencing child management problems like yours"; "We've worked with many couples who have experienced similar conflicts" help establish the credibility of the therapist and the program without offering promises that can't be fulfilled. Truthful, realistic encouragement is crucial.

To facilitate credibility, it is important to explain to family members what will occur during counseling. Describing the process of defining problems, developing a specific intervention program for the family to function more effectively and thus alleviate the problem, and regularly assessing progress generally develops a sense of confidence in the program and the therapist.

A number of clinical skills have been identified as particularly appropriate for social learning family therapists to use in their work with families (Fleischman et al., 1983, pp. 48–49):

Building the Relationship
   Communicate empathy
   Provide reassurance and normalize problems
   Use self-disclosure
   Define everyone as a victim
   Emphasize positive motivation
   Establish positive expectations for change
   Match your communication style to the family
   Use Humor
Gathering Information
   Use open-ended questions

Paraphrase and summarize

Gather information about what people do

Gather information about cognitive/
emotional reactions

Gather information about sequences and
patterns

Maintaining Structure

Share the agenda

Deal with one issue or task at a time

Break complex problems into manageable
units

End sidetracking

Give everyone a chance to participate

Teaching New Skills

Describe skills in specific, nontechnical
language

Provide rationales

Model the skill

Check for comprehension

Couple negative feedback with positive
statements

Insuring Implementation of Skills

Personalize in-session rehearsals

Preproblem solve potential difficulties

Solicit and anticipate concerns

Predict feelings and behavior changes

Promoting Independence and Generalization

Encourage client initiative

Reinforce client initiative and give credit
for positive changes

Interpret situations from a social learning
perspective

Handling Resistance

Determine why clients resist

Make sure it is not a comprehension problem

Discuss client concerns

Relate tasks to client goals

Modify tasks and assignments

For elaboration of therapists skills, with
explanations and examples, see Fleischman et al. (1983).

APPLICATION

Defining the Problem

Every person or family that enters therapy does so because there is a problem—
no one enters therapy because they are
feeling or doing too well. Most often
there is an identified patient, a person
who has brought attention to him- or
herself through behavior that others find
offensive or worrisome. During the assessment phase of treatment, several
questions must be addressed: What is the
presenting problem? (e.g., a child is having difficulty in the home, at school, and
in the neighborhood.) Does this call for
a first-order (behavior) or second-order
(family system) change? Is the problem
resident in an individual (autism, attention deficit disorder with hyperactivity),
or is it a family problem, or both?

Assessment from a social learning approach examines the problem from a variety of positions. First, *interviews* take
place generally including all who are involved in the situation. In the case of a
disruptive child, for example, the therapist would be interested in interviewing
the child, the parent(s), siblings, and related persons such as live-in relatives and
teachers. The interview would generally
take several forms, with some being done
individually ("Billy, there seems to be
some problems in your family. Could
you tell me about what is happening?"),
some conjointly with various members
of the problem represented, and some
with the whole group involved.

A second aspect of assessment is the
use of *standardized instruments*. A variety of measures have been developed to
help define different problems. For marital conflict, for example, measurements
such as the Dyadic Adjustment Scale
(Spanier, 1976), the Marital Adjustment
Scale (Locke & Wallace, 1950), or Stuart's Marital Precounseling Inventory
(Stuart & Stuart, 1972) may be used; for
family functioning, measures such as the
Family Environment Scale (Moos, 1974)
might be applied. For assessing the
child's behavior, the Child Behavior
Checklist (Achenbach & Edelbrock,

1983) may be used, or the Perceived Competence Scale for Children (Harter, 1982), depending on the nature of the problem and the type of changes that may be necessary.

A third level of assessment is *observational data*. Observational data may be collected in the clinical setting by having family members demonstrate ways they handle problems and carry on conversations, but they are more useful if gathered in a more natural environment such as the home or school. A number of observational data-collecting systems are available, including the Spouse Observation Checklist (Weiss, Hops, & Patterson, 1973), the Parent Daily Report (Patterson, 1982), the Family Problem Solving Scale (Nickerson, Light, Blechman, & Gandelman, 1976), or some form of classroom observation system. The primary advantage of observational systems is that they provide information about what people actually do in situations and thus a better understanding of the interactional nature of the behavior since it is possible to see people interact over time and in response to actual situations. The drawback is that the process is time- and resource-consuming.

The fourth area of assessment is the collection of *baseline data* for specific areas to be targeted. How many times does the spouse do/not do what is desired? How many aggressive acts per day does the antisocial child commit? The baseline data are used to identify the extent of the problem—is there a high rate performance of the aggressive behavior, or do parents have exceptionally and unrealistically high expectations for their child? They also serve as a thermometer of change as the treatment program is put into effect.

Assessment has always been a major component of behavioral approaches to treatment. A difficulty arising in much of the early work, however, was that although detailed assessment of the presenting problem was conducted, little effort was made to determine whether the presenting problem (e.g., an acting-out child) was the primary problem. Early failures in social learning family therapy have been attributed to moving too quickly to treat the presenting problem without determining whether other problems were more appropriate for attention (marital discord that upsets a child, causing him to behave aggressively). This would be analogous to providing physical treatment for a headache without attempting to determine why the patient has a headache in the first place. The thorough evaluation of family interactions should answer these questions.

Frameworks for Treatment

The nature of social learning family therapy lends itself to developing frameworks or models for treatment programs. The models may take the form of decision trees in which decision points are made and treatments are provided based on the answers at each decision point. Brown and Christiansen (1986), in their discussion of behavioral family therapy, used the guiding questions provided by Blechman (1981) to develop a flowchart for making decisions relative to involving the child in treatment and assessing parental functioning, marital conflict, self- or life-support ability, and resources available for treatment. Liberman, Mueser, and Glynn (1988) have presented clinical decision trees for behavioral marital therapy and the treatment of depressive and schizophrenic disorders, including points for family involvement and exclusion.

A conceptual framework developed by Horne, Norseworthy, Forehand, and Frame (1990), presented in Figure 3, ad-

Figure 3. Conceptual framework for development and prevention
of serious conduct disorders in children.

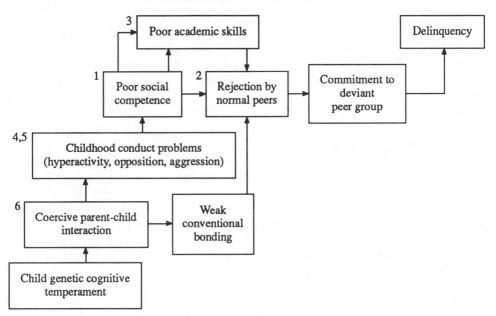

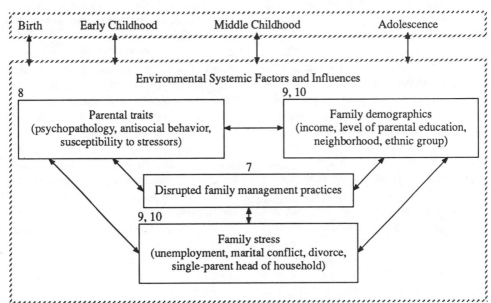

Potential Interventions:

1. Social competence enhancement (four levels)
2. Peer counseling
3. Academic remediation
4. Behavioral self-control strategies
5. Training teachers-educators in
   behavior-management strategies

6. Parent training in child management skills
7. Social learning family therapy
8. Parent individual therapy
9. Couple/single-parent counseling
10. Parent education/career-vocational/financial

dresses the development of delinquency and defines points of intervention to attempt to prevent the antisocial behavior from developing.

The center line represents the developmental period from birth through adolescence. The model can be broken into two broad components. First, the child's developmental progression is presented. It depicts the child as having certain genetic predispositions, cognitive potential, and temperament, which may lead to initial conduct problems directly or indirectly through the development of coercive parent-child interactions. If a coercive interactional style is maintained, the child develops only weak bonding to conventional societal norms, increasing the probability of rejecting, and being rejected by, normal peers. At the same time, the child's conduct problems develop into displays of poor social competence (including attributional bias of hostility toward peers, lack of perspective taking, failure to consider alternative solutions to social problem situations, selection and enactment of inappropriate behaviors), which also result in the child being rejected by normal peers. When peer rejection is sustained over several years, the child will seek a commitment to a deviant peer group in early adolescence. If the child also has failed to develop appropriate academic skills over the grade-school years due to time spent off-task (and perhaps preceding cognitive deficits), by the time she or he reaches adolescence the student won't be invested in school, nor will there be a success experience there. The combination of academic failure and association with a deviant peer group provides the final impetus for serious antisocial and illegal behavior.

The second component, represented in the bottom half of the figure, illustrates the environmental systemic factors that influence families. The parental and family factors may further contribute to the development of chronic conduct disorder in youth, such as existing psychopathology, poor family management practices, economic stressors, and marital conflict.

Each point in the model is amenable to intervention, and a listing of potential interventions is provided at the bottom of the figure, with the numbers indicating where interventions would occur to be effective in altering the development of antisocial, delinquent behavior. Every one of the areas in which a child and the family exhibit difficulties must be treated in order to reduce the risk of chronic antisocial behavior beyond only temporary time periods. However, children and their families should receive treatment only for those areas in which they demonstrate deficits.

The prevention model has been depicted in a linear fashion in order to illustrate the developmental nature of conduct problems. In actuality, the factors that contribute to the development of delinquency do not develop linearly; rather, they are acting at different levels of intensity at different times. Figure 4 illustrates a conceptual model that demonstrates the interactive nature of the factors contributing to an antisocial outcome. These factors occur across time, conditions, and family characteristics and may differentially influence the child's development in various ways at different points.

The following sections further illustrate therapeutic interventions that may be used at strategic points for impacting the family, depending on their needs at that particular developmental stage.

Figure 4. Development of conduct disorders in children (cut-away view).

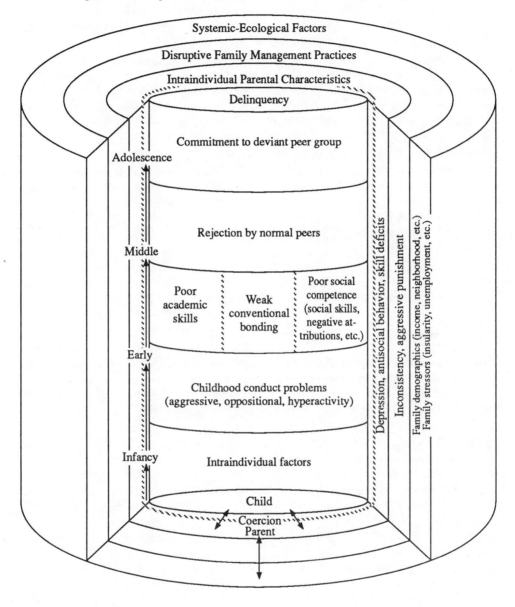

CASE EXAMPLE

The Falsch family was referred for treatment through the Child Protective Services (CPS) of the local Department of Public Welfare. The information provided by CPS was that Bill, age 12, had been hit by his father Robert, 40, after Bill had been arrested for shoplifting. Apparently Bill had been at a discount department store and took a tape without paying for it. When he was apprehended, he initially refused to give his name but finally provided it. Robert was called at home and had to come get Bill, who was released to his father without charges being filed. When they got home, Robert attempted to spank Bill, who refused to accept the punishment. A fight erupted between the two, with Robert hitting Bill several times on the body and once in the face. Bill went to school the next day, and his teacher reported the bruised appearance to the school counselor, who contacted the CPS. CPS met with the family and informed them that an informal adjustment would occur, with charges not being filed if the family successfully participated in family therapy.

Initial Interview

During the initial contact, all members of the family residing together came for the session. Besides Robert and Bill, this included Lois, the mother, age 38; sons Bob, 15, and Donny, 8; and daughter Betty, 4. Lois and Robert reported considerable stress in the family and indicated they had trouble with all their children. All of the children, except perhaps Betty, were angry about having to come in for counseling. Bob was experiencing difficulty in school and was considering dropping out when he reached 16. He had been in fights and antisocial activities throughout his school career, and he hung out with a group of other students who experienced academic and behavioral problems, several of whom had already left school.

Bill, the identified patient, said that he had just "forgotten" to pay for the tape he took, and he indicated that Robert was way out of line for thinking he

could spank Bill, for Bill saw himself as too old for that type of punishment. Besides, Bill insisted no punishment was deserved since it was only an accident. He reported that teachers didn't like him and that a lot of kids didn't either. The parents reported that Bill had an extensive history of fighting and lying.

Donny, the third child, was also described as difficult to parent, though he was very cooperative in the interview. The parents said he teased a lot, was constantly whining and doing other things for attention, but wasn't as mean as the two older boys. He was not doing well at school, but the teachers hadn't reported any extensive trouble yet.

Betty, the youngest, was ignored by the family. She wandered around and pretty much left the family alone as they presented their concerns. She did get irritable toward the end of the interview and began crying when the family wouldn't take her home when she wanted to go. The parents offered her a reason to cry: "You keep that crying up and I'll give you something to cry about...Is that what you want?"

Robert was a truck driver who was on the road about 5 days, 4 nights each week, leaving Monday mornings and returning Friday evenings. He saw the child management issues as not a father's role and mostly Lois's responsibility since he was home so little. Sessions were scheduled on a late Friday afternoon to accommodate his schedule.

Lois worked in a school cafeteria, so she was able to be home to see the children off to school in the morning and generally was home when they got home, though she often was visiting her parents, who lived next door, or friends in the neighborhood. Lois reported she didn't know what to do with the kids, that they had all been born particularly active and had been acting out ever since they learned to walk and talk.

Overall, the picture of the family was one of dysfunction: the children had never had very close monitoring, all but the youngest had experienced difficulty in school, and they all engaged in arguing and criticizing one another during the initial session. Several assessment instruments were given, including a Locke Wallace Marital Adjustment Scale and the Family Environment Scale, and the Child Behavior Checklist was completed for each child by the parents, with the therapist's assistance. The assessment instruments indicated there were considerable problems in the family, including marital disagreements, poor parenting skills, and inadequate and ineffective family interaction dynamics.

The parents expressed concern and some anger about being involved in therapy. They thought that, if anything, the children should be seen but that since *they* hadn't done anything wrong, they should't be forced into therapy. The therapist explained that since they had more potential for contact with the children than the therapist and since the material to be shared with them could be taught to be used with all the children, they would benefit more from counseling than if just their children participated. Since the family was there under order from the CPS, it was pointed out that they really would have to go along with the program.

Therapist: Mr. and Mrs. Falsch, I understand your being upset about being forced to come here when you don't think you really did anything—that the children are the ones who should be seen. What we do here, though, is work with the whole family to do two things. First, we teach the family more effective ways of working and living together. This includes how to get kids to mind a little

better, how to talk with each other so that everyone feels better, and so on. The second point is we get the CPS off your back if you work cooperatively with us and apply the skills we teach. We can't guarantee that everything will work, but we've had lots of experience with families similar to yours and by and large we've had good success. There's no guarantee, of course, but what I'd like to propose is that you give us a few sessions and let's see how it works out. If it does not work, you won't have lost anything but a little time, and you can still deal with the CPS as you'd like to. If it does work, then CPS will be off your back and the kids will also be more enjoyable to be with. You two might even find life a little better for you. Would you like to try it, or do you prefer to contact CPS and deal with them?

The family agreed to participate in therapy.

Addressing Parent-Child Conflict

The Falsch family had many areas that needed attention. It was decided that the initial intervention would be working with child management concerns, helping the parents learn to deal more effectively with their children. The model used was one presented in *Troubled Families* by Fleischman et al. (1983). The following sections detail its use with the Falsch family.

Assessing the Presenting Problem.

In this phase of treatment, clear definitions of the problem are sought. In the Falsches' case, it was decided that treatment programs needed to be developed such that all of the children would receive attention in the treatment program. To do this, each child was interviewed, discussing changes they would like to see in the family: "If you could make changes you would like, how would you like to see your family be different? Who would have to change and what would the changes be? If they made some changes, would you also be willing to make some so that not only they, but you too, would be cooperating more?" Once clear goals were established for each person in the family, a goal scale was completed that spelled out what the current level of behavior to be addressed was, what an expected behavioral goal would be, and what an even greater than expected outcome would be. Each person agreed to the goals as defined and was given tracking sheets to take home to monitor their behavior for a week to see what the baseline of behavior was.

Setting Up for Success. The next phase, setting up for success, means identifying what behaviors are being addressed and trying to understand the ABCs of the situation (antecedent, behavior, consequence), that is, to see how the consequence for one behavior may be an antecedent for another. When Bill teases Donny (behavior) and Donny gets angry (consequence), Donny's anger may be an antecedent to the next behavior (hitting Bill), which may provide another consequence (Bill and Donny fight), which may lead to yet another behavior (Lois yells at both boys and bans them from the TV room, a consequence), which may in turn be the antecedent for the next round of interaction.

It is important for the family to understand the way each person impacts on the others. All claim innocence in behavior, but all are instigators as well as victims. They receive an explanation of how problems escalate until someone is hurt, loses, or gives up. Alternative ways of handling conflicts are sought, but the important point at this level of intervention is to understand how each affects the others.

A second component to setting up for success is for the therapist to identify ways the family may handle daily routines differently. This includes:

- rearranging the environment to make positive behaviors easier to accomplish;
- examining family routines and developing more consistent patterns;
- teaching parents and children how to speak to each other in such a way that they are better understood and there is no room for ambiguity (get the child's attention, say exactly what you want, say when you want it, be polite but firm); for instance, "I want Bob to clean up the kitchen after dinner and before any TV tonight"; "I want Bill to take out the garbage before any TV"; "Donnie is to feed the dogs before dinner";
- teach new skills (to aid the children if they don't know how to do specific things requested of them);
- treat each other with care, respect, and love (treat the children as you would a valued neighbor or stranger);
- strengthen marital ties (identify things the couple can do now to improve the marriage: "Tell me about what you two did when you first got married... have you done that lately?");
- improve parental coordination; and
- encourage parental growth and well-being, a particularly important activity for stressed parents.

Learning Effective Self-Control. It is unreasonable to expect children to be able to demonstrate a skill that the parents don't have. Depression leading to giving up on working with children and excessive force in disciplining children (as Robert had done with Bill) are both examples of poor self-control skills. Teaching self-control involves training in (a) calming methods (modified relaxation training), (b) cognitive restructuring (using one of two forms: Ellis's rational thinking process or Glasser's steps of reality therapy), and (c) stepping out of the immediate conflict. Skills are also taught to the children for them to use both at home and in school.

Our experience in working with several hundred families is that by the time the first components have been introduced to the family (setting up for success and self-control), approximately half of the antisocial behavior that had been originally targeted has disappeared. We have found that children can be most cooperative and amenable to treatment if two conditions exist: (a) they believe the changes are real and dependable and (b) they believe the changes are fair, even if they don't agree that they want to make the changes asked of them. Another way of stating this: Children cooperate in this model of treatment if they are treated fairly and with respect and dignity. Without these characteristics, the program doesn't work.

Discipline. By and large, parents of acting-out children do not know how to apply discipline skills effectively. Too often there is too much, too late. That is, they ignore inappropriate behavior a number of times, in essence reinforcing the behavior, and then reach a point where they are no longer able to ignore the child and then come down much harder in their discipline than the act deserves. This extreme punishment then results in anger and a desire for revenge on the part of the children and a sense of guilt about their own behavior on the part of the parent.

The method of discipline that the therapist uses with the parent for implementing with children varies, depending on the nature of the behavior to be changed. The methods generally fall into one of the following categories:

- Withholding attention
- Grandma's law (Premack Principle: Eat your peas, then you may have dessert)
- Natural and logical consequences
- Time-out
- Assigning extra work
- Taking away privileges

Sometimes a combination of methods is used, depending on the nature of the behavior and the level of cooperation from the child. Using disciplinary methods is important because merely reinforcing appropriate behavior alone does not reduce the number of aggressive acts.

Reinforcement. While the earlier phases of treatment have already included a number of reinforcing methods, special attention must be paid to this area, for it is important that parents learn to "catch their kids being good" as well as be able to define the inappropriate behavior already addressed. As with discipline, the method of reinforcement is tailored to the needs and interests of the child. For younger children, including Betty and Donny in the Falsch family, a program of reinforcement using a token system may be highly effective. The use of stars, smiley faces, or other tokens provided in a reasonable manner catches the attention of the child and seems to be highly motivating. For other children, particularly as token systems lose their reinforcing capacity, other methods are needed. For Bill Falsch, an allowance system was established, since young adolescents respond particularly well to monetary reinforcers. An even more advanced form of reinforcement, contracting, in combination with an allowance system was used with Bob. Contracting is a quid pro quo method of working with people: "You cut the grass on Friday, and you may go out to the dance on Friday night"; "You help me with the construction work I'm doing on the house and I'll give you the money to buy the boom box you've wanted."

Communication. All of the phases of treatment up to this point have emphasized improving communication (giving clear commands, specifying what is wanted, clarifying contingencies of discipline and reinforcement), but at this phase of treatment specific training in communication is done. There has been ample opportunity to observe the family and to define how the family communication pattern breaks down. In this phase, specific communication recommendations, based on the family deficits in this area, are presented.

Generalization. Up to this point, the therapist has played a major role in guiding the therapeutic process. An analogy for the process would be that initially the therapist is like a teacher, specifically telling each member what to do. After the family has experienced success and moved through helping children make changes in the initial phases, the therapist acts more like a coach, helping the family define what is needed next (what are the next problems to be dealt with), working with them to develop an intervention program, and coaching them as they apply the methods. During the generalization phase, the parents have successfully changed some of the defined troublesome behaviors in the family, and the therapist coaches them on ways to generalize to other problem areas. Later, after the family has experienced success and there is a move toward termination, the therapist moves from a coaching role to a consultant role, letting the family make decisions about what needs to be done when.

School Problems. All of the children in the Falsch family, except the youngest, had school problems. School difficulties are generally held off for treatment until the family has experienced some success in working with the children at home: If parents can't control their children in the home setting, they certainly can't control them away from home when they aren't even present, as in the school.

It is important to meet with teachers, identify problem areas, and begin to develop a plan for how to help the child in the school setting. Often the therapist must serve as a liaison with the school to the parents because many parents have difficulty working with teachers and school systems. We have experienced that the parents often are correct believing that teachers don't like their kids, for many of the kids are not likable at the beginning of therapy.

The school program involves developing a Daily Report Card that the teacher, in a matter of 2 to 3 minutes daily, completes on the child. The child then takes the Daily Report Card home, and the parents provide the consequences: positive for a good day, negative for a bad one. Teachers frequently need support and help in applying treatment interventions in the classroom similar to what the family has been using at home.

Termination. After the family has experienced success working with the home and school setting as well as generalizing to other settings, termination occurs. Termination generally comes about through reduced visits, changing from weekly to bimonthly, to monthly, and then finally to very irregular contact. It is important that therapists not just quit completely; it has been our experience that families will have a relapse, generally in about the third month after stopping. Having contact with the family will allow the therapist to recognize the relapse and get the family back in for "booster sessions" to get them back on track.

Marital Therapy

Lois and Robert Falsch had marital conflict as well as having the other family problems described earlier. As part of the social learning family therapy program, they were involved in marital therapy that addressed their specific problems.

The couple was initially seen together to discuss how they had scored on the Locke Wallace Marital Adjustment Scale and to discuss problems they saw in the relationship. They agreed that there were differences on the level of importance they placed on various activities in the relationship: Lois wanted more social time, more support in managing the children, and more affection from Robert. Robert, on the other hand, wanted less fussing and arguing, less conflict in the relationship, and a better appreciation of the demands his work put on him.

Following a joint session, each spouse was seen individually to identify issues that were impinging on the relationship but that had not been presented in the conjoint session. Lois's anger at Robert for not helping more with the children came out, and Robert expressed concern about staying in the relationship since he enjoyed being on the road in his truck more than he enjoyed coming home. He had not previously thought about reasons why, but in the session he began to explore difficulties he had being expected to manage the children when he was home so little and to be involved in social activities every weekend when he was tired.

The clinical interview provides the therapist with information about the development of the relationship: what was reinforcing about it initially, what had happened over time, and whether other circumstances are influencing the relationship (extramarital affairs, drug or alcohol abuse, in-law problems, financial difficulties). No specific difficulties were presented related to the Falsch family, and so couples counseling began.

Following the first couples interview, initial expectations were presented. The first was to set expectations for couples in therapy, in part based on Stuart's (1980) model of therapy:

1. Make a commitment to change.
2. Act as if change will occur.
3. Be willing to be the first to make change.
4. Take small steps.

Lois and Robert agreed to these guidelines, and then they worked with the therapist to pinpoint areas of the relationship that they particularly enjoyed and wanted to enhance. Lois particularly liked Robert's sense of humor and his touches and wanted to experience more of those. Robert enjoyed the physical closeness of Lois and prized the private times they had. Steps to increase these behaviors were defined. A guideline similar to the one used with children was implemented: Catch your spouse doing what you like, and let him or her know you like it. This process helps partners give immediate feedback on what they like and cues each to look for what they find pleasing in the relationship. Jacobson (1981) has indicated that expectations during this time are fragile, so the process should not pressure either partner into concessions in areas where there is strong disagreement. The behaviors should be easily understood and highly likely to take place. The emphasis is on triggering positive behaviors, not decreasing undesirable ones.

Following the above phase of behavior exchange, communication skills were introduced. The model used here included two approaches, that spelled out by Gottman (Gottman, Notarius, Markman, et al., 1976) and that presented by Ohlsen (1979). Of primary emphasis in Gottman's work is helping couples understand the concept of intent and impact in messages. Clear communication occurs when the intent of the sender has the effect on the receiver that the sender intended. This process helps couples understand the filters that may occur in communicating, resulting in messages not having their intended impact.

Ohlsen's process, called a *triadic interview*, involves teaching the couple to listen and restate messages much as counselors in training learn to listen for the content and affect of client messages in beginning therapy. Many people have never learned to communicate affectively, and the process is particularly important in couples therapy. The process involves going from only minimal expression of affect in the initial phases of counseling to more intensive levels of expression by the time therapy concludes.

Problem-solving training is the next phase of couples therapy. In this process, couples are taught the steps of problem solving as outlined by Baruth and Huber (1984):

Discuss only one problem at a time.
Paraphrase or clarify communications.
Avoid "mind reading."
Avoid abusive exchanges.
Begin with positives.
Be specific.
Encourage expression of feelings.
Validate feelings.
Own mutual responsibilities.
Focus on finding solutions.
Base final solutions on mutuality and compromise.
Make final agreements specific. (pp. 102–104)

Following the problem solving, Lois and Robert developed contracts that they carried out during their homework assignments. The marital therapy was conducted conjointly with the parent training/family therapy that was addressing larger family issues. It took 6 weeks to accomplish the goals set for them.

Other Treatment Populations

The treatment of other populations and problem areas has expanded dramatically in the past decade. Areas previously considered beyond the scope of behavioral family therapy are now regarded as routine: schizophrenia, anxiety disorders, the developmentally disabled, obsessive-compulsive behavior, and drug and alcohol abuse. The basic theoretical model holds for each application, but specific application procedures vary substantially among the various treatment populations. As additional research and clinical experience contribute to the growing knowledge in the field, additional populations will be added in the near future.

EVALUATION

Research and program evaluation have been a hallmark of the behavioral approaches to therapy from the very beginning. Data collection is an integral component of the treatment program, with intensive assessment and ongoing baseline and progress data collection seen as an essential component of therapy. Evaluation is not an added feature; it is built into the system of therapy. That being the case, there has been substantial documentation of the effectiveness of social learning family therapy for the two decades that it has been a major model of treating families. It is unknown whether social learning family therapy is more effective than other treatment modalities available, for such comparative work is still being carried out. It is fairly established now that for populations investigated (particularly families with conduct-disordered or oppositional defiant children and marital conflict, as well as sexual dysfunction), social learning family therapy is an effective intervention approach.

The summary position of program effectiveness presented by Falloon supports the premise that social learning family therapy is as effective as, or more so, than the few models it has been compared to. There still is much to be done, though, in order to provide clear guidelines of the clinical skills necessary, combined with appropriate intervention strategies, for specific family needs under particular environmental conditions.

Much of the process thus far still relies on the "artistry" of the therapist, and this comes from experience and personal factors that are difficult to build into a treatment model.

SUMMARY

Social learning family therapy is an approach to helping people that emphasizes principles of learning. Dysfunctional behavior is assumed to be learned through reinforcement of inappropriate behavior, through modeling and imitation, and through shaping via extensive learning experiences. Treatment involves assessing the environmental, behavioral, and cognitive factors that contribute to maintaining the inappropriate interactions people have developed; it provides for the development of intervention programs based on principles of reinforcement. People presumably engage in activities that provide the greatest payoff and avoid those that lead to cost or pain. Social learning family therapy uses a psychoeducational approach to help people learn more effective ways of achieving the goals they have established. The approach is effective for treating a number of problem areas, particularly families with aggressive children, marital issues, and sexual dysfunctioning.

ANNOTATED SUGGESTED READINGS

Bandura, A. (1986). *Social foundations of thought and action: A social cognitive theory.* Englewood Cliffs, NJ: Prentice Hall.

Not specifically related to treating families or family systems, but a thorough introduction to the current theoretical base of social learning theory and therapy.

Falloon, I. (1988). *Handbook of behavioral family therapy.* New York: Guilford.

Eighteen chapters by leading research and clinical behavioral therapists who take the theoretical and conceptual base of behavior therapy and apply it to family therapy. The text presents current literature describing innovative clinical procedures and defines the process of treating the family as a system while using a behavioral orientation and technology.

Fleischman, M., Horne, A., & Arthur, J. (1983). *Troubled families: A treatment program.* Champaign, IL: Research Press.

A manual developed for therapists treating families with acting-out, aggressive children. The material presents a step-by-step program identifying clinical skills, defining steps for joining the family in treatment, and developing procedures for change. The book includes intake and assessment procedures, specific therapy guidelines, and generalization and maintenance methods.

Horne, A. & Sayger, T. (1990). *Treating conduct and oppositional defiant disorders in children.* New York: Pergamon Press.

A family therapy intervention approach for working specifically with families that have children who are conduct disordered. There is an extensive review of the family basis for conduct disorder along with specific treatment intervention for helping the families.

Patterson, G. R., & Forgatch, M. (1987). *Parents and adolescents living together.* Champaign, IL: Research Press.

Offers specific guidelines for dealing with adolescents' negative behavior and addresses ways families may work to have more effective family lives. The book provides numerous examples of effective and ineffective parenting exchanges.

Stuart, R. (1980). *Helping couples change.* New York: Guilford.

Presents an excellent rationale for treating couples and describes an extensive treatment model that has been supported by extensive research and clinical experience.

REFERENCES

Achenbach, T. M., & Edelbrock, C. (1983). *Manual for the child behavior problem checklist.* Burlington: University of Vermont.

Arnold, J., Levine, A., & Patterson, G. R. (1975). Changes in sibling behavior following family intervention. *Journal of Consulting and Clinical Psychology, 43,* 683–688.

Azrin, N. H., Naster, B. J., & Jones, R. (1973). Reciprocity counseling: A rapid learning based procedure for marital counseling. *Behavior Research and Therapy, 11,* 365–383.

Bahm, A., Chandler, C., & Eisenberg, L. (1961). *Diagnostic characteristics related to service on psychiatric clinics for children.* Paper presented at the 38th Annual Convention of Orthopsychiatry, Munich, Germany.

Bandura, A. (1969). *Principles of behavior modification.* New York: Holt Rinehart & Winston.

Bandura, A. (1977). *Social learning theory.* Englewood Cliffs, NJ: Prentice Hall.

Bandura, A. (1986). *Social foundations of thought and action: A social cognitive theory.* Englewood Cliffs, NJ: Prentice Hall.

Bandura, A., & Walters, R. (1963). *Social learning and personality development.* New York: Holt, Rinehart & Winston.

Baruth, L., & Huber, C. (1984). *An introduction to marital theory and therapy.* Monterey, CA: Brooks/Cole.

Bateson, G., Jackson, D. O., Haley, J., & Weakland, J. (1956). Toward a theory of schizophrenia. *Behavioral Science, 1,* 251–264.

Beach, D., & Laird, J. (1968). Follow up

study of children identified early as emotionally disturbed. *Journal of Consulting and Clinical Psychology, 32,* 369–374.

Birchler, G., Weiss, R., & Vincent, J. (1975). A multimethod analysis of social reinforcers exchange between maritally distressed and nondistressed spouse and stranger dyads. *Journal of Personality and Social Psychology, 31,* 349–360.

Blechman, E. (1981). Toward comprehensive behavioral family intervention: An algorithm for matching families and interactions. *Behavior Modification, 5,* 221–236.

Boardman, W. K. (1962). Rusty: A brief behavior disorder. *Journal of Consulting Psychology, 26,* 293–297.

Brown, J. H., & Christensen, D. N. (1986). *Family therapy: Theory and practice.* Monterey, CA: Brooks/Cole.

Colpe, L. (1990). *The relationship between mothers' self percepts of efficacy and family problem solving behaviors.* Unpublished doctoral dissertation, Indiana State University, Terre Haute.

Eideson, B. (1968). Retreat from help. *American Journal of Orthopsychiatry, 38,* 910–921.

Falloon, I. R. (1988). *Handbook of behavioral family therapy.* New York: Guilford.

Fleischman, M. (1976). *The effects of a parenting salary and family SES in the social learning treatment of aggressive children.* Unpublished doctoral dissertation, University of Oregon, Eugene.

Fleischman, M., & Horne, A. (1979). Working with families: A social learning approach. *Contemporary Education, 1,* 66–71.

Fleischman, M., Horne, A., & Arthur, J. (1983). *Troubled families: A treatment program.* Champaign, IL: Research Press.

Goldiamond, I. (1965). Self-centered procedures in personal behavior problems. *Psychological Reports, 17,* 851–868.

Goldstein, M. K. (1971). Behavior rate change in marriages: Training wives to modify husbands' behavior. *Dissertation Abstracts International, 32* (1-B), 559.

Gottman, J., Markman, H., & Notarius, C. (1977). The topography of marital conflict: A sequential analysis of verbal and nonverbal behavior. *Journal of Marriage and the Family, 39,* 461–477.

Gottman, J., Notarius, C., Gonso, J., & Markman, H. (1976). *A couple's guide to communication.* Champaign, IL: Research Press.

Gottman, J., Notarius, C., Markman, H., Bank, S., Yoppi, B., & Rubin, M. (1976). Behavior exchange theory and marital decision making. *Journal of Personality and Social Psychology, 34,* 14–23.

Harter, S. (1982). The perceived competence scale for children. *Child Development, 53,* 87–97.

Henggeler, S. W., & Borduin, C. M. (1990). *Family therapy and beyond.* Pacific Grove, CA: Brooks/Cole.

Horne, A., Norseworthy, K., Forehand, R., & Frame, C. (1990). A delinquency prevention program. Athens, GA: University of Georgia.

Horne, A., & Sayger, T. V. (1990). *Treatment of conduct and appositional defiant disorders of children.* New York: Pergamon Press.

Hunt, R. (1961). Age, sex, and service in a child guidance clinic. *Journal of Child Psychology and Psychiatry, 2,* 185–192.

Jacobson, N. (1978). A review of the effectiveness of marital therapy. In T. J. Paolino & B. S. McCrady (Eds.), *Marriage and marital therapy: Psychoanalytic, behavioral, and systems perspectives.* New York: Brunner/Mazel.

Jacobson, N. (1981). Behavioral marital therapy. In A. S. Gurman & D. P. Kniskern (Eds.), *Handbook of family therapy.* New York: Brunner/Mazel.

Jacobson, N., & Margolin, G. (1979). *Marital therapy: Strategies based on social learning and behavior exchange principles.* New York: Brunner/Mazel.

Jones, M. C. (1924). A laboratory study of

fear: The case of Peter. *Journal of Genetic Psychology, 31,* 308–315.

Lazarus, A. A. (1968). Behavior therapy and group marriage counseling. *Journal of the American Society of Psychosomatic Medicine and Dentistry, 15,* 49–56.

Lederer, W., & Jackson, D. (1968). *Mirages of marriage.* New York: Norton.

Levitt, E. (1958). A comparative judgemental study of defection from treatment at a child guidance clinic. *Journal of Clinical Psychology, 14,* 429–432.

Levitt, E. (1971). Research on psychotherapy with children. In A. Bergin & S. Garfield (Eds.), *Handbook of psychotherapy and behavior change* (pp. 474–494). New York: Wiley.

Liberman, R. P. (1970). Behavioral approaches to family and couple therapy. *American Journal of Orthopsychiatry, 40,* 106–118.

Liberman, R. P., Mueser, K., & Glynn, J. (1988). Modular behavioral strategies. In I. Falloon, (Ed.), *Handbook of behavioral family therapy* (pp. 27–50). New York: Guilford.

Locke, H. J., & Wallace, K. M. (1959). Short-term marital adjustment and prediction tests: Their reliability and validity. *Journal of Marriage and Family Living, 21,* 251–255.

Lovibond, S. H. (1963). The mechanism of conditioning treatment of enuresis. *Behavior Research and Therapy, 1,* 17–21.

Meltzoff, J., & Kornreich, M. (1970). *Research in psychotherapy.* New York: Atherton Press.

Moos, R. H. (1974). *Family environment scale.* Palo Alto, CA: Consulting Psychologists.

Moos, R. H., & Moos, B. S. (1981). *Family environment scale manual.* Palo Alto, CA: Consulting Psychologists.

Morris, H. (1956). Aggressive behavior disorders in children: A follow-up study. *American Journal of Psychiatry, 112,* 991–997.

Nichols, M. (1984). *Family therapy: Concepts and methods.* New York: Gardner Press.

Nickerson M., Light R., Blechman, E., & Gandelman B. (1976, Winter). Three measures of problem solving behavior: A procedural manual. *ISAS Catalog of Selected Documents in Psychology* (M51190).

Ohlsen, M. (1979). *Marriage counseling in groups.* Champaign, IL: Research Press.

Overall, B., & Aronson, H. (1963). Expectation of psychotherapy in patients of lower socioeconomic class. *American Journal of Orthopsychiatry, 33,* 421–430.

Patterson, G. R. (1974a). Interventions for boys with conduct problems: Multiple settings, treatments and criteria. *Journal of Consulting and Clinical Psychology, 42,* 471–481.

Patterson, G. R. (1974b). Retraining of aggressive boys by their parents: Review of recent literature and follow-up evaluation. *Canadian Psychiatric Association Journal, 19,* 142–161.

Patterson, G. R. (1975). *Families: Applications of social learning theory to family life.* Champaign, IL: Research Press.

Patterson, G. R. (1982). *Coercive family process.* Eugene, OR: Castalia.

Patterson, G. R. (1988). Forward. In I. Falloon (Ed.), *Handbook of behavioral family therapy* (pp. vii–x). New York: Guilford.

Patterson, G. R., & Brodsky, A. (1966). A behavior modification programme for a child with multiple behavior problems. *Journal of Child Psychology and Psychiatry, 7,* 277–295.

Patterson, G. R., Cobb, J., & Ray, R. (1973). A social engineering technology for retraining the families of aggressive boys. In H. Adams & I. Unikel (Eds.), *Issues and trends in behavior therapy* (pp. 139–224). Springfield, IL: Charles Thomas.

Patterson, G. R., & Gullion, M. E. (1971). *Living with children: New methods for parents and teachers* (rev. ed). Champaign, IL: Research Press.

Patterson, G. R., & Hops, H. (1972). Coercion: A game for two. Intervention techniques for marital conflict. In R. Ulrich

& P. Mountjoy (Eds.), *The experimental analysis of social behavior.* New York: Appleton-Century-Crofts.

Patterson, G. R., Jones, R., Whittier, J., & Wright, M. (1965). A behavior modification technique for a hyperactive child. *Behavior Research and Therapy, 2,* 217–226.

Patterson, G. R., McNeal, S., Hawkins, N., & Phelps, R. (1967). Reprogramming the social environment. *Journal of Child Psychology and Psychiatry, 8,* 181–195.

Patterson, G. R., Reid, J., Jones, R., & Congers, R. (1975). *A social learning approach to family intervention.* Eugene, OR: Castalia.

Patterson, G. R., Shaw, D., & Ebner, M. (1969). Teachers, peers, and parents as agents of change in the classroom. In F. A. M. Benson (Ed.), *Modifying deviant behaviors in various classroom settings* (No. 1, pp. 13–47). Eugene: The University of Oregon Press.

Reid, J. (1967). *Reciprocity and family interaction.* Unpublished doctoral dissertation, University of Oregon, Eugene.

Reid, J., & Patterson, G. R. (1976). The modification of aggressive and stealing behavior of boys in the home setting. In A. Bandura & E. Ribes (Eds.), *Behavior modification: Experimental analyses of aggression and delinquency.* Hillsdale, NJ: Lawrence Erlbaum Associates.

Risley, T. R., & Wolf, M. M. (1967). Experimental manipulation of autistic behaviors and generalizations in the home. In S. W. Bijou & D. M. Baer (Eds.), *Child development: Readings in experimental analysis* (pp. 184–194). New York: Appleton.

Roach, J. (1958). Some social psychological characteristics of child clinic caseloads. *Journal of Consulting Psychology, 22,* 183–186.

Robins, L. (1966). *Deviant children grown up: A sociological and psychological study of psychopathic personality.* Baltimore: Williams & Wilkins.

Sayger, T. V. (1987). *The maintenance of treatment effects for families of aggressive boys participating in social learning family therapy.* Unpublished doctoral dissertation, Indiana State University, Terre Haute.

Sayger, T. V., Horne, A., Passmore, J. L., & Walker, J. M. (1988). Social learning family therapy with aggressive children: Treatment outcome and maintenance. *Journal of Family Psychology, 1,* 261–285.

Spanier, G. B. (1976). Measuring dyadic adjustment: New scales for assessing the quality of marriage and similar dyads. *Journal of Marriage and the Family, 38,* 15–28.

Stuart, R. B. (1969). An operant interpersonal treatment for marital discord. *Journal of Consulting and Clinical Psychology, 33,* 675–682.

Stuart, R. B. (1980). *Helping couples change.* New York: Guilford.

Stuart, R. B., & Stuart, F. (1972). *Marital pre-counseling inventory.* Champaign, IL: Research Press.

Teuber, H., & Powers, E. (1953). Evaluating therapy in a delinquency prevention program. *Psychiatric Treatment, 21,* 138–147.

Thibault, J., & Kelley, H. H. (1959). *The social psychology of groups.* New York: Wiley.

Wahler, R. (1976). Deviant child behavior within the family: Developmental speculations and behavior change strategies. In H. Leitenberg (Ed.), *Handbook of behavior modification and behavior therapy.* Englewood Cliffs, NJ: Prentice Hall.

Walker, J. M. (1984). *A study of the effectiveness of social learning family therapy for reducing aggressive behavior in boys.* Unpublished doctoral dissertation, Indiana State University, Terre Haute.

Walter, H., & Gilmore, S. (1973). Placebo versus social learning effects in parent training procedures designed to alter the behavior of aggressive boys. *Behavior Therapy, 4,* 361–374.

Watson, J., & Raynor, R. (1920). Conditioned emotional reactions. *Journal of*

Experimental Psychology, 3, 1–14.

Weiss, R. I. (1978). The conceptualization of marriage from a behavior perspective. In T. J. Paolino & B. S. McCrady (Eds.), *Marriage and wanted therapy.* New York: Brunner/Mazel.

Weiss, R. L., Hops, H., & Patterson, G. R. (1973). A framework for conceptualizing marital conflict, a technology for altering it. Some data for evaluating it. In L. A. Hamerlynch, L. C. Handy, & E. T. Mash (Eds.), *Behavior change: Methodology, concepts and practice.* Champaign, IL: Research Press.

Williams, C. D. (1959). The elimination of tantrum behavior extinction procedures. *Journal of Abnormal and Social Psychology, 59,* 269.

Wills, T., Weiss, R., & Patterson, G. R. (1975). A behavioral analysis of the determinants of marital satisfaction. *Journal of Consulting and Clinical Psychology, 42,* 802–811.

Wiltz, N., & Patterson, G. R. (1974). An evaluation of parent training procedures designed to alter inappropriate aggressive behavior in boys. *Behavior Therapy, 5,* 215–221.

CHAPTER 17

Transactional Analysis and Family Therapy

RICHARD G. ERSKINE

DEFINITION

The family is a group of two or more persons who have a commitment to one another over time and who share resources, responsibility for decisions, values, and goals. It is the unit of persons one "comes home to," regardless of the biological or legal ties, adoption, or marriage. The basis for the life of a family is the communication and interaction that occur between individuals in the family. Clear communication contributes to the family's well-being and growth, while faulty communication is a hazard to the psychological and physiological health of each member of the family.

Transactional analysis (TA) is a theory of personality that focuses on communication. This model of personality describes each personality as being composed of three ego states. Each ego state organizes external and internal stimuli in a specific way, resulting in uniquely different communication. The analysis of the transactional patterns that appear using this model provides a tool to understand and to change interpersonal and intrapersonal dynamics that may block effective communication.

The tendency of a person to favor any one ego state as a basis for communication is determined in part by the life script. A script is a life plan decided upon in childhood as a way to fit into the family. It is formulated out of what the child hears, experiences, and perceives as possible options.

Transactional analysis provides family members with a cognitive understanding of the dynamics of family scripts, the functions of personality and transactional patterns. The counseling methodology encourages each person to take responsibility for him- or herself consistent with developmental age, to express the emotions that are often held back or are ineffectively communicated, and to focus on specific behavioral changes that can improve family life.

The work of the TA therapist is to provide the environment and means whereby persons are free to make meaningful contact with others and to respond to problem solving without preconceived ideas or plans that limit interpretation of the situation and restrict behavior choices.

HISTORICAL DEVELOPMENT

Beginnings

Transactional analysis began with the San Francisco Social Psychiatry Seminar in the late 1950s. Eric Berne, a leader of the seminar, was interested in the social aspects of psychiatric problems. He believed that if the client's problem could be resolved at the social level, it would lead to more rapid and effective intrapsychic cure. He encouraged his clients to work in a group setting, facing each other in a circle of chairs, and to engage in communication. He focused on the transactions between the people in the group and provided them with an understanding of their behavior and an opportunity to experiment with behaving differently.

TENETS OF THE MODEL

In the 1950s and early '60s, Berne wrote a series of papers on intuition (Berne, 1949, 1952, 1953, 1955, 1957, 1962) and communication wherein he developed a model of personality providing a structure for understanding an enormous variety of human behavior. The theory was aimed at extracting a simple set of concepts for people at all levels of development based on developmental psychology and Freudian theory.

Basic to this model was Paul Federn's (1952) concept that psychological reality was based on unique and discrete ego states. Eduardo Weiss (1950) also detailed evidence on the existence of ego states. Federn and Weiss both maintained that hypnosis, dreams, and psychosis prove that ego configurations of earlier age levels remain in potential existence throughout life (Dusay, 1971).

These theoretical concepts were supported experimentally in the work of Wilder Penfield (1952), a neurosurgeon who used an electronic probe to stimulate the temporal cortex of epileptic patients. The electrical stimulation awakened in the person not only the memory of past events but also the total reexperiencing of all sensing and feeling associated with past experiences. At the same time, the patient was aware of being on the operating table undergoing a procedure.

Ego States

Drawing from the theoretical work of Federn and Weiss, Berne postulated that in Penfield's patients there was a sense of

self (an *ego state*) that was conscious as an observer and a separate archaic ego state that was reexperienced. He began to realize the similarities between this idea and the observation that many of his clients who were reporting difficulty in interpersonal relations were at times relating to people as rational adults and at other times feeling and behaving just the way they had when they were young children; in essence, they were functioning from two different ego states (1957).

In his initial model, Berne identified two ego states that had a separate system of feelings related to a set of thoughts and corresponding behaviors. The archaic aspects of the personality became the *Child* ego state, distinguished by relics of beliefs, behavioral patterns, and feelings carried over from childhood. The Child ego state is not just the thoughts, feelings, and behavior that resemble children but *are* from childhood. They are *fixations* of an earlier developmental period. Berne called the observant, rational sense of self the *Adult* ego state, composed of thoughts, actions, and feelings that are self-developed responses to the current situation.

In later psychotherapeutic group work, Berne began to realize that people have not only an ego state that is an observer and participant in current reality and an archaic ego state but also an ego state that feels, thinks, and behaves much like their parents. This introjected or exteropsychic aspect of the personality was described as the *Parent* ego state (see Figure 1).

The Parent ego state is not what resembles parental behavior but is an actual historical *incorporation* of the feelings, attitudes, and behavioral patterns of one's own parents or other significant parental figures. Each personality has all three aspects of "self," colloquially re-

Figure 1. Ego states.

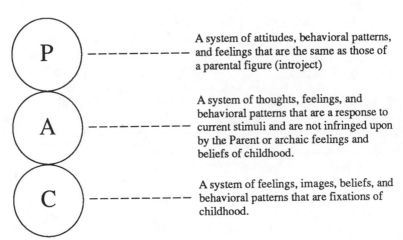

A system of attitudes, behavioral patterns, and feelings that are the same as those of a parental figure (introject)

A system of thoughts, feelings, and behavioral patterns that are a response to current stimuli and are not infringed upon by the Parent or archaic feelings and beliefs of childhood.

A system of feelings, images, beliefs, and behavioral patterns that are fixations of childhood.

ferred to as Parent, Adult, and Child.

Berne (1961) used the term *ego state* to describe a state of mind with a coherent system of internal feelings and thoughts and a corresponding system of postures, facial expressions, speech patterns, voice tones, and other external behaviors. The two together—the behaviors and the state of mind—form the active ego state.

It is from these active ego states that people communicate. Sometimes people talk to others from their Parent with all the feelings, attitudes, and expressions that their mother or father used years before; at other times they may react as a little child, perceiving the situation as they did when they were only 5 or 6 years old. They may then switch to the Adult ego state and react to the communication with the emotions, ideas, and behaviors that are situationally and developmentally appropriate and unencumbered with that which is borrowed from parents or a fixation from childhood.

Ego states are not related to the psychoanalytic concepts of id and superego but only with the concept of ego—

defined here as the self that is knowable. Each person's identity of self is comprised of all three states of the ego, and transactions with others can come from any one of the three ego states, often without the awareness of which state of the ego is active.

Phenomenologically, the Parent ego state is experienced as a structure for living (a set of values and rules) and is manifested as controlling or nurturing behavior. The Adult ego state is experienced as the here-and-now integration of perceptions, thoughts, and feelings and is evidenced behaviorally as problem solving appropriate to the person's developmental stage. The Child ego state is experienced as a state of feelings, needs, wants, and fantasies and is manifested as either adapted behavior or spontaneous, natural behaviors from previous developmental periods.

Dysfunctions

Psychological problems emerge when the introjected or archaic ideas, images, and emotions contaminate the here-and-

Figure 2. Contaminations.

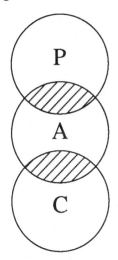

now perceptions of the Adult ego state. When Adult ego state *contamination* exists, the phenomenological experience of the person is that they are processing current stimuli, accounting for current sensations and feelings, and are behaving appropriately to the situation when, in fact, this is not so. The person is unaware that the introjected ideas and emotions or the childhood decisions and feelings are infringing on present perceptions (see Figure 2). These contaminations function as a delusion or prejudice in processing current thoughts, feelings, and perceptions. An example of contamination is Bob's statement, "We don't have any problems" (Transaction 48).* His Parent view that the role of a father was to work hard distorted his ability to process information about his relationships with his wife and children.

———

*The numbered transaction to which a statement refers can be found in the transcript of the family therapy session appearing as the Case Example of this chapter.

Transactions

When two people contact each other, the unit of social intercourse is called a *transaction*. Each of us has the potential to transact with another person from one of three ego states.

Complementary transactions occur when one addresses an ego state in another person and the response is from the same ego state. As long as transactions are complementary, communication can continue indefinitely with the response of each person serving as the stimulus for the next transaction. When transactions are crossed—that is, a different ego state than that addressed responds—communication stops or the subject changes. The most common crossed transactions involve an Adult to Adult stimulus and a Child to Parent response or a Parent to Child response (see Figure 3). Transactional analysis involves analyzing which ego states are used to communicate and to which ego states they are directed and then teaching the client how to choose the most effective way of transacting.

Figure 3. Transactions.

COMPLEMENTARY TRANSACTION

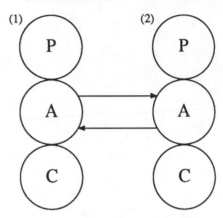

1. Did you take the garbage out?

2. I took it out after dinner.

CROSSED TRANSACTIONS

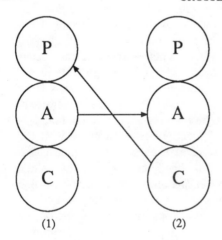

1. Did you take the garbage out?	1. Did you take the garbage out?
2. You're always picking on me!	2. You should have done it yourself.

Sometimes a stimulus is directed at more than one ego state, in which case an *ulterior transaction* exists, as in Jean's communication with her husband where, at the social level, she says, "I would like to go away for a weekend" (51, 55). Simultaneously, she shrugs her shoulders and laughs, directing a message at the ulterior or psychological level that implies "I won't get what I want." Bob responds

Figure 4. Ulterior transaction.

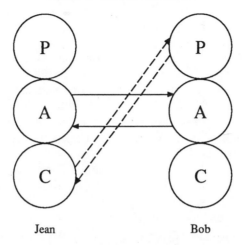

Jean   Bob

Jean: I would like to go away for a weekend.
      Psychological: I won't get what I want.

Bob: I have to work in the store.
      Psychological: My work is more im-
        portant than your wants.

socially with "I have to work in the store" and ulteriorly with "Work is more important than your wants" (85; see also Figure 4).

When there is an ulterior message, it is the psychological level of communication that determines the outcome of that communication. People often think that their communication is at the social or content level and are unaware of the ulterior level of transaction. The function of the therapist is to make the ulterior messages explicit, allowing the psychological message to be dealt with openly.

Strokes

A transaction consists of a series of *strokes* or units of recognition. A stroke can be a verbal or nonverbal indication of recognizing another's existence: a hello, a smile, a pat on the back, a letter in the mail. The psychological strokes are an outgrowth of what each person needs in infancy in the form of physical stroking and is an important component in the survival of all infants. In addition, the way in which an infant is stroked often affects the view that that child will have of the world—gentle, rough, reliable, unpredictable. As children grow, they develop preferences for different kinds of strokes, preferences that are generally present throughout life. Sometimes these preferences are based on the kinds of strokes available. For a child who lives in a family where the predominant kind of strokes is negative, the learned preference may be for negative strokes, resulting in the child acting out, agitating, or being disruptive. Negative strokes are better than none at all and provide at least some stimulation for survival. Besides being positive or negative, strokes are either conditional or unconditional—that is, recognition for specific behaviors or lack of behaviors or recognition for being.

A major focus in family therapy is understanding and, if necessary, changing the stroking patterns of a family. In some families, members have to compete for strokes by outperforming each other or by having the greatest need, such as through sickness, accidents, or getting in trouble. In other families, strokes are given only indirectly through a third person, as when Mother strokes Billy by telling the neighbors how well he did in school. Some families stroke only through giving objects such as food or gifts; in other families, a parent gives strokes only when he has been drinking alcohol or is high on drugs.

In all of these cases, what the therapist looks for are patterns of who strokes whom, when, under what conditions, how, and the kinds of strokes exchanged. A family with an enuretic child experienced significant change by giving the child a back rub every night before sleep. This provided an opportunity for the child to get physical strokes, to have 15 minutes alone with one parent, and have an opportunity to discharge tensions left from the day by talking to that parent.

Games

A specific series of transactions that serve to provide negative strokes and maintain the script is called a *game*. A game is a series of complementary ulterior transactions leading to a well-defined payoff (Berne, 1964). The ulterior or psychological level of these transactions is always out of awareness, while the overt communication is experienced as real and ego-syntonic. The underlying attempt in each of these games is to meet some need. For example, a child who habitually plays a game where

he ends up getting some form of negative recognition, referred to in Berne's (1964) catalog of games as "Kick Me," is probably attempting to fill a need for strokes and possibly to resolve an earlier developmental need to be accepted in spite of negative behavior.

There are many colloquial names ascribed to the various games to make them easier to identify with and to assist people in being able to smile at their own foibles. Examples of games are "Now I've Got You, You SOB," "Courtroom," "Why Don't You," "Yes But," and "Ain't It Awful."

The family therapist will often identify the dominant family games, look for what need is attempting to be met, and teach the family new ways of asking for and responding to needs so that they can be satisfied without collecting bad feelings in the process and thereby reinforce script beliefs and behaviors.

A way of looking at games is through the social roles of Persecutor, Rescuer, and Victim (Karpman, 1968). When functioning from the limitations of script, people have a tendency to transact socially from one of the three positions. These positions behaviorally either defend against or support the script beliefs. Victims habitually see themselves as helpless in the world and will go in search of Rescuers to assist them. Often in the process, Victims will stimulate a response in others to persecute as a way of defending against their own sense of helplessness.

An important element in games is the switch in social roles, which leads to the negative payoff. A mother who starts the day giving and giving to her family without taking for herself (Rescuer) may be in tears by nighttime, accusing her family of not loving or appreciating her (Victim). She ends up feeling mistreated and sad, and the family members may end up feeling annoyed or guilty.

CURRENT STATUS AND OTHER SYSTEMS

Script

Much of the current work of transactional analysis focuses on life script. *Script* is a life plan formulated from what one experiences as a child and decisions made under stress. A script limits spontaneity and flexibility in problem solving and in relating to people because the story, including the ending and all the major events, is already written in early childhood. In essence, the script answers the question "What does a person like me do in a family like this with people like you?"

The script can be established in either of two ways. One, a child may *introject* implicit or explicit messages and behavioral patterns from parents in order to be accepted and loved by them (Steiner, 1971, 1974). For example, a mother may say to her child, "You don't need anything," and the child may accept it literally, developing a life plan of denying wants and needs. Or the message can be inferred, as when a boy whose father continually ignored him concluded that father was saying to him, "Don't exist."

A second way in which a script is formed is through the child's *decisions* about life, which are based on perceptions of which options are open. These decisions may be about the child, other people, and the quality of life. When these decisions are made by a person under pressure, they emerge later in life as beliefs that inhibit personal relationships, communication, and problem solving.

These script beliefs begin developing when a child is under pressure from parental programming (Berne, 1972; Steiner, 1974) or from environmental trauma where expressing feelings does not result in needs being met (Erskine, 1980). Through the process of cognitive mediation, the child attempts to explain the experiences and the unmet needs through decisions about self, others, and the quality of life. These script beliefs are usually expressed in concrete terms consistent with the thinking levels of which young children are capable (Piaget, 1952).

Mary was extremely quiet and uncommunicative to others about her wants and needs. In therapy she reexperienced having to suppress her joy and enthusiasm for life as a young child living in a home with a bedridden grandmother who spent several years in pain. Mary's noise often wakened the grandmother, so she decided as a young child, "My wants will hurt people." She continued to live out this decision years later with her own husband, children, and friends.

The early script decision (script belief) is described as though it occurs at one particular time in a child's life. It is important to keep in mind that these may occur over a period of time and may be the result of fantasy as well as of an actual occurrence.

To the child, the decisions that are made seem to be the best possible choice in the circumstances to solve the immediate problem. Once adopted, the script beliefs influence what experiences are attended to, how they are interpreted, and whether or not they are regarded as significant by the individual.

The life script is maintained as the person grows older in order not to reexperience the unmet need and the feelings suppressed at the time of script decision and to provide a predictive model of life and interpersonal relationships. Although the script is often personally destructive, it does provide psychological homeostasis. Any disruption in this predictive model produces anxiety (Epstein, 1972); therefore, perceptions and experiences will be organized to maintain the script beliefs.

During childhood, a whole range of behaviors is tested to elicit strokes while maintaining compatability with the script beliefs. The child experiments to find which behaviors will elicit responses in others that will confirm what she or he is believing. Parents and other significant figures also influence the child's choice of behaviors through instructions ("Be good"); prohibitions ("Don't cry"); stroking ("You're so cute when you pout"); attributions ("He's the toughest kid in the neighborhood"), and modeling (Dad's temper tantrum always gets everyone's attention). Eventually the child settles on a specific group of behaviors, including displays of emotion, and uses them repeatedly, especially in situations that may confront the script beliefs.

As a child, Jean decided "I won't get what I want" and learned to laugh rather than feel the discomfort of not getting what she wanted (55). As an adult, Jean seldom asks for what she wants and whenever she does ask, she covers it with a laugh.

Racket System

Script refers to a longitudinal life plan. A way in which the script is lived out day by day is detailed in "The Racket System" (Erskine & Zalcman, 1979). It describes a one-act scene demonstrating how the script plot is reinforced and how others are manipulated into the roles the script requires. Identifying a client's

racket system provides useful guideposts for therapeutic intervention.

The racket system is defined as a self-reinforcing, distorted system of feelings, thoughts, and actions maintained by individuals who are functioning in script. The racket system has three interrelated and interdependent components: the script beliefs and feelings, the rackety display, and the reinforcing experiences.

When needs are not met in life today, the script beliefs and related feelings will be stimulated as they were at the time the script was written in early childhood. The person is then likely to engage in behaviors that will verify the script decision, referred to as the *rackety display.* This may include *observable behaviors* (choice of words, sentence patterns, tone of voice, displays of emotion, gestures and body movements) that are a direct manifestation of the script beliefs and feelings (the intrapsychic process). A person may either act in a way defined by the script beliefs, that is, saying "I don't know" when believing "I'm stupid"; or they may act in a way which socially defends against the script beliefs, that is, excelling in school and acquiring numerous degrees.

An individual may also have a physiological reaction in addition to or in place of the overt behaviors. These *reported internal experiences* are the behaviors that are not readily observable but on which the person can give a self-report, such as fluttering in the stomach, muscle tension, headaches, colitis, and all the somatic responses to the script beliefs-feelings. Persons who have many somatic complaints or illnesses frequently believe "Something is wrong with me" and use the physical symptoms to reinforce the belief.

Rackety display also includes *fantasies* where the individual imagines behaviors, either his or her own or someone else's that lend support to the script beliefs. These fantasied behaviors function as effectively in reinforcing script beliefs-feelings, and in some instances even more effectively, than the overt behaviors.

When the other 8- or 9-year-old children were not playing with Karen, she imagined them having fun together and laughing at her for not being like them. She used the fantasy to reinforce her beliefs that "I don't belong" and "No one likes me" (14).

Any rackety display can result in the collection of *reinforcing experiences,* which are the recall of selected events during a person's lifetime. Reinforcing experiences are a collection of emotional memories of transactions and the reactions, either real or imagined, of other people; recall of internal bodily experiences; or the retained remnants of fantasies, dreams, or hallucinations. Reinforcing experiences serve as a feedback mechanism to reinforce the script beliefs.

Since script beliefs function to maintain psychological homeostasis, only those memories supporting the script belief are readily accepted and used as reinforcement. Those memories that negate the script beliefs are often rejected or forgotten since they would challenge the prejudice. They may also be distorted through fantasy to create script-syntonic memories. A memory or response that is dystonic may be negated by switching to another script belief. This is identical to the function of contamination of ego states where the Parent's beliefs or the Child's perceptions interfere with Adult processing of information.

Bob's script beliefs were "Life is hard and difficult" and "No one understands me." When the therapist suggested that he ease the pressure on himself by picking a date for a weekend alone with his wife, his response was, "Life doesn't work that way, unfortunately. That's too easy" (89). This maintained his belief about life and indirectly also reinforced that, again, no one understands him.

The following example of the racket system illustrates how the client maintained script through script beliefs-feelings, rackety displays, and reinforcing experiences.

Beginning with the birth of her first sibling, Louise made a decision, based on the care her sick sibling received and her being "pushed off," that she was not important. At this time her mother was under great emotional pressure and was psychologically unavailable, while her father was frequently away. The early decision "I'm not important" was reinforced with each successive sibling and in every traumatic home situation where, being oldest, Louise's needs were ignored. Louise reported in therapy that she often experienced her parents' nonverbal attitude as an injunction: "Don't be important." At an early age, she discovered that one solution to the problem of not being important was to take care of others—siblings and parents—which would make it possible for some of her needs to be met.

In adult life, this decision was observable in her choice of a helping profession. Her general demeanor was quiet and withdrawn, deferring to others. The social response from others was that she was ignored and often did not get what she wanted, thereby reinforcing her belief that she was not important, was unwanted, and others were more important. Her affective behavior was one of sadness with periods of depression and/or severe headaches.

Her fantasy life often centered around the belief that if she were good enough

Figure 5. Louise's racket system.

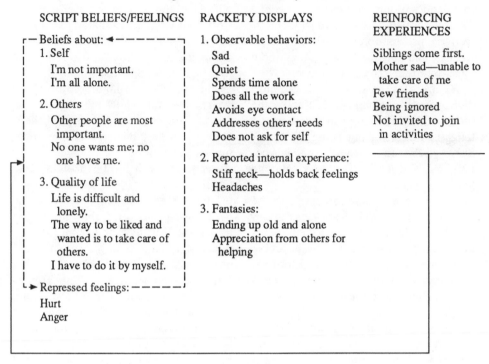

SCRIPT BELIEFS/FEELINGS	RACKETY DISPLAYS	REINFORCING EXPERIENCES
Beliefs about:	1. Observable behaviors:	
1. Self	Sad	Siblings come first.
I'm not important.	Quiet	Mother sad—unable to
I'm all alone.	Spends time alone	take care of me
	Does all the work	Few friends
2. Others	Avoids eye contact	Being ignored
Other people are most	Addresses others' needs	Not invited to join
important.	Does not ask for self	in activities
No one wants me; no		
one loves me.	2. Reported internal experience:	
	Stiff neck—holds back feelings	
3. Quality of life	Headaches	
Life is difficult and		
lonely.	3. Fantasies:	
The way to be liked and	Ending up old and alone	
wanted is to take care of	Appreciation from others for	
others.	helping	
I have to do it by myself.		
Repressed feelings:		
Hurt		
Anger		

to someone else, they would love her and take care of her. To support this belief she also occasionally fantasized ending up alone, poor, and unloved.

The model of the racket system in Figure 5 describes how Louise lived out her old script decisions day by day. Within a family context the behavior of other family members is used either to reinforce or to extinguish script beliefs. When a family system is dysfunctional, family members are in script and are reinforcing each other.

Interlocking Racket System. In a dysfunctional family, awareness of each person's needs and desires is avoided or concealed and family problems are met with rigidity and manipulation. The dynamics of a dysfunctional family are illustrated in the *interlocking racket sys-*

tem as various family members attempt to live out their scripts.

The model of the interlocking racket system describes how the script of each family member is intricately woven into a family pattern. Each person influences and is influenced by the behavior of others in the family who provide reinforcing experiences that confirm the script beliefs. In family therapy, the therapist will watch for the transactions (or lack of appropriate transactions) that are script reinforcing for someone in the family.

In Louise's case, her behavior often consisted of long periods of silence, often without initiating contact with her husband, and spending time alone reading. Louise's husband, Bill, in wanting contact with Louise, would use Louise's behavior as a reinforcing experience to confirm his script belief "There is something wrong with me." During the periods of Louise's silence, Bill would fantasize a variety of things that he might have done wrong to lead Louise to avoid him. In each fantasy he would collect further evidence to support the script belief. He then would defend against the belief by angrily telling his wife and son all that they had done wrong. Louise would then use the memory of Bill's angry criticism to reinforce "I'm not important" and would withdraw, providing further evidence for Bill's script belief. While Louise was at work she would repeatedly remember Bill's criticism of the night before, each memory serving to stimulate her childhood sadness and anger and old script decisions. To repress the old feelings she would work harder to please Bill, anticipating all the things she could do to please him.

In response to his father's criticisms, Ron, who is 10 years old, came to the conclusion as a younger child that "something is wrong with me." Each angry criticism of Bill would serve to reinforce Ron's script belief. His pattern of behavior included doing poorly in school, breaking neighbors' windows, stealing and getting into trouble with grown-ups. Each problem behavior proved to him that there was something wrong with him. Bill, in turn, would use Ron's behavior to reinforce that something was wrong with him as a father and would then give his son even more negative strokes. Louise would use Ron's discipline problem to reinforce her beliefs that she was unimportant and could not make an impact on her son to control his behavior. The behaviors of each family member interlocked with the others' racket systems to maintain each person's script (see Figure 6).

The interlocking racket system demonstrates in operation how each family member supports and helps others to carry out their own script decisions in day-to-day life and describes both the interpersonal and intrapersonal dynamics of a dysfunctional family. Each person's script beliefs provide a distorted framework for viewing self, others, and the quality of life. In order to engage in a rackety display, individuals must discount other options and frequently will maintain that their behavior is the "natural" or "only" way they can respond. When used in social transactions, rackety displays are likely to produce reinforcing experiences that, in turn, are governed by and contribute to the reinforcement of the script beliefs and rackety displays. Thus, each person's racket system is distorted and self-reinforcing through the operation of its three interrelated and interdependent subsystems: script beliefs-feelings, rackety displays, and reinforcing experiences.

APPLICATION

Clients for Whom the Model Is Especially Effective

Transactional analysis is a psychotherapy that has been used in a broad range of cultures and socioeconomic groups. The client populations to which TA has been applied have varied from people seeking personal growth to people requiring treatment for severe pathologies. Clinical transactional analysis has been effective in the treatment of schizophrenia (Schiff, 1970), alcoholism (Steiner, 1971), drug addiction (Windes, 1973), and in inmate populations in prisons (Corsover, 1979; Groder, 1977). Elementary and high schools have used TA to improve student behavior and self-concept (Erskine & Maisenbacher, 1975). When used in family therapy, TA provides the tools for understanding the in-

Figure 6. Interlocking racket systems.

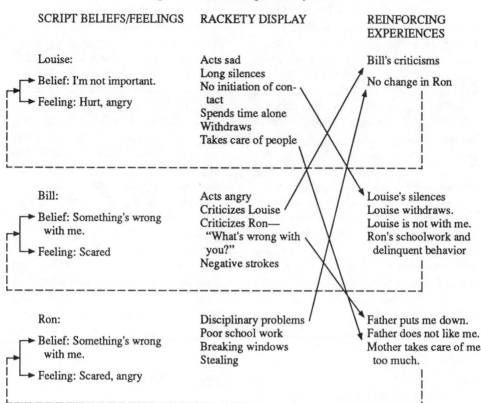

SCRIPT BELIEFS/FEELINGS   RACKETY DISPLAY   REINFORCING
                                                EXPERIENCES

Louise:

Belief: I'm not important.

Feeling: Hurt, angry

Acts sad
Long silences
No initiation of con-
   tact
Spends time alone
Withdraws
Takes care of people

Bill's criticisms

No change in Ron

Bill:

Belief: Something's wrong
   with me.

Feeling: Scared

Acts angry
Criticizes Louise
Criticizes Ron—
   "What's wrong with
   you?"
Negative strokes

Louise's silences
Louise withdraws.
Louise is not with me.
Ron's schoolwork and
   delinquent behavior

Ron:

Belief: Something's wrong
   with me.

Feeling: Scared, angry

Disciplinary problems
Poor school work
Breaking windows
Stealing

Father puts me down.
Father does not like me.
Mother takes care of me
   too much.

terpersonal and individual dynamics and the methodologies for effective intervention (Bader, 1980).

The personality adaptation of each individual will determine to a large degree how they will respond to psychotherapy. Under psychological stress or in response to unmet needs, people foster personality adaptations to protect against what they experience internally as vulnerable. Some people will present themselves to the world in an intellectualizing way, others will be emotive, and still others will be highly active. In order to be effective with various personality adaptations that can be present in family therapy, the theoretical concepts and methodology of

the psychotherapy need to address the cognitive, affective, or behavioral levels of personality adaptations of each person as well as provide a protective means to reach the person in his or her vulnerable areas.

For the person who presents her- or himself as highly intellectual, the therapeutic goal may be the comfortable expression of feelings. However, to press for feelings too quickly may be very threatening. In understanding the client's personality adaptation, the therapist would make contact first at the level she or he was most comfortable, moving toward making behavioral changes, and finally dealing with the threat of emotional display after the therapeutic alliance is strong and positive results have been experienced in the therapy.

A particular advantage of TA in family therapy is that it is flexible and adjustable to a wide variety of problem areas clients present. It provides therapeutic options for working with people affectively, behaviorally, and cognitively (Erskine, 1975). Some clients may be resistant to behavioral changes until they first receive cognitive information that explains the problem or their psychodynamics. Others may need to express pent-up emotions before they can process information about their dynamics. Still others may need to change behavior first and then later cognitively process their effect on other family members. Some TA therapists also include a focus on physical stroking and body constrictions as an important area of therapy (Cassius, 1975; Erskine, 1980).

Goals of the Therapeutic Process

The aim of family therapy is to meet the contracts for change that each family makes with the therapist. The aim of the contract in most cases is to create a functional, interdependent family structure. This is accomplished through creating changes in the communication patterns and the interrelationships of family members so that needs are met in a cooperative way. For families who decide not to live together, the contract may be to make the separation process nontraumatic and to provide for the optimal welfare of each person involved.

Dependence. Three types of family relationships are identified. The first type is one of dependency where boundaries between individuals or between family roles may be distorted or unde-

fined. For example, one person may function in a problem-solving capacity while the other person may continually focus on personal feelings and needs to the exclusion of others. This symbiotic relationship is dramatically expressed in the hardworking wife and the alcoholic husband. There is often a shift of feelings and responsibility for behavior from one person to the other, exemplified by the statement "She made me do it." The goal in therapy for a symbiotic family is to help each individual function independently, consistent with their developmental level. The aim is for each person to take responsibility for their own thoughts, feelings, and behaviors.

Independence. In the process of family therapy, independence can be a phase between dependence and a final goal of interdependence. However, some families come to therapy with relationships that are so rigid and independent that they cannot rely on each other for meaningful contact and mutual need fulfillment. The final therapeutic goals for both types of family are the establishment of interdependence.

Interdependence. In a functional, interdependent family there is an acknowledgment that each person has an impact on the other. In order to live comfortably and cooperatively together, individual feelings and needs have to be accounted for and responded to in some meaningful way. Interdependence is a combination of the autonomy of independence and the acknowledgment of the responsibility and dependency each person experiences in relation to others with whom he or she is living for the satisfaction of some emotional and physical needs. The aim is to have family members actively ask for and negotiate to get what they want while also learning to give without resentment and hidden "you owe me's."

Learning. An early treatment goal in this change process is to teach family members a framework for understanding themselves and a simple language to describe their internal experiences and the dynamics that occur in the family relationships. An additional goal is to instruct individuals in identifying needs and making a distinction between thoughts, feelings, and behaviors so that they can develop effective ways of communicating and problem solving. In some families, a goal may be for parents to learn about developmental needs of children and to identify ways of meeting those needs, either directly or by helping the child develop internal or other external resources.

Intrapsychic Therapy. Once family members have an understanding of their own ego states, transactional patterns, and their effects on others, the goal may then be in-depth intrapsychic therapy. This process may include examining, exploring, or reexperiencing early life experiences that have led to present-day problems. In reliving old scenes, the goal is to release repressed emotions, identify the decisions that were made at that time, and make redecisions that disconnect the old beliefs and feelings from their current situation (Erskine, 1974; Goulding & Goulding, 1979).

Script redecision work may be useful for adults or older children where script patterns have already been established. This level of therapy may be done in individual or couple sessions or within an ongoing therapy group as well as within the context of the family sessions. For

younger children, it is often sufficient to provide information, develop options, and give permissions that will lead to a change in script beliefs and enable them to get what they need. In a situation where a 7-year-old girl was in a symbiotic relationship with her mother, evidenced by school phobia, the child was frequently given permission by the therapist (and later in therapy by the mother also) to have her own feelings, which may be different from Mom's. The mother was encouraged in the session to talk to the child about what she was feeling and to provide information to the child that she would be home and available at specific after-school hours.

Integration. A final treatment goal is to integrate each individual's personal changes into a healthy family structure. This includes supporting changes in script beliefs, developing options for new behavior patterns, and maintaining family dynamics that allow for joyful, spontaneous, intimate, and creative living.

Client's Responsibility

Transactional analysis is based on a contractual model of therapy in which the client is responsible for identifying personal goals and investing the energy necessary to accomplish those goals. Goals are frequently formulated in clearly defined behavioral terms so that the client can experience success and active participation in his or her own growth. The contractual model also allows a balance of power between the therapist and clients so that all are equally responsible for the progress of therapy.

In family therapy, clients are asked to take responsibility for being open to confrontation and feedback and to respond to others with their thoughts and feelings honestly and with care for themselves and others.

Members of the family are also asked to take responsibility for their own behavior and how their behavior contributes to the well-being of the family or causes conflict. This is particularly important for parental figures who by their behavior may be contributing to script formation in a child. It becomes the parents' responsibility to identify the needs of their children and what they can do to satisfy those needs. For example, for the child with unsatisfied security needs, the therapist may encourage the parents to make more physical contact with the child—holding on their laps, cuddling before bedtime—or to find ways to share more information, like having short talks before going to school each day. They are also taught to recognize the clues in the child that he or she is experiencing this need in order to respond to it effectively. In some situations, the parents' responsibility may be to teach children to care for themselves.

Family members are also equally responsible for identifying the completion of the contract and either establishing a new contract or terminating the therapy.

Therapist's Role and Function

Resource.   The role of the TA therapist is primarily to provide a resource for the family to help solve its communication difficulties and for each member of the family to resolve intrapsychic problems that contribute to dysfunctionality within the family.

Safety.   Often the first task of the therapist is to provide safety for each person. In families where physical violence or sexual abuse exists, protection needs to be established so that each person can express him- or herself freely in the therapy process. This may involve specific contracts with the abusive person that they will not threaten or engage in such behavior. In one case where the mother continually inflicted beatings on a 7-year-old girl, the therapist assumed a child-advocate position and informed the parents that they would be reported to legal authorities if the child was beaten again. Several months later the mother reported to the therapist that the strong child-advocate position of the therapist was what she had needed as a child to protect her from her parents. Although she had been angry at the therapist for taking "the kid's side and not mine," she did honor the contract not to hit the child. At first the contract was made out of fear, but after doing some regressive therapy, the contract was from awareness of her daughter's needs for security and affection.

In families that are verbally abusive, the therapist needs to work to establish a contract that what is said in the therapy session will not be used in a hurtful way outside. This level of protection to be free to express what one is thinking and feeling is necessary before the therapist can begin to work with the family on meaningful contact and any individual therapy.

Contact.   An important early role of the therapist is to make contact with each family member and then to use the contact between each person and the therapist to open communication between family members. This is often done early in therapy by having the family talk about themselves and by not focusing on the identified "problem" person. When the focus is on the family dynamics, family members have to communicate with each other and can no longer use the "problem" person as a refuge from relating to each other.

Contract. The therapist is responsible for having clear contracts as to his or her role in the therapy process. This includes a precise statement of involvement in solving the dynamic problems of the family as well as the type of investment in working individually with each person. This may begin with a role of helping participants clarify what they want from the therapy. Often families come for therapy out of desperation or by referral and have very little idea of what possibilities for change lie ahead. Other times family members come reluctantly because they were brought by someone else. The therapist needs to establish a straightforward relationship with each family member and to help them identify the changes they want.

In addition to the therapy contracts, the therapist must establish administrative contracts regarding appointments, fees, availability in crisis situations, and other procedural matters related to the therapy.

Termination. An important function of the therapist is to help families determine when they have gotten the maximum from the therapy and to plan a goal for termination. This may include getting a commitment from each member that he or she will not quit before the specified therapy work is finished.

Skills. The ongoing responsibility of the therapist is to use the training and skills in opening the communication process within the family and in providing direct feedback so that they can each

step out of their internal frame of reference and see themselves from a new perspective. Since a TA approach to family therapy often involves a great deal of investment on the part of the therapist in the dynamics of the family, the therapist's responsibility includes a commitment to seek supervision and peer feedback on the therapy approach and the nature of the therapist's involvement in the therapy process.

Primary Techniques Used in the Treatment Process

The primary techniques in the transactional analysis approach to family therapy vary with the stage of family therapy. McClendon (1977) has identified three stages of therapeutic work with a family: (a) determining the dynamics of how the whole family relates, (b) practicing therapy with each individual, and (c) reintegrating the whole family with a focus on creating healthy family dynamics.

In the initial stage, the therapist encourages each family member to talk about the family, why they came to therapy, and the goal they wish to achieve. The object of this stage is for the therapist and the family to gain an understanding of the transactional dynamics that make life within the family uncomfortable for some members. This is done by the therapist taking these observations of the behavior of each family member and relating it to the theories of ego states, the concepts of transactions, and the dynamics of interlocking scripts to develop hypotheses in formulating specific treatment interventions. A premise of the TA approach to therapy is that awareness is an important first step and support for change. In the early process of family therapy many of the techniques are aimed at increasing the family members' awareness of the problems and options for change.

Having gathered an essential amount of information, each family member may develop a contract with the therapist for what they want to accomplish. Change for any person depends on the goals that that person sets and on his or her willingness to make and follow through on decisions necessary to meet the goals. Contracts may be for generalized changes or for specific, observable behavioral changes.

As some members begin to initiate changes, the therapist needs to be particularly aware of how other family members react to these changes and the subtle invitations back to the homeostasis of the old structure. At this point the therapist may need to share information about why people do what they do, pointing out transactional patterns and how communication can be more effective, and, specifically, about the racket systems of each individual and how they connect with each other, forming the structure of the family.

Stage 1: The Family Dynamics. During this first stage of therapy, the focus of the interventions is on the stroking patterns and transactions of the whole family and not specifically with the "problem member." This is intended to get each family member involved in identifying their respective roles in the dynamics of the *family's* problem.

Therapeutic Operations. In the process of collecting information and effecting change, the therapist makes use of several therapeutic operations (Berne, 1966).

1. *Interrogation* involves the gathering of information from each member in the family. This may be done by asking questions about how each one experiences him- or herself and transactions within the family or by having the family discuss among themselves how they handled a particular situation (see beginning of the Case Example transcript and Transactions 116, 130, 139, 177b).

2. *Specification* is a statement or question designed to elicit more detailed information and to provide the family with certain sets of information that may be significant. The therapist may make comments describing the dynamics among family members such as "When Father talks, Mother crosses her arms and legs and Susan looks the other way." Specification may also involve questioning other family members in order to verify information about one member's perceptions or beliefs (73, 98, 120, 128).

3. *Explanation* is the sharing of information with either the whole family or an individual regarding their behavior and how it may be affecting others in the family. This usually involves some teaching about TA concepts. Examples are used that have already occurred in the therapy to explain ego states, crossed or ulterior transactions, or games. Together with the clients, the therapist will explore options for behaving differently. Homework assignments, which may include popular reading on TA (Babcock & Keepers, 1976; Harris, 1967; James & Jongeward, 1971), may be given to increase a person's understanding (56a, 78, 132, 177, 183).

4. *Illustration* is the therapist's use of a story or metaphor that describes the family dynamics or change possibilities. It is used particularly effectively with young children or where members of the family are resistant to explanation (92).

5. *Direction* is a statement or permission by the therapist that guides a person to a behavior they are not initiating on

their own. It should only be used after a good therapeutic relationship is established (56b, 107, 143, 164).

6. *Confrontation* is a statement or question used by the therapist to bring into the client's awareness a discrepancy in their perceptions and behaviors or between beliefs and actual events. Confrontation can be of two types: (a) to foster awareness, so the person gains greater insight into their discrepancies, which may lay the groundwork for later change (52, 80, 82, 96, 105); or (b) to effect immediate behavioral change (86, 90, 94, 118, 154). Family therapy involves a continual balance between confrontation and support—alternately intervening into the dynamics and supporting each individual in their change process.

Specific Interventions. There is a wide range of specific interventions that the TA therapist may use. These may include having each speaker state the psychological level of communication overtly, as in the expression of expectations and resentments. Once resentments are expressed, the therapist may have the person contract not to bring them up again, particularly if resentments are used either to distance or punish another or to reinforce internally the script beliefs. The therapist will usually interrupt blaming anger such as "You never..." and direct the person to express the anger in a problem-solving way, such as "I want..." (148).

The therapeutic procedures are aimed at making explicit what is implicit through identifying how the family members are adapting or not adapting to each other and the possible advantages and disadvantages (177, 183). The assumptions of one member may not be known by another. When one member is expressing what he or she is thinking and

feeling, the therapist will encourage other family members to respond with their internal response.

Much of the work involves showing people how to ask directly for what they want. This may involve explaining about the needs for physical and unconditional strokes and teaching people to be sensitive to others' stroking needs. Initial work with stroking problems usually begins by directing people to look at the person to whom they are talking and to speak directly to that person rather than about them to someone else. The therapist may also direct the person to verbalize the appreciations that are unexpressed. When appreciations are not stated openly, often only the negative thoughts or feelings about the other get communicated. This is a beginning step in changing a negative stroke or non-stroking family pattern to a positive pattern.

Another approach may involve having people specify their different frames of reference. For example, when someone in the family says they want another member to be close, the therapist may ask the person to describe specifically what "close" means so that others will know exactly what is wanted.

Stage 2: Therapy with Each Individual. Many of the approaches used in the initial stages of therapy are used in the second stage, except that the focus of the second stage is on individual intrapsychic and script dynamics. In this intrapersonal stage, the therapist may do individual work with each person within the context of the family, may work with one person in extensive individual therapy, may have another member attend a therapy group, or work conjointly with the couple. The division between stages is not discrete but is thought of by the therapist primarily for treatment planning. In practice there is some shuttling back and forth between Stage 1 and 2. In Stage 2 work, as one family member makes a change, it may reveal family dynamics that had not emerged earlier and the therapist may again focus on the whole family.

Racket System Therapy. For each individual, any therapeutic intervention that interrupts the flow in the racket system will be an effective step in changing the script and therefore the family dynamics. Contracts to alter the overt behavior related to the rackety display will most likely result in different social responses from other family members and, hence, a change in either one's own or someone else's reinforcing memories.

Even when overt behaviors are changed the racket system may be maintained by imagining script-related behaviors and collecting reinforcing memories as a result of fantasy. For some clients it is important, therefore, for the therapist to check if the script is being lived out in fantasy. This is often apparent in dreams. One man maintained continual anger and a belief of rejection by imagining his wife having sex with each man she met. When he changed his fantasies by intentionally creating images of building a new house, he related to his wife with much less anger and more joy.

The somatic level of the rackety display can be dealt with in therapy through techniques designed to change the body or physiological level of script. Such approaches may include deep muscle massage, biofeedback, bioenergetics, meditation and yoga, or physical exercise such as expressive dancing.

Reinforcing experiences will no longer have an effective role in maintainng the system when people live in the here and now and do not dwell on old memories or fantasized memories of events that are yet to come. A specific therapeutic intervention may involve the confrontation of discrepancies between what the client remembers and what actually took place and the meaning of what occurred, as well as what was anticipated to happen in the future.

The script beliefs themselves can be challenged directly, sometimes through a question like "Is this belief really true in your life today?" This frequently produces the insight that the client is operating from old perceptions or misconceptions and has been living life based on script beliefs that originated in early childhood. For some clients, the only thing needed at this point is an invitation to drop the script beliefs and to live with an awareness of other possible options that are available.

Where trauma has played a significant part in forming the script, clients have made major changes by focusing on the unexpressed affect that was present and suppressed at the time of script decision. The release of repressed emotion through cathecting to an early age and the expression of primal feelings often leads to a redecision about one's self, other, or life (Erskine, 1974; Goulding & Goulding, 1979).

The therapeutic focus may then become cognitive and/or behavioral as the person decides to change his or her script beliefs. The racket system concepts may be taught to clients so they have a conceptual tool for understanding how they have maintained script, and contracts for new behavior may be negotiated to support their decision to change their beliefs.

However the therapist decides to intervene—at the level of script beliefs, the repressed script feelings, the various rackety displays, or the reinforcing experiences—any change that stops the flow in the system can stop the script. The more aspects of the racket system there are on which the therapist focuses (thereby dealing with the behavioral, cognitive, and affective level), the greater the probability is that the client will create functional and healthy family dynamics.

Stage 3: Developing a Functional Family. The final stage of family therapy is a reintegration process aimed at developing a family structure in which each person will have needs met and live in supportive harmony, which will provide for maximum personal development of each family member.

The therapist may make use of the techniques of direction, explanation, or illustration to guide a family in developing interdependence. This is the acknowledgment that each person has an impact on the other and that in order to live comfortably and cooperatively together, individual feelings and needs must be accounted for and responded to in some effective way. In this stage, family members actively ask for and negotiate to get what they each want while also learning to give freely.

CASE EXAMPLE

Mrs. Brown initially made an appointment by phone stating the school psychologist had referred her 8-year-old adopted daughter, Karen, and the family for therapy. Karen was doing poorly in school, was not paying attention in class, and had no friends among the other children and in the neighborhood. The appointment had to be rearranged three different times because the father was unable to find time to get away from the store he owns.

The initial session began with the therapist asking each member of the family to introduce themselves and to state why they had come for family therapy. The family consists of the father, Bob, aged 36; the mother, Jean, 33, who has been married to Bob for $10^1/_2$ years; Roberta, the 15-year-old daughter by Bob's first marriage who lived with her mother after the parents' separation from age 3 to 8 and then came to live with Jean and Bob (who report that they took her because her mother was neglecting her); Karen, 8, a child Jean and Bob adopted when she was 2 after they had been married 4 years and were unsuccessful in having a child of their own; and two daughters, Denise 4, and Tina, 14 months, who are home all day with Jean.

Bob described the problem as Jean and the two older children not getting along and as Jean, who was always upset with the children, calling him at work. Roberta reported that there really were no problems in the family except that her stepmother always bossed her around, but that that wasn't much of a problem. During this time, Jean held the two youngest children, attempting to entertain them both. In order to free Jean to talk, the therapist invited 4-year-old Denise to play with crayons and paper. Jean described the family problem, with laughter, as an overwhelming one, with two older children not cooperating. She said that Karen often would not talk. When Karen was asked why she had come to family therapy she answered, "I don't know." Several additional questions elicited the same response. A large portion of this session was spent in having the family talk among themselves about what they wanted to accomplish by coming for family therapy. Bob, Jean, and Roberta discussed chores not being accomplished, while Karen remained quiet and uninvolved in the conversation. The therapist then asked the two adults to develop a contract that would establish the goal of this therapy session as well as forthcoming therapy. Bob and Jean set an overall contract to lessen the stress in the family and to enjoy being together. They each agreed to do whatever personal therapy that was needed. Although this aspect of the contract seemed to be an adaptation to the therapist on their part, the therapist accepted it as a tentative statement of willingness. Both parents then stated that their goal for this session was for the therapist to work directly with Karen to resolve the problems she was having.

Therapist (to Jean): When you and I first talked on the phone, you told me that Karen was having problems in school and that's why you wanted family therapy. Will you tell me more about that? 1

Jean: Well, the teachers and school psychologist say she daydreams in school all day and that she doesn't play with or get along with the other kids. She does the same thing after school—she won't play with anyone, except she bothers her sister, Roberta, while she's doing her homework. 2

Therapist (turns to Karen): Will you tell me what you think about what your mother has just said? 3

Karen: I don't know. 4

Therapist: If I really listen to you...and if you really think about school, what do you feel when you're there? 5

Karen: The kids just don't want to play with me...just leave me alone. They don't like me that much. 6

Therapist: And what do you do? 7

Karen: I just stay away from them. 8

Therapist: And what do they do? 9

Karen: They just ignore me and take other kids to play with. 10

Therapist: And what do you do when they play with someone else? 11

Karen: I go away from them. (Pause) And I keep thinking about them and how they all like each other and not me. 12

Therapist: And what else? 13

Karen: I think about them having fun playing together and laughing at me for not being like them. 14

Therapist: What do you feel inside then? 15

Karen: I feel hurt. 16

Therapist: And then? (Long pause) 17

Karen: Roberta pushes me out of her room too (begins to tear, but no audible cry). 18

Therapist: And what do you feel? 19

Karen: I don't belong with her either. 20

Therapist: Is that like with the other kids? 21

Karen: I don't know. 22

Therapist (softly): Well, your tears look like they know. What do you feel? 23

Karen: I just don't belong—I just go away from them. 24

Therapist: And what do you feel inside when you believe you don't belong? 25

Karen: Well, I usually go upstairs and cry or something. 26

Jean (to therapist): She usually gets in a bad mood, then Roberta gets upset 'cause she pesters her, then I get upset 'cause there's more for me to do, then Dad gets upset because I don't have things ready the way he wants them, then we're all in a bad mood all night. 27

Therapist (to Karen): Would you like me to explain how this problem works so you can change it? 28

Karen (Nods.) 29

Therapist: Come over here to this pad of paper, and I'll draw a little diagram to show you what I think is happening. (Both go to a large pad on the floor.) What do you say to yourself when you think of the kids? 30

Karen: There's no one who likes me. 31

Therapist: So one of the things you believe is that "no one likes me"? (Karen nods.) And what do you feel when you believe this? 32

Karen: I'm in a bad mood. 33

Therapist: What does that mean? (Pause) Is a bad mood like feeling mad or sad or scared? 34

Karen: I don't know—I think I'm sad. Sometimes when I come home I don't want to do anything. 35

Therapist: Is that when you go to Roberta's room? 36

Figure 7. Karen's racket system.

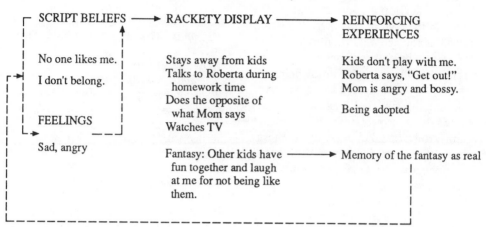

Karen: Yes, but she tells me to get out. 37

Therapist (while drawing the racket system): And then what do you feel? 38

Karen: That I don't belong anywhere. 39

Therapist: And then what do you do? 40

Karen: Mom tells me to do something, but I just go watch TV or say the opposite of anything anyone says to me, but mostly I just watch TV. 41

Therapist: And what do you feel inside? 42

Karen: I'm sad—'cause the only reason she wants me is to boss me around. 43

Therapist: And what do you think about then? 44

Karen: No one likes me (begins to cry hard). 45

Therapist: And what else? 46

Karen: I don't belong in this family. 47

The therapist explained each item of the racket system to Karen and continually checked for her understanding of each element and how they fit together (see Figure 7).

After explaining the racket system, the therapist asked Karen what she wanted to change and together they identified several behaviors that she made a contract to do differently and to report on them the following week.

These behavioral change contracts were more specific than the general overall contract at the beginning of the therapy. At one point Karen said that she did not know how to get attention from her sister, so the therapist worked with Karen and Roberta to arrange ways to spend time together. Roberta made a contract to spend 20 minutes of play time with Karen each day.

The therapist then worked with Bob regarding his lack of contact with each of the children in the family. He explained the importance of physical stroking as a psychological message of security to children and supported Karen in asking Bob to hold her. Four-year-old Denise also curled up in Bob's lap while Jean continued to hold the sleeping 14-month-old, Tina. The session ended with Jean and Bob agreeing to read *Born to Win* (James & Jongeward, 1971) before the next session.

In the initial session just described, the therapist worked with the identified "problem" member of the family in regard to her internal beliefs and feelings related to not belonging, resulting in the relationship problems at school and at home. Change in the family dynamics was initiated by encouraging immediate changes in Karen's transactional and stroking patterns with Roberta and with Bob and by facilitating Karen's receiving direct information from her parents about their wanting to adopt her and that she belongs in the family.

In the second session, Karen reported that she and Roberta were spending time together and that she had brought a friend home from school one day. Jean interrupted to add that on Sunday Karen was back in the old pattern, but that the rest of the time there had been a definite improvement.

Bob: You are all good kids—you won't grow up drinking and smoking dope. (To therapist:) We don't have much problems. Just the problem that's solved with Karen and friends and school. We are the kind of family they put on TV. (To the kids:) You are all working well now. 48

Jean (to Bob): But it's not working. (To therapist:) He's just away all day and doesn't see it. I am involved with the problems and as great as the girls are, we have a lot of problems. 49

Therapist: Talk directly to Bob. 50

Jean: You're never home to see—I have to handle it all. You're never really involved. (Turns to therapist.) He won't even go away with me (laughs). 51

Therapist: In your laughter, Jean, there seems to be a lot of pain behind it. 52

Jean: I'm dead serious, though. He won't take me away even for one day. 53

Therapist: Look at Bob and tell him what you want. 54

Jean: I have—he knows. I'm very serious. I would like to go away—without the kids, though (laughs). 55

Therapist: Stop there for a moment. That's a family pattern—"He knows," "They know" (a dynamic that occurred frequently in the first session). Will you assume each time that the other person does not know?

Every time that you use "He knows" and tell it to me, it is a distancing process. 56a Will you start over again and assume he doesn't know and tell him this time so he really hears you? 56b

Jean: You promised me (laughs) that you would take me (laughs) away for a weekend without the kids (laughs). (Long pause) I still want to go! (said seriously) 57

Bob: Yes, I promised. 58

Jean: And I still want to go (pleadingly). 59

Bob: Yes, I did (curtly). 60

Jean: . . . without the kids. 61

Bob: Yes, I will (5-second pause). . . in due time. 62

Karen: Where are you going to put us? 63

Jean (simultaneously with Bob): I don't care! (angrily) 64

Bob (simultaneously with Jean): In a home. 65

Jean: I really don't care! (angrily) 66

Roberta: I want to know what due time is. 67

Jean: This summer! That's what I call due time. (Date of session is early May.) I give only till this summer (crying). 68

Therapist: What do you mean, Bob, by "due time"? 69

Bob: I will say within the calendar year. 70

Roberta: (Gasps for breath; long pause.) 71

Jean: (Looks down, then up with a smile.) 72

Therapist: Jean, right now I suspect you are angry inside and are covering it up with a big smile. Are you? 73

Jean: I'm really not angry. I just know that if we don't go in the summer, we don't go. (Pause) So if we don't go by the end of summer, I know I'm not going—and so does he. (Turns to Bob.) Right? 74

Bob: Not necessarily. 75

Jean: Yes! (angrily) That's how it is. 76

Bob: OK. That's your opinion. . . you're entitled to it. (Pause) 77

Therapist: If you continue like this, what will happen is that you will get further and further away from each other. 78

Jean: We have been at it (laughs) a long time. (Laughs) This is just a continuation. 79

Therapist: And what I observe you doing

right now, Jean, is to laugh and shrug your shoulders. The implication is that there will be no change. 80

Bob (to therapist): She is entitled to her opinion. I don't want to sit here and stamp on her and say "Shut up." 81

Therapist: No, but you can give her a date. 82

Bob: Oh, well.... (Roberta and Karen pull together on the couch.) 83

Jean: You could give me...84

Bob:...no offense, but that's easy for you to say, but not easy for me to pick a date. Impossible for me to pick a date, because I have people that work for me. I have schedules. I have a manager that's out. I work many days I'm not supposed to. Because when you are the guy that owns the joint, you are the last guy on the list. You are meaner and lousier and worse and harder on yourself than on *any* of all the other people that work for you! 85

Therapist: It doesn't have to be that way. 86

Bob (pause): Well, I have to agree with you on that. Which is one of the reasons I would like to change my business, but...87

Therapist: One way to be easier on yourself is to pick a date to be with your wife. And then you make it happen. 88

Bob (pause): Life doesn't work that way, unfortunately. That's too easy. 89

Therapist: I think that *you* could make it work that way. 90

Bob: It could be, I guess...but then, again, I know it's hard for you to understand. Sometimes it...ah...you just can't. 91

Therapist: I've been in a similar position in my work. The change came for me when I made a decision and stuck to it. 92

Bob: You can't...you're supposed to...ah ...ah...keep to the work. I mean, I wanted to just do all the things around the house this week. Things that have waited a long time. It just happened that somebody else had to go on vacation, now, cause they were in the dumps. So I said, "OK," and I stayed and I worked 14 days in a row for him. 93

Therapist: It does not have to be that way. You could say "No" and arrange the way you run the store differently. 94

Bob: No, it could cost me....95

Therapist: Yes; and are you willing to pay for it in the relationship with your wife? 96

Bob: I've gotten to a conclusion that the retail business...I don't know anybody in business that's happily married or has a happy family relationship with their kids. What I'm trying to do is to work to...97

Therapist (interrupting): Bob, do you want to go on a weekend with Jean? 98

Bob: Oh, I'd love to, so long as she...ah ...ah...don't...ah...ah...(Long pause) 99

Therapist: My impression is that you don't want to go. 100

Jean: Mine too. 101

Bob: No, that's not true. 102

Therapist: You've given excuse after excuse. 103

Bob: Not true, not true, no. If you are trying to pin me down and are talking about this summer I won't say yes. I don't know. Probably. We might be able to...then again we might not. I have this...ah...my problem ...I have...ah...ah...priorities. I always feel the kids first and Jean and I second. You see, and if I have 3 days I really want all of us to go someplace. Which is entirely opposite to what she wants to do. What she wants to do is to get the hell away from them. And I don't blame her, but...104

Therapist: Will you consider that Jean wants to be with *you*? (very softly) There is a big difference between wanting to be alone with you and getting away from the kids. (Long pause) (To Jean): Say what you are thinking, Jean. 105

Jean (laughs): I'm thinking that he (laughs) would never think of that (laughs). That's what I'm thinking (laughs). 106

Therapist: Then you need to talk to him so he knows from you. 107

Jean: He knows. I would like to be away with him...and without the kids; that would be a second bonus. 108

Therapist: Tell *him*. 109

Roberta: Come on, Mom. Tell him. 110

Jean (laughs): Oh,...111

Bob (interrupts): In reality we don't have that many problems. When we take the disagreements about the kids...how to raise the kids...we don't have any problems together. 112

Roberta: When was the last time you were together, Daddy? 113

Jean: We don't. We don't ever go away together. We are never without the children! It never happens! 114

Bob: I don't know...we go to the movies occasionally. 115

Therapist (to Jean): What are you feeling when you say that? 116

Jean: Resentment. I resent it. I resent it (laughs). (Long pause) 117

Therapist: Last week you talked about Karen not talking when she had a problem. My impression is that you also don't talk about what is really significant. 118

Jean: I do...but I'm put off so much. I'm usually understanding about being put off, because I know what his priorities are. 119

Therapist: And what are yours? 120

Jean: Mine get mixed. I really can't say to him we should go away for a weekend and spend $500 when I know somebody might need braces or something. So I'm in conflict with myself, and I know that. The kids come first. They are more important. However, if it's them going away for a weekend or me going away for a weekend than I would take the priority. I'm not that totally screwed up (with disgust). (Long pause) 121

Therapist (to Jean): I think that you, for a long time, have taken on a pattern of adapting all the time. You don't say clearly what you want. You laugh off your requests. Then I imagine you resent not having your requests fulfilled and the resentment comes out in picky little fights, the content of which is not significant. 122

Bob: Hey, let's give that a hand (laughs and claps hands to applaud). 123

Jean (to Bob): The content is not always insignificant either. That's why I'm angry. I'm a very fair person and if I'm angry and looking for a fight I *will* find something appropriate. I don't do it without cause. 124

Therapist (to Jean): And is the cause in part from the stored-up anger?

Jean: Yes (begins to cry).

Therapist: And it seems that you get reasonable to cover up your sadness and anger. (Pause) I suspect that you did the same as a young child. (Jean nods.) My observation of the way you perpetuate the problem is that you are not straight and clear with what you want from Robert—clear all the way to the point of making it happen. The net result is that you are hurt and angry about not getting what you want. You used the term resentment—that resentment will seep into your relationship in lots of other places.

Jean: Yeah, it shows up over little arguments that could be quick to solve in other ways—but that's a way to let it out. 127

Therapist: How else? 128

Jean: In our affection—I'm not turned on (long pause). 129

Therapist (to Jean): What are you thinking? 130

Jean: I'm trying to remember when it started. 131

Therapist: Jean, the starting with Bob is probably so small that there is no place to pinpoint it. And I suspect it's a pattern that you did before—as a child—of adapting to please. 132

Jean: I'm tired of it. 133

Therapist: Do you know what the end of this scenario is like? How it progresses from here? 134

Karen: Yeah, I do (sounding scared). 135

Bob: Yeah. The kids all get married and move away, and I'll retire and her and I will go to Europe. 136

Jean: We'll get divorced! 137

Bob: Take your pick. 138

Karen: No! What about us kids? 139

Jean: It's a 50-50 chance (laughs). 140

Therapist (to Roberta, Karen, and Denise, who are cuddled together on the couch between mother and father and are whispering): Say it out loud, girls. 141

Roberta: We didn't say anything. 142

Therapist: I think what you said must be important. Say it out loud. 143

Roberta: What I said was that it (crying) could come a lot sooner than before any of us could get married. That's one thing I don't need. 144

Karen: Where will we go? 145

Therapist (to Jean): Say it out loud. 146

Jean (to Bob): What I'm saying is that if we don't have any kind of relationship together, if the kids are here or not, when they go we two have nothing. (Loudly) When they go you and I will have *nothing!* 147

Therapist (to Jean): And what I want... 148

Jean: I want to have something *now.* 149

Bob (to therapist): I love this lady. I've been married to her for 10 years, and I'll love her 20 years from now. 150

Jean: If I'm still around. 151

Roberta: Oh, wow! 152

Bob: Stop trying to scare me. 153

Therapist: Bob, Jean is telling you she wants a change. She is changing and growing. She wants a relationship with you. 154

Bob: If she is changing, then she will have to deal with the change, and I will then make up my mind if I will stand for the change or not stand for the change. 155

Therapist (to Bob): Who is that talking now? 156

Bob: It's me. 157

Therapist: Who else would talk that way with those kinds of words and that tone? 158

Bob: I suppose my father would. (Pause) Is that my Parent ego state or whatever? 159

Therapist: I think so. I suspect you spend a lot of time relating to Jean the way your father related to you. 160

Jean (to Bob): For the past 10 years, I've been willing to not take the time with you. I've been willing to give up the time. The only thing that's changed is that I'm no longer willing to give up the time because right now the most important thing to me, now, is time with you (starts to cry and holds back). 161

Therapist: Let it go, Jean. You don't need to hold back. 162

Karen: Let it out, Mom. (Jean cries for about 1½ minutes.) 163

Therapist: Come back and continue talking to Bob. It is important that you carry all the way through on what you want. 164

Jean: No, there is nothing worth saying. 165

Therapist: And what happens when you hold it in? 166

Roberta: She is mad at 3:00 in the afternoon and nobody knows why. 167

Therapist: You do. 168

Roberta: I know it's not us kids. Me, just because I didn't put the vacuum away or left the mayonnaise jar out. But, sometimes I think it's my fault. 169

Jean: Sometimes it is your fault. 170

Roberta: I can tell. If you stop being mad in less than half an hour, it was probably my fault. If you're still mad 3 days later, it's not us—it's you and him. 171

Therapist: Are you two willing to look at the dynamics going on between you? 172

Bob: Yes. 173

Jean: OK, 'cause I've got to figure out what goes wrong. 174

Therapist: Did you begin to read *Born to Win?* Did you understand the basic ideas? 175

Bob and Jean: (shake their heads, yes.) 176

Therapist: Both of you transact from what appears on the surface to be Adult—that is, logical communication. (Therapist draws diagram on pad of paper; see Figure 8.) Jean, you say, "I would like to go away for a weekend" and Bob responds with, "I have to work in the store." I think that the problem in your communication is at the psychological level where your Child ego state sends a message "I won't get what I want" to Bob's Parent, and Bob responds with a psychological message from his Parent ego state, something like, "Work is more important than your wants." Bob, does that seem right to you? 177a

Bob (long pause): That's how my father treated me. 178

Therapist: OK, let's assume for now that that is the psychological response you send back to Jean from your Parent whenever she asks for something. Then you (to Jean) use the message to feel... 179

Jean: Hurt and angry. 180

Therapist: ...and then that is your payoff. And then you probably confirm your Child's position, "I won't get what I want," and you wind up feeling victimized again. 181

Jean: Yeah, that happens all the time. 182

Therapist: I think it happens because you send a psychological message when you

Figure 8. Jean's and Bob's transaction.

Jean's Social Message
Adult to Adult:

"I'd like to go away."

Bob's Social Response
Adult to Adult:

"I have to work at the
   store."

Jean's Psychological Message
Child to Parent:

"I won't get what I want."

Bob's Psychological Message
Parent to Child:

"Work is more important
   than your wants."

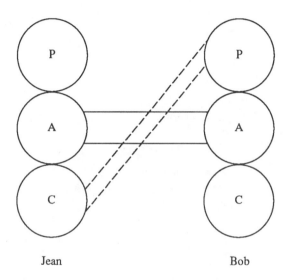

Jean   Bob

shrug your shoulders or laugh or smile, the few times when you do ask for what you want. 183

In the second session, it became apparent that part of Karen's anxiety about not belonging in the family and believing no one likes her is related to the problems between her mother and father that Bob had been denying and Jean had been displaying indirectly in her anger and bossiness with the children. Until this problem is brought into the open and resolved, there may not be adequate resolution of Karen's beliefs and fears. The result of this session was that Jean decided to join a woman's group to gain support for her continued growth, and

both parents decided to work on their relationship as a couple before continuing work as a family.

As we attempted to resolve Bob's resistance to spending time with Jean alone, it became apparent that Bob was working himself harder and harder, following a script pattern learned from his father to work himself to death. This became evident as Bob talked about his diminishing sexual interest and his concern that if he and Jean went away together for a weekend his decreased sexual interest would be obvious to both of them and could no longer be excused by the children and work.

Further therapy included teaching

Figure 9. Brown family interlocking racket system.

SCRIPT BELIEFS AND FEELINGS	RACKETY DISPLAY	REINFORCING EXPERIENCES
Jean: I won't get what I want. I don't belong.	Does not make direct demands from Robert Laughs to cover up feelings beneath requests Acts reasonable about the denial of own wants "I don't care"—to Karen. "The kids come first; they are more important."	Bob is never home. Bob does not keep his promises. Bob always has an excuse. Bob grants special requests to others. We never go away together. Kids always come first.
Bob: Life is hard and difficult. (No one understands me.)	Spends most of the time at work Makes promises without a specific way in which they will be kept "(You will be put) in a home"—to Karen. Excuses to Jean's requests Grants special request to co-workers She wants to "get the hell away from them." Works self harder than anyone else	Tired much of the time Demands from Jean
Karen: I don't belong. No one likes me.	Quiet, withdrawn No friends at school or in the neighborhood	Father says, "In a home." Mother says, "I don't care." Father says, "Mother wants to get away from us."

Bob about ego states and script and how he had incorporated a pattern of working hard and keeping distant from the family that had been his father's. In regressive work with Bob's Child ego state, he recalled an early childhood scene where, in order to get his father's approval, he decided to be just like his father, even if it killed him. In crying out the repressed emotions of his childhood, Bob made a redecision to live, not to have to work hard like his father, and made an Adult commitment to spend more time with his wife and children and to hire an assistant to help manage the store.

Jean did more work on her Child being dependent, a pattern that she had learned in her family of origin, and on her beliefs of not belonging and "I won't get what I want." She was encouraged to find more ways to actualize herself outside of the home.

Bob and Jean currently are in couples therapy once a week and Jean is in an ongoing TA group for women. Plans include working with the entire family again when school starts in September. (Figure 9 illustrates the Browns' interlocking racket system as it appeared for the Case Example here.)

EVALUATION

Contemporary literature on transactional analysis consists primarily of case studies wherein clinicians report positive outcomes. Some families have provided self-reports of long-term positive changes in relationships among family members after TA family therapy (Kadis & McClendon, 1980). Few scientific evaluations have been done on the effectiveness of TA therapy, and only one study (Bader, 1976) has investigated the effects of a TA approach to family therapy. Bader investigated change in both the family system and each individual and compared five control families with five families who attended a week-long family therapy session.

Both the experimental and control families were white middle-class and were selected from among those who had expressed a desire for intensive family therapy. A pretest, posttest, and a 3-month follow-up test were conducted on both experimental and control families. Bader used the Family Environment Scale to evaluate the family dynamics or system. The California Psychological Inventory and the Personal Orientation Inventory were used to determine change in each individual. At the end of an intensive week of family therapy the five families in the experimental group showed positive gain in cohesiveness and expression of a range of feelings and positive increase in the amount of independence. During this same pre- to posttest period the control group showed no changes on any of the scales.

At the 3-month follow-up testing, the experimental group had maintained the changes gained in the intensive TA family therapy session and the control group continued to show no changes. An interesting change also occurred in the follow-up testing where a significant positive change on the California Psychological Inventory in Constructive Dominance for the experimental families indicated that individuals were taking increased responsibility for their own behavior. The control families showed no change.

There are still no studies of family therapy where TA has been compared with other methods. As with all therapy approaches, the effectiveness of the model depends on the skill, personality, and enthusiasm of the therapist using the model. Effective therapy is an interaction between the method, the person using it, and the readiness of the clients.

The International Transactional Analysis Association has attempted to ensure a high caliber of TA therapy (International Transactional Analysis Association, 1772 Vallejo Street, San Francisco, CA 94123). Certified clinical members are required to have didactic training in TA theory and other psychotherapy approaches, training in the clinical application of TA to groups and/or families, and regular ongoing supervision of their clinical work. Before clinical certification as a transactional analyst, the trainee is required to pass a written examination and an oral examination where audiotaped samples of their therapy are reviewed by a board of examiners to determine clinical competence.

SUMMARY

Family therapy can be done effectively using transactional analysis as a model for intervention. Family therapy was illustrated using the basic concepts of strokes, transactions, and script. Demonstrating the use of the interlocking racket system with an actual family, the chapter described both the interpersonal and intrapersonal dynamics of a dysfunctional family.

ANNOTATED SUGGESTED READINGS

Babcock, D. E., & Keepers, T. D. (1976). *Raising kids ok*. New York: Grove Press.

A simple review of transactional analysis, plus a discussion of normal psychological development over the entire life span, emphasizing healthy family functioning. The authors focus on an understanding of children's needs in terms of emotional stroking and time structuring, with emphasis on recognizing "games" that families may play and the detection of life scripts. This book is often used as a valuable homework source for parents who need information about effective parenting.

Bader, E., & Pearson, P. T. (1988). *In quest of the mythical mate*. New York: Brunner/Mazel.

The diagnosis and treatment of relationship problems, using the model of Margaret Mahler's stages of early child development as a metaphor for understanding stages of couplehood.

Berne, E. (1961). *Transactional analysis in psychotherapy*. New York: Grove Press.

Berne's original concepts of ego states and the consequent development of transactional analysis theory. It is a good book for the reader interested in a more advanced study of ego states and ego state pathology.

Berne, E. (1972). *What do you say after you say hello?* New York: Grove Press.

A review of the basic concepts of transactional analysis and their application to the development of script theory. The greatest portion of the book is devoted to the detailed analysis of scripts. This is recommended reading for both professionals and laypersons for understanding life scripts.

Erskine, R. G., & Moursund, J. P. (1988). *Integrative psychotherapy in action*. Newbury Park, CA: Sage Publications.

A valuable book for understanding how theory is applied in clinical practice. Integrating transactional analysis and other therapeutic modalities, the authors present a framework for choosing therapeutic interventions with a wide variety of client problems. Particularly applicable to the intrapersonal dimension of family therapy are the several chapters that include actual transcripts of the treatment of parental introjections.

McClendon, R., & Kadis, L. (1983). *Chocolate pudding and other approaches to intensive multiple-family therapy*. Palo Alto, CA: Science & Behavior Books.

An important book for understanding the relationship between intrapersonal change and structural change in a family. It is based on a therapeutic format involving four families living and working together with the authors for a week of intensive multiple-family therapy. Using techniques from transactional analysis, family systems, and Gestalt therapy, the families are guided through a three-stage model of family therapy, including (a) analysis of the system; (b) redecision of childhood script decisions that interfere with present effectiveness; and (c) reintegration of individual and systemic changes.

REFERENCES

Babcock, D., & Keepers, T. (1976). *Raising kids OK*. New York: Grove Press.

Bader, E. (1976). *Redecisions in family therapy: A study of change in an intensive family therapy workshop*. Doctoral dissertation, California School of Professional Psychology. (*Dissertation Abstracts International, 1976, 37B,* 5, 2491. University Microfilms, No. 76-25, 064.)

Bader, E. (1980). A cured family has problems. *Transactional Analysis Journal, 10,* 2.

Berne, E. (1949). The nature of intuition. *Psychiatric Quarterly, 23,* 203-226.

Berne, E. (1952). Concerning the nature of diagnosis. *International Record of Medicine, 165,* 283-292.

Berne, E. (1953). Concerning the nature of communication. *Psychiatric Quarterly, 27,* 185-198.

Berne, E. (1955). Intuition IV: Primal images and primal judgment. *Psychiatric Quarterly, 29,* 634-658.

Berne, E. (1957). Intuition V: The ego image. *Psychiatric Quarterly, 31,* 611-627.

Berne, E. (1961). Transactional analysis in psychotherapy. New York: Grove Press.

Berne, E. (1962). Intuition VI: The psychodynamics of intuition. *Psychiatric Quarterly, 36,* 294-300.

Berne, E. (1964). *Games people play.* New York: Grove Press.

Berne, E. (1966). *Principles of group treatment.* New York: Grove Press.

Berne, E. (1972). *What do you say after you say hello?* New York: Grove Press.

Cassius, J. (1975). *Body scripts: Collected papers on physical aspects of Transactional Analysis.* Private circulation.

Corsover, H. (1972). Life scripts of Asklepieion therapeutic community. *Transactional Analysis Journal, 9,* 2.

Dusay, J. (1974). Eric Berne's studies of intuition 1949-1962. *Transactional Analysis Journal, 1,* 1.

Epstein, S. (1972). The nature of anxiety with emphasis upon its relationship to expectancy. In C. C. Spielberger (Ed.), *Anxiety, current trends in theory and research* (Vol. 2). New York & London: Academic Press.

Erskine, R. (1974). Therapeutic intervention: Disconnecting rubberbands. *Transactional Analysis Journal, 4,* 1.

Erskine, R. (1975). The abc's of effective psychotherapy. *Transactional Analysis Journal, 5,* 2.

Erskine, R. (1980). Script cure: Behavioral, intrapsychic and physiological. *Transactional Analysis Journal, 10,* 2.

Erskine, R., & Maisenbacher, J. (1975). The effects of a TA class on socially maladjusted high school students. *Transactional Analysis Journal, 5,* 3.

Erskine, R., & Zalcman, M. (1979). The racket system: A model for racket analysis. *Transactional Analysis Journal, 9,* 1.

Federn, P. (1952). *Ego psychology and the psychoses.* New York: Basic Books.

Goulding, M., & Goulding, R. (1979). *Changing lives through redecision therapy.* New York: Brunner/Mazel.

Groder, M. (1977). Asklepieion: An integration of psychotherapies. In G. Barnes (Ed.), *Transactional analysis after Eric Berne.* New York: Harper & Row.

Harris, R. (1967). *I'm ok, you're ok.* New York: Harper & Row.

James, M., & Jongeward, D. (1971). *Born to win.* Reading, MA: Addison-Wesley.

Kadis, L., & McClendon, R. (1980). Project: Family "cure". *Transactional Analysis Journal, 10,* 2.

Karpman, S. (1968). Fairy tales and script analysis. *Transactional Analysis Journal, 7,* 26.

McClendon, R. (1977). My mother drives a pickup truck. In G. Barnes (Ed.), *Transactional analysis after Eric Berne.* New York: Harper & Row.

Penfield, W. (1952). Memory mechanism. *Archives of Neurology and Psychiatry, 67,* 178-198.

Piaget, J. (1952). *The origin of intelligence in children.* (Margaret Cook, Trans.). New York: International Universities Press.

Schiff, J. (1970). *All my children.* New York: M. Evans.

Steiner, C. (1971). *Games alcoholics play.* New York: Grove Press.

Steiner, C. (1974). *Scripts people live.* New York: Grove Press.

Weiss, E. (1950). *Principles of psychodynamics.* New York: Basic Books.

Windes, K. (1973). Transactional analysis with addicts. *Transactional Analysis Journal, 3,* 3.

CHAPTER 18

Integrative Family Therapy

BRUCE R. LORIA

DEFINITION

Many models of integrative and eclectic family therapy exist. Some combine major family therapy schools, such as a Bowenian-Minuchin approach; others combine and apply major theories of individual therapy, as in a psychodynamic-behavioral model. Two points emerge: (a) no consensus among clinicians can be reached regarding the primacy of one model, and (b) eclectic and integrative family therapies will continue to proliferate. This chapter presents integrative family therapy (IFT), a dynamic, evolving model of clinical theory and practice. IFT draws upon many diverse schools of individual, group, and family therapy and avoids competition over which model is best by placing all contributing schools under an epistemological umbrella of constructivism.

For several hundred years, constructivism has advanced the theory that reality is not discovered but is created: it does not exist, nor is it separate from its observer. In therapy, clients, problems, and solutions come into existence through the meaning-making activities of all concerned parties. This process is referred to as *languaging*.

IFT avoids monological definitions and meanings and instead operates on the premise that what constitutes reality is constructed through the dialogue of the therapeutic conversation. Each voice in the session conveys a unique picture of reality for that participant, regardless of their age, sex, or family position. Central to IFT is the hope that each person is willing to participate in the therapeutic conversation that generates the consensually defined problems, goals of the therapy, and what will constitute the processes and end points of therapy. Discrete definitions for major terms or concepts of IFT are not particularly useful or possible. From constructivism, it is deemed arbitrary and controlling to impose one person's definitions on others. IFT prefers to avoid the trap of struggling over whose definition is correct and who is holding onto false beliefs. All definitions are considered equally valid in continuing the conversation of therapy. Emphasis is directed at understanding the personal significance of each definition. Working meanings emerge from the interchanges during the conversation. IFT's truths and tenets exist only as long as they remain consensually viable and facilitate the construction of meaning. Its dogma evolves from the languaging of its proponents and its critics. IFT does not seek a position apart from other therapies as one that is more effective or correct, as this would be an attempt to lay claim to objectivity or reality existing separately from the observer.

The model is replete with clinical metaphors offered by the therapist to the family as aids in the coconstruction of meaning. Many of these metaphors are familiar as they serve organizing functions in other theories and therapies. In IFT, they are not reified into free-standing absolutes that replicate reality, nor do they enjoy the "robes of certainty" they are often granted. Instead, they are considered clinically useful metaphors. Therapy stops and the dynamic evolution of meaning ceases when therapists seek to impose their subjective definitions on families.

An additional premise guiding IFT is that theorists can only develop and practice from uniquely subjective perspectives. The implications are that (a) the personal and developmental experiences of theorists become inseparable from their theories, and (b) no two theorists or clinicians can ever share completely the same representational system of theory or treatment. These systems are always filtered through the subjectivity of the individual.

IFT seeks to be inclusive, making room for all theories and clinical approaches that demonstrate utility. At times, IFT is experienced as a gentle, delicate, and subtle model of therapy, while at other times, it is emotionally charged, vigorous, and confrontive. A continuum of theories and techniques is constructed based on the needs of each family and the experience of the therapist. Hence, this model—IFT—is recommended to clinicians with some experience in family therapy.

Constructivism serves as the metatheory guiding the integration of all components of IFT. The model strives to facilitate the intrapsychic integration of therapists and all family members. The metaphor of autonomy is used as a guiding construct, as are the metaphors of blockages and disowned aspects of the self. The reclaiming of full cognitive, affective, behavioral, physiological, and systemic domains of functioning is a principle aim of IFT. These domains can be considered as manifestations of au-

tonomy when demonstrated through effective action and the capacity for full contact.

IFT also provides a system of explanations from which therapists integrate their observations, experiences, theories, hypotheses, and interventions. This is a recursive process that maximizes the options available for the continuance of the therapeutic process.

IFT addresses several domains of integration—(a) theoretical, (b) practical, (c) personal, and (d) systemic—while maintaining the highest regard for the integrity of all participants.

HISTORICAL DEVELOPMENT

Precursors

Interventions to alleviate discord in relationships and families have been a necessary component to the socialization of humanity. Presumably, tribal and clan chiefs, rulers, priests, shamans, medicine men, and other figures of social authority served as the first family counselors and mediators. It was not until early in the 20th century that working with relationships and families was approached scientifically and systemically. Since that time, the field of family counseling and therapy has evolved to its current level of theoretical complexity and widespread applicability.

The first integration of diverse systems of therapy was considered over 50 years ago when French (1933) presented a paper at the 1932 meeting of the American Psychiatric Association addressing similarities between Pavlovian conditioning and psychoanalysis. It met with an understandably cool reception, yet it was to be the beginning of an inquiry that continues to blossom today. Corsini (1981) identified over 250 distinct models of psychotherapy, and by 1986, Karasu identified over 400 therapies from the literature. This number is likely to be conservative and increasing steadily.

The interest in eclecticism and the integration of the psychotherapies has resulted in specialized journals, associations, conferences, and a wealth of literature. Norcross (1986) presents a comprehensive text covering the field of eclecticism and integrationism. He believes that while all integrationists are eclectic, all eclectics are not integrationists. Definitions of each term are required to understand his context. The common usage of the term *eclectic* refers to the approach of selecting and using what seems best from a number of systems. Lazarus (1967) termed this "technical eclecticism" in which techniques are used from different sources without the user needing to subscribe to the theories the techniques were drawn from. Norcross (1986) states, "For Lazarus and other technical eclectics, no necessary connection exists between metabeliefs and techniques" (p. 10). The promise of eclecticism and integrationism is that as growing numbers of therapies emerge and as society continues to accept the value of therapy, more diverse types of clients presenting a variety of problems will seek assistance. Hence, practitioners able to match their clinical approach to the client type and presenting problems are likely to be more effective than those who become monogamously wedded to a single theory.

Integration is presented in the literature as referring to more of a theoretical synthesis rather than a technique blending. It appears to be striving to create a meta-approach to therapy by providing the structure that links component theories. Norcross and others have reported that there is an emerging preference for

such theoretical synthesis or integrationism and a lessening of investment in technical syntheses or eclecticism (Norcross & Prochaska, 1988; Norcross, Strausser, & Faltus, 1988).

Useful questions to ask are "Why this blossoming interest in integration?" and "Why now?" London (1983), Norcross (1986), and Goldfried and Newman (1986) offer a number of self-reinforcing factors that have contributed to the development of integrative approaches. Foremost is the continuing proliferation of approaches to treatment, with none demonstrating a clear superiority over others. Also, the growing recognition that no one theory meets the needs of all clients favors the pursuit of integrationism. The centrality of theory and technique is giving way to evidence that what the client brings to therapy and what characteristics the therapist possesses are more important in predicting outcome. Theorists and practitioners from diverse schools continue to discuss the commonalities of effective therapy across schools of thought, which fosters the spirit of integrationism. Also, all theories have their share of successes and failures, whether this conclusion is drawn from research findings or clinical experiences. What can be concluded is that the integration of models of psychotherapy meets the needs of many clinicians and will continue to attract new followers in years to come.

Beginnings

The roots of integrative family therapy are diverse and reach deeply into the past of several fields of knowledge. Certainly acknowledgment is due Sigmund Freud for his contributions in the development of psychoanalysis. IFT makes use of a number of his core concepts, although in

IFT they are considered "clinical metaphors" rather than concrete entities. Theorists following in Freud's tradition also have made contributions to IFT. Anna Freud's work on defense mechanisms (1936), Paul Federn's writings on different states of the ego (1952), Wilhelm Reich's theories of character structure and body armor (1945), Frederick Perls's work in Gestalt therapy (Perls, Hefferline, & Goodman, 1958), Fairbairn's contributions to object relations theory (1952), and Eric Berne's development of transactional analysis (1961) all have found a place in integrative family therapy. The influence of Kohut's self psychology (1971, 1977, 1984) is also significant in clinical practice, as is the work of Fred Pine in integrating drive theory, ego psychology, object relations theory, and self psychology into a clinical synthesis (1985). These theorists are predominantly recognized as intrapsychically oriented. The rapprochement currently underway within family therapy is recognizing the need to make use of the valuable experiences and constructs of the individual therapists.

Additionally, IFT draws upon the founders of family therapy and the contributions of those theorists influenced by the masters. Ackerman (1958); Satir (1967, 1972); Bowen (1978); Haley (1963, 1971); Minuchin (1974); and Bateson, Jackson, Haley, and Weakland (1956) all have influenced thousands of family therapists, and the merits of their seminal contributions are integrated into IFT. A number of these theories have been considered incompatible, such as Minuchin's structural approaches with Satir's process level approach. Yet within IFT, each finds utility and makes theoretical contributions. The emphasis on integration within the field of family therapy continues to expand and is likely to be the dominant trend in the coming years (Feldman 1982, 1985; Friedman, 1981; Gurman, 1981; Kantor & Neal, 1985; Kaslow, 1981; Lebow, 1984, 1987a, 1987b; Moultrup, 1981; Pinsof, 1983; Pinsof & Catherall, 1986). Lebow (1987a) believes that the integration of theories and clinical practice is still in an early stage of development and focuses on two central questions: Which of the schools of family therapy need to be included for a model to be considered "integrative," and "What constitutes unity of approach?" (p. 585). This chapter's model of IFT deals with both questions by seeking a position that is "meta" to previous models and discussions. Using a constructivistic model of domains of knowledge, IFT seeks to include as many theories and modes of practice as are specified by the practitioner and are useful in meeting the needs of the client family. Synthesis is not a desired aim at the theoretical level because that brings about a new theory set. Rather, keeping the previous models intact and creating a structure that grants all theories equal access is preferred. Regarding "unity of approach," IFT grants that different theories contain different beliefs and presuppositions, yet it is not necessary to exclude a model because of its theory. If the practitioner finds utility in a model, no matter how far from the mainstream of family therapy it is, room is created in this model for its acceptance. The fluidity of shifting from model to model or from technique to technique is similar to the discussion of technical eclecticism, yet the tenets of constructivism serve as the overarching construct for synthesis.

In order to accomplish this integration of theories, IFT draws upon some of the tenets of constructivism. Constructivism can be traced to Giambattisa Vico, the 18th-century historical philosopher.

Watzlawick (1984) discusses Vico's influences in founding constructivism and cites Vico's famous quote from his 1710 text: "Verum ipsum factum—the truth is the same as the made" (p. 27). Following Vico in the development of constructivistic thought were Berkeley, Kant, Hume, Dilthey, Husserl, Wittgenstein, Dewey, Piaget, and Kelly. Recently, from the field of cell biology, constructivism has received increasing visibility from the theories of Humberto Maturana and Francisco Varela (1987) and the theory of "structure-determined organisms." Although this material is complex and philosophical, it also provides the best opportunity to date to provide the social sciences a foundation in biological science.

Current Status

This model of integrative family therapy is evolutionary. As such, its components of theory and practice are continually being refined and revised. Currently, there are several veins of interest being pursued. Kelly's Personal Construct Psychology (1955) contributes to the overarching framework of constructivism. Also, there is interest in the works of infant researchers like Stern (1985) and Sameroff and Emde (1989) who are providing revisions of previously revered stage theories. Such material is useful from both a theoretical level and practical level. Kohut's writings of self psychology, particularly from the perspective of his students like Rowe and MacIsaac (1989), are also finding prominence in the furthering development of IFT. As new vantage points for understanding the human experience emerge, they will be studied and if found useful, incorporated into the body of IFT.

In conclusion, Neimeyer (1988), con-structivistically states that "there are potentially as many integrative approaches to psychotherapy being practiced as there are practitioners doing the integrating" (p. 284).

TENETS OF THE MODEL

Three focal points are central to this section: (a) tenets derived from constructivism that address the limits, methods, nature, and origins of knowledge, the epistemological domain; (b) tenets derived from integrative psychotherapy addressing the technotheoretical domain; and (c) tenets that attend to the needs of the therapist to maximize effectiveness and personal and professional development, the subjective domain.

Constructivism

"Everything said is said by an observer to another observer who may be him- or herself" (Maturana, 1988a). Maturana's often-quoted phrase holds a significant position in the formation and application of integrative family therapy. It challenges the belief in an independent reality and that knowledge and objectivity exist separately from observers. Maturana's theory is called *structure determinism* and states that it is the structure of an organism that specifies how it will interact with its environment, and not the environment that specifies how the organism will respond. For practitioners of IFT, this means that we are always observers of our own self-created realities and to the realities of clients. We can never say we *know*, with certainty, why a family functions as it does. All that we create is a world of explanations that emerges from our effective actions. All acts of knowing are synonymous with effective action. Acts of knowing are acts like specifying criteria of distinctions among different domains of knowledge or striving to understand the realities families bring to therapy.

Therapy or *counseling* are terms in IFT that specify a plan and activity in which meaning will be cocreated by all participants. The term *languaging* is central to this discussion. Languaging is not simply talking with families; it is a process of performing coordinations of actions either by an observer with him- or herself or with others. Languaging creates a world of experiences, and observers cannot be separated from their experiences until *after* they have happened. Maturana states that the experiences of living "happen" in language. They do not exist until they are languaged about. All actions that result in experiences are part of languaging. According to constructivists, we are always in dialogue, even when languaging with ourselves.

An important constructivistic point is that the observer cannot distinguish between perception and illusion until after the moment of experience. An example is that therapists have no way of knowing whether an intervention will work with a family until after it has been used. This renders *all* therapeutic interventions educated guesses at best, or experiments conducted to see if the family responds to the perturbance with a structural reorganization.

Maturana and Varela (1987) begin with cellular biology and build their theory up through higher order mammals to congregates of animals and societies. Maturana's (1988) diagram of his "Explanatory Pathways of Objectivity" aids in understanding the differences between experiences that happen in language from what we do with such experiences (see Figure 1). The observers experience

life as it happens to them in language. If it does not happen, no experiences are experienced and there is nothing to language about. Although we commonly collapse our experiences with our explanations, Maturana, and subsequently Dell (1986, 1989), present the differences between experiences, explanations, and descriptions. In doing so, Dell clarifies the confusion between epistemology and clinical practice with respect to lineal or unilateral causality. Said succinctly, experience always "just happens" to us and must precede explanations. Explanations are attempts to provide the causes or reasons why experiences happened. They are always offered by either subjectively experiencing observers or detached observers. IFT practitioners understand that they participate with families from both positions of observerhood and develop skill and comfort in shuttling between the two. Descriptions are reports of what observed events constituted the experience and address the question "*what* happened?" Dell states that explanations always function at a level different from both descriptions and experiences.

In Maturana's Explanatory Pathways of Objectivity, what I label as "Path A" represents the pathway in which the question "How does the observer know what he claims to know?" is never asked. Path A explanations are accepted as the truth or as what is real. Possessing independent knowledge is also accepted as reality, and as such, no need exists to specify criteria of acceptance for all explanations. The observer believes he is independent from what he claims to know or what he experiences. In Path A, claims to know the "right" diagnosis, the "correct" way to treat families, or the "real" reason why a family missed an appointment are made while believing in

Figure 1. Maturana's Explanatory Pathways of Objectivity.

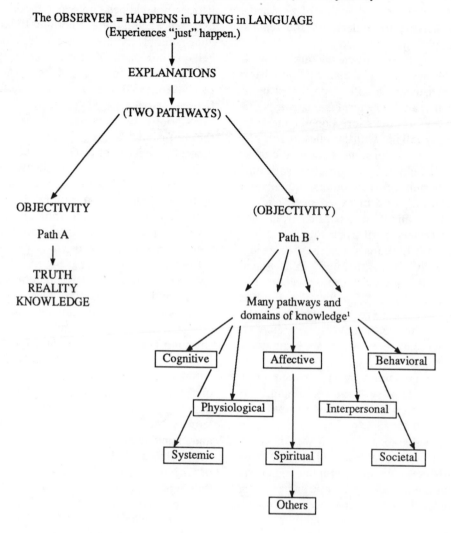

The OBSERVER = HAPPENS in LIVING in LANGUAGE
(Experiences "just" happen.)

EXPLANATIONS

(TWO PATHWAYS)

OBJECTIVITY   (OBJECTIVITY)

Path A   Path B

TRUTH
REALITY
KNOWLEDGE   Many pathways and
                               domains of knowledge[1]

Cognitive   Affective   Behavioral

Physiological   Interpersonal

Systemic   Spiritual   Societal

Others

[1]These are examples. There are as many domains as are specified by the criteria.

a privileged access to illusory independent reality: knowledge that is independent from the therapist. Additionally, the pathway of objectivity (Path A) makes a demand for obedience from the family. The therapist speaks from a position of fictional certainty, assumes he is "right" in his assessment and the family is "wrong." Families get labeled as resistant or as poor candidates for therapy. It is never considered that something might be inaccurate with the explanation created by the therapist. Also, therapists making claims to independent knowledge also evade any personal responsibility because what they say are not opinions but facts or absolute realities. This approach leads to competition between parties and a negation of the family and their realities. In Path A, the belief in objective facts leaves the family either to submit to the reality of the therapist or continue therapy knowing that they are being tolerated. Often, such a stance replicates what happened to family members in their families of origin. Maturana (1988) calls this unidimensional view of reality a "domain of universum."

In contrast, Path B is a "multiversum" where all domains of knowledge are equally valid yet different. Maturana calls this "Objectivity in Parentheses," meaning that these explanations are always reformulations of experiences of the therapist or family members. Path B makes no assumption that reality or objectivity exist independently from what observers do. Path B's acceptance of many theories and approaches to treatment makes it absurd to compete over which model is correct. Each domain of knowledge in Path B is considered a domain of operational coherence. This means that each treatment approach and theory is based on distinct criteria of acceptability specifying unique domains of knowledge. Maturana and Flores (1988) believe that knowledge is an assessment of the behaviors of others. The assessment is made by an observer who decides whether the behaviors are acceptable and fit that domain of knowledge. An example is when a therapist and family address the domain of protecting children. Through the therapeutic conversation, meaning regarding this domain is cocreated, and the family reports their experiences in this domain in the next session. Based on the previously specified criteria of what constitutes this domain, the participants are able to determine if what took place provided protection to the children or not. An expert does not place judgment on the family; rather, using cocreated criteria, the therapist and family jointly arrive at conclusions.

Integrative Psychotherapy

The preceding section has addressed the metalevel concerns of the epistemologist seeking an overall understanding of the nature of knowledge, objectivity, and realities in the field of family therapy. This section attends to a subordinate level of clinical practice and theoretical diversity found in many integrative models. It seeks to avoid the competition for "Who's approach is right" by blending Maturana's Pathway of Objectivity with a multiverse of theories and clinical approaches. While this may seem like a violation of classes and a mixing of models, it actually is a means to organize the theoretical and interactional facets of family counseling.

In 1972, Richard Erskine began teaching his model of integrative psychotherapy. It represented his understanding of diverse theories and techniques he had studied and used. To him, "integrative" referred to a synthesis of cognitive, affective, behavioral, and physiological theories and approaches to clinical treatment and to the integration within the client of "the fragmented or fixated aspects of the personality" (Erskine & Moursund, 1988, p. 8). His model focuses on the defense mechanisms employed by clients and makes use of the Gestalt therapy concept that defenses limit the capacity for contact. From Reich, Erskine derived the importance of the body in psychotherapy. The body is the repository of the muscular inhibitions that accompany repression and support the avoidance of full awareness and contact. The early writings of Eric Berne, founder of transactional analysis, are of equal importance to the influence of Frederick and Laura Perls. To Erskine and his students, transactional analysis is an ego psychology that was developed by Berne from his studies of Paul Federn, a psychoanalyst. (Readers are encouraged to study the two chapters on Gestalt therapy and transactional analysis as a prelude to this chapter.)

Integrative psychotherapy believes that therapists derive personal benefit from their investment in studying various approaches. Therapists also are able to match the needs of clients better than unidimensional practitioners. Erskine's model was originally based on integrating theories and approaches from four major domains:

1. The *cognitive* domain of knowledge that generally addresses the question of "Why?" (i.e., "Why is this a problem?" or "Why is this happening to me?")
2. The *affective* domain and the question of "How?" (i.e., "How are you feeling?" or "How do you experience me?")
3. The *behavioral* domain and the question of "What?" (i.e., "What do you want to change?" or "What needs to stop happening for your family to fight less?")
4. The *physiological* domain and the question of "Where?" (i.e., "Where in your body do you hurt?" or "Where do you experience yourself tightening up when you talk about incest?"

These four domains of knowledge serve as reference points onto which various discrete schools of therapy are placed. Some therapies are pure: psychoanalytic

therapy is considered a cognitive model and Gestalt therapy is an affective model. Other therapies can be plotted at varying points between these domains: transactional analysis is considered a cognitive-affective model. This valuing of multiple approaches provides the therapist many options for joining the client and maximizing therapeutic fit.

Erskine has two guiding principles of integrative psychotherapy: "an enduring commitment to positive life change" instead of symptomatic relief and "respecting the integrity of the client" (Erskine & Moursund, 1988, p. 43). Positive life change is arrived at through resolving barriers to contact and the script beliefs and feelings that bind together the beliefs, symptoms, somatic complaints, fantasies, and memories clients or families experience. Contact refers to the simultaneous attention to internal and external experiences and the fluid shifting between these two domains. Contact focuses on the internal thoughts, needs, perceptions, awarenesses, and emotions, what is taking place in the environment and what our experience is of others. Integrative psychotherapy emphasizes the development of an interpersonal relationship that affirms the client's integrity and never forces more openness on clients than they demonstrate an ability to handle. In Erskine's integrative psychotherapy, rather than attempt to neutralize client resistances to changes resulting from therapy, client resistances are encouraged and supported. Clients have found meaning in their lives through their holding onto past patterns of thinking, feeling, and behaving. Their resisting alternative frames to their existence is a statement about some facet of their integrity. Metaphorically, before clients can be expected to lessen the energy invested in maintaining their self-protective postures, no matter how self-destructive they appear, they must have the experience of being understood emphatically and accepted as they currently are. To not do this is to increase the risk of unwittingly re-creating an archaic injury from their family of origin.

Regressive therapy is a major clinical component of this model. This approach supports clients in going back in time metaphorically to the times of archaic injuries and trauma, encountering those situations and people differently, and creating new meanings. Regressive techniques combine all four major domains. Clients are empathically supported in telling family secrets, helped to create new meanings or constructs about themselves and how they fit into their world, supported in affectively and behaviorally confronting in fantasy their past aggressors, and helped to release body inhibitions and character armor.

Integrative psychotherapy takes place across the four major domains. At times, attention is directed to other domains, such as the spiritual domain, if they appear to be central organizing domains within a particular client. The domains are assessed, an intervention plan formulated that assists in achieving the client's stated goals, and a plan included to facilitate the attainment of integration. The overall goals are to assist clients in removing barriers to full contact; regain flexibility and spontaneity in their lives; resolve the life-distorting archaic constellations of beliefs, attitudes, and behaviors; and foster autonomy. Attaining autonomy means that clients have neutralized the harmful effects of introjects of significant others, resolved problematic fixations stemming from archaic unmet needs, and developed a high degree of skill in contact making.

Every family seeking therapy will not respond to a behavioral approach or to a strategic approach. Some may be manifesting what are termed affective blocks, and Satir's Process Model might provide a better fit for the family. Other families struggling with extended family involvements might derive a maximum fit from a Bowenian approach or Minuchin's structural approach. Hence, it becomes incumbent on therapists seeking to practice IFT to develop a solid theoretical base and practical experiences in a number of diverse schools of family and individual therapy. Integrative family therapy becomes a continuing commitment of therapists to their profession and to their clients.

Subjective Considerations

It must be emphasized that proficiency in integrative family therapy carries a weighty responsibility. It is not solely a didactic endeavor, nor is it mastered by amassing a requisite number of seminar hours. It is a competency-based model that assesses therapist effectiveness through what takes place during therapy; how the therapist languages about theories, approaches, and facets of therapy; and how contactfully the therapists conduct themselves at all times. It encompasses all aspects of therapists' personal and professional lives. There is a strong expectation for therapists to do personal therapy to resolve whatever blocks to contact and limits to their personal autonomy they experience. Some therapists demonstrate a sensitive ability to be empathic toward a client or family but do not get confrontive when that seems called for. Others are adept at being cognitively oriented but experience discomfort when powerful emotions emerge in a session. Integrative family therapy clinicians, by virtue of enduring in-depth training and commitment to personal therapy, develop a multiplicity of options for engaging clients and families in all aspects of psychotherapy. Heinz von Feorster's ethical imperative is "Always act to increase options" (Segal, 1986 p. 4). Von Foerster considers it a sign of health for people to possess a wide range of options. In IFT, this applies equally to therapists and families.

Integrative family therapists are invested in continuously advancing their knowledge and clinical skills. Almost all practicing integrative psychotherapists are involved in ongoing training programs, therapy experiences, and professional development seminars. Such rigorous standards are accepted as necessary in order to respect clients for their trust. Anything less than this diminishes the honor of being invited into the most private and vulnerable parts of client lives.

Using Figure 1, the many domains of theoretical and practical knowledge find a place in Path B, the domain where knowledge does not exist apart from the using therapist. Here, each domain of therapy finds an accepted place so long as its criteria of distinction can be specified. This means that the therapist needs to be able to specify what constitutes the theory and practice of each theory (i.e., cognitive therapy, structural family therapy, paradoxical therapy, and all others). By specifying the criteria of distinction, the therapist sets up the parameters that invite further discussion with either colleagues or clients. Therapists who do not specify the criteria that constitute a particular domain of knowledge create barriers to languaging about that domain. This means that the necessary discussion regarding when to use or not use a model, why it is advantageous, and what pitfalls must be considered cannot be ad-

dressed. Instead, others must accept reality as presented by the construing therapist.

Relevant questions surface regarding how integrative family therapy is taught. In keeping with the integrative thrust, this model uses a developmental model that builds knowledge and skills from less complex tasks to more complex multitheoretical perspectives. Erskine (1982) provides one framework for matching the focus and depth of supervision to the trainee's developmental level of professional skill and experience. Attention is continually directed to any issues in the therapist that replicate the issues in the family or client. Any domains of integrative practice that are consistently avoided by the therapist are addressed.

Initially, inexperienced therapists are encouraged to focus their time and attention on the development of their *observational* abilities. This pertains to attending to all facets of the client or family system. It includes registering what is happening on all sensory systems, what is not happening, the posturing of the family, seating arrangements, and overall transactional style of the family among themselves and with the therapist. Beginning IFT therapists spend a significant amount of time refining their ability to observe the experiences of families and formulate descriptions of what is observed.

They then articulate *theories* to explain what they observed. These theories are general and address all people in that culture rather than a particular client or family. The descriptions of the family's experiences are translated into as many theories as are mastered by the therapist. Therapists versed in only one theory translate all client experiences into that one theory. IFT therapists consider the multiverse of theories they understand. Having multiple theoretical sets available means that the therapist is not constrained by an unnecessarily narrow field of observation. This is not a linear process, as these two initial phases influence each other recursively. What the therapist observes and describes is influenced by the theories the therapist holds, and what theory the therapist chooses is influenced by what is selectively attended to. Both are influenced by the subjective life experiences of the therapist, the degree of training, personal therapy, and a number of other factors.

A second set of explanations are then formulated by the therapist. These are *hypotheses* that address this particular client or family. "Why is *this* family manifesting these behaviors?" is an example of a question used in formulating hypotheses. Again, IFT therapists endeavor to formulate multiple hypotheses for *each* theory from which they operate, again striving to create maximum options for engaging the family system. After hypotheses have been crystallized, the therapist is ready to focus attention to the level of *techniques* or interventions used to carry out the therapy. IFT therapists will develop several techniques from each hypotheses previously formulated. Any technique that does not sufficiently "perturb" the family system into making some internal adjustment means that the intervention "didn't work." The therapist now has the option of either (a) selecting another technique from the same hypotheses subset, (b) considering another hypothesis for why the family is functioning as it is, (c) switching to an alternative theory for organizing experience, or (d) attending to the observations and reevaluating this data. This process is depicted in Figure 2, referred to as the "Integrative Psychotherapy Treatment Planning Sequence." Each therapist's diagram will be unique, as no two therapists can formulate this process in the same way. IFT clinicians do not conduct therapy in a step-by-step manner. Rather, the diagram serves as a model of the internal map a therapist can use to understand the family and the process of therapy.

APPLICATION

Clients for Whom the Model Is Especially Effective

Integrative family therapy evolved out of a desire to facilitate the development of "autonomy" in family systems and in all of their members. It also seeks to increase the options available to the therapist working with a family. The types of problems that concern families take many forms. The family's subjective conceptualizations of problems brought to therapy serve as a starting point for the therapeutic conversation. If families can demonstrate their congruence by entering into a mutually agreed-on therapeutic contract and then take the necessary steps to begin resolving their presenting problems, there are likely to be few impediments to what they determine to be a satisfactory experience. Therapists with narrow theoretical bases, limited clinical experiences, and many personal obstacles to full contact are likely to be less effective in working with families.

Attention to the congregate domains of knowledge leading to autonomy in either the therapist or the family members is a focus of IFT. The domains specified thus far are

- cognitive,
- affective,
- behavioral,

Figure 2. Integrative Psychotherapy Treatment Planning Process.

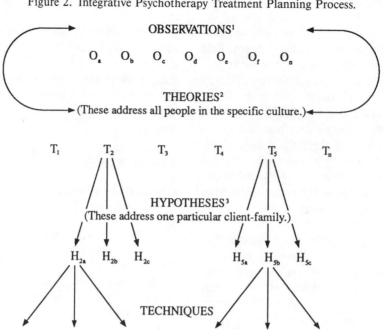

OBSERVATIONS[1]

O_a O_b O_c O_d O_e O_f O_n

THEORIES[2]
(These address all people in the specific culture.)

T_1 T_2 T_3 T_4 T_5 T_n

HYPOTHESES[3]
(These address one particular client-family.)

H_{2a} H_{2b} H_{2c} H_{5a} H_{5b} H_{5c}

TECHNIQUES

$T_{2a\text{-}1}$ $T_{2a\text{-}2}$ $T_{2a\text{-}3}$ $T_{5b\text{-}1}$ $T_{5b\text{-}2}$ $T_{5b\text{-}3}$

[1]Observations are as numerous as specified by the observer.
[2]Theories are only limited by the knowledge of the observer.
[3]The diagram depicts an example of the flow. The full trail of each theory and hypothesis to all possible techniques is too expansive for this diagram.

- physiological,
- interpersonal,
- spiritual, and
- societal.

If awareness of the value of any of the domains is not present or if the person excludes that domain from his or her functioning, the therapist, client, or family can be considered to be experiencing some blockage. Whether the explanation created deals with "affective misattunement during childhood" (Stern, 1985, p. 138), parental unavailability in the current family because of physical or emotional trauma, rigid family dogmatism, impaired reality testing, obtrusive character armor, prevalence of defense mechanisms, or the inability to establish or maintain contact, the IFT therapist has a theoretical-technical matrix available to formulate explanations. Hence, it is likely that the only problems or clients that will not benefit from IFT are (a) problems that therapists and concerned family members cannot reach consensual agreement on and (b) clients who do not experience problems in their lives or families. Again, there are no problems in existence until the family and therapist conjointly agree to create them through languaging.

No preexisting limitations are placed on clients in IFT. There are no entrance hurdles for families to surmount such as bringing a prerequisite number of family members or stopping the abuse of alcohol or drugs prior to the start of sessions. All that matters is that the family demonstrates a willingness to enter into a contract for therapy and then perform their parts of the contract in a manner consistent with their current level of autonomy.

Two distinctions have been offered to explain the goals of clients and families. *Social control* is a term used by Holloway (1974) to describe clients and families seeking symptomatic relief. Other clients or families seek autonomy with the aim of reclaiming or establishing full mastery over all facets of personal and family life. Both are fully acceptable in IFT. There are no preordained expectations that families are expected to meet. It is acceptable if families choose to end therapy prior to demonstrating the attainment of what is defined as autonomy.

Therapy is not a static event in a family's life cycle. It is expected that families may return for additional therapy at later points in their lives. IFT seeks to remain respectful of the family's current level of development and helps each member experience therapy as a positive process.

IFT has been used with all types of family concerns. Generational and boundary issues, competitive family structures, the symptomatic child, and the myriad of family construct issues have been attended to and resolved. Additionally, IFT is particularly suited for dealing with "intrapsychic family therapy" in which the archaic thoughts, feelings, behaviors, and bodily expressions or the introjections of significant others are manifested within the current family at problematic levels. Somatic expressions of emotional problems, disruptive fantasies, or repetitive relationship patterns that are experienced as toxic or unfulfilling are also within the realm of IFT. Overriding this discussion is the belief that people can create new meanings in their lives and eliminate the problems they bring to therapy by creating new personal and family constructs.

Goals of the Therapeutic Process

Establish Rapport and Contact with the Family. The establishment of rapport and contact with family members is a necessary prerequisite for having a therapeutic conversation; without it, the family may not return for a second session. Therapists need to suspend clinical judgments and not begin making direct therapeutic interventions until the family decides whether they want to participate in therapy and the therapists demonstrate successfully to the family that they are capable of languaging cooperatively with the family about their concerns. "Empathic attunement" (Rowe & MacIsaac, 1989 p. 16), a concept central to Kohut's self psychology, is a skill IFT clinicians must develop and use frequently and is a process that starts with the initial contact with the family member, continues through the contracting discussions, and is important throughout the family's participation in therapy. This means that therapists metaphorically attempt to place themselves within the shoes of the clients in every possible respect. Contact with them is made through the use of experience-near questions that convey to the family that the therapist is affectively pacing the flow of therapy.

Therapists demonstrate to the family that they understand the family's situation, the problems they are concerned about, how each family member is experiencing the effects of the concerns, and what will be necessary for the family to determine that therapy was successful. Attainment of family goals is accomplished across the domains of knowledge. The therapist focuses on domains that are problematic to family members, domains they are adept at using, or domains excluded from their personal repertoire.

A therapist's education is not complete unless time is devoted to Saturday cartoons, MTV and VH-1, Double Dare, the sports pages, and whatever else is likely to be central in the lives of clients. Such an investment enables the therapist to join with each family member.

Attention to contact is another major focus for therapists. Contact is the paying attention to one's inner experiences and external stimuli and then shifting back and forth between the two as a means of establishing meanings and realities between parties. The absence of contact results in a stopping of the flow of the therapeutic conversation. When family members break contact, they rely on "private realities": meanings constructed in isolation. These are common occurrences in therapy and family life. For example, a son wants to go out with his friends to a movie but in the absence of contact with his parents, he does not ask permission. He concludes instead that they will turn him down. So, rather than ask, he either may drop his plans to be with his friends or sneak out to join them. Therapists could intervene by asking the son to discuss the incident and his "private realities" with his parents. As a result, he may understand them better, they may gain insight into what he believes about them, and the family may create a "shared reality" regarding future situations.

Establish a Mutually Agreed-upon Therapeutic Contract. The contract demonstrates the therapist's understanding of the family, the family's willingness to enter into the therapeutic conversation, and the degree of the therapist's autonomy and self-care; and it attends to the necessary administrative details. It is integrative, and it is not only a behavioral agreement. Contracts attend to all facets of the two parties being together, including personal comfort and preference matters, and they need to answer all of the questions the therapist and family members have. This includes criteria for addressing questions not yet created.

Maintain Flexibility throughout the Therapeutic Conversation. Therapists create problems for themselves by "getting married" to a particular theory or clinical approach. IFT stresses that there is a cornucopia of theories and approaches available to use in continuing the therapeutic conversation. Theories and interventions support the process of creating meaning but do not take prominence over languaging with the family. One theory or clinical approach is as valid or "correct" as the next, provided the criteria of acceptance are specified. Hence, retaining as many options as are available based on the therapist's knowledge base, clinical experience, and personal integrity provides a rich matrix for the cocreation of meaning with families.

Continue the Therapeutic Conversation for As Long As the Family Experiences Problems. When the family no longer experiences the problems for which they sought therapy, it is time to negotiate a new therapeutic contract or end therapy. If the therapist has concerns that the family is ending therapy before the problems have been resolved, the therapist addresses these directly yet respectfully. Therapists must ensure that they remain honest with themselves and with the families by saying what they feel a need to say regardless of whether the family likes them. Therapy is not a popularity contest. As long as therapists continue to like themselves, they are free to say what they think to families. This is not a license to be condescending, abrupt, evasive, or unkind toward them. Rather, too many therapists shackle themselves by being overly concerned for the feelings of the family at the expense of themselves. Sharing thoughts and feelings with a family announcing their intent to end therapy is both diagnostic and contact maintaining. A family can use the therapist's information as a basis for their next step. Ending therapy with the door left open for a family's possible return is deemed more advantageous than strongly encouraging them to remain in therapy past a comfortable point. Therapists who try to hold clients in therapy may win the battle but lose the war. Nothing is served by not respecting a family's wishes and trying to convince them to stay in therapy.

Maximize Opportunities for Languaging. Families language on many channels and levels simultaneously. IFT encourages therapists to use whatever is observed in the service of continuing the therapeutic conversation. In essence, the phrase "Everything is grist for the mill" guides attention to family verbal and nonverbal communications. For example, if an IFT clinician is discussing a problem with a family member and notices body movements, eye glances, sighs, or similar signals from other members, a decision to focus attention on under-

standing that gesture before continuing the previous discussion must be made. This is because the signal may be part of the larger conversation, a sign of a shift to a different topic, or a random event. The current topic may trigger archaic internal conversations in a family member that may impede the person from full contact in the present. If so, these other conversations should be noted and a decision made about what the client would like to do about them.

Keep Therapist Self-Worth Separate from Family Satisfaction. Therapists are not responsible for curing the family. They are there to conduct a therapeutic conversation with the family about problems jointly specified to be of concern. They provide clients time and attention because therapy is an endeavor they like to do not because they believe they can help, heal, cure, or fix. Therapists do not issue guarantees with their work that problems will never return. If families revert back to previous ways of relating and langauging, problems can certainly return. Therapists participate in the creation of meaning through language with families, make interventions that hopefully trigger internal reorganizations in family structure, and meet with the family until they agree that their concerns have dissipated. IFT clinicians do homework, whether it is reviewing tapes of their work, obtaining supervision, or learning more about the theories and practice of family therapy. They do not take home the emotional residue of sessions or allow doubts about themselves to consume their free time. These are indicators that the boundaries between the therapist and the family may be blurry or that some personal constructs the therapist holds about him- or herself are being activated by counseling. This means it is time to seek out a mentor and resolve these internal issues that are impediments to autonomy.

Client's Primary Responsibilities

Although it sounds provocative, families are not responsible in integrative family therapy for anything until they agree on what constitutes "responsible." This is accomplished through conversation with the therapist. All families are responsible to do is "do themselves." From a structure-determined perspective, this is all a family can do. They only have one way to be, and that is how they present themselves in therapy. To ask a family to be other than they are is to make a demand for obedience from them. If this is done because the therapist determines that something is wrong with the family, then the therapeutic conversation in an IFT perspective has ceased and has changed into an attempt at controlling the family. There are times when therapists must make demands similar to this, as when parents are using physical pain as a means of obtaining obedience from their children or when a parent uses a child as a sexual object. In IFT, at such times, the therapist possesses full awareness of his or her subjective values and the guiding ethical parameters and takes personal responsibility for whatever action taken. However, other than in extreme situations where laws or the safety of the family is in jeopardy, the IFT therapist must be led by the principle that families are free to stay as they are. It is their absolute right to not move in any direction the therapist values or desires. As it is the family's responsibility to remain congruous with their demonstrated level of functioning, it is also the therapist's task to not accept responsibility in

those situations where the family chooses not to continue the therapeutic conversation.

It must be remembered that from a constructivist perspective, it is the therapists-as-observers who attach subjectively construed labels on families because the families demonstrate behaviors unacceptable to them. Such a process is of little benefit and has nothing to do with the primary objective of continuing the conversation of therapy. Nor does it have anything to do with reality as experienced by the family. It is another example of how therapists for the past 90 years have believed they possessed the independent knowledge that justified their specifying the realities of others.

A Chinese proverb states, "Only the fish does not know it is wet." This is how it is for the families we treat. While they may experience their lives differently from how they construed them to be, they do not generally know they are enmeshed, resistant, disengaged, or triangulated. A primary goal of integrative family therapy is the attainment of individual and family autonomy. Von Foerster refers to autonomy as the regulation of regulations. This recursive statement is another way of stating that autonomy is self-regulation (Segal, 1986) and that all organisms function according to the postulate of cognitive homeostasis, which states, "the nervous system is organized (or organizes itself) so that it computes a stable reality" (Von Foerster, in Watzlawick, 1984, p. 58). This implies that families, regardless of the assessment placed on them by external observers, have established a stable reality for themselves. Families seek therapy when their realities are experienced as unstable or, from Kelly's perspective, their core constructs are threatened. In integrative family therapy, autonomy is used as a metaphor rather than a description of experience. It refers to the capacity to demonstrate self-regulation in the major domains of knowledge: cognition, affective experience and expression, behavior, physiology, interpersonal relating, spiritual meaning making, and societal fit. From this perspective, autonomy represents one possible end point of therapy.

At times, a family's definition of self-regulation does not match with society's definitions. Schools, law, and health officials will take definite action when parents use physical punishment in ways the community considers excessive or abusive. In many instances, families referred for family therapy by community agencies are not those who function with full respect and dignity for all members. Rather, a number of families practice their self-regulating in a manner that was demonstrated by previous generations or as a result of current environmental stressors. It becomes the IFT clinicians' major task to help these families make meaning out of the referral to therapy. Also, therapists will need to be empathetic and convey understanding for the families' experiences as a prelude to any changes.

Families in IFT remain active participants in the conversations that bring problems into existence. They also remain active in discussing the ending of therapeutic discourse when problems are no longer a concern. In line with the metaphor of personal and family autonomy we can expect that families in contact with their thoughts, feelings, and behaviors and having the skills to continue languaging about the problems among themselves will not need the conversation of therapy. They will feel congruent and comfortable about discussing the end of therapy.

Additionally, it is sometimes humorous to observe how upset some therapists make themselves over a family's failure to keep an appointment. Some therapists expect that such action means that the family does not like or value the therapist, that they are resisting therapy, or some other construction of the therapist's private reality. This event is only a problem if the therapist has some unresolved questions about his or her ability, is operating on limited information, or is experiencing more investment in the family's therapy than the family. If the therapist has taken care to establish a clearly defined, mutually agreed-on contract, then the family's behavior of not attending a session is nothing more than an indication that the family is somewhere else. There is no way the therapist can know *why* the family is not at the appointment until the conversation is resumed between parties. Therapists can be quick to ascribe meaning to such events or even lay claim to the true meaning of such behavior. Families arrive in our offices because that's where we find them. We do not know they are coming until they arrive. Therapists create needless roadblocks to the creation of meaning by pretending to know why a family did not keep a therapy appointment.

A family is free not to show up for a session as long as the therapist and family are in explicit agreement about what happens in such situations. The term *resistance* does not apply as there is nothing to resist. The family is simply functioning in a manner consistent with its current level of organization.

The therapist and involved family members agree during the first few sessions on a number of salient points:

- How frequently will sessions be held and for what duration?

- Where will they be held? In the therapist's office, the family home, a school, some other neutral site?
- What will be the currency of exchange for the therapist's time?
- Who is in the family, who would the parents like to bring, who is involved in what becomes defined as the "problems"?
- Who would the therapist like to talk to?
- How are abrupt cancellations or missed appointments handled?
- What happens if the family or therapist go on vacation?
- What recourse does the family have if the therapist runs overtime with a previous session or shows up late?
- How is therapy ended? Who takes responsibility for initiating the discussion of termination?
- How are problems identified? How are goals set?
- Are there any overarching concerns in the family regarding the problems, the therapy, or the therapist?
- What are the therapist's ethics, preferences for conducting therapy, and relevant likes and dislikes?
- Are there any "ground rules" to discuss and agree on, such as who's job is it to chase down toddlers running in the offices; are there any off-limits areas; and what does the therapist prefer that the family do with disposable diapers after the baby has been changed?
- How does the contract get revised and renegotiated?
- How are sensitive topics like "family secrets" to be handled by the therapist and the family?

This is not an inclusive list of *all* questions needing attention during the contracting phase but examples for therapists to use and modify.

Families are "responsible" to the extent that they demonstrate understanding of what the contract means and are willing to accept the parameters of the contract.

Therapist's Role and Function

A primary therapist role in integrative family therapy is to be the "manager of the conversation" (Loos & Epstein, 1989, p. 161). The therapeutic conversation is the medium through which meanings are made and problems come into existence. These problems are discussed until the family and therapist consider them resolved. The term *manager* is not synonymous with keeper of the truths or other traditional roles therapists have occupied. Rather, the therapist participates in the ongoing conversation designed to language problems out of existence. This is not to imply that the therapist talks the family into submission or into accepting her definition of reality, but rather that in a facilitative mode, the therapist does what is necessary and realistic to keep the parties in conversation. Additionally, the therapist serves as the primary source of "therapeutic perturbations"—another name for interventions or techniques designed to trigger changes in the family's organization. Families will continue their "drift" until they experience some perturbation that is of sufficient magnitude to their organization that they accommodate to the stimuli and evolve into a new family structure.

Therapists need a map to organize their experiences of a given family, the jointly created problems, and the theories and interventions to be used to trigger family reorganization. Included in this map is attention to the distance the therapist maintains with each family member, awareness of each family member's definitions of reality and problems, and attention to the contact points available. This is also referred to as "therapist positioning" (Loos & Epstein, 1989, p. 162; Anderson, Goolishian, & Winderman, 1986; Watzlawick, Weakland, & Fisch, 1974). The distance therapists maintain with each family member is seldom fixed; it is fluid and changes from person to person, from session to session. The decision is based on the problems being languaged, who feels centrally involved, and where the therapist believes the most impact on the family system can be made by either moving in closely or occupying a distant or detached stance. Also, positioning requires the maintenance of a multiverse of theoretical and clinical perspectives to prevent becoming channeled into a narrow clinical path. It is the therapist's collective understanding of the family and the process of therapy that is shared with whomever the family brings to sessions through languaging about family concerns.

The therapist strives to understand how each family member creates his or her world and how these separate world views merge to form the family's view. Also, the therapist assesses his or her ascribed role in the client's or family's construct system. The acceptance of this role is dependent on whether it is within the therapist's personal ethics, professional judgments, and encompassing values. Sometimes, a family member will ascribe to the therapist the role of a "missing historical parent figure" and relate to the therapist accordingly. At other times, the therapist accepts both "positive and negative transferences" of family members. Therapists are often granted knowledge and authority by families, even before the therapeutic conversing begins. Then, it is up to the

therapist to retain this privilege by demonstrating behaviors that the family considers competent.

Therapists have the responsibility to be a representative of the community in child welfare, law, health, and other extrafamilial interactions with society. This requires that therapists be clear about laws governing the reporting of violations, clinical practice, and the lines of communications between referring agencies. Of equal importance is the internal clarity therapists need to have regarding their responsiveness to incidents requiring reporting. Sometimes, therapists feel an inner conflict between their allegiance to a family and the requirements of law. This is an example of a dilemma to be brought to supervision, and if there is a personal therapy issue attached to it, it needs attention and resolution.

Part of therapeutic languaging is designing experiments with the family. As meanings are cogenerated by family and therapist, so are resolution strategies. The therapist looks continuously for opportunities to provide families with reformulations of their experiences from the vantage point of a different observer. The therapist offers experiments to the family to do either in session or between sessions, as a means of continuing the conversation about the family's reality and as another avenue to challenge their current construction of reality. "Reframing" is a technique common in many schools of therapy. In IFT, reframing is another way to challenge the family to begin considering alternative ways for constructing their reality.

It is common for parents in families participating in therapy to report having had "perfect parents." Such parents were people who never admitted to making mistakes during their child-rearing years, never did anything to their children that warranted an apology and request for forgiveness, and always knew the "right" way. As one mother reported, "I may not always be right, but I'm never wrong." Therapists do well to remember that they are people, and as such, they will make mistakes, oversights, or conversational blunders with families. For families to have the experience of a therapist who admits mistakes, apologizes, asks if apologies are accepted, and admits when questions are beyond his or her current comprehension is to provide families with alternative role modeling and possibly a corrective experience. This is especially true if the parents in the session are still carrying on the traditions established by their parents. The therapist's behaviors in sessions provide the family with continuous opportunities for self-regulation and assessment of therapist congruence. If the therapist is available and contactful with all family members and demonstrates congruence in expressions of thinking, feeling, and actions, the family is likely to experience the therapist in a positive and impactful way. At times, some therapists engage in practices that alienate or discount family members. Examples are claiming to be an expert or behaving in ways that the family regards as condescension. In these instances, it is likely that there will be serious interruptions to contact between key family members and the therapist, therapy may be shortened, or the therapeutic conversation will cease.

Some families prefer to focus on selected aspects of themselves to the exclusion of others. At such times, integrative family therapists metaphorically hold up the mirror before the family at strategic times during the therapeutic conversation. If the family is concerned about the school performance of an intelligent child now doing average work and are not concerned about another child who comes home at odd hours or Father's alcohol consumption problems, the therapist has the responsibility both to respect the family's current conception of reality while simultaneously providing experiments that will allow them to open up the family lens to obtain a wider-angle view of themselves. This can be accomplished by exploring the unexpressed domains of functioning, such as the feelings experienced by the drinking father or the child coming in late, or by focusing on the behaviors that the family considers acceptable for all members.

The therapist will experience an easier time sustaining conversations by continually striving to advance his or her personal level of autonomy. Also, in addition to being more effective with families, therapists placing a high value on self-development in both the personal and professional domains are likely to experience well-being and satisfaction.

"Being popular" is an inconsistent aim for IFT practitioners. This does not mean that IFT clinicians have license to be as provocative as they wish. Some schools of therapy sanction provocativeness or confrontiveness in therapists. Supervisors behind the mirror instruct student therapists in being more challenging to the family's frame of reference, focusing on the desired systemic change at the expense of the emotional experiences of family members. The old adage that "sticks and stones may break by bones, but names can never hurt me" is obsolete in a constructivist theory of family treatment. Names, verbal assaults, and attacks on the character of family members are perturbances to the current organization of that person. If these are of sufficient magnitude, the triggers will lead to a variety of painful or negative experiences for the listener. It is doubly injurious if the verbal assailant is a parental figure or trusted therapist. The degree of provocativeness, like silence, closeness, or distance, must fit into the overall integrative schema of integrative family therapy. The therapist needs to be able to formulate an explanation acceptable to the listener for why a particular affect or style of relating is used.

Primary Techniques Used in Treatment

Integrative family therapy meets many of the criteria for being a model of technical eclecticism. Whatever techniques therapists use in continuing the therapeutic conversation are acceptable. However, techniques as discrete components do not hold a position of prominence. IFT's reliance on constructivism for its epistemology renders techniques to a minor role.

In this model, techniques are narrow slices of the therapeutic conversation specified by the therapist as important. At work here is the dynamic of punctuation (Minuchin & Fishman, 1981). Punctuation in family therapy is used as a metaphor from grammar, where certain marks such as periods and commas set off segments of text from others. Families and therapists punctuate life according to their respective realites. This means that they break up the continuum of life into segments according to their personal or family constructs. Therapists intentionally change the punctuation of the therapeutic conversation in order to change the width of the field of vision in use. Some therapists punctuate the process at a transaction-by-transaction level, while others focus on much broader patterns of family interac-

tions. An example of a broader pattern is focusing on the multigenerational transmission of family norms and rules.

Concerns for the developmental needs of therapists is another reason techniques are not a major focus in this model. Many therapists begin their training by amassing and relying on a collection of techniques without an appreciation for the broader context-guiding utilization. At other times, therapists employ techniques to avoid experiencing discomfort. Therapist uncertainty is part of the process of working to understand family complexities. Techniques used to "sterilize" therapy of such affects are considered counterproductive.

In IFT, techniques refer to those sequences of activity initiated by therapists to achieve several aims. These aims are considered IFT's "function and form" and include (a) facilitating meaning making and the construction of therapeutic realities, (b) fostering contact, (c) perturbing family structures, and (d) conducting experiments that challenge family constructs. Hence, any sequence of behaviors that is directed at any of the above four aims would constitute a technique in this model.

CASE EXAMPLE

Introduction

IFT and case studies are strange bedfellows. Case studies are generally written from the perspective of the therapist and seldom enlist input from the family members. In IFT, a full case study is the cocreation of all involved family members and therapists. Each session, each topic, and even each transactional exchange is reviewed to elicit the thoughts, feelings, conclusions, and impressions of all. A consensus emerges from this process. The therapist is only one of the observers and has no claim to being right. His or her observations and explanations represent subjective experiences of the session, filtered through layers of private realities and lived experiences.

The family discussed here was not involved in as thorough an analysis as presented. Each member reviewed this section, provided feedback, and offered alternatives that were discussed. The added fictional qualities of this family were also discussed and agreed to in the service of anonymity.

Initial Contact

The caller identified herself as Monika L., calling on behalf of her son Jeremy, age 7, who was being referred for family counseling by his school psychologist. Her accent sounded German. My guess was that she had met and married her husband while he was stationed overseas. If this was correct, she was here probably without her family or a support system. She stated that her first-grader was "not listening to his teacher" and "not taking school seriously." At home, he told lies, disappeared for hours without permission, and threw temper tantrums. She then asked for an appointment on Wednesday at 5:00 P.M., as that was the only time she and her husband could attend. This was an unusually specific request. I wondered if their lives were that busy and, if so, could this be some contributing factor. I wondered if they might be overly rigid or controlling people and whether that might become a factor in the therapy. I also wondered if they were perhaps feeling somewhat entitled because her husband Jules, age 40, was a lieutenant colonel and held a very visible and responsible position at the

nearby Army base. Fortunately, I had an opening at that time and offered it to her. She asked if I wanted to see everyone in their family. I told her that only those family members involved and concerned about this matter need attend.

IFT clinicians make mistakes from the outset if they presume to know what the problems are, why the families act as they do, or how things will turn out. Initially, it is better to answer questions directly and obtain information necessary to determine if therapy is warranted. Therapist time is better spent attending to the observations of the family that lead to multiple theories and hypotheses.

First Session

The family that arrived for the first session consisted of Monika, 26, Jules, and Jeremy. All were available for contact, emotionally expressive, and pleasant. They reported that two other sons—Jim, 17, and John, 16—were still at school or off at work. There was an older daughter—Jackie, 18—now attending college, who otherwise lived with her maternal grandparents. The older three children were from Jules's first marriage that ended 10 years previously when his wife died of cancer. I wondered about the emotional toll on the family and how that tragedy altered their lives.

Jeremy was the only child from Jules's second marriage that lasted just over 2 years. It ended when his second wife admitted having several extramarital sexual encounters, experimented with drugs, and wanted out of the marriage. Jules explained that he realized that he married too soon after the death of his first wife, that his second wife really didn't know what military life was like, and that she had a number of "emotional problems" surface. I felt somewhat sad as I thought of this period in Jules's life. Just a few years after the death of his first wife, which left him with three small children, he put himself in another marriage that also dies. His toddler, Jeremy, accompanied his mother to California, but, according to Jules, her drug involvement and her need for psychological help continued. Jules obtained custody and brought Jeremy to live with him. Jeremy, who had been quiet and seemed attentive, suddenly piped in with "My mother kidnapped me and my father had to come and get me back." This outburst took everyone by surprise. Monika's response was immediately to tell the boy about interrupting, speaking when spoken to, and about "knowing better." I was struck by how she did not seem upset or emotionally triggered in some way by Jeremy's comment. To me, it seemed like an automatic reflex on her part. I wondered if her reaction was common in their family, what Jules was thinking about his son's statement and Monika's response.

Jules almost immediately began to explain that what Jeremy referred to was not as dramatic as the boy reported. In a calm, assured voice, he reported that his ex-wife had a 1-month visit with the boy and at the end of the month could not bring herself to send him back. To secure the child, Jules had to fly to California with custody papers to bring his son home. Yet, this incident in session struck me for several reasons. It sounded like the episode had become a central narrative in this family, one that got repeated often at family gatherings. I also sensed that Jules possibly was not in tune with his son's emotional experiences regarding the incident. Perhaps to a 5-year-old, it *did* seem like he was being kidnapped, and to him, it *was* a dramatic event in his life. Also, if the grown-ups often remem-

bered this time, that could serve as reinforcement for the importance of this event for the boy. This led me to wonder if the discounting of emotions and experiences was common in this family and somehow a contributing factor to their concerns. While it was too premature to delve into this subject, I did hear how Jules dealt with the death of his first wife and the feelings of betrayal by his second. Also, Monika's life in Germany sounded like she was a parental child needed to care for her three younger brothers most of the time because her parents were butchers and ran a shop in town for long hours. Her relationship with her parents sounded stormy. Overall, it seemed that minimizing the importance and value of the affective domain was possibly quite common in this family.

The discussion regarding Jeremy's problems seemed to split the couple. Monika seemed more animated and involved in explaining the boy's problems, while Jules seemed more accepting of what the boy did. I asked if it was possible that only one parent experienced a problem with Jeremy. With Monika looking at him, Jules said that while he sees that something isn't working well with Jeremy, the boy is probably going through a normal phase of childhood and Monika was much more concerned. I asked Monika if she agreed with what her husband said and whether she could offer any explanation for why this was the case. She agreed and added that Jules did not see much of what Jeremy did. The boy acted out mostly when around her. Also, she was the point of contact for calls from the school. I asked her if she ever felt taken advantage of by her situation, and she denied any experience of this. Rather, she expressed acceptance of this role for her in the family. This exchange led me to question whether Jules might be minimizing the seriousness of what Jeremy was doing and what his wife's feelings were, and if so, what messages or permissions might Jeremy be concluding.

I asked about discipline, consequences, and punishments, because thus far in the session, no one had mentioned this subject. It was refreshing to hear that they both did not believe in physical punishment, although they admitted to wanting to resort to it at times. Instead, they used a variety of restrictions and consequences. Monika usually administered them and reported to Jules on the events. She also gave "talks" to him. I asked what this meant, and again Jeremy jumped in with the answer: "Whenever I'm bad, my mom gives me a talk to help me be good." Monika then confirmed that she believes in talking directly to the child to help him understand what he was in trouble for, why he was being punished, what he could do differently next time, and how important it was for him to learn these things as a child. On the surface, this sounded great. It sounded like a modern approach to an age-old problem of helping children understand about consequences, yet I wondered if it worked. I asked the parents if they had seen desired results from the "talks." Jules looked to Monika to answer, and she stated that they do work. Here was a word I could assume we all understood, but instead, I asked for her meaning of "work." She said it meant that Jeremy would listen and then do things better next time and that the talks work, but not as she had hoped. This led me to ask her what happens instead of the talks working. Monika replied that Jeremy joins in the talks freely, asks questions, discusses the subjects, yet she is left feeling that nothing really sunk in. I pursued this final phrase because I was

again in search of her private meaning to this. Monika continued and described the step-by-step account of the talk with Jeremy. What surfaced was that Jeremy would engage her rapidly with questions, and on the surface, they appeared to be part of the conversation. It also seemed like Jeremy was gradually leading Monika away from her subject, question by question, to a point of distraction. Since Monika placed value on having these talks, and she wanted her son's participation, she fully participated in these meandering conversations. Only afterward did it dawn on her that she was feeling unfulfilled from her talks. Having described her experiences, Monika began to make new meanings about the efficacy of her talks as they currently took place.

It was interesting to observe how active and vocal Jeremy became as Monika began to reflect on what usually happens and how she winds up feeling led astray. The explanation I offered was that perhaps Jeremy was doing, in session, what took place between them during talks. Perhaps he was seeking to interrupt her, distract her, or shift the focus to himself instead of allowing her to complete her train of thought. I asked Jules to attend to his son, and this was easily accomplished. Jules validated what Monika was describing about the process of the talks. He reported that for him, the talks went far too long and that he soon lost interest in being part of them. I asked him what did he feel when Monika and Jeremy began a talk, and he replied that he felt "unneeded," "a spectator," and eventually "bored." Monika seemed surprised and stated that she never knew this about Jules. I suspected that this may be much more of a pattern between them rather than an incident. I decided not to interject my agenda into the discussion at this point, and instead, wait for a more relevant time to open this subject. We focused the conversation on whether Jules's experiences were unusual or probable. If they were not unusual, did Monika or Jeremy share any of these feelings? Jules and Monika talked about this and arrived at the conclusion that maybe Jeremy was quickly "tuning out" his mom because he knew what he was in for. I suggested that the family continue to talk about the talks between sessions and attempt to come up with alternatives, and even conduct and experiment with Jeremy to see if any other results could be obtained. The family decided that they would do this.

Part of this initial session was spent discussing our definitions and expectations for therapy. I explained my philosophy and canon and asked them to share any assumptions or expectations about our process. They seemed aware of the rudiments of family counseling and their expectations. They wanted to obtain help in understanding Jeremy's behaviors and in developing more effective ways to deal with him. There were no unresolved issues regarding other aspects of the contract, and I accepted their expectations as an initial working treatment contract.

Jeremy participated throughout this session by asking questions, speaking out in the midst of someone's answer, and frequently correcting his mom. To me, it seemed like an ingrained pattern to their relationship. I asked if Jeremy exhibited any "perfectionistic" tendencies, such as never using the eraser end of a pencil, throwing away a paper if he made a mistake, and becoming upset at dinner if his green beans touched his rice on his plate. The parents laughed and reported that Jeremy did do things like that, which led them to frustration. But, they added, "We have just come to live

with these things." I thought that such an approach was basically fine. I wasn't going to make any pronouncements of "psychopathology" on the boy if the family did not experience these as problems. The only part of this that did concern me was his frequent corrections of Monika, even when he was factually wrong. I told myself that I would be irritated if he did it to me, and yet, Monika seemed to allow him to do this often. I wondered why would she allow this and asked her to help me make sense of this. She replied that Jeremy "had a habit" of doing this and that she had tried, without success, to get him to stop. Jules added that he is aware of Jeremy's habit, but added that the boy doesn't do it much with him. He sees this basically as a problem between Monika and Jeremy. I asked the family if Jeremy did this anywhere else, and Jeremy replied that he did it with his teacher in school, but "only when she is wrong."

The laughter from the parents did not abate my growing concern that this boy's charm and wit may be serving several purposes. At times, it may be something that triggers parental pride and love, while at others, it may be a form of "entertainment" for the parents. It appeared that this 7-year-old was being talked to like one of the older children. This led me to wonder if Jeremy was getting mixed messages about being a 7-year-old who was allowed and expected to talk to his parents as equals. I wondered if the way the parents conversed with Jeremy sustained the behaviors they called problems. What they chose to attend to and ignore was used by the boy to make meanings out of his parents' responses to him.

This initial session ended with all of us reviewing our experiences in the conversation. I also asked them if they had made a decision whether they wanted to return to continue our conversation. They talked briefly, mostly about conflicting schedules, and decided to return in a week.

Subsequent Sessions

The family attended 10 sessions spanning 6 months. Their attendance was generally in accordance with our contract; there were only two occasions when they did not keep an appointment. One was a conflict with the parents' work schedules, and the second was a time when Jeremy took off for 2 hours instead of waiting outside as the family prepared to come to the session. After a few weeks of weekly sessions, we began to space them out to twice monthly, then monthly visits.

The second session was dominated by Jules's feelings of anger and distrust toward his second wife, Jeremy's mother, who was requesting an extended visit with her son in California. The family experienced this request as creating several problems for them: (a) They didn't trust her enough to send Jeremy there; (b) they were being asked to pay all air fare for Jeremy, which they thought was unfair; (c) they could not obtain any assurances from Jeremy's mother's probation officer or psychiatrist that she might not again attempt to prevent Jeremy from returning home; and (d) Jeremy felt conflicted in both wanting to stay in New Jersey and also wanting to see his mother. Everyone took part in the discussion of perceived problems and possible alternatives. Jeremy made it clear that if he went, a month was too long for him. He preferred to go for 2 weeks. The parents decided to offer his mother a plane ticket to New Jersey if she would pay for a reduced-rate motel room on the Army base. They would

lend her a car for the days, but Jeremy would sleep at home. They considered flying Monika and Jeremy to California for 2 weeks and having Jeremy sleep in the motel at night. They expressed a concern that Jeremy was getting too old to sleep with his mother in her bed. Later, it was learned that Jeremy's mother rejected all options and decided a summer visit would not take place.

In this session, time was spent discussing Jeremy's fears about being "kidnapped." Jules took the stance that Jeremy was old enough to know what to do; he knew how to make collect phone calls, knew both parents' work numbers, and knew his father would come for him if that happened. Again, I was concerned that although all of this was factually true, it may not have addressed the emotional concerns of a 7-year-old boy facing a transcontinental flight into a possible "kidnap" situation with a person about whom he had heard a number of distressing things. Monika was triggered by Jeremy's concerns and became very animated. She wanted me to tell them what they should definitely do, whether they should defy the court order, or what would happen if they sent Jeremy. I asked her a number of questions in attempting to make meanings from what she was saying. It was clear that Monika's foremost thoughts concerned the safety of Jeremy and that this was based on the previous incident. She was clear in expressing her love for the boy, and it was clear that a very strong bond existed between them. She also added that she knew how Jules had been hurt by the past incident and how their lives were thrown into turmoil.

This discussion seemed particularly significant to me, because it indicated how sensitively aware she was of Jules's pain, even though his style is to suppress it. Out of a tangential curiosity, I asked her if this incident reminded her of any other similar experiences she had in her life. She reported that when she was 13 and in charge of the daily care of her three younger brothers, one was injured and needed to be taken to the doctor. Her parents were away in a neighboring town on business and could not be reached. She remembered feeling the total responsibility for her younger brother and how hard it was for her to get him to the doctor's and get the adults there to take her seriously. I acknowledged how difficult that must have been for her and decided to wait and see if any patterns emerged from other discussions.

During the fifth session, we discussed how Jules and Monika arrived at consensus in their discussions. At one point, Jules said emphatically, "She just won't sit down and talk to me!" Monika reeled back in her chair and put her hands up, palms outward before her face, as if to ward off an attack. Her response seemed fearful, despite the absence of any overt anger or rage coming from Jules. Somehow, this behavioral gesture did not fit the current context. I asked Monika to notice her body posture and allow herself to be aware of what she experienced when Jules spoke out. She replied that she got afraid at that moment and that she is often scared that Jules will blow up in anger at her. This was surprising because they never reported any marital strife, nor did Jules's temper ever surface as a concern. Thus far, my experience of him was as a person who tended to suppress affect, remain primarily cognitive, and invest energy in task-oriented problem solving. Jules expressed some awareness of Monika's concerns but added that they had never discussed it nor had they argued. I asked Monika a question from a different theory: "Who's face

might you be putting on Jules when he sounded as he did to you?" This was aimed at eliciting any archaic memories being triggered by Jules's emotions and words. Monika thought for a moment and then replied that Jules reminded her of her father who would fly into fits of anger when anyone did something he considered a mistake. She remembered being afraid of him because he would escalate his anger until he would hit someone, usually Monika or her mother, and that nothing was ever talked about or resolved. It was due to her father's behaviors that she married at 18, even though she did not love her husband. She saw this as her opportunity to get out of his house and away from the chaos.

I asked Jules how Monika's memories had touched him. He directed his response to her and, with a previously unrevealed tenderness, spoke to her of how she had helped him realize what life must have been like for her in Germany. He added that he understood why they never got into serious discussions and why she took so much of the burden on herself. He put his arms around her and held her while she softly cried. Jeremy remained wide-eyed and speechless throughout this exchange. Later, Monika added that this conversation had helped her make sense out of her avoidance of any conversation she believed would result in an argument. We discussed ways she could experiment with desensitizing herself to arguments and anger. Everyone in the family agreed to help her in her homework.

The parents began talking about other things in sessions. They no longer came to the sessions preoccupied with what Jeremy had done at home or at school. I asked what they experienced as different in their lives. Jules reported that he was coming home earlier from work whenever he could to be with Monika and spend more time with Jeremy. Monika reported that the "talks" had ended, that she and Jules now practiced saying what they expected of Jeremy concisely and without discussion. Jeremy reported that his activities were progressing nicely. He still thought his teacher was "weird," but he had significantly curtailed his oppositional posture toward her.

Follow-up of this family at 3 months revealed no return of initial problems. Jules reported that he felt happier for the first time in a long while. Monika was feeling less burdened and was getting results without overworking herself. Jeremy was doing well in school and enjoying his time there. At times, he still sought to sidetrack Monika, although she was ever vigilant to his tactics. There were a number of individual issues that surfaced from the sessions that could have been the focus of attention in other theories. Jules and Monika were aware of these possible directions and that they could be discussed later if deemed a problem. The two older boys remained minimally involved, contributed to changes within the family, and did nothing to impede the conversations within the family. The family experienced the emergence and cessation of problems in their lives. It was not the place of the therapist in this model to create problems for them that they were not experiencing. This is an essential component of integrative family therapy.

EVALUATION

Outcome research supports the conclusion that family therapy helps clients obtain desired results. Yet, a great deal of the research is of an empirical nature and pursues "historical truth" (Spence, 1982) that is generally context-free. This is

adopted from the natural sciences and seeks to elucidate "universal truths" in language free from contextual influence. However, an equally valid alternative, "narrative truth," also exists and is grounded in the field of hermeneutics. It draws conclusions from the lived experiences of participants, makes meaning from the subjective discourse of those centrally involved, and fits closely with the theory of IFT.

The domain of "research" is of value in other theories. In IFT, research only exists among the participants who cocreate the therapeutic conversation. Other detached observers could monitor IFT and offer conclusions and evaluations. Yet their findings hold no greater validity because they were not involved in creating the problems or solutions. In this model, reality testing is consensus testing. Spence (1987) devotes considerable text to how the subjectivity of therapy is studied and reported. The standard approach is to present case studies, interpretations, and articles written exclusively from the perspective of the therapist. In IFT, such a voice is only one of many observers of the process. The subjective experience of each participant, on a transaction-by-transaction level, must be languaged in order to create conclusions or evaluations of the therapy. This means that the evaluation of a 7-year-old "identified patient" is as "real" and as "valid" as the evaluation of the PhD therapist.

In IFT, therapy is cocreated by therapists and clients bringing their subjective agendas, concerns, and skills to the conversation. Making the determination that therapy was successful can only be based on the criteria all participants agree to. Because this is an intersubjective matrix of meanings, relationships, and outcomes, evaluations are an internal process. In this model, it is doubtful if external research would be useful. If the external research conclusions indicate that changes took place in the family's attitudes or behaviors and that the family did not experience any significant lessening of their problems, then the question of "who's reality is real?" surfaces. This runs counter to the coconstructive process of meaning making that is so central to IFT. Maturana's maxim that "everything said is said by an observer to another observer who may be him- or herself" helps with the dilemma of evaluations. There will be as many unique evaluations of one session as there are observers. Valid evaluations of therapy are obtained only when all active participants agree on one set of conclusions.

What can be shared regarding evaluation comes from what we as therapists experience and from what our families tell us. To our emipirical colleagues, such measures are not reliable or valid. When people leave therapy using IFT, they report a cessation of their initial concerns. They report feeling different; therapy was not what they expected it to be. They report that they expected to be changed by an expert; they did not expect to become equal participants in conversations with someone who they come to respect and who respects them. In IFT, relationships develop that span many years. Follow-up visits to the same therapists for other problems are routine. Families report that the overall quality of life improves. The therapists enjoy their work, despite the demands of the discipline and the constant flood of families. These comments do not imply that IFT is the only way to obtain such results; again, IFT emphatically supports that there is no one approach to family therapy.

SUMMARY

The notion that family therapy is a positivist science capable of discovering direct knowledge of the world is not viable. Emerging family therapy literature suggests that metaphors like "families are homeostatic systems" or "families need and make their symtoms" are losing favor. Instead, attention is turning to constructivistic thought, the role of empathy in therapy, the importance of the relationship between therapist and clients, and integrative and eclectic models.

Integrative family therapy is a theory and model of clinical practice built on the tenets of constructivism. Reality, objectivity, and truth are created, not discovered, and are subjectively experienced and intrinsically linked to the life experiences of people using these terms. Reference to such terms cannot exist apart from the people who talk about them. Clinically, the implications in this model are that problems and solutions do not exist until they are cocreated through the therapeutic conversation by participants. Some take the title of therapist, and others accept the role of client. Together, they participate in a coordination of interactions that brings forth domains of knowledge through languaging until problems cease to exist. Technically, this means that therapists perturb families in ways that trigger structural family reorganization. The result of this triggering is that the family no longer languages about previous problems; when they cease languaging about their problems, the problems are no longer granted existence.

This model shares many similarities with Lazarus's technical eclecticism, except that techniques do not play a significant role in the therapeutic conversation. Attention is directed toward domains of knowledge: cognitive, affective, behavioral, physiological, spiritual, interpersonal, and societal to determine if clients demonstrate effective action in each. This is not a complete or exhaustive listing of domains. It represents those specified for this chapter. Demonstrating effective action in each of these domains cumulates metaphorically and is referred to as *autonomy*. Being autonomous means having a range of options for problem solving and contact making.

IFT blends individual intrapsychic therapy with facets of group and family systems therapy and affords therapists a multitude of options for languaging with families. Maturana's concept of "objectivity in parentheses" refers to there being no one right way to do therapy and to there being as many domains of theoretical and clinical relevance as are specified. Hence, multiple theoretical and clinical pathways to knowledge exist and are available for therapist selection.

Finally, IFT accepts that being a therapist is a weighty responsibility. Great emphasis is placed on continuous personal and professional development of therapists throughout their life cycle. Therapy, supervision, and training are regular components of this process. Accepting such obligations maximizes respect for families and demonstrates therapist congruence and integrity. From this approach, new meanings can be created that trigger the dissolution of family problems.

ANNOTATED SUGGESTED READINGS

Watzlawick, P. (Ed.). (1984). *The invented reality.* New York: Norton.

A good beginning into constructivism that includes chapters by some of the foremost thinkers, including von Glaserfeld, von Foerster, and Varela. It is not easy reading but will provide a foundation.

Segal, L. (1986). *The dream of reality: Heinz von Foerster's constructivism.* New York: Norton.

A logical next step into constructivism. This book presents many of von Foerster's articles in a logical fashion, capturing von Foerster's brilliant and elegant thought.

Maturana, H., & Varela, F. (1987). *The tree of knowledge.* Boston: New Science Library.

Dell once wrote that "it hurts to read Maturana." This work is a testament to that statement. Careful and systematic reading will take a reader interested in constructivism into its depths. The diagrams, sidebars, and drawings all enhance the systematic building of the theory of structure determinism.

Erskine, R., & Moursund, J. (1988). *Integrative psychotherapy in action.* Newbury Park, CA: Sage Publishing.

An excellent "transcript" text. It has a beginning theoretical chapter and 11 transcript chapters of actual work, interspersed with explanations and the therapists' rationales for their work. An instructive text for seasoned clinicians and beginners, it is powerful reading and provides an accurate view of this model.

O'Hanlon, B., & Wilk, J. (1987). *Shifting contexts.* New York: Guilford Press.

A worthwhile work for demystifying the

process of therapy. It will perturb readers in some ways as it presents the authors' approach, "clinical epistemology," focusing on "video descriptions" of happenings. It is refreshing and holds merit for all readers.

REFERENCES

Ackerman, N. W. (1958). *The psychodynamics of family life.* New York: Basic Books.

Anderson, H., Goolishian, H., & Winderman, L. (1986). Problem determined systems: Toward transformation in family therapy. *Journal of Strategic and Systemic Therapies, 5* (4), 1–14.

Bateson, G., Jackson, D., Haley, J., & Weakland, J. (1956). Toward a theory of schizophrenia. *Behavioral Science, 1,* 251–264.

Berne, E. (1961). *Transactional analysis in psychotherapy.* New York: Grove Press.

Bowen, M. (1978). *Family therapy in clinical practice.* New York: Jason Aronson.

Corsini, R. J. (Ed.). (1981). *Handbook of innovative psychotherapies.* New York: Wiley.

Dell, P. (1986). In defense of "lineal causality." *Family Process, 25,* 513–521.

Dell, P. (1989). Violence and the systemic view: The problem of power. *Family Process, 28* (1), 1–14.

Erskine, R. (1982). Supervision of psychotherapy. *Transactional Analysis Journal, 12* (4), 314–321.

Erskine, R., & Moursund, J. (1988). *Integrative psychotherapy in action.* Newbury Park, CA: Sage Publishing.

Fairbairn, W. (1952). *Psychoanalytic studies of the personality.* London: Routledge and Kegan Paul.

Federn, P. (1952). *Ego psychology and the psychoses.* New York: Basic Books.

Feldman, L. (1982). Dysfunctional marital conflict: An integrative interpersonal/intrapsychic model. *Journal of Marital and Family Therapy, 8,* 417–428.

Feldman, L. (1985). Integrative multi-level therapy: A comprehensive interpersonal and intrapsychic approach. *Journal of Marital and Family Therapy, 11,* 357–372.

Friedman, P. (1981). Integrative family therapy. *Family Therapy, 8,* 171–178.

French, T. M. (1933). Interrelations between psychoanalysis and the experimental work of Pavlov. *American Journal of Psychiatry, 89,* 1165–1203.

Freud, A. (1936). *The ego and the mechanisms of defense. The writings of Anna Freud* (Vol. 2, rev. ed.). New York: International Universities Press.

Goldfried, M., & Newman, C. (1986). Psychotherapy integration: An historical perspective. In J. Norcross, (Ed.) *Handbook of eclectic psychotherapy* (pp. 25–61). New York: Brunner/Mazel.

Gurman, A. (1981). Integrative marital therapy: Toward the development of an interpersonal approach. In S. Budman (Ed.), *Forms of Brief Psychotherapy.* New York: Guilford Press.

Haley, J. (1963). *Strategies of psychotherapy.* New York: Grune & Stratton.

Haley, J. (Ed.). (1971). *Changing families.* New York: Grune & Stratton.

Holloway, W. (1974). Beyond permission. *Transactional Analysis Journal, 4* (2), 15–17.

Kantor, D., & Neal, J. (1985, March). Integrative shifts for the theory and practice of family systems therapy. *Family Process, 24,* 13–30.

Karasu, T. B. (1986). The specificity versus nonspecificity dilemma: Toward identifying therapeutic change agents. *American Journal of Psychiatry, 143,* 687–695.

Kaslow, F. (1981). A dialectic approach to family therapy and practice: Selectivity and synthesis. *Journal of Marital and Family Therapy, 7,* 345–351.

Kelly, G. (1955). *The psychology of personal constructs* (2 vols.). New York: Norton.

Kohut, H. (1971). *The analysis of the self.* New York: International Universities Press.

Kohut, H. (1977). *The restoration of the self.* New York: International Universities Press.

Kohut, H. (1984). *How does analysis cure?* Chicago: The University of Chicago Press.

Lazarus, A. A. (1967). In support of technical eclecticism. *Psychological Reports, 21,* 415–416.

Lebow, J. (1984). On the value of integrating approaches to family therapy. *Journal of Marital and Family Therapy, 10* (2), 127–138.

Lebow, J. (1987a). Developing a personal integration in family therapy: Principles for model construction. *Journal of Marital and Family Therapy, 13,* 1–14.

Lebow, J. (1987b). Integrative family therapy: An overview of major issues. *Psychotherapy, 24* (3S), 584–594.

London, P. (1983). Ecumenism in psychotherapy. *Contemporary Psychology, 28,* 507–508.

Loos, V., & Epstein, E. (1989). Conversational construction of meaning in family therapy: Some evolving thoughts on Kelly's Sociality Corollary. *International Journal of Personal Construct Psychology, 2* (2), 149–167.

Maturana, H. (1988). *The world according to Humberto Maturana.* Paper presented at the Horsham Clinic Symposium, Horsham, PA.

Maturana, H., & Flores, F. (1988). *The social construction of reality.* Paper presented at the Logonet Symposium, New York, NY.

Maturana, H., & Varela, F. (1987). *The tree of knowledge.* Boston: New Science Library.

Minuchin, S. (1974). *Families and family therapy.* Cambridge, MA: Harvard University Press.

Minuchin, S., & Fishman, H. C. (1981). *Family therapy techniques.* Cambridge, MA: Harvard University Press.

Moultrup, D. (1981). Toward an integrated model of family therapy. *Clinical Social Work Journal, 9,* 111–125.

Neimeyer, R. (1988). Integrative directions in personal construct therapy. *International Journal of Personal Construct Psychology, 1,* 4.

Norcross J. (Ed.) (1986). *Handbook of eclectic psychotherapy.* New York: Brunner/Mazel.

Norcross, J., & Prochaska, J. (1988). A study of eclectic (and integrative) views revisited. *Professional Psychology: Research and Practice, 19,* 170–174.

Norcross, J., Strausser, D., & Faltus, F. (1988). The therapist's therapist. *American Journal of Psychotherapy, 42,* 53–66.

Perls, F., Hefferline, R. F., & Goodman, P. (1958). *Gestalt therapy.* New York: Julian Press.

Pine, F. (1985). *Developmental theory and clinical process.* New Haven, CT: Yale University Press.

Pinsof, W. (1983). Integrative problem-centered therapy: Toward a synthesis of family and individual psychotherapies. *Journal of Marital and Family Therapy, 9,* 19–35.

Pinsof, W., & Catherall, D. (1986). The integrative psychotherapy alliance. *Journal of Marital and Family Therapy, 12,* 137–152.

Reich, W. (1945). *Character analysis.* New York: Farrar, Strauss, and Giroux.

Rowe, C., & MacIsaac D. (1989). *Empathic attunement: The "technique" of psychoanalytic self psychology.* New York: Aronson.

Sameroff, A., & Emde, R. (Eds.) (1989). *Relationship disturbances in early childhood.* New York: Basic Books.

Satir, V. (1967). *Conjoint family therapy* (rev ed.). Palo Alto, CA: Science & Behavior Books.

Satir, V. (1972). *Peoplemaking.* Palo Alto, CA: Science & Behavior Books.

Segal L. (1986). *The dream of reality: Heinz von Foerster's constructivism.* New York: Norton.

Spence, D. (1982). *Narrative truth and historical truth*. New York: Norton.

Spence, D. (1987). *The Freudian metaphor: Towards paradigm change in psychoanalysis*. New York: Norton.

Stern, D. (1985). *The interpersonal world of the infant*. New York: Basic Books.

Watzlawick, P., Weakland, J., & Fisch, R. (1974). *Change: Principles of problem formation and problem resolution*. New York: Norton.

Watzlawick, P. (Ed.). *The invented reality*. (1984). New York: Norton.

Name Index

Abrahms, E., 405, 422, 432
Achenbach, 479, 492
Ackerman, N., 209, 414, 431
Adler, A., 6, 16, 305, 384, 385, 386, 388, 400, 405, 431
Akerman, 535, 563
Akhilananda, S., 298
Alexander, F., 405, 414
Allen, D., 416, 431
Aderson, C., 258, 260
Anderson, W., 328, 330, 342, 551, 563
Andolfi, M., 88, 104
Annon, J., 408
Antoninus, M., 437, 461
Aponte, H., 79, 88, 104
Arbuckle, T., 357, 382
Ard, B., 408, 431
Ard, C., 408, 431
Arnold, J., 492
Arnold, L., 431, 469
Aronson, H., 469, 494
Arthur, J., 470
Ashby, W., 359, 381
Aspy, D., 338, 342
Assigioli, R., 16
Atwater, M., 357, 381
Aurelius, M., 404
Azrin, N., 471, 492

Babcock, D., 515, 528
Back, J., 309, 343
Bader, E., 510, 527, 528
Bahm, A., 492
Bahm, S., 466
Baisden, H., 407, 431
Baker, L., 80, 81, 102, 104, 105, 106

Baldwin, M., 15, 19, 20, 21, 24, 25, 26, 29, 31, 32, 33, 43, 44, 45
Balint, M., 211, 212, 232
Bandler, R., 43, 348, 350, 351, 353, 354, 355, 356, 358, 359, 360, 370, 372, 377, 379, 380, 381, 382
Bandura, A., 6, 404, 465, 466, 470, 472, 473, 477, 491, 492
Banmen, J., 44
Barbach, L., 408
Barcai, A., 81, 105
Barnard, C.P., 210, 232
Barnes, G., 529
Barrett-Leonard, G., 316, 338, 342
Barrows, S.E., 238, 260
Baruth, L., 416, 433, 490, 492
Basmania, B., 22, 44
Bateson, G., 16, 22, 43, 44, 111, 147, 149, 177, 181, 182, 205, 237, 238, 239, 241, 243, 246, 248, 249, 260, 355, 360, 361, 376, 381, 415, 472, 473, 492
Beach, D., 466, 492
Beavin, J., 144, 148, 178, 204, 237, 261, 359, 382
Beck, C., 357, 381
Beck, E., 357, 381
Beevar, R., 161, 166, 170, 171, 173, 178
Bell, N., 217, 234
Benjman J., 160, 178
Benjamin, M., 161, 168, 178
Bergin, A., 416, 433
Berkley, 536
Berman, J., 407, 433
Bernard, M., 433
Bervar, D., 161, 166, 170, 171, 173, 178
Berger, H., 88, 104

567

Berne, E., 16, 405, 498, 499, 500, 504, 505, 515, 528, 529, 535, 540, 563
Bernheim, H., 405
Betoff, N., 88, 104
Bion, W., 213, 232
Birchler, G., 475, 483, 493
Bitter, J., 13, 16, 21, 33, 44, 45
Blanck, G., 230, 232
Blanck, R., 230, 232
Blazier, D., 408, 431
Blechman, 470, 480, 493
Bluestein, J., 441, 461
Boardman, 467, 493
Bodin, A., 157, 178, 182, 189, 205
Bonner, J., 73
Bordvin, C., 8, 12, 472
Boscolo, L., 149, 238, 239, 240, 241, 243, 248, 249, 250, 251, 252, 259, 260
Boszormenyi-Nagy, I., 209, 214, 232, 234, 260
Bowen, M., 16, 22, 25, 41, 44, Ch. 3 (pp. 48–75), 48, 49, 50, 51, 54, 57, 60, 61, 62, 64, 74, 75, 148, 208, 209, 214, 217, 231, 232, 415, 416, 431, 535, 563
Bozarth, J., 321, 343
Brenner, C., 210, 232
Breurer, J., 209, 232, 405
Brill, A., 209, 232
Brody, W., 22, 44
Brodsky, G., 467, 468, 494
Brooks, M., 356, 357, 381
Bross, A., 161, 168, 178
Brown, J., 172, 175, 178, 480, 493
Buber, M., 223, 232, 237, 304
Buckner, M., 357, 380, 381
Bynner, W., 303, 343

Cady, D., 357, 382
Cain, D., 309, 338, 342, 343
Calhoun, J., 51, 75
Cameron-Bandler, L., 348, 349, 357, 358, 360, 362, 364, 368, 372, 376, 377, 381
Campbell, D., 261
Campbell, J., 139, 304, 343
Caplow, T., 25, 44
Carlson, J., 387, 401
Cassius, J., 511, 529
Castanada, C., 125, 140
Catherall, D., 535
Cecchin, G., 149, 238, 240, 243, 244, 259, 260
Chambers, N., 309, 342
Chandler, C., 466, 492
Chaney, R., 235

Chilman, C.S., 4, 5, 11
Christianson, D., 172, 175, 178, 480, 493
Cirillo, S., 245, 260
Cobb, J., 468, 494
Colapinto, J., 77, 101, 104
Collins, L., 441, 461
Colpe, 465, 493
Combs, A., 310, 321, 325, 343
Conger, J., 468
Congers, R., 495
Cooper H., 8, 12
Corey, G., 386, 401
Cornelison, A., 233
Corrales, R., 209, 210, 232
Corsini, R., 385, 401, 432, 533, 563
Corsover, H., 509, 529
Coulson, W., 307, 308, 318, 319, 336, 339, 340, 343
Cox, F.M., 4, 5, 11
Coyne, J., 161, 178

Dearwin, C., 48
Day, J., 140, 209, 234
Davison, G., 404, 407, 408, 433
Deardorff, M., 205
Dejerine, J., 405
DeLozier, J., 348, 350, 382
Dell, P., 537
Deming, W., 440, 461
Devereux, G., 111
Dewey, J., 305, 313, 439, 536
Diaz-Guerrera, R., 405
Dicks, H., 210, 213, 217, 230, 231, 232
Diekstra, R., 407, 433
DiGiuseppe, R., 406, 407, 429, 431, 432, 433
Dilthey, 536
Dilts, R., 348, 350, 351, 353, 357, 359, 360, 361, 362, 363, 364, 375, 376, 377, 381
DiMattia, D., 406, 431, 432
Dinkmeyer, D., 384, 386, 387, 388, 389, 390, 391, 392, 394, 395, 399, 400, 401
Dinkmeyer, D. Jr., 387, 400, 401
Dodson, L., 16, 44
Dollard, J., 405
Dorn, F., 357, 381
Downing, G., 16
Draper, R., 261
Dreikers, R., 384, 385, 396, 401, 419, 431
Dryden, W., 404, 405, 406, 412, 413, 416, 420, 431, 432
Dubois, P., 405, 437
Dusay, J., 499, 529
Dymond, R.F., 338, 345
Dysinger, B., 22, 44

Ebner, M., 468, 495
Edelbrock, 479
Edelwich, J., 442, 461
Eelan, P., 433
Ehrenwald, J., 128, 140
Eideson, B., 469, 493
Einspruch, E., 380, 381
Eisenberg, J., 408, 431
Eisenberg, L., 466, 492
Elgin, S., 349, 350, 353, 358, 382
Ellickson, J., 357, 382
Ellinwood, C., 318, 342, 343
Elliot, S., 408, 431
Ellis, A., 385, 404, 405, 406, 407, 408, 410,
    411, 412, 413, 415, 416, 417, 420, 421,
    422, 427, 428, 429, 430, 431, 432, 433,
    434
Emerson, R., 304
Emoe, R., 536
Engels, G., 407, 433
Englund, S., 441, 461
Epictetus, 404, 433
Epstein, S., 506, 529, 550, 551
Erickson, M., 16, 147, 158, 149, 157, 178,
    179, 181, 182, 204, 205, 350
Erikson, E., 217, 232
Erskine, R., 505, 506, 509, 511, 512, 517,
    528, 529, 539, 540, 542, 561, 562, 563
Eysenck, H., 8, 11

Fagan, J., 298
Fairbairn, W., 210, 211, 220, 231, 232, 535,
    563
Falloon, I., 471, 491, 492, 453
Faltus, F., 534
Federn, P., 499, 529, 535, 540, 563
Feldman, L., 535, 563
Fellner, C., 124, 140
Ferenczi, S., 210, 211, 232
Finklerstein, L., 208, 212, 220, 221, 230,
    231, 232
Fisch, R., 149, 151, 157, 178, 182, 183, 184,
    189, 198, 204, 205, 551
Fishman, H., 82, 86, 88, 104, 105
Fishman, M., 553
Flack, S., 209, 233
Fleischman, M., 469, 470, 478, 479, 485,
    492, 493
Flores, F., 509
Folen, V., 214, 215, 232
Fontaine, O., 433
Ford, E., 438, 439, 441, 461, 462
Forehand, 470, 480
Forman, B., 380, 381
Foster, C., 309, 343

Fowles, J., 135, 140
Frame, 480
Framo, J., 214, 217, 231, 232, 233, 248, 260
Franco, J., 234
Frank, J.D., 6, 7, 11, 405
Frankl, V., 405
Freeman, A., 408, 433
French, T., 405, 414, 533, 563
Freund, S., 48, 49, 209, 210, 211, 212, 215,
    216, 232, 233, 386, 405, 414, 433, 534,
    535, 563
Friedman, L., 535, 563
Fromm, E., 405, 414
Fry, W., 22, 147

Galanter, E., 362, 382
Ganahl, G., 144, 146, 157, 178
Gandelman, 480
Garcia-Marquez, G., 139
Garfield, S., 417, 433
Gaukler, E., 405
Gaullion, 468
Gaylin, N., 321, 325, 343
Gendlin, E., 305, 307, 342, 343
Gerber, J., 44
Gerson, R., 32, 44
Gilligan, C., 220, 233
Gilmore, E., 470, 495
Glass, G., 434
Glass, R., 407, 408, 433
Glasser, N., 441, 462
Glasser, W., 6, 385, 436, 437, 438, 439,
    440, 441, 442, 444, 448, 459, 460, 461,
    462
Glynn, J., 480, 494
Goetz, S., 431
Golden Triad Films, 34, 44
Goldenbera, H., 143, 151, 172, 178
Goldenberg, I., 143, 151, 172, 178
Goldfreid, M., 404, 534, 563
Goldiamond, I., 470, 493
Goldstein, K., 266, 298
Goldstein, M.K., 470, 493
Gonso, 471
Good, 441, 462
Gooliehian, H., 551, 563
Goodman, P., 535
Gordon, D., 358, 377, 381, 382
Gordon, T., 339, 343
Gottman, J., 471, 475, 490, 493
Gottman, M., 408, 433
Goulding, M., 512, 517, 529
Goulding, R., 512, 517, 529
Govinda, L., 16
Graziano, 470

Green, A., 16
Green, E., 16
Grieger, R., 405, 412, 422, 431, 432
Grinder, J., 43, 348, 349, 350, 351, 353,
    354, 356, 358, 359, 360, 362, 370, 372,
    377, 379, 380, 381, 382
Grinker, R., 116, 140
Groder, M., 509, 529
Guerin, P., 205
Guerney, B., 79, 104, 105, 325, 339, 343
Guerney, L., 325, 343
Gullion, M., 494
Guntrip, H., 211, 213, 222, 231, 233
Gurman, A., 8, 11, 108, 148, 175, 176, 178,
    535, 563
Gyarfas, K., 21

Haaga, D., 407, 408, 433
Haley, J., 9, 11, 22, 41, 43, 44, 79, 80, 104,
    139, Ch. 6 (pp. 141–78), 142, 143, 144,
    145, 146, 147, 148, 149, 150, 151, 152,
    153, 155, 156, 157, 158, 159, 160, 161,
    162, 163, 164, 165, 166, 167, 168, 169,
    170, 171, 172, 173, 174, 176, 177, 178,
    181, 182, 204, 205, 215, 238, 260, 415,
    416, 433, 472, 535, 563
Hansen, J., 144, 146, 157, 178
Harper, R., 404, 408, 412, 413, 427, 432
Harrington, G., 303, 437, 438
Harris, R., 515, 529
Hart, J., 338, 345
Harter, S., 480, 493
Hauck, P., 408, 433
Hawkins, N., 467, 495
Hayakawa, S., 16, 22
Hayward, M., 111
Hazelrigg, M., 8, 12
Heard, D., 106
Hefferline, R., 535
Heider, J., 303, 320, 322, 324, 328, 343
Henggeler, S., 472, 493
Herzberg, A., 405
Hirsch, S., 140, 209, 234
Hoebel, F., 190, 205
Hoffman, L., 143, 148, 149, 152, 170, 173,
    177, 178, 238, 259, 260
Hofstadter, D., 220, 233
Hollingworth, L., 305
Holloway, W., 545, 563
Hops, H., 475, 480, 494, 496
Horne, A., 1, 14, 44, 178, 332, 344, 470,
    473, 480, 492, 493, 495
Horney, K., 384, 385, 405, 414
Huber, C., 416, 433, 490
Huebner, B., 338, 345

Hume, 536
Hunt, R., 469, 493
Husserl, 536
Huxley, A., 349, 382

Jackson, D., 16, 22, 43, 44, 83, 104, 105,
    111, 144, 147, 148, 149, 177, 178, 181,
    182, 204, 205, 209, 237, 238, 260, 261,
    359, 382, 415, 472, 475, 494
Jacobsen, E., 421, 428, 433
Jacobsen, N., 404, 408, 433, 471, 475, 490,
    493
James, M., 515, 520, 524
James, W., 437
Jereb, R., 357, 381
Johnson, V., 408
Johnson, W., 5, 12
Jones, A., 298
Jones, M., 466, 493
Jones, R., 467, 468, 471, 495
Jongeward, D., 515, 520, 529
Jorgens, B., 338, 345
Jorm, A., 407, 433
Jourard, S., 315, 343
Joy, B., 16
Jung, C., 16, 137, 140

Kadis, L., 527, 528, 529
Kaiser, W., 437, 462
Kant, 536
Kantor, D., 535, 563
Karasu, T., 534
Karpman, S., 504, 529
Kaslow, F., 535, 563
Keepers, T., 515, 528
Keith, D., Ch. 5 (pp. 107–40), 111
Kelly, G., 405, 429, 433, 536, 548, 563
Kelly, H., 471, 474, 495
Kempler, W., 266, 267, 298, 299
Kernberg, O., 213, 216, 218, 233
Kerr, M., 48, 49,. 50, 54, 74, 75
Kierkegard, S., 304
Kiesler, P., 307
Kilpatrick, A., 207
Kilpatrick, E., 207
Kilpatrick, W., 305
Kirschenbaum, H., 342
Kirschner, S., 106
Kleiman, J., 106
Klein, M., 108, 140, 210, 211, 212, 216, 217,
    231, 233
Knaus, W., 428, 432
Kniskern, D., 8, 11, 108, 148, 175, 176, 178
Kohut, H., 220, 233, 535, 536, 545, 564
Konner, M., 73

Kornreich, M., 466, 494
Korzybski, A., 353, 382, 421, 433
Krestensen, K., 21, 33, 44, 45
Kripner, S., 16

L'Abate, L., 144, 146, 157, 171, 178, 448
Laird, J., 466, 492
Land, D., 308
Langs, R., 230, 233
Lankton, C., 351, 354, 356, 358, 359, 360,
   382
Lankton, S., 348, 351, 352, 354, 356, 357,
   358, 359, 360, 370, 373, 374, 375, 382
Lawe, C., 332, 344
Lazarus, A., 310, 343, 404, 408, 413, 433,
   470, 494, 534, 561, 564
Lebeau, M., 358, 377, 381
Lebow, J., 535, 564
Lederer, W., 475, 494
Levant, R., 316, 321, 342, 343
Levinas, E., 299
Levinue, F.M., 5, 12
Levine, A., 469
Levitt, E., 466, 469, 494
Liberman, R., 470, 480, 494
Lidz, T., 209, 233
Liebman, L., 80, 81, 85, 102, 104, 105, 106
Light, 480
Lindblad, M., 88, 105
Locke, H., 479, 494
London, P., 534, 564
Loos, V., 550, 551, 564
LoPiccolo, J., 408
Lord, S., 364
Lovibond, S., 467, 494
Low, A., 405
Lowe, R., 385, 401
Lowen, A., 16
Luce, G., 10, 12
Luepnitz, D., 219, 233

MacIsaac, D., 536, 545
Madanes, C., 143, 145, 149, 150, 153, 154,
   155, 156, 170, 171, 173, 177, 178
Mahler, M., 217, 230, 233
Mahoney, M., 404
Maisenbacher, J., 509, 529
Makower, J., 353, 382
Malcolm, J., 79, 105
Malone, T., 110, 139, 140
Manaster, G., 401
Margolin, G., 408, 433, 470, 475
Margulis, J., 356, 382
Markman, H., 470, 475, 490
Marsh, S., 217, 234

Maslow, A., 25, 44
Masters, W., 408
Matorana, H., 536, 537, 538, 539, 561, 562,
   564
Maultsby, M., 404, 410, 422, 433
McCleary, R., 310, 343
McClellan, T., 408, 433
McClendon, R., 514, 527, 528, 529
McGoldrick, M., 32, 44

McGovern, T., 407, 433
McGrady, B., 418, 433
McInerney, J., 431
McKay, G., 387, 395, 401
McLuhan, M., 439
McNeal, S., 467, 495
Mead, M., 182
Meador, B., 308, 338, 342, 344
Meara, N., 357, 381
Mearns, D., 321, 344
Meichenbaum, D., 404
Meissuer, W., 220, 233
Meltzoff, J., 466, 494
Metcoff, J., 138, 140
Middlefort, F., 115, 140
Miller, G., 358, 362, 363, 382
Miller, N., 405, 407, 431
Miller, R., 407, 433
Milman, L., 80, 81, 104, 105
Minuchin, S., 6, Ch. 4 (pp., 77–105), 78, 79,
   80, 81, 82, 86, 89, 92, 95, 102, 104,
   105, 106, 117, 140, 146, 148, 149, 178,
   209, 415
Moos, R., 479, 494
Moreno, J., 16
Montalvo, B., 79, 80, 104, 105, 148
Morris, H., 466, 494
Morris, S., 153, 178
Moseley, S., 408, 432
Moskowitz, L., 88, 105
Moultrup, D., 535, 564
Moursund, J., 528, 539, 540, 562, 563
Moyers, B., 304, 343
Mowatt, D., 106
Mueser, K., 480, 494

Nag Hammadi, 304
Napier, A., 111, 139
Naster, B., 471, 492
Natiello, P., 342
Neal, J., 535, 563
Neimeyer, G., 536, 564
Neja, P., 338, 345
Nevin, W., 33, 43, 44
Newman, 534

Nichols, M., 208, 209, 216, 214, 219, 233, 472, 494
Nickerson, M., 480, 494
Norcross, J., 9, 12, 534, 564
Norseworthy, 480
Notarius, C., 470, 475, 490
Nunnally, E.W., 4, 5, 11

O'Donnell, D., 439, 462
O'Hanlon, B., 562
O'Leary, C., 315, 344
O'Leary, D., 470
O'Leary, S., 470
Ohlsen, M., 14, 44, 178, 323, 332, 344, 490, 494
Olson, D., 319, 339, 345
Ornstein, R., 304, 344
Overall, B., 469, 494

Pagels, E., 304, 344
Palazzoli, M., 149, 260
Paolino, T., 414, 433
Papero, D., 47, 74
Papp, P., 170, 171
Passmore, J.L., 1, 470, 495
Patterson, C., 320, 321, 344
Patterson, G., 466, 467, 468, 469, 470, 472, 474, 475, 480, 494, 495, 496
Payne, R., 73
Pearson, P., 528
Pell, P., 563
Penfield, W., 499, 529
Penn, P., 238, 259, 260
Perls, F., 16, 264, 265, 266, 267, 286, 299, 350, 535, 540, 564
Perls, L., 540
Peters, M., 217, 234
Peters, T., 217, 234
Phelps, R., 467
Phillips, L., 405
Piaget, J., 505, 529, 536
Piercy, F., 217, 233
Pine, F., 535, 564
Pinsof, C., 564
Pinsof, W., 535, 564
Powers, E., 466, 495
Powers, W., 440, 460, 462
Prata, G., 149, 238, 240, 260
Pribram, K., 16, 362, 382
Prochaska, J., 7, 8, 9, 12, 534, 564
Pursglove, P., 299

Rabkin, R., 149
Rablen, R., 338, 346
Raimey, V., 404

Rami, S., 16
Rank, O., 110, 140, 306, 344
Raskin, N., 321, 338, 339, 344
Ray, R., 468, 494
Raymor, R., 466, 495
Reese, E., 357, 381
Reese, M., 357, 381
Reich, W., 535, 539, 564
Reid, J., 467, 468, 470, 475, 495
Richardson, J., 356, 382
Riley, P., 106
Riskin, J., 22
Risley, T., 467, 495
Roach, J., 466, 495
Robbins, A., 373, 374
Robins, L., 466, 468, 495
Robinson, H., 139
Roebuck, F., 338, 342
Rogers, C., 5, 16, 44, 118, 302, 303, 304, 305, 306, 307, 308, 309, 310, 313, 314, 316, 318, 320, 321, 327, 328, 330, 331, 333, 336, 338, 341, 344, 345, 416, 433
Rogers, N., 342
Rolf, I., 16
Rosen, J., 111, 182
Rosenberg, J., 88, 105
Rosman, B., 79, 81, 95, 102, 104, 105, 106
Rossi, E., 178
Rotter, J., 405
Rowe, C., 536, 545, 564
Ruesch, R., 184, 205
Russell, B., 404
Russell, R., 357, 381
Ryckoff, I., 140, 209, 234

Salter, A., 405
Sameroff, A., 536, 564
Sampson, E., 416, 433
Sampson, H., 223, 233
Sandeen, E., 5, 12
Satir, V., 5, 6, Ch. 4 (pp. 13–45), 15, 16, 20, 21, 23, 24, 25, 26, 29, 30, 31, 32, 33, 40, 42, 43, 45, 148, 149, 178, 181, 182, 209, 350, 379, 381, 399, 400, 535, 541, 564
Saxon, W., 408, 434
Sayger, T., 470, 495
Scharff, D., 212, 213, 214, 215, 218, 219, 222, 230, 231, 233
Scharff, J., 212, 213, 214, 215, 218, 219, 222, 230, 231, 233
Schiff, J., 509, 529
Schumer, F., 79, 104, 105
Schwarz, J., 16
Scott, S., 88, 104, 106

Segal, H., 211, 233
Segal, L., 148, 178, 179, 204, 542, 548, 562, 564
Selvini, M., 236, 237, 245, 260
Selvini Palazzoli, M., 238, 239, 240, 241, 242, 245, 246, 247, 250, 252, 253, 259
Selye, H., 16, 26, 45
Shah, I., 304, 345
Shanks, A., 321, 343
Sharpley, D., 356, 380, 382
Shaw, D., 468, 495
Sheeley, N., 16
Shepherd, I., 298
Sherman, R., 384, 386, 387, 388, 389, 390, 391, 392, 394, 401
Schilson, E., 141, Ch. 6 (pp. 141–78)
Shlien, J., 338, 345
Shmurak, 408, 433
Sichel, J., 406, 421, 427, 431, 432, 434
Sih, P., 303, 346
Silverman, M., 407, 433
Siminston, C., 16
Siminton, S., 16
Simkink, J., 266
Simmel, E., 110
Simon, F., 218, 220, 233
Simon, R., 149, 178, 245, 248, 261
Singer, A., 237, 261
Slavson, S., 110
Slipp, S., 208, 209, 210, 215, 216, 221, 222, 223, 224, 225, 230, 232, 233
Smith, M., 407, 434
Snyder, M., 345
Snygg, D., 310, 343
Sonstegard, M., 385, 401
Sorrentino, A., 245, 260
Spanier, G., 479, 495
Spark, G., 232
Speed, B., 259, 261
Spence, D., 560, 565
Spinoza, 404
Sprenkle, D., 217, 233
Stachowiak, J., 26, 44
Standal, S., 310, 311, 312, 338
Stanton, D., 88, 106, 148, 150, 153, 154, 165, 167, 175, 178
Steed, S., 408, 434
Steiner, C., 505, 509, 529
Stekel, W., 405
Stephenson, W., 338, 345
Stern, D., 536, 544, 565
Stevens, B., 307
Stewart, R., 217, 222, 225, 230, 234
Stieper, D., 408, 433
Stierlin, H., 208, 218, 233, 234

Strausser, 534, 564
Strode, O., 309
Strupp, H., 7, 8, 12
Stuart, R., 471, 475, 479, 495
Sullivan, H., 384, 385, 414
Suomis, 73
Suomi, V., 73
Sweeney, T., 401
Swenson, G., 309, 342
Szykula, S., 153, 161, 178

Taft, J., 306, 345
Taschman, H., 26, 45
Tannenbaum, B., 16
Taschman, H., 44
Taylor, E., 111
Terry, D., 209, 233
Teuber, H., 466, 495
Thayer, L., 303, 310, 325, 345
Thibaut, J., 471, 474, 495
Thorne, B., 321, 344
Thorne, F., 405
Thomason, T., 347, 382
Thunder, R., 16
Todd, T., 80, 81, 88, 104, 105, 106
Toffler, A., 358, 382
Toman, W., 59, 75
Tomlinson, T., 338, 345
Tomm, K., 259, 261
Trexler, L., 407, 431
Truax, C., 307
Tsoi-Hoshmand, L., 408, 434

Umbarger, C., 104

Van der Veen, F., 319, 338, 339, 344, 345
Van Deusen, J., 106
Van Feoster, 542, 548
Varela, F., 536, 537, 562, 564
Vasconcellos, J., 309
Vico, 536
Vincent, J., 475, 493
Vivekananda, S., 265, 299
Vogel, E., 217, 234
Von Foerster, H., 204

Wachtel, P., 414, 434
Wahler, R., 473, 474, 495
Walker, A., 338, 346
Walker, J., 470, 495
Wallace, K., 479, 494
Walter, H., 470, 495
Walters, R., 470
Warkentin, J., 109, 110, 111
Warner, M., 325, 346

Watson, L., 466, 495
Watts, A., 22
Watzlawick, P., 144, 149, 151, 157, 178, 180, 181, 182, 183, 189, 192, 197, 204, 205, 237, 261, 359, 382, 415, 536, 548, 551, 565
Weakland, J., 22, 44, 147, 148, 149, 151, 157, 177, 178, 180, 181, 182, 183, 184, 189, 193, 204, 205, 238, 260, 472, 535, 551, 563
Wedding, D., 432
Weeks, G., 171, 178, 448, 462
Weiner, W., 440, 460, 462
Weiss, E., 471, 475, 479, 493, 496, 499, 529
Weiss, J., 223, 233
Weiss, R., 408, 433
Wessler, R., 420, 434
Whitaker, C., Ch. 5 (pp. 107–40), 110, 138, 139, 140, 209
Whiteley, J., 309, 342, 346, 405, 407, 410, 412, 429, 431, 432
Whittier, J., 467, 495
Wilk, J., 562
Williams, C., 467, 496
Wills, T., 475, 496
Wilson, E., 73
Wiltz, N., 470, 496

Winderman, L., 551, 563
Winders, K., 509, 529
Winnicott, D., 114, 119, 140, 211, 212, 213, 218, 234
Winter, J., 41, 43, 45
Wittgenstein, 536
Wolberg, L., 405
Wolfe, J., 405, 408, 432
Wolfe, M., 467, 495
Wolpe, J., 417, 434
Wright, M., 467, 495
Wu, J., 303, 346
Wubbolding, R., 437, 441, 442, 444, 448, 450, 451, 459, 462, 461
Wynne, L., 125, 140, 209, 217, 218, 233, 234, 237, 261

Yeager, R., 406, 431, 432, 433

Zalcman, M., 506, 529
Zeia, J., 45
Zeno, 404
Zilbergeld, B., 408
Zimring, F., 338, 345
Zingle, H., 408, 431
Zunin, L., 437, 438, 462
Zuk, G., 232

Subject Index

ABCs of emotional disturbance, 411–12
Accidental learning, 474
Activating events, 419
Active ego state, 500
Actualizing tendency, 310, 315
Analogical expression, 354, 355, 359
Anchoring, 376, 377
Anorexia nervosa, 81, 236
Assertive training, 422
Autonomy, 543, 545, 548–49, 562
Avanta network, 41
Awareness, 264, 265, 266, 272, 311

Basic encounter, 332
Belonging, 440, 443, 447, 460
Bioenergetics, 16
Biofeedback, 16
Biological predispositions, 409
Birth order, 389
Body therapies, 16, 23
Booster treatments, 469
Boundaries, 25, 83, 143, 148, 389
Boundary making, 95
Brief Therapy Center, 180, 183, 204

Catharsis, 8
Center for Family Studies, 237, 242
Change, 83
Child Guidance Center, 384, 385
CHOICE Program, 441
Circularity, 144, 241
Circulation through another, 278, 279
Classical conditioning, 466
Cotherapy, 109, 111, 123, 125, 126, 127
Coaching, 63, 123
Coalition, 144, 148, 389

Coercion, 475
Cognitive behavior therapy, 404, 408
Cognitive distraction, 421
Cognitive restructuring, 407
Communication skills, 392–93
Complementarities, 389
Complementaries—roles, 389, 391
Complementarity, 83, 93
Conditional stimuli, 8
Confrontation, 332, 516
Congruence, 312
Cojoint family therapy, 15, 23
Constructivism, 217, 532, 533, 535, 536–39
Contact, 312, 546
Contamination, 501, 507
Contingency control, 8
Contingent attention, 467
Contract, 511, 513, 514, 515, 517, 520
Contracting, 422
Control theory, 436, 440, 442, 460
Counseling vs. therapy, 4
Counterparadox, 238
Cues, 473
Cybernetics, 180, 187, 204

Detriangled, 62, 64
Deep structure, 353
Defense mechanisms, 539
Deletion, 353, 354, 370–71
Dependence, 511
Desensitization, 422
Developmental phases, 476
Devil's pact, 170, 196
Diagnosis, 272, 283
Differentiation, 52, 54, 269, 270
Digital expressions, 354, 355

Directives, 144, 168, 170
Discordant psychological process, 269
Disengaged families, 84, 117
Distancing mechanisms, 275
Distortion, 353, 354, 370, 371
Distressed process, 271
Drama, 32

Eclecticism, 534
Ecological trap, 51
Ego state, 498, 499–500, 526
Emotional cutoff, 49, 59
Emotional system, 50
Empathic understanding, 302, 318, 321, 323, 330, 338
Empathic attunement, 545
Empathy, 314
Enactment, 94
Encouragement, 394
Enmeshed families, 54, 117
Esalem, 22, 23
Exchange theory, 471, 474
Extinction, 470

Facilitation conditions, 315
Fading, 472
Failure identity, 439
Family actualization, 324
Family atmosphere, 388
Family concept, 338
Family constellation, 59, 386, 398
Family diagram, 49, 65, 66
Family Education Center, 385
Family life cycle, 113, 148, 157
Family life fact chronology, 21, 32
Family maps, 32
Family of origin, 113
Family projection process, 57
Family reconstruction, 21, 33
Fantasy, 275
Feedback, 144, 181
Flooding, 422
Formative tendency, 302, 340
Four-tuple, 351, 375–76
Freedom, 440, 443, 444, 447, 460
Full personal expression, 278
Fun, 440, 443, 447, 460
Fusion, 49, 55
Future-pacing, 377

Games, 504
General semantics, 16, 421, 428
Generalization, 353, 354, 355, 370, 371, 472
Generation, 145
Genograms, 32, 65

Genuineness, 318, 321
Gestalt family therapy, 264, 265, 267, 270, 281
Gestalt therapy, 16, 22
Goal-directed behavior attention, 387
Goal-directed behavior power, 387, 389, 390
Goal-directed behavior revenge, 387
Goal-directed behavior inadequacy, 387

Habituation, 361
Hermeneutics, 560
Hierarchy, 145, 148, 155
Homeostasis, 83, 145, 181
Homework, 150, 168, 198, 422, 428
"Hot seat," 266, 267
Human validation process model, *see* Ch. 2
Humor, 33, 62
Hypothesizing, 240
Hypnosis, 16

I-position, 63
Iatrogenic, 10
Id, 209
Identity needs, 439
Illinois State Psychiatric Institute, 21, 22
Imaging, 421
Imbroglio, 245, 246
Immediate existence, 265, 266
Implosion, 422
Incongruence, 360, 363
Independence, 511
Individual psychology, 384
Insight, 412
Instigation, 246
Intergenerational coalitions, 84
Integrative family therapy, 532, 534–36, 561
Integrative psychotherapy, 539–41
Integrationism, 534
Intensionality, 312
Intensity, 96
Interdependence, 511
Interlocking racket system, 509–510, 527
Internal maps, 351
Interactional, 473
Introjection, 211, 216
Invariant prescription, 244, 245
Irrational beliefs (iB's), 404, 406, 413, 416, 427
Isomorphisms, 220

Joining techniques, 91, 127

Languaging, 532, 537, 547, 551, 561
Laws of evaluation, 324
Libido, 209, 210

Life-posturing reintegration, 16
Life style, 389
Locus of control, 448, 449
Logico-empirical method, 421

Map, 353
Menninger Foundation, 48, 49
Mental Research Institute, 22, 148, 180, 182, 183, 204, 238
Meta-model, 350, 354, 370-74
Metaphor, 32, 148, 154, 171
Modeling, 457, 491
Milan approach, Ch. 9 (pp. 235-61)
Milan associates, 242, 243, 258
Mimesis, 92
Multigenerational transmission process, 56, 58
Multiversum, 539
Myths, 389

National Institute of Mental Health (NIMH), 22, 49, 50, 51, 147
Negative reinforcement trap, 414
Neurolinguistic programming, 348
Neutrality, 242
Nominalization, 359
Nuclear family emotional system, 49, 55-57

Oak Ridge Hospital, 109
Object relations family therapy, Ch. 8 (pp. 207-34, 237)
Operant learning, 470
Ordeal technique, 173
Organismic valuing, 313, 314
Overadequate-inadequate reciprocity, 49

Palo Alto Project, 147, 153
Paradox, 145, 171, 182, 185, 187, 198, 204, 238
Paradoxical intention, 395, 422, 428
Parental child, 145
Parts party, 33
Perception, 446, 447
Philadelphia, 79, 80, 82, 102, 148, 149
Play therapy, 108, 109, 110
Point system, 467
Polarities, 327
Polarization, 265, 273, 276
Positioning, 172
Positive regard, 302, 313, 321, 322, 338
Positive reinforcement trap, 473
Power, 440, 443, 447, 469
Predicate usage, 357
Prescribing the symptom, 172, 198
Primary survival triad, 20

Private logic, 389
Private realities, 546
Process, 269, 270, 271, 272, 273, 276
Process for family development, 319
Process for problem solving, 319, 324
Projection, 211, 217
Psychoanalysis, 208
Psychodrama, 16
Psychosynthesis, 16
Punctuation, 95, 96
Punishment, 470

Quality time, 447, 450, 459

Racket system, 506-508, 517, 518, 520
Rackety display, 506
Rational-emotive family therapy, 404, 407, 414, 417, 430
Rational-emotive imagery, 422, 428
Rationality, 410
Reality family therapy, 447
Reality therapy, 437, 442
Reciprocal interaction, 473, 475
Reciprocity, 475
Reframing, 33, 92, 145, 169, 551
Regressive therapy, 541
Reinforcement, 470, 487
Reinforcers, 473
Reintegration, 279
Relaxation, 421, 428
Relabeling, 145, 169
Reluctant clients, 159
Renegotiation, 280
Representational systems, 351, 360
Resistance, 146, 148, 169, 288, 396, 539
Responsibility, 437, 459
Role playing, 288, 422, 428
Role reversal, 395
Ropes, 32
Rules, 389

Scripts, 498, 504-506, 514, 517, 526, 527
Sculpting, 15, 20, 32
Self-actualization, 310
Self-awareness, 265
Self-concept, 272, 311, 322
Self-disclosure, 123, 124, 271
Self-efficacy, 465
Self-esteem, 23, 24, 32
Sensate focus, 421
Sensory representational system, 352
Sex therapy, 408
Sibling position, 59
Significance, striving for, 388
Social control, 545

Social interest, 388–89
Social learning, 464
Social meaning, 386–87, 388
Social learning family therapy, 464, 466, 470, 471, 474, 491
Splitting, 215, 279
Strategic Therapy Institute, 149
Stress, 16
Strokes, 503–504, 506, 515, 527
Strokes—positive, 503
Strokes—negative, 503, 516
Strokes—conditional, 503
Strokes—unconditional, 503, 516
Structure determinism, 536
Structural family therapy, Ch. 4 (pp. 77–105)
Structure, 146
Subjective perception, 388
Subsystem, 146
Success identity, 439
Surface structure, 353, 366
Symbiosis, 54
Symptom(s), 146, 271, 273, 297, 394, 460
Symptom assessment, 31
Travistock Clinic, 230
Theory, 3
Therapeutic perturbations, 550
Therapist positioning, 551

Time-out, 467
"Top dog," 266, 267
TOTE, 362–65, 370
Touch, 33
Tracking, 92
Transaction, 501, 508, 514, 515, 527
Transaction—complimentary, 501
Transaction—crossed, 501
Transactional analysis, 16, 22
Transactional patterns, 498
Transference, 219, 237
Triangles, 49, 54–55, 146–48

Ulterior transactions, 502, 504
Unbalancing, 93, 96
Unconditional regard, 302, 318, 321, 322
Unconscious, the, 209
Undulation, 269
Union, 270, 279
Universum, 539

Visual accessing cues, 356

Wants, human, 444
WDEP, 449–52, 458–59, 460
Working point, 258, 286
Wiltwych School for Boys, 78, 79, 80

THE BOOK'S MANUFACTURE

Family Counseling and Therapy,
Second Edition, was typeset by
Point West, Inc., Carol Stream, Illinois.
The typefaces are Times Roman for text
and Stymie for display.
Printing and binding were done by
Arcata Graphics, Kingsport, Tennessee.
Cover design and book design by John B. Goetz,
Design & Production Services, Co., Chicago.